HISTORY OF
THE MANCHESTER REGIMENT
(63RD AND 96TH REGIMENTS)

Printed and bound by Antony Rowe Ltd, Eastbourne

N. Osborne Barnard, M. Gen'l.
Colonel The Manchester Reg't.

(1904–1920).

[*Frontispiece.*

HISTORY
OF THE
MANCHESTER REGIMENT
(LATE THE 63RD AND 96TH FOOT)

COMPILED BY
COLONEL H. C. WYLLY, C.B.

WITH ILLUSTRATIONS BY
GERALD C. HUDSON

VOL. II

1883—1922

LONDON
FORSTER GROOM & CO. LTD.
15 CHARING CROSS, S.W.1
1925

BRIG. GEN. WILLIAM LOWRY AUCHINLECK, COMMANDED 63RD (WEST SUFFOLK) REGIMENT IN AFGHANISTAN, 1880.

THIS HISTORY

OF

THE MANCHESTER REGIMENT

FORMERLY

THE 63RD (WEST SUFFOLK) AND 96TH REGIMENTS

IS MOST RESPECTFULLY

DEDICATED

BY GRACIOUS PERMISSION

TO

HIS MAJESTY KING GEORGE V

Capt. Lt. C. Henderson. Capt. Lt.
Phillips. Lt. Stracey. Lt. Dawson. Ridley. Pearce.
Capt. Maj. Rus- Lt. Quin.
Lt. Vizard. Simpson. sell Jones. Capt. Tenison. Lt. Ternan.
Lt.-Col. Maj. Lt.-Col. Lt. Henderson.
Capt. Capt. Barnard. Marryat. Auchinleck. Q.-M. Facer. Lt. Graham. Maj. Saportas.
Lt. Capt. Chevers. Cooke. Maj. Maj. Studdy. Capt. Lt. Bertram. Lt. Codrington. Lt. Wilson. Lt. O'Brien.
Capt. Prioleau. Reay. Kirwan. Lt. Watson. Newbigging. Moores. Thomas. Lt. McIvill. Lt. Stubbs.
Capt. C.pt. Rowbottom. Lt. Maxwell. Lt. Uternarck.
Rochfort-Boyd. Capt. Nash. Moores.

THE OFFICERS, 1ST AND 2ND BATTALIONS, AT RAS-EL-TIN PALACE, ALEXANDRIA, EGYPT, 1882.

vij

CONTENTS

	PAGE
DEDICATION	v
BATTLE HONOURS	xiv

CHAPTER XVI
THE 1ST BATTALION IN THE SOUTH AFRICAN WAR, 1883–1900. SIEGE OF LADYSMITH 1

CHAPTER XVII
THE 1ST BATTALION IN THE SOUTH AFRICAN WAR, 1900–1903 . . 18

CHAPTER XVIII
THE 2ND BATTALION, 1885–1901 34

CHAPTER XIX
THE 2ND BATTALION IN SOUTH AFRICA AND M.I. COMPANY, 1900–1902. THE 3RD AND 4TH BATTALIONS, 1900–1906 50

CHAPTER XX
THE 1ST BATTALION, 1903–1914—THE 2ND BATTALION, 1902–1914. THE EVE OF THE GREAT WAR 67

CHAPTER XXI
THE OPENING OF THE GREAT WAR—THE 2ND BATTALION, AUGUST TO DECEMBER 1914 85

CHAPTER XXII
THE 1ST BATTALION 106

CONTENTS

CHAPTER XXIII
THE 2ND BATTALION IN FRANCE, JANUARY 1915–AUGUST 1917 . . 126

CHAPTER XXIV
THE 1ST BATTALION IN MESOPOTAMIA, JANUARY 1916–MIDSUMMER 1917 147

CHAPTER XXV
THE 2ND BATTALION IN FRANCE AND FLANDERS, AUGUST 1917—THE ARMISTICE 168

CHAPTER XXVI
THE 1ST BATTALION IN MESOPOTAMIA AND PALESTINE, JULY 1917—THE ARMISTICE 185

CHAPTER XXVII
THE 1ST BATTALION, 1918–1922 202

CHAPTER XXVIII
THE 2ND BATTALION, 1918–1921 213

CHAPTER XXIX
NOTES ON UNIFORM, COLOURS, BADGES, ETC., BY THE LATE D. HASTINGS-IRWIN, ESQ. 224

APPENDICES

APPENDIX I
DOCUMENTS RELATIVE TO THE CAPTURE OF THE STANDARD BY ANTHONY LUTZ 269

APPENDIX II
THE FLEUR DE LYS 272

APPENDIX III

THE BRUNSWICK STAR OF THE 63RD AND 96TH REGIMENTS . . 280

APPENDIX IV

SUCCESSION OF COLONELS, 63RD, 96TH, AND MANCHESTER REGIMENTS 282

APPENDIX V

ALPHABETICAL ROLL OF ALL OFFICERS WHO HAVE JOINED 63RD, 96TH, AND MANCHESTER REGIMENTS 283

APPENDIX VI

DECORATIONS AND HONOURS ROLLS 318

APPENDIX VII

ROLL OF OFFICERS KILLED IN ACTION IN THE GREAT WAR . . 330

APPENDIX VIII

THE ROYAL MILITARY COLLEGE MEMORIAL TABLET . . . 332

APPENDIX IX

CASUALTIES IN ALL RANKS OF ALL BATTALIONS OF THE MANCHESTER REGIMENT IN THE GREAT WAR 334

APPENDIX X

THE CENTENARY CELEBRATIONS—2ND BATTALION—JUBBULPORE, INDIA, MARCH 1924 336

APPENDIX XI

(a) ARMY LIST, AUGUST 1881, ON THE AMALGAMATION OF 63RD AND 96TH REGIMENTS AS THE MANCHESTER REGIMENT . . . 340

(b) ARMY LIST, NOVEMBER 1906, THE LAST OF THE FOUR LINE BATTALIONS 341

APPENDIX XII

THE REGIMENTAL GAZETTE 342

APPENDIX XIII

THE MARCHES PAST . . . . *Facing* 342

APPENDIX XIV

THE REGIMENTAL AID SOCIETY 343

INDEX 345

The coloured plates in this reprint are placed after page XIV

LIST OF ILLUSTRATIONS

COLOURED PLATES

	FACING PAGE
1ST BATTALION, LADYSMITH—NATAL, 1899	12
96TH FOOT, FIELD DAY ORDER, ALDERSHOT, 1880	34
THE RETREAT FROM MONS, 1914	90
1914–1918	128

PORTRAITS AND ILLUSTRATIONS

MAJOR-GENERAL WILLIAM OSBORNE BARNARD, COLONEL, 1904–1920	*Frontispiece*
	FACING PAGE
BRIGADIER-GENERAL WILLIAM LOWRY AUCHINLECK	iv
OFFICERS, 1ST AND 2ND BATTALIONS, RAS-EL-TIN, ALEXANDRIA, EGYPT, 1882	vi
THE DRUMMERS, 1ST BATTALION, LIMERICK, 1893	2
(*a*) 1ST BATTALION MEMORIAL ON CÆSAR'S CAMP, LADYSMITH, 1899	14
(*b*) SOUTH AFRICAN WAR MEMORIAL, ST. ANN'S SQUARE, MANCHESTER	14
2ND BATTALION—QUEEN EMPRESS' BIRTHDAY, CHAKRATA, N.W.P., INDIA, 1893	40
2ND BATTALION—QUARTER GUARD AT GNATONG, TIBETAN FRONTIER, INDIA, 1894	42
3RD (LINE) BATTALION—PRESENTATION OF COLOURS, ALDERSHOT, 1902	62
4TH (LINE) BATTALION—PRESENTATION OF SOUTH AFRICAN WAR MEDALS, KINSALE, IRELAND, 1901	64
1ST BATTALION, GIVENCHY, DECEMBER 20TH, 1914	110

LIST OF ILLUSTRATIONS

	FACING PAGE
2ND BATTALION, FRANCILLY-SELENCY, APRIL 2ND, 1917	144
1ST AND 2ND BATTALIONS—MEETING—FARNHAM PARK, OCTOBER 13TH, 1919	204
THE FIFTEEN RECIPIENTS OF THE VICTORIA CROSS OF ALL BATTALIONS OF THE REGIMENT.	318–324
MEMORIAL TABLET—ROYAL MILITARY COLLEGE—THE GREAT WAR, 1914–1918	332
UNVEILING MEMORIAL—THE GREAT WAR—ST. ANN'S SQUARE, MANCHESTER, 1924	334
2ND BATTALION CENTENARY CELEBRATIONS, JUBBULPORE, C.P., INDIA, 1924	336

MAPS AND PLANS

SKETCH. MOVEMENTS OF 2ND BATTALION ON WESTERN FRONT, 1914 . *p.* 89

SKETCH. POSITION OF LE CATEAU (2ND BATTALION, 1914) . *p.* 93

NO. 1. SOUTH AFRICA (SHOWING ITINERARY OF 1ST AND 2ND BATTALIONS, 1899–1902)

NO. 2. LADYSMITH (JANUARY 6TH, 1900)

NO. 3. WESTERN THEATRE OF WAR (1914–1918)

NO. 4. LOWER MESOPOTAMIA (1916–1918)

NO. 5. PALESTINE (1918)

NO. 6. MESOPOTAMIA (2ND BATTALION IN THE INSURRECTION, 1920)

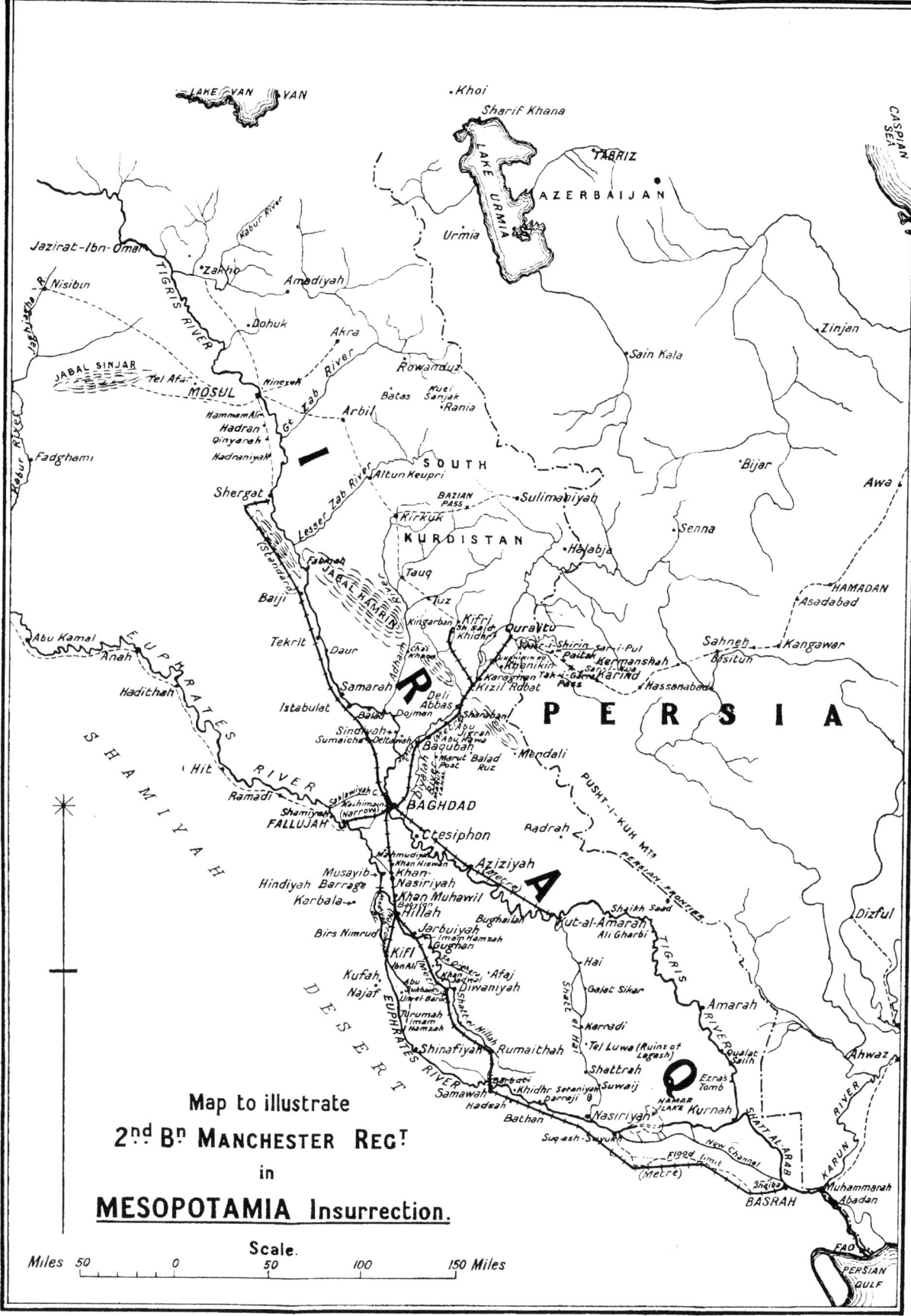

63ᴿᴰ   **96**ᵀᴴ

The Manchester Regiment

BATTLE HONOURS

The SPHINX, superscribed "EGYPT."

"GUADALOUPE, 1759," "EGMONT-OP-ZEE," "PENINSULA," "MARTINIQUE, 1809," "GUADALOUPE, 1810," "NEW ZEALAND," "ALMA," "INKERMAN," "SEVASTOPOL," "AFGHANISTAN, 1879–80," "EGYPT, 1882," "DEFENCE OF LADYSMITH," "SOUTH AFRICA, 1899–1902."

THE GREAT WAR—42 BATTALIONS

"MONS," "Le Cateau," "Retreat from Mons," "Marne, 1914," "Aisne, 1914," "La Bassée, 1914," "Armentières, 1914," "GIVENCHY, 1914," "Neuve Chapelle," "YPRES, 1915, 1917, 1918," "Gravenstafel," "St. Julien," "Frezenberg," "Bellewaarde," "Aubers," "SOMME, 1916, 1918," "Albert, 1916, 1918," "Bazentin," "Delville Wood," "Guillemont," "Flers–Courcelette," "Thiepval," "Le Transloy," "Ancre Heights," "Ancre, 1916, 1918," "Arras, 1917, 1918," "Scarpe, 1917," "Bullecourt," "Messines, 1917," "Pilckem," "Langemarck, 1917," "Menin Road," "Polygon Wood," "Broodseinde," "Poelcappelle," "Passchendaele," "St. Quentin," "Bapaume, 1918," "Rosières," "Lys," "Kemmel," "Amiens," "HINDENBURG LINE," "Épéhy," "Canal du Nord," "St. Quentin Canal," "Beaurevoir," "Cambrai, 1918," "Courtrai," "Selle," "Sambre," "France and Flanders, 1914–18," "PIAVE," "Vittorio Veneto," "Italy, 1917–18," "Doiran, 1917," "MACEDONIA, 1915–18," "Helles," "Krithia," "Suvla," "Landing at Suvla," "Scimitar Hill," "GALLIPOLI, 1915," "Rumani," "Egypt, 1915–17," "MEGIDDO," "Sharon," "Palestine, 1918," "Tigris, 1916," "Kut-al-Amara, 1917," "BAGHDAD," "Mesopotamia, 1916–18."

(The Battle Honours which have been selected to be borne on the Colours or Appointments are printed in CAPITAL LETTERS.)

1ST BN., LADYSMITH—NATAL, 1899.

96TH FOOT, FIELD DAY ORDER, ALDERSHOT, 1880.

THE RETREAT FROM MONS, 1914.

1914—1918.

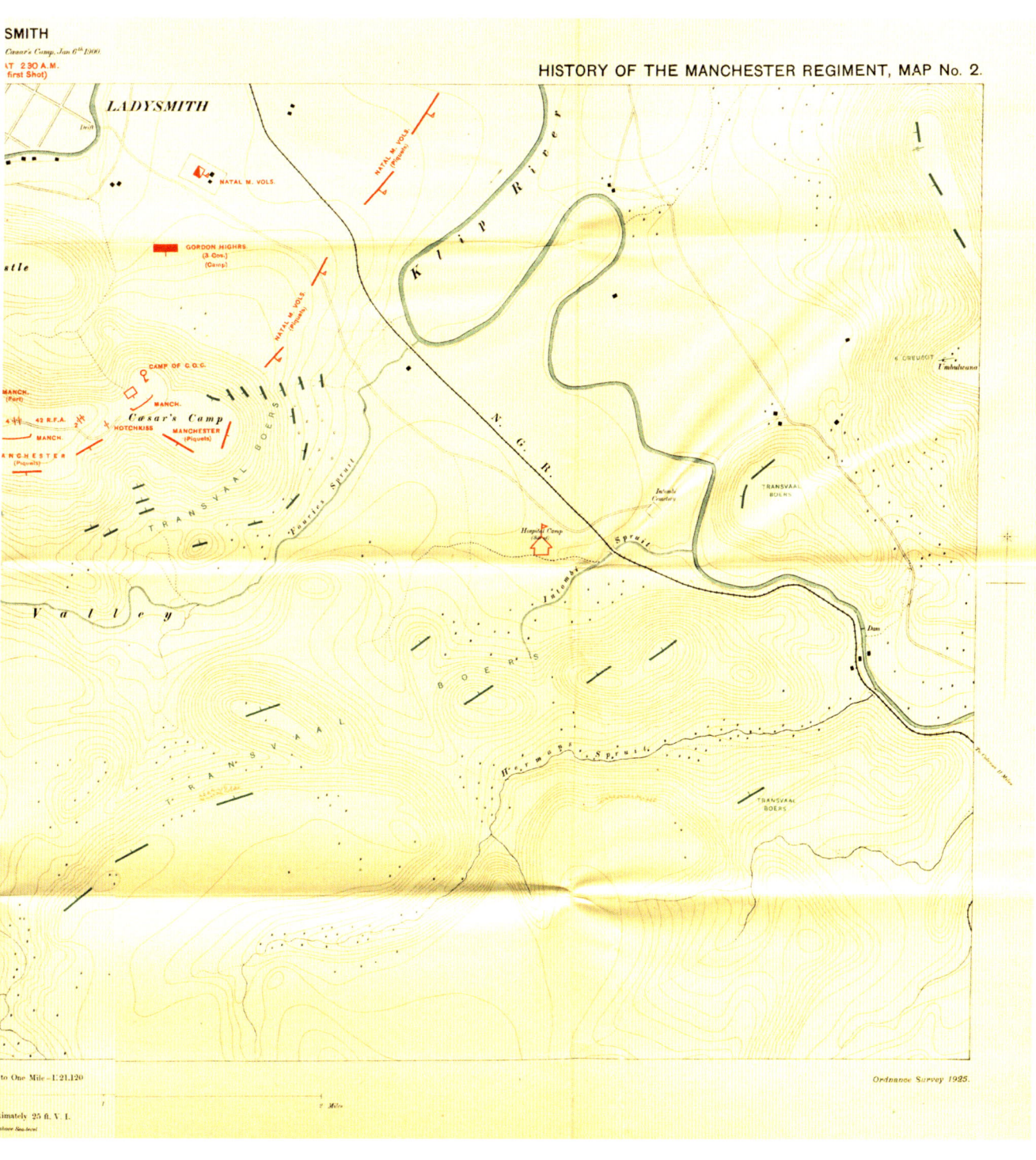

HISTORY OF THE MANCHESTER REGIMENT, MAP No. 2.

HISTORY OF THE MANCHESTER REGT.

MAP N° 3

HISTORY OF THE MANCHESTER REGT.

LOWER MES[OPOTAMIA]
BETWEEN BAGHDAD AN[D ...]

SOPOTAMIA
D THE PERSIAN GULF

MAP No. 4

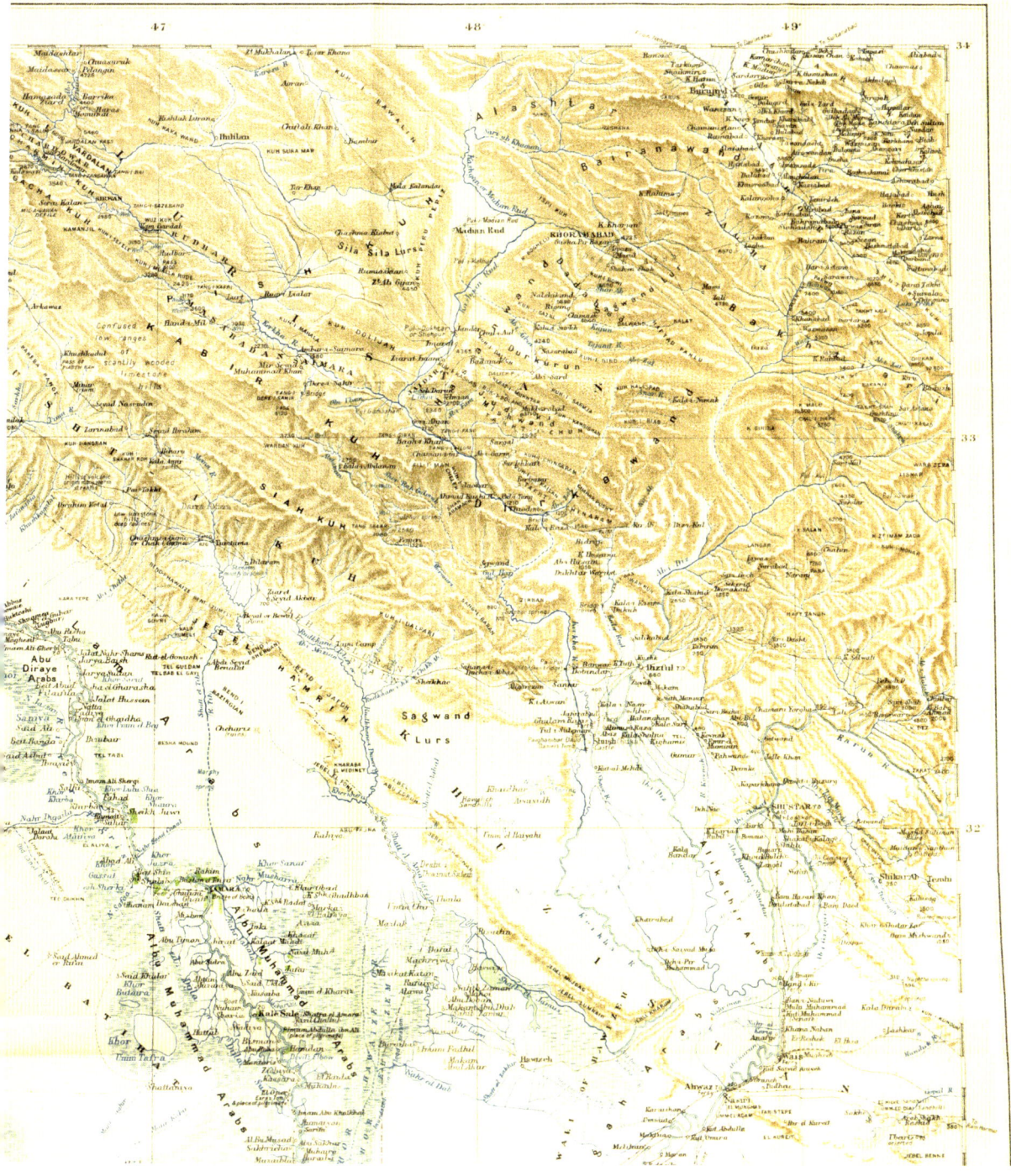

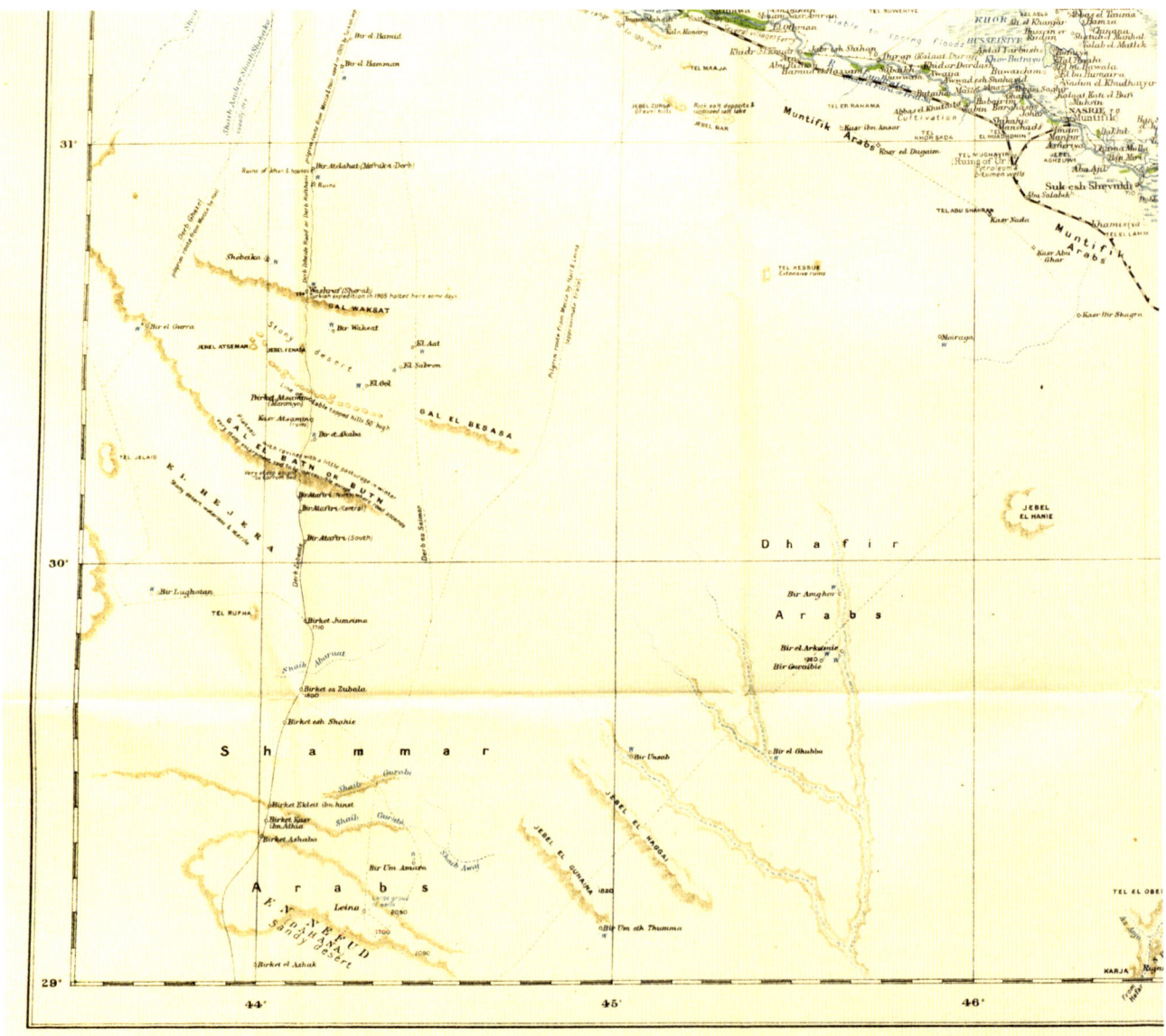

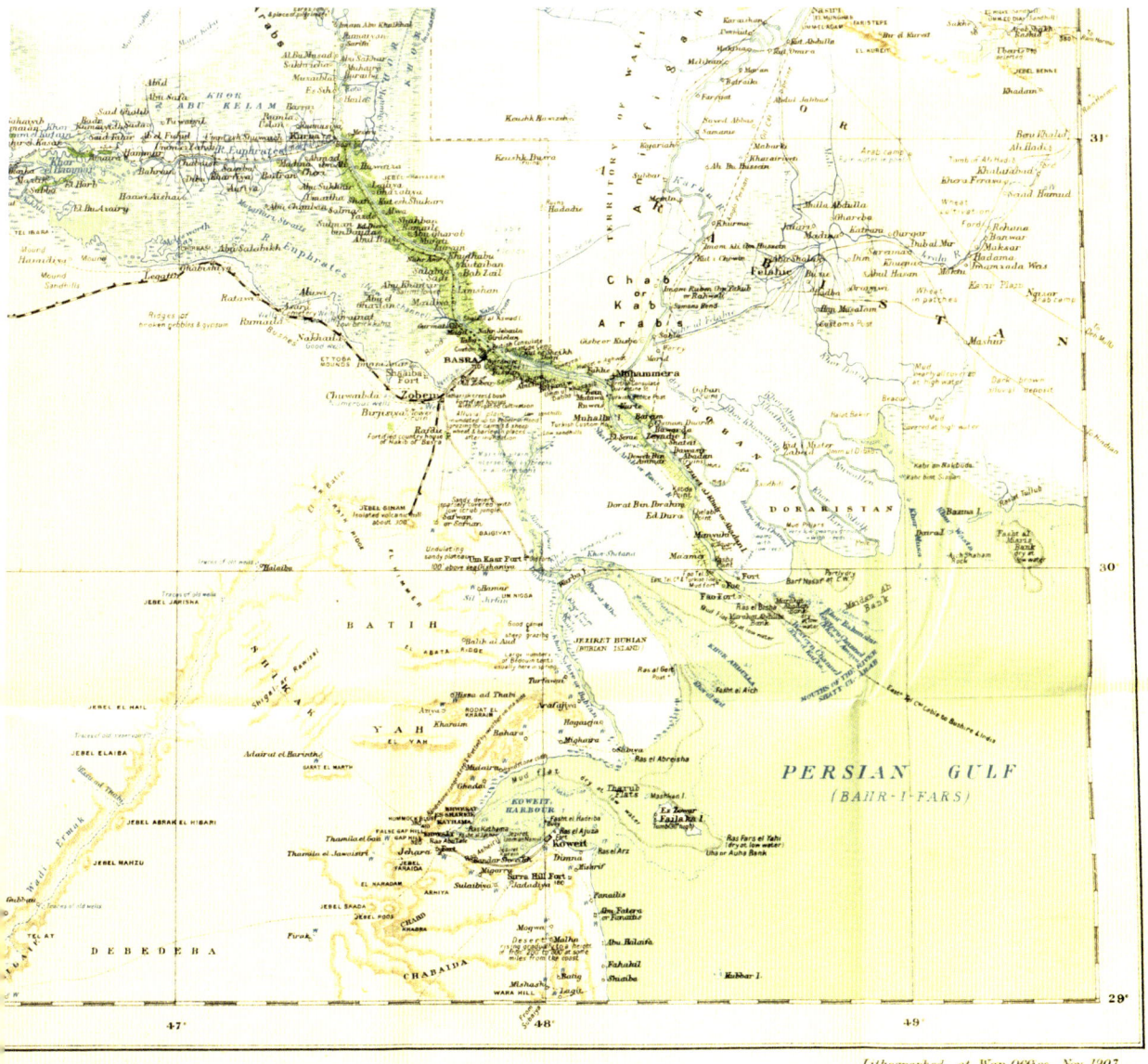

Lithographed at War Office Nov. 1907
Additions & Corrections, Aug 1916.
Railways revised Nov. 1919

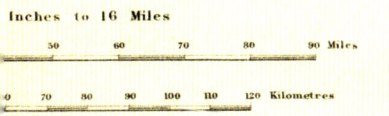

Inches to 16 Miles

SOURCES OF ADDITIONAL INFORMATION

River Euphrates by Sir W. Willcocks 1909
Indian Degree Sheets
Map of part of country round Koweit by Capt. W.H.I. Shakespear 1910
Map of North East Arabia showing route of Capt. G.E. Leachman 1910
Sketch of El Batin near Zobeir by Major Knox 1908
Routenkarte von Bagdad nach Siraz 1907
Information supplied by the Anglo-Persian Oil Company 1910

A telephone runs along the Anglo-Persian Oil Company's pipe line

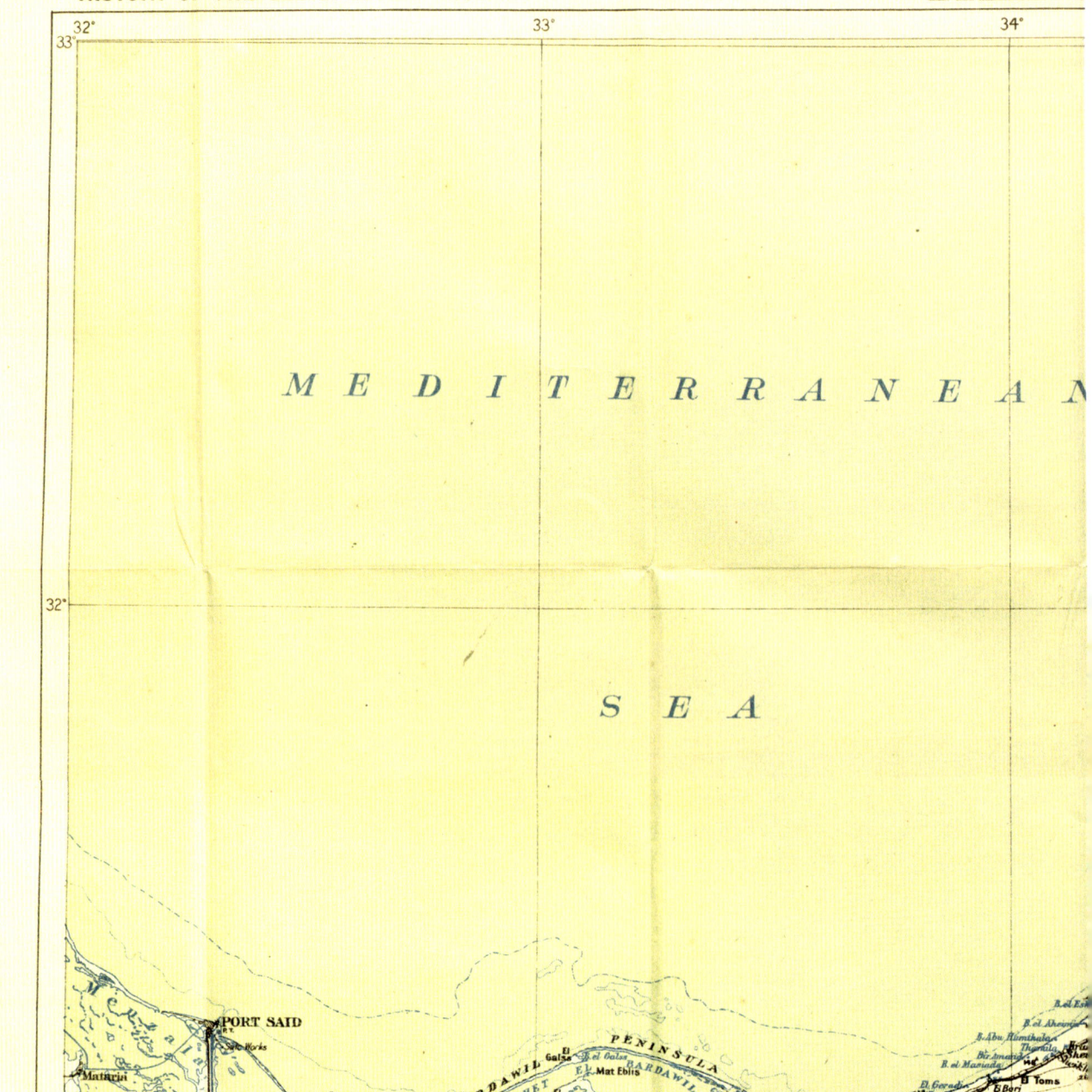

HISTORY OF THE MANCHESTER REGT.   PALES

MAP No 5

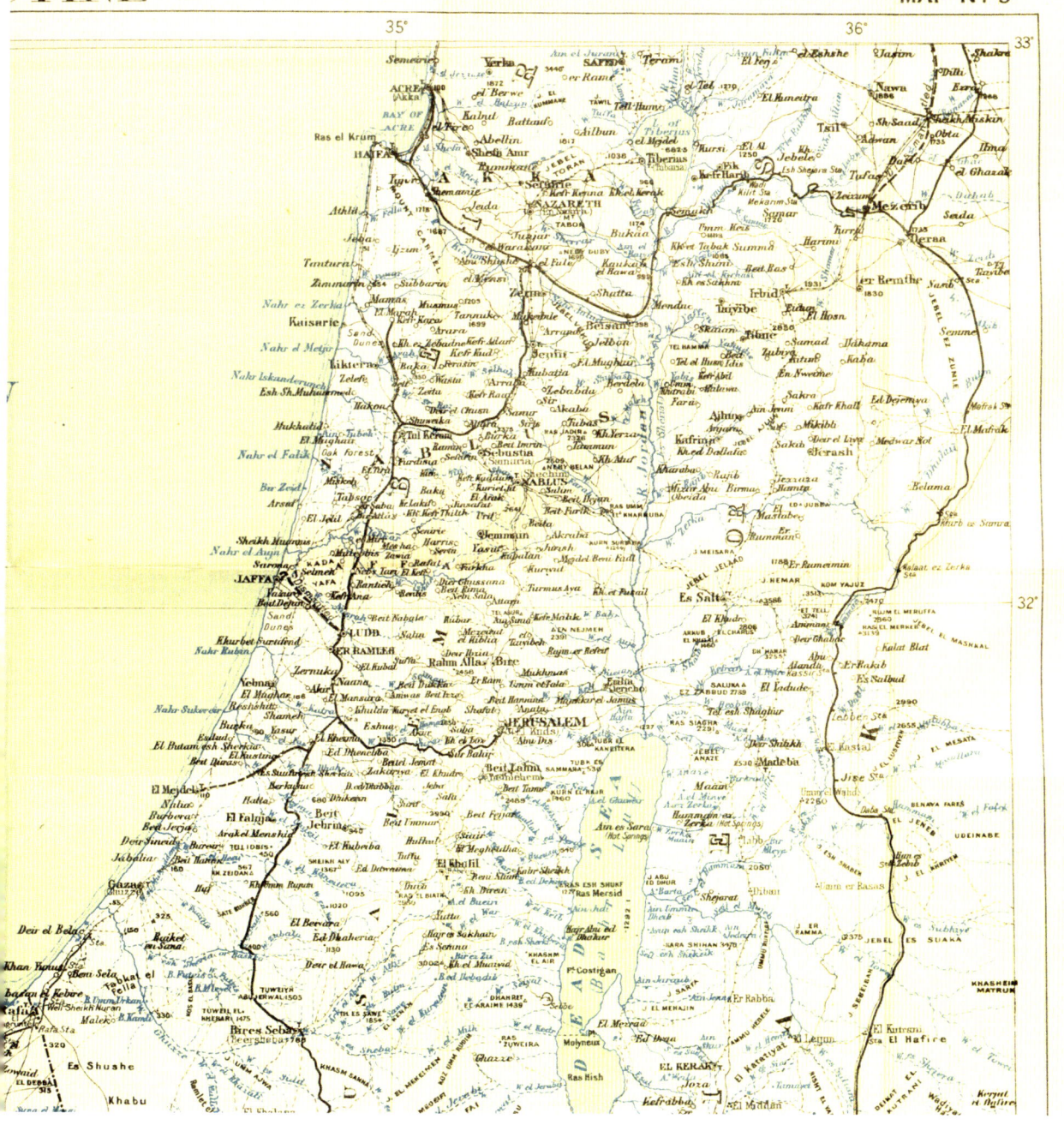

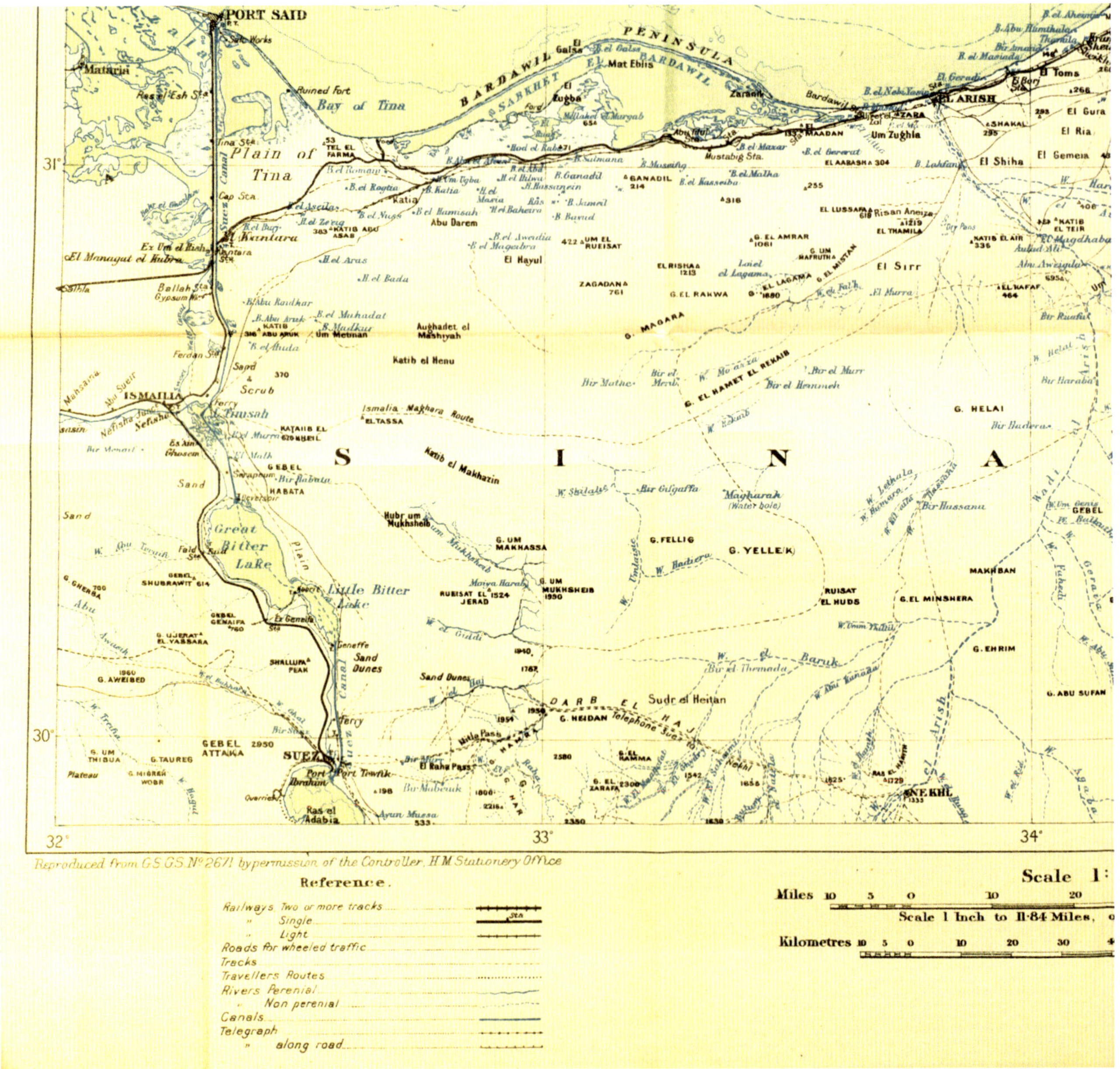
PORT SAID
Matarieh
Ras el Esh Sta.
Ruined Fort
Bay of Tina
BARDAWIL
PENINSULA
SABKHET EL BARDAWIL
Mat Eblis
Zaranik
EL ARISH
El Toms
El Gura
El Ria
El Gemeia
El Shiha
Um Zughla
Mustabig Sta.
Plain of Tina
Tina Sta.
TEL EL FARMA
Katia
Cap Sta.
Kantara
El Managat el Kubra
Abu Darem
El Hayul
ZAGADAN
Ballah Sta.
Gypsum Wks
Ferdan Sta.
Sand & Scrub
ISMAILIA
L. Timsah
Katib el Henu
Aughadet el Mashiyah
Um Metnan
Ismalia Maghara Route
G. MAGARA
G. EL HAMET EL REKAIB
G. HELAI
El Sirr
G. EL LAGAMA
G. EL RAKWA
S I N A I
Katib el Makhazin
Hubr um Mukhsheib
G. UM MAKHASSA
GEBEL HABATA
Serapeum
Great Bitter Lake
Little Bitter Lake
Maghara (Water hole)
G. FELLIG
G. YELLEK
RUISAT EL HUDS
G. EL MINSHERA
MAKHBAN
G. EHRIM
G. ABU SUFAN
Sand Dunes
Geneffe
SHALLUFA PEAK
G. AWEIBED
Sudr el Heitan
DARB EL HAJ
G. HEIDAN
Telephone Suez to Nekhl
Mitla Pass
El Raha Pass
GEBEL ATTAKA
SUEZ
Port Tewfik
Port Ibrahim
Ras el Adabia
Ayun Musa
NEKHL
Wadi el Arish
Suez Canal
31°
30°
32°
33°
34°
Reproduced from G.S.G.S. No 2671 by permission of the Controller, H.M. Stationery Office
Reference.
Railways, Two or more tracks
Single
Light
Roads for wheeled traffic
Tracks
Travellers Routes
Rivers Perenial
Non perenial
Canals
Telegraph
along road
Scale 1:
Miles 10 5 0 10 20
Scale 1 Inch to 11·84 Miles
Kilometres 10 5 0 10 20 30

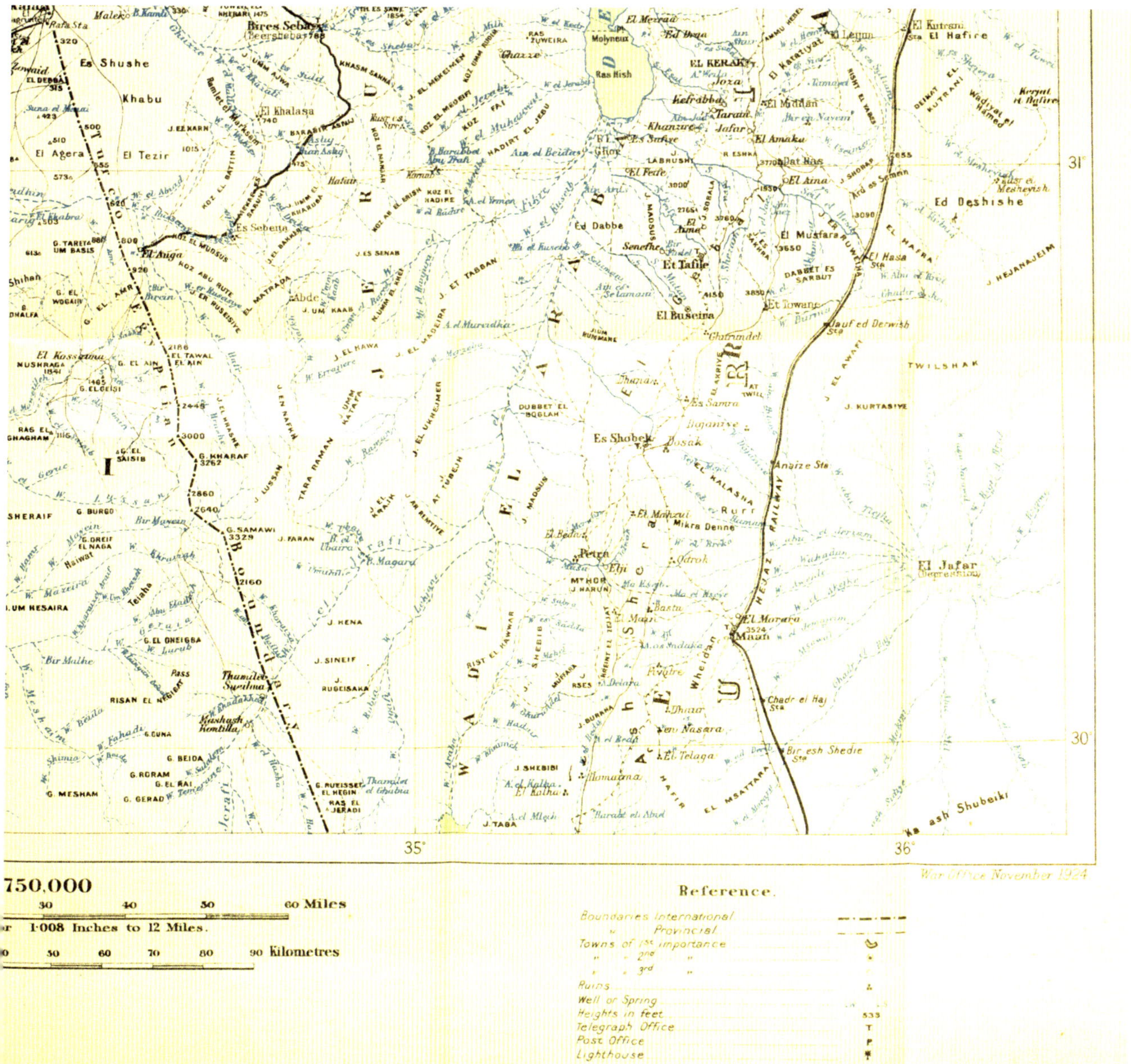
Bir es Seba
El Khalasa
Es Shushe
Khabu
El Agera
El Tezir
El Auja
Es Sebeita
Abde
Ras Hish
Molyneux
El Mezraa
EL KERAK
Kefrabba
Taraun
Jafar
El Amaka
Dat Ras
El Aina
Ed Deshishe
Ed Dabbe
Senefhe
Et Tafile
El Buseira
El Musfara
El Hasa Sta
Et Towane
Jauf ed Derwish Sta
El Kutrani Sta
El Hafire
El Lejjun
TWILSHAK
J. KURTASIYE
Es Shobek
Anaize Sta
Mikra Denne
Petra
Elji
J. HARUN
El Jafar
El Marara
Maan
HEJAZ RAILWAY
Chadr el Haj Sta
Bir esh Shedie Sta
EL MSATTARA
Ra ash Shubeiki
J. TABA
G. SAMAWI 3329
G. KHARAF 3262
RISAN EL NEGIEB
G. MESHAM
G. BEIDA
G. RORAM
G. GERAD
G. EL RAI
Kushash Kontilla
Thamilet Sudma
J. SINEIF
J. HENA
31°
30°
35°
36°
750,000
30 40 50 60 Miles
1·008 Inches to 12 Miles.
50 60 70 80 90 Kilometres
War Office November 1924
Reference.
Boundaries International
Provincial
Towns of 1st importance
2nd
3rd
Ruins
Well or Spring
Heights in feet
533
Telegraph Office
T
Post Office
P
Lighthouse

HISTORY OF THE MANCHESTER REGIMENT

(FORMERLY 63RD AND 96TH)

CHAPTER XVI

THE 1st BATTALION IN THE SOUTH AFRICAN WAR
1883–1900
SIEGE OF LADYSMITH

ON the 11th August 1883 the headquarters and left wing of the 1st Battalion Manchester Regiment returned to Warley from the Tower of London,

1883 leaving two companies at Gravesend and two more at Colchester, but these all returned to Warley before the end of September. It was not long, however, before a move was made, and in April 1884 the

1884 battalion, for the second time since its arrival in England, was stationed at the Tower, where on the 19th July it was inspected by H.R.H. the Duke of Cambridge, prior to its transfer to Shorncliffe camp on the 28th of the following month.

The battalion remained the greater part of two years at Shorncliffe, where on the 1st January 1886 the strength was 599 warrant, non-commis-

1886 sioned officers, and men out of an establishment of 658; but by an Army Circular of the 1st June the establishment was augmented to 24 officers, 2 warrant officers, 40 sergeants, 40 corporals, 16 drummers, and 710 privates.

In October of this year the First Battalion was moved to Aldershot, taking up its quarters in the East Infantry Barracks, and on the 9th July

1887 formed part of a body of some 56,000 men which was reviewed by Her Majesty at Aldershot in celebration of the fiftieth year of her reign. On the same occasion the battalion furnished a Guard of Honour on Her Majesty's arrival at the Royal Pavilion, as well as the Royal Guard, consisting of 1 captain, 1 subaltern, 1 sergeant, 1 corporal, and 24 privates, mounted at the Pavilion during Her Majesty's stay.

On the 4th April 1888 the battalion left Aldershot for Portsmouth by train and embarked in H.M.S. *Assistance* for conveyance to Ireland; it disembarked at Queenstown on the 9th and went by rail to Tipperary, there to be stationed, providing a detachment of one company at Clonmel. The marching in state was 17 officers, 35 warrant officers, staff-sergeants, and sergeants, 31 corporals, 13 drummers, 548 privates, 38 women and 48 children.

The stay of the battalion at Tipperary was an unusually long one, extending to close upon three years, for it was not until the 5th February 1891 that the headquarters moved to Kinsale, sending two companies to Fort Camden. At this new station also the battalion was quartered for nearly as long a period, not leaving Kinsale until the 31st October 1894, when it was sent by train to Queenstown and there embarked in the hired transport *Warwick Castle*, but owing to the very heavy gale that was raging the vessel was not able to leave port until very early on the 1st November. Liverpool was reached the next morning, and from here the battalion proceeded by train to Fulwood Barracks, Preston, sending one company to Castletown in the Isle of Man.

In November 1895 a change of station saw the battalion at Aldershot, occupying Barrosa Barracks, Stanhope Lines, South Camp; and after two years in this command the battalion moved still further afield, being sent on the 17th November 1897 to Southampton, where it embarked in the hired transport *Nubia* for conveyance to Gibraltar. The embarking strength was 19 officers and 568 other ranks.

Gibraltar was reached on the 22nd, and, disembarking, the battalion took over the Grand Casemate Barracks, where the strength was almost immediately increased by the arrival of upwards of 200 young soldiers whom the 2nd Battalion had dropped at Malta on its way home from India.

The First Battalion Manchester Regiment had been stationed at " the Rock " for rather less than two years when the long-standing disagreement between the British and the Transvaal Governments led, first to a condition of intense tension, and finally to the outbreak of war. The Transvaal Government had preferred a claim which had been definitely refused by the British Cabinet in September 1899, to be considered as a Sovereign State, and in consequence of this refusal had incontinently rejected all the counter-proposals which the British Government had earlier put forward. The Cabinet now seemed to realise that hostilities were not impossible and that our garrisons in South Africa

DRUMMERS, 1ST BATTALION, LIMERICK, 1893.

were perilously depleted in face of the warlike attitude of the Transvaal and the uncertainty as to the views of her sister State. Reinforcements, none too many, were therefore sent to South Africa from Europe and 5,000 British troops were ordered from India to Natal: these all reached their destinations before the end of September.

That month had no sooner closed than the Orange Free State made it clear that in the event of war its assistance would be whole-heartedly afforded to the Transvaal; on the 9th October a Proclamation was issued in England calling out the Army Reserve; and on the same day the President of the Transvaal Republic presented an ultimatum to our representative requiring an answer within forty-eight hours. Her Majesty's Government refused so much as to discuss this ultimatum, and on the 11th October the sister Republics declared war against Great Britain and sent their forces across our border from north and west.

Two infantry battalions only had left their British garrisons while negotiations were still in progress and before any mobilisation order had been issued; these were the 1st Battalion Manchester Regiment and the 1st Battalion Royal Munster Fusiliers, the one from Gibraltar, the other from Fermoy, intended for Natal and Cape Colony respectively.

On the 5th August 1899 a telegram was received at Gibraltar from the War Office containing instructions that the 1st Battalion Manchester Regiment was to be held in readiness to proceed to the Cape at an early date. The work of preparation was at once commenced, and in accordance with orders later received, the battalion embarked in the Union Castle steamship *Goth* on the 23rd August—strength 23 officers, 1 warrant officer, and 954 non-commissioned officers and men. The following are the names of those officers who sailed with the "First Manchesters" to South Africa: Lieutenant-Colonel Curran, Majors Simpson and Watson, Captains Melvill, Vizard, Marden, Bridgford, Menzies, and Newbigging (adjutant), Lieutenants Tillard, Crichton, Danks, Hardcastle, Hunt-Grubbe, Dunlop, and Roe, Second Lieutenants Coghill, Deakin, H. Fisher, Creagh, E. Fisher, and Eddowes, Lieutenant and Quartermaster Bankes—the three last-named having come out in the *Goth* from Southampton.

The ship touched on the 26th at Teneriffe and arrived off Cape Town on the 15th September, anchoring in Table Bay and entering the harbour early next morning. About midday the battalion landed and marched to the Grand Parade for inspection by General Sir F. Forestier Walker, commanding the troops in Cape Colony. But instructions coming to hand that the battalion was to go on to Natal, it was re-embarked and the *Goth* left at 12 noon on the 17th for Durban, arriving there on the 20th, when the battalion, having landed, proceeded in three trains to Pietermaritzburg, and there took over quarters in Fort Napier from the Royal Dublin Fusiliers.

The next three weeks were fully occupied in drawing equipment and clothing and stores of all kinds; a mounted infantry company was detailed under Captain Bridgford, with Lieutenants Crichton and Creagh as his subalterns, and horses, many of them practically unbroken, had to be drawn and trained. Lieutenant Dunlop was appointed transport officer, while Lieutenant Hunt-Grubbe assumed charge of the Maxim gun.

On the 7th October Lieutenant-General Sir George White, who had been detailed to command the troops in Natal, landed at Durban, and by this date the worst of the crisis was over, since the greater part of the force ordered from India had arrived, while the remainder was close behind. It was no easy matter to protect Natal from the invasion by which on almost every side it was threatened, and Sir George, seeing the impossibility of holding all Natal up to Newcastle, resolved to concentrate his whole force upon Ladysmith and abandon to the enemy all Natal north of the Biggarsberg.

Instructions that the 1st Battalion Manchester Regiment would proceed by march-route to Ladysmith had been issued on the 5th October, and on the morning of the 9th the tents being sent on by train, the battalion started on the first stage of its march—to Howick, a distance of 16 miles, uphill all the way and the heat very great. The Mounted Infantry Company followed the battalion later, and 2nd Lieutenant Coghill remained behind at Pietermaritzburg in charge of some 80 sick and other details.

On the 10th the journey was continued to Dargle Road, a short march of no more than 7 miles, but a very unpleasant one, a dust-storm raging all the time, changing to rain just as camp was reached. That night the Commanding Officer received a telegram informing him that as the battalion was urgently needed in Ladysmith it would be necessary to entrain for that place as soon as the required rolling stock could be made available, leaving the mounted infantry and transport to come on by road. About 2 a.m. on the 11th two troop trains arrived at Dargle Road and the battalion entrained by half-battalions at short intervals. The journey was a very cold one, the men being accommodated in open cattle-trucks, and the line attaining an altitude of between 4,000 and 5,000 feet above sea-level about Mooi River. Ladysmith was reached at 10.30 a.m. this day and the battalion marched to the Hutments, spending the night in bivouac.

On the 12th Captain Paton joined headquarters from England. In the course of the morning the tents came up and camp was pitched, and later official information was received that a state of war existed as from 5 p.m. the previous day, with the result that two companies of the battalion were detailed for outpost duty for the first time during the campaign.

At 8 o'clock that evening commanding officers were informed by Major-General Hunter, chief of the staff to Sir George White, that a large force of Transvaalers was within striking distance of Laing's Nek, and that two enemy columns from the Free State had entered Natal by Van Reenan's and Tintwa Passes, while the patrols of the Natal Carabiniers reported that the Free Staters were steadily advancing in considerable numbers. Accordingly Sir George White decided to move out at once to check this advance, but having proceeded some nine miles with the greater part of his Ladysmith troops without seeing the enemy, who was still at some distance, the whole force returned to camp, which was reached about 4 p.m. on the 13th.

On the following day it was given out that the 1st Battalion Manchester Regiment, with the 1st Battalion Devonshire Regiment, the 2nd Battalion Gordon Highlanders and the 2nd Battalion Rifle Brigade—this last not yet arrived from Crete—was to form the 7th Brigade of the 4th Division. The Divisional Commander was General Lyttelton, and the Brigadier was, later, Brigadier-General Kitchener, but pending his arrival the command of the 7th Brigade was assumed by Colonel Ian Hamilton, who remained in command until the beginning of March 1900.

The Mounted Infantry Company of the battalion arrived on the 17th at Ladysmith, and during the next two days the battalion was engaged in practising the attack over the ground near camp and in taking up a less extended position for the defence of the town.

On the 20th the Boers, making a sudden dash to the south, captured the railway station at Elandslaagte, seizing a supply train which was on its way to the advanced British force at Glencoe under General Symons; but much about the same time news coming in of a British success in the north at Talana, the purely partial success of which was not at the moment understood, Sir George White determined to attack those Boers at Elandslaagte, who appeared to be in some danger between the main force at Ladysmith and General Symons' victorious troops at Glencoe. Early on the 21st, therefore, Major-General French, who had only reached Ladysmith the previous day, moved out against Elandslaagte with 5 squadrons Imperial Light Horse and the Natal Field Artillery, followed a couple of hours later by the headquarter wing of the First Manchesters, some R.E. and Railway Detachments. The companies detailed were C, D, F, and G, the officers being Lieutenant-Colonel Curran, Major Watson, Captains Melvill, Marden, Paton, and Newbigging (adjutant), Lieutenants Danks,

Hardcastle, Deakin, Fisher, with Lieutenant Hunt-Grubbe in charge of the Maxim, the " other ranks " numbering 330.

D Company was in the armoured train which led the way up the line, the other three companies following in a train composed of open cattle-trucks. Modderspruit was reached, and here the Boer artillery, having out-ranged and out-shot the Natal 7-pounders, turned their fire on to the detraining infantry ; but the practice, though excellent, was not particularly effective, and no casualties were here sustained by the battalion. Orders were now given to retire a short distance and await reinforcements for which General French had asked from Ladysmith. The battalion accordingly occupied some slightly rising ground covering Modderspruit station.

Reinforcements gradually came up and it was nearly 3 p.m. before the following had joined General French's little force : 1 squadron 5th Dragoon Guards, 2 squadrons 5th Lancers, the 21st and 42nd Batteries R.F.A., 7 companies of the Devonshire Regiment, and 5 companies of the Gordon Highlanders. The force now advanced about a mile up the line, the infantry in their trains keeping level with the mounted troops whose patrols were gradually clearing the ridges on the right.

The infantry, under Colonel Hamilton, now detrained and formed a line of quarter-columns, the Devons on the right, Gordons in the centre, and the Manchesters on the left ; the objective was pointed out and the advance commenced, the four companies of the Manchesters leading, the Devons being in support, and the Gordons in reserve. The advance had not made much progress when Lieutenant-Colonel Curran was ordered to take his men to the high ground on his right, making a flank attack on the Boer left, while the other two battalions made the frontal attack. But later these orders were cancelled and the Manchesters, supported by the Gordons, were directed to carry out the main attack on the enemy left, while the Devons held him in front.

The battalion covered a front of some 600 yards, the firing line being composed of C and D companies with F and G in support ; the scouts, under Lieutenant Deakin, were some 400 yards in front.

To the S. and S.W. of Elandslaagte the open veldt is broken by three spurs jutting out to within about 2,000 yards of the railway line from the high ground running roughly parallel to it ; this high ground falls away very gently to the S. and S.E. The eastern spur is considerably higher and more clearly defined than either of the other two, and formed the main Boer position ; it consisted of a long, steep, broad-topped kopje, joined at its northern end by a nek to a slightly lower round kopje. Close to this nek and on the east side of it, there rises a steep conical hill, and in the hollow thus formed lay the Boer laager. The crest of the main kopje is about 350 feet above the level of the surrounding veldt, and close to its northern end the Boers had placed their guns. The whole of this group of stony hills was strewn with large rocks and loose stones providing excellent cover, and in fact the whole position was one of great natural strength and was in every way suitable to the force defending it.

As the firing line of the Manchesters crossed the crest of the most westerly of the three spurs a party of mounted Boers was seen retiring about 3,000 yards to the right; these had evidently been outflanked by British cavalry some distance further south. As the support line came on to the skyline the Boer guns opened fire, and the half-battalion was ordered to halt until our guns could better support the infantry, who were now exchanging shots at 1,700 yards with their admirably concealed enemy.

The 21st Field Battery galloped up and came into action on the left of the Manchester line, and soon had the range of the Boer guns, which were not, however, silenced until the 42nd Battery also opened on the left of the 21st. The British guns now turned their fire on to the Boer riflemen on the right front, causing these hurriedly to retire on their main position.

The infantry was then ordered to move forward to the high ground to the right front, and then "to push on and carry the position at all costs." The halt in the open had lasted some seventeen minutes and four men had been hit. It was now 4.15 p.m.

As the advance began again a heavy storm of rain, thunder, and lightning broke over the attackers, who were soon all drenched to the skin. As C and D companies pushed on they came under a heavy long-range rifle fire and casualties began to occur, so the two supporting companies commenced to reinforce the firing line, which now halted and opened independent fire. The further advance was by short rushes, the "going" being very bad over rough ground, with, however, good cover.

About half-way down the slope of the central spur a high barbed wire fence was met with; this had evidently been carefully ranged on by the Boers, but the officers cut pathways through it with the wire cutters with which they had been provided. It was after passing through this fence that Captain Paton was hit.

The Gordon Highlanders now advancing somewhat obliquely from the right rear, the two regiments got much intermixed and the front became somewhat contracted. The advance had been rapid and the ground difficult and the men were much out of breath, but they were not to be held back; the rushes became sharper and the independent fire heavier while our shrapnel was bursting continuously along the crest in front, and single Boers could be seen leaving their position and hurrying away to the rear.

The casualties in the Manchester companies were increasing, and it was during the ascent of the final slope that Lieutenant-Colonel Curran and Captain Melvill were both hit. Bayonets were now fixed, the charge was sounded and taken up by the pipers of the Highlanders, and with loud and prolonged cheering the infantry swept over the crest and into the position, where the more determined of the defenders made a last stand and many were captured or shot down. Two Boer guns came into view on the left front and Captain Newbigging and Lieutenant H. Fisher were the first to reach them.

For the moment it seemed that all opposition was at an end, and the " cease fire " was sounded by order of the Brigadier, who had detected the raising of a white flag in the enemy camp. The call was repeated along the line and an order was passed " Cease fire and give the cavalry a chance." The cessation of fire, however, had the sole effect of causing the Boers occupying the conical hill behind the camp to open a heavy fire on the British infantry, while others of the enemy, who had remained under cover on the reverse slope of the main position, now rushed up and fired at point-blank range. For a moment the line wavered and fell back, but rallying at once, the men charged forward again, the lost ground was recovered, and the line advanced down to the laager in the hollow below.

The Devons now came up the northern slope of the main ridge.

The time was 5.40 and it was getting dark; those of the enemy who had not surrendered retired on their ponies towards the Newcastle road, where they were intercepted and repeatedly charged by the squadron of the 5th Dragoon Guards and one of the 5th Lancers.

The action was over, the victory complete; the Boers lost 67 men killed, 108 wounded, and 188 prisoners, their guns and their camp equipment. The casualties among the British amounted to 263 of all ranks killed and wounded, the losses in the First Battalion Manchester Regiment being:

Killed or died of wounds: Lieutenant Danks, Lance-Corporals Delaney and Poyser, Privates Butler, Dewhurst, Harper, Heath, Major, Murphy, Newton, Robinson, Stevenson, Taylor, and Williams.

Wounded: Lieutenant-Colonel Curran, Captains Melvill, Newbigging, and Paton, Sergeant Woods, Lance-Corporal Pimm, Privates Anchor, Bradshaw, Brown, Burke, Chapman, Crawford, Dainty, Davies, Evans, Fenton, Flanagan, Hall, Hemingway, Houston, Jones, Lugood, McCarthy, Mellor, Moran, Pegg, Rogers, Sillifont, and Vayro.

During that night the four companies of the battalion occupied the Boer position, the other two infantry regiments bivouacking in the laager.

Sir George White had no intention of holding the ground that had been won, since it had no strategical or tactical importance, while in view of the presence of strong hostile forces it was necessary to concentrate rather than detach. General French was therefore instructed to withdraw his force to Ladysmith, and on the morning of the 22nd the retirement began, the Manchesters, escorting 40 prisoners, being the last to leave by train at 3.20 p.m., while the 5th Dragoon Guards formed the rear-guard by road.

Captain Marden was appointed to act as adjutant *vice* Captain Newbigging, wounded ; on the 22nd October another officer joined from home in the person of Second Lieutenant Merriman.

Early on the 25th a wing of the battalion marched out to Modderspruit to help in Colonel Yule's column retiring from Dundee ; the wing bivouacked at Modderspruit and next day provided the rear-guard to the retreating column.

General French took out a brigade of cavalry on the 27th from Ladysmith and scouted along the Newcastle and Helpmakaar roads, establishing the numbers and general dispositions of the enemy, while some little time later Colonel Hamilton marched out to the Neks between Gun Hill, Lombard's Kop, and Umbulwana with five infantry battalions and four batteries Royal Field Artillery. The 1st battalion Manchesters furnished the advanced guard and the escort for the guns, and the whole force, deploying in support of the cavalry reconnaissance, caused the enemy to disclose 15 guns and 10,000 men in expectation of attack, when Sir George White, having obtained the information he wanted, ordered his force to withdraw, and the whole returned to camp next morning.

On the 30th October General Sir George White decided to assume the offensive and attempt the capture of Long Hill and Pepworth Hill, the resulting action being that known as Lombard's Kop. He made use of all his available troops, sending two battalions with a mountain battery to cover his left flank, seize and hold Nicholson's Nek, and there intercept the enemy when they should fall back. His cavalry was to reach the neighbourhood of Gun Hill before dawn and cover the right ; while the main attack upon, first Long Hill, and secondly Pepworth Hill, was to be carried out by the five battalions and four batteries of the 8th Brigade, supported by the four battalions of the 7th Brigade with the remainder of the mounted men and a brigade division of artillery.

What happened to the Nicholson's Nek party is a matter of history, and was one of the first of the " regrettable incidents " of the war.

The First Battalion Manchester Regiment, less half a company remaining on outpost under Second Lieutenant Eddowes, left its camp at 3 a.m. and already *en route* to the place of brigade-rendezvous met several stragglers from the Nicholson's Nek party, whose stories made it clear that all was not well. Limit Hill, the rendezvous, was reached before dawn, and shortly after the artillery opened fire. As the day brightened the left party could be seen heavily engaged three or four miles away, and the battalion was ordered to move off to its assistance, but, fortunately perhaps for the battalion, this order was almost at once cancelled, and the Manchesters were moved to the right flank, divided into half-battalions, and told off as escort to the guns.

The right wing under Major Watson was then sent off about a mile and a half to the right and occupied successive ridges below Lombard's Kop, and was later directed by General French to line a ridge in the front to cover his cavalry which was massed in a hollow in rear. Here this wing seems to have remained until about 1 p.m., when, being the most advanced of all the troops and somewhat isolated, Major Watson was ordered to fall back, which was done by successive companies from the left over very rough ground and under shell fire.

In the meantime the left half-battalion, commanded by Major Simpson, had accompanied the artillery into the open and sustained most of the casualties that day suffered by the battalion.

The retirement now began, successfully covered by the fire of the naval guns which had only that morning arrived in Ladysmith from Natal, and by about 3 p.m. the whole force was back in camp.

The casualties in the battalion this day were : *died of wounds*, Private Coulter ; *wounded*, Lance-Corporal Lewis, Privates Archer, Brown, Nicholls, and Wilson.

The events of the 30th October had caused General Sir George White to decide to make of his troops a garrison for the defence of Ladysmith, holding the shortest line of kopjes round the town which gave the best field of fire and kept the enemy's artillery at a reasonable distance. The perimeter was divided into four sections, known as A, B, C, and D, under command of Colonel Knox, Major-General Howard, Colonel Hamilton, and Colonel Royston respectively.

Section A extended from Devonshire Post on the northern edge of the Ladysmith plain to Cove Redoubt, some three miles to the west, and was held by the Devons and portions of the Liverpool and Gloucester Regiments and 1st Battalion King's Royal Rifles.

Section B was manned by the Leicesters, two battalions Royal Rifles and Rifle Brigade, and extended from Leicester Post to Range Post on the right bank of the Klip River.

Section C was the longest and most weakly held of all, being continued S.E. from Range Post up to Cæsar's Camp, the latter held by the Manchesters, and the other points by half the Gordons and the two surviving companies of the Royal Irish Fusiliers.

Section D from Cæsar's Camp to Devonshire Post was picqueted and patrolled by the Natal Volunteers.

The total length of the perimeter was nearly 14 miles and the force available for its defence, including the reserve, amounted to over 13,000 men.

The battalion moved on the 31st October to the position assigned to it on Cæsar's Camp, and for the next few days was very busily engaged in clearing the ground, building sangars and other defences, in improving the water supply, and in laying in stores of all kinds.

On the 2nd November the battalion was under shell fire more or less all day, a cross fire from the south shoulder of Umbulwana and from another high hill to the south-west, and in consequence the camp was shifted to a more sheltered spot. On this day Lieutenant-Colonel Curran, who had been wounded on the day of Elandslaagte, rejoined the battalion from hospital, receiving a great reception from all ranks.

On the next day Private Harries of the battalion was wounded in an action in which some companies of the Manchesters supported a mounted column which went out towards Lancers' Nek.

The tactics of the enemy now became bolder and their infantry seemed on occasion inclined to advance against the outlying positions of the camp under cover of their artillery, and on the 7th some Boers appeared to the south and south-east, engaging at long range the picquets of the battalion. Later the enemy worked round from east to west and to the number of some 800 massed on Middle Hill, threatening the right flank. Captain Menzies accordingly pushed out with H Company to Wagon Hill and checked any further advance. On this day Second Lieutenant Eddowes, Privates Barrett and Gee were wounded.

There was considerable shelling by the enemy again on the 8th, in the course of which Private D'Arcy was severely wounded by shrapnel, and it was evident that the Boers were contemplating a more serious attack. Early on the morning of the 9th they started a heavy bombardment from four sides, and then made a sudden attack on the left of the position held by the battalion, galloping into the low ground and engaging No. 2 Picquet, furnished by half C Company under Major Watson. The enemy also pushed west up the valley, engaging No. 1 Picquet provided by the other half of the company under Lieutenant H. Fisher, who at 11.45 signalled for reinforcements.

The garrison of No. 3 Sangar—part of G Company under Second Lieutenant Merriman—proceeded to reinforce, its place being taken by half D Company, the other half also reinforcing the firing line.

The firing at this time, both from guns and small-arms, was very heavy, but the 42nd Battery R.F.A. now coming into action the enemy's fire was to some extent checked, while A Company of the battalion under Captain Vizard had been pushed under cover well round the left and supported the left front with a party under Second Lieutenant E. Fisher.

Firing continued fairly severe all day, but after dark the advanced companies were drawn in, and the dead and wounded collected. It was only now that Lieutenant H. Fisher reported himself as wounded; it appeared he had been hit about 11 a.m., but had remained all day under fire with his men. The Boers were noticed all the night through searching for their dead with lanterns.

The casualties in the battalion were : *Killed or died of wounds :* Lance-Corporal Whitehead, Privates Jackson, Butterworth, and McCabe. *Wounded:* Lieutenant H. Fisher, Second Lieutenant Merriman, Sergeant Danvers, Drummer Higgins, Privates Fitton, Forshaw, Harper, Harris, Hughes, Josephs, Leach, McCarthy, Marsland, Quinliven, Stewart, Townhill, and Yates.

The following message reached the battalion in the evening from the Brigadier : " Deeply regret so many hit ; I have informed Chief how excellently well your regiment behaved under trying circumstances."

For some days after this affair the enemy was comparatively quiet, though spasmodic shelling and sniping continued, and on the 27th November three of the battalion—Sergeant Chandler, Privates Tumelty and Whitehead—were wounded, while three weeks later—on the 18th December—Privates Dance and Abbott were wounded by pom-pom fire, the last-named mortally. On the 20th Private Evans was hit.

And so the long siege of the little town went on, the defenders being nowhere safe from enemy fire, and the picquet duty being heavy, while the scanty news that filtered through from the outside, of the efforts being made for relief by the forces under General Sir Redvers Buller, was of a very contradictory and not especially cheering character.

On the 6th January 1900 another and a very much more serious attack was made upon the defences of Cæsar's Camp. At 3 a.m. heavy firing opened against Wagon Hill, and three-quarters of an hour later very severe gunfire developed against the south-east corner of Cæsar's Camp, where was C Company with A in support. Here the losses were exceptionally heavy, nearly all the men in the left section and the adjacent groups being killed within the first half-hour. It appears that the Boers had crept up during the darkness round the left flank, between the Manchesters and the Natal Police, coming up a gully on to the crest line, when challenged passing themselves off as the " Town Guard," and then shooting down the British from behind.

They succeeded in getting into the sangars on the left, where they remained until 5.30 p.m.; they were also for some time among the rocks near the east crest until ejected by a bayonet charge by a company of the Gordons; and Lieutenant Hunt-Grubbe, who was moving about inside our picquet line trying to find out the facts of the situation, was captured by the Boers and held prisoner for nearly three hours. These Boers were finally turned out by the well-directed fire of the guns of the 53rd Battery.

A very hot rifle fire was maintained all day, and the serious nature of the situation may be gauged by the fact that at 5 a.m. the Manchesters were reinforced by one company of Highlanders, at 11.30 by four more, and later again by six companies of the Rifle Brigade; and that of these by the evening only one company was left in reserve. On Cæsar's Camp, where Colonel Curran was in command, there were the 1st Battalion Manchester Regiment and its Mounted Infantry Company, five companies of the Gordons, six of the Rifle Brigade, and the Mounted Infantry Company of the Liverpool Regiment. The shelling by the enemy was not so severe as on previous occasions, so far as regards the actual number of shells and weight of metal fired, but this attack stood out pre-eminent for the strength and determination of the enemy and the heat and accuracy of his rifle fire.

The battalion had 34 men killed and 40 wounded: the names of the casualties are as follows: *Killed or died of wounds:* Colour-Sergeant Johnson, Sergeants Connor, Williams, and Woods, Lance-Sergeant Walsh, Lance-Corporals Butterworth, Granger, and Leach, Privates Ashley, Bartley, Bird, Bostock, Bradshaw, Broadwater, Brownhill, Cheatham, Cluer, Dalby, Davenport, Farmer, Frampton, Gee, Green, Guttery, Hanley, Hartley, Kelly, Lindsay, Loftus, Longbottom, Milton, Murphy, Parker, and Porle. *Wounded:* Major Simpson, Captains Marden and Menzies, Second Lieutenant E. Fisher, Band Sergeant Waddington, Sergeant Wilkinson, Corporals Bramwell and Crouch, Lance-Corporals McDowell, James, Kennett, and Lacey, Privates Beattie, Bentley, Bond, Bowers, A. Brown, J. Brown, Castle, Coalin, Gibbon, Glyn, Gough, Green, Gregory, Hancey, Harrison, Jagger, Jones, Kane, Kelly, Maloney, Ogden, Parker, Pownall, Scott, Snelling, Tetlow, Urquhart, and Vanryne.

The following letter was received on the 8th January from the Brigadier:

"The Officer Commanding 7th Brigade wishes to convey to all ranks of the Manchester Regiment his admiration of the courage and determination displayed by them in the action of the 6th January 1900, the casualty list testifies to the severity of the fighting, and the fact that all the positions were maintained shows how complete was the victory.

"The Brigadier is proud to have been so long associated with the Battalion which has invariably come to the front when called upon to show the enemy and the world at large how stubbornly an Englishman can fight."

It was to this stubborn fight on Cæsar's Camp that Sir George White made allusion when entertained at Cape Town prior to his departure for England; speaking of the Boer attack of the 6th January 1900, he said:

"During the attack on Cæsar's Camp a remote corner was held by sixteen of the Manchester Regiment who fought from three in the morning until dusk, when the Devonshires reinforced them. Fourteen of the little band lay dead and of the two survivors one was wounded—but they still held their position."

The men of the Manchester Regiment were occupied during the next day or two in burying their dead; there was a general quiet, though spasmodic shelling by the Boers still went on, while in the distance could be heard the guns of General Buller's force which was trying to fight its way to Ladysmith, and occasionally the bursting of their shells could be seen from the high ground outside Ladysmith.

A stray copy of the *Standard and Digger's News* came through to the besieged town, and from its columns the battalion learnt that the Boers admitted only 17 casualties on the 6th January, while the Manchester Regiment was reported as having had a thousand men killed and wounded!

Sunday the 28th January a bread ration was for the last time issued and the besieged were placed on a reduced scale of rations; the weather turned very wet; and the news of the attacks at Potgieter's Drift and Spion Kop was not of an especially cheering character.

Sniping and shelling continued, but there were few casualties; news came through on the 13th February that Lord Roberts had entered the Free State; in the besieged town the price of luxuries rose to fabulous heights—a packet of American cigarettes, usually threepence, cost £1 5s., a tin of Capstan tobacco was three guineas, a pot of jam cost three-and-twenty shillings, eggs were £2 8s. a dozen and not easy to come by, while matches cost more than one shilling a box.

SOUTH AFRICAN WAR MEMORIAL, (1899-1902), ST. ANN'S SQUARE, MANCHESTER.
Erected by the City.

1ST BATTALION MEMORIAL, ERECTED ON CÆSAR'S CAMP, LADYSMITH, NATAL, IN MEMORY OF THOSE FALLEN IN THE DEFENCE OF THAT TOWN, 1899.

On the 17th February the garrison was cheered by the receipt of the tidings of the relief of Kimberley; next day it was seen that Buller's men had captured the hill Cingolo, and parties of Boers seemed to be trekking homewards from Buller's front; on the 23rd the small arms of the Relief Force could be heard in action, and on the 28th it was announced that on the day previous—Majuba Day—Lord Roberts had effected the surrender of Cronje and the whole of his force. Then on the evening of this ever-memorable day some mounted scouts were seen on a hill about two miles south of No. 5 Picquet and preparations were made to lay a gun on them, when it was realised that they were actually our own troopers, and something like an hour later three squadrons of Natal Carabiniers and Imperial Light Horse rode joyously in through Intombi and were enthusiastically received.

Huge Boer convoys could be seen at dusk trekking away on the Elandslaagte road beyond Gun Hill.

Early on the morning of the 1st March more British mounted troops came in, and later a column from the garrison composed of Gordons, Devons, and Liverpools, with all available mounted men and guns, marched out viâ Limit Hill to Pepworth to engage and harass the retiring Boers, but men and horses were too weak to go far afield. Bulwana, whence the town had so often and so heavily been shelled, was found to be deserted by the enemy.

The siege of Ladysmith was now practically at an end, and it may be well here to give some account of the position which the Manchester Regiment so long and so gallantly held, and of the methods of its successful defence. Cæsar's Camp Ridge, then, viewed in profile resembles the usual field fortification trace. At the Ladysmith side it is very steep and the top flat, but slopes gently towards the enemy. The front crest was edged mostly with mimosa trees about 20 feet in height, and the soil was very rocky though not much broken. Continuous lines of trench were therefore out of the question, and since large works drew fire and were moreover open to enfilade from three directions, small rifle pits were preferably dug and sangars erected, each some ten or twenty yards apart, accommodating three or more men each, and provided with head cover. Owing to the growth of bushes and grass these defences do not seem ever to have really been properly located by the Boers, who fired mainly at the stronger works on the rear crest and flanks, and which being very substantially built—stone-faced, 16 feet thick, with several feet of head cover and loopholed—were never seriously damaged.

Owing to this wise defence system the battalion suffered but very few casualties from the severe and continuous shelling, but the field of fire was rather interfered with by the high grass which grew on the exterior slope of the ridge, and which being required for grazing purposes was not allowed to be burnt down.

Cæsar's Camp was generally recognised as the key to Ladysmith, and the battalion was proud of having so long held it. In January the Brigadier offered to relieve the Manchesters by troops from easier and less exposed positions, but the offer was declined for reasons which will be appreciated.

At the end of the siege the battalion was badly off for boots and clothing, all ranks were weak from short rations, and practically everybody, officers and men, was suffering from dysentery or fever—or both.

On the 3rd March the battalion, with the remainder of the 7th Brigade, lined both sides of Lime Street to greet General Sir Redvers Buller and his troops who marched through the town. The day was very hot, and after two hours' marching and four hours of standing, the men, who were very weak, were greatly exhausted.

Captain and Adjutant Newbigging, who on his discharge from hospital on recovery from his wound had been attached to the M.I. of the relief force, now rejoined his battalion; Lieutenant-Colonel Curran went to a convalescent home and Lieutenants Hunt-Grubbe and Dunlop were admitted to hospital; and Colonel Knox assumed command of the 7th Brigade from Colonel Hamilton.

On the 9th March the battalion received an unexpected and unusual gift through the General Officer Commanding the Lines of Communication: it was a cheque for £7 which had been handed to the Under-Secretary for Native Affairs by N'geeda of Chief N'Dunge's tribe, who wished the money to be expended " especially for the benefit of the Manchesters who defended Ladysmith."

On the night of the 15th a Manchester Volunteer Service Company joined the battalion at Cæsar's Camp; it was composed of three officers—Captain Heywood, Lieutenants Howe and Darlington—and 112 non-commissioned officers and men, and was drawn from the 1st (Wigan), 2nd (Manchester), 3rd (Ashton-under-Lyne), and 4th (Manchester) Volunteer Battalions of the Manchester Regiment.

As soon as war seemed inevitable in 1899 many offers to raise companies and battalions of Volunteers for service in South Africa had been made to the authorities. These, however, were all declined on the grounds that there was no likelihood of Volunteers being needed until the Militia Reserve was exhausted. About the middle of December, however, the Government sanctioned volunteering for service abroad or embodiment at home of a limited number of militia battalions, with in addition the formation of a strong force of volunteers from the yeomanry and a contingent of carefully selected volunteers for service in South Africa. These last were to be formed as Service Companies of a strength of 114, including four officers, and were to be attached to Regular Battalions at the front to make up for those of their own companies which had been converted into mounted infantry.

By the end of April 1900 about sixty-eight Service Companies had reached South Africa, while during the course of the war some 16,500 Volunteers went to the front in such Companies.

The two months that followed the relief of Ladysmith were a time of comparative inaction for the Natal Army. The infantry of the Ladysmith garrison was sent to recruit at Arcadia, a few miles to the west of Ladysmith, and to Colenso, and to Arcadia the 1st Battalion of the Manchester Regiment proceeded on the 16th March, the 7th Brigade, now taken over from Colonel Knox by Brigadier-General Kitchener, being here concentrated. On the 11th May the battalion moved to a camp near Ladysmith and ten days later was joined by a large draft of men from the Militia Reserve—3 sergeants, 5 corporals, and 211 men.

CHAPTER XVII

THE 1st BATTALION IN THE SOUTH AFRICAN WAR

1900–1903

WHEN at last General Buller felt himself able to move northwards, he marched rapidly and with decision, sending forward Dundonald's cavalry and the 2nd Division. Dundee was occupied on May 15th and three days later the vanguard of the Natal Army was in Newcastle, the 4th and 5th Divisions slowly closing up in rear. Botha's Pass was captured on June 5th and Alleman's Nek on the 8th, after which the Boers evacuated Volksrust and Laing's Nek, Buller occupying the first-named place on the 12th June. In these operations the 4th Division and the Manchester Regiment in particular had no part, and when Buller's advance on Standerton commenced Lyttelton's division was left in charge of the lines of communication from Laing's Nek to Newcastle.

1900

So large a portion of Buller's forces had been left behind in Natal, tied down to the lines of communication, that the number of troops actually in the advance was comparatively small, and about the 20th July it becoming necessary to call up more men from the rearward services to assist to clear away some troublesome commandos at Graskop near the Natal border, three battalions of Lyttelton's Division and two companies of his mounted infantry were placed at the disposal of General Hildyard, commanding the 5th Division. The three battalions thus employed were the 1st Battalion King's Royal Rifles, the 1st Battalion Manchester Regiment, and the 2nd Battalion Gordon Highlanders.

For the past month the battalion had formed part of the Drakensberg Defence Force, with the 5th Lancers, 13th Hussars, two field batteries, and the Gloucester Regiment and Inniskilling Fusiliers, and more recently had been quartered about Elandslaagte and Junono's Kop; but on the night of the 19th July orders were received for the battalion to move north by rail next day. Proceeding by train viâ Charlestown the battalion—strength 20 officers and 868 other ranks—reached Zandspruit in the Transvaal early on the morning of the 21st July, and, marching thence some five miles, joined a composite force of the 7th and 8th Brigades under Major-

General Howard. The whole force to be employed was commanded by Lieutenant-General Hildyard, who had with him a column operating on his right under General Talbot Coke, and another on the left under General Brocklehurst, to which the Manchester Mounted Infantry Company under Captain Bridgford was attached.

At 8.30 a.m. on the 22nd the 7th Brigade under Howard moved out to attack the enemy in position on Graskop, the Rifles being in the front line, the Highlanders in support, while the Manchesters, with a half-battalion of the Leicester Regiment, formed a third line. In supporting the Gordons the battalion came under fire, but did not at this time experience any loss and the withdrawal began about 4 p.m., when Colonel Curran was directed to occupy a line of kopjes to the right front as an outpost line. In moving to this position the battalion—three companies in front and three in support —came under a sharp musketry fire and had two men hit, Private Holland, a militia reservist, being mortally wounded, dying the same night, and Private Brown (No. 4100) severely wounded.

The Boers who, to the number of some 250, were holding the position were finally driven out, and the battalion occupied the ground during a very wet, cold, and windy night.

Next day the Regiment moved off to join General Brocklehurst's column, and was under a good deal of fire on this day and on the 24th, when Private Broadbent of the Mounted Infantry Company was severely wounded. This column remained at a place called Meerzicht, near Paardekop, from the 24th July to the 7th August, and during that time a wing of the battalion under Major Watson formed part of a reconnaissance sent towards Amersfoort and had three men wounded, Privates Evans, Fletcher, and Whitehead, the first named dying of his injuries.

Moving in a north-easterly direction Buller's troops occupied Amersfoort on the 8th, Ermelo on the 12th, the Komati River was reached on the 15th, and Van Wyk's Vlei on the 21st August: during this last day's march the mounted infantry on the right flank was engaged with the Boers, and Private Hannon of Captain Bridgford's company was badly wounded. The column halted at Van Wyk's Vlei during the 22nd, and the battalion, with the Devonshire Regiment, was ordered out to attack a Boer position. The battalion on this occasion was much broken up; three companies were detached as escort for guns, three others were sent off to hold a flat-topped ridge, while these were covered as to their eventual retirement by the remaining two companies occupying a position about 1,500 yards in rear. A Maxim gun on tripod mounting was this day for the first time in action with the battalion, manned by Sergeant Wood, Privates Forrester and Price, and did excellent service. The enemy could not readily be seen, but his fire was heavy and accurate as the casualties in the battalion show: there were killed or died of wounds, Privates Barnes, Commerford, and Lally, and wounded, Privates Archibald, Davies, Mitchell, and Page.

Geluk was reached on the 23rd, and here a halt was made for three days, but on the 26th and 27th, while marching to and camped at Bergendal Farm, there was a good deal of opposition and the battalion had 25 casualties in the two days: Lance-Corporal Munro, Privates Fisher and Williams were killed, Sergeant Richmond, Lance-Corporal Chaundy, Privates Clarke, Hoffmann, Holmes, Ives, Jackson, Parsons, Pilkington, Ratcliffe, Roscoe, Scott, Spencer, Stirling, Toole, Van Dort, Walsh, and Wood wounded, and Privates Claber, Niblick, Russell, and Thorpe taken prisoners.

Of the action at Bergendal Farm General Buller stated that "the battalion had rendered valuable service in holding the right flank so firmly, for he had since learnt that the Boers had contemplated delivering a strong attack on that flank, but had been unable to do so as the position was so tenaciously held."

On the 28th the column reached Dalmanutha *en route* to Machadodorp, and here the Manchesters were left in garrison with a small body of cavalry, some engineers, and two 4.7 guns; but on the 2nd September one wing went on to Helvetia, where the other wing under Major Watson joined it on the 17th. In some fighting on the 3rd, the Mounted Infantry Company had four men wounded—Sergeant McDermott, Lance-Corporal Sharkey, Privates Johnson and Cummins.

Early in October General Buller handed over his command to Lieutenant-General Lyttelton and left Lydenburg on the 6th; the headquarters of the 7th Brigade was now at Lydenburg and Major-General Kitchener was in command from that place to Schoeman's Kloof, about eight miles north of Helvetia. The 1st Battalion Manchester Regiment guarded the road between these two places with posts at Witklip, Badfontein, and Schoeman's Kloof. The Devons and 2nd Battalion Rifle Brigade were in Lydenburg, while General Lyttelton's headquarters was at Middelburg.

In this district the battalion remained for several months, doing heavy and harassing work in providing picquets for the road and in escorting convoys; the Boers hereabouts were very active, there were much "sniping," many attacks, and many more threats of attacks upon the different posts held by the troops. The majority of the casualties incurred were naturally among the men of the mounted infantry company of the battalion; thus, on the 7th November Private Salt was killed and Private Sowden was wounded; on the 13th February 1901 Captain Crichton was mortally wounded and Private Joyce was hit in an action fought by Major-General Kitchener to the west of Helvetia; while on the night of the 29th–30th November 1900 the tent of one of the companies was struck by lightning, when Private Makin was killed and the following men were all more or less injured—Lance-Corporal Hall, Privates Davey, Kershaw, Piggott, and Steele. Again, on the 30th March 1901, when on escort duty with a convoy, Private Gilligan was killed and Private Stewart wounded—both of the Battalion Mounted Infantry Company.

Early in April the battalion was ordered to move to Lydenburg, and having called in all detachments, except a company and a half which remained for a short time longer at Witklip, the battalion was concentrated at its new station by the 13th April 1901.

On the 22nd May the officers of the battalion were thus distributed:

At Lydenburg: Lieutenant-Colonels Curran and Watson, Major Hudson, Captains Marden, Menzies, Newbigging, Lieutenants Deakin, H. Fisher, Eddowes, Stuart, and Hardman (Volunteer Company), and Lieutenant and Quartermaster Banks.

Hospital, Lydenburg: Lieutenant Murphy (Militia) and Second Lieutenant Dann.

At Mission Camp: Captain Dunlop.

At Strathcona's Hill: Captain Hunt-Grubbe.

At Witklip: Captain Paton, Lieutenants Roe and Terry.

At Badfontein: Captain Tillard and Lieutenant Clarke (Militia).

Hospital elsewhere: Captain Heys (2nd Volunteer Company) and one subaltern Volunteer company.

M. I.: Witklip and Machadodorp: Lieutenants Merriman, Knox, and Stirling (Dublin Fusiliers, attached) and Second Lieutenant Hovell.

Elsewhere in South Africa: Captains Bridgford and Vaughan and Lieutenant Vanrenen.

For many weeks the same round of duties continued—constant convoy duty, clearing of neighbouring farms, raids against positions said to be in the occupation of the enemy, while there were frequent threats, which only very occasionally materialised, of Boer attacks upon some one or other of the posts held by the battalion. Then the telegraph line was often cut and picquets were attacked, and on the 3rd June Private Broadbent of the battalion was slightly wounded. And so the long-drawn-out war went on, until in the middle of December the battalion, less three companies which remained behind, was ordered to move out with a column which, under Colonel Park, had for some considerable time past been operating in the Lydenburg district.

The column left Lydenburg on the 18th December and marched to Witklip, where it bivouacked for the night. On the next morning B and C Companies under Major Hudson left camp before dawn and proceeded to crown the heights commanding the Wemmershoek Valley, while the remainder of the column, marching an hour later, passed through the valley and "outspanned" about two and a half miles beyond Wemmershoek Farm. While here a report came in that the mounted infantry was heavily engaged near Elandspruit, and G and H Companies with a pom-pom moved forward in support, causing the Boers who were engaging the M.I. to retire.

The column then moved on to and bivouacked at Elandspruit in a hollow almost entirely surrounded by a chain of low rocky kopjes, broken only on the east where the ground fell away gently; but these kopjes as well as the bivouac were entirely commanded by the high ridge on the north-east, where most of the camp picquets were posted. At 8.30 p.m. the camp was roused by a heavy outburst of fire from the north-west and south.

The Boer plan of attack was somewhat as follows: a pom-pom on the road about 3,500 yards south-west of the camp shelled the kopjes round the camp; a rocky hill about 800 yards south of the drift was occupied by Muller's commando, which kept up a very heavy fire on the bivouac and the low kopjes surrounding it; while a body under Commandant Trichardt worked round to the west with the apparent intention of rushing the picquets on the high ridge, from which, once in their possession, they could completely command the camp; this they made a very determined attempt to achieve. The Boers got right round E Company's picquet on the left, and when within twenty-five yards of the sangars opened a heavy fire and then tried to rush them; but E Company stood its ground admirably and returned an equally heavy fire. Captain Deakin was almost at once shot through the throat and Sergeant Danvers was also wounded. The command of the picquet now fell to Second Lieutenant Gordon, who succeeded in repelling the attack, when the enemy withdrew leaving four dead and three wounded close to the sangars, while they were seen to carry off others of their wounded.

When Captain Deakin was being carried down the hill by Privates Carter and Stevenson a party of Boers stopped them; Carter made his escape, but Stevenson was stripped while Captain Deakin was robbed, the latter being eventually carried in by Sergeant Derbyshire.

While this attack was taking place, another was made on the two picquets on the right under Lieutenant Terry. These picquets were commanded respectively by Sergeants Ford and Chase, and when the former was killed and the latter severely wounded their picquets were driven in, 1 man being here killed and 5 wounded.

The fire directed on the camp had been very heavy, several casualties had taken place, and a very large number of transport animals had been hit. On information being received that the picquets of A Company had been driven in, the commanding officer sent Captain Menzies and a small party to try to recover the ground lost, and these were almost at once followed by a larger party under Major Hudson. This officer, leaving some men to reinforce Second Lieutenant Gordon's picquet, made his way along the line until nearly opposite the site of A company's picquets, where they were received with a volley at very close range, whereby Major Hudson, Colour-Sergeant Martin, Sergeant Davies, and a private were knocked over. At this moment a very thick fog rolled up over the position, under cover of which the enemy withdrew, but the same mist made the recovery of the dead and wounded very difficult and some of the latter remained out until daybreak next morning.

The total casualties suffered by the battalion in this affair were :

Killed or died of wounds : Major Hudson, Colour-Sergeant Martin, Sergeants Davies and Ford, Privates Bohin, Brandreth, Frost, Holmes, and Redford.

Wounded : Captain Deakin, Lieutenant Terry, Second Lieutenants Gordon and Prince, Sergeants Chase, Danvers, and Hart, Lance-Corporal Dyson, Privates Armitt, Berry, Driscoll, Fleet, Jones, Hilton, Smith, Stuart, and Walker.

The following was published in Column Orders next day by Colonel Park :

"*The Officer Commanding the Column wishes to thank the officers, non-commissioned officers, and men of the Manchester Regiment which held the top of the hill last night, for the gallant way in which they defended their posts against heavy odds and inflicted great loss upon the enemy. The Officer Commanding will not fail to bring their good services to the notice of the Commander-in-Chief.*"

The column moved on viâ Dullstroom and Vlakfontein to Helvetia, which was reached on Christmas Day, and here Colonel Park found orders awaiting him to move on to Machadodorp *en route* for the Belfast district ; so marching on again the same day Belfast was finally reached at midday on the 27th December. Here on the 4th January 1902 the battalion received the following parting telegram, sent off from Durban :

"All ranks First Manchesters from all ranks First Devons; Good-bye and good luck from your Comrades of the old Seventh Brigade."

During the next few days the combined columns of Colonels Park and Urmston engaged in certain operations against different Boer commandos with varying success, some few prisoners being here and there rounded up, and captures of arms, ammunition, horses, cattle, and supplies being made. Casualties were naturally sustained, though these were happily not many, but on the 21st January the battalion experienced a serious loss. Orders had been issued for an attack upon certain enemy positions at Paardeplatz, and A and K Companies of the battalion with 2 of the Royal Scots, 2 battalions mounted infantry, and 2 guns, the whole under Colonel Curran, moved out at 5 a.m. by the Witpoort road, while E and H Companies with a battalion M.I., two guns, and a pom-pom, worked up the valley to the east of Paardeplatz. The Boers at once fell back before this advance and were pursued by the mounted infantry as far as Windhoek, but on the retirement commencing the enemy followed up, the firing on both sides becoming very heavy. E and H Companies of the battalion with some M.I. were sent out against the Boers, and while H Company was moving from one kopje to another a hot fire was opened upon them at 1,400 yards, when Captain Menzies, who was leading his men, was mortally wounded, dying early the next morning.

On the 24th Colonel Park's column marched to Houtenbek, experiencing considerable opposition *en route,* as was indeed the case almost daily, and on the 29th the column, with the battalion, was back again at Lydenburg. The stay here did not, however, extend much beyond ten days, for on the 12th February the column moved off again, being at Helvetia on the 13th, Machadodorp 14th, Dalmanutha 15th, Belfast 16th, and Pan on the 18th. From here Colonel Park, in conjunction with two other columns, operated against the commandos of Hinton and Trichardt, many prisoners, wounded and unwounded, were taken and many important captures of stock were made; the battalion suffered no casualties.

The Boer Government, at this time a very peripatetic cabinet, was known to be moving about the district, and parties were constantly out in all directions in the hope of rounding them up, entailing a very great deal of exhausting marching and counter-marching about the country. Then on the 21st March, while Colonel Park's column was at a place called Onvervacht, orders were received directing the column to take part in a "drive," of which the following was the scheme: By the night of the 23rd three columns—those commanded by Colonels Wing, Williams, and Park—were to be formed on a line drawn east and west through Bethel, Wing's left to rest on the Ermelo–Standerton blockhouse line, while Park's right was on the Brugspruit–Waterval blockhouse line. A continuous line of outposts was to be held, and on the 24th the whole line was to move forward and drive in a south-westerly direction to the Natal railway.

Colonel Park's force paraded at 7 p.m. on the 22nd and marched 18 miles to Uitkyk, bivouacked there from 4.30 a.m. till 10 a.m., and then marched another 12 to 16 miles to take up the allotted position on the general outpost line. B and K Companies of the battalion with two companies M.I., under Lieutenant-Colonel Watson, held the right section, while D and F with some more mounted infantry, with Colonel Curran, were in the centre, and G and H and two companies of the 4th Battalion Mounted Infantry held the left under Major Marden. The guns and baggage, escorted by A Company of the battalion, was in rear of the centre ; Park's column covered a front of 12 miles.

Owing to the capture of a native runner taking orders to Colonel Wing, that officer did not receive his orders until 2 a.m and consequently was unable to arrive at his place on the left of Colonel Williams until 7, by which time it was feared that many Boers had escaped through the gap thus left. The line began to move forward at 6.30 a.m., Park's force having an extended line of mounted men, supported by half-companies of infantry at intervals of about one mile. The general direction was admirably maintained, except that a portion of G Company under Lieutenant Murphy lost touch by reason of a delay caused by two men fainting and falling out, and by the end of the day the infantry, marching magnificently, had covered 34 miles—altogether 75 miles in 60 hours. Part of the column camped at 10 p.m. at Vlaklaagte Station, but several of the companies of the battalion bivouacked where they happened to strike the railway. The captures this day were insignificant, amounting only to seven Boers, a few rifles, some stock, and 30 horses.

On the 25th March Colonel Park published the following in Column Orders :

"*The Colonel Commanding wishes to express to all ranks of the column his thanks for the excellent manner in which the orders for yesterday's drive were carried out, and his admiration for the splendid marching powers displayed by the Manchester Regiment, all of whom covered distances of more than 60 miles during the 48 hours. It has been a great pleasure to the O.C. Column to be able to bring this very fine performance to the notice of the General Commanding in Chief.*"

The column left Vlaklaagte on the 30th March and, moving north, marched by New Denmark, Vrischgewaagte, Bethel, Ermelo, Roodepoort, Nooitgedacht to Eikeboom, which was reached on the 10th April, and hence the column, in accordance with orders received from Lord Kitchener, moved into position in readiness to take part in a " drive " to the south. The following was the scheme drawn up for these operations : eight different columns, those of Park, Williams, Wing, Mackenzie, Spens, Allenby, Stuart, and Lawley, all under the general direction of General Bruce Hamilton, were to form up in one long line with their backs to the Delagoa railway, and start on the 12th April to drive southwards, the right of the long line, where was Park's column, resting on the Witklip–Vaal Constabulary line of posts, and the left on the Wonderfontein–Standerton blockhouse line, the drive terminating on arrival at the Natal railway. On the 11th the right column started in the order in which squadrons and companies would rest on the line, the front taken up being about six miles. The 8th Hussars, with A, D, and F Companies of the battalion took the three miles on the right, while G, H, and K with the 4th, 18th, and 19th M.I. covered the three miles on the left of the column-front. By 3 p.m. all were in position ; each picquet consisted of 15 men and was self-contained, having each its own wagon ; the intervals between wagons was about 150 yards and each picquet threw out an intermediate post of 5 men 75 yards in front. Then all the wagons were linked together by a wire fence running out to salients in front of the intermediate posts. All the companies occupied and strengthened their front in this way, so that on each night of the drive a continuous wire fence about 50 miles in length was put up.

The whole line advanced at 6.30 a.m. on the 12th, 75 per cent. of the infantry riding in their wagons at a time ; there was a halt from 10.30 a.m. to 12.30 p.m., when the advance was renewed ; and on the new outpost line being reached about 3.30 in the afternoon, picquets were thrown out, trenches dug, and the wire fence put up.

The line of the Natal railway was reached on the 14th April after a march of 55 miles, the oxen and mules much knocked up, and the column went into camp near Vaal Station, when it was found that the result of the drive was 1 Boer killed, 1 wounded, and 134 prisoners, with 85 rifles, nearly 5,000 rounds of ammunition, and a considerable number of horses captured.

On the 15th April a new Volunteer Company under Captain Eaton—3 officers and 88 other ranks—arrived from England and became M Company of the battalion.

The column marched 16 miles to Vaalbank on the 16th and began at once to take part in further operations under the following " General

Idea ": The tract of country on the west of the Constabulary line of posts was to be driven south to north by seven columns, the right resting on the Constabulary line, which was to be strengthened by the columns of Colonels Park and Wing, these two moving on ahead of the driving line, covering a distance from south to north of about 16 miles. At night these columns were to face west, put out picquets, dig trenches, and erect wire fences as before.

Colonel Park's force started to move at 6.30 a.m. on the 17th April, and that day the battalion covered 12 miles to Wildebeestfontein, the companies on arrival spreading out and occupying a front of 5 miles. These operations were continued until the 13th May, the whole district being thoroughly and carefully searched, and in the course of these Sergeant Chandler, mess sergeant of the battalion, was mortally wounded on the night of the 26th–27th April, dying on the 4th May.

Belfast was reached on the 13th May, and a few days later orders were received that the Liverpool Regiment would relieve the 1st Battalion Manchester Regiment in Colonel Park's column, and that the battalion was to take over the stations and blockhouses at Waterval Boven, Waterval Onder, and Nooitgedacht—affording the prospect of a rest which was by no means unwelcome, since while the headquarters of the battalion had been " on trek " it had marched over 1,300 miles and done very much hard work. The following appeared in Column Orders of the 18th May;

" On the departure of the 1st Battalion Manchester Regiment, the O.C. Column wishes to convey his personal thanks to Lieut.-Colonel Curran and all ranks of the Battalion for the admirable manner in which his orders and wishes have at all times been carried out, and for the cordial support he has at all times received during the eight months in which the Battalion has been under his command. During this period the Battalion has had a great deal of hard work and some stiff fighting, and has performed many long and arduous marches. The gallantry and determination displayed by all ranks during the attack on the camp on the 19th December 1901, were beyond praise, and were the means of saving the column from very serious loss; while their power of endurance during long and continuous marches has been a constant source of pleasure and admiration to the O.C. Column. Colonel Park wishes the whole Battalion the best of good luck wherever they may be, and trusts before long they will be able to enjoy a well-earned rest and all the comforts of peace."

G and M Companies now proceeded to Nooitgedacht under Major

Marden, A, F, and half D under Colonel Watson to Waterval Onder, while B, H, and the remainder of D were sent with headquarters to Waterval Boven.

On the 31st May Lieutenant-Colonel Curran handed over command of the battalion to Brevet Lieutenant-Colonel Watson on completion of his tenure of command of the battalion, and left the same day for Pretoria *en route* to England. Colonel Curran had taken the 1st Battalion of the Manchester Regiment out to South Africa at the very commencement of the war, and he had, as it happened, actually seen the whole campaign through to its close—for on the next day the following telegram was received from the Chief Staff Officer at Middelburg :

" Lord Kitchener telegraphs peace was signed last night "—

and so at long last the three years' war came to an end.

On the 2nd June the following party left by special train for Cape Town *en route* for England to take part in the ceremonies of the Coronation, which unfortunately had eventually to be postponed owing to the sudden and serious illness of King Edward VII : Lieutenant Gordon, Sergeants Norton and Potts, Corporal Duncan, Privates Bounds, Hancock, Huggins, Keetch, Kilcoyne, Mountford, and No. 3512 Private Smith.

Congratulations on the close of hostilities were now coming in from all sides, and on the 3rd and 6th the following telegrams were received from General Lord Kitchener :

"*Please communicate to your troops the following gracious message I have received from His Majesty the King, and for which I have thanked him in the name of all concerned : Begins : Heartiest congratulations on the termination of hostilities, and also congratulate my brave troops under your command for having brought this long and difficult campaign to so glorious and successful a conclusion.*"

"*The following telegram from the Secretary of State for War is published for your information : Begins : 4th June, His Majesty's Government offer to you their most sincere congratulations on the energy, skill and patience with which you have conducted this prolonged campaign, and would wish you to communicate to the troops under your command their profound sense of the spirit and endurance with which they have met every call made upon them, of their bravery in action, of the excellent discipline preserved, and of the humanity shown by them throughout this trying period.*"

The casualties suffered by the battalion in this campaign were heavy : 4 officers and 75 non-commissioned officers and men had been killed, 15 officers and 145 other ranks had been wounded, 1 officer and 93 non-commissioned officers and men had died of disease, and 408 men had been invalided, making a grand total of casualties of 20 officers and 721 other ranks.[1] Three officers of other corps had also been wounded while attached to the battalion.

The following were the different decorations, " mentions in despatches," and promotions won by the battalion during the campaign :

The Victoria Cross was conferred upon Privates R. Scott and J. Pitts for gallantry as under : " During the attack on Cæsar's Camp in Natal, January 6th 1900, these two men occupied a sangar on the left of which all our men had been shot down and their positions occupied by Boers, and held their post for fifteen hours without food or water, all the time under an extremely heavy fire, keeping up their fire and a smart look-out, though the Boers occupied some sangars on their immediate left rear. Private Scott was wounded " (*London Gazette*, 25th July 1901).

Mentioned in Despatches : Lieutenant-Colonel Curran, Majors Watson, Melvill, Vizard, and Hudson, Captains Marden, Bridgford, Menzies, Newbigging, Vaughan, and Hardcastle, Lieutenants Deakin, H. Fisher, and Merriman, Second Lieutenants Gordon and Buchan, Quartermaster and Hon. Lieutenant Bankes, Sergeant-Major Haddon, Quartermaster-Sergeants Jones and Pike, Colour-Sergeants Bassett, Connery, Finney, Gleeson, Lloyd, Martin, Rhind, Scott, and Wilcock, Sergeant-Cook Davies, Sergeants Burke, Carter, Croasdale, Fagan, Grant, Gresty, Hill, Lloyd, Morris, Murphy, and Wood, Corporals Brookes and McDowell, Lance-Corporals Harris, Hudson, and Preston, Privates Bateman, Bell, Conroy, and Newton.

Brevet Promotion : The following officers were promoted brevet lieutenant-colonels : Majors Watson and Vizard ; Captains Marden and Vaughan were promoted brevet majors ; while Quartermaster and Hon. Lieutenant Bankes was promoted Honorary Captain.

The Distinguished Service Order was conferred upon Brevet Major Marden, Captains Hardcastle, Bridgford, Newbigging, and Fisher, and Lieutenant Buchan.

The Medal for Distinguished Conduct in the Field was bestowed upon the following warrant officer, non-commissioned officers, and men : Sergeant-Major Haddon, Colour-Sergeants Finney and Scott, Sergeants Carter, Grant, Gresty, Hall, and Lloyd, Corporals Richardson and Brookes, Lance-

---

[1] *The Official History of the War*, vol. iv, p. 696, gives killed or died of wounds 5 and 70, died of disease 0 and 78, wounded 16 and 117, captured 0 and 4, missing 0 and 1, making a total of 291 casualties—exclusive of " invalided."

Corporals Harris and Preston, Privates Bateman, Bell, Cummings, Forshaw, Ladley, McKinley, and Newton.

The First Battalion was serving at Standerton, and had received from the Second Battalion 65 non-commissioned officers and men, when on the 16th January 1903 it was placed under orders to embark for Singapore on or about the 8th March. Punctually to the date mentioned the battalion entrained for Durban, at a strength of 20 officers and 420 other ranks, under the command of Lieutenant-Colonel Maxwell. The port of embarkation was reached on the 10th and the troops at once proceeded on board the s.s. *Dilwara*, being received on that ship by a draft of 114 non-commissioned officers and men who, with 11 women and 14 children, had come out from England under Captain Creagh.

Singapore was reached on the 30th March and, disembarking, the battalion occupied Tanglin Barracks.

THE FIRST VOLUNTEER ACTIVE SERVICE COMPANY MANCHESTER REGIMENT

The record of the work of the Regular Battalions in the South African War could not be considered to be complete were not something to be said about the services of the Volunteer Companies which were attached for duty.

Something has already been stated as to the circumstances and conditions under which the offers of the Volunteer Battalions were accepted, and as to the remarkable response which was made by the citizen-soldiers of the United Kingdom to the invitation issued by the War Office. The war had only been something like four months in progress when a Volunteer Active Service Company was formed for attachment to the 1st Battalion Manchester Regiment, and on February 9th 1900 the company furnished by the 1st, 2nd, 3rd, and 4th Volunteer Battalions was mobilised at Ashton-under-Lyne, being made up as under:

1st Volunteer Battalion, Wigan District, 29 non-commissioned officers and men.
2nd Volunteer Battalion, Manchester District, 29 non-commissioned officers and men.
3rd Volunteer Battalion, Ashton-under-Lyne District, 28 non-commissioned officers and men.
4th Volunteer Battalion, Manchester District, 27 non-commissioned officers and men.

Total: 113 non-commissioned officers and men

The officers detailed were Captain B. C. P. Heywood, 2nd Volunteer Battalion, in command, with Lieutenants E. H. Howe, a captain in the 3rd Volunteer Battalion, who had waived his rank in order to see service, and H. C. Darlington of the 1st Volunteer Battalion.

The company sailed from Southampton on the 14th February in the *Greek* and joined the 1st Battalion at Ladysmith on the 14th March.

The company remained in the neighbourhood of Ladysmith until the 20th July, and during that time was joined by a draft from the 5th and 6th Volunteer Battalions which came out from home in charge of Lieutenant P. Bamford, a captain in the 6th Battalion; the draft was 20 strong, each of these battalions providing 10 non-commissioned officers and men.

When the 1st Battalion moved forward the Volunteer Company went with it, taking its full share of reconnaissance and outpost work; and on the 30th July in the affair near Meerzicht the company sustained its first casualties in the campaign, Privates Fletcher and Whitehead being wounded, while on the same day, after return to camp, Private Ball was so badly burnt in attempting to save the camp kit of his officers during a veldt fire that he died a few days later.

On the 26th August the battalion was engaged near Geluk, the Volunteer Company forming the right of the firing line, and having Lance-Corporal Munro killed and Privates Holmes and Wood wounded; while on the following day, when there was fighting near Bergendal, the company was in support and Private Sterling belonging to it was wounded.

When on the 16th September the battalion was stationed at Schoeman's Kloof orders were received for the Volunteer Company to proceed to Pretoria preparatory to return to England, and the following appeared in Battalion Orders of the 9th October 1900:

"*On the occasion of the departure of the Volunteer Company en route for England, the Commanding Officer feels that all ranks of the 1st Battalion Manchester Regiment will share his great regret at losing this Company of whose services he cannot speak too highly.*

"*Captain Heywood, his officers, non-commissioned officers and men have shown a knowledge of their work which has surprised him, and they have on all occasions proved themselves gallant comrades in the field, while their conduct in camp has been exemplary.*

"*It is certain that Manchester will know how to appreciate the deeds of men who have willingly left home and employment to take up arms for their Country, and it must remain a source of gratification that a lasting bond of union has been established between the Line and Volunteer Battalions of the City."*

The company left the battalion on the 11th October and marched to Machadodorp, proceeding thence by rail on the 17th to Pretoria, camping at Arcadia with other volunteer companies, and shortly hearing that the order for its return home had been cancelled. On October 25th it took part in the Annexation Parade and the march-past before Field-Marshal Lord Roberts.

On the 29th October the company entrained for Elandsfontein, remaining as part of the garrison of this place until the 26th March 1901, being stationed at the Simmer and Jack Mine. It was then sent to Natal Spruit, near the junction of the Cape and Natal Railways, relieving a company of the Railway Pioneer Regiment, and the garrison including 1 sergeant and 10 men of the Carabiniers for scouting purposes. It was while quartered at Natal Spruit that definite and final orders were received for the company to return home.

Leaving Natal Spruit on the 16th April and travelling via Greylingstad, Zandspruit, and Ladysmith, Pietermaritzburg was reached on the 20th, and after a stay here of four days for collecting kits, etc., the company went on to Durban, whence it sailed on the 26th April in the *Englishman*, reaching Southampton on May 22nd and Ashton-under-Lyne on the day following. Lieutenant Howe remained behind in South Africa, having obtained a company in the 3rd Battalion Railway Pioneer Regiment, in which he served out the remainder of the war.

Colour-Sergeant McCabe and Sergeant Stirke of the Volunteer Company were " mentioned " in Lord Roberts' despatch of the 4th September 1901.

The following Order was sent to the Officer Commanding 63rd Regimental District by Major-General Barton, under whom the company had served during the last six months of its stay in South Africa:

" The Volunteer Service Company of the Manchester Regiment having now been ordered to England, I wish to put on record the excellent services they have rendered while under my immediate command, in charge of various important posts, and the soldierlike qualities exhibited by all ranks under conditions rendered most trying by an active enemy and severe weather.

" It has given me special pleasure to observe that these Manchester Volunteers maintained in the field the good feeling, born of discipline and esprit de corps, *that I had noticed in their Volunteer Battalions when serving recently as Chief Staff Officer in the North Western District.*

" Captain B. C. P. Heywood has commanded the company with great

success and has been indefatigable in his care for the good name and the well-being of all ranks.

"*Lieutenant E. H. Howe is well qualified for higher rank and would have commanded a company with credit and advantage.*

"*The other subaltern officers, Lieutenants H. C. Darlington and P. Bamford, have supported their captain well in all respects.*

"*The Non-commissioned officers and Men were gallant in the field, indifferent to hardships, and in every way a credit to their Corps and the great City whence they came.*

"*Elandsfontein,
    Transvaal, 12th April 1901.*"

CHAPTER XVIII

THE SECOND BATTALION

1885–1901

EARLY in 1885 a war with Russia seemed by no means an unlikely contingency. For some little time past a British and a Russian commission **1885** had been engaged on the spot in conducting the demarcation of the Afghan northern frontier, and matters had been increasingly complicated by the incursions made into territory in dispute by the Russian Governor of Merv. At last on the 29th March the Russians made an entirely unprovoked attack upon an Afghan post on the Khusk River, cutting up its defenders almost to a man, and occupying the Penjdeh district. The news of this affair produced intense excitement in England, and scarcely less in India, where it arrived just after the Amir of Afghanistan, Abdur Rahman, had joined the Viceroy at the Grand Durbar at Rawal Pindi, where negotiations between the two Governments were about to be concluded. In India two army corps were at once mobilised; the European portion of the permanent garrison was ordered to be raised by 10,000 men, and additions were made to the Indian cavalry and infantry; some of the latter were rearmed with the Martini-Henry rifle, arrangements were made with the Nepal Durbar for a larger supply of recruits for Gurkha regiments, and in view of a probable advance to assist the forces of the Amir, Sir Charles Macgregor, then Quartermaster-General in India, selected a site for an entrenched camp in the Pishin Valley.

On the 10th March of this year the 2nd Battalion Manchester Regiment —strength 825 of all ranks—left Multan to join the Camp at Rawal Pindi, where some 18,500 troops had been assembled to do honour to the Amir, and on arrival was posted to the 3rd Brigade, 1st Division. The ceremonies incidental to the meeting of the Viceroy and the Amir were, however, speedily interrupted by the news of the happenings in northern Afghanistan, preparations were made for war, and the battalion was warned for active service and told off to the 1st Army Corps.

It left Rawal Pindi on the 12th April by train on return to Multan and remained here on a war footing until the 24th September, when instructions were issued that any likelihood of war had disappeared and that the battalion need no longer be held in readiness for active service.

During the next cold weather a camp of exercise was held at Ambala, whither the Second Battalion proceeded on the 9th November, arriving here on the 11th December after a march of 371 miles, and being attached for duty to the 1st Brigade of the 2nd Division.

The manœuvres were on a larger scale than had ever before been attempted in India, and were attended by a considerable number of officers of foreign armies who came out specially from Europe. The camp broke up early in 1886, and on the 21st January the battalion paraded in review order at H.E. the Commander-in-Chief's camp at Delhi for the presentation of Colours by General Sir Frederick Roberts, Commander-in-Chief in India. The strength of the Second Battalion on this historic occasion was 21 officers, 2 warrant officers, 33 staff-sergeants and sergeants, 36 corporals, 10 drummers, and 563 privates. The officers were Lieutenant-Colonel W. O. Barnard, Majors Marryat, Thomas, Anstruther, and Ridley, Captains Simpson, Maxwell, Anderson, Lang, Henderson, Melvill, and Vizard, Lieutenants Prioleau, Moore, Fitton, Johnson, Boileau, James, and Dennys, Captain and Adjutant Rochfort-Boyd, and Quartermaster Facer.

The field officers who received the Colours were Majors Marryat and Thomas, the lieutenants for the Colours were Lieutenants Henderson and Melvill, while the officers of the escort were Major Ridley and Lieutenant Prioleau.

The Colours having been consecrated by the Rev. J. Adams, V.C., Chaplain to the Forces, they were presented to the Regiment by Sir Frederick Roberts, who made the following address:

"*Soldiers of the Manchester Regiment!*

"*This is the first occasion at which I have had the pleasure of being present at such an interesting ceremony as this. I am particularly proud of attending this parade to-day and I feel highly gratified at the compliment you have paid me in expressing a wish that I should present the new Colours to your Regiment. I can assure you that I consider it a great honour to perform this very agreeable duty.*

"*I can claim a somewhat lengthy acquaintance with this distinguished Battalion. It was in the year 1852 that I first met the old 96th, and I am glad to find that the Regiment is in the same good order now that it was then, and that it has clung to its old traditions for smartness and discipline. Not only have you gained a good name for yourselves in quarters, but you have taken a high place amongst the best shooting regiments in India.*

"*I congratulate you, Colonel Barnard, your officers, non-commissioned officers and men, on the very efficient state of the Regiment. I can well understand how keenly you feel having to sever your connection with a corps in which you have served for more than thirty years, but it must be a great satisfaction to you to know that when you give up the command your successor will take over the Battalion in the most admirable order.*

"*The Battalion, though now called the 2nd Battalion of the Manchester Regiment, dates its origin, curiously enough, from the island of Minorca. It was there at the close of the last century that a regiment of foot was raised which the following year served with distinction in Egypt, and at the Battle of Alexandria a private soldier of the Regiment, named Anthony Lutz, captured a standard of Napoleon the Great, a standard which was known as the Invincible. Since those days, under different names and in different lands, the Regiment has taken its part in many a hard-fought action, and the long list of battles inscrolled on your Colours—commencing with Egmont-op-Zee and ending with the Egyptian campaign of 1882—shows that wherever hard work had to be done or glory to be won the Manchester Regiment has been well to the front and has borne its full share in the several wars in which it has been engaged.*

"*In the name of Her Most Gracious Majesty the Queen I now entrust these Colours to your care, and though it is impossible to foretell over what future battle fields they may wave, I feel confident that the men of the Manchester Regiment will ever prove true and loyal to their trust, and that when duty demands they will lay down their lives cheerfully and willingly in defence of their Colours —Colours which they bear as the proud emblem of the Queen they serve and of the country to which they belong.*"

Colonel Barnard made the following reply:

"*Sir,*

"*On behalf of the officers, non-commissioned officers and men of the Second Battalion the Manchester Regiment which it is my pride to command, I beg to thank your Excellency for the honour you have done us by presenting our new Colours to-day. I have also to thank you for the kind and complimentary manner in which you have spoken of the Battalion.*

"*I can assure your Excellency that all ranks in the Battalion will experience the utmost gratification at hearing your words, and that they will travel to the First Battalion in England and be received there with pride and pleasure.*

"*It is a matter for regret to my brother officers and myself that owing to being on the line of march and other circumstances we are unable to commemorate this auspicious event by some entertainment befitting the occasion.*

> "*I feel certain that the strong feeling of* esprit de corps *and devotion to our Queen, our country, and our Colours which animates all ranks in the Battalion will be still further stimulated by the fact that our Colours have this day been presented to us by a distinguished soldier.*"

The battalion left Delhi on the 25th January for Agra, arriving at that station on the 5th February after a march of 140 miles. The marching-in strength was 20 officers and 613 other ranks, but three days after reaching its new station the battalion was joined by a draft from the depot of 2 officers and 123 non-commissioned officers and men.

Colonel Barnard left the battalion in March on completion of his period in command, and by desire of all ranks he took charge of the old Colours presented in 1825 and 1861 and conveyed them to England. On the 21st June these two stands of old Colours were handed over to the Dean and Chapter of Manchester Cathedral by Colonel Barnard in person and were placed on either side of the Great Arch of the Lady Chapel, immediately behind the reredos at the east end of the cathedral.

The 2nd Battalion Manchester Regiment remained quietly at Agra for nearly four years, and only during the latter part of its stay in this station were the companies in any way dispersed; in March 1888 two companies were sent for a short time to Fatehgarh, and again just before leaving Agra two companies were ordered on detachment to Delhi. The departure from Agra took place on the 18th December 1889, one company under Captain Sitwell proceeding by rail direct to Sialkote, the new station, while the remainder of the battalion —17 officers and 484 other ranks—commanded by Colonel Saportas, marched in the first instance to Meerut where a camp of exercise had been directed to assemble. On arrival here on the 31st December it was found that the camp of exercise had been cancelled, but the battalion was detained at Meerut for garrison duty until the 4th February 1890, when the march to Sialkote was resumed. Amritsar was reached on the 1st March, and here two companies, those of Captains Graham and Ward, were dropped, and the headquarters arrived at Sialkote on the 10th of the month. Since leaving Agra the battalion had marched a distance of close upon 470 miles.

During the year 1891 there were two punitive expeditions to the Miranzai Valley, both under the command of Brigadier-General Sir William Lockhart. The first expedition had been undertaken in January for punishing and enforcing the submission of some six sections of the Orakzai tribe, a considerable force had been employed, the recalcitrant tribesmen had submitted and for the most part had paid up the fines demanded of them; while they had also agreed, though with considerable reluctance, to our terms, which included the establishment of three posts on the Samana Ridge for the more effectual protection of the Miranzai border. The original Miranzai Field Force had only just been broken up, when a tribal combination was reported, having for its object the prevention of the construction of the posts; and on the 4th April there was a concerted attack upon a party of the 29th Bengal Infantry working upon the roads leading to the Samana Ridge, which was driven off, but not without considerable loss. On this Colonel Reid, 29th Bengal Infantry, who was commanding on the Samana, heliographed a message to Kohat stating that the rising appeared to be general and that strong reinforcements were at once required.

The troops detailed for the second Miranzai Expedition comprised 6 squadrons of cavalry, 15 mountain and 3 heavy guns, 1 company of Bengal Sappers, and 10½ battalions of infantry; the force was divided into three columns, concentrating the one at Hangu, the other two at Darband, and the whole numbered something under 8,000 men.

Notification early reached the Second Battalion Manchester Regiment at Sialkote that it was required to furnish 300 bayonets for the expeditionary force, and on the 6th April A, B, and G Companies were placed under orders for active service, and on the receipt of telegraphic orders on the 26th these companies paraded at 10 p.m. and entrained for Rawal Pindi; the strength was as under:

Major Barlow in command, Captains Graham, Abbot-Anderson, and Watson, Lieutenants Plunkett, Gunning, Hughes (transport officer), and Stevens (acting adjutant), Second Lieutenants Sealy and Menzies, Lieutenant and Quartermaster Stewart-Wynne, and 300 non-commissioned officers and men.

Rawal Pindi was reached at 2 p.m. on the 27th, and the detachment left again by train for Khushalgarh at 5.30 the same evening. On arrival here Major Barlow received instructions that, owing to an unexpected attack upon Kohat, he must push on and reach that place, 31 miles distant, before dark on the 28th without fail. In consequence of this the little party started from Khushalgarh at 4 a.m. on the 28th, halted for a couple of hours *en route* at Gumbat, where it was overtaken by a heavy thunderstorm, and marched into Kohat about 5.30 p.m., having covered the 31 miles in 13½ hours, including halts. The companies were played into Kohat by the bands of the 3rd Sikhs and 1st Battalion 4th Gurkhas.

The Detachment remained at Kohat until the 3rd May, being joined while there by Major Ridley from Amritsar.

On the 3rd May Major Barlow's party marched viâ Hangu to Mastaon on the Samana Ridge and joined the column under Colonel Brownlow, which was composed of 3 guns No. 2 Mountain Battery, the 6th Punjab Infantry, and 19th and 29th Bengal Infantry.

On the 7th the Detachment marched to Gulistan—where a fort has since been erected, and remained there in bivouac during the two following days, the weather being very inclement, but some of the men of the Punjab Infantry gave up a certain number of their tents for use by their British comrades.

On the 10th May the detachment joined a column commanded by Colonel Turner, and accompanied by Sir William Lockhart, which marched from Gulistan to Kharappa. The column was composed as under:

4 companies 1st Battalion King's Royal Rifles.
3 companies 2nd Battalion Manchester Regiment.
4 guns No. 3 Peshawar Mountain Battery.
No. 5 Company Bengal Sappers and Miners.
3rd Sikh Infantry.
2nd Punjab Infantry.
6th Punjab Infantry.
29th Bengal Infantry.

Six days' supplies for men and two days' for animals were taken. The main body marched down the Margharu-Talai spur, while Sir William Lockhart, with the 3rd Sikhs, 6th Punjab Infantry, some Sappers, and the whole of the baggage, followed the longer route by the Chagru Kotal, camp being pitched a mile from Kharappa at the junction of the Khanki and Kandi valleys. The force remained halted here during the 11th, while Sir William interviewed certain *jirgas* and informed them that as a public token of their submission the force would march through their country—a condition which was to the tribesmen an especially bitter humiliation.

In pursuance of this resolve, on the 12th, the column, less the Sappers, and two Indian regiments which remained at Kharappa, marched to Sadarai, a large village on the left bank of the Khanki stream, and on the 13th Mamuzai Bazar was reached. From here Sir William made a reconnaissance for survey purposes, and Captain Watson's company formed part of the escort.

The tribesmen having now all tendered their submission, Colonel

Turner's column returned on the 14th to Kharappa and on the next day to Gulistan; here Lieutenant Baldwin joined the Manchester detachment from headquarters.

The field force now began to be broken up, ceasing officially to exist on the 8th June; on the 17th May the detachment was back again at Hangu, but had no sooner arrived when it was ordered back to Mastaon on the Samana, a hot and fatiguing march. Arriving here on the 18th, it remained until the 21st, when it moved viâ Darband, Hangu, Chilabagh, Kohat, and Gumbat to Khushalgarh, which was reached on the 26th. Owing to the heat the marching was done at night.

At 4 a.m. on the 27th the three companies entrained and left for Rawal Pindi and Sialkote, arriving at this latter station early the next morning. During an absence of something less than five weeks the detachment had marched nearly 250 miles over a mountainous and little-known country.

In Army Order 252 of December 1891 it was announced that "the Queen has been pleased to command that the India Medal of 1854, with a clasp inscribed 'Samana 1891' shall be granted to all troops employed in the late Miranzai expedition," those being eligible who formed part of the Field Force between the 5th April and 25th May 1891.

On the 18th November 1892 the headquarters and six companies of the battalion, strength 17 officers and 523 non-commissioned officers and men under Lieutenant-Colonel Barlow, proceeded by march-route to Amritsar *en route* to Meerut, there to be stationed, and also to take part in the district concentration of troops there arranged to take place. At Amritsar the two companies on detachment were picked up and the united battalion was then sent by rail to Meerut, arriving there on the afternoon of the 29th. Three weeks later two companies were detached for duty at Delhi.

On the 19th February 1893 Major-General Nairne, C.B., commanding the Meerut District, presented the medals and clasps for the Miranzai Expedition of 1891 to those of all ranks entitled to the same, and complimented the officers and men decorated on the good work they had performed while serving with the Field Force. The following are the names of the officers who received medals: Lieutenant-Colonel Barlow, Majors Ridley and Graham, Captains Watson and Abbot-Anderson, Lieutenants Plunkett, Gunning, Stevens, and Hughes, 2nd Lieutenants Sealy and Menzies, Captain and Adjutant Baldwin, and Lieutenant and Quartermaster Stewart-Wynne.

Lieutenant-Colonel Barlow received the clasp, inscribed "Samana 1891," only, having been already awarded the India Medal for 1854 for

2ND BATTALION FIRING A FEU-DE-JOIE AT CHAKRATA, N.W.P., INDIA, ON QUEEN EMPRESS' BIRTHDAY, 1893.

service in the Hazara Expedition of 1888 as D.A.A.-General of the Second Brigade of the expeditionary force.

The stay of the battalion at Meerut lasted barely six months, for on the 20th March 1893 it marched out—strength 19 officers and 868 other ranks—and proceeded to Chakrata, which was reached on the 1st April and where the battalion remained throughout the hot weather, providing a detachment of 50 men under Captain James at Gnatong in Independent Sikkim. Chakrata was left again on the 13th November, when the Second Battalion Manchester Regiment went by march, river, and rail to Dinapore, where the Regiment had already twice previously been quartered.

During the stay in this garrison the battalion lost 1 sergeant and 14 men in an outbreak of cholera which occurred in August 1894, and which occasioned a move into cholera camp.

In 1897 while the battalion was quartered at Dinapore the frontier troubles became very acute, the border for 400 miles was in a blaze, and a larger force was mobilised for service than had ever before been placed in the field in India for any lesser operations than those of an actual campaign. The 2nd Battalion Manchester Regiment was not so fortunate as to be selected for service, but several officers took part in the expedition, Captain Plunkett, Lieutenants Weston and Stevenson being employed as transport officers, and Lieutenants Godbold and Wright were attached for duty to the 2nd Battalion Argyll and Sutherland Highlanders while that regiment was employed with the Tochi Field Force.

The battalion had still to complete another twelve months of foreign service before it could expect to be sent to England, and this last year was to be spent at Aden. Accordingly on the 4th November 1897 it left Dinapore—15 officers, 793 other ranks, 20 women and 44 children—under command of Lieutenant-Colonel Ridley, for Bombay, where it arrived on the 11th and embarked the same day in the hired transport *Dilwara*. Aden was reached on the 21st, and while 254 men of between three and five years' service went on in the ship to Gibraltar for transfer to the 1st Battalion, the remainder of the officers and men landed, headquarters and five companies proceeding to the barracks at the Crater, while the three other companies were accommodated in those at Steamer Point.

During the battalion's stay in Dinapore it had lost by death two officers—Major Graham and Captain Ward—8 non-commissioned officers, 46 men, and 7 children.

The battalion, under command of Lieutenant-Colonel Ridley, embarked at Aden in the transport *Dunera* on the 14th November 1898 for conveyance to England, being relieved at Aden by the 2nd Battalion Derbyshire Regiment. The embarking strength was 18 officers, 553 other ranks, 13 women and 28 children. At Malta 25 young soldiers were put on shore for transfer to the 1st Battalion at Malta, and the *Dunera* then proceeding on her voyage arrived on the 2nd December at Southampton, whence headquarters and four companies went by rail to Manchester and the rest of the battalion to Lichfield, at the former place being received with great enthusiasm.

The 2nd Battalion had been only exactly a year in Manchester and Lichfield when, on the 8th December 1899, it was concentrated at Holyhead, where it embarked for Dublin in relief of the 2nd Battalion Bedfordshire Regiment, being quartered on arrival in the Royal Barracks; but the recent outbreak of the war with the Dutch Republics had greatly dislocated all ordinary arrangements for relief, and on the 10th January 1900 the commanding officer received orders directing the battalion to prepare for early embarkation for Egypt. These instructions were cancelled on the same evening, and the fresh orders now issued directed that the 2nd Battalion Manchester Regiment was to proceed on the 19th to Aldershot, there to mobilise for active service in South Africa, having been posted to the 17th Brigade, 8th Division, South African Field Force.

The 8th Division was placed under command of Lieutenant-General Sir H. Rundle and was composed as under:

16th Brigade: Major-General Campbell; 2nd Battalion Grenadier Guards, 2nd Battalion Scots Guards, 2nd Battalion East Yorkshire Regiment, and 1st Battalion Leinster Regiment.

17th Brigade: Major-General Boyes; 1st Battalion Worcestershire, 2nd Battalion Royal West Kent, 1st Battalion South Staffordshire, and 2nd Battalion Manchester Regiments.

Also the 1st, 4th, and 11th Battalions Imperial Yeomanry, the 5th Company Royal Engineers, and the 2nd, 75th, and 79th Batteries Royal Field Artillery.

An advance party of 2 officers and 25 non-commissioned officers and men left Ireland on the 15th January, and on the 19th the remainder of the battalion followed, reaching Aldershot next day and being quartered at Oudenarde Barracks, North Camp. The marching-in strength was 25 officers, 685 other ranks, 25 women and 52 children.

Mobilisation began at once and demands were made upon the depot for all reservists of Sections A, B, and C of the Army Reserve at once to

D COMPANY, 2ND BATTALION, QUARTER GUARD, AT GNATONG, JALEP LA—TIBETAN FRONTIER, 1894.
(11,000 feet altitude.)

rejoin the headquarters. Trained men were urgently required, since upwards of 200 men then serving with the battalion were either under the age-limit for active service or were medically unfit. During the next ten days 375 reservists joined in parties of varying size : and it being decided that one company of the battalion should be trained and equipped as a Mounted Infantry Company, H Company was selected for this service and proceeded for training to the Army Service Corps barracks ; the officers with this company were Captain and Brevet Major Goldfinch, Lieutenant Trueman, and 2nd Lieutenants Thornycroft and de la Penha.

In Army Order 50 of March 1900 it was announced that " Her Majesty the Queen has been graciously pleased to approve of each of the undermentioned regiments of infantry being increased by two line battalions, which will be numbered the 3rd and 4th Battalions respectively :

> " The Northumberland Fusiliers.
> The King's (Liverpool Regiment).
> The Worcestershire Regiment.
> The Duke of Cambridge's Own (Middlesex Regiment).
> The Manchester Regiment.
> The Royal Munster Fusiliers."

This arrangement naturally entailed the renumbering of certain Militia Battalions, and as a consequence the 3rd and 4th Battalions of the Manchester Regiment now became the 5th and 6th. On this augmentation Majors Gethin and Melvill—the latter temporarily—were posted to command the new 3rd and 4th Battalions respectively, while to each were sent 113 non-commissioned officers and men, and all men who would ordinarily have been left behind in England on the departure of the battalion on active service.

On the 16th March the 2nd Battalion Manchester Regiment left Aldershot in two special trains and embarked at Southampton on the *Bavarian*, sailing at 4 p.m. the same day for South Africa. The embarking strength of the battalion was 27 officers and 858 non-commissioned officers and men ; the following officers left England with headquarters :

Lieutenant-Colonel C. T. Reay, Majors A. B. Maxwell and J. H. Abbot-Anderson, Captains H. L. James, W. H. Williamson, G. C. Rynd, and G. Cooper-King, Captain and Brevet Major W. H. Goldfinch, Captain and Adjutant J. H. M. Jebb, Lieutenants A. G. Sharp, J. D. B. Erskine, F. H. Dorling, C. F. H. Trueman, and F. S. Nisbet, Second Lieutenants W. G. K. Peirce, W. C. N. Hastings, C. M. Thornycroft, P. D. de la Penha, C.

Richardson, and K. E. Kirkpatrick, Hon. Captain and Quartermaster O. Stewart-Wynne, Sergeant-Major W. I. Cordon. Attached: Captain C. A. Vanderzee (5th Btn. Militia), Captain D. C. Ansted (5th Btn. Militia), Lieutenant C. O'Hagan (6th Btn. Militia), Lieutenant Middleton-Stewart, Surgeon-Captain Black, attached R.A.M.C.

Cape Town was reached on the 6th April, and here the battalion was joined by Lieutenant Baker, who had proceeded to South Africa in the previous December attached to the Duke of Cornwall's Light Infantry. At Cape Town orders were received that the battalion was to go on to Port Elizabeth.

The greater part of the 8th Division was now in South Africa, embarkation having begun on the 10th March, though the last unit did not leave England until the 18th April.

The battalion disembarked at Port Elizabeth on the 9th April, and the following day was occupied in completing equipment and preparing for the field. Captain Vanderzee, 5th Battalion, and 23 non-commissioned officers and men were detailed to remain at Port Elizabeth as a depot and to have charge of all the regimental baggage.

On the 11th April the 2nd Battalion Manchester Regiment left Port Elizabeth for the front in two special trains, and on reaching Edenburg on the afternoon of the 13th orders were received to detrain and to march the same night to Reddersburg. At Edenburg fifty ponies were drawn for the battalion mounted infantry company, and the battalion left at 8 o'clock that night, arriving on the 14th at daybreak at Reddersburg and marching out the same afternoon to Mostert's Hoek, about five miles distant.

The 8th Division had been ordered to concentrate at Edenburg and was now pushing forward to the relief of Wepener, a small town in the south-eastern part of the Orange Free State, where a portion of the Colonial Division was at this time besieged by De Wet, and to relieve which Lord Roberts had directed two columns to converge upon the town from the west and south. The southern column which started from Aliwal North was commanded by Major-General Hart, while the other column under Rundle contained the 8th Division, a brigade of the 3rd, and some Yeomanry under Brabazon.

By the 17th April Rundle, who had been ordered to move on Dewetsdorp so as to cut off the Boer forces moving north from Wepener, now about to be relieved by Hart, had concentrated the following troops at Rosendal: the 17th Brigade under Major-General Boyes, 1 battalion of the 16th Brigade, 3 batteries, and 2 battalions of yeomanry—in all, with the troops from the 3rd Division, some 12,000 men with 24 guns ; 2 battalions of the 16th Brigade with a battery and some mounted men were left to keep up communication with the railway.

De Wet, hearing of Rundle's advance, sent a force of some 2,500 men with guns, under his brother, Piet de Wet, to occupy a defensive position on the semicircle of hills under which the town of Dewetsdorp lies.

The force under Rundle left Rosendal on the 19th April and bivouacked that night at Oorlog's Poort, about 12 miles from Dewetsdorp, the yeomanry and M.I. moving on next morning to reconnoitre the Boer position and coming on the enemy near the farm of Wakkerstrom, three miles from Dewetsdorp. The infantry of the British force was coming up in rear, and it seems possible that had they been immediately pushed forward Dewetsdorp might at once have been carried. At this period of the war, however, frontal attacks had been found to be very costly, and Lord Roberts had issued a warning against their too general employment, while Rundle's yeomanry was rather raw, and a wide turning movement—the only alternative—might have been risky.

Any attack was therefore withheld until more British troops had been collected, but the Boers did not stay for the arrival of these and evacuated Dewetsdorp on the 24th, moving north towards Thaba' Nchu.

During these operations the battalion was entrenched under enemy fire for fifty hours, but suffered no casualties.

Marching on in the track of the retreating Boers, the 17th Brigade and the Manchester Battalion reached Thaba' Nchu on the 27th April, Houtnek on the 8th May, and Senekal on the 25th, and here it was found that the enemy, having withdrawn from the town, was occupying a strong position at Biddulphsberg about 8 miles to the east ; but in the action which ensued on the 29th May the brunt was borne by the 16th Brigade, and the battalion was not engaged, though five companies had marched through Senekal on the 28th and had taken up and entrenched a position on the Lindley road.

On the 4th June a mixed force marched to Ficksburg, there to remain in occupation ; the force was commanded by Lieutenant-Colonel Reay, who had with him five companies of his battalion, which on arrival camped under Imperani Mountain, one mile to the north-east of the town and commanding the Fouriesburg and Senekal roads. The enemy held positions at Commando Nek some seven miles to the north-east, and the battalion was occupied in strengthening the defences and in patrolling the neighbourhood of the town ; during one of these reconnaissances Corporal Clark of the 2nd Battalion Manchester Regiment was slightly wounded.

On the 30th June the battalion left Ficksburg for Hammonia, and on the 1st July its members were distributed as under :

At Hammonia : 19 officers and 701 non-commissioned officers and men.
At Bloemfontein : 5 officers and 71 non-commissioned officers and men.
At various places : 1 officer and 16 non-commissioned officers and men.
Sick, detached : 1 officer and 54 non-commissioned officers and men.
Missing : 2 non-commissioned officers and men.
En route to England : 1 officer and 5 non-commissioned officers and men.
Staff employ : 2 officers and 7 non-commissioned officers and men.
Making a total of 29 officers and 856 non-commissioned officers and men.

On the 3rd July at Hammonia some welcome reinforcements in officers and men were received, Captain Vanderzee and 21 other ranks rejoining from the base at Port Elizabeth, while Lieutenant Mansergh, 6th Battalion, and Second Lieutenant Eykeyn, 5th Battalion, came out from home in charge of one hundred Militia Reservists of these battalions ; about the same date Second Lieutenants Woodhouse, Boone, and Crozier joined on first appointment.

On the 24th July General Rundle, with the 8th Division, initiated an attack upon the enemy's position from Ficksburg, Willow Farm, and Hammonia, D, F, and G Companies of the Manchesters, with the Queenstown Volunteers, being sent to seize a hill above Ward's Farm to cover the left of the advance. The operations were protracted until the 26th, when the Boers evacuated their positions and fell back in a north-easterly direction upon Fouriesburg, which they merely passed through in their retreat, leaving upwards of a hundred British prisoners behind them.

The 17th Brigade was in Fouriesburg on the 30th July and then marched on the 1st August for Slaap Krantz in the Caledon Valley, reaching Naauwpoort Nek on the following day, only to learn of the surrender a few days previously of 4,000 of the enemy under Commandant Prinsloo, who had been hemmed in in the Brandwater Basin by the 8th Division on the south, the 10th on the west, by the Colonial Division and 21st Brigade on the north, while Basutoland lay to the east beyond the Caledon River.

The 17th Brigade left Naauwpoort Nek on the 3rd August and reached the Wilge River, four miles short of Harrismith, on the 6th : here the battalion was joined by half A and half E Companies, which had up to this remained behind at Hammonia. Reitz was occupied by the brigade on the 14th without opposition, and the few days' rest which was here obtained was very welcome, for supplies had been so scarce that the 8th Division had been on short rations, the clothing of the men was completely worn out, and many men in the battalion were without serviceable boots. Men who for this reason were unable to march were sent back from Reitz to Harrismith under Lieutenants Nisbet and de la Penha. Many questions were asked in the House of Commons as to the extent and preventability of the privations suffered by those under General Rundle's command, and in a divisional order of the 11th August General Rundle acknowledged that in carrying out the instructions he had received his force had undergone "exceptional privations," and thanked all ranks for the hearty co-operation they had afforded him.

The brigade, and with it the battalion, continued for some considerable time longer to operate in this district, occasionally marching from one part of it to another in pursuit of an elusive enemy, only to find on returning to its former haunts that towns which had been occupied had, in the absence of the British column, been reoccupied by the Boers. Thus on the 17th August the 17th Brigade marched into Vrede, was at Bethlehem on the 11th September, and then, retracing its steps towards Senekal, found on arrival in the vicinity on the 15th that the enemy was in occupation and that it was necessary to evict him. In the operations that here resulted the battalion took no very active part, being detailed as escort to the guns; but on the 17th, when Rundle's force moved towards Ventersburg, the enemy was found at Bronkhartsfontein and an engagement ensued, during the course of which the battalion endeavoured, but unsuccessfully, to cut off the enemy's retreat.

On the 19th September the battalion was back again at Senekal, where it was joined by a welcome draft of 180 Militia Reservists, some of these from the 5th and 6th Battalions of the Regiment and others from the 3rd and 4th Battalions of the Suffolk Regiment: the following officers joined with this draft: Captain Noble on promotion, Lieutenant Harris, 5th Battalion, and Second Lieutenants Anderson and Waters on first appointment.

The column reached Bethlehem again on the 22nd, and between that date and the 30th September when it returned to Reitz it was on two occasions engaged with the enemy, but the battalion suffered no casualties.

The battalion remained at Reitz the best part of a fortnight, arriving at Harrismith again on the 14th October, the Mounted Infantry Company of the battalion, however, remaining behind at Reitz attached to the Imperial Yeomanry.

On the 3rd November a force left Harrismith with a convoy for Vrede; it was under the command of Major-General Boyes and was composed of the 2nd Battalion Manchester Regiment, a wing of the 2nd Battalion East Yorkshire Regiment, and 4 field guns; it was attacked in front and flank on the march, a man of the Battalion M.I. Company, which had by this rejoined from Reitz, Private Hall, being severely wounded. There was opposition again on the 7th and 8th; and on this latter date, while a wing of the battalion was engaged in clearing some heights on the right flank, Second Lieutenant Woodhouse, who had only joined the previous May, was dangerously wounded and died the next morning.

Vrede was reached on the 9th, and Standerton on the 12th, the march on each day being hotly opposed. The column left Standerton again for Vrede on the 15th, and on the next day a determined attack was made upon the left flank protected by F Company under Captain Noble, by whom the enemy was completely held in check, though our men were out in the open without shelter of any kind. The battalion suffered several casualties, Private Percival being killed, Private Murden mortally wounded, while Privates McNicholls, Johns, and Carey were also hit.

During the time that F Company was under fire the following non-commissioned officer and man behaved with very conspicuous coolness and courage: Corporal Richardson and Private Haines several times volunteered to bring in two men of the company who, by reason of the heavy fire of the enemy, were unable to rejoin their company, but they were not allowed to do so as at the time it was believed that the two men had been killed. The names of both the corporal and the private were brought to the notice of the Divisional Commander, while Civil Surgeon Moon, who had relieved Lieutenant Black at Harrismith in medical charge of the battalion, was also mentioned for conspicuous bravery "in recovering the body of a man who had been killed, though the Boers were firing at him at 300 yards' range."

The column reached Vrede in safety and was back again at Harrismith on the 23rd November, where on the 27th a draft of 41 Militia Reserve men joined the battalion.

On the 3rd December a column, of which the 2nd Battalion Manchester Regiment formed part, left Harrismith and moved via Reitz to Senekal; this town had been in occupation of the enemy, but on the approach of the British the Boers cleared off, the column marching in on the 15th. A stay of only four days was here made, when the force moved out again, was at Winburg on the 22nd, and back again at Senekal on the 1st January 1901. Here three companies of the battalion were left in garrison under Major Vizard, while the remainder marched out again with the force on the 4th and reached Reitpan on the 6th, when the enemy made a determined attack on the rear-guard, composed of A, B, C, and F Companies of the battalion, 50 men of Bethune's Horse, and 2 guns. A section of A Company, which was some distance in rear, was for some time in a very critical position, and Private Collier showed great gallantry and was brought to the notice of the General for taking, under heavy fire, a message from Captain Noble to Lieutenant Mansergh, commanding the isolated section. In carrying out this duty Private Collier was wounded.

The section was extricated with no little difficulty, and in the course of the action the following casualties occurred in the battalion: *killed*, Private Shawcross; *wounded*, Lance-corporal Chapman, Privates Collier and Hancock.

During the next few days' marching there was constant fighting, and on the 21st, in an engagement at Vlakplaats, Lance-Corporal Sullivan, of the battalion, was wounded.

Eland's River Bridge was reached on the 23rd January, on which date the battalion was thus distributed:

Present at headquarters and fit for duty	473
Unfit to march	149
Sick in various hospitals	181
Detached on various duties	252
Making a total strength of the battalion of	1,055

In the previous November Lord Roberts had been summoned to England to take up the high office of Commander-in-Chief of the British Army in succession to Field-Marshal Viscount Wolseley, and on the 29th of that month he issued his famous order thanking his troops for the great services they had rendered to their Queen and Country, and announcing that he had given up the command of the army in South Africa into the able hands of General Lord Kitchener of Khartoum.

The beginning of the New Year brought news from England to the army which filled the heart of every member of it with the deepest possible sense of personal loss, news which was communicated to the Officer Commanding at Harrismith on the 24th January 1901 in the following telegram from General Rundle:

"*Please place in orders that the Lieutenant-General has received the following message from Army Headquarters:*

"'*An official announcement of the death of Her Majesty the Queen at 6.30 p.m. yesterday has been received. All flags to be flown half-mast until further orders.*'

"*The Lieutenant-General in publishing this news to the troops feels that all ranks will join him in the deepest feelings of sorrow which no words can express.*"

CHAPTER XIX

SECOND BATTALION IN SOUTH AFRICA AND M.I. COMPANY
1901-1902
THE THIRD AND FOURTH BATTALIONS (1900-1906)

AFTER a very brief halt at Eland's River Bridge the 2nd Battalion of the Manchester Regiment marched on again and reached Bethlehem on the 28th January, having marched 400 miles since the 3rd of the preceding month; the defences of the town were taken over from the 1st Battalion Worcester Regiment, and the remainder of the 17th Brigade left on the 31st for Ficksburg.

1901

The command of the garrison was assumed by Lieutenant-Colonel Reay of the battalion; his staff officer was Captain and Adjutant Jebb, while Captain Noble took over the duties of Intelligence Officer, Major Vizard taking command of the battalion with Lieutenant Hastings as Adjutant.

The distribution of the battalion on the defences was as under:

A Company, Captain Erskine, Worcester Hill, Southern Line.
B Company, Lieutenant Nisbet, Manchester Hill, Southern Line.
C Company, Captain Rynd, flats commanding Harrismith Road.
D Company, Captain James, Stafford Hill, Northern Line.
E Company, Captain Williamson, Worcester Ridge, Southern Line.
F Company, Second Lieutenant Boone, Headquarter Camp.
G Company, Captain Cooper-King, Town Hall, Southern Line.

The Mounted Infantry Company of the battalion, under Captain and Brevet Major Goldfinch, proceeded to Ficksburg with the 17th Brigade.

During the next few weeks Lieutenant-Colonel Reay organised several minor expeditions in which companies and parties of the battalion joined the Yeomanry in the endeavour to round up isolated bodies of Boers on outlying farms, to bring in grain, etc., and in one of these expeditions Captain Noble received an injury to the head from the butt of a Boer rifle. Rumours too were occasionally raised that the enemy was collecting to attack Bethlehem, but nothing of so serious a character transpired.

On the 24th April General Rundle came in with Campbell's brigade and supplies and mails; these last were specially welcome as the troops in Bethlehem had been without letters for three months. Rundle's column had met with persistent opposition the whole way from Harrismith from a party of 300 Boers who had hung upon its flanks throughout the march.

On the 29th in heavy rain and deep mud General Rundle left again with Campbell's column to work within the Brandwater Basin, a special force composed as under being placed under Colonel Reay's command:

A, B, D, and F Companies 2nd Battalion Manchester Regiment.
Two companies of Details.
62nd Company Imperial Yeomanry.
2 Guns Field Artillery.
1 pom-pom.

C, E, and G Companies remained in Bethlehem under Major Vizard.

Retief's Nek was occupied without opposition, and the whole force then marched on to Fouriesburg, which was reached on the 2nd May. On the way the column spent a couple of days in clearing Snyman's Hoek, when large supplies of grain and several carts and wagons were destroyed; there was a certain amount of opposition, and Lieutenant Boone, who commanded F Company in these operations, was specially mentioned for gallantry. During the next fortnight the troops were employed in clearing the country about Heynsberg, Commando Nek, Brindisi, and Bamboosberg. Back again at Fouriesburg on the 15th May, the force left once more on the next day for Theron's Mill, where there was considerable opposition, and Brindisi Poort, and the ground was found to be so difficult for wheeled traffic that all tents and heavy kits were sent into Bethlehem on the 23rd May with the 16th Brigade, and for the next three weeks the force bivouacked.

The Division, the 16th Brigade excepted, now marched on the 1st June to Golden Gate, Colonel Reay's force acting for the first portion of the way as advance guard and thereafter taking over the protection of the right flank. Golden Gate was reached on the 5th, the enemy offering but small resistance to the advance, though continuously harassing the flanks and rear, but the battalion suffered no casualties. The road was so bad that two companies of infantry were kept constantly at work repairing it, while other companies had to man-handle and drag the wagons, and on one day only three miles could be covered.

The column arrived at Harrismith on the 8th, heavily fired on up to the last, and here during the 10th–12th June the battalion was refitted, and the kits and stores, which had been sent for safe custody to Bloemfontein on the arrival of the corps in South Africa, were now brought up to Harrismith. The battalion moved about the neighbourhood during the next few days, driving in cattle and escorting convoys; here too C, E, and G Companies rejoined from Bethlehem on relief by the 2nd Battalion East Yorkshire Regiment; while about this time the following officers came to the battalion on first appointment: Second Lieutenants Holberton, Lawson, Foord, and Fowke, and also Second Lieutenant Rackham-Bullard attached for duty from the 6th Battalion of the Manchester Regiment.

On the 4th July all ox-transport having been exchanged for mules, the following units were detailed as a mobile column under command of Lieutenant-Colonel Reay, with Captain Noble of the battalion as Intelligence Officer and Assistant Provost Marshal:

> 2nd Battalion Manchester Regiment.
> The Battalion M.I. Company.
> 2 squadrons Imperial Yeomanry.
> 2 guns R.F.A.
> 1 pom-pom.
> Detachments R.E. and R.A.M.C.

A combined sweep northwards on a large scale was now commenced under General Elliott, who controlled several columns on the west bank of the Wilge River, Colonel Reay's little force being next him just east of that river, while the 16th and 17th Brigades prolonged the line to the east. On the 5th Reay's column moved forward to Mill River Drift, encountering there some 50 of the enemy who were at first mistaken for our own men, but were very soon driven from their position, two or three being hit as they fell back. On the 17th Standerton was reached, the force marching via Brakspruit, Venterspruit, and Roberts' Drift over the Vaal River. Here Second Lieutenant Tylden-Wright joined the battalion on first appointment.

Only one clear day was passed at Standerton, which the column left again with the 16th and 17th Brigades on the 19th July, reaching the neighbourhood of Vrede on the 24th. Here a party of 40 Boers crept up in a dense fog close to C Company's picquet line, capturing Corporal Peacock, Privates Kelly, Kirwan, and Rawlings, who were, however, all released a few days later.

Lieutenant-Colonel Reay marched his column to Strydplaats on the 26th and on the next day to Witkopjes, where a large number of horses, cattle, and sheep was captured; but on the 27th Captain and Quartermaster Stewart-Wynne was severely wounded and taken prisoner while endeavouring to get a wagon and a Cape cart out of a drift some distance out on the flank. Corporal Fletcher of the Battalion M.I. Company and Private Coggan (Quartermaster Stewart-Wynne's groom) were also captured, as was a man of the South Stafford M.I.—attached to H Company; the two privates were released the same day and the two others on the 28th.

Moving on again, Colonel Reay's force joined the 17th Brigade in camp three miles south of Harrismith on the 3rd August; the trip had been a very successful one so far as regards clearing the country of live stock. On the 4th August the 3rd Volunteer Service Company joined the battalion; it contained 101 non-commissioned officers and men with Captain Lupton, Lieutenants Cronshaw and Routley; Second Lieutenant Harrison also joined on first appointment.

On the 5th the battalion took over the defences of Harrismith from the 2nd Battalion Grenadier Guards and 1st Battalion Leinster Regiment, when the different companies were distributed as under:

A Company : Plattberg and Underberg.
B   ,,   Town.
C   ,,   Basuto Hill.
D   ,,   Headquarters.
E   ,,   Waterworks and Natal Hills.
F   ,,   half at Bloemfield, half at headquarters.
G   ,,   Underberg.
Volunteer Company : half on Natal Hills, half on Vrede and Reitz Hills.

While the battalion was at Harrismith the usual excursions were made to bring in cattle and grain, and a second Mounted Infantry Company was formed from F Company, which was made up to a strength of 130 non-commissioned officers and men with Captain Noble, Lieutenants Richardson, Holberton, and Tylden-Wright.

On the 1st September the battalion was relieved at Harrismith by the 1st Battalion South Staffordshire Regiment, and the following force was then placed under the command of Lieutenant-Colonel Reay:

> 2nd Battalion Manchester Regiment.
> 250 mounted men, including H Company.
> 3 guns Royal Field Artillery,

and this little column left on the 4th with a convoy for Bethlehem, being joined *en route* by two battalions of Imperial Light Horse. Bethlehem was reached on the 7th and left again on the 9th, the column being back again at Harrismith on the 12th. A good many of the enemy were seen, but offered no opposition. On the 16th Lieutenant-Colonel Vizard was selected to superintend the building of a line of blockhouses from Harrismith to Olivier's Hoek, and to remain in charge of the line when completed. The column was for some days held in readiness to move out at the shortest notice, as reports were rife that the Boers intended invading Natal. It left again for Bethlehem on the 23rd September, and on this trek no Boers were seen as other British columns were in the neighbourhood; but on the return journey, when encumbered with many civilians who had been removed from Bethlehem, a party of Boers fired heavily upon the mounted men of the rear-guard composed of the 62nd Company Imperial Yeomanry. Three yeomen were left behind in some kraals without their horses, and Lieutenant Thornycroft and Private Archibald, of H Company of the battalion, went back to look for them, the latter riding up and down under a very heavy fire, calling out to the men to retire. This they succeeded in doing covered by fire from H Company. Private Archibald was brought to the notice of the Commander-in-Chief for gallantry, and the sequel was the appearance of the following in District Orders of the 28th October:

" The General Commanding in Chief has been pleased to sanction the promotion of the undermentioned non-commissioned officers and men for distinguished gallantry in the field, such promotion to take effect from the date of performance of the act. They will be borne supernumerary to the establishment of their units and will be absorbed into vacancies at the first opportunity :

.   .   .   .   .

2nd Battalion Manchester Regiment.
No. 3292 Private D. Archibald to be Corporal.
Date and particulars, Tyger Kloof, Orange River Colony. On September 29th 1901 volunteered to look for three missing men and did so successfully under fire of forty Boers."

.   .   .   .   .

On the next day, the 30th September, some 70 of the enemy attacked the rear-guard furnished by F Company of the battalion and some of the Yeomanry, when Privates Doran and Gilligan were wounded, the latter mortally. On the 5th October G Company and half D were mounted under Captain Noble, and provided an escort for a convoy conveying supplies to the columns of Colonels Broadwood and de Lisle. There was much of this convoy work at the time, and on the 13th at Austin's Drift Private McCarty was wounded, while on the 16th, close to Harrismith, Private [...] taken prisoner by the enemy but was released the next day.

On the 31st Lieutenant-Colonel Reay's column went into Be[...] taking a convoy and having orders to bring away all the civilian inhab[...] On the return journey, on the 6th November near Hathingsdal, as the col[...] was about to march off, a large number of the enemy appeared all roun[...] the camp and " sniped " the outposts, and when the advance guard reached Tyger Kloof it was heavily fired on, while a still more determined attack in greater strength was made upon the rear-guard, and part of F Company under Second Lieutenant Tylden-Wright was successfully rushed, when the following casualties were incurred :

Killed : Privates Ishmael, Taylor, and Bates (3rd Volunteer Company).

Wounded : Second Lieutenant Tylden-Wright, Lance-Corporals Dualey and McCarthy—these last both taken prisoners.

Prisoners : Sergeant O'Donnell, Lance-Corporal Hepworth (Volunteer Company), Privates Duncalf, Dawson, Durham, Green, Taylor, Townsend, Turner, Collins (Volunteer Company), and McCormick.

The Boers refused to release the prisoners at the time, but took them over the Basutoland Border and then set them all free, with the exception of Corporal Dualey, who was wounded, and whom they handed over to the Imperial Light Horse in camp north of Bethlehem.

Orders were now received to hold a line from Eland's River Bridge to Bethlehem to prevent the Boers from breaking south, and E Company, under Captain Williamson, entrenched and occupied a position at Eland's River Bridge, the remainder of the column moving on the 9th November to Tweefontein, where Captain Rynd with C Company entrenched another post. Marching on again on the 10th the advance guard was fired into at very short range near Hathingsdal, when the horses of Lieutenant Thornycroft and Corporal Archibald were killed under them and Private Jackson was severely wounded.

A few days later, on the 12th, near the Langberg, about 400 of the enemy were found in position ; they offered a very determined resistance, and a party of 20 men under Captain Noble was surrounded on three sides by about 70 of the enemy ; the following were our casualties :

Wounded : Captain Noble, mortally, dying the same day, Second Lieutenant Holberton, Privates Connery, Murray, and Ruskin. Returning to Tweefontein early next morning, the rear-guard again came in for some fighting and was followed up for several miles, having Private Parker wounded.

as now placed in command of a blockhouse
...ek and Albertina–Van Reenan's Pass,
..., Harrismith District"; A, C, D and E
...ith–Olivier's Hoek line, F and G, having
...Albertina, the Volunteer Company was at
...y and Battalion Headquarters were at
...any was divided up between these three
...mber, however, headquarters was moved
...dge was found inconvenient.
... joined about this time on first appoint-
... December a draft of 99 non-commissioned officers and
men arrived from the 3rd Battalion; and on the 9th Sergeant Francis of
the battalion was unfortunately shot dead by a sentry at Albertina.

Early in the year 1902 the Harrismith–Van Reenan's Pass Blockhouse
Line was greatly strengthened and pushed forward, while the number of the
blockhouses on the Olivier's Hoek line was increased from 16 to
36; and when in February there was a big drive from the north
up to Van Reenan's Pass, 750 unwounded and 110 wounded Boers were
captured.

On the 3rd March Second Lieutenant Marsh joined on first appointment.
In the middle of this month G Company was relieved at Albertina by
a company of the 2nd Battalion East Yorkshire Regiment, and proceeding
to Basuto Hill there took over the blockhouses from the 1st Battalion Black
Watch. The Van Reenan's Pass line from now on formed no part of
Lieutenant-Colonel Reay's command, which then ran from the Wilge
River to Olivier's Hoek, being known as Section A2. A new fort was built
at Bughtie for Battalion Headquarters. On the 20th F Company was
relieved at Van Reenan's Pass, taking over the blockhouses between
Bughtie and Harrismith; and at the end of April the battalion was thus
distributed:

Present on blockhouse line	. . . .	23 officers and 549 other ranks.
In hospital	. . . . .	1 ,, ,, 86 ,, ,,
On command	. . . . .	1 ,, ,, 97 ,, ,,
In prison	. . . . .	5 ,, ,,
M.I. Company	. . . .	4 ,, ,, 82 ,, ,,
Making a total of	. . . .	29 officers and 819 other ranks.

The long-drawn-out war was now coming to an end; on the 20th
May the Volunteer Company was relieved on the blockhouse line, and next

day entrained at Harrismith *en route* for the port of embarkation preparatory to proceeding to England. On the 1st June news was received that peace had been signed, and Lieutenant-Colonel Vizard, 3 non-commissioned officers, and 7 other ranks left Harrismith and sailed for England on the s.s. *Bavarian* to represent the battalion at the Coronation of King Edward VII, a ceremony which had to be postponed owing to His Majesty's sudden and very serious illness.

On the 16th of the month the battalion was ordered to evacuate the blockhouse line and concentrate at Harrismith, whither the different companies moved during the next two or three days, the mounted infantry company only remaining out to guard the blockhouses from theft and damage.

The men of the Army Reserve now began to leave for home in parties of one hundred; the first party left headquarters on the 7th July under Lieutenant Richardson, embarking on the 12th in the s.s. *St. Andrew*; the second sailed from Durban on the 31st under Captain Cooper-King, D.S.O.; and the third left Harrismith on the 14th August in charge of Captain Erskine and Second Lieutenant Mansergh; on the 18th August the officers and men of H Company returned their horses "to store" and resumed ordinary battalion duty.

Intimation was received on the 21st September that the battalion would shortly sail for home in the s.s. *Michigan* with battalions of the Scots Guards and Munster Fusiliers, and accordingly on the 24th the 2nd Battalion Manchester Regiment entrained for Durban at 5.30 p.m. at a strength of 17 officers and 419 non-commissioned officers and men; but on it being stated that there was accommodation for nine officers only of the battalion in the *Michigan*, the following embarked with the battalion; Lieutenant-Colonel Reay, Major Melvill, Captains Nisbet, Cockburn, and Hastings, Lieutenants Abbot-Anderson, Oliver, Lawson, and Holberton. The following seven officers sailed as follows: in the *Orient*: Lieutenants Ellershaw and Captain and Quartermaster Stewart-Wynne, in the *Kinfauns Castle* Captains Hardcastle and Sharp, Lieutenants Boone, Fowke, and Foord.

Durban was reached at 7 a.m. on the 26th, when the battalion at once went on board, sailing for Southampton at midday on the 27th.

During the South African war the battalion had marched upwards of 2,600 miles, had been repeatedly engaged with the enemy, and although it had taken no part in any of the so-called great actions of the campaign the casualties had been fairly heavy; they were as under: [1]

---

[1] The *Official History*, vol. iv, Appendix 17, gives: killed or died of wounds, 2 officers and 7 other ranks; wounded, 5 officers and 19 other ranks; captured and missing, 20 other ranks; and died of disease, 39 non-commissioned officers and men, or a total of 92 casualties as against 141 in the battalion list.

Killed in action : 9 non-commissioned officers and men.
Died of wounds : 3 officers and 2 non-commissioned officers and men.
Wounded : 4 officers and 28 non-commissioned officers and men.
Taken prisoners or missing : 1 officer and 38 non-commissioned officers and men.
Died of disease : 56 non-commissioned officers and men.

The following were the different " mentions," decorations and promotions won by the battalion during the campaign :

Mentioned in despatches : Lieutenant-Colonel Reay, Majors Maxwell and James, Captains Goldfinch, Cooper-King, Jebb, Noble, Brindley, and Hastings, Lieutenants Thornycroft and Baker, Second Lieutenants Boone and Waters, Sergeant-Majors Prosser and Burke, Colour-Sergeants Kennedy and Walker, Sergeants Burke, Clarke, Lindsay, McKenzie, Price, and Wood, Lance-Sergeants Richardson and Robertson, Privates Archibald, Collier, Howard, Gough, Newton, and Pearson.

The Companionship of the Bath was conferred upon Lieutenant-Colonel Reay.

The Distinguished Service Order was bestowed on Lieutenants Hastings and Jebb.

A Brevet Lieutenant-Colonelcy was given to Major Maxwell and Private Archibald was promoted Corporal.

The Medal for Distinguished Conduct in the Field was given to the following warrant officer, non-commissioned officers, and men : Sergeant-Major Prosser, Colour-Sergeants Kennedy and Walker, Sergeants Morris and Barton, Privates Archibald and Collier.

M.I. Company, Second Battalion Manchester Regt.

Soon after the arrival of the Second Battalion at Aldershot in January 1900 to form part of the 8th Division prior to going to South Africa, H Company was told off as a Mounted Infantry Company under Captain and Brevet Major W. H. Goldfinch. The subalterns of the company were Lieutenant C. F. Trueman, Second Lieutenants C. M. Thornycroft, and P. de la Penha. The N.C.O.s and men were chosen as far as possible from men who had either been through an M.I. course or who had had something to do with horses in civil life.

Soon after its formation the company was detached from the Regiment and proceeded to South Camp, Aldershot, where it was attached to the A.S.C. For the first month it was simply learning the mounted drill on foot, and it was only two weeks before embarkation that the company received 50 cobs, and its saddlery, etc., the result being that when the company rejoined the battalion on the day of embarkation the men had only a very sketchy idea of riding and horse-management in general.

On disembarking from the *Bavarian* at Port Elizabeth on 9th April, the company proceeded with the first part of the battalion to Edenburg, reaching there about 11 a.m. on 13th April. Orders were received to draw 50 cobs and to be ready to move off that night to Reddersburg, about 16 miles away. The cobs were all Argentine ponies, half-broken, and had arrived that morning, having only been off the ship a few days, most of which had been spent in the train, and as can be imagined were not half fit. There was great difficulty in getting them saddled up, as all the saddlery was new and in the time it was impossible to fit it properly. Besides this, there were dozens of things to be attached to the saddles, such as bayonets, cold-horseshoe cases, rifle buckets, etc. etc.

The company managed to get away from Edenburg at 8.30 p.m. and the column reached Reddersburg without mishap, at 5.30 a.m. next day. After a few hours' rest the company again moved off to Masserbock Farm, where it remained for a couple of days, and then on the 17th moved to Rosendal, where it stayed till the morning of the 19th. From the 14th to 18th it rained hardly without stopping. During the next two days the column moved towards Dewetsdorp, and on the 21st the company came under fire for the first time. The next four days were spent in shelling the Boer position, the mounted troops being sent to reconnoitre the flanks each day.

On the 28th, General French having come out with a column from Bloemfontein, an attempt was made to surround the position; but on the movement being duly completed, it was discovered that the enemy had all disappeared during the night. All the mounted troops were at once moved off to Wepener, but the Boers had raised the siege there and retired.

At the beginning of May the company left the battalion and was attached to a regiment of M.I. belonging to the 3rd Division. The next fortnight was spent in and around Dewetsdorp, and on the 20th May the column moved to Bloemfontein, arriving there in time for the official annexation of the Orange Free State, the company taking part in the parade in the square. On 31st May the company was ordered to proceed to rejoin the 8th Division; Second Lieutenant C. M. Thornycroft was left behind in hospital with dysentery.

The company overtook the 8th Division near Thaba 'Nchu, and together with the Yeomanry formed the mounted troops of the 17th Brigade. From now for several months the movements of the M.I. Company corresponded to those of the 2nd Battalion, i.e. moving about between Thaba 'Nchu, Senekal, Bethlehem, Winburg, and Harrismith, taking part in the Wittebergen operations and convoying supply columns from Harrismith to Bethlehem. In November the 17th Brigade operated over the country between Harrismith and Standerton and back again to Harrismith. On the 3rd December the column again left Harrismith and moved by Reitz and Senekal to Winburg, arriving there on the 23rd December. Only one night was spent there, and then it moved out towards Spitz-Kop and from there to Senekal. Half the battalion and 20 M.I. were left at Senekal for ten days, whilst the remainder of the column operated in the neighbourhood in conjunction with Colonel Knox and Colonel White's columns.

On their return Senekal was again evacuated and the column moved to Eland's River, near Harrismith. Everyone was now hoping for a rest in Harrismith, as since the 3rd December the column had been steadily on the move, a tremendous number of men had gone sick (the M.I. Company instead of being 130 strong was only 60, and the battalion could only muster about 300), all clothing was in a very bad state, and horses and men were getting worn out. However, it was not to be, and after a night's rest at Eland's River the column moved back once more to Bethlehem. Here the battalion was left to garrison the town, and the mounted troops (Yeomanry and M.I.), Stafford and Worcester Regiments were sent through the Brandwater Basin to Ficksburg, on the border of Basutoland, arriving there on 3rd February.

"Here at last was a welcome rest for men and horses, and the M.I. Company stayed here for a month. Every now and then raids were made on mills and farms in the neighbourhood where the Boers kept supplies, otherwise most of the time was spent in recreation—cricket, tennis, sports, etc.—and in getting the men and horses fit again. On 5th March a column composed of the M.I. Company and the Worcester Regiment was sent off to Ladybrand via Basutoland; here we received orders to strengthen the line between Ladybrand and Thaba 'Nchu and prevent the Boers from breaking through. After a few days we were rejoined by the rest of the troops from Ficksburg. Unfortunately this drive was a failure, all the Boers slipping through, and we returned to Ficksburg, arriving there on 3rd April, and once more enjoyed a peaceful time, interlarded with expeditions into the Brandwater Basin collecting supplies and cattle. On all these expeditions we generally ran across the enemy and there was usually a good deal of rifle fire and a few casualties on each side.

"On 12th May the column left Ficksburg with many regrets and joined up with the remainder of the 8th Division under General Rundle, spending the next four weeks in the Brandwater Basin rounding up farms and taking away all women and children, cattle, horses, supplies, etc., and burning what could not be taken away. This was a very cold trip, as there were no tents and only two blankets per man and it was freezing nearly every night. The country was very mountainous, and it was hard work on both men and horses; and the enemy, although they never attacked in force, were worrying us the whole time. On 9th June we got to Harrismith, and here to everyone's great regret we had to say good-bye to our old friends the Yeomanry, who were going home. On 12th June the M.I. Company was once more off to Bethlehem with a convoy, returning again to Harrismith on 26th June. On 3rd July a column under Lieutenant-Colonel Reay, consisting of the 2nd Battalion Manchester Regiment, 250 mounted troops, two 18-pounder guns, and one pom-pom, left Harrismith and proceeded in the direction of Vrede. The M.I. Company were on their own most of this trek about seven miles west of the main column. The fourth day out a laager was captured, but the men all got away; but the next day the M.I. Company rounded up about 5 prisoners and 300 head of cattle. Standerton was reached on 16th July and after two days' rest the column returned to Harrismith. Here at last the company got a good rest, as it was not till 5th September that it started again, once more doing convoy work to Bethlehem. This was a very uneventful trek, our casualties being only 2 men slightly wounded and 3 horses killed. On 20th September the same was again repeated, our casualties this time being 2 killed, 1 wounded, and 1 taken prisoner. The next moves were two short ones taking supplies to Colonel Broadwood's column about thirty miles out of Harrismith, and they were very peaceful ones.

"Owing to rinderpest breaking out all the oxen had to be inoculated, with the result that there was nothing doing for ten days.

"On 25th October the mounted troops joined Colonel Broadwood's column for six days, most of the work consisting of rounding up farm-houses, but the results were poor, only 3 prisoners being taken. A convoy to Bethlehem was the next job, and the new I.Y. let 150 Boers rush their rear-guard one day, taking 12 prisoners, killing 3 men, and wounding 1 officer and 2 men. On our return journey fresh supplies met the column at Eland's River Bridge, and we turned again towards Bethlehem. The column nearly got into a tight corner as it ran up against General Prinsloo's commando of about 500 strong, and our strength was only about 300. However, we managed to get back, but with 1 officer killed (Captain Noble) and 1 wounded (Lieutenant Holberton) and about 12 men wounded.

"The horses of the M.I. got mange rather badly at this time, and the company was told off for a rest and to do garrison duty. The company was split up at Bloemfield Bridge and Albertina, and there it remained till 20th December, when it moved to Olivier's Hoek. Our duties now were helping to guard the block-house line, and hereabouts the company stayed till the end of the war, except for one or two short expeditions for a couple of days at a time rounding up farm-houses and preventing small parties of Boers from breaking through into Natal. During 1901 Second Lieutenant A. G. Foord joined the company on first appointment and also Second Lieutenant Crozier.

"Lieutenant Trueman proceeded home on promotion."

THE THIRD BATTALION

As already elsewhere stated, the new Third (Line) Battalion of the Manchester Regiment was raised at Aldershot on the 1st March 1900, Lieutenant-Colonel Gethin from the 2nd Battalion being appointed to command a fortnight later. Within some nine months at most of the creation of the new battalion it had already begun to be called upon to furnish officers and men to comply with the incessant calls for both from the seat of war in South Africa. Thus, on the 2nd January 1901, 18 men left for South Africa to form part of a composite company of mounted infantry; again, on the 6th May 1 officer and 17 other ranks embarked for the war with No. 6 Composite Mounted Infantry Company; No. 7 Company of the same arm took away 1 officer and 32 men from the battalion on the 7th October; a month later a draft of 103 "other ranks" embarked for the war; and finally on the 7th February 1902 15 men sailed with No. 18 Aldershot Company Mounted Infantry for service at the front.

During the stay of the battalion at Aldershot the 3rd Battalion was, on the 24th May 1902, presented by Field-Marshal Lord Roberts with its first set of Colours, the religious part of the ceremony being performed by Bishop Taylor Smith, Chaplain-General to the Forces.

The 3rd Battalion was now to proceed on its first tour of foreign service, and being railed from Aldershot to the port of embarkation it there embarked on the 28th July in the hired transport *Dominion* for St. Helena at a strength of 15 officers, 2 warrant officers, 37 sergeants, 23 corporals, 16 drummers, and 418 privates. On arrival at the island on the 12th August the battalion disembarked and proceeded to Longworth Camp, in relief of the 3rd Battalion Wiltshire Regiment.

PRESENTATION OF COLOURS TO 3RD (LINE) BATTALION AT ALDERSHOT BY FIELD-MARSHAL EARL ROBERTS, 1902.

The battalion made a stay of no more than four and a half months at St. Helena, when, leaving behind B and C Companies, it embarked in the *Plassey* on the 31st December for Cape Town, landed there six days later and was sent by rail to Middelburg, Cape Colony, arriving there on the 9th January 1903, and relieving the 1st Battalion Royal Inniskilling Fusiliers : 4 officers and 103 men from the 4th Battalion joined on board ship prior to leaving St. Helena.

Of the officers whom the battalion had sent to the war Captain Hopkins was mentioned in despatches.

Two drafts now reached the battalion in quick succession, 157 men coming in February from the 4th Battalion, and 139 from the 2nd, now at home again; with the arrival of this last draft the strength of the 3rd Battalion, including the two companies detached at St. Helena, now reached a total of 1,118 all ranks, and of these 134 men were in April sent to reinforce B and C Companies at St. Helena; but within rather less than a year—on the 16th January 1904—these two companies rejoined headquarters in South Africa, their strength being 4 officers, 206 other ranks, with 3 women and 11 children.

At the end of January a draft of 9 officers and 200 men proceeded to Singapore to join the 1st Battalion.

In February 1904 Lieutenant-Colonel Gethin on completion of four years in command was placed on half-pay, and was in the following May succeeded by Lieutenant-Colonel J. Abbot-Anderson.

During the ensuing six months two drafts came out from home— one arrived in July and contained 1 officer and 104 other ranks, the other came out in January 1905 and was composed of 114 men.

In January 1906 headquarters proceeded to Middelburg, Transvaal, detaching half the battalion to Barberton, there to be quartered, and during this year drafts of a total strength of 183 non-commissioned officers and men were received from the 2nd and 4th Battalions.

On the 13th September the following Special Army Order was published :

" Reduction in Establishments.

" His Majesty the King has been graciously pleased to approve of the following battalions of the Foot Guards and Infantry of the Line being reduced :

Foot Guards—

3rd Battalion Coldstream Guards.
3rd Battalion Scots Guards.

Infantry of the Line—

3rd and 4th Btns. Northumberland Fusiliers.
3rd and 4th Btns. Royal Warwickshire Regiment.
3rd and 4th Btns. Lancashire Fusiliers.
3rd and 4th Btns. Manchester Regiment.

" These reductions will be carried into effect under instructions that will be issued from time to time. The reduction of the 3rd Btn. Coldstream Guards will be postponed for the present."

On the 22nd October the battalion, under Major James, who had assumed command in the month previous on Lieutenant-Colonel Abbot-Anderson being appointed Commandant of the Legation Guard, Peking, embarked at Cape Town in the *Braemar Castle* and sailed for Southampton, which was reached on the 19th November. Here the battalion was put on board the freightship *Frederica*, 4 officers and 130 men proceeding to Alderney and 16 officers and 299 other ranks to Guernsey. The disbandment of the battalion which had already begun now went rapidly forward, the non-commissioned officers and men being transferred to the 2nd Battalion, and by the 1st December the disbandment was completed, only the battalion staff remaining.

On the 6th December Colonel W. G. Gwatkin, Director of Operations and Staff Duties, Canadian Militia, and formerly of the Manchester Regiment, arrived with War Office authority to enlist men for the Canadian Military forces, and 120 men of the disbanded battalion volunteered for service in the Royal Canadian Regiment. This is the first instance of men being enlisted from the Imperial Forces for the Canadian service.

On the 14th December the Commanding Officer and Battalion Staff, having handed over all records, etc., at Preston, reported for duty to the 63rd Regimental Depot.

The Fourth Battalion

Raised on the same date as the Third, the Fourth Battalion Manchester Regiment came into existence at Aldershot, and for a short time Lieutenant-Colonel Gethin remained in charge of both, but on the 1st May Lieutenant-Colonel L. L. Steele was brought in from the Wiltshire Regiment to command the 4th Battalion.

The summer of this year was passed at Aldershot, and then on the 4th and 5th December the battalion left by rail in two parties and proceeded

PRESENTATION OF SOUTH AFRICAN WAR MEDALS TO 4TH (LINE) BATTALION (RAISED 1900—DISBANDED 1906) BY MAJ.-GEN. SIR H. McCALMONT, K.C.B., KINSALE, IRELAND, 1901.

(Lieut.-Gen. Vere Hunt Bowles, C.B., late 63rd Foot, Colonel of the Regiment, in the foreground.)

to Portland, taking over quarters in the Citadel. During its brief existence the 4th Battalion seems to have been regarded by the authorities purely as a draft-producing unit, and from first to last it gave no fewer than 32 officers and 1,726 non-commissioned officers and men to other corps, mainly of course to the 1st and 2nd Battalions of the Regiment.

On the 6th May 1901, 1 officer and 44 other ranks of the 4th Battalion embarked for South Africa with No. 2 Composite Company, Mounted Infantry; and when in July the battalion moved from Portland to Kinsale in relief of the 3rd Battalion Dorsetshire Regiment, it contained 12 officers, 2 warrant officers, and 370 non-commissioned officers and men.

1901

At the end of this year the calls for drafts began to be very insistent, and during the next five years the response was as follows:

Date	officers	other ranks	to
9th November 1901	0	103	1st and 2nd Batts.
27th July 1902	1	63	3rd Battalion.
15th December 1902	1	103	3rd ,,
7th January 1903	1	154	3rd ,,
7th February 1903	1	185	3rd ,,
7th February 1903	1	70	1st ,,
3rd March 1904	2	166	1st ,,
23rd December 1904	0	114	3rd ,,
1st March 1905	0	9	1st ,,
2nd June 1905	0	7	3rd ,,
14th October 1905	0	101	3rd ,,
8th December 1905	0	60	1st ,,
28th February 1906	0	40	1st ,,
16th March 1906	1	62	3rd ,,
7th November 1906	0	50	1st ,,

Of the 4th Battalion officers who served in the South African War, Captains Terry, Toogood, and Crichton and Second Lieutenant Wickham were mentioned in despatches; Captain Terry was promoted to a brevet majority.

On the 4th February 1902 headquarters and four companies moved from Kinsale to Cork, and here on the 31st July 1903 H.R.H. Field-Marshal the Duke of Connaught presented its first Colours to the battalion, while on the day following the battalion assisted to line the streets on the occasion of His Majesty the King's first visit to Cork since his accession.

1902
1903

1904 Lieutenant-Colonel Steele's four years in command came to an end on the 24th February, when he was succeeded by Lieutenant-Colonel C. C. Melvill.

1905 On the 20th October 1905 the 4th Battalion—strength, 23 officers, 2 warrant officers, 527 other ranks, 50 women and 99 children—left Ireland for Aldershot, and on arrival there was quartered in Corunna Barracks.

1906 In the following year the order for disbandment, already quoted in the case of the 3rd Battalion, was published, and the 4th Battalion was thereupon thus disposed of :

To the 1st Battalion in India, 50 privates.
To the 2nd Battalion in Guernsey, 23 officers and 311 other ranks.
To the Depot, 16 non-commissioned officers and men.
To other Corps, 18 non-commissioned officers and men.

The Colours of both the 3rd and 4th Battalions of the Manchester Regiment are now in the Town Hall, Manchester.

CHAPTER XX

THE FIRST BATTALION, 1903–1914
THE SECOND BATTALION, 1902–1914

THE EVE OF THE GREAT WAR

THE FIRST BATTALION

On the 17th April 1903 the 1st Battalion was inspected by Brigadier-General Sir A. Dorward, K.C.B., D.S.O., commanding the Straits Settlements,

1903 who took the opportunity of presenting the officers and men with the Queen's South African Medal; while on the 20th October all ranks entitled thereto received the King's South African medals from the same general officer.

Early in the next year two large drafts were received by the battalion; the first, composed of 205 non-commissioned officers and men, arrived

1904 on the 3rd March from the 3rd (Line) Battalion in South Africa, while on the 9th of the same month Second Lieutenant Sharland brought out 350 non-commissioned officers and men—the latter mostly recruits—from England.

On the 13th December the battalion, under command of Colonel Maxwell, embarked on the *Avoca* and sailed for Madras on the following day; reaching its destination on the 19th, it landed next morning and proceeded in two trains to Secunderabad, being quartered on arrival in the Entrenchment Barracks. The embarking strength at Singapore was 18 officers, 2 warrant officers, and 739 non-commissioned officers and men, with 7 women and 10 children.

1908 The 1st Battalion remained close upon five years at Secunderabad, moving in October 1908 to Kamptee in parties as under:

On the 9th October . 2 officers and 214 other ranks.
  ,,   26th   ,,   . 6   ,,   ,, 412   ,,   ,,
  ,,   27th   ,,   . 5   ,,   ,, 293   ,,   ,,

and on the departure of the battalion the General Officer Commanding the 1st Infantry Brigade, Secunderabad, published the following in brigade orders:

"*In bidding farewell to Colonel R. D. Vizard and all ranks of the 1st Battalion Manchester Regiment the Brigadier-General desires to record his high appreciation of the great keenness and efficiency displayed by the Battalion enlisted under his command, both when engaged in field manœuvres and in the field of sport. The good wishes of the Brigadier-General and those of the remainder of the Brigade accompany the Battalion to its new station.*"

In the Annual Inspection Report of the battalion of the 7th August 1909, Lieutenant-General Sir E. Barrow, K.C.B., Commanding Southern Army, stated of the 1st Battalion Manchester Regiment:

1909

"*A very good Regiment. Perhaps for physique, smartness and general 'turn out' the best Infantry battalion in the Southern Army.*"

At the Southern India Army Rifle Association Meeting held in September of this year at Bangalore, Colour-Sergeant Goodson of the battalion won the "Staff" Cup, and a team composed of Colour-Sergeant Goodson, Colour-Sergeant Eldon, Band-Sergeant Kennedy, Sergeants Robinson and Sutton won the "Wolfe-Murray" Cup. The non-commissioned officers and men who competed at this meeting won, in addition to the abovementioned cups, Rs. 713 in money prizes. Lance-Corporal Cummings and Private Rounds fired for the Army Team against the Volunteers, Lance-Corporal Cummings making the highest score for the Army.

On the 24th March 1910 Colonel Vizard with Captain Eddowes, Sergeant-Major Pike, 1 colour-sergeant, 1 sergeant, 2 corporals, and 3 privates proceeded from Kamptee to Trimulgherry to represent the battalion at the unveiling of a Memorial Brass Tablet which had been erected in All Saints' Church to the memory of the officers, non-commissioned officers and privates who died at Secunderabad during the stay of the battalion at that place in 1904–1908. The ceremony was attended by the Hon. Sir Charles Bayley, K.C.S.I., Resident of Hyderabad, and many old friends of the battalion.

1910

Towards the end of the year 1911 notification was received that the battalion would shortly effect a change of quarters, moving from Kamptee to Jullundur, and on the 11th and 12th October, E Company at a strength of 105 rank and file, under Captain Creagh, with Lieutenant Scully, proceeded to Jullundur, there to form a depot pending the arrival of the remainder of the battalion. At the same time the band

1911

—1 warrant officer and 42 other ranks—was sent from Kamptee to Delhi to form part of the massed bands there assembling for the approaching Coronation Durbar.

The battalion remained at Kamptee until the 23rd November, on which date, under command of Lieutenant-Colonel Baldwin, who had succeeded Colonel Vizard rather more than a year previously, it was dispatched by train to Delhi, which was reached on the 25th November. Here the Manchesters formed part of the 8th Brigade (Major-General Powell, C.B.) of the 3rd Division under Lieutenant-General Sir A. Pearson, K.C.B. The 8th Brigade was composed of the 1st Battalion Manchester Regiment, the 28th Punjabis, and the 47th and 53rd Sikhs, and it took part in all the Durbar ceremonial parades, including the State entry of their Imperial Majesties, on which occasion the Brigade lined the route in the Chandni Chowk.

On the 10th December there was an open-air divine service parade on the Maidan, at which their Majesties were present; the 12th was the day of the Durbar—Captain Hastings, D.S.O., Lieutenants Heelis and Tillard, with 72 other ranks representing the battalion in the Durbar Amphitheatre; on the 13th the King-Emperor visited the different camps; and on the 14th there was a Grand Review attended by some 49,000 troops, British and Indian. Of this Review the King expressed himself as follows to H.E. the Commander-in-Chief:

"*It gave me great pleasure to see so many of my troops on parade yesterday, including Imperial Service Troops, commanded in many cases by their own chiefs. I wish you to convey to all ranks, British and Indian, Volunteers and Imperial Service, my entire satisfaction with their appearance and steadiness under arms. I realise that much hard work was entailed by the preparations for the Durbar, and by the ceremonials connected with it, and I fully appreciate the efficient manner in which these arduous duties have been carried out by the men themselves and by the staff, both executive and administrative.*"

The battalion paraded this day 637 all ranks.

During the Durbar period the 1st Battalion Manchester Regiment was required to furnish many Guards of Honour:

On the 2nd December on the arrival of H.E. the Lieutenant-Governor of Burma; Captain Bates, Second Lieutenant Shaw, and 50 other ranks.

On the 8th a Guard from C Company under Captain Bates with Second Lieutenants Bostock and Shaw.

On the 9th a Guard was provided by B Company under Captain Dunlop with Lieutenant Fox and Second Lieutenant Hickie.

On the 11th a Guard was furnished by A Company under Captain Hastings, D.S.O., with Lieutenant Brown and Second Lieutenant Shipster.

On the 15th one of D Company under Major Walker with Lieutenants Mair and Musson.

On the 16th December, the date of the State departure from Delhi, the streets were again lined, the battalion being stationed inside the Kashmir Gate of the Fort opposite the church.

During the Durbar two silver cups were offered for competition, one for the best band present at the ceremony, the other for the best hockey team, and the band of the 1st Battalion Manchester Regiment won them both.

At the conclusion of the Durbar concentration 26 Durbar Coronation Medals were allotted to the battalion—4 to the officers, 6 to the band, and 16 to the warrant officers, non-commissioned officers, and men. Before the camp broke up Lieutenant F. Handley, late sergeant in the Manchester Regiment and now of the Ordnance Department, was presented with the Albert Medal, 1st Class, by His Imperial Majesty the King-Emperor in recognition of his gallant conduct in connection with the explosion of cordite in the Ferozepore Arsenal on the 31st August 1906.

On the 20th December the battalion left for Jullundur by train, arriving there the same day and detaching two companies to Amritsar.

During the summer of 1912 three companies with headquarters proceeded to Dalhousie, and in the autumn of this year the battalion was rearmed with the new short M.L.E. Mark III rifle.

In January 1913 the following letter, No. 090/2169 (A.G. 1), dated the 13th January, was received from the Secretary, War Office:

"*I am commanded by the Army Council to inform you that His Majesty the King has been graciously pleased to approve of the 8th (Southland) Regiment, formerly the 8th Regiment (Southland Rifles), New Zealand, being shown in the War Office Army List as allied to the Manchester Regiment.*"

The following correspondence passed in connection with the above:

"*To the Officer Commanding 1st Btn. Manchester Regiment.
From the Officer Commanding 8th (Southland) Regiment.*

"*Invercargill Club,
Invercargill, New Zealand.
24th June 1913.*

" *Sir,*

"*I have the honour to acknowledge the receipt of your very kind letter of the 22nd March and to convey to you on behalf of my officers and myself, our* grateful thanks for the kind expressions and good wishes contained therein, and for your kind invitation to us to consider ourselves honorary members of your Mess; should the opportunity present itself we should be most happy to avail ourselves of this privilege.

"Belonging as we do to a citizen army and consequently having no regular mess, we cannot offer you and your officers a similar compliment, but we hope if any of our comrades of the Manchester Regiment should visit New Zealand that they will favour us by calling at our Regimental Headquarters in this town, so that we may have the pleasure of meeting them and extending to them any attention and hospitality in our power.

"We are proud of the honour of being officially allied to your distinguished Regiment.

"With friendly greetings to yourself and your officers,
"I am,
Yours very sincerely,
J. E. Watson, Major,
Commanding 8th (Southland) Regiment."

"*To Major-General W. O. Barnard, Colonel of the Manchester Regiment. From the Officer Commanding 8th Southland Regiment.*

"*Invercargill Club,
Invercargill, New Zealand.
"24th June 1913.*

"Sir,
"I have the honour to acknowledge receipt of your very kind letter of 19th April, and to convey to you on my own behalf, as well as on behalf of all ranks of my Regiment, our very sincere and grateful thanks for the kind expressions and good wishes contained therein.

"We are very sensible of the honour so graciously conferred upon our Regiment by His Majesty the King in approving of the arrangement to officially affiliate us with so distinguished a Regiment in His Majesty's regular army.

"If any of our comrades of the Manchester Regiment should visit this outpost of the Empire, we hope they will favour us by calling at our Regimental Headquarters in this town, so that we may have the pleasure of meeting them and doing our best to show them some hospitality.

"Believe me, dear Sir,
Yours sincerely,
J. E. Watson, Major,
Commanding 8th (Southland) Regiment."

1914 The strength of the 1st Battalion Manchester Regiment on the 1st January 1914 was officers 25 and other ranks 1,003.

During 1914 the battalion was issued with the 1908 Web Infantry Equipment and the sword bayonet and scabbard pattern 1907.

In the autumn of this year came the swift sequence of events which led to the outbreak of the European war—a war in which India was to play a notable part and to share in which she hastened to send to Europe of her bravest and best. In a leading article in *The Times* of the 15th September the following fine passage describes how India came to the assistance of England in the mighty struggle upon which she had entered :

" In all its long annals the House of Commons has never been more moved than it was yesterday upon the reading of the wonderful message from the Viceroy of India. The Indian Empire has overwhelmed the British Nation by the completeness and the immensity of its enthusiastic aid. India is sending 70,000 men—horse, foot and artillery, British and Indian, Rajput and Gurkha, and Sikh and Pathan, a formidable fighting force trained and maintained in constant readiness for warfare—to fall into line beside their brethren and the French. The proudest Princes of India have buckled on their swords and are hastening to battle in the fair land of France. At their head comes the gallant Sir Pertab Singh, the Nestor of Rajput chivalry, who vowed long ago that he would not die in his bed, and at seventy years of age claims to face the foe once more upon the battlefield. With him is the knightly figure of the Maharaja of Bikanir; the young Maharaja of Patiala, the head of the Sikhs; the heir apparent of Bhopal, the hope of a powerful Musulman ruling family; the Maharaja of Jodhpur, another famous Rajput ruler; and many more representatives of the most ancient and honoured princely families of India. Seven hundred Princes and Chiefs of India have placed the whole of their resources at the disposal of the King-Emperor. They have offered their swords, their treasuries, their troops, their lives. The peoples of British India—the innumerable millions under the sole control of the Government—have been equally lavish in their outpourings and their demonstrations of loyalty. From the grim Khyber, from far Baluchistan, from the mountain heights of Chitral, promises of assistance and appeals for enrolment are being pressed upon the Government of India. Nor is this all. The Prime Minister of Nepal, the great Gurkha state, has offered the formidable troops he controls, an offer of inestimable value. Such is India's glorious answer to the Kaiser and his misguided dream of revolt in the East. Asia has joined in the battle against brutal lust for power, and her weapons are turned against him. . . . The Kaiser has lighted a torch indeed, for he has set the West and East alike afire against him."

The Second Battalion

1902 On reaching Southampton from South Africa about the end of September 1902, the 2nd Battalion Manchester Regiment proceeded to and was quartered at Aldershot, where it remained for exactly two years.

In June 1903 the battalion took part in a review of the First Army Corps by His Majesty the King and M. Loubet, President of the French Republic; in September manœuvres were held in the counties of Hampshire, Bedfordshire, Oxfordshire, and Surrey, and at the close of these the commanding officer was requested by the major-general commanding the brigade to convey to all ranks of the battalion under his command that " Lieut.-General Sir John French appreciated highly the marching and leading of the troops under his command, and that he would desire nothing better than to command the Army Corps in the event of active service."

1903

In June 1904 there was again a review of the First Army Corps on Laffan's Plain—this time before the Archduke Franz Ferdinand of Austria; and at the close of the Aldershot training for the year the battalion attended manœuvres in Essex, leaving Aldershot on the 1st September and marching via Alton and Avingdon Park to Southampton. Here on the 5th the battalion, in company with the 2nd Battalion Durham Light Infantry, embarked under command of Lieutenant-Colonel Watson, who in the previous October had taken the place of Lieutenant-Colonel Reay, C.B., in the *Consuelo*, and sailed for Spithead. The whole of the 6th was spent at sea, and on the 7th the battalion disembarked and marched the same evening towards Colchester, being temporarily attached to the 3rd Infantry Brigade. The battalion was at Stanway on the 9th, at Little Bentley the 10th and 11th, returning to Clacton on the 12th. Next day was the last day of the manœuvres and the battalion was on board ship again late on the night of the 13th, spent the 14th and 15th at sea, and, disembarking on the 16th, proceeded back to Aldershot by rail. Within a fortnight the 2nd Battalion was on the move again, leaving Aldershot in two trains on the 28th and embarking for the Channel Islands: headquarters with B, C, D, and H Companies went to Guernsey to be stationed at Fort George, while A, E, F, and G Companies disembarked at Alderney under Major Baldwin and were accommodated in Forts Albert and Château à l'Etoc.

1904

On leaving Aldershot the commanding officer received a private letter from Brigadier-General Belfield, of which the following is an extract:

"*I am very sorry to lose you and your Battalion from this brigade, not only for social reasons, but far more because you and yours have always played the game by me and I could always rely on you and I am grateful for the support you gave me. I wish you and yours the very best of luck.*"

Field-Marshal H.R.H. the Duke of Connaught, Inspector-General of the Forces, visited the island of Guernsey from the 23rd to the 25th September 1905, on which occasion the battalion furnished a Guard of Honour and was inspected. H.R.H. expressed his gratification at all he saw and was enabled to make a satisfactory report to His Majesty the King.

1905

When at the end of 1906 orders, which have already elsewhere been quoted, were issued for the disbandment of the 3rd and 4th Battalions of the Regiment, all the supernumerary officers, non-commissioned officers and men—exclusive of staff—were posted to the 2nd Battalion pending absorption. The residue of the 4th Battalion left Aldershot on the 15th November 1906 and proceeded to Alderney, the strength being 21 officers and 304 other ranks. The 3rd Battalion having arrived from South Africa in the *Braemar Castle*, on the 19th of the same month joined that part of the 2nd Battalion then quartered in Guernsey: the strength of the 3rd Battalion was 22 officers and 413 non-commissioned officers and men.

1906

With a view to the reduction of the Manchester Regiment the following steps were taken:

1. Bounties were offered to men transferring to other Lancashire Regiments for service in India.
2. Extensions of service were for the present to be in abeyance.
3. A number of men were, as already stated, discharged and allowed to accept service under the Canadian Government.
4. Men were permitted to pass prematurely to the Army Reserve provided they were assured of civil employment.
5. Continuance in the Service was held for the time in abeyance in the case of non-commissioned officers, and those who had already been allowed to continue in the Service received four months' notice.

On the 1st December 1906 there were on the strength of the 2nd Battalion no fewer than 63 officers and 1,041 non-commissioned officers and men, but by the 31st March 1907 these figures had been reduced to 51 and 764 respectively.

1907

The following officers were attached to the 2nd Battalion pending absorption:

From the 3rd Battalion: Major Weston; Captains Cooper-King, D.S.O., Jebb, D.S.O., Sowray, Chute, and Gillam, D.S.O.; Lieutenants de Lancy Forth, Stapledon, Rose, de Putron, Bolton, Stanley-Murray, Minogue, Ainsworth, and Frisby; Second Lieutenants Fulda, Clegg, Morris, Harrison, and Harper.

From the 4th Battalion: Majors Marden, D.S.O., and Walker; Captains Tillard, Trueman, Deakin, Bathurst, Merriman, and Terry; Lieutenants Morley, Bayley, Heelis, Irwin, Reade, Guinness, Thomas, and Woods; Second Lieutenants Dearden, Dean, Boutflower, Sotham, and Cates.

In the autumn of 1907 the 2nd Battalion was placed under orders to leave the Channel Islands and return to England when, through the Bailiff, Sir H. A. Giffard, the Royal Court of Guernsey forwarded the following letter, dated the 28th September, to the commanding officer:

"*Sir,*

"*I have the honour to inform you that at a special sitting of the Royal Court, held yesterday, the Court expressed its regret at the coming departure of the Battalion under your command, and paid a high tribute to the exemplary conduct of the Regiment whilst in garrison in this island. The Court further expressed its belief that these sentiments were shared by the public generally, and that it was fitting that a memorial thereof should be entered upon the Public Records.*

"*The Court therefore upon the motion of the Crown Officers orders its Resolution to be embodied in an Act of Court, and I was requested, as Bailiff, to transmit a copy thereof under the seal of the Bailiwick to yourself as Commanding Officer, together with this letter in which I have endeavoured to express to you for communication to the officers, non-commissioned officers and private soldiers under your command the high satisfaction with which the Court has witnessed the excellent order and irreproachable conduct which have distinguished the Battalion, and the excellent relations which it has established and maintained with the inhabitants of the Island generally.*

"*A copy of the Act of Court, duly sealed and authenticated, will be forwarded to you in due course.*"

The companies from Alderney, under Major Baldwin, embarked in the *Alberta* on the 1st October, and the headquarter wing, under Colonel Watson, in the *Vera* on the 2nd of the month, the two parties reaching Portsmouth on the 2nd and 3rd respectively; the battalion was quartered on arrival in the Cambridge Barracks and formed part of the 9th Infantry Brigade.

Soon after arrival the following were awarded the medal for Long Service and Good Conduct: Sergeant-Major Prosser, Sergeant Master-Tailor Holloway, Sergeants Watkins and Worley, Lance-Sergeants Rowley and Varney, and Private Dennerley.

In November 1907 His Imperial Majesty the German Emperor visited England, and on his being received on landing at Portsmouth Dockyard by H.R.H. the Prince of Wales, the battalion furnished a Guard of Honour of 100 non-commissioned officers and men under Captain Jebb, D.S.O., with Lieutenants Bayley and C. Abbot-Anderson, the last-named carrying the King's Colour. His Imperial Majesty was pleased to confer upon Captain Jebb on this occasion the Third Class of the Prussian Order of the Crown.

In the year following the battalion was again detailed to find a Guard of Honour—on the 18th June 1908 when H.R.H. the Duchess of Albany visited Portsmouth; the Guard was commanded by Captain Hopkins, the subalterns being Lieutenants Reade and Sotham.

Since the close of the South African War a movement had been on foot in the City of Manchester to raise a memorial to commemorate the services of the different battalions of the Regiment in that campaign and to perpetuate the names of those who died. Monday, 26th October 1908 was the day fixed for the unveiling of the Memorial, and at ten the previous evening a special train left Portsmouth conveying a Guard of Honour of the 2nd Battalion under Captain Paton, with whom were Lieutenants Foord —carrying the Regimental Colour—and C. Abbot-Anderson, Sergeant-Major Connery, the Band, and Sergeant-Drummer Pearce with a party of buglers. Ashton-under-Lyne was reached early the next morning, and from here the party proceeded to Manchester for the unveiling ceremony which took place in the afternoon.

The Memorial, the work of Mr. Hamo Thornycroft, stands in St. Ann's Square facing Exchange Street, and represents a soldier of the Manchester Regiment standing with bayonet fixed at the "ready," while a wounded comrade at his feet hands him a cartridge to continue the fight. On the different sides of the plinth are recorded the names of those who gave their lives in the South African War, and these number:

```
1st Battalion   4 officers and 148 non-commissioned officers and men.
2nd     ,,      3    ,,     ,,   84        ,,            ,,       ,,   ,,
5th     ,,      1    ,,     ,,    7        ,,            ,,       ,,   ,,
```

6th Battalion	0 officers and	18	non-commissioned officers and men.
1st Vol. ,,	0 ,, ,,	4	,, ,, ,, ,,
7th R.G.A. Vol.	0 ,, ,,	1	,, ,, ,, ,,
77th Co. I.Y.	0 ,, ,,	7	,, ,, ,, ,,
2nd Vol. Batt.	0 ,, ,,	6	,, ,, ,, ,,
3rd ,, ,,	0 ,, ,,	3	,, ,, ,, ,,
4th ,, ,,	0 ,, ,,	2	,, ,, ,, ,,
5th ,, ,,	0 ,, ,,	2	,, ,, ,, ,,
6th ,, ,,	0 ,, ,,	20	,, ,, ,, ,,
R.A.M.C. Vol.	0 ,, ,,	7	,, ,, ,, ,,

At 2.30 p.m. the Lord Mayor, General Sir Ian Hamilton, the Bishop of Manchester, Lieutenant-General Sir C. Burnett, Major-General W. O. Barnard, the Colonel of the Manchester Regiment, Brigadier-General W. Fry, and others entered the enclosure in the Square and proceeded to the platform. Here the Mayor made a brief speech, saying that the Memorial to be unveiled recorded the names of over 300 men who gave their lives in South Africa in defence of King and Country; he trusted that the Monument would not only perpetuate their noble work, but that it would be an everlasting reminder to others of their duty to their King and Country.

The Memorial was then dedicated by the Bishop of Manchester, who offered up a prayer concluding with the words:

"*To the Glory of God and in memory of the officers and men of the Manchester Regiment, Imperial Yeomanry, and Manchester Volunteers, who fell in the South African War, we dedicate this memorial in the Name of the Father, of the Son, and of the Holy Ghost. Amen.*"

General Sir Ian Hamilton, Colonel 3rd Battalion Manchester Regiment, being called on by the Lord Mayor to unveil the statue, spoke as follows:

"*My Lord Mayor and Citizens of Manchester and you Soldiers who are proud to wear the word 'Manchester' on your insignia and titles,*

"*I shall in the fewest possible words try to tell you something of these men to whose memory we meet together to-day. They had a quality, these men, which was nobly and clearly brought out under the stress of war; the quality of grit and of endurance, which brought them through hard times and difficult situations. If the Manchesters got into a tight corner, they meant fighting.*

"*At Elandslaagte these lads advanced over the open for a mile under a storm of shell and bullets, and turned out from their cover the most dangerous* shots in the world. Let me tell you something about that same fight of Elandslaagte, not like a military study drawn to scale, but more as a picture which, viewed from afar, gains in truth precisely what it loses in detail.

"At Elandslaagte, as I say, these boys advanced with the greatest bravery. There never was a fairer stand-up fight than Elandslaagte; there was no thought on either side of giving way; each side steeped in the most desperate endeavour—the Boers with no idea of going back, the British with no idea of stopping, but only of going forward. I remember the loud crack of the bullets on the stones and the crack of the bursting shell; I remember the long shout, the strong shout, of 'Majuba' from the Gordons; I remember Chisholm, flag in hand, waving on the Imperial Light Horse; and I remember the Manchesters fixing bayonets, and then the headlong simultaneous desperate rush on to and over the guns. Then came that incident of the white flag—the hurrahs when we thought the victory was won—and then the Boers, proud men in the prime of life, aristocrats, farmers, landowners, astonished and surprised to find themselves routed, the best of them rallying, refusing defeat; no surrender, ignoring death, charging up that strong kopje. I remember our left wavering with awful hesitation, and the slow, reluctant ebb of the human tide, the Boer guns abandoned, and the example and entreaties of our officers, and the Devons pouring in on the left flank. The Manchesters advanced with a yell, and then once more that wild cry, 'Majuba,' echoing out over the darkening veldt, proclaiming the victory and the honour of the Army achieved. There, on that bloodstained kopje, lie some of your best and bravest. Afterwards came Ladysmith, and the Manchesters had to stand the slow and sapping struggle against starvation at Cæsar's Camp, where want, like an armed man, rushed on your lads and struck them down even as they were staggering forward to meet the bullets of the foe. The Manchesters covered themselves with glory there. They never did better.

"They fought against starvation from 2.30 on the morning of the 6th January till 5.30 in the afternoon. Those starving, ragged lads kept back the Boers from the vitals of the town.

"Here stands the monument of those who fell, not only at Elandslaagte and Ladysmith, but in remote, desolate spots scattered east, west, north and south over the kopjes and dongas of that far South African land. We lament their loss, but we do not in lamenting forget that Manchester has also cause for deep pride and thankfulness at the thought that she could, were it needed, call up battalion after battalion to fight in a just cause—battalions who would be inspired by the memory and example of these heroic comrades of theirs who have gone on before. Yes, Manchester laments her dead, but accepts their gifts of love and life; she would have it no otherwise, and would not, if she might, take again the purple of their blood out of the cross on the breastplate of England."

Sir Ian Hamilton then unveiled the Memorial, the Guard of Honour presented arms, the buglers of the 2nd Battalion sounding the "Last Post," and the proceedings then came to an end.

Major-General Barnard, the colonel of the regiment, wrote to the Commanding Officer : "*I congratulate you on the very smart appearance and excellent turn-out of your Guard of Honour. I can assure you I felt very proud of the old Regiment.*"

The battalion remained at Aldershot until the autumn of the following year, when at the conclusion of the manœuvres at the end of September it moved to Mullingar in Ireland, speeded on its way by the following valedictory letter from the Brigadier :

"*The Brigadier-General commanding 9th Infantry Brigade regrets the Battalion is leaving his command, and in bidding farewell desires to express his appreciation of the manner in which the Battalion worked during the manœuvre period, and his satisfaction at the conduct, soldierly bearing and turn-out of the men during the time they were in the garrison at Portsmouth.*"

On the 6th March 1910 there occurred at Buckingham Palace the lamented death of His Majesty King Edward VII, and on the occasion of the funeral of the deceased monarch the battalion sent a memorial wreath to Windsor Castle which was deposited, with other floral tributes, in the precincts of St. George's Chapel. On the proclamation of the accession of His Majesty King George V, by the High Sheriff of County Westmeath, the battalion furnished a Guard of Honour under command of Major Weston, consisting of 100 rank and file, with Lieutenants C. Abbot-Anderson and Wright, the first-named carrying the King's Colour.

The following parties proceeded to London on the 13th June to take part in the Army Pageant : Captain Hardcastle, D.S.O., and 16 non-commissioned officers and men to represent the 63rd Regiment as the "Green Horse" in the American War of Independence, and Lieutenant C. Abbot-Anderson and 10 other ranks to represent the 96th Regiment of the period 1779—"the British Musketeers"—with the Regimental Colour of that date.

On the occasion of the Coronation of their Majesties King George V and Queen Mary in June 1911, orders were issued for the formation of composite battalions to line the streets in London. Lieutenant-Colonel Westropp, commanding 2nd battalion, was appointed to command E Composite Battalion, forming part of the 20th Provisional Brigade under Brigadier-General Gorringe, C.M.G., D.S.O. The following of the battalion formed Colonel Westropp's staff: Lieutenant and Adjutant Reade, Lieutenant and Quartermaster Connery, Sergeant-Major Lindsay, and Quartermaster-Sergeant Connery. The Composite Battalion was made up of 3 officers and 50 other ranks from the following corps:

1st Batt. The Buffs, Dublin.	3rd Batt. Worcestershire Regt., Dover.
1st Batt. Cheshire Regt., Belfast.	
2nd Batt. Essex Regt., Curragh.	1st Batt. K.O. Shropshire L.I., Fermoy.
2nd Batt. Wiltshire Regt., Dublin.	
1st Batt. King's Liverpool Regt., Fermoy.	2nd Batt. Manchester Regt., Mullingar.

Captain Hardcastle, D.S.O., commanded the detachment representing the battalion, and had with him Lieutenants Abbot-Anderson and Bolton. The various detachments concentrated in London on the morning of the 21st June, the battalion when formed being encamped in the Regent's Park; next day it lined the streets from Downing Street to Margaret Street, and on the 23rd June from the National Gallery to Duncannon Street; on this evening the battalion was broken up, and the various detachments rejoined their corps.

In the following month their Majesties paid a visit to Ireland, and on the 7th July the battalion—20 officers and 570 other ranks under Lieutenant-Colonel Westropp—left Mullingar by rail and proceeded to Ashtown near Dublin, and thence by march-route to the Phœnix Park, and encamping near Castleknock, formed with battalions of the King's, Scottish Borderers, and South Lancashire Regiments, a brigade under Brigadier-General Wilson, all of which, with also the 2nd Battalion Connaught Rangers, were to receive new Colours from His Majesty the King. On the 8th the King and Queen landed in Ireland, when the battalion assisted to line the streets in Dublin; on the 9th there was a Church Parade for all troops on the "Fifteen Acres"; on the 10th there was a levée, and on the 11th took place the presentation of Colours to the five battalions above mentioned.

On this day the battalion—18 officers and 422 non-commissioned officers and men—paraded at 8 a.m. for the ceremony. On arrival on the ground their Majesties were received with a Royal Salute, and the King then inspected the troops, returning to the saluting base to witness the march-past. This concluded, the five battalions formed up in line of quarter-columns in a hollow square, the drums being piled in front of the centre. The new Colours for the 2nd Battalion Manchester Regiment were brought from the rear cased and laid on the drums by Colour-Sergeants Ogden and

Parker. His Majesty then presented the Colours after consecration, the officers concerned in the ceremony, on the part of the battalion, being Majors James and Weston, Lieutenants Abbot-Anderson and Holberton. The ceremony ended, the commanding officers approached His Majesty—Major-General Barnard accompanying Lieutenant-Colonel Westropp—and were handed an address which, for the 2nd Battalion Manchester Regiment, reads as follows :

"*Lieut.-Colonel Westropp, officers, non-commissioned officers and men of the 2nd Battalion Manchester Regiment.*

"*To take part in the ceremony of the presentation of new Colours is an occasion which must appeal not only to the Regiment but to all who are imbued with the true military spirit. It is the commencement of a new chapter in the life of the Regiment, when all ranks—and especially the young soldiers—should remember those names and mottoes borne on its Colours, recalling as they do the history of the Regiment, its victories, its leaders, and those who in the past have fought and died on the field of battle.*

"*Your Battalion has seen active service in New Zealand, Egypt, India and South Africa, and I know you will always be ready to obey the call of duty.*

"*Though no longer led to the attack by your Colours, their consecration to-day will remind you that God's blessing is not denied to those who give their lives for their Country and its freedom. Every man knows that he has them in his special keeping, and by his action he can secure to them new lustre.*

"*With such feelings I have much pleasure in confiding these Colours to your charge.*"

The new Colours were then accorded a " General Salute," the troops advanced in review order, saluted the Sovereign, and then marched to quarters.

This was the third presentation of Colours to the battalion which had been attended by General Barnard, and among other former officers present on this day were Colonels Church, Barlow, and Agnew, and Quartermaster and Hon. Captain Bankes : the serving officers present with the battalion on this historic occasion were : Lieutenant-Colonel Westropp, Majors James and Weston, Captains Hardcastle, Theobald, and Nisbet, Lieutenants Abbot-Anderson, Holberton, Rose, Ellershaw, Reade (adjutant), Thomas, Dearden, Humphreys, and Harper, Second Lieutenants Freeman, Mardall, Vanderspar, and Nepean, and Quartermaster and Hon. Lieutenant Connery.

The Officer Commanding the Forces in Ireland received the following letter from His Majesty the King, dated the 11th July :

"*It has given me much pleasure to have had the opportunity of seeing the troops under your command. I desire to express to you my entire satisfaction with the smart appearance under arms of all the units on parade to-day.*

"*I greatly appreciated the excellent manner in which the Presentation of Colours to five different Regiments was arranged.*"

On the 19th August the battalion returned hurriedly to Mullingar on account of expected trouble due to labour disputes.

The King's Coronation Medal was conferred on Colonel Westropp, Sergeant-Major Lindsay, and Private Mayes.

On the 6th October the following officers of the 2nd Battalion proceeded to Ashton-under-Lyne, there to deposit the old Colours in the Parish Church: Lieutenant-Colonel Westropp, Captains Dorling, Hardcastle, D.S.O., and Nisbet, Lieutenants Abbot-Anderson and Holberton, with Sergeant-Major Parker, Colour-Sergeants Ogden and Carter. The ceremony took place on Sunday the 8th and was attended by the Mayor and members of the Town Council, many residents in the town and neighbourhood, while the following officers, with 120 rank and file, paraded from the depot: Major Vaughan, Captains Jebb, Fisher, and Wymer, Lieutenant and Adjutant Foord, and Lieutenants Woods and Harrison. In September the battalion moved to the Curragh.

Towards the end of the year parties were sent to Portarlington, Kildare, and Newbridge in anticipation of disturbance caused by labour troubles,

1912 but nothing transpired; and in February 1912 the battalion went for a couple of days to Belfast, where there was an assembly of troops.

In March 1913 Lieutenant-Colonel James—who thirteen months previously had succeeded Lieutenant-Colonel Westropp in command of the

1913 battalion—proceeded to London, accompanied by Colour-Sergeant Carter, Sergeant Doran, Lance-Sergeant Kelly, Privates Mayes and Smyth, to represent the 2nd Battalion at the funeral of Field-Marshal Viscount Wolseley in St. Paul's Cathedral.

On the 11th July a Guard of Honour for His Majesty King George V on the occasion of his visit to Manchester, left the Curragh and proceeded to Hulme Barracks, Manchester, where the following were accommodated: Captain Nisbet, Lieutenants de Putron and Humphreys—the latter carrying the King's Colour—Sergeant-Major Parker, Bandmaster Hoyle, and 154 non-commissioned officers and men. On the 14th the Guard marched to Albert Square and took up its post in front of the Town Hall, where it was inspected by His Majesty, who expressed himself as being very pleased with its smartness and fine appearance.

On the 1st October, in accordance with the terms of a Special Army Order dated 16th September, a four-company formation was adopted in the battalion:

A and B Companies became A Company
C ,, D ,, ,, B ,,
E ,, F ,, ,, C ,,
G ,, H ,, ,, D ,,

At the beginning of 1914 Ireland began to be seriously disturbed owing to the controversy due to the Home Rule Bill, and it was considered necessary that all magazines, ordnance, and other stores should be adequately guarded; consequently at the Curragh the guards mounted at the magazine and ordnance stores were provided with twenty rounds of ball ammunition per man. In March rumours reached London that many officers serving at the Curragh, particularly those of the 3rd Cavalry Brigade there stationed, had resigned to avoid serving against Ulster should any attempt be made to coerce the Loyalists of that province, and many Unionists in England believed that British troops were to be ordered to shoot down the Ulster volunteers at once. On the 20th the Officer Commanding the 2nd Battalion Manchester Regiment received the following communication from the General Officer Commanding the 5th Division (Sir Charles Fergusson):

"*In view of the possibility of active operations in Ulster the War Office has authorised the following communication to officers: (1) Officers whose homes are actually in the province of Ulster, who wish to do so, may apply for permission to be absent from duty during the period of operations and will be allowed to 'disappear' from Ireland. Such officers will be subsequently reinstated and will suffer no loss in their career. (2) Any other officer who from conscientious or other motives is not prepared to carry out his duty as ordered should say so at once. Such officers will at once be dismissed from the Service.*

"*As regards (1) the words underlined are to be taken literally and strictly, and brigadiers and officers commanding units are responsible under penalty of court-martial that only such officers as come under that description are allowed to forward applications to disappear.*

"*As regards (2) it is hoped that very few cases will be found of officers who elect to sever their connection with the Service.*"

The reply of the Officer commanding the 2nd Battalion Manchester Regiment was as follows:

"*After most seriously and loyally considering the duty of the Army to His Majesty and the Empire, I now know that my officers would prefer to resign in one body or be dismissed the Service rather than have to throw in their lot in Civil War.*"

On the 26th March the Prime Minister stated in the House of Commons that there had been a "misconception," and as a result what was known at the time as "the Curragh incident," and which had aroused very strong feeling both in the nation and the Army, was thereupon closed.

The trouble in Ireland and symptoms of unrest in other parts of the United Kingdom were not for some considerable time allayed, but already in July all domestic difficulties were rapidly obscured and effaced by the gathering of war-clouds in Central Europe. The heir to the thrones of Austria and Hungary was murdered in Serajevo on the 28th June; the Government of the Dual Monarchy addressed an ultimatum to Serbia, and the reply to this was known in England on the 26th July to have been rejected. The British Foreign Minister made every effort to convene a conference of Ambassadors, Austro-Serbian operations being meantime suspended; but Germany refusing the invitation, Austria-Hungary at once declared war on Serbia, and Russia on the 28th mobilised fourteen of her army corps. On August 1st the European situation became worse: German troops were preparing to invade France; Russia had proclaimed a general mobilisation; Germany announced her intention of doing the same; in Great Britain steps were taken to guard magazines, tunnels, and dockyards; steps were also taken to defend our ports by means of booms; while cables came to hand from all parts of the British Empire containing offers to aid the mother country by sending troops.

On the 2nd August the Naval Reserve were called out; next morning's papers announced Germany's violation of the neutrality of Luxemburg, her invasion of France, and ultimatum to Belgium; on the 4th was published the King's Proclamation calling out the Army Reserve and embodying the Territorial Force; an ultimatum was sent to Berlin from London "asking for the unequivocal assurance that Germany would respect the neutrality of Belgium, identical with that given the week before by France both to Belgium and to Great Britain, and for a satisfactory reply by midnight to it. . . . Otherwise, the British Ambassador was instructed to make what was, substantially, a declaration of war. Late that night this request was refused; and on Wednesday morning, 5th August, Great Britain found herself called to be once more the saviour of Europe."[1]

[1] *Annual Register* for 1914, p. 174.

CHAPTER XXI

THE OPENING OF THE GREAT WAR

THE SECOND BATTALION AT MONS AND LE CATEAU, AT THE MARNE AND THE AISNE, AND ON THE LA BASSÉE AND MESSINES FRONTS

AUGUST TO DECEMBER 1914

1914 On the day—the 4th August—that England declared war on Germany, the mobilisation of the Regular Army, Special Reserve, and Territorial Force was ordered; and on the following day a Council of War, attended by nearly all the members of the Cabinet, and by—among other soldiers—Field-Marshal Sir John French, Commander-in-Chief elect of the British Expeditionary Force, was held at No. 10 Downing Street, when the following subjects were discussed:

1. The composition of the Expeditionary Force.
2. Its point of concentration on arrival in France.

It was generally believed that it had been mutually agreed that in the event of certain circumstances arising, necessitating the British nation affording material assistance to the French, we should send a cavalry division and six divisions of all arms across the Channel; but this arrangement was naturally liable to modification according to the number of troops considered necessary to retain in the United Kingdom to guard against invasion and maintain order. After considerable discussion it was decided that two divisions must for the present at any rate remain behind, and that the remaining four, and the cavalry division, should proceed to France as early as possible. This made up an army of approximately 100,000 men.

The point of concentration was then discussed, but the question was not at this meeting finally settled. At previous consultations between the British and French General Staffs, the area of concentration for the British Forces had been fixed on the left flank of the French, and the actual detraining stations were in the country lying between Maubeuge and Le Cateau. Lord Kitchener then considered that this placed the concentration position too far forward, and was of opinion that it should be further back—in the neighbourhood of Amiens—but the arrangement originally made was adhered to.

The Expeditionary Force which left England in the early part of August 1914 consisted of two Army Corps, each of two divisions, and a cavalry division. The First Army Corps comprised the 1st and 2nd Divisions and was commanded by Lieutenant-General Sir Douglas Haig, while the Second was made up of the 3rd and 5th Divisions, and was in the first instance placed in charge of Lieutenant-General Sir James Grierson, who, on his death in the train very soon after landing in France, was succeeded by General Sir Horace Smith-Dorrien. The commander of the Cavalry Division was Major-General Allenby.

At 5.25 p.m. on the 4th August 1914 the 2nd Battalion Manchester Regiment received orders to mobilise for active service, and during the ten days that elapsed prior to embarkation all ranks worked at very high pressure. The battalion was to form part of the 14th Brigade, 5th Division, Major-General Sir Charles Fergusson commanding the division and Brigadier-General S. P. Rolt the brigade, which was made up of the following units:

> The 2nd Battalion Suffolk Regiment.
> The 1st Battalion East Surrey Regiment.
> The 1st Battalion Duke of Cornwall's Light Infantry.
> The 2nd Battalion Manchester Regiment.

On the 5th August Captain Hardcastle and Second Lieutenant Dixon arrived from the depot to take charge of details; on the 6th Captain F. H. Dorling was appointed Staff Captain of the brigade, and Lieutenant Scully of the Regiment, but then with the West African Regiment, was attached for duty to the battalion; on the 7th Major B. L. Anley was appointed Assistant Provost-Marshal, 5th Division, and Lieutenant Brodribb joined with 200 Reservists; next day Captain Ford and Lieutenant Butler came with 400 more; and on the 9th and 12th the following officers proceeded to the depot—Captain Irwin, Lieutenants Sotham, Crawhall, Green, and Wilson, these two last-named of the Special Reserve.

On the 13th the battalion entrained for Dublin in two trains; on arrival there it was accommodated for the night in the Royal Barracks, and left Ireland on the 14th August in the *Buteshire* in company with the 2nd Battalion King's Own Yorkshire Light Infantry of the 13th Brigade. The embarking strength of the 2nd Manchesters was 27 officers, 1 warrant officer, 50 staff-sergeants and sergeants, and 927 other ranks. The following are the names of the officers who left for the front with the battalion:

Lieutenant-Colonel H. L. James, Major R. S. Weston, Captains C. F. H. Trueman, H. C. Theobald, D.S.O., F. S. Nisbet (adjutant), G. P. Wymer, H. Knox, A. G. Foord, C. Morley, and M. C. Fowke, Lieutenants W. G. Mansergh, A. F. Thomas, J. H. L. Reade, N. W. Humphrys, J. S. Harper (machine gun officer), E. R. Vanderspar, V. A. Albrecht, A. G. M. Hardingham, A. J. Scully, R. F. G. Burrows, J. H. M. Smith, A. G. B. Chittenden, W. E. Butler, R. T. Miller, and R. Brodribb, Lieutenant and Quartermaster W. L. Connery and Captain Brown, R.A.M.C., attached.

The *Buteshire* arrived off Havre at 4 p.m. on the 16th; disembarkation and landing of stores commenced the same night and was completed by ten o'clock on the morning of the 17th; that night the battalion entrained and left via Rouen and Amiens for Le Cateau, which was reached at noon, and the troops then marched ten miles to Landrecies, where they arrived at 8 p.m. and were billeted. Here a halt was made for two days and the divisional commander, Sir Charles Fergusson, took the opportunity of visiting his brigades in their billets, giving the men many " tips " about the Germans and their wiles.

The general situation was by no means yet clear, and such as it was it was known only to a comparatively few; all that was common knowledge was that when the march began northward the 3rd Division would be on the right while the First Corps was further still to the east; but there was no information forthcoming as to the position either of the enemy or of the French. On the 21st the 14th Brigade marched fifteen miles to St. Vaast–Le Bavai; the weather was fine, the country clean and smiling, and the villagers most hospitable, freely offering fruit and drink to the thirsty men.

On the 22nd the battalion marched another fifteen miles to Hainin, and " rumours of the approach of the Germans soon began to come in, and were substantiated by the receipt of orders from the Second Corps for the 3rd and 5th Divisions to hold the straight reach of the Mons–Condé Canal running due west from Mons. The left of the 5th Division was to be on the Pommerœuil–Thulin road, the right at Mariette in touch with the 3rd Division. The front was divided up between the 13th Brigade on the right and the 14th on the left, while the 15th Brigade remained in reserve and prepared a defensive line about Wasmes in case the Canal line was forced back."[1]

The morning of the 23rd August opened misty and wet, when the 14th Brigade moved out to take up the position told off to it. The Duke of Cornwall's Light Infantry and the East Surrey Regiment were on the canal,

[1] *The Fifth Division in the Great War*, p. 3.

the Suffolks and Manchesters in reserve in rear; but later in the day the battalion entrenched the line of the Hainin River, which here runs generally parallel to the Canal—fairly broad with a good field of fire to the canal from half a mile to a mile distant; but the view here and there was obstructed by undergrowth and buildings. The main road, bordered by the usual poplars, was absolutely straight to and commanded the canal bridge, which, as well as that over the Hainin River, had been prepared for demolition.

When in the afternoon the troops at the canal salient at Mons had commenced to fall back by reason of the German penetration near Obourg, the enemy pressure came against the left flank of the 5th Division, and it was for this reason that the advanced troops of the 14th Brigade were withdrawn from the actual line of the canal to that of the Hainin River. The Duke of Cornwall's Light Infantry were retired from the canal bridge, which was then blown up: the East Surreys, more to the right, did not get away so easily, for one company, left to cover their retirement, was overwhelmed after giving a very good account of itself.

The 2nd Battalion Manchester Regiment now put in some very useful work; the machine guns, under Lieutenants Harper of the battalion and Darwell of the East Surrey Regiment, did considerable execution among the enemy, engaged in crossing by the wrecked canal bridge. The main force of the German advance came against the battalion left, where were Captains Theobald and Foord, and Lieutenant Reade, assisted until dark by some of de Lisle's cavalry. The Hainin bridge was blown up by our Engineers about 6.30 p.m. and the line was held until 11 o'clock, when orders were received to fall back to a prepared position north of Wasmes.

An officer of the battalion who was present has recorded in his diary:

" At midnight, 24th August, we passed through Thulin again and a piteous sight it was: all our friends who had shown us so much hospitality when we advanced only a few days before, were now fleeing southward with what few belongings they had been able hurriedly to collect. The road was blocked, not only by the inhabitants but by de Lisle's cavalry, by guns, and by every conceivable form of military impedimenta which could not be moved southward earlier in the evening. Very old men and women were being hurried along by the younger generation, children and babies in arms, together with perambulators containing household goods, provisions and clothing, carts loaded with people belonging to them and forage both for the horse and ox-teams were mixed up with the troops on the road. The cry—' the Germans are coming '—was heard incessantly along the

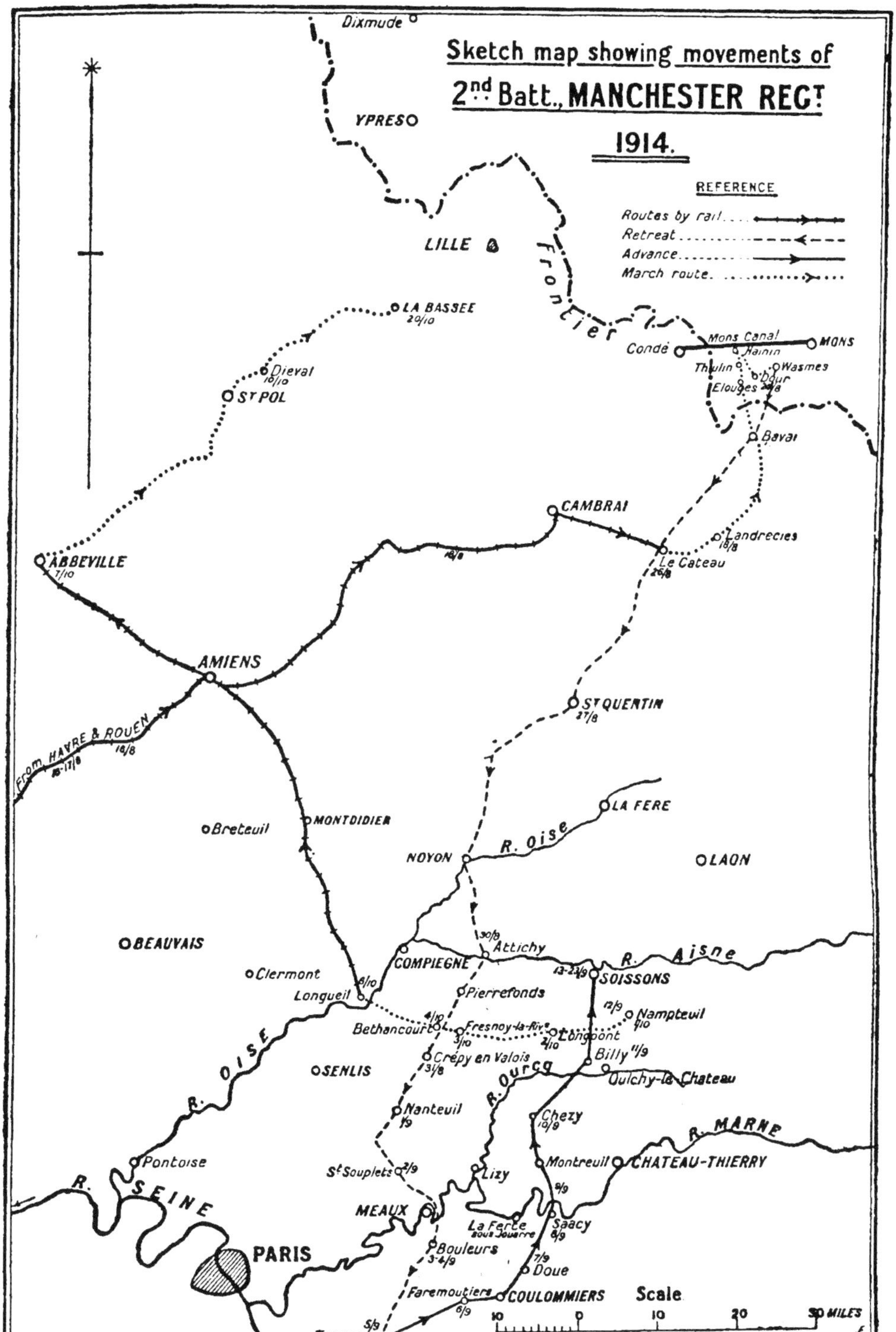

Sketch map showing movements of
2nd Batt., MANCHESTER REGT
1914.
REFERENCE
Routes by rail
Retreat
Advance
March route
Dixmude
YPRES
LILLE
Frontier
LA BASSEE 20/10
Dieval 16/10
ST POL
ABBEVILLE 7/10
AMIENS
From HAVRE & ROUEN 15-17/8
16/8
18/8
CAMBRAI
Le Cateau 26/8
Landrecies 18/8
Bavai
Conde
Mons Canal
MONS
Hainin
Thulin
Wasmes
Dour
Elouges 24/8
ST QUENTIN 27/8
LA FERE
R. Oise
NOYON
LAON
Breteuil
MONTDIDIER
BEAUVAIS
Clermont
COMPIEGNE
Attichy
30/9
R. Aisne
13-23/9
SOISSONS
Pierrefonds
Longueil 6/10
Bethancourt 4/10
Fresnoy-la-Rive 3/10
Longpont 2/10
Nampteuil 1/10
12/9
Billy 11/9
Crépy en Valois 31/8
SENLIS
R. Ourcq
Oulchy-le-Chateau
R. OISE
Nanteuil 1/9
Chezy 10/9
R. MARNE
Montreuil
CHATEAU-THIERRY
Pontoise
St Souplets 2/9
Lizy
R. SEINE
MEAUX
La Ferte sous Jouarre
Saacy 8/9
9/9
PARIS
Bouleurs 3-4/9
Doue 7/9
Faremoutiers 6/9
COULOMMIERS
Tournan 5/9
Scale
10
0
10
20
30 MILES

route. . . . The sadness of it all I shall never forget, as the advance of only 48 hours or so previously was so marked by the joy of the populace on the arrival of *l'armée anglaise.*"

During the operations of the 23rd the casualties in the battalion amounted to 12 killed and wounded.

Dours was reached about 2.30 a.m. on the 24th August, but the little town was so full of troops that the men rested where the halt found them until 4 a.m., when the battalion moved to the position allotted to it, some 3½ miles off among the mines and dumps about Wasmes. The position required much strengthening and all ranks set to work at once, but there was not time to effect much before, at 5.30 a.m., the enemy's guns opened fire. Of the 14th Brigade the Manchesters, D.C.L.I., and Suffolks were in the first line with the East Surreys in reserve.

" At first our artillery and rifle fire proved too much for the Germans, and they suffered heavy casualties without achieving much result, but the right soon became outflanked, and, under the ever-increasing pressure, began to retire. On the left, too, the situation was threatening, the 14th Brigade being violently attacked about Dours station. A message was received at this time from General Allenby to the effect that his orders were to retire to a line some miles back, but the danger of the 5th Division left being enveloped was so evident, that Sir Charles Fergusson, who had been ordered to hold on in order to cover the withdrawal of the 3rd Division, pointed out in reply that it was of vital importance for the Cavalry to prevent the Germans outflanking us. The Cavalry responded splendidly to this appeal, with great gallantry standing their ground until the retirement was well under way."[1]

At 11.30 a.m. the Brigade received orders to retire, but these failed to reach the battalion, which up to this had not been heavily engaged—the total casualties in the Manchesters were this day not more than six; and the battalion was still in position when the Germans opened a very heavy shell-fire on to one of the batteries of the 28th Brigade R.F.A., and the presence and help of the battalion enabled this battery to get away with all its guns after an hour and a half's fighting. The battalion then withdrew, covered by Captains Knox's and Trueman's companies and part of Captain Foord's, to Dours, whence the whole division retired to the St. Vaast–Bavai line, the 14th Brigade taking the outposts facing north

[1] *The Fifth Division in the Great War,* p. 7.

with the East Surrey Regiment and two companies of the battalion under Major Weston.

"At 4 a.m. on the 25th," writes the same officer from whose diary extracts have already been given, "we stood to arms and the outposts were to cover a further retirement for the 14th Brigade. Shortly after 4 the remaining two companies of the battalion, under Lieutenant-Colonel James, were ordered out to continue the line to the right at Bavai and reinforce, if necessary, with the other two Manchester companies. This turned out to be a useful move. Our outpost line was roughly from St. Vaast to Houdain—the East Surreys at St. Vaast, the two companies Manchester Regiment on or about the Houdain road; the line of general retirement for the 5th Division was Bavai–Montay–Le Cateau. The 14th Brigade eventually furnished the rear-guard."

It had been hoped that the rear of the 5th Division would have cleared Bavai by 9 a.m. at latest; but the congestion of the roads—due to the hurried retirement of the previous day and the intermingling of units—was so great that this hope was not fulfilled, and an unexpected delaying action had to be fought.

The battalion, near Houdain, north of Bavai, came in touch with the advanced German troops, and, being reinforced by its other two companies, prolonged the line with the 1st Battalion Berkshire Regiment of the 6th Brigade. The Germans for some reason did not press the attack, but contented themselves with artillery fire which did little damage. The orders were for the outposts to retire through Bavai, but Major Weston suggested that the East Surreys should retire direct from St. Vaast on Louvignies, south of Bavai on the Jolinette–Peix–Montay road. This was done, and the D.C.L.I. then took up a covering position at Bavai, the Suffolks one near Louvignies, while the East Surreys held a further southward position near the road.

During the retirement from Bavai many men of the battalion, including the medical officer and the grooms with the led horses, took the wrong road, eventually "fetching up" with some of the First Army Corps at Landrecies, and not being able to rejoin the battalion again for some six weeks.

On arrival near Montay about 6 p.m. the battalion, with the Suffolks and the Brigade R.F.A. under Lieutenant-Colonel Onslow, was ordered to take up an outpost position covering the north of Le Cateau, but later this order was cancelled and the battalion moved on through Le Cateau to its bivouac; there were three casualties this day in the Manchesters.

"Le Cateau lies in the valley of the Selle River, which is little more than a stream; the rolling, billowy nature of the country, cut up here and there into deep valleys, made the position a difficult one to defend. A spur lay to the east of the village running in a northerly direction, parallel to the stream, and a similar spur with a branch towards Troisvilles lay on the western side. The country was principally cornfields, but the corn was nearly all cut and stood in stooks; the only restriction to free movement of all arms was an occasional wire fence."

The battalion bivouacked in a field, the wagons along a narrow road, by which troops, guns, and vehicles of all kinds were constantly moving. There was little chance of sleep for anybody that night, and at dawn Quartermaster Connery came up with the supply carts and some hot soup was hurriedly issued, when the wagons left again, and almost immediately afterwards the battalion fell in to continue the retreat southward as was the intention, in accordance with very clear orders issued by the Commander of the British Expeditionary Force, and much of the impedimenta of the 5th Division was already some miles away on the road.

The reasons which induced the commander of the Second Corps to disregard the orders he had been given and to stand and fight at Le Cateau are very clearly stated in a paper [1] which appeared in one of the periodicals in 1919, entitled "Why did Smith-Dorrien stand at Le Cateau?" "The first question of interest requiring an answer would seem to be this: When did Smith-Dorrien finally decide to stand his ground? The answer to this is no secret, for the orders of each of the divisions then under the command of the G.O.C. Second Corps clearly show that G.H.Q. order for the continuance of the retreat was to be carried out, and the divisions only received the counter-order to stand and fight between 4 and 6 a.m. on the 26th. This counter-order was issued from Second Corps H.Q. as soon as Smith-Dorrien had got in all the reports from his scattered units. At a conference held at headquarters at Bertry at 2.30 a.m. on the 26th—a conference attended by the G.O.C. Second Corps, the G.O.C. Cavalry Division, and the G.O.C. Third Division with their General Staff Officers—the facts of the situation were laid bare, and it was upon these facts as here revealed that Smith-Dorrien based his conclusions that retreat without a fight was impossible; with this Allenby was in full accord, and he agreed to act under Smith-Dorrien's orders. The *decision* was Smith-Dorrien's—when announced all present expressed themselves relieved. . . . The advice General Allenby gave was that '*unless the march could be resumed during the night, battle must be accepted*

---

[1] *United Service Magazine*, September.

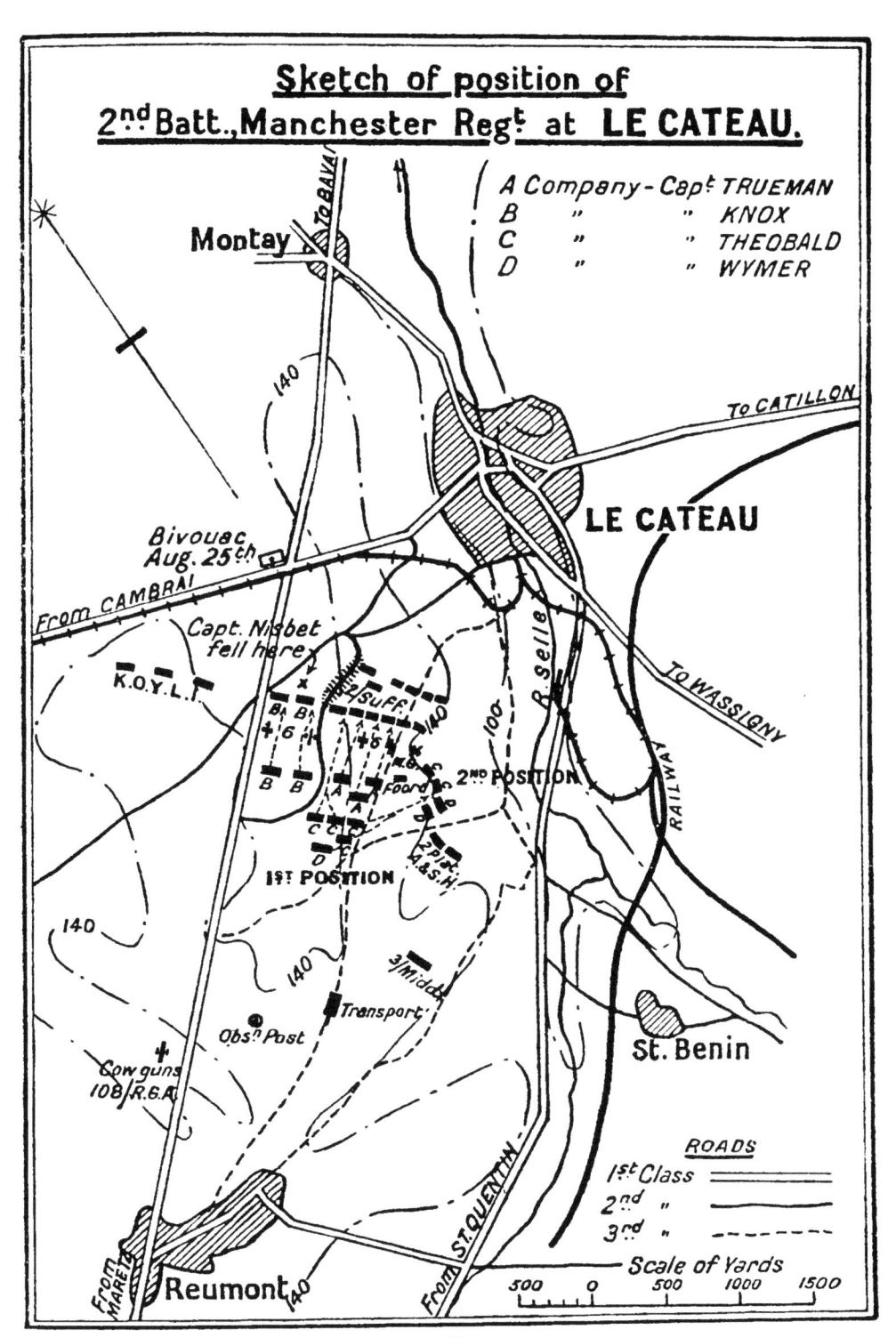

Sketch of position of 2nd Batt., Manchester Regt at LE CATEAU.

A Company — Capt. TRUEMAN
B   "   "   KNOX
C   "   "   THEOBALD
D   "   "   WYMER

ROADS
1st Class ―――
2nd   "   ――
3rd   "   - - -

Scale of Yards
500 0 500 1000 1500

at dawn.' " Further on it is stated that on the afternoon of the 25th " but few indeed of the Second Corps had reached Le Cateau at all. The troops came into that place utterly exhausted, some were not in until after midnight, others not until 4 a.m. on the 26th ; while the three brigades of the 4th Division, which had gone towards Sollesmes to help in the 3rd Division, the 19th Brigade, and the Cavalry Division, did not get back to the Haucourt–Caudry line until after daylight on the 26th August."

The change in the orders gave new life to the troops, and about 6 a.m. the concentration of all fighting bodies was carried out. The line taken up by the Second Corps ran, on the right, from a little beyond the Reumont–Le Cateau road to Troisvilles ; from that place to Caudry it was held by the 3rd Division, and from Caudry to Haucourt by the 4th Division, just arrived from home ; of this line the right sector was allotted to the 5th Division, and the 14th Brigade took up its position on the right—half the Suffolks south of the Reumont road, half the East Surreys and the Manchesters in support. The D.C.L.I. and the remaining companies of the East Surreys and Suffolks had bivouacked to the south-east of the town, and on trying to rejoin the Division in the morning were intercepted by the Germans, and only got back by making a long detour to the south.

To quote again from the diary of the officer of the Manchesters : " All I know is that the Suffolk Regiment had to take up the advanced fighting trenches south of Le Cateau, while the Manchester Regiment behind them in reserve prolonged to the right and held some advanced ground with part of Captain Foord's company thrown slightly back. The left of this line was strengthened by the machine-gun section under Lieutenant Harper, and the rest of the battalion dug in on a central reserve position with Captain Wymer's company echeloned slightly to the right. On the right front of the battalion were two of our batteries, nearly all the guns of which were ere long knocked out by the German artillery." The enemy attacked all along our line, but his chief efforts, on the 5th Division front, were against the right and right centre. This was the vulnerable flank, for beyond Le Cateau there was nothing except the 1st Cavalry Brigade, which could give but little help.

About 10 a.m. the Germans pressed the attack against the Suffolk Regiment and the two batteries, and the battalion was ordered to support. A Company under Captain Trueman went to the right, Captains Knox and Nisbet went to the left with B, while the rest of the reserve—half C under Captain Theobald and a portion of D with Second Lieutenant Smith—was brought forward by Colonel James, and the remainder of D under Captain Wymer had been sent to reinforce the right. Up to 11 o'clock we seemed to be holding our own; such guns as remained in action were now able to be withdrawn owing mainly to the stubborn resistance offered by Lieutenant Harper with his machine guns and by the officers and men of C Company. But as the fight developed on the right front the shallow trenches became quite untenable, the casualties mounted up in an alarming way, strong hostile columns were advancing against the whole British front, and it was evident our line was being outflanked. Some time after 4 in the afternoon the retirement began, the dispersed men of units were collected by any officer who happened to be at hand, and the wounded, who had been placed in a temporary hospital, were hurriedly evacuated, but very many men, killed, wounded, and missing, had to be left behind on the field.

In the Manchester Regiment there were 14 officers and 339 other ranks killed, wounded, and missing; of the former Captain and Adjutant Nisbet was killed, while the following were wounded: Captains Trueman,[1] Fowke,[1] Theobald, Wymer, Knox, and Morley, Lieutenants Thomas, Albrecht, Burrows, Miller, Butler, Brodribb,[1] and Mansergh.[1]

The retreat once begun was continued through Maretz, where rolls were called and checked, and only 8 officers and some 339 other ranks were found to be with the battalion, others rejoining later; then by way of St. Quentin to Pontoise, which was reached on the 28th. The following day Carlepont was reached, and on the 30th August the battalion, with the D.C.L.I., took up an outpost line Attichy–Bitry, north of the Aisne. " The hungry and exhausted men plodded along in a hopeless way, many men lying down by the roadside utterly worn out and broken, and every carriage was crowded with wounded, the artillery outriders and even the horses of the teams being used to carry them. To make matters worse a steady rain set in and continued throughout the pitch-dark night."

Moving on by Crépy en Valois, Sablières, and Nanteuil, the battalion crossed the Marne at Esbly and reached Boulers at 6 on the evening of the 3rd: here Lieutenant Scully rejoined the battalion with 20 men of C Company, having been away six days owing to not having been relieved on outpost at Bretigny. On the 4th the division had a trying night march to Tournan, only 15 miles from Paris, arriving at 8 a.m. on the 5th, to learn late that afternoon the joyful news that the long retreat was at last at an end; the effect on the spirits of the men was electrical, and the change in their bearing was most marked.

Here Colonel James received the following very appreciative letter from Brigadier-General Headlam, commanding the artillery 5th Division:

---

[1] These four were missing and were later assumed to have been killed at Le Cateau.

"MY DEAR JAMES,

"I told you that it was only owing to the somewhat 'occupied' life we have been leading that I had not written before to thank you for what your Regiment has done for the Divisional Artillery. By two of the Brigades have I heard of the magnificent way the Manchesters stood by them; and though I have not words to express my gratitude at all adequately, I should like to put it on record. It will never be forgotten by the Brigades, nor, you may be sure, by myself."

The advance began on the 6th at 7 a.m. : reaching Château St. Avoe that night, the Grand Morin was crossed on the 7th, and the battalion moved forward through Coulommiers, Pontmoulin, to Rougeville, and passed the Marne again on the 9th at Saacy without difficulty; but when the advance guard—the battalion at the head of the 14th Brigade—reached the plateau near Le Limon, it was met with heavy artillery and rifle fire, both from Hill 189, south-east of Montreuil, and from the left front. The position of the 5th Division was at the north end of a big loop of the Marne, 3 or 4 miles in advance of the Third Corps on the left, and the Germans on the ridge running from La Ferté to Montreuil were able to enfilade the left flank of the Division with impunity. What followed is thus described by an officer of the battalion:

"The Germans had taken up a position at Prisseloup; they were shelling the road below us and I can't help thinking they imagined troops were on it. The ground just here was difficult and they, fortunately for us, had taken a false crest to shell, so all shots were falling short. Our heavy battery was well to the right and back and came into action, giving much help, but still had not located the guns giving trouble, although they had silenced one German battery more to the right. I was now told by the Brigadier to continue the advance as soon as the advanced company, under Lieutenant de Putron,[1] had moved round the corner of the village of Le Limon on the main road. Shelling now began and we could not move—had, in fact, to fall back. A battery of ours now came up under Major Ballard, but did not come into action as the Germans could not be located.

"A change of march was ordered and the 14th Brigade dropped down from the plateau through woods into a valley below Prisseloup, where we were pointed out a farm-house about 500 feet on the forward slope, from which our attack was to be delivered. . . . Half left of the farm was a small wood running generally S.W. to N.E., and roughly a mile from this

---

[1] This officer had arrived from the base with the first reinforcement on the 5th September.

point the Germans had an entrenched position and 4 guns across the valley to our left. The D.C.L.I. moved forward half left, the Suffolks started through the wood, but worked to the right and then into the open field again on the right. . . . What actually happened on the left I can't say, but the right got hung up and the 3rd Division came along and was also delayed. I found that the Dorsets had come up on our right, but the line could not advance and remained in position until dark, our chief obstacle not being fire from the direct front, but enfilade rifle fire from the woods on our right. Our losses at this point were small, but to the left I heard that the fighting was severe. We had Lieutenants Smith and Chittenden and 8 men killed, Captain Foord and 37 men wounded. Smith had got as far forward as possible and was shot with only 6 men killed around him. The killed were buried in the wood on the following morning, when Captain Foord was brought in having lain out all night. . . . After dark we sorted ourselves out and bivouacked on our ground ; we had had little food all day as the supplies and ambulances had been shelled. The Germans retired during the night."

The Battle of the Marne was over, and during the next few days, though there was fighting on either flank, the battalion was not actually engaged. On the 10th it marched to Chézy-sur-Ourcq, where Second Lieutenants Moore and Walker joined with reinforcements amounting to 176 non-commissioned officers and men ; on the 11th the battalion was at Billy-sur-Ourcq, and on the 12th at Chacrise, near the edge of the plateau overlooking the Aisne valley, beyond which, two miles or more on the northern side, the Germans held a strong position. " The Aisne is a sluggish river, 60 or 70 yards broad ; on the north side the hills stand out like a wall, with the thickly-wooded spurs dipping down sharply into the valley, while on the south of the river lay the heights of Champagne, practically a tableland, whence a series of ridges sloped down towards the river. . . . The German guns posted on the heights commanded all the crossings, and the enemy was fully prepared to hold up by every means the advance of the British. . . . Definite orders, however, were received from Corps H.Q. that the advance was to be pushed on strenuously."

The Germans in their retreat had destroyed most of the bridges over the Aisne, but there was one left standing at Condé which had been allotted for the crossing of the 5th Division ; this, however, was held by the Germans.

On the 13th September the 14th Brigade was advance guard, and on nearing Jury orders were received to reconnoitre the Aisne for a crossing and to hold the high ground on the south. It was known that the Germans had destroyed the bridge at Venizel on the left, where later the 4th Division crossed the river, that the bridge at Missy had gone, that the cavalry were over the Aisne at Braine holding the north bank, and that the 3rd Division was about to force a passage at Vailly.

The 14th Brigade crossed the river on rafts between Missy and Venizel—the 2nd Battalion Manchester Regiment leading, followed by the East Surreys—and was then ordered to advance on St. Marguerite, the attack commencing about 3.30 p.m. There was some shell and rifle fire, but the objective was reached with little or no loss, and the battalion was then ordered back as being no longer needed, but had no sooner withdrawn than two companies had to go forward again. At dusk the battalion was again withdrawn, but then relieved the Lancashire Fusiliers of the 12th Brigade on outpost about Chivres. From this date until the 20th the battalion held on to the west side of the wood at Chivres, trying to improve the position, though digging trenches was impossible owing to the ground being so low-lying; the Germans had command of fire and casualties took place frequently: Captain Brown, the medical officer, established a collecting station in a barn at St. Marguerite; in some places the advanced trenches were only 200 yards from those of the Germans; and many casualties were incurred in bringing up rations and other supplies from the pontoon on the Aisne, two miles in rear, mainly under cover of darkness.

On the night of the 20th the battalion was relieved by the D.C.L.I. and withdrew into bomb-proof trenches at St. Marguerite, where it remained until the 24th, when it recrossed the Aisne to Jury to a well-earned rest. In one day of the week spent in Chivres wood the battalion had 15 men killed and 47 wounded, and during that time 170 non-commissioned officers and men joined as reinforcements with the following officers: Captains Hardcastle, Evans, Tillard, and Peirce, Lieutenants Balshaw and Bentley, and Second Lieutenant Davidson, with Second Lieutenants Price and Waller of the York and Lancaster Regiment.

The Battle of the Aisne may be said to have come to an end on the 28th, and of the share taken in it by the 5th Division the Field-Marshal wrote in his despatch: "With great skill and tenacity Sir Charles Fergusson maintained this position throughout the whole battle, although his trenches were necessarily on lower ground than those of the enemy on the southern slope of the plateau which was only 400 yards away."

At the end of the month orders came that the whole of the Second Corps was to be moved to another sphere of operations, and there was much surmising where this was likely to be. The trenches were taken over by the 6th Division, and on the 1st October some of the regiments of the

5th Division started for their destination. The battalion marched from Jury to Nanteuil, thence by way of Longpont, Fresnoy-la-Rivière, Bethancourt, St. Mies, and Longueil, thence by train to Abbeville, and from Fallières to Dieval by motor-buses. Here was the concentration area of the 14th Brigade, and it was reached on the 9th October. On the 11th the Brigade was at Hinges in touch with the 3rd Division on the left and took up the line of outposts Pont d'Hinges–Locon–Pont Tournant–Le Quesnoy.

" On the 12th October the Battalion formed the advance guard to the Brigade and marched off at about 5 a.m. from Hinges, passing through our outpost line. . . . The morning was foggy and we couldn't see any distance in front of us, but we knew the Germans were all along this line and expected to meet them at any moment. . . . Near Le Touret I met the cavalry brigadier of French cavalry with some Cuirassiers. He told me all sorts of places on our right and front were held by his cavalry patrols, but our own cyclist companies told quite a different tale—that the Germans were all over the place and that our 3rd Division was held up and could not get up on our flank for some hours. . . . We had to take up a defensive line for the night which was roughly Rue des Chavattes–Rue l'Epinette. The Germans shelled us a little in the morning along the advance and it was here that I saw a bomb dropped for the first time. The East Surreys occupied the left, we were centre and the D.C.L.I. on the right: our fourth battalion, the Devons, was kept back as divisional reserve, so we really had no reserve."

The country north of the La Bassée Canal was perfectly flat, only rising very slightly at Givenchy; near the Canal on both sides were some swampy woods, but further north the land is mostly arable, intersected with muddy dykes and rows of trees much impeding the view. To the south were the villages of Cuinchy and Cambrin and the mining village of Annequin with its big slag-heap; further on towards Vermelles the ground is of chalky formation and becomes more undulating.

On the 13th a general attack was ordered and the battalion advanced on Richebourg l'Avoué, but the forward movement was slow, for every yard of ground, every hamlet, every house had to be fought for. The western end of the village was occupied, and here the battalion dug in for the night, with the Germans doing the same some 200–250 yards in front: " King-Peirce's company on the left, Evans centre, Tillard right and Hardcastle and Hd.-qrs. about a quarter of a mile behind; the left had the hardest fighting and was most exposed." The casualties this day were Major Weston, Lieutenant Vanderspar and Second Lieutenant Davidson and 4 sergeants and 36 men wounded, while 10 men were killed.

On the 14th and 15th there was little, if any, change in the situation; the German shell fire was heavy and fighting went on all day and all along the line. " In the advanced trenches you could hear the German officers cursing and trying to get their men on. Our fire must have been very good, it certainly was incessant, and the sending up of fresh ammunition was dangerous to the carriers but was very well done. . . . The village of Richebourg l'Avoué suffered most frightfully and there was hardly a house in the place which was left whole. . . . Harper had his machine gun up in the window of a loft in the next house to our headquarters, but I am afraid did little good, though he tried over and over again to switch on to the Germans."

On the 14th 8 men in the battalion were hit, one dying of his wounds, and next day Second Lieutenant Blane arrived with a welcome reinforcement of 95 men.

On the 16th British patrols reported the withdrawal of the enemy, and this day and the next a certain advance was achieved; Givenchy, Rue d'Ouvert, Violaines, and Beau Puits all fell into our hands, and by the 18th it seemed as though La Bassée itself was almost within our grasp. On the 19th the battalion reached Les Trois Maisons and held that place for the night; but it was becoming evident that the Germans had been greatly reinforced by troops set free by the fall of Antwerp, and on the 20th the whole British line was violently attacked. About 9 a.m. the enemy came on against the front and left and heavy fighting ensued; two gallant bayonet attacks of A Company, Manchester Regiment, were led by Captain Tillard and Second Lieutenant Dixon when the enemy had arrived within 200 yards, but the men of the Manchesters were caught in enfilade and lost considerably. Fighting went on until dusk, when the battalion withdrew to the support trenches covering Lorgies; and for the time the German pressure was removed.

During the three days' fighting—from the 18th to 20th—the battalion had suffered the following casualties : *killed*, 11 non-commissioned officers and men; *wounded*, Second Lieutenants Walker (died of wounds), Price, and Waller—both the two last attached from the York and Lancaster Regiment —and 127 other ranks; *missing*, Captain Tillard, Second Lieutenants Balshaw and Dixon, and 70 men.

Lieutenant-Colonel James was sent to hospital on the 18th and thence to England, Captain Hardcastle assuming temporary command of the battalion.

At 4 a.m. on the 21st the battalion was relieved in the forward trenches by the East Surrey Regiment and D.C.L.I., and was ordered back to

Festubert, but had only gone a mile in the direction of Richebourg when it was directed to support the 13th Brigade. Owing, however, to a strong German offensive from Violaines the 13th Brigade retired and the battalion was moved up again into the firing line, when it had 1 man killed and 3 wounded. At midnight the Manchesters were withdrawn to take up a new line, which had previously been prepared by the R.E., and which extended half a mile along the road leading north from the cross roads one mile east of Festubert.

"The next seven days," writes the author of *The 5th Division in the Great War*, " were a lively period for the 5th Division. In the space of 60 days it had fought at Mons, stood the brunt of the battle of Le Cateau, taken part in the terrible retreat, fought again on the Marne and the Aisne, and already on this front had almost reached its limit; it was now holding a long line with worn-out and exhausted troops, with no reserves, and was attacked all day and every day. . . . The two most critical periods were on the 26th and 29th October."

Captain Gauntlett (King's Regiment), Second Lieutenant Williamson, and 77 men joined on the 25th October, and on the 26th the line began to feel the advantage of the arrival on this sector of some of the troops of the Indian Army Corps—the 1st Battalion taking over trenches on the left of their comrades of the 2nd—this being the first time that the two battalions had met for thirty-two years, the last occasion being in 1882 at Alexandria. Shelling and fighting continued, the casualties mounted up daily, and on the 29th the enemy, having shelled the trenches of the battalion vigorously since daylight, made a rush in overpowering strength against the centre and right of the Manchesters and against the Devons on their right. The Germans succeeded in occupying the Manchester centre forward trench in charge of Second Lieutenant Leach; but the right forward trench, under Captain Evans, repulsed the attack made upon it. Here Second Lieutenant Bentley was killed, and Lieutenant and Acting Adjutant Reade also fell in assisting to stem a rush made against the supporting trench by the Germans, who were finally stopped only ten yards from it. It was now determined to try and retake the trench occupied by the enemy. Two attempts failed to dislodge them, and then about 3.30 p.m. Second Lieutenant Leach and Sergeant Hogan went forward and, creeping up the communication trench, they gradually drove back the Germans, fighting from traverse to traverse until they had forced them to the extremity of the trench, killing 8 and capturing 14 unwounded and 2 wounded Germans.

Some companies of the Bedford Regiment and Munster Fusiliers came up in support of the Manchesters, and about midnight, the line of trenches having been taken over by the 2nd Battalion 8th Gurkhas, the battalion retired to the Rue l'Epinette.

The following message was sent to the 14th Brigade from General Sir H. Smith-Dorrien, commanding Second Army Corps, dated the 29th October:

"With reference to action on the 29th October please convey to Second Manchester Regiment and Devons the Corps Commander's high appreciation of the splendid manner in which the two regiments repelled the enemy's attacks to-day."

For their services on this day Second Lieutenant Leach and Sergeant Hogan were both awarded the Victoria Cross in the *London Gazette* of the 22nd December.

During the fighting from the 21st to the 29th October inclusive the battalion suffered the following casualties: *killed*, Captain Peirce, Lieutenants Reade and Bentley, 48 non-commissioned officers and men; *wounded*, Captain Gauntlett, Lieutenant Harper, and 48 other ranks; *missing*, 28 men. Captain Hardcastle was admitted to hospital owing to injury to his eye from dust thrown up by a bullet, and Captain Evans thereupon assumed command of the battalion.

At the end of October the Germans commenced their great offensive at Ypres, and the 5th Division, without time for rest or recovery, was taken from the La Bassée front and sent up north. Battalions were attached for a day or two to any division or brigade needing support, and it was not until the end of November that the units of the division came together again. The 14th Brigade was at first kept back as a reserve to the Indian Corps, but on the 7th November it was sent up north to take over trenches at Laventie, relieving the 8th Brigade on part of the Indian front. The fire trenches were in fair order, but there were no communication, support, or reserve trenches, and no wire in front. The line ran along the Rue Tilleloy, from near Fauquissart on the left to the cross-roads of Chapigny on the right. On the 15th the Brigade left and marched to Meteren with orders to take over the trenches east of Wulverghem from the 39th French division, running from the Wulverghem–Messines road to the Messines–Wytschaete road; but on the 28th November the 14th Brigade was relieved by the 15th and sent to the reserve area at St. Jan Capelle.

During this period the battalion received several drafts, while some officers belonging to it joined and some of other corps were attached for duty : Major Weston came back from hospital and Captain Irwin arrived from the depot, while the following were attached : Lieutenants Nicholson (Cheshire Regiment), Murray (North Stafford), Abercrombie (Queen's), Elliot (King's), Horridge (4th Battalion), Farrar (Leicester Regiment), and Clarke, Haller, and Geary (all of the East Surreys) ; reinforcements came out in parties of 55, 117, and 127 non-commissioned officers and men.

The casualties during November were not so heavy as during the previous month, though severe enough : thus, Lieutenants Nicholson, Caulfeild, and Horridge with 8 other ranks were killed, while 41 non-commissioned officers and men were wounded.

At the beginning of December the battalion was resting in billets at Dranoutre, where on the 2nd a draft of 125 men joined under Captain Sayers, East Surrey, and Second Lieutenants Green of the battalion and Martin of the King's Royal Rifles.

On the 5th December the battalion went into the trenches again east of Wulverghem—the division holding a line from La Petite Douve in a north-west direction up the slope to the Wulverghem–Messines road, and thence along the crest east of Wulverghem to Hill 75, a frontage of some 3,500 yards. The German line ran roughly parallel at a distance varying from 30 yards on the left to 800 on the Messines road. Owing to the waterlogged nature of the ground trenches could not be dug and cover was obtainable only from breastworks, while wire entanglements were practically non-existent. The Messines Ridge completely overlooked the forward area and rendered movement by day impossible without grave risk ; two miles behind the British lines rose the wooded slopes of Kemmel Hill, affording good observation over the German lines.

The winter was very cold and wet, and consequently the men lived in trenches half full of knee-deep mud and water, and the complaint of " trench-feet " became common. The ground leading to and near the trenches quickly became a morass, making difficult the movements of reliefs and ration parties. The fighting activity, once the opposing armies had settled down to trench warfare, was small, but there were casualties almost daily and raids were undertaken against the enemy's lines. On the 7th December Lieutenant Williamson with a patrol located by night an enemy trench about 300 yards on the left front, and two days later the same officer moved out with 45 men at 6.30 p.m. The party failed to surprise the enemy owing to the presence of wire, heavy fire was directed upon them and they were compelled to retire, Lieutenant Williamson and 1 man being wounded while 3 men of the party were missing.

On the 15th December Colonel James rejoined from England, and

Christmas Day found the battalion in the trenches, but everything was quiet by reason of the much-debated truce which the fighting men on either side arranged mutually. On that day every officer and man received a Christmas Card from Their Majesties and a few days later a present from Princess Mary. There were many telegrams from friends at home, from the 1st Battalion, from the depot, and from Major-General Barnard, the Colonel of the Manchester Regiment, while the following Special Order of the Day was issued by the Commander-in-Chief:

"*In offering to the Army in France my earnest and most heartfelt good wishes for Christmas and the New Year, I am anxious once more to express the admiration I feel for the valour and endurance they have displayed throughout the campaign, and to assure them that to have commanded such magnificent troops in the field will be the proudest remembrance of my life.*"

Since the campaign opened there had been many changes in commands. Major-General Sir Charles Fergusson was promoted Lieutenant-General at the end of October and appointed later to the command of the Second Army Corps, being succeeded in the 5th Division by Major-General Morland. About the same time Brigadier-General Rolt handed over command of the 14th Brigade to Brigadier-General Maude; while at the end of 1914 the Commander of the Second Corps was promoted to command one of the two armies into which the British Expeditionary Force was then divided, and published, on the 1st January 1915, the following special farewell order:

"*The day has arrived when with much regret General Sir H. L. Smith-Dorrien, having assumed command of an Army, has to relinquish that of the Second Corps, and he cannot do so without expressing to all ranks his gratitude for the loyal support which they have given him during the eventful months which have elapsed since the commencement of the war. During these months the Corps has been engaged day after day, and night after night, in desperate fighting, continuous to a degree never known before in the history of the world, against a very brave and resourceful enemy.*

"*General Smith-Dorrien is indeed proud of the grand name which the Corps has earned for itself whether in advance or retirement, attack or defence, if not always decisively victorious, yet invariably holding its own and never defeated. He is in the very deepest sympathy with all ranks in the heavy losses which they have suffered, and it is satisfactory to know that the casualties, great as they have been, are nothing to what the enemy has experienced, and without them this war would never have progressed as it has towards the successful issue which is in view.*

"*It is indeed a great honour to have commanded such magnificent troops, who, under every sort of trying conditions, nerve-shaking shell-fire, overwhelming fatigue, extreme heat and cold, continual rain, mud, frost, snow, have always maintained an indomitable fighting spirit, and have not only never complained but have shown cheerfulness which at such times they can hardly have felt. The one dominating aim of each individual man has been to sink all personal feelings to defeat the enemy.*

"*It is a satisfaction to Sir Horace to hand over the command to Lieut.-General Sir Charles Fergusson, who has added so much to the credit of the Corps by the handling of the 5th Division, which he had to relinquish on promotion some two months ago. It is a further satisfaction to him that, as the Corps forms part of his new Command, he by no means severs connection with it.*"

CHAPTER XXII

THE FIRST BATTALION

AUGUST 1914–DECEMBER 1915—ARRIVAL IN FRANCE—AT FESTUBERT—THE BATTLES OF GIVENCHY, NEUVE CHAPELLE, SECOND BATTLE OF YPRES, LOOS—FRANCE TO MESOPOTAMIA.

1914 When on the 8th August 1914 orders were received for the 1st Battalion Manchester Regiment to mobilise for active service, it was distributed as follows:

Headquarters, B, D, and E Companies at Dalhousie.
G and H Companies at Amritsar.
A, C, and F Companies and machine gunners at Jullundur,

and instructions were at once issued to the battalion to concentrate at the last-named station.

The Dalhousie party, having stored all spare baggage at that hill station, started for the plains on the 11th, and, after a march in great heat and much heavy rain, reached Pathankote very early on the 13th and, entraining here, arrived the same evening at Jullundur, where the Amritsar detachment had also joined the same day; and it was now learnt that the battalion was to leave Jullundur for Karachi on the night of the 17th August.

The contingent which India was to send to the war consisted of two Infantry Divisions, those from Lahore and Meerut, each composed of three brigades, each containing four infantry battalions—one British and three Indian—and the brigades being known, not by numbers, but by the names of their headquarters in India. Thus the 1st Battalion Manchester Regiment formed part of the Jullundur Brigade, commanded by Major-General Carnegy, in the Lahore Division under Lieutenant-General Watkis. The other three regiments in the brigade were the 15th and 47th Sikhs and the 59th Scinde Rifles of the Punjab Frontier Force.

The Indian Army Corps was completed by four brigades R.F.A. and a Heavy Battery, a regiment of Indian Cavalry, two companies R.E. and an Indian Infantry Battalion per division. The Army Corps Commander was Lieutenant-General Sir James Willcocks of the British Service.

On the 15th August Captain Buchan, D.S.O., Sergeant Morris, and 12 men of the battalion transport establishment left Jullundur for Karachi to take over transport ; Captain Hastings, D.S.O., embarked this day at Bombay for a destination which was not disclosed ; and the following regimental appointments appeared in orders :

"To be Signalling Officer, Lieut. S. S. Norman.
,, ,, Sergeant, Sergeant Hudson.
,, Machine Gun Officer, Lieut. W. N. Shipster.
,, ,, ,, Sergeant, Sergeant Reynolds."

On the 16th August machine guns were received from the Ferozepore Arsenal to replace any which had become unserviceable ; and on the following day the battalion, being now practically complete, left Jullundur for Karachi at 9.57 p.m., reaching Karachi at 6 a.m. on the 20th after a very hot and trying three-days' rail journey. The battalion remained in the relief camp until the 27th, on which day it embarked in the *Edavana*, which also accommodated the 1st Battalion Connaught Rangers of the Ferozepore Brigade. The *Edavana* finally sailed about 1 p.m. on the 29th August in company with seven other troopships.

The total embarking strength of the battalion was 16 officers and 891 other ranks, of whom 1 officer—Lieutenant Shipster—and 18 other ranks, composing the machine-gun detachment, sailed in the *Sangola*.

The following are the names of the officers who left India with the 1st Battalion Manchester Regiment for the Great War :

Major H. W. E. Hitchins (in command), Captains Dunlop, Fisher, Buchan, and Heelis (adjutant), Lieutenants Browne, Paulson, Norman, and Lynch, Second Lieutenants Parminter, Masse, Connell, and Henderson, Quartermaster O'Brien, Captain Seaver, R.A.M.C., and Assistant Surgeon Maguire, I.S.M.D.

The distribution of the battalion on leaving India, including Captain Hastings and a few men attached to other services in the field, was as under :

Proceeding on service . .	17 officers and	914 other ranks.
Remaining at depot (India) .	2[1] ,, ,,	110 ,, ,,
On leave in England . .	5[2] ,, ,,	5 ,, ,,
To join at port of Disembarkation . . .	2 ,, ,,	0 ,, ,,
Total . . .	26 ,, ,,	1,029 ,, ,,

[1] These were Lieutenant Harrison and Second Lieutenant Saportas.
[2] These were Major Walker, Captains Creagh and Tillard, Lieutenants Mair and Davidson.

The ship was very full, there being 1,800 British soldiers and 72 Indians of the Supply and Transport Corps on board, and the monsoon was still active, so that the first five or six days were passed in very considerable discomfort. Suez was reached on the 13th September, and the battalion disembarked and proceeded by train to Cairo, being there quartered in the barracks at Abbassieh, where Lieutenant-Colonel E. P. Strickland arrived on promotion and appointment from the Norfolk Regiment and took over command of the battalion; on the following day Lieutenant Davidson rejoined from leave in England.

Nine men of the battalion were left in hospital in Cairo when on the 18th it was sent by rail to Alexandria, embarking there in the *Edavana* and sailing next day. The fleet of transports and escort now numbered 23 ships.

Marseilles was reached on the 26th September, and here the remaining four of the five officers who had been in England on leave rejoined. The battalion disembarked at once and marched to camp at Borély, where English clothing was drawn, Mark VI ammunition was returned to store and Mark VII issued in lieu, all rifles were exchanged for Mark III*, and new machine guns were drawn.

The journey was renewed on the 30th, when the battalion proceeded by train to Orleans and marched to Camp Cercottes, where until the 16th all ranks were busily engaged in training and in completing equipment. Here Captain Hastings came back to the battalion for duty, the Rev. H. K. Foster was attached as Church of England Chaplain, Lieutenant Carr reported himself as interpreter, while two French soldier interpreters—Corporal Gourdon and Private Compte Calix—were also attached.

On the 17th October orders were received that the battalion was to go north, and, moving by rail and road, the Lahore Division, less one brigade which had remained in Egypt guarding the Suez Canal pending the arrival of Territorials from England, reached the region of Ypres in the third week in October, the 1st Battalion Manchester Regiment arriving at Estaires on the morning of the 23rd and then, marching on to Picantin, was employed with the 47th Sikhs, the remainder of the Jullundur Brigade being detached. The battalion was in reserve to the French cavalry and this day came under fire for the first time in the war.

For the next two days there was not much doing, but on the 26th October the battalion marched early to Gorre, where the greater part of the day was spent, and then in the late afternoon was sent to relieve the Bedfordshire Regiment in the trenches three-quarters of a mile east of Festubert; here, as elsewhere related, the two battalions of the Manchester Regiment met for the first time since 1882. In the course of the relief two men of the 1st Battalion were slightly wounded, and during the next two days, until relieved early on the morning of the 29th by the Devons, 7 men were killed and 13 wounded either by shell fire or by snipers. The battalion had expected to go into billets at Le Touret, but on the afternoon of the 29th it marched to Estaires, left there again the next day and moved to a point south-west of Picantin and took over trenches from the 15th Sikhs and 34th Pioneers near the Rue Tilleloy. These trenches were held by the battalion until the 13th November; the battalion was constantly under fire and there were many casualties: on the 1st November Colonel Strickland and Lieutenant Masse were wounded, as was also Lieutenant Davidson, though he made no report until next day; on the 8th Captain Dunlop was killed by a sniper, while of other ranks 3 were killed and 10 wounded.

On the 16th the battalion moved to Le Couture and rested there in billets till the 22nd, when it returned to the trenches, relieving part of the Meerut Division about La Quinque Rue, and on the 23rd Lieutenant Davidson was mortally wounded by a sniper and died next day. On the 26th and 27th there was some hard fighting, for their share in which the First Manchesters got great praise.

A plan had been devised for attacking the enemy's sap-heads—for his sap had a double head to it, and in one place had encroached to within some 20 yards of the battalion trenches opposite No. 3 Company. The plan was for this company to evacuate their trenches, leaving only a few men behind who, by keeping up a fire, should lead the enemy to think the trench was held in the usual strength. Meanwhile the British guns were to bombard the sap-heads and advanced trenches for about half an hour—from 11.30 p.m. to midnight. When this bombardment ceased, No. 1 Company was to send out parties to investigate the sap-head and to break up any mining arrangements that might be found. At the last moment the operation was postponed to the following night, but the Germans seem to have suspected something, for they opened a heavy shell and machine-gun fire and the battalion sustained several casualties.

At 11.30 p.m. on the 27th the artillery bombardment began as arranged, but it lacked volume and did not appear to be very effective. Captain Creagh sent out two parties from No. 3 Company and these found some 60 yards of enemy trench unoccupied, and returned having 3 men wounded. Captain Tillard—right centre company—also sent out two parties each of 10 men, to each sap-head, where the enemy were found at work and some 40 Germans were killed, the rest escaping down the sap. Lieutenant Connell was in charge of both parties, and having searched the saps and partially filled in one of them, he gave the order to fall back. One party, under Colour-Sergeant Heywood, got back without loss, but that with which was Lieutenant Connell was caught by machine-gun fire as it left the sap, and the officer and 5 of his men were killed and 3 wounded.

The battalion was back in rest billets again at Le Couture from the 3rd to the 10th December, and was inspected on the 6th by General Sir James Willcocks, who congratulated all ranks on their services on the night of the 27th November.

While "resting" there arrived from the base a draft of 154 men, of whom 36 had either been previously wounded and had now recovered, or who had been left in various hospitals since the battalion had sailed from India.

During the next ten days the battalion was constantly in and—for very short periods—out of the trenches, incurring casualties daily in officers and men—Captain Fisher being killed on the 15th December; and then on the 20th while in billets at Bethune orders were received in the morning about 11 o'clock to march at once to Gorre and report to the G.O.C. Sirhind Brigade. The reason for this was the following :

"The Germans had occupied the whole of the Sirhind Brigade front, and the brigade had fallen back to the Festubert road. The enemy had also occupied the left or northern part of the line held by the Ferozepore Brigade, while Givenchy village was itself also in the hands of the Germans."[1]

The battalion marched off at noon, but on the way the orders were changed and it was now directed to march to Pont Fixe, where it was to be met by the Brigade-Major. The route led along the Bethune–La Bassée Canal and on arrival at Pont Fixe Colonel Strickland received orders to deliver an attack on the enemy's trenches east of Givenchy.

"The Manchesters began their attack shortly after 3 p.m. and found on reaching the village that it was held in unexpected strength by the enemy. Rough and tumble hand-to-hand fighting took place, the Germans holding their positions house by house, and they were not cleared out until it had become too dark to distinguish the features of the country or to locate the position of the hostile trenches, which were the next objective. The desperate nature of the fighting can be gauged from the fact that only 12 prisoners were taken. The village was held during the night.

"At 6.30 a.m. on the 21st Colonel Strickland launched his attack, but immediately came under a withering fire from rifles and machine guns, which proved particularly deadly, as every movement of our men

[1] *The Indian Corps in France*, p. 176.

1ST BATTALION AT GIVENCHY, DECEMBER 20TH, 1914.

was clearly shown up by the blaze of two haystacks which were burning furiously behind them. The Manchesters, however, are a regiment which takes a good deal of stopping, as the enemy to his cost has learnt on many occasions in this campaign. For over an hour they made desperate efforts to reach the German trenches, but against the torrent of bullets and shells little progress could be effected, and men were everywhere falling fast.

"It was becoming evident that the attempt could not succeed, when at 11 a.m., after the village and our trenches had been vigorously shelled for 45 minutes, the enemy made a strong attack. The Manchesters held firm, and the attack was on the verge of being repulsed, when the French on the left were forced out of their position, leaving our flank in the air. The enemy seized his advantage, and began to work round the Manchesters' left, which was compelled to retire through the village on to the road. At the same moment the Germans heavily attacked the centre and right. The situation appeared to be rapidly becoming untenable and it was decided to retire the left supports to a position in rear, in order to cover the withdrawal of the centre and right.

"The gallant Manchesters, a regiment of Ironsides, had, however, not yet shot their bolt. They held on so tenaciously that Colonel Strickland decided on a further attempt. By a splendid rush the original trenches were re-occupied, the enemy being driven back on the left at about 2 p.m.; but this was our last expiring effort. Soon after 3 p.m. the Germans delivered a sharp attack from the front, while large bodies appeared on the right flank and rear. At the same moment machine guns opened on us, enfilading our line from the right.

"There was nothing for it but to retire; the casualties had been very heavy and the men were utterly done. There were only three officers left with the companies, and in some companies there were hardly any non-commissioned officers. The centre and right held on with the utmost obstinacy, while the remainder, with whom were Colonel Strickland, the adjutant, and a few non-commissioned officers, took up a position in the rear, the firing line then falling back after a furious hand-to-hand fight on the road.

"The retirement to Pont Fixe was conducted with the greatest steadiness, a quality for which, under all circumstances, this splendid regiment has always been known. Many wounded men were carried back under heavy shrapnel and machine gun fire. By their wonderful staunchness the Manchesters had given time for reinforcements to be brought up, and the arrival of the Cameron Highlanders of the 1st Brigade, 1st Division, righted the situation at this point.

"The losses of the Manchesters were heavy: Captain Creagh, Lieutenant Norman and 64 men were killed, Major Hitchens, Captain Rose, Lieutenant Lynch and 123 men were wounded, while 46 men were missing. There was, however, the satisfaction of knowing that our mark had been left still more deeply on the enemy. Of this Regiment it may be said once for all that none more devoted and none more valiant has passed in this war through the Valley of the Shadow of Death." [1]

The Jullundur Brigade now went back into billets and while "resting" the battalion was visited both by the Divisional and Corps Commander, who heartily congratulated all ranks of the First Manchesters on the splendour of their achievements on the 20th and 21st December: the following speeches were made:

By Lieutenant-General Watkis

"Colonel Strickland, Officers, N.C.O.'s and men of the 1st Manchester Regiment.

"It gives me great pleasure to come and speak to you this morning. I want to tell you how very pleased I am with the work you did on the 20th and 21st inst. Yours was the Battalion detailed to carry out the attack on the village of Givenchy, and from all accounts I learn that it was a magnificent piece of work. I have not heard this from your own Officers, but from others, and all the time you were doing your duty I was receiving wires telling of the splendid way you were behaving, and in my reports to higher Authorities I could only use the term ' Gallant Manchesters.'

"You went into the attack steadily, you carried the village, also the trenches, and held them all night in the rain and mud. Next day you were subjected to a Hell of a bombardment, still you hung on, and when you had to retire you did so in the same way that you advanced. When you were called upon to go back, by God, men, you went back. Perhaps you do not know exactly what you did, but I may tell you that at that particular period, the village of Givenchy was the most important point, not only in your Brigade or Division or Corps, but of the whole British Line, and had you given way God only knows what would have happened. I thank you from the bottom of my heart. You are a very brave set of men."

By General Sir J. Willcocks

"Colonel Strickland, Officers, and men of the 1st Manchester Regiment,

---

[1] *The Indian Corps in France*, pp. 177 et seq.

"I want to thank you for your very fine bit of work in the last fight. You are a very gallant Battalion. You were holding the most important point on the right of the British Line, and by your gallant conduct in holding on to it, you rendered greater services than you probably realise.

"I want to tell Colonel Strickland in front of you all what I think of him. He is a first-class Soldier, and you a brave lot of men. I shall not fail in my report to the C.-in-C. to bring to notice your conduct and of those recommended for reward, and shall do my best to obtain some suitable reward for them."

Speech by Major-General P. M. Carnegy, Commanding Jullundur Brigade.

"Colonel Strickland, Officers, N.C.O.'s and men of the 1st Manchester Regiment,

"I am very pleased to be able to speak to you this morning, and to personally thank you for your splendid behaviour at Givenchy.

"You did your work magnificently and saved what was becoming a very serious situation. You are what I consider the finest fighting soldier in the World—the British Soldier—and by your behaviour at Givenchy you have still further heightened the reputation of the British Soldier as a fighting man.

"Again I thank you and say how proud I am of you."

On the 29th a draft of 86 non-commissioned officers and men joined the battalion under Lieutenant Vanderspar.

Early in January 1915 Colonel Strickland was appointed to command the Jullundur Brigade with the rank of Brigadier-General, Captain Buchan assuming command of the battalion; but at the end of the month he was relieved by Major Anley, who had been D.A.A.G. 3rd Division.

The months of January and February passed without any special incident on the Indian Corps front, but though the troops were not seriously engaged they were not idle, and every opportunity was taken of filling up gaps, exercising in the use of trench mortars and rifle grenades, the handling of bombs, and other methods incidental to the new warfare. Heavy rain fell, accompanied by high, cutting winds, and snowstorms were frequent; the whole country became a wilderness of mud and offensive operations were thus impossible for both sides, but casualties continued to mount up, and by the 1st February the losses in the Indian Corps totalled 1,429 killed, 5,989 wounded, and 2,335 missing.

The position on the northern front at the beginning of March was as follows : the line from Dixmude southwards to the apex of the Ypres salient was held by French troops with some British cavalry. To the south again was the 5th Corps, in touch with which was the 2nd. The 3rd Corps occupied its old position opposite Armentières, whence the line was continued southwards from Estaires to the west of Neuve Chapelle by the 4th Corps. Thence the Indian Corps held the line as far as Givenchy, where it linked up with the 1st Corps, which was in touch with General Maud'huy's 10th French Army across the La Bassée Canal.

On the 10th March the Jullundur Brigade, now under Brigadier-General Strickland, consisted of the 1st Battalion Manchester Regiment, 4th Battalion Suffolk Regiment (Territorials), the 47th Sikhs, and 59th Rifles, the 15th Sikhs, whose place the Suffolks had taken, having been transferred to the Sirhind Brigade.

The French had lately had some important successes in Champagne, the effect of which had been to divert German units from the British front, and it was considered that the moment was opportune for here taking the offensive and straightening out the enemy salient at Neuve Chapelle. The scope of the proposed operations was defined in an order issued on the 9th March—the attack on Neuve Chapelle was to be undertaken by the 4th and Indian Corps, the 8th Division of the former and the Meerut Division of the latter forming the assaulting troops. " The immediate objective was the enemy's trenches W. of Neuve Chapelle, and the occupation of a line to the E. of the diamond-shaped figure formed by the main road from Estaires to La Bassée, the road by Fleurbaix to Armentières, and that which connects the two. In the northern angle of this diamond lies the village of Neuve Chapelle. The general object of the attack was to enable the 4th and Indian Corps to establish themselves on a more forward line to the E., the ultimate objective being the high ground on which are situated the villages of Aubers and Ligny-le-Grand, with the intention finally of cutting off that portion of the enemy's troops which held the line between Neuve Chapelle and La Bassée."

The battalion was at Le Couture in billets on the 10th March, when it received orders to march at 12.30 p.m. as advance guard to the Jullundur Brigade, which at 2.30 had arrived 300 yards S. of Richebourg St. Vaast, where for a time it halted. At 4 p.m. the battalion received orders to proceed with the 47th Sikhs via La Bassée Rue to the cross roads 700 yards S.E. of Neuve Chapelle to protect the right flank of the Dehra Dun Brigade of the Indian Corps, which was then about to attack the Bois de Biez. The battalion moved forward in rear of the 47th Sikhs, coming under shellfire, and had got some distance when information was received that no more troops were needed, and that the Jullundur Brigade was to go into billets for the night in the ruined houses near the junction of the Rue des Berceaux and La Bassée Rue.

On the 11th the battalion again moved forward and formed up in rear of the battered houses of Neuve Chapelle, and while here was ordered to advance on the left of the second line on the 59th attacking. The enemy were firing freely on the village with guns and rifles, and while the line was being pointed out to the officers, Lieutenants Mair and Holness were wounded and several men were killed and others wounded. Later the enemy turned their guns on to the houses behind which the battalion was sheltering, and it accordingly moved into the open and lay down in extended order, when Second Lieutenants Bettington and James were hit. An attack was ordered and later cancelled, the battalion finally moving back after dark to the previous night's billets.

At 5 a.m. on the 12th the Brigade, the Manchesters leading, moved off again towards Neuve Chapelle, the road swept with intensely heavy shell-fire, the battalion first sheltering in some trenches and then advancing to the Neuve Chapelle Road. Here Lieutenant Curtis was killed. On reaching the trenches S.W. of the village they were found to be occupied by Indian troops, therefore Nos. 1 and 2 Companies were extended in rear of the trench S.E. of the road, while Nos. 3 and 4 and the machine-gun section were left in trenches on La Bassée Rue.

At 9 a.m. orders were received to attack the Bois de Biez, when the battalion was thus distributed: No. 1 Company under Captain Browne on the left of the first line was to advance in an easterly direction; No. 2 under Lieutenant Gwyther on the right of No. 1, which was to direct; No. 4 under Captain Phillips formed the second line to follow 200–300 yards in rear of the centre of the first line; while No. 3 Company under Lieutenant Parminter formed the third line and was to follow behind the left of No. 4 carrying shovels and sandbags. Battalion Headquarters moved with No. 3 and the machine-gun section followed No. 4 Company.

It had originally been intended that the Jullundur Brigade should attack on a front of three battalions—the Manchesters on the left in touch with the 8th Division, the 47th Sikhs in the centre, and the Suffolks on the right, with the 59th in reserve. It was, however, discovered that, owing to the losses under the previous day's shell-fire, the Suffolks and 59th Rifles barely numbered 265 rank and file all told; consequently in order to fill up the front allotted to the Brigade the 59th had to be brought up into the front line and there was then no brigade reserve.

The attack, originally ordered for 9 a.m., was postponed.

"At 12.30 p.m. our artillery poured a very heavy shrapnel fire into the Bois de Biez, and at 1 p.m. the infantry attack commenced. The Manchesters, heroes of Givenchy, advanced with their accustomed determination and steadiness, but the moment the first line of two companies appeared, the enemy opened a staggering fire, and Captain Brown, commanding No. 1 Company, was wounded, while men were falling fast. By 1.30 p.m. the leading companies of the Battalion had succeeded in reaching the front line trenches held by the Garhwal Brigade, but here they became mixed up with the 2/3rd Gurkhas, while the first and second lines and the communication trenches had become completely blocked by troops.

"The remainder of the Battalion was held up for some time, owing to the necessity of crossing gaps in the trenches where roads and ditches intersected them. These gaps were marked down by the enemy and swept by machine-gun fire, all attempts to pass them ending only in heavy casualties. The Manchesters, however, are hard to beat, as the enemy has so often found to his cost, and Nos. 3 and 4 Companies eventually made a most gallant rush and reached the front line, but with much-diminished ranks." [1]

The Jullundur and Sirhind Brigades this day failed, it is true, to reach their objectives, in spite of the great dash and bravery with which the attack was carried out, but this was due to the fact that the brigade of the 8th Division on their left was unable to advance, and the enemy could thus bring oblique and enfilade fire on the Indian Corps. It had been intended that the attack on the Bois de Biez should be still pressed, but General Willcocks decided against it in view of the darkness and of the fact that the ground was quite unknown.

The Battle of Neuve Chapelle then ended with a loss to the Indian Corps of 835 killed, 3,083 wounded, and 315 missing.

The battalion was withdrawn from the line between 3.15 and 4.30 on the morning of the 13th and returned with the Brigade to divisional reserve about Richebourg St. Vaast. On the 28th March it was visited and inspected by General Sir James Willcocks, commanding the Indian Army Corps, who addressed the battalion as follows:

"First Manchesters!

"Once again how gloriously you have fought in front of the enemy! The Battle of Neuve Chapelle was a hard one, but bravely you faced it. I have been requested by the Commander-in-Chief to visit you personally and thank you for your gallant work. You are a credit to the country to

---

[1] *The Indian Corps in France*, pp. 260, 261.

which you belong; and you have gallantly maintained the splendid traditions of your Regiment. How proud and pleased I am to have such a splendid Regiment under my command, and every man here should be proud to belong to it."

The remainder of March passed without special incident, but the enemy continued to shell heavily the British trenches and back areas, without, however, drawing any very effective reply, as particular economy in gun-ammunition expenditure had been enjoined.

On the 21st March the Indian Corps took over that portion of the front hitherto held by the 4th Corps, being itself relieved by the 1st; while a week later the brigades of the Indian Corps were reorganised and the Jullundur Brigade received a fifth battalion—the 40th Pathans, which was due to arrive on the 8th April from China.

No events of special importance took place on the Indian Corps front during the first three weeks of April, but on the 24th the Lahore Division, now commanded by Major-General Keary, was ordered up to the Ypres sector, where, by the German gas-attack on the evening of the 22nd April, the situation east of the Ypres Canal had become very critical and most difficult to deal with; and thus again, as during the first battle of Ypres in October 1914 and later in the same month at La Bassée, the Indian Corps was called upon to step into the breach.

Leaving its billets at L'Epinette on the afternoon of the 24th April, the battalion marched $23\frac{1}{2}$ miles to Boeschepe, which was reached before midnight, and leaving again at 6 a.m. on the 25th it moved by way of Vlamertinghe to Wieltje, arriving about 10.30 a.m. on the 26th, and being there greeted by an enemy shell which fell on the battalion, killing and wounding 12 men.

On this march the 1st Battalion again met the 2nd, which was then near Ypres.

At 12.30 p.m. the Lahore Division moved out to its position of deployment, the Jullundur Brigade, with its right resting on a farm slightly west of Wieltje, occupying a front of 500 yards, and its front line units being thus disposed from right to left—Manchesters, 40th Pathans, 47th Sikhs, while in the second line, 400 yards behind, were the 59th Rifles in rear of the Manchesters and the Suffolk Regiment in rear of the 47th.

The battalion attacked over a distance of about 1,600 yards, on a front of two companies in four lines, and came at once under very heavy shrapnel, machine-gun and rifle fire, losing many officers and men; but succeeded in reaching to within 70 yards of the enemy's trenches, where the battalion lay until dark, unable to get further without reinforcements. The attack of the battalion is thus described in *The Indian Corps in France*:

"The enemy's guns were very active from the beginning of the attack, and when the troops reached the crest they came under a perfect inferno of fire of all kinds, machine gun, rifle and every variety of shell, many of which were filled with gas. On crossing the ridge the Manchesters at once began to feel the effects of the fire, officers and men falling everywhere.

"At about this time Lieutenants Huskinson, Crawhall and Robinson were wounded. This left only one officer, 2nd Lieutenant Williamson-Jones, with No. 1 Company. Shortly afterwards he too was hit, and Captain Buchan, D.S.O., commanding the firing line, was gassed by a shell, but saved himself to a great extent by covering his mouth and nose with a wet handkerchief. Going up the final slope Captain Paulson and Lieutenant Roberts were wounded, the latter in five places. He died shortly afterwards.

"Corporal Issy Smith won the Victoria Cross by his devotion in leaving his company and going far forward towards the enemy's position to assist a severely wounded man, whom he carried for a distance of 250 yards into safety, although he was all the time exposed to heavy machine-gun and rifle fire. Subsequently Corporal Smith voluntarily helped to bring in many more wounded men, and attended to them regardless of danger. . . .

"The Manchesters, as stubborn and superb here as at Givenchy, still pushed on, the casualties increasing with every yard gained, until they reached a road at a distance of only some 60 yards from the German trench. . . . The adjutant of the Manchesters, Captain Heelis, was wounded during the afternoon while taking a message to Brigade Headquarters under heavy fire, and at about 9.30 p.m. Lieut.-Colonel Hitchins, commanding the Battalion, was killed by a stray bullet while crossing the ground between the French and British trenches." He had only rejoined the battalion on the 15th April on recovering from the wound received at Givenchy.

It was a great satisfaction to the battalion that the promotion of Major Hitchins to Lieutenant-Colonel was announced the day the battalion had left Epinette for Ypres.

"During this battle the Manchesters sustained and, if possible, increased their splendid reputation, but at a great cost, their casualties amounting to 1 officer and 15 men killed, 11 officers and 206 men wounded, and 56 men missing."

At about 3 a.m. on the 27th the Jullundur Brigade was relieved and withdrew to reserve trenches at La Brique, where next day a draft of 65 non-commissioned officers and men under Second Lieutenant Ruddy joined the battalion, and another of 20 under Second Lieutenant Pembroke. By the end of May the total reinforcements received by the battalion amounted to 38 officers and 1,449 other ranks—after no more than eight months of war!

The Jullundur Brigade remained at La Brique for 8 days and was heavily shelled; on the night of the 2nd May it commenced its march through Ypres at night by the only route by which ammunition, rations, etc., could be sent to troops in the salient, and this was an experience that none who went through are likely to forget. The enemy was fully aware of the stream of troops and transport going through by night, and was most attentive in the way of shell-fire. Ammunition columns went by at a canter, and the situation of infantry was precarious in the extreme. The battalion, and in fact the whole Brigade, was most fortunate as very few casualties were incurred.

The battalion was specially mentioned for the " great service " it had performed in the second Battle of Ypres by General Smith-Dorrien, commanding the Second Army, while the Commander of the Indian Corps has placed on record his opinion of the battalion : " I have known," he writes, " many splendid corps in the Army, but not one to beat the 1st Manchesters," and elsewhere he mentions " the fiery zeal with which they always advanced." [1]

During June, July, and August the battalion remained on the same sector of the front, taking part in no operations of the first importance, but losing men steadily not only on every tour in the trenches, but even when nominally in " rest " billets, from the long-range shelling of the enemy. Here is the record of one day—the 25th July—from a private diary:

" One shell hit the parados of the fire-trench. Although the parados was 5 feet high it was entirely demolished and two dug-outs destroyed. One man was killed and several buried. One man when extricated was badly shaken, but the other two shook themselves and laughed. A few minutes later another shell hit four dug-outs of the reserve company; here two men were blown to pieces, another had his arm blown off at the shoulder, and a fourth was badly shaken. Although about twenty shells were fired, no other damage was done. During the previous night a man in No. 1 Company was killed by a bullet coming through a loophole."

[1] *With the Indians in France*, pp. 172, 249.

On the 13th June Lieutenant-Colonel Crawford arrived and assumed command of the battalion, while early in September Lieutenant-General Anderson succeeded General Sir James Willcocks at the head of the Indian Army Corps.

In September the decision was come to that offensive operations on a large scale should be undertaken, and Champagne was chosen as the area for the main attack; in conjunction with these there were to be a number of subsidiary actions to prevent the enemy from sending substantial reinforcements to Champagne, and the Indian Corps was to operate in the vicinity of Neuve Chapelle. Three objectives were laid down for the Corps:

(*a*) To attack the enemy's line between Sunken Road and Winchester Road, and to establish a line along the road running from Mauquissart to the " Duck's Bill."

(*b*) To press on, with the left in front, until the high ground between Haut Pommereau and La Cliqueterie Farm was gained.

(*c*) To continue the advance from that point in a S.E. direction in order to assist the main offensive in the south by turning the La Bassée defences from the north.

The attack was to be delivered by the Meerut Division, the Lahore and 19th Divisions holding the whole of the front except that portion from which the attacking division was to advance. The operations that now ensued have been given the name of the Battle of Loos.

A bombardment began on the 21st September and was kept up for four days; on the 22nd the Lahore Division made a feint of attacking, raising bayonets over the parapets of the trenches, holding up dummy heads, and shouting, thus causing the Germans to crowd their trenches in anticipation of an attack—with satisfying results to our artillery.

The weather, which had latterly been very fine, now changed, heavy rain fell, the trenches filled with water and movement became very difficult. Early on the 25th a German bomb burst in a projecting portion of trench known as the " Duck's Bill," blowing off the heads of several gas cylinders, the vapour filling the front and support trench and putting many men out of action, including a bombing party of the 1st Manchesters which had been sent to the " Duck's Bill " preparatory to the attack.

The following from a private diary of one of the battalion gives in brief the story of these days:

" *September 24th.*—Bombardment more intense. One man in the Regiment carrying bombs to the front line was blown up in the air by a shell, but discovering himself uninjured, picked up his box of bombs and went on

"*September 28th.*—Assault on enemy's position by Meerut Division, preceded by the explosion of a mine in their front, which was immediately followed by a heavy bombardment by our guns. In front of the Meerut Division poisonous gas was used by us, and in front of the Lahore Division smoke bombs. Our front was immediately obscured by the cloud raised, and the Garhwal Brigade of the Meerut Division advanced at 6 a.m. behind it. Two lines of the German trenches were taken and 8 officers and 200 prisoners of other ranks sent back. However, by 10 a.m. the Garhwal Brigade had been counter-attacked by bombs and driven back to their original line. Before this strong patrols of the 1st Btn. Manchester Regiment approached the German trenches in our front to find them strongly held. Lieutenants Findlater and Lane preceded our left patrol and the former began cutting the German wire, while the latter directed bombs to be thrown into the German trench to cover the retirement of their patrol. Lieutenant Heywood took another patrol out and reached the German wire, but was killed and the patrol retired. Several of our bomb-throwers were gassed. About 9 a.m. one of our Maurice-Farman aeroplanes, manœuvring over the German lines, was surprised by a German 'Aviatik,' which suddenly appeared out of a cloud above it, and opened fire with his machine gun. After some exciting manœuvres our aeroplane was forced to descend inside the German lines. About 4 p.m. the rain came down in torrents, and our trenches were soon flooded and active operations suspended. Our casualties amounted to 56."

The question of reinforcements for the Indian regiments of the Indian Army Corps had from the first been a constant source of anxiety, and matters came to a head at the beginning of this winter. The reserve organisation had broken down, there had been heavier casualties in the Indian ranks than could adequately and promptly be filled, while it was impossible to keep up a satisfactory reinforcement of British officers. The Corps made its first appearance in the front line on the 22nd October 1914, and already by the 1st December the casualties numbered 4,863 of all ranks. As time went on and wastage increased battalions became mere skeletons, and of the truth of this statement two instances may suffice. By the beginning of November 1915 the 47th Sikhs had but 28 *men*—no British or Indian officers—of those who had landed with it in France, while the 59th Rifles had no British, 4 Indian officers, and 75 other ranks of their original numbers.

" For some time past during the autumn of 1915 rumours had been current of the impending transfer of the Corps to other theatres of war less remote from its original base. It was therefore without surprise that information was received on the 31st October that the Indian Corps would be required to embark at Marseilles in the near future," leaving behind it the Special Reserve and Territorial units which had joined it during recent months.

On the 4th November the relief in the trenches of the Indian Divisions commenced, on the 7th the Meerut Division began to entrain for Marseilles, and on the 9th December the first detachments of the Lahore Division followed.

The battalion was in billets at Quernes when, on the 16th November, the following letter was received by the Commanding Officer from Brigadier-General Strickland, on giving up the command of the Jullundur Brigade:

"*I wish to express to you and to all ranks of the Battalion the very deep regret I feel at leaving you, but though I shall not be serving with you I shall have the honour of still belonging to the Regiment. I joined you 15 months ago, at the commencement of this great war, and you had the disadvantage of going into action under a commanding officer you did not know.*

"*I shall never forget, or cease to be deeply grateful for, the loyal spirit you showed. Through pride in the fine Regiment you belong to, you gave me such support and loyalty that could not have been exceeded had we known one another for years. It was owing to that that the Regiment has so distinguished itself, and leaves the name it does behind it in France for gallantry, determination, indifference to, and cheerfulness under, the most adverse conditions.*

"*I regret that there are so few left now who arrived in France with the Battalion, but those who have fallen have left their mark behind them; and let their deeds here be an example for those now serving to follow, and so maintain, and if possible add to, the grand traditions of the Manchester Regiment.*

"*I wish you all God-speed. I shall follow your doings with the greatest confidence and interest, and hope that the day may come when we shall once again serve together.*"

On the 22nd November the following special order of the day was issued by Field-Marshal Sir John French:

"*On the departure of the Indian Corps from my command under which you have fought for more than a year, I wish to send a message of thanks to all officers, non-commissioned officers and men for the work you have done for the Empire. From the time you reached France you were constantly engaged with the enemy until the end of last year. After a few weeks' rest you returned to the trenches, and since then you have continually held some portion of the front line, taking part in the important and successful engagements of Neuve Chapelle* and of Richebourg, and in the heavy fighting at the end of September. The Lahore Division was also engaged in the severe actions near Ypres in April and May. That your work has been hard is proved by the number of your casualties. The British troops of the Corps have borne themselves in a manner worthy of the best traditions of the army.

" The Indian Corps have shown most praiseworthy courage under novel and trying conditions, both of climate and of fighting, and have not only upheld, but added to, the good name of the army which they represent. This is all the more praiseworthy in view of the heavy losses amongst British officers having deprived the Indian ranks of many trusted leaders whom they knew well, and of the fact that the drafts necessary to maintain your strength have frequently had to be drawn from regiments quite unconnected with the units they were sent to reinforce. You have done your work here well, and are now being sent to another place where an unscrupulous enemy has stirred up strife against the King-Emperor. I send you all my good wishes for success in the part you will now be called on to play in this great war. I thank you for the services you have rendered while under my command, and trust that the united efforts of the Allies may soon bring the enemy to his knees and restore peace to the world."

Then on the 25th November a parade of representatives of the Indian Army Corps—to which the 1st Manchester Regiment sent a contingent of 23 officers, non-commissioned officers and men—was held at Château Mazinghem, at which the following message from His Majesty the King-Emperor to the British and Indian troops of the Indian Corps in France was read by H.R.H. the Prince of Wales :

" *Officers, Non-Commissioned Officers, and Men of the Indian Army Corps !*

" *More than a year ago I summoned you from India to fight for the safety of my Empire and the honour of my pledged word on the battlefields of Belgium and France. The confidence which I then expressed in your sense of duty, your courage, and your chivalry you have since then nobly justified.*

" *I now require your services in another field of action, but before you leave France I send my dear and gallant son, the Prince of Wales, who has shared with my armies the dangers and hardships of the campaign, to thank you in my name for your services and to express to you my satisfaction.*

" *British and Indian comrades-in-arms, yours has been a fellowship in toils and hardships, in courage and endurance often against great odds, in deeds nobly done and days of memorable conflict. In a warfare waged under new conditions and in particularly trying circumstances, you have worthily upheld the honour of the Empire, and the great traditions of my Army in India.*

"*I have followed your fortunes with the deepest interest and watched your gallant actions with pride and satisfaction. I mourn with you the loss of many gallant officers and men. Let it be your consolation, as it was their pride, that they freely gave their lives in a just cause for the honour of their Sovereign and the safety of my Empire. They died as gallant soldiers, and I shall ever hold their sacrifice in grateful remembrance. You leave France with a just pride in honourable deeds already achieved and with my assured confidence that your proved valour and experience will contribute to further victories in the new fields of action to which you go.*

"*I pray God to bless and guard you, and to bring you back safely when the final victory is won, each to his own home—there to be welcomed with honour among his own people.*"

On the 8th December the 1st Battalion Manchester Regiment paraded at 12.30 a.m. at Beaumetz-les-Aires, where for the previous forty-eight hours it had been billeted, and marched to Berguette, a distance of 14 miles, on a very wet night. Berguette was reached at 6 a.m. and the battalion entrained, leaving about 10 o'clock for Marseilles. This port was reached late on the night of the 10th December and the men at once detrained and marched straight on board the transport *Huntsend*—a captured German liner formerly named the *Lützow*—which also accommodated the 1st Battalion Connaught Rangers. The embarking strength of the Manchesters was 28 officers, 7 warrant officers, and 812 non-commissioned officers and men.

The following are the names of the officers who sailed with the battalion for an "unknown destination": Lieutenant-Colonel Hardcastle, D.S.O., Major Browne, Captains Vaudrey, Lynch, Parminter (adjutant), Henderson, and Cosgrove, Lieutenants R. W. Smith, A. G. Smith, Ruddy, and Campbell, Second Lieutenants Marley, Assig, Davis, Wilkins, Butterworth, Bedford, Morris, Adams, Lane, and Gaukroger, Lieutenant and Quartermaster O'Brien, and Captain Spackman, R.A.M.C. Lieutenant Baxter joined the battalion at Port Said and Lieutenant Burdon sailed in the *Georgian*; Captain Holmes sailed with the divisional transport.

Steaming steadily eastward, the *Huntsend* was off Koweit late on the afternoon of the 6th January 1916, and next day, the troops having been transhipped to the *Pentakota*, that vessel sailed about 5 p.m., anchored for the night off the Shatt-el-Arab lighthouse, finally reaching Basra on the morning of the 8th January.

The " unknown destination " had at last been reached and the battalion was now definitely committed to take part in the campaign in Mesopotamia, where the situation had arrived at a somewhat critical stage.

In this theatre of war two Commanders-in-Chief had already resigned, and a third, General Sir Percy Lake, had only arrived in the country a very short time before the Indian divisions from France had reached their new scene of operations. The forward movement of Major-General Townshend had been checked and he had fallen back upon and was now besieged in Kut, and at this time there were in Mesopotamia, besides the division locked up in Kut, nothing more than the remains of the 12th Division, greatly reduced by the fatigues of a hard campaign, and " burdened with the duty of policing nearly 400 miles of river, as well as the occupation of a province nearly as large in area as Great Britain."[1]

When Sir Percy Lake landed at Basra from India he brought with him General Sir F. Aylmer, lately Adjutant-General in India, who had been appointed to command what was called the " Tigris Corps," and which, reinforced by the troops now arriving from France and Egypt, was to attempt the relief of Kut and the re-establishment of British prestige.

[1] Dane, *British Campaigns in the Near East*, vol. i, p. 135.

CHAPTER XXIII

THE 2ND BATTALION IN FRANCE

JANUARY 1915–AUGUST 1917

AT the end of the year 1914 we left the 2nd Battalion in billets at Dranoutre, where was the brigade reserve, and for some considerable time the battalion took no part in operations on so large a scale as those in which during the earlier months of the campaign it had been so conspicuously engaged.

1915 During January 1915 several officers joined the battalion on first appointment or attached from other corps, some who had been otherwise employed or had previously been wounded came back to serve with it again, while drafts arrived from the base to make good the wastage which was always going on; thus on the 4th January Captain Thornycroft, Lieutenant Albrecht, and 125 men joined; on the 6th Second Lieutenant Davies was attached from the 3rd Battalion East Surreys; on the 7th Lieutenants Pomfret and Henderson joined; on the 13th Captain Parker and Second Lieutenant Martin-Smith brought a reinforcement of 60 men; and on the 20th Second Lieutenant Mackay, 5th Battalion Worcesters, came with 30 more. The trench line occupied by the battalion during January was about La Petite Douve Farm, and towards the end of the month the billets were at Neuve Eglise.

In February and March there was not very much doing, but the casualty list continued to mount up, and during the last turn of duty in the trenches in March the battalion had 8 men killed, Lieutenant Boyle, Second Lieutenant Gudgeon, and 27 other ranks wounded.

At the beginning of April the 5th Division was relieved on the Wulverghemr front, and moved to a sector in the Ypres salient, the new line running from the east of the Mound at St. Eloi by the Bluff, Hill 60, and Zwartelen, to the western end of Armagh Wood, the 14th Brigade being at first in reserve.

On the very day—April 7th—that the battalion marched to Ypres Captain Anthony was wounded, and during the first four days in the " Bloody Salient " 6 men were killed, Second Lieutenant Owen and 32 men were wounded.

On taking over the new sector preparations for the attack on Hill 60 were proceeded with, and the infantry were called upon to provide large working parties to carry up stores, etc., so that by the middle of April all was ready for one of the most sanguinary and hard-fought encounters of the war, but in which the battalion was not specially engaged, although, during the period of its continuance, the losses were heavy.

Prior to the attack on Hill 60 brigade reliefs had been carried out, and on April 16th the 14th Brigade was holding the right sector of the Divisional front, and the 15th Brigade the left sector, around Hill 60. The attack was mainly conducted by the 13th and 15th Brigades, but at different times nearly all the battalions of the 14th Brigade were " lent " to one of the other two for support at critical moments.

The battle of Hill 60, which began on the 17th April, endured with great violence for three weeks, and at the end of it we had lost rather than gained ground ; but what was known as the Second Battle of Ypres went on during the whole of May. During these two months the battalion was constantly in the trenches, even while " resting " losses did not abate, and the roll of killed and wounded was daily added to. In the month of April the casualties amounted to 27 killed and Captain Anthony, Second Lieutenants Owen, Martin-Smith, Raphael, and 158 men wounded, while in May Second Lieutenants Gudgeon, McKiever, and 28 men were killed and Captain Pomfret, Lieutenant Albrecht, Second Lieutenants Gwyther, Grindel, Mackay, Price, and 181 non-commissioned officers and men were wounded.

" Towards the end of May the units of the Division had been reorganised into their proper formations, and the 13th Brigade held the sector S. of Woormezeele through St. Eloi ; the 14th Brigade the sector in the centre astride the Comines Canal ; and the 15th Brigade the Hill 60—Armagh Wood sector. The fighting on our own front had died down and the period until the end of July was one of comparative quiet, if such a term can be applied to the salient at this time ; but to our left fighting occurred at Hooge from time to time." [1]

The battalion held " the Bluff," a high piece of ground which was the point of attraction for all enemy gun-fire, causing many casualties. The reverse slope was covered with fir trees and the only protection for the company in local reserve was in shelters.

" Comparative quiet " is, of course, under the circumstances a relative

---
[1] *The 5th Division in the Great War*, p. 78.

term, for in Sector B, where was the 2nd Battalion Manchester Regiment, that condition of affairs did not mean that men were not being almost hourly killed and wounded; and from the beginning of June until the 25th July, when the Division was relieved and proceeded to the Somme area, the casualties in the battalion made the following total :

Killed: Lieutenants Saportas and Vanderspar (died of wounds) and 25 men. *Wounded*: Second Lieutenants Guinness and O'Leary and 131 other ranks.

At the end of July the Division was relieved by the 46th Division and withdrawn to the area between Poperinghe and Hazebrouck, the marching being done at night. The battalion was relieved by the 1st Battalion Gordon Highlanders on the 25th July *after having completed eighty-seven days in the trenches*, and marched to huts at Rening Helst, resting there for the day, and moving on at night with the rest of the Brigade to Caestre, arriving in billets at 4 a.m. on the 26th.

Major-General Morland was now promoted to the command of the Tenth Corps, then in course of formation, his place in command of the Division being taken by Major-General Kavanagh.

On 27th July General Plumer, who was now commanding the Second Army, came to see the 14th Brigade before it left, and in the course of his remarks to the troops said,

"*he had not come there that morning to hold an inspection parade, but rather to say a few words to the Brigade before it left to join the new Army to which it was being transferred. He was glad to say that the long period during which the men had been engaged in trench warfare had not caused them to forget how to stand still and to handle their arms; their clothing was against them and it would not have pleased those who were used to Aldershot parades, but those who really knew soldiers were able to judge in spite of clothing, and the Brigade had turned out as it ought to have done. The General went on to say that he need not remind his hearers of what they had done in the past, for that would be found written in the records which would form the History of the War. Those, however, who were acquainted with the facts knew the part which the 5th Division and the 14th Infantry Brigade had taken in the early part of the war, and they knew that that part had been at least an arduous one. During the period that the Brigade had been in the sector which it was then leaving, it had been occupied with trench warfare rather than with active operations against the enemy; with one or two exceptions, when although not actually employed as a brigade, two of its battalions—the Devons and the East Surreys—had been very hotly engaged at Hill 60, and by their efforts had contributed very greatly to the reduction of that Hill. Since that time the Brigade had continued to be engaged in trench warfare, but trench warfare was not to be rated the dull sort of fighting that some are prone to think, as Army Commanders know full well. Comparisons, the General remarked, were odious, but he had no hesitation in saying that, so far as the Second Army was concerned, and for that matter, as far as the Expeditionary Force was concerned, no brigade had won so high a reputation for trench warfare as had the 14th Brigade under General Maude. During the operations which had taken place in the Ypres Salient, the 14th Brigade had been engaged in fighting, which might be characterised as ' dull ' from the newspaper point of view, but the General reminded his hearers that unless a Commander can rely on the troops that are holding the line, he cannot withdraw troops, as he otherwise might, for fighting elsewhere. Whilst the 5th Division was there he knew that the Line occupied by the Brigade was absolutely safe, and, he added, it was to the Officers, Non-commissioned Officers and Men whom he was addressing that he ascribed as much credit as he did to those who were engaged in the more active fighting.*

" The Army Commander concluded by saying that the Brigade was going to a new Army under General Monro, and to a new Corps under General Morland, both of whom knew full well the reputation of the Brigade. On those whom he was addressing would devolve the responsibility of living up to the reputation which they had made, and of forming the nucleus of the new Army, for they would be the veterans, and the 14th Brigade standard would be the standard which the other Brigades would emulate ; it must and would be a high one, and if all the other brigades reached it both the Army and the Corps Commander would have confidence.

" The General then expressed his sorrow that the Brigade was parting from the Second Corps and the Second Army, and wished it the best of luck."

On the 1st August the move actually commenced, the battalion entraining at Godewaerswelde and proceeding via Calais and Abbeville to Corbie, whence it marched to billets at Vecquemont, where on the 3rd the Brigade was inspected by General Sir C. Monro, commanding the 3rd Army. On the 4th the march was resumed to Morlancourt, and after spending two clear days here it went on to Suzanne, from where on the 9th August the Manchesters marched to Maricourt and took over trenches from the 2nd Battalion of the 99th French Infantry Regiment. The 14th Brigade held the right sector " from the Somme near Frise, to a point N.W. of Maricourt, the 13th Brigade thence to the top of the ridge overlooking Mametz, and the 15th Brigade the left sector through the Bois Français to the Tambour between Fricourt and La Boisselle. On our right the French held the line S. of the Somme, and on our left were the 51st Highland Division, who, with ourselves, formed part of the newly formed Tenth Corps.

"The terrain was the typical undulating country of Picardy, open, with woods dotted about here and there. Our extreme right rested on the marshes of the Somme at the Moulin de Fargny, where the river makes a horse-shoe bend towards the N.; on the left bank of the Somme lies the village of Frise, which was held by the French, and on the right bank lie the villages of Vaux and Curlu, facing each other either side of the horse-shoe, while at the top is the Moulin de Fargny. . . . From the Moulin de Fargny northwards runs a ravine, known, owing to the shape of a wood situated therein, as ' Y ' wood ravine. Along the west side of this ravine ran our line." [1]

The trenches taken over from the French were very good and, while giving a large measure of protection, permitted also great freedom of movement. At first the situation on this front was comparatively quiet, shells were few and far between, and practically no sniping was done, and this relatively peaceful state of affairs lasted throughout the month of August, during which time the casualties in the battalion were few—2 killed and 7 wounded—but this included one officer, Lieutenant Martin, who was killed in action on the 13th.

In connection with the Loos offensive in September the Division was to have carried out an attack on some rising ground in front known as the Pommier Ridge, but owing to the failure of the operations at Loos the Pommier Ridge project was abandoned, and the front was again held by the three brigades, the 14th on the right, the 13th in the centre, and the 15th on the left, and this disposition was maintained until the end of the year.

During the month of October the battalion moved from the trenches to billets at Suzanne or Maricourt and had 1 man killed and Lieutenant-Colonel Weston (who was now commanding), Major Luxmoore, Devon Regiment, attached, and 21 non-commissioned officers and men wounded.

In November there were no big actions or operations of serious importance on this front, but there was considerable activity on the part of the British in the endeavour to harass the enemy and bring down his *moral*. Thus on the 13th, it being noticed that the Germans had had the temerity to display a flag in front of their wire, Lieutenants Gwyther and Williamson

[1] *The 5th Division in the Great War*, pp. 82, 83.

of the battalion went out at night to bring it in. They failed that night and again on the 14th to find the flag in the darkness, but made a third attempt in the half-light and found that it was a trap covering a mine. They succeeded, however, in cutting loose the flag and bringing it in, without exploding the mine. On the 19th it was noticed that the Germans had put up a new flag, and that night the same two officers went out again and found that the flag was secured to a large grenade. Cutting the contact wire and securing the flag, they then attached a wire to the German wire, retired about 20 yards, and pulled the wire, thus exploding the bomb. The enemy then opened a rapid fire, and Lieutenants Gwyther and Williamson, having waited until this had died down, then returned in triumph to the trenches with the flag.

On at least two other occasions during this month did these two daring young officers patrol up to the enemy's wire, as did Lieutenant Glover, Second Lieutenants Lewtas and Shacklady, and the trench warfare on this front provided very many opportunities for distinction for enterprising subalterns.

On the night of the 25th–26th November a combined bombing operation was carried out along the brigade front, each company in the trench sections A 2, A 3, and A 4 sending out a party simultaneously to bomb the enemy's trenches and gather what information they could. The first party consisted of Second Lieutenant Evill, Lance-Corporal Keelan, and 3 men of the battalion who went out from No. 20 Fire Trench. About 30 yards from the German trenches the party came upon a number of empty bottles, evidently put out on purpose to cause a noise and prevent surprise, when four rifles opened fire from a spot some 10 or 15 yards in front of the enemy's trenches. Lieutenant Evill's patrol threw four bombs at this post, when fire was again opened from the same spot and from the flanks, but on the patrol throwing several more bombs in the same direction, all firing ceased and the patrol then withdrew, reaching our lines without casualties, although a machine gun opened on it as it was retiring.

Another party went out from No. 26 Fire Trench, composed of Second Lieutenant Haigh-Wood, Corporal Herbert, and 3 men. On two bombs being flung into the enemy sap, a heavy fire commenced and Corporal Herbert was at once hit, and was only brought in with great difficulty by his party.

The casualties in the battalion during November were as follows : 7 men killed, Second Lieutenants Lewtas and Williamson and 14 non-commissioned officers and men wounded.

Since the formation of the 14th Brigade several changes had taken place in its composition ; originally composed of the 2nd Battalion Suffolk,

1st Battalion East Surrey, 1st Battalion D.C.L.I., and 2nd Manchester Regiment, the 1st Battalion Devons had been added to the Brigade before the end of 1914, in 1915 the battalion of the Suffolks had been transferred and two Territorial Battalions—the 5th Battalion Cheshires and the 9th Battalion Royal Scots—had joined, making a brigade of six battalions. By the end of 1915, however, battalions of the New Army were coming out from home in constantly increasing numbers, and it was considered desirable, at any rate at first, to divide the New Army troops amongst those more experienced in war. Consequently when in December of this year the 95th Infantry Brigade of the New Army came out from England, it was sent to take the place of the 14th Brigade in the 5th Division, the 14th retaining three only of the battalions then with it.

At the beginning of January 1916 the battalion was in billets at Sailly Lorette, but on the 3rd of this month it left with the 14th Brigade for Henencourt, there to join the 32nd Division, commanded by Major-General Rycroft, in the 10th Corps under General Morland. The 32nd Division was now composed of the 14th, 96th, and 97th Brigades, and in the 14th Brigade were the following regiments under Brigadier-General Compton :

      1st Battalion Dorsetshire Regiment.
      2nd Battalion Manchester Regiment.
      5/6th Battalion Royal Scots (Territorials).
      15th Battalion Highland Light Infantry (New Army).

At Henencourt the battalion took over billets from a battalion of the King's Own, Royal Lancaster Regiment, and remained here until the 10th, on the afternoon of which day it marched via Millencourt and Albert to Authuille, where it was distributed as follows :

    One platoon at Gordon Castle.
    One officer and 25 other ranks at " A " Keep.
    One officer and 25 other ranks at " B " Keep.
    One non-commissioned officer and 20 men at Mill Post.
    A Company in garrison at Authuille.
    B and D Companies on the left section of Authuille defences.
    C Company in reserve dug-outs by the River Ancre, S. of the Cemetery.

In this neighbourhood the 2nd Battalion remained during the ensuing six months, occupying billets when out of the line at Authuille, St. Gratien,

Contay Wood, Aveluy, and other places, and taking its turn of trench duty. During the early part of the year the casualties were not so heavy as they had been on other portions of the front where at different times the battalion had been stationed.

" In the middle of March the pressure upon the French at Verdun had become severe, and it was determined to take over a fresh section of line so as to relieve troops for the north-eastern frontier. General Foch's Tenth Army, which had held the section opposite to Souchez and Lorette, was accordingly drawn out and twelve miles were added to the British front. From this time forward there were four British armies, the Second (Plumer) in the Ypres district, the First (Monro) opposite to Neuve Chapelle, the Third (Allenby) covering the new French sector down to Arras, and the Fourth (Rawlinson) from Albert to the Somme."[1] Under Rawlinson's immediate command there were five corps—from left to right, the 8th under Hunter-Weston, the 10th under Morland, the 3rd under Pulteney, the 5th under Horne, and the 13th under Congreve, while in rear of these was the nucleus of the 5th Army, mainly composed at this time of cavalry, under General Gough.

The German pressure about Verdun continued so long and had by June become so serious that, in order in some measure to relieve it, it was decided to make an allied attack at the western end of the line, and the British share in it was allotted to the Fourth Army under General Rawlinson. The actual attack had been planned for the 28th June, but the weather was so tempestuous that it was put off until it should moderate, and it commenced on the 1st July, which was calm and warm with a light south-westerly breeze. During the course of the preceding winter the British had gradually wrested from the Germans their early superiority in number of guns and supply of ammunition, and the opening of the attack by the British had been prefaced by a very heavy and long-continued bombardment whereby the German trenches had been virtually obliterated, while the villages in which their supports and reserves sheltered had been reduced to mere heaps of rubble.

General Morland's Tenth Corps consisted of the 36th, 49th, and 32nd Divisions, and covered a front from a mile north of Hamel to a mile north of Ovillers. At its northern end it was crossed by the River Ancre, a sluggish, canalised stream, running between two artificial dykes which the Germans periodically cut with their artillery fire. This sector of attack presented peculiar difficulties to the assailants, as the ground sloped upward to the strong village of Thiepval with the ridge behind it, from which the German guns could sweep the whole long glacis of approach. The German

---

[1] Conan Doyle, *The British Campaign in France and Flanders*, vol. iii, p. 11.

first position, which was the first aim of the British, ran from north to south as follows : " It covered Gommecourt, passed east of Hébuterne, followed the high ground in front of Serre and Beaumont Hamel, and crossed the Ancre a little to the north-west of Thiepval. It ran in front of Thiepval, which was very strongly fortified, east of Authuille, and just covered the hamlets of Ovillers and La Boisselle. Then it ran about a mile and a quarter east of Albert. It then passed south round the woodland village of Fricourt, where it turned at right angles to the east covering Mametz and Montauban. Halfway between Maricourt and Hardecourt it turned south again, covered Curlu, crossed the Somme at the wide marsh near the place called Vaux, covered Frise and Dompierre and Soyecourt, and passed just east of Lihons."[1]

The 2nd Manchesters were in billets at Bouzincourt, when on the 27th June they were moved to Aveluy Wood in readiness for action on the following day. Owing to the state of the weather, operations were, however, postponed until further notice, and the battalion was sent back again to billets in Senlis, where it was resting on the eve of the great battle. During the past fortnight all ranks had been much occupied, furnishing working parties day and night, the men coming off one duty and after a very brief rest going on to another. They were really almost worn out, and all welcomed the day of battle as a rest from incessant toil.

On the night of the 30th June the Brigade moved into assembly position at Black Horse Shelters and Crucifix Corner with two companies of the 2nd Manchesters in the line. " Zero hour " was early on the morning of the 1st July and was announced by a deafening roar of artillery, and the battalion was shortly after ordered up into Authuille Wood, where it awaited further orders. On the advance commencing the 96th and 97th Brigades led the 32nd Division, the 14th Brigade following the 97th ; in the 14th the 1st Battalion Dorsets led followed by the 19th Battalion Lancashire Fusiliers—which had recently relieved the Royal Scots battalion in the brigade—by the 2nd Battalion Manchesters, and 15th Battalion Highland Light Infantry in the order named, the Brigade forming two columns of attack, the right being under the commanding officer of the Lancashire Fusiliers, the left under Lieutenant-Colonel Luxmoore, commanding the Manchesters.[2]

As the leading battalions left the shelter of Authuille Wood and attempted to advance across the open they were met by a very heavy fire, inflicting severe losses, and the Dorsets and Fusiliers suffered many

---

[1] Buchan, *History of the War*, vol. xvi, pp. 35, 36.
[2] It has been no easy matter to compile anything like a coherent account of the part played by the battalion in the Battle of the Somme ; few private diaries are in existence and no battalion diary for July is now forthcoming.

casualties. It appears that the Germans had galleries running out from their dug-outs at the end of which a shaft was sunk just within or without their wire. In this a narrow loophole was made from which a machine gun fired ; these could not be seen by our troops and were untouched by our artillery fire.

After some considerable difficulty the 97th Brigade, with some officers and men of the 14th, managed to cross the enemy's line, but nobody was able to get very far. The intention had been that after the enemy's line had been broken, the 14th Brigade should advance past Mouquet Farm and take certain strong points beyond it, sending out patrols and consolidating the position. But only little, if any, ground was gained, and bombing attacks went on all day. Later in the afternoon, so Colonel Luxmoore states, " I was sent for by Brigade Headquarters and was ordered to take the battalion to the left and hold the Leipzig Salient, the edge of which had been captured. By this time our own trenches had been battered, the enemy having brought up their guns again and opened a heavy bombardment ; on both flanks of the Leipzig Salient and in rear of it were Boches. . . . The salient was one mass of dead and dying ; we had little ammunition and no one knew when the Boche would counter-attack. It was getting dark, so that all I could do was to get what men I could, relieve the other brigade (the 97th) and hope for the best."

At nightfall the Dorsets and Lancashire Fusiliers were withdrawn to reorganise ; the night passed fairly quietly, though but very little consolidation could be done owing to shell-fire. Early on the morning of the 2nd July the Germans made a counter-attack upon the advanced position held by the Manchesters, but these were on the alert and the enemy was driven off ; on this night the battalion was relieved by the Highland Light Infantry, who on the 3rd attempted to gain more ground, but though at first partially successful they were eventually driven back by heavy machine-gun fire ; at night the 14th Brigade was relieved by the 7th and moved back to Senlis, which was reached early on the morning of the 4th. Here casualty returns were called for, when it was found that in the Brigade these amounted to about 1,270.

On arrival at Senlis, writes Colonel Luxmoore, " he discovered that Regimental Sergeant-Major Hastewell had not turned up ; he, however, came later and stated that a shell had buried him and another man, and they had had to dig themselves out ! "

The Brigade moved on the 5th to Forceville, a poverty-stricken and dirty village, and here next day orders were received that the Brigade was to be in corps reserve for an attack next day on Ovillers–la Boisselle and that it was to be in position at Bouzincourt and Senlis by 8 a.m. on the 7th. Under later and revised orders the 14th Brigade concentrated on that date at Bouzincourt, and while there the 2nd Battalion Manchester Regiment was lent to the 36th Brigade, 12th Division, and moved off to join about 10 a.m.

The battalion joined the 36th Brigade at Ovillers Post, and, so records its commanding officer, " we spent the rest of the night in trying to find dugouts and getting a little sleep. On the 8th we reconnoitred the ground and while doing so noticed that ' Sausage ' and ' Mash ' Valleys were littered with the bodies of dead and wounded from the attack which failed. . . . Our one weak battalion relieved the 36th Brigade, consisting of the Essex, Middlesex, and East Surrey Regiments. The place was a heap of ruins, and the Boche had a position round the ruins of the church in the shape of a horseshoe."

On the night of the 8th the remainder of the 14th Brigade moved up to the Manchesters' position, and on the 10th carried out an attack by three of its battalions only, the Lancashire Fusiliers being held in reserve. The attack was successful and the ground won was consolidated. The Dorsets and Manchesters returned to Bouzincourt on the 11th, but the whole Brigade was up in the line again by the 14th, and of that period in Ovillers we are told that " a Boche shell struck the side of the entrance to the Battalion Headquarter Dug-out. If it had gone down there would have been an end to all of us below. Being a Boche dug-out the entrance was towards the enemy and all dug-outs were of course well known to his gunners. Through all this trying time the officers and men never wavered and carried out all their duties cheerfully." And then follows in lighter vein : " In Ovillers the Dorsets were on our right and apparently had found a supply of good German soda water. When the O.C. Battalion relieving them was given a drink he hoped to finish up the soda water, but found none. To his surprise when the Dorsets again relieved him he was given some more soda water—the Dorset messman had hidden his supply under a dead Boche in the next dug-out ! "

On the 19th July the units of the 14th Brigade having been collected together marched by way of Moncheaux, Monchy-Breton, Conchy à la Tour to Haillicourt and Houchin, at each of which places two battalions were installed by the 26th, and here on the 28th the Brigade was inspected by General Sir Charles Monro, commanding the First Army. Next day the headquarters of the Brigade moved to Bethune, whence the 2nd Battalion Manchesters and 15th Battalion Highland Light Infantry were lent for work to other divisions. At this time the 19th Battalion Lancashire

Fusiliers left the 14th Brigade on conversion into Pioneers, their place being taken by the 5/6th Royal Scots.

At the beginning of August the battalion was in billets at Le Préol and Annequin, with 250 men and officers detailed for working parties with the Royal Engineers; but on the 5th August the Brigade took over the line in the Cambrin sector with its left on the La Bassée Canal, two battalions being in front, one in support and one in reserve. In this neighbourhood the 14th Brigade remained until the beginning of October, when orders were received for its return to the Somme area, where fighting had been practically continuous ever since the Brigade had left it at the end of July. On the 10th the battalion marched to Busnes, where some days were spent in training and where reinforcements to the number of 219 joined, and then moving on on the 15th via Raimbert, Roellecourt near St. Pol, Le Breuve, Beauval, and Warloy to the neighbourhood of Albert, where a draft of 210 non-commissioned officers and men reached the battalion.

From the 26th October to the 13th November, when the Manchesters moved to their old quarters at Bouzincourt, they were in billets at Contay. "We had," writes a battalion diarist, "just received a large draft of men from England who in spite of training were very soft, and on the first march, when the weather was rather warm, about seventy fell out. It was the same with all the regiments in the Brigade. By the end of the five days' march, when march discipline was enforced, the battalion arrived at its camp at Contay without a single casualty."

The fighting which began in July and came to a temporary close at the end of October, and the operations connected with which are generally known as the Battle of the Somme, had been so far successful that a wide semicircle of country to the east of Albert had been wrested from the enemy, but the German front before Beaumont Hamel and Serre had proved unexpectedly strong, and there here remained a deep wedge-shaped re-entrant in our line bisected by the River Ancre. "All the slopes were tunnelled deep with old catacombs, and these had been linked up by passages to constitute a subterranean city. There were endless redoubts and strong points armed with machine guns . . . and the wire entanglements were on a scale which has probably never been paralleled. . . . Very strong too were the sides of the Ancre, should we seek to force a passage that way."[1]

The attack was mainly entrusted to the Fifth Army under General Gough, but it was arranged that the gap between his army and the Fourth Army under General Rawlinson should be filled by the 32nd Division, which

[1] Buchan's *History of the War*, vol. xvi, pp. 150, 151.

should push in the direction of Pys. The 14th Brigade was not engaged in the earlier operations of the Battle of the Ancre, and in a diary of an officer dated the 13th November we read : " Attack this morning fairly successful, resulting in capture of Beaumont Hamel and St. Pierre Divion and about 1,500 prisoners—prisoners look a wretched lot and show signs of having been confined to dug-outs for some time " ; and then on the 15th, " moved to Mailly-Maillet to take over part of the line from the 99th Brigade."

For the part taken in the ensuing action by the 2nd Battalion Manchester Regiment and other battalions of the 14th Brigade it is proposed to draw on Colonel Luxmoore's account of what passed, supplemented by such special details as are to be found in other histories of the war :

" On the 17th November I was told that we were to attack the following day. As we were very short of bombs I sent back to Brigade Headquarters to send some up. At midnight—17th–18th—I received my orders to attack at 6 a.m. Still no bombs ! I then heard that they had reached the 15th Highland Light Infantry who were on our left rear, and I sent a party under an officer to fetch them, but he was so long finding his way that he only returned after the attack had begun, and with the news that all our bombs had been taken by other regiments. We therefore had to go into action with only a very few bombs, most of which were German ones found in the dug-outs. The trenches to be attacked were very awkward, as we had to attack outwards in two directions from Lager Alley. The K.O.Y.L.I. of the brigade on our right had constructed a trench from which to kick off, and the left of their advance was to be along the Lager Alley.

" A German patrol was reported in Lager Alley, so Captain Gwyther was ordered to clear it, which he did nearly to the dug-out at the end of the trench forming part of the enemy's front line. Our orders were to form up in Lager Alley and attack Munich Trench and also another, No. 28 ; only $3\frac{1}{2}$ companies were available, half of A Company having been left in our original front line. Half a company was sent up Serre Trench to protect our flank and also to keep touch with the 15th H.L.I., who were attacking on our left and trying to take the Heidenkop Redoubt ; the trenches, however, were full of water and when they tried to advance over the open they were driven back. The half company that went up the trench met with strong resistance, and if it had not been for a non-commissioned officer who got out into the open with a Lewis Gun and outflanked the enemy's bombers, they would have got through, and as no reserves were immediately available for us we should have been in a bad way.

" To return to the main part of the battalion : they were formed up correctly, and just before 'zero hour' some snow began to fall; they went over the top punctual to the second."

The rest of the narrative is from a sergeant who got cut off and was able to relate what happened :

" The Manchesters gained their objective and were the only regiment to do so. The company which was keeping touch with the K.O.Y.L.I. advanced as long as they did, but instead of halting at their objective they went on to a trench called Ten Tree Alley ; the dug-out at the end of Lager Alley was not mopped up, so that when the men had passed beyond it the Boches came out and cut off their retreat. In the meanwhile the company that had got into Munich Trench and Trench 28 could neither advance nor withdraw ; bombs were scarce, the Germans were on both sides of them and advancing up a trench in front of them ; while a dug-out caught fire and the smoke was so dense that the men had to put on their gas masks. This party was either all killed, or wounded, or taken prisoner, while the fate of those who went on too far was as tragic as it was glorious and was equal to the splendid traditions of the Manchester Regiment. They halted on a small rise, and, refusing to surrender, fought it out to the last. The place was found afterwards with the bodies all grouped together."

The diary of the Brigade Commander for the 18th November contains the following terse account of the day's doings : " Attack this morning fairly successful at first, but resulted in the Second Manchesters having very heavy casualties and being practically wiped out." And the two days' record may be completed by the account of another historian,[1] who writes :

" This movement "—the filling by the 32nd Division of the gap between Gough's and Rawlinson's armies—" gave rise to some severe fighting in which the historical 14th Brigade sustained some heavy losses. The immediate obstacle in front of the division was a powerful system of trenches amid morasses caused by the recent heavy rains, and known as the Munich Line, with the Frankfort line behind it. Upon 17th November the division took over the advanced trenches, while the 18th Division side-stepped to the left. The 32nd Division had formed its line for attack with the 14th Brigade upon the left and the 97th upon the right, the leading battalions from left to right being the 15th Highland Light Infantry, the 2nd Manchesters, the 2nd Yorkshire Light Infantry, and another battalion of H.L.I. The advance was to have been on the 17th, but from the beginning a series of misfortunes occurred, arising largely from the weather,

[1] Conan Doyle, vol. iii, pp. 322, 323.

the condition of the trenches, and the severe German barrage behind the line, which made all preparations difficult and costly. The ground behind the troops was so awful that one mile an hour was considered remarkable progress for an unladen messenger ; while the enemy's fire was so severe that of six runners sent with a despatch only the last arrived unwounded. The Germans in front appeared to be both numerous and full of fight, and upon the 17th they made a vain attack upon the advanced line of the 14th Brigade. Two companies of the Manchesters sustained upon this day the losses of half their number as they lay, an object lesson in silent patient discipline, in the muddy bottom of a shell-swept ditch. The attack was postponed until the 18th, and even then the advancing battalions were short of bombs, without which trench fighting becomes impossible.

"At 6.10 in the morning of the 18th an advance was made, but the bomb supplies had not yet come up and the disadvantages were great. None the less, the first line of German trenches was successfully carried by the Manchesters, but the 15th Highland Light Infantry were held up by wire and were unable to get forward, while the Yorkshire Light Infantry upon the right got through at some points and were held at others. The Manchesters even penetrated to the second line of trenches and sprang into them, but the fatal want of bombs tied their hands, and a counter-attack of the Germans retook the position. The Highland Light Infantry had fallen back upon Serre Trench, and were hard pressed by a party of the enemy, but fortunately some of the 1st Dorsets came up from the rear with some bombs, and the situation was saved. In the meantime the position of those Manchesters and Yorkshiremen who had got forward as far as the second trench, and were exposed without bombs to a bombing attack, was very serious. They had taken a number of prisoners, and some of these they managed to send back, but the greater part of the British were bombed to pieces, and all died where they fought or were taken by the enemy. A single survivor who returned from the final stand made by these gallant men stated that he was the last man who had crawled out of the trench, and that his comrades lay dead or dying in a group in front of a blazing dug-out, the woodwork of which had taken fire. A patrol next day came upon the bodies of an officer and forty men who had died, fighting to the last, in a single group."

The remnant of the battalion remained all the 19th in the line, was relieved on the 20th by the 1st Battalion Dorsetshire Regiment, but came back to the line on the next day in support. Then on the 23rd the Manchesters went into billets at Mailly-Maillet, finally moving back on the

24th to the training area about Halloy. Both General Rycroft and Brigadier-General Compton had now left their commands, and in a battalion diary we read : " On our way back we were met by the new divisional general, who, as our 6 officers and 150 men and transport went by, complained that I had no intervals. I informed him that what he was looking at was the battalion ! "

Brigadier-General Compton's place was taken by Colonel W. W. Seymour, Rifle Brigade, and when in the spring of 1917 Colonel Seymour went to hospital, the command of the 14th Brigade was assumed by Colonel Lumsden, V.C., of the R.M.L.I., who had been G.S.O.I. of the division. Major-General Rycroft was succeeded by another cavalry officer, Major-General R. W. R. Barnes, C.B. ; he did not, however, remain very long, and when he left the command of the Division fell to Major-General Shute.

About Halloy the battalion remained until the end of the first week in January 1917 " licking its wounds after the recent severe fighting and preparing for the greater fighting to come." During the winter drafts or reinforcements to the number of 527 joined the 2nd Battalion Manchester Regiment, so that it was practically a new battalion, but possessing the indomitable spirit of the old one, which was ready for the fighting of the new year.

At a conference of allied commanders held in November 1916 a great combined attack had been fixed for the coming spring, in the form of an assault by the British armies on the German salient between the Scarpe and the Ancre by the Third Army from the north and the Fifth Army from the south. By the end of January Beaumont Hamel had been captured, and during the next three weeks further ground had been gained, so that by the 25th February the enemy was found to have evacuated all his positions in front of the Le Transloy–Loupart line and north of the Albert–Bapaume road. Further still was the enemy gradually forced back, until by the 10th March it was clear that he was contemplating an even greater withdrawal, in fact to the new position which had been created in rear and which was known to the Germans as the Siegfried and to our soldiers as the Hindenburg line.

The 2nd Battalion Manchester Regiment left Halloy on the 6th January 1917, marching to Beauval, and moving thence by motor-bus to Bertrancourt. In this neighbourhood it remained until the middle of February, when it found itself again on the move, and eventually on the 25th the Brigade of which it formed part took over the line from the French near Fresnoy, occupying dug-outs at Bouchoir or billets at Beauvois. The front of the 32nd Division was to the immediate west and north-west of St. Quentin, and with the 35th and 61st Divisions it was now—early in April—called upon to assist in pressing back the German line. The account of the share which the battalion played in the events of the first week in April is taken from one contributed to the *Manchester Regiment Gazette* by Lieutenant-Colonel Luxmoore, who at that time was in command of the 2nd Manchesters:

"On the morning of April 1st the battalion was ordered to move" (from Beauvois) "to a village about five miles distant on our right flank called Germaine. Billets were allotted and it was expected that we should stay there for at all events the night. This, however, was not to be, for at about one o'clock an order came for the Brigade to move at once and rendezvous at a place called Château Pomery. The distance was only about two miles, but owing to unavoidable delays the battalion did not start until 5.30 p.m., soon after which hour it became dark. The place, although imposing enough on the map, was in reality a few hedges and trees marking no doubt a once magnificent château. The Brigade halted here and made itself as comfortable as it could, resting and having some food in preparation for the work in the near future.

"In the meanwhile the commanding officers reported at Brigade Headquarters for orders. At the conference we were informed that the 97th Brigade had captured the village of Savy in the morning, whilst in the afternoon Savy Wood was taken by the 96th Infantry Brigade. This latter brigade was, however, unable to emerge from the wood and capture the Quarry which was situated about 500 yards up a glacis slope from the forward edge of the wood. In 1918 this quarry was known as 'the Manchester Quarry' because another battalion of the Manchester Regiment—the 16th—held it during the Boche offensive. It is rectangular in shape, about 250 yards long by 150 broad, with steep sides in which were dug-outs. It was known that the Germans were holding it strongly with machine guns firing to the front and flanks.

"Our orders were to move to Savy Wood that night and attack at 5 a.m. on April 2nd. The dispositions and objectives were as follows: right, 15th H.L.I. the Quarry; centre, 2nd Manchesters, Francilly–Selency and Selency; left, 1st Dorsets, Holnon; 5/6th Royal Scots in reserve. It was explained that the villages could be distinguished by the fact that one possessed a spire and the other a tower, but as neither village was at that time more than about eight feet high, this information was not of much assistance in finding our objectives! In order to allow for possible delays and for the men to have as long a rest as possible after the march, the Brigade moved off at midnight, the battalion following the Dorsets who were leading. The only incident on the march was that as we neared Savy a shell burst on the road and caused two casualties.

"After passing through Savy the column moved across open fields along the W. edge of Savy Wood, and halted behind the railway embankment. Leaving the battalion to get some rest, I went along the line to the right to obtain information as to the situation. The plan of attack had been slightly altered, as the H.L.I. were not to advance on our right, but to move in echelon; this meant that our right flank would be exposed and two platoons of A Company were detailed to watch this flank; the companies were told off as follows: 1st line: right, B Company under 2nd Lieutenant R. E. Prouse; left, C Company under Captain G. M. Glover; 2nd line: right, A Company under 2nd Lieutenant A. Heydon; left, D Company under 2nd Lieutenant D. H. Briggs.

"The railway ran through Savy Wood, but as the part N. of the railway had been cut down, it was very difficult to find the position of deployment which was along the northern face of the wood. Beyond the railway the ground is open grass land which rises gently for about 1,000 yards to Francilly-Selency. After this the ground slopes down into a shallow valley and again rises rather steeply to Selency, which was the final objective and which was connected by a road from St. Quentin to Holnon. To the E. of this valley there is a short and broad gorge on the top of which is the Bois des Roses. This was about 900 yards from Selency and was held by the enemy.

"Punctually at zero hour, with the first streak of dawn, the line advanced to the attack, and was immediately met by heavy rifle and machine gun fire. This came principally from the Quarry and therefore A Company suffered most. Second Lieutenant Taylor, who was in command of the two platoons of A Company, at once changed direction half right, and successfully attacked the Quarry on the flank, taking four machine guns, and in addition two more machine guns in a trench adjoining the Quarry. This success materially assisted the H.L.I. to advance. These two platoons did not remain here, but, in spite of losing touch with the company on their left, pushed on until brought up short by a huge crater at the outskirts of St. Quentin itself. They took up a position in the crater, and, under a very heavy rifle fire remained there until darkness enabled them to withdraw. A message was sent back to battalion headquarters, but no assistance could be sent by day.

"The attack on Francilly-Selency was successful, but when the advance was continued C Company and part of B Company suddenly came upon a battery of 77 mm. guns on the low ground N.E. of the village which was firing at point-blank range. Captain Glover, by attacking both in front and on the right, captured the battery after a hand-to-hand fight with those gunners who remained. An escort was left with the battery, the advance was resumed, and Selency—about 1,250 yards beyond Francilly-Selency—was captured by 6 a.m. or 1½ hours after zero hour. The line was reorganised by 2nd Lieutenant Briggs and the position consolidated.

"Owing to the enemy still holding the Bois des Roses our right flank went back to Francilly-Selency, forming a right angle, which, with the few men available, was very vulnerable, and had the Germans launched a counter-attack instead of contenting themselves with spasmodic shelling they might have made it very unpleasant for us.

"During the night efforts were made by the Adjutant, Lieutenant G. R. Thomas, to draw the guns out of their position with the aid of men and drag ropes, but this proved to be impossible. On the night of the 3rd April the G.O.C. 32nd Division ordered Major Lumsden, G.S.O.2 of the division, to withdraw them with the assistance of teams furnished by the artillery and a covering party of the H.L.I. which was now holding that portion of the line. It appears that the enemy had selected this night to endeavour to recapture the guns, for after some of the guns had been withdrawn he put down a very heavy barrage and attacked with a company of infantry. The H.L.I. put up a stout resistance, and although a few of the enemy were able to blow up the breech of the last gun, they were driven off and all the guns were withdrawn. The following night the limbers were got away by the battalion, assisted by teams from the artillery, but there was not much shelling.

"On the night of 4th April the Battalion Transport Officer, Lieutenant D. C. Pearse, brought out the signalling limber wagon, thus completing the withdrawal of the whole battery. The battalion remained in this position until relieved on April 8th, when it withdrew to Beauvois for a rest. Our total trophies were: 8 machine guns, 6 guns, 77 mm., 6 ammunition wagons, and 1 battery signalling limbered wagon complete with signalling stores. . . . Private C. E. Overton, signaller of A Company, was recommended for the Victoria Cross for repeatedly repairing the telephone line and carrying wounded back under a very heavy fire, but was awarded the D.C.M. instead. Captain Glover was wounded early in the fight, but refused to leave his company until after he had completed his task. On his way back to the Regimental Aid Post he encountered two Germans whom he captured with the aid of an empty revolver.

CAPTURE OF A GERMAN 77-MM. BATTERY BY C COMPANY, 2ND BATTALION, APRIL 2ND, 1917, AT FRANCILLY-SELENCY.

From the painting by R. Caton Woodville, presented to the Officers' Mess, 2nd Battalion.

"The guns were awarded as follows: 2nd Manchesters 2 guns, 15th H.L.I. 1 gun, 161st Brigade R.F.A. 1 gun, 125th Heavy Battery 1 gun, 159th Brigade R.F.A. 1 gun.

"Our casualties were: *killed*, 2 officers—Second Lieutenants Gaukroger and Winch (London Regiment, attached)—and 10 other ranks; *wounded*, 7 officers—Captain Glover, Second Lieutenants Wilkins, Heydon, Smith, Tooley, Eady (London Regiment), Nibbs (London Regiment)—and 52 non-commissioned officers and men."

The battalion remained in billets in Beauvois until the 12th, when it was moved to Savy and was accommodated in cellars and trenches round the village.

During the 12th instructions were received that the French intended to attack St. Quentin, and in the event of their being successful two battalions of the 14th Brigade—the Manchesters and H.L.I.—were to protect their left flank, while the Dorsets were to maintain connection between the British and French. These orders were modified and their execution postponed until the 14th, when the battalion moved forward to Savy Wood, but in proceeding thence to the assembly position some very open ground had to be crossed. "Immediately the first wave passed over the crest of the hill the enemy placed a hurricane barrage on the ground to be crossed with 10·5 cm. and 15 cm. high explosive shells. Though this barrage was straight in the middle of the battalion they moved forward through it as steadily as on parade, each wave keeping its dressing and distance and every carrier retaining his load. By the grace of God alone only 30 men were lost in this barrage."

The trench to be attacked was found to be empty, but the battalion remained in the main line digging, connecting, and wiring until the 21st, when it was relieved by a battalion of the 182nd Brigade, moving then to Quivères, where it was quartered in cellars, and in this neighbourhood the Brigade remained for some weeks. Then on the 1st June the battalion entrained at Marcelcave and proceeded to Bailleul, occupying billets in this area and "standing-by" during the Messines battle which opened on the 7th of this month. On the 13th there was a further move, this time to the Eecke area, the battalion being housed in billets and tents at Tergedem, but on the 15th the Manchesters went by train and motor-bus to Nieuport, which was reached on the 17th. Here the battalion remained for some time, taking its share of trench duty and carrying out occasional raids. In August the 14th Brigade was finally taken out of the line for a real and prolonged rest, being sent to La Panne, where training was carried on under battalion and company arrangements, and where on the 12th the battalion was inspected by Her Majesty the Queen of the Belgians.

Here, then, for the present we may leave the 2nd Battalion enjoying a well-earned relief from the discomfort of the trenches, while we go back to see how their comrades of the 1st Battalion are faring in another and distant theatre of the war.

CHAPTER XXIV

THE 1st BATTALION IN MESOPOTAMIA

JANUARY 1916 TO MIDSUMMER 1917

It was stated in Chapter XXII that the 1st Battalion had arrived at Basra late on the afternoon of the 8th January 1916, and little time was here **1916** lost in equipping officers and men for the wholly novel warfare in which they were now about to take part. The 9th and the early part of the 10th were taken up in drawing tentage, ammunition, and stores, and on the afternoon of the last-named date headquarters with Nos. 3 and 4 Companies and the machine-gun detachment were transhipped to barges and proceeded up the Shatt-el-Arab, the remainder of the battalion following later under Captain Vaudrey. All the transport and the mules were left behind at Basra. Qurnah was reached on the 11th, Amara about 2 p.m. on the 14th, heavy rain and wind impeding the progress of the flotilla up-stream and necessitating tying up to the bank more than once during the journey. At Ali Garbi, where the battalion headquarters was delayed for a couple of hours, an unfortunate accident happened, Sergeant Hurst falling overboard and being drowned in the river. On the 18th Shaik Sa'ad was reached in driving rain and after a short delay the troops disembarked and marched to camp, arriving there about midnight.

The 1st Battalion Manchester Regiment now found itself attached to the 7th Brigade, composed of the 1st Battalion 1st Gurkhas, the 1st Battalion 9th Gurkhas, and the 93rd Burma Infantry.

While the battalion was completing the final portion of its long voyage from France to Mesopotamia heavy fighting had been in progress with the object of effecting the relief of the troops shut up in Kut under General Townshend. General Aylmer's force had advanced from Ali Garbi, on the 8th January, after two days' fighting had captured the Turkish position at Shaik Sa'ad, had fought another battle on the Wadi River on the 13th and 14th, forcing the enemy to retreat to an entrenched position across the Umm-el-Hannah defile; and on the date when the 1st Manchesters joined the army in camp the bulk of General Aylmer's force was on the left bank of the Tigris above the Wadi River, while the advanced troops were in touch with the Turks entrenched in their Umm-el-Hannah position.

"Situated between a flooded swamp and the great waterway, the Turkish position at Hannah consisted of five lines of trenches, each line some 200 yards behind the other and connected by numerous saps. This formidable maze had to be attacked after very inadequate artillery preparation." [1]

At 10 a.m. on the 19th No. 4 Company of the battalion under Captain Brown left camp as rear-guard to the Brigade advancing westward along the south bank of the Tigris, while No. 3 Company occupied itself in unloading barges and furnished the camp guard. The Brigade was this day ordered to attack an Arab village and clear the ground on the right bank immediately opposite the main Turkish position situated on the left bank of the river, so that this could be enfiladed when the real attack commenced. The Arab village was successfully carried by the Gurkhas and 93rd Burma Infantry, one company of the 1st Battalion 1st Gurkhas and a platoon of No. 4 Company Manchesters being in reserve

At about 3.30 p.m. a cavalry sowar reported that he had been fired on by Turks on the right or south bank of the river directly opposite the enemy's position, and the Manchester Company and one from the 1st Gurkhas were ordered to turn them out. No. 4 Company advanced with No. 16 Platoon leading, under Lieutenant Wilkins, closely supported by Nos. 14 and 15 platoons, No. 13 being in echelon on the right to protect that flank. The attack was pushed with great vigour, the Turks opening fire at 900 yards and the advance being over ground wholly without cover of any kind. It was estimated that two Turkish battalions were in position and firing was kept up till dark, when the company of the Manchesters was relieved by the 93rd.

The casualties this day in the Manchester Regiment were 2 men killed and 8 wounded; the medical officer of the battalion, Captain Spackman, R.A.M.C., was also wounded.

On the 20th the company had 1 man wounded by shrapnel.

The 21st was the day when the main attack was delivered against the Hannah position, but on the south bank the battalion took little part in the operations, No. 3 Company being employed partly on outpost near camp, guarding the shipping in the river, and providing parties for fatigue duty, while No. 4 was held in reserve ready to follow up any Turks falling back from the main attack, and was afterwards ordered to protect the British

---

[1] Dane, *British Campaigns in the Near East*, pp. 140, 141.

guns immovable in the marshy ground, and passed a miserable night in pouring rain.

The attack on the Hannah position was a failure; though in places the enemy's front line was penetrated and some of his trenches occupied, these could not be held, and when the Turkish counter-attacks developed, our successful troops were overwhelmed by numbers and obliged to retire, having suffered heavy losses. Thus the first attempt at the relief of Kut had failed.

On the 22nd the remainder of the 1st Battalion Manchester Regiment rejoined headquarters, and the whole crossed the river to the left bank, going into reserve trenches about three miles from camp in very boggy ground. On the 24th the battalion took over the front line of trenches from the Connaught Rangers and 107th Indian Infantry, the Turkish lines being about one thousand yards distant. This day the first mail was received since leaving France. The strength of the battalion on this date was 30 officers and 881 other ranks.

On the 5th February a move was made to a camp on the south bank of the river, where a draft of 131 men joined; but next day the battalion moved again to another camp about a mile further up the same bank.

During the next few weeks nothing of any outstanding importance took place; the battalion took its turn of trench duty and was twice employed on reconnaissances in strength; on at least three different occasions a Turkish airman passed over the column in which part of the battalion was serving or over the camp or trenches in which it happened at the time to be, but no damage was done to any of the personnel of the Manchesters, two pack mules only being killed. The casualties up to the beginning of March were but slight, 2 men being killed and Second Lieutenants Butterworth and Marley and Lance-Corporal Pickering being wounded.

On the 3rd March the battalion was thus distributed:

In the trenches at Abu Roman 23 officers and 641 other ranks.
In the Arab village, 5 officers and 217 other ranks.
In Camp C, 3 officers and 222 other ranks.

On the 4th a draft of 202 men arrived with Captain Shipster, Lieutenant Owen, and Second Lieutenant Nicholas.

" The situation at the end of February was briefly as follows: On the left bank the enemy, having been reinforced, still held the Hannah position in force; further in rear were other defensive lines at Falahiyah, Sannaiyat, Nakhailat and along the northern part of the Es Sinn position. All except the last-named had been constructed since the battle of Hannah on 21st January. They were all protected on both flanks by the Tigris and the Suwaikeh Marsh respectively. On the right bank the Es Sinn position constituted the Turkish main line of defence with an advanced position near Beit Aiessa. The right flank of the Es Sinn position rested on the Dujailah Redoubt, which lay some five miles south of the river and fourteen S.W. of the British lines on the right bank. It was decided to attack the Turkish right flank and Dujailah Redoubt as the first step towards the relief of Kut before the arrival of the flood season about the middle of March." [1]

"The central point of support in the Turkish defences between the Tigris and the Shatt-el-Hai was a considerable work called the Dujailah Redoubt. At this point the line of the Turkish defences was crossed by the bed of an ancient tributary of the main river, dry in the summer season, but a sinuous swamp during the wet months, and the Dujailah Redoubt was situated at the point of one of the bends, and on the further side, so that it was partly surrounded by a sort of natural ditch. Both the apparent security of the position, and the difficulty of obtaining on the spot a supply of drinking water, had led the enemy so far to hold the redoubt lightly. If he could be surprised, and the bend or peninsula on which the redoubt was built seized, his line west of the Tigris would be effectually broken and the siege of Kut would have to be raised." [2]

When on the afternoon of 7th March General Aylmer assembled his subordinate commanders to receive his final orders, he laid great stress on the fact that the operation was to be of the nature of a surprise, and that the capture of the Dujailah Redoubt was to be pushed through with the utmost vigour.

His dispositions were as follows: the greater part of a division under General Younghusband, assisted by gunboats, was to contain the enemy on the left bank, while the remaining troops, formed in two columns under Generals Kemball and Keary, were to attack the redoubt from the south and east respectively. The night march whereby the position was to be reached undiscovered was a very delicate operation, and only one of the two columns was in position at daybreak, Kemball's force not reaching the point selected for deployment until more than an hour later. When General Keary's column reached the neighbourhood of the redoubt, it was still only very lightly held by the Turks and might well have been captured by prompt and energetic action. But General Aylmer decided to wait until

---

[1] General Sir Percy Lake's despatch dated 12th August 1916.
[2] Dane, *British Campaigns in the Near East*, p. 145.

his whole force was in position, whereby the advantage of a surprise was lost and the garrison of the redoubt was substantially reinforced.

On the night of the 7th–8th March the 3rd Division marched from Abu Roman Camp towards the Es Sinn position, the 1st Battalion of the Manchester Regiment being now back again with its own—the 8th—Brigade. In the original orders it had been directed that the troops should march off at 9 p.m., but the start was actually not made until 10 o'clock by reason of the late arrival of three batteries of artillery intended to accompany the column. The position was reached at daybreak and, after moving on about a mile in support of the guns, the 8th Brigade "dug in" at 8 a.m.

"Owing to a stoppage in the pumps near Thorny Nullah the 8th Brigade had left camp the night before without filling their water-bottles. They had been digging themselves in, supporting the artillery; covering the flank, now of the 7th, now of the 37th Brigade; advancing and demonstrating and retiring all day. At 4.9 p.m. they were ordered to attack the Dujailah Redoubt and to push the assault home at all costs. The artillery would support the attack by bombarding the redoubt, lifting their fire at 5.15 p.m. The 37th Brigade (two battalions) on the left would go in at the same time. . . . The brigade formed up, the Manchesters and 59th Rifles in the first line (the Manchesters on the left), the 2nd Rajputs in support, and the 47th Sikhs forming a third line prepared to act against a counter-attack from the enemy's left. The 36th and 28th Brigades, under General Kemball's command, were ordered to support the 8th Brigade by attacking the redoubt from the south, but they were held up by the forward trenches in front of the position." [1]

A front of 400 yards was allotted to the Manchesters and the firing line consisted of No. 1 Company on the right, No. 2 on the left, supported by No. 3 four hundred yards in rear, with No. 4 in local reserve six hundred yards behind No. 3. The battalion directed the advance, during the first thousand yards of which it was not found necessary to extend, but then a Turkish battery, firing from the direction of Sinn Aftar Redoubt, brought a heavy enfilade fire to bear on the firing line and the first casualties were incurred. Later the companies came into a cross-fire from the enemy trenches flanking the redoubt on either side, and which received little or no attention from the British guns, these concentrating their fire on the redoubt itself; further, the fire from the supporting brigade failed to keep down the enemy's fire, while an enemy machine gun to the left rear caused many casualties.

Of the men of the firing line, writes a historian,[2] "they were steady as

[1] Candler, *The Long Road to Baghdad*, vol. i, pp. 152, 153.   [2] Candler, pp. 153, 154.

a machine, and did not stop to pick up their wounded or dying. No one seeing them could have imagined them other than confident. But it was discipline and soldierly virtues that gave them the air. . . . At 5.20 the Manchesters and 59th Rifles gained a footing in the redoubt, followed closely by the 2nd Rajputs and a thin line of Gurkhas and Somersets from the left. Two lines of trenches were occupied. They were found to be very deep, with a firing step and no parapet; they were almost invisible, and every advantage had been taken of the glacis slope leading up to them. Our artillery can have had little effect on these defences."

The battalion diary records that "Lieutenant Morris and Sergeant Duffy were the first to enter the trenches, two lines of them being quickly occupied while the supporting companies followed up in a few minutes. . . . The trenches were bombed along for some distance, but the supply of bombs being limited was soon exhausted; the sun, moreover, was low and full in the eyes of the attackers, and as they swept over the crest of the redoubt they were enveloped in thick clouds of dust and smoke caused by the shell and machine-gun fire. In the meantime our machine gunners reached a position about 500 yards from the redoubt and maintained fire until ordered to withdraw by the Brigade Machine Gun Officer. At 5.45 p.m. a heavy counter-attack developed chiefly from the left flank, where, being able to approach under cover, it was not noticed until too late and the Turks were able to use their bombs with great effect. At the same time the flanking fire re-doubled and the position became untenable and the force was ordered to withdraw. . . . All ground gained was finally abandoned at dusk, but all through the night large parties were out collecting and bringing in the wounded."

"The 8th Brigade had gone into action 2,301 strong; they came out 1,127. In the attack 33 British and 23 Indian officers fell; the 2nd Rajputs lost all their 10 British officers (6 killed), their medical officer, 12 out of 16 Indian officers (7 killed), and 302 (110 killed) out of 534 rank and file."[1]

The casualties of the 1st Battalion Manchester Regiment were as follows:

Killed or died of wounds   6 officers and 31 N.C.O.'s and men.
Wounded . . . 2 ,, ,, 286 ,, ,,
Missing . . . 5 ,, ,, 130 ,, ,,

Total casualties . 13 ,, ,, 447 ,, ,,

[1] Candler, p. 155.

Many of the missing must of course unfortunately be added to the roll of dead, and the following are the names of nine officers of the battalion who fell this day: Captains Lynch and Ewen, Lieutenants Baxter, Burdon, Wilkins, and Bedford, Second Lieutenants Davis, Morris, and Lane.

"The troops, who had been under arms for some 30 hours, including a long night march, were now much exhausted, and General Aylmer considered that a renewal of the assault during the night of the 8th–9th March could not be made with any prospect of success. Next morning the enemy's position was found to be unchanged, and General Aylmer, finding himself faced with the deficiency of water already referred to, decided upon the immediate withdrawal of his force to Wadi, which was reached the same night."[1]

The 3rd Division moved on the 9th by a long, tiring, and waterless march of 16 miles in the sun to Orah Camp, and while here the battalion was gratified by the publication of the following letter from Major-General Keary to Lieutenant-Colonel Hardcastle:

"Headquarters, 3rd Division, Tigris Army Corps.
23rd March 1916.

"*Dear Colonel Hardcastle,*
"*I wish to put on record my very high appreciation of the conduct of your Battalion in common with the other battalions of the 8th (Jullundur) Brigade at the action of the 8th March 1916.*
"*The attack on the Dujailah Redoubt was most gallantly carried out and its capture was a most notable achievement. The withdrawal from it was a military necessity which the 8th Brigade could not have averted. The steady manner in which the withdrawal was carried out is a further proof of the quality of the Officers and Men engaged.*
"*I have already thanked you on parade, and conveyed to you the Corps Commander's appreciation. Your achievement is honourable not only to yourselves but to the Division which I have the honour to command.*
"*Yours sincerely,*
H. D. Keary, Major-General,
Commanding 3rd Division."

However gratifying the praise of a soldier's superiors, it is at least a matter of almost equal interest to know what value our opponent places upon the effect of our efforts against him; and the battalion was afforded an opportunity of gauging the weight of their achievement in the receipt

[1] General Sir Percy Lake's despatch of 12th August.

of the following extract from a letter written home by an officer of another corps serving in Mesopotamia ; he wrote as follows :

"A Turkish officer (German educated), who was afterwards taken prisoner, said of that attack of the Manchesters : ' You English talk about Balaclava, *that* was six Balaclavas ! I was standing by my general, Suleiman Bey, and he said : " Thanks be to God I have been spared to fight against such men as these ! " ' "

For some days now there was nothing done by the Brigade, except to move camp once or twice to escape from the now rapidly rising river. Between the 26th and 28th March four young officers reported their arrival —Second Lieutenants Moorhead, Thornton, Bourne, and White, while on the 3rd April a draft of 29 men arrived with Captain O'Meara, Lieutenant Jackson, Second Lieutenants Barker, Graham, and Atkin.

Ere this Major-General Gorringe had succeeded General Aylmer in command of the Tigris Army Corps, fresh troops had begun to arrive up the river—among these being the 13th Division, now commanded by the Manchesters' late Brigadier in France, General Maude, and it was determined to renew active operations with the least possible delay. The feasibility of an advance on Kut by the right bank from Shaikh Sa'ad was considered, but the idea was abandoned, and the decision was then come to for an attack on the Hannah position and an advance by the left bank of the river.

On the 1st April the 13th Division was moved up to the front trenches preparatory to an attack, but owing to the heavy and continuous rain which now fell the attack was postponed until the 5th, when the 13th Division rushed the Hannah trenches at daybreak, finding the Turks asleep and putting them to flight. " Meanwhile, on the right bank," writes General Lake in his despatch from which quotation has already been made, " the 3rd Division had been gaining ground. In the morning the 8th Infantry Brigade, led by the Manchesters, captured the Turkish position on Abu Roman mounds. An attempt by the enemy to recapture this position in the afternoon was beaten off."

A patrol from No. 1 Company of the battalion, under Lieutenant Ruddy, was first into the position, capturing some Turkish prisoners; Captain Shipster was this day wounded. The troops now entrenched themselves on the Abu Roman position.

The following congratulatory message was received, from the Corps Commander through the Division : " *Well done ; please tell 8th Brigade how pleased I am at their capturing Abu Roman position. The G.O.C. adds his congratulations."*

It now became a matter of extreme urgency to capture the Falahiyah and Sannaiyat positions, three and six miles respectively west of the Hannah position, before the rising river should enable the Turks to flood the intervening country by breaking the *bunds*; but in the initial operations the 8th Brigade was not actively employed. The Falahiyah position was captured by the 13th Division, but two attacks upon the Turks at Sannaiyat failed mainly because the Tigris broke the *bunds* and flooded the trenches, and when the attack was renewed on the 9th it was not possible to carry any more than the first line of enemy trenches.

The next thrust was now made on the right bank, where was a network of Turkish trenches as well as two lines known as Beit Aiessa and Chalela, before any advance could be made on the main position at Es Sinn. After the operations of the 5th progress on this bank had been very gradual, there had been many small actions and the Turk had been forced back to his prepared position at Beit Aiessa. The 3rd Division gained a footing here on the 15th April, when the outworks were captured at dawn after an advance in a violent thunderstorm through a swamp.

Lieutenant-Colonel Hardcastle was wounded about 10 a.m., Captain O'Meara assuming command of the battalion, and No. 2 Company was ordered to advance and capture the enemy's picquets which had been located to their front. This was carried out in conjunction with the 47th Sikhs and 59th Rifles, and our picquet line was pushed forward some 400 yards. One of the battalion machine gunners was killed and Second Lieutenant Barker and Sergeant Flanagan were wounded.

All was tolerably quiet during the early part of the 17th, but at 5 p.m. the enemy's artillery commenced to bombard Beit Aiessa and to establish a barrage in rear of the 3rd Division, sweeping the passage through the swamps along which its communications lay. An hour later a very strong counter-attack came from the south-west, "half the garrison of Es Sinn was brought up, and the assault was launched by the famous 2nd Division of Constantinople, veterans of the Balkan War, our opponents in Gallipoli, and generally reckoned the pick of the Turkish Army.

" In spite of heavy shelling the attack was pressed home against the 9th Infantry Brigade, from which a double company had been pushed forward to guard two captured guns which could not be brought in during daylight. In retiring the double company masked our fire; the 9th Infantry Brigade was pressed and gave ground, exposing the left of the 7th

Infantry Brigade, which was also forced back. Our troops rallied on the 8th Infantry Brigade, which was holding its ground firmly on the left of the line, and on a portion of the 7th Infantry Brigade." [1]

An eye-witness of the fight describes as follows the part played by the regiments of the 8th Brigade : [2]

"To turn to the 8th Brigade who held the line on our left flank. Assault after assault was launched on them, six distinct attacks in mass before three o'clock, as well as sporadic rushes. But they never yielded an inch through the whole night. Acting on the first hint of the attack, the Staff Captain had sent for more ammunition ; this new supply came in the nick of time. Every man who could hold a rifle, clerks, signallers, orderlies, was sent to the firing line to hold the parapet until the attack had failed. Even the ammunition bearers were ordered to stay in the trench and to eke out the thin line. The two battalions of 59th Rifles and 47th Sikhs, who held this line, were a bare 800 rifles. To these were added during the night, to fill gaps in the line and to extend it to the left, two battalions of the 40th Brigade who had come to reinforce the 9th, 100 rifles of the 2nd Rajputs held in reserve, and a company of the Manchesters. *It was the Manchesters and the 47th Sikhs who blocked and held the north end of the Trench X, and saved the right of the Brigade which was at one time in extreme danger. The enemy were coming on thickly here. Had they broken through, transport, guns and Brigade Headquarters might have been lost. . . . We killed more Turks at Beit Aiessa than at Sheikh Sa'ad, the Wadi, El Orah and Falahiyah combined. And the repulse of the counter-attack at night was really a greater coup than the taking of the position in the morning, for it put out of action the best part of two Turkish divisions.*"

The Manchester Company here mentioned was No. 2. The battalion bombers captured a Turkish machine gun which was brought in by Captain Parminter.

At dawn on the 18th things were fairly quiet, but about 6 a.m. large parties of Turks who had lain concealed in the scrub began to retire and offered a splendid target. The battalion diary records that "the 47th Sikhs were issuing rations, but they dropped these and commenced to wipe out the retiring Turks. The sight of dead and wounded was one to be remembered, the ground in front being strewn with them. Our casualties were 1 killed, 14 wounded and 3 missing, most of the losses occurring among our first-line transport-men who were in great demand,

---

[1] General Lake's despatch. [2] Candler, vol. i, p. 195.

and their work of man-handling ammunition up to the firers was splendid, some of them joining in the actual fighting. At noon we were relieved and the rest of the day was quiet."

Considering that the Turkish losses were estimated at between 4,000 and 5,000, those of the battalion may be considered as being remarkably low, since between the 4th and the 18th April the casualties in the 1st Battalion Manchester Regiment were: *killed or died of wounds*, 7 rank and file; *wounded*, 3 officers and 29 other ranks, and 1 man missing.

The following message from the Brigade-Major, 8th Brigade, was received on the 18th April: "*Manchesters. Express to all ranks the G.O.C.'s appreciation of their real gallantry*"; while on the 21st Major-General Keary, commanding the 3rd Division, visited the battalion and warmly congratulated No. 2 Company on its good work on the night of the 17th–18th, and that company was also mentioned in the "Order of the day."

In General Lake's despatch of the 12th August he wrote:

"General Gorringe's troops were nearly worn out. The same troops had advanced time and again to assault positions strong by art and held by a determined enemy. For 18 consecutive days they had done all that men could do to overcome, not only the enemy, but also exceptional climatic and physical obstacles—and this on a scale of rations which was far from being sufficient in view of the exertions they had undergone, but which the shortage of river transport had made it impossible to augment. The need for rest was imperative."

But by this time the long-enduring garrison of Kut was virtually at the end of its resources. One final effort to reprovision the besieged was made by the *Julnar*, which, laden with a cargo of supplies, attempted to run the blockade. It was a daring but a vain endeavour. The ship was raked by fire from the Turkish Fort Magasis, the vessel was sunk, and her gallant crew were killed or captured; and then at last on the 29th April, after a siege of five months, the British flag at Kut fluttered down and the white flag was raised.

On the 22nd April Second Lieutenant White of the battalion was hit in the head by the bullet of a sniper, dying the same night; on the 2nd May Captain Vaudrey died of cholera; while on the 16th Lieutenant-Colonel Hardcastle returned from hospital and resumed command.

From the fall of Kut until the month of August operations were both of a minor character and in the main defensive, for neither the numerical strength nor the health of the troops allowed of much being attempted beyond the work of regularising the occupation of the wide territory now under British control. Fatigues were very heavy, the heat of summer came on rapidly, and a good deal of sickness prevailed.

On the 19th May it became apparent that the enemy, under the pressure of the Russian advance from Persia towards Baghdad, had withdrawn from their advanced positions at and in front of Es Sinn on the right bank, though the lines of Sannaiyat were still strongly held. In consequence of this retirement the 7th and 8th Brigades of the 3rd Division moved off at 3.30 a.m. on the 20th and occupied the Dujailah Redoubt while the brigade of cavalry reached the Hai, the river which joins the Tigris just above Kut. Of the 8th Brigade the Manchesters and the 47th Sikhs started at 2 a.m.; the heat during the day was very great, water was scarce, and 15 men were struck down by the sun. The Brigade bivouacked about 4 in the afternoon, and marching again at 4 the next morning, eventually formed a camp between the Dujailah Redoubt and the river, and remained here from the 22nd to the 29th; then on the 30th the battalion took over the front line from the Devons.

During the latter part of June and the first week in July the battalion received some much-needed reinforcements; on the 24th June the strength of the battalion was 19 officers and only 367 other ranks, but Captains Irwin, Close-Brooks, and Atherley, Lieutenant Paterson, Second Lieutenants Yates, Cooper, Rigby, and Purcell joined, while on the 30th Second Lieutenant Gwynne arrived with a draft of 170 non-commissioned officers and men; on the 3rd July three more officers joined—Captain Bostock and Second Lieutenants Marriott and Adamson, so that by the 19th July, in spite of a good deal of sickness that was prevalent, the battalion was at a strength of 25 officers and 496 other ranks.

The temperature in July and August was very high, being on some days as much as 124° F. in the shade.

On the 29th September the Division moved to Sinn Aftar, taking over the river line as far as the mouth of the Nasafieh Canal, and the battalion was employed during the greater part of the month of October in making new roads to various points on the river. Nothing of any importance transpired during November, but early in the month following some 212 non-commissioned officers and men joined the battalion in drafts of varying strength, thus making good to some extent the wastage of the summer. Stores, ammunition, and supplies were rapidly accumulating at the front, communications were now secure, and Lieutenant-General Sir Stanley Maude, who at the end of August had taken over the command from Sir Percy Lake, judged that the time had arrived again to undertake offensive operations.

"At the beginning of December the enemy still occupied the same positions on the Tigris front which he had occupied during the summer. On the left bank of the Tigris he held the Sannaiyat position, flanked on one side by the Suwaikeh Marsh and on the other by the river. In this position he had withstood our attacks on three occasions during the previous April. Since then he had strengthened and elaborated this trench system, and a series of successive positions extended back as far as Kut, fifteen miles in the rear. The river bank from Sannaiyat to Kut was also entrenched. On the right bank of the Tigris the enemy held the line to which he had withdrawn in May when he evacuated the Es Sinn position. This line extended from a point on the Tigris three miles N.E. of Kut in a S.W. direction across the Khaidari Bend to the River Hai, two miles below its exit from the Tigris, and thence across the Hai to the N.W. . . . The enemy occupied the line of the Hai for several miles below the bridgehead position with posts and mounted Arab auxiliaries. On the left bank of the Tigris our trenches were within 120 yards of the Turkish front line at Sannaiyat. On the right bank our troops were established some eleven miles from those of the Turks opposite the Khaidari Bend, and some five miles from his position on the Hai."[1]

The operations which were now to be undertaken were in order as follows :

1. To secure possession of the Hai.
2. To clear the Turkish trench systems on the right bank of the Tigris.
3. To sap the enemy's strength by constant attacks.
4. To endeavour to compel him to give up the Sannaiyat position.
5. To cross the Tigris and sever his communications.

The army had by this been reorganised, the Tigris Corps being split into two Army Corps, becoming the 1st Indian Army Corps (3rd and 7th Divisions) under General Cobbe, and the 3rd Indian Army Corps (13th and 14th Divisions) under General Marshall. "As regards general distribution, the 1st Corps was to be on the right on both sides of the river, with the 3rd Corps on its left, the latter taking over some of the ground previously held by troops of the 1st Corps as soon as the 13th Division came up to the front from Amara."[2]

Marshall's force was concentrated before Es Sinn on the night of the 13th December, crossed the Hai at 6 the next morning, and moving north

---
[1] Sir Stanley Maude's despatch of the 10th April 1917.
[2] Caldwell, *Life of Sir Stanley Maude*, p. 250.

drove in the enemy's advanced posts : by the 18th December the 3rd Corps Commander had extended his grip on the Turkish defences and had cut in opposite Kut between the outer Turkish defences east of the Hai and those west of it. In the meantime Cobbe had been engaged in heavily bombarding the Sannaiyat position, in bridging the waterway, and in making new roads, in spite of the heavy rain which had been almost incessantly falling.

It was, however, the 5th January 1917 before anything further could be attempted, and these operations that then followed " took the form of a prolonged attack by portions of the 1st Corps upon the elaborately constructed system of defence works stretching across the Khaidari Bend, which secured to the Turks a footing on the right bank of the Tigris below Kut."

1917

Between January 5th and 7th General Cobbe's troops had dug some 25,000 yards of saps and trenches and had advanced to within 200 yards of the position to be assaulted, which was the section of the defences, 600 yards in length, nearest the Shatt-el-Hai, in the bend of the river N.E. of Kut.

The intelligence reports furnished to the 3rd Division stated that the enemy lines in the immediate front were held by 3 battalions of the 142nd Regiment of the 45th Turkish Division with 4 machine guns. The position of any guns had not been disclosed, but it was known that heavy guns could be so directed as to assist the defence with their fire.

The dispositions for the attack by the 8th Brigade on the early morning of the 9th January were as follows : the assault was to be made by the 1st Battalion Manchester Regiment in six lines, the 59th Rifles participating but on a very much narrower frontage ; the 47th Sikhs were to support the attack by covering rifle and machine-gun fire, while the 124th Baluch Light Infantry were to be in brigade reserve.

No. 4 Company of the battalion, with the battalion and company bombers, formed the 1st and 2nd waves, No. 2 Company the 3rd and 4th, and two platoons of No. 1 the fifth, while one and a half companies provided the battalion reserve.

Prior to the attack the following message was received from General Cobbe :

"*Following message from General Maude begins : please convey to General Keary and the 3rd Division my best wishes for an overwhelming success, and tell them that I feel confident that the old Lahore Division will worthily maintain and even enhance the splendid record for dash and determination which it has so constantly upheld. I have no doubt as to result.*"

It happened unfortunately that the morning of the 9th opened in thick mist, which, while it helped the first rush of the attackers, hampered the artillery support and enabled the enemy to prepare and launch a counter-attack. The following account is collated from the reports of the company commanders of the battalion.

The waves pushed over the trench well together, but, owing to excitement or a desire to get at the enemy, the men broke into a double too soon and consequently reached the Turkish trench before the artillery barrage had lifted. The enemy had up to this fired no shot, and a machine gun which was captured by the battalion showed no signs of having been in action. Very few of the enemy seemed to be in occupation of the trench, and such as were seen were bayoneted or captured, while some who later made their appearance from the nullahs and ditches in rear were disarmed and sent back under escort. No. 4—the leading—Company had then begun to reverse the parapet and consolidate the captured trench, when a rapid fire broke out and it was learnt that the enemy was outflanking the right, and No. 2 Company swung back and extended to the right at right angles to meet this attack. This company was, however, forced back, fighting hard, to its original front line, where, joined by some of the 34th Pioneers and helped by the fire of a Lewis gun handled by Sergeant Humphreys, the company attacked in its turn and finally consolidated on the Turks' front line.

Nos. 3 and 4 Companies were now taking up any positions they could, consolidating small nullahs across the trench and opening fire to the flanks and down the sides on the advancing enemy, and the fight swayed backwards and forwards till about midday. The British batteries dropped four shells in Nos. 3 and 4 Companies, causing many casualties, but they shortly got the range more accurately, and covered by their fire the battalion pushed forward, and the Turkish attack being now spent, everything was consolidated for the night.

The above account may well be supplemented by that given by the " Official Eye-witness in Mesopotamia,"[1] who writes as follows of this fight :

" The Manchesters had attacked on a 200 yards front and got in with few casualties, close up to our barrage, before an enemy head had emerged from behind the parapet. . . . Once in the enemy's first lines the bombing parties of the Manchesters worked along the trench on both flanks, on the left to join up with the H.L.I., who were bombing up from the river ; on the

[1] Candler, vol. ii, pp. 20, 21.

right to extend the position gained another 300 yards and there to form a block, while other parties worked up to points in the brushwood nullahs between the first and second Turkish lines, which were to be converted into communication trenches by our sappers and pioneers. It was down these nullahs that the enemy counter-attacked in overwhelming numbers and enveloped a party of the Manchesters. There was a thick fog, very favourable to a surprise, and the Turks who had been lying up in the scrub suddenly loomed out of the mist like a football crowd. The Manchesters were pinned into a trench from which it was difficult to use their rifles, their Lewis gun jammed with dirt, but the small party hung on, cut off from all support, and fought to a finish with bomb and bayonet until they were practically exterminated; the Turkish dead found on the spot next morning outnumbered ours. The wave swept on and caught a second party of the same regiment on the flank, driving them back to the trench we had captured, where it was held up.

"In the meanwhile the Turks were pressing down the trench on our right. It was here that a small working party of Pioneers, a mere platoon, under a young subaltern, Lieutenant Gordon, of the 34th Sikh Pioneers, found themselves with a handful of the Manchesters in the crisis of the action. They held the breach, built up a block, and bombed the Turks lustily for hours. Other Manchesters joined them. Captain Close-Brooks was killed as he stood on the parapet and directed the bombing. Pembroke, a second lieutenant, succeeded him and fell badly wounded. Yates, a second lieutenant, succeeded him and was killed in the trench. Hardman and Walker, both second lieutenants, took over in turn and were both killed. Henderson survived. . . . Here, too, he and one other officer of the Manchesters, Major Brown, returned unwounded. . . .

"The day's work had given us the whole of Kut East Mounds, part of the west side of the Mahomed Abdul Hassan loop, extending by 600 yards the gap we held between the two Turkish positions on the right bank of the river, and 1,000 yards of the first line trench which lay astride the bend. We captured 7 officers, 155 other ranks, 1 machine gun, and buried a trench full of Turkish dead."

The casualties in the 1st Battalion Manchester Regiment were heavy:

Killed or died of wounds: 7 officers—Captains Jackson and Close-Brooks, Second Lieutenants Graham, Yates, Walker, Hardman, and Swift —and 80 other ranks.

Wounded: 5 officers—Lieutenants Holmes, Pembroke, Moore, and

Marley, and Second Lieutenant Atkin—and 136 non-commissioned officers and men.

Missing: 10 men.

For the next few days the battalion was in reserve, employed mainly in salvage work and in clearing up generally, but on the 14th January all ranks were heartened by the receipt of the following message from General Maude:

" *Please convey to General Keary and Third Division my appreciation of excellent work done since 9th inst. Blow so successfully struck is bound to lower enemy's moral whilst heavy casualties inflicted on him are most creditable to fighting powers of Division. Am confident that remnants of enemy will be driven across river within next few days.*" To this General Cobbe, the Corps Commander, added: " *Please express to all ranks my admiration of gallantry shown. I am confident that they will always carry out whatever may be required of them.*"

Writing home on the 21st General Maude said: " *The 3rd Division did most of the fighting and did it splendidly. As you know the Turks are very stubborn fighters, especially in trenches; but our men fairly beat them at their own game, and with bomb and bayonet drove them steadily back, foot by foot. . . . The men are tremendously pleased with themselves—as well they may be, for their conduct has been splendid.*"

Fighting went on every day, the enemy being driven back trench by trench; on the 11th January the town of Hai was occupied by the cavalry, and one by one the enemy's advanced posts were captured. The final assault was to have been made on the 19th, but during the previous night the enemy, under cover of rifle and machine-gun fire, retired across the river.

General Marshall's Corps was now ordered to capture the defences across the mouth of the Hai, and his operations culminated on the 15th February in the successful assault upon the Dahra Bend defences. While this was in progress General Cobbe had been keeping the enemy on the *qui vive* in the Sannaiyat lines, helping to distract the attention of the Turks; and General Maude now issued instructions that the formidable position on the left bank of the Tigris, already three times unsuccessfully attempted in April 1916, should be attacked on the 17th February.

On this day, therefore, the 21st Brigade attacked the left flank of the Sannaiyat position on a front of 350 yards, the 8th Brigade assisting by rifle and machine-gun fire from the opposite bank. The Turkish first- and second-line trenches were captured, but retaken by an enemy counter-attack;

for three days the troops remained inactive and then the attack was renewed on the 22nd; and finally on the 24th the Turks were forced out of their positions at Sannaiyat, Nakhailat, and Suwada, and the left bank as far as Kut was cleared; on the same day the passage of the Tigris was secured at Shumran.

In these operations the battalion was not specially actively employed, on the 24th February being placed at the disposal of the 7th Division and moving at 2 p.m. on the extreme right to protect that flank. On this night the Manchesters halted near the Dahra Canal, marching early next morning to rejoin the 3rd Division, which was finally linked up with the 27th N.E. of the Shumran Bend about 1,000 yards from the river. Here for some ten days or more the battalion was very busily engaged in salvaging war material of all kinds left by the retiring enemy, an enormous quantity of shells and rifle ammunition lying about and bearing witness to the very hurried retreat of the Turks.

" So rapid had been the enemy's flight that on the evening of February 27th his troops reached Aziziya, 50 miles from Kut. They had covered that distance in two days. Nevertheless, all through the 27th the British gunboats had hung on to and shelled them from the river, while the British cavalry harried them on the flank, and when the retreating army reached Aziziya and streamed through that place it was as a broken, demoralised and, in part, unarmed mob." [1]

On the 5th March the Brigade containing the 1st Battalion Manchester Regiment marched by Shedhaif-ash-Sharqui and Um-al-Tubal to Aziziya, which was reached on the 7th March, and here the battalion took over the defences. In the meantime the whole force had gradually been closing up to the front in anticipation of a fresh advance. On the 5th General Marshall's Corps moved forward 18 miles to Zeur, his cavalry a further 7 miles to Lajj, and these troops had some heavy fighting about the Diala River, which joins the Tigris on its left bank some 8 miles below Baghdad.

On the 14th the battalion marched by the eastern wall of the city, which was on the next day visited by some of the officers and men, and on the 18th the Brigade reached the Diala, crossing the river in pontoons holding 10 men at a time.

The 8th and 9th Brigades under General Keary, now composing what Edmund Candler [2] calls " the Khanikin Column," pushed out from Baghdad " in the hope of intercepting the Turk and crushing him between the British and Cossack nutcrackers." There was at first but little opposition, the

[1] Dane, p. 272.   [2] *The Long Road to Baghdad*, vol. ii, p. 136.

column concentrating on the 20th at Baquba, the centre of a district rich in supplies, and, moving on to Abu Jisra, the troops were by the 21st in touch with the enemy. On the 23rd the Turks were shelled out of a position they had taken up at Shahraban, when they slowly fell back upon a strong natural position on a long, low range of hills known as Jebel Hamrin, through which the Khanikin road passes to the Persian frontier. The Turks were here in strength with their right on the Diala River and their left two and a half miles east of the road, the front being covered by the Ruz Canal, a high-banked waterway 30 feet wide. Facing the road were three tiers of traversed fire trenches with a line of picquet posts thrown forward.

" On the night of the 23rd General Keary's plan of operations was to work round to the east with the 9th Brigade, capture the Jebel Hamrin heights and roll the enemy back on the Diala, leaving the 8th Brigade to press in frontally as soon as this movement had become effective."

Actually the two British brigades were scarcely strong enough for the task demanded of them and success could only have resulted from a surprise attack, which was impossible, and already on the evening of the 23rd the battalion had had 16 men wounded, 1 of whom died, from the very heavy and effective artillery fire opened by the Turks. On the early morning of the 24th the 8th Brigade made a feint attack on both sides of the Khanikin road to distract the attention of the Turks from the movements of the 9th Brigade which had marched during the night to attack the enemy's right. By daybreak on the 25th our infantry had established themselves in the foothills and the advance to the main ridge began. Hostile picquets were driven in and the lower crest of the hills was gained, but beyond this another crest rose 2,500 yards away, and the intervening country was much broken with hillocks and ravines. The advance continued towards the line held by the enemy about 1,000 yards north of the captured crest, but as he now began to show considerable strength it was deemed inadvisable to press the advance further.

At this period of this day's fighting the battalion seems to have been in divisional reserve, but it was now ordered to assist to cover the general retirement. " The Manchesters on the right, the 93rd in the centre, and the 124th Baluchis on the left, fought a steady rear-guard action. The enemy made one attempt to follow up the withdrawal of the infantry, whose retirement they covered, but it was easily repulsed. At 3.30 the Turkish cavalry on our right had formed and were preparing to charge, but were dispersed by the rifle and machine gun fire of the 13th Lancers and the battery protecting their flank. Our infantry had three miles of plain to cover swept by the enemy's shell-fire"[1]—and the 1st Battalion Manchester Regiment sustained many casualties before at dark it rejoined its own Brigade and was placed in reserve. During the operations of the 24th and 25th these were as follows :

Killed and died of wounds : Second Lieutenant Hussey, 3rd Battalion Devonshire Regiment (attached) and 11 other ranks.
Wounded : Second Lieutenants Atkin, Holden, Flood (3rd Battalion Connaught Rangers), Huggard (3rd Battalion Connaught Rangers), and 73 other ranks.
Missing : Lieutenant Butterworth (also wounded) and 16 men.

The battalion received many messages of thanks for and congratulations on the fine fight it had put up ; Brigadier-General Campbell, commanding the 9th Brigade, wrote as follows to the commander of the 8th Brigade :

"*My dear Edwards,*
"*Will you kindly convey my thanks to the Manchesters for the help they gave to my Brigade. They were most steady, and their steadiness and gallantry during the retirement undoubtedly saved us many casualties.*
"*Yours sincerely,*
Leslie Campbell."

This was forwarded to Lieutenant-Colonel C. D. Irwin, commanding the battalion, endorsed as under by Brigadier-General Edwards :

"*Dear Irwin,*
"*It gives me much pleasure to forward the note over leaf. Well done !*
"*Yours sincerely,*
S. M. Edwards."

While on the 27th the following message was circulated to the troops :

"*Please inform troops that Army Commander appreciates very highly their gallantry and stubborn fighting in yesterday's battle in which they appear to have punished the enemy severely. He regrets the casualties incurred*"— which amounted in the two brigades to 1,177, more than a third of the numbers engaged.

[1] Candler, vol. ii, pp. 143, 144

Finally in General Sir Stanley Maude's despatch of the 10th April 1917 he wrote :

"*The Manchesters specially distinguished themselves by their gallantry and steadiness on this occasion.*"

The two or three days immediately following the action were employed in making reconnaissances in the Jebel Hamrin Hills, from which on the 31st March it was found that the Turks had finally withdrawn. On the 2nd April, having advanced the previous day to Kizil Robat, the 8th Brigade met the detachment of Cossacks which had been sent forward from the Russian main body to establish communications ; the object of the movement in this direction having now been attained, the force under General Keary returned to Baghdad, where the battalion arrived early on the 7th.

The 8th Brigade was not actively engaged again for some considerable time ; it was held in reserve throughout the operations conducted during April, and then when the hot weather commenced the battalion was quartered about Istabulat. During the summer leave was opened to India of which all ranks took advantage, drafts arrived in the country, and training of all kinds was seriously taken in hand, while occasionally some punitive expeditions were organised for the punishment of a recalcitrant village or having for their object the capture of some troublesome or truculent sheikh. The summer of 1917 passed very much more comfortably than had that of the preceding year : large tents were brought up from the rear, encampments were laid out on carefully selected sites, well-organised canteens were provided, supplies of comforts were distributed, and provision for the recreation of officers and men was not forgotten ; while the river transport was now in thorough-going order, and had been supplemented by the laying of a narrow-gauge railway between Kut and Baghdad.

Here, then, this chapter may fittingly end, leaving the 1st Battalion of the Manchester Regiment preparing for the operations which were to conclude its service in Mesopotamia, preparatory to undertaking fresh ones in a wholly different and unknown theatre of war.

CHAPTER XXV

THE 2ND BATTALION IN FRANCE AND FLANDERS

AUGUST 1917 — THE ARMISTICE

AT the end of August 1917 the rest period enjoyed by the 2nd Battalion at La Panne came to an end, and on the 27th it relieved the 2nd Battalion Royal Welch Fusiliers in the Nieuport defences, which at this time comprised the following works, viz. the Sardinière, Novel Trench, Canal Bank Trench, Howitzer Pits and dug-outs, with the Presculle defences, the battalion head-quarters being at New Parade; but on the 1st September it went into the trenches in the Lombartzyde sector, and here on the 5th Second Lieutenant Horby and 1 private were killed. Some time was spent on this part of the line, in the Coxyde area, or in the St. George's defences, casualties occurring tolerably regularly if in small numbers—on the 21st September, the Rev. R. Gillanders, the chaplain to the battalion, being wounded, while 3 other ranks were killed and 4 wounded.

Towards the end of this month the enemy showed unusual activity; on the early morning of the 27th September he commenced a heavy bombardment of the battalion trenches S. of Lombartzyde, the left divisional front being also shelled. Our artillery replied and later the bombardment died down. But on the next evening the Germans opened fire again, shelling the Oost-Dunkerke cross roads and killing the adjutant, Second Lieutenant F. M. Nicholas, and 1 private of the battalion.

By the 1st October the Manchesters were back again in the Nieuport neighbourhood, remaining here until the 6th, when, having been relieved by the 10th Battalion Manchester Regiment, they marched via Coxyde to Adinkerke, where they embarked on barges and proceeded by way of the Canal as far as Chapeau Rouge and Rosendpel, and disembarking here marched by way of Dunkerke and St. Pol to Petite Synthe, arriving about 11.30 p.m. and being accommodated in billets.

Here the battalion remained until the 26th October, when it marched back to the Arneke area, where on the 1st November Colonel Vaughan, D.S.O., took over command from Major Whittaker, M.C., 1st Battalion Dorsetshire

Regiment, who in the previous May had relieved Lieutenant-Colonel Luxmoore of the Devonshire Regiment.

About the 12th November another move was made, this time to the Poperinghe area, where the battalion was housed in tents and huts at Tunnelling Camp and where a very strict training in day and night operations was carried out; this came to an end on the 24th, when the battalion marched to Poperinghe, where it entrained, detrained again at Brielen and marched to the Yser Canal, occupying dug-outs on the east and west banks. Here for some days all ranks were busily employed in providing working-parties for making new trenches up to the front line, in carrying ammunition and stores, and in erecting and strengthening dug-outs.

The Manchesters were now some distance away from the fighting with which the year 1917 closed further south, but there was always a certain " liveliness " in their front, and on the 1st December they were brought nearer to the front line in connection with certain operations about to be undertaken by the 97th Brigade of the 32nd Division, and were ordered to be ready to move at fifteen minutes' notice to exploit any success gained or to repel any counter-attacks that might be made. In the early hours of the 2nd December news was received that the attack by the 97th Brigade had been successful and that all the objectives had been gained. Later, however, a message came in to say that the 97th Brigade had been compelled to fall back, and in consequence the battalion moved off at 11 p.m. and marched to Belle Vue.

On arrival here early on the 3rd it was learnt that the situation was very bad and the battalion was placed under orders to be ready to move at a moment's notice : while waiting orders, however, the enemy shelled Belle Vue heavily, killing 2 and wounding 4 men. At 10.30 p.m. the Manchesters moved up to the left sub-sector and relieved the 15th Battalion Lancashire Fusiliers, the front held being an organised system of shell-holes, and battalion headquarters being at Pill Box No. 88. Here the battalion remained under intermittent but heavy shelling until the night of the 5th–6th, when, on being relieved in the left sub-sector by the 5th/6th Royal Scots, it fell back to Belle Vue, relieving there the 15th Highland Light Infantry. Belle Vue also was under shell-fire, but the Manchesters remained here until the 9th (when they were withdrawn to dug-outs at Canal Bank), mainly engaged in salvage operations and in providing fatigue parties for taking food and stores to the battalions in the front line. During this week the casualties were 9 killed and 40 wounded, among the latter being Lieutenant Haynes.

From this date until the end of the year the 2nd Battalion Manchester Regiment remained in this sector, moving up in its turn to the line or

" resting " in the dug-outs at Canal Bank or in huts at Hospital Farm, and during this period it incurred a further loss of Second Lieutenant Rowley and 5 men killed and 9 men wounded; Second Lieutenant Cassidy distinguished himself on Christmas Eve by capturing two German prisoners.

On the 1st January 1918 the 2nd Battalion Manchester Regiment marched to St. Jean station, entraining there for Audruicq, on arrival at which place it moved on to Listergaux, and here it remained, carrying on routine training, undergoing inspections and lectures on all kinds of the latest weapons of war. At Listergaux—on the 11th January—a belated Christmas Day, impossible of recognition at Canal Bank, was celebrated, the men's dinners being served in the Y.M.C.A. hut at Audruicq, followed by a concert.

After a peaceful three weeks at Listergaux, the battalion took the train for Elverdinghe and marched to some hutments bearing the unattractive title of Dirty Bucket Camp, being concentrated here by the 23rd January; but on the 30th it was again on the move and marched to Emile Camp in the Boesinghe N.2 Area, and was placed in the Divisional Reserve with orders to be ready to move at two hours' notice. Here Captain Watts and Second Lieutenant Lowther and 69 other ranks, who had been attached to the 173rd Tunnelling Company, rejoined their battalion.

In February the battalion was transferred from the 14th to the 96th Infantry Brigade, consequent upon the very extensive reorganisation which was now made, for so great had been the drain upon the man-power of the nation that it was found necessary to reduce the number of battalions in a brigade from four to three, and as a result the brigades had to be rearranged. On the 5th February the General Officer Commanding the 14th Brigade inspected the 2nd Battalion Manchester Regiment and presented the ribbon of the " 1914 " Star to those present with the battalion who were entitled to it. He then wished the battalion " good-bye," and in so doing expressed his thanks for all the good work that it had done in the past, and his regret at its now severing its connection with the 14th Brigade.

The 96th Brigade was composed of the 2nd Battalion Manchester Regiment, the 15th and 16th Battalions Lancashire Fusiliers, and the 96th Trench Mortar Battery.

From Emile Camp the battalion was moved up at regular intervals into the front line, and as usual the casualties at once recommenced—not, of course, in the same number and to the same extent as those suffered by other regiments engaged in the general actions which during this year were fought at more distant parts of the long line—but providing always a general drain upon the best manhood of the battalion. Thus on the 7th

February 3 men were killed and 5 wounded ; on the 9th, in an enemy raid upon our line, 1 man was killed and 4 wounded, mainly by enemy bombs, while another man of the battalion was killed on the following day.

By the 11th February the Manchesters were withdrawn again to brigade reserve to huts at Abri Wood, and during this month a party of 119 non-commissioned officers and men and 4 officers—Captain McKenzie, Lieutenant Bennett, and Second Lieutenants Burton and Berry—joined the battalion from the 23rd Battalion of the Regiment lately disbanded.

On the 15th a move was made to the Support System, and thence in turn to the Front System of the Forward Zone, Houthulst Forest Sector, the battalion Headquarters being at Caledonian Club—where the amenities were probably less conspicuous than the name would seem to indicate ! Early on the morning of the 20th the enemy shelled Veldhoek, killing 1 man and wounding 2 in the battalion, while an enemy patrol attempted to raid the right post on the front of the right company, but was driven off, 2 prisoners being captured. Later the shelling became more violent and 10 men were wounded. The 21st was tolerably quiet, and many patrols went out from our lines at night with the object of finding out the positions of the enemy machine guns and the condition of the German wire. On the 22nd the battalion was relieved in the front line, but it was for the enemy a day of rather extra activity, shelling being heavy, and there being also increased aerial offensive, several enemy aeroplanes flying low over the British lines and several bombs being dropped—happily harmlessly so far as the Manchesters were concerned.

On the 27th the battalion was back again in the front line, and was disposed as follows : Battalion Headquarters and B Company at La Chaudière, A Company at Colonel's Farm, C Company in Corps Line as permanent garrison, and D Company in Corps Line.

This night a raid was carried out by a party of the battalion 110 strong under Captain Kay, who had with him Lieutenant Bennett, Second Lieutenants Thomas, Surkitt, Brady, Hollins, and Parker. The little force was divided into eight different parties from 6 to 20 strong and the objects of the raid were as under :

1. To locate the position of the enemy's main line of resistance.
2. To find out what works the enemy was carrying out in Owl Wood.
3. To capture any of the enemy found in the area raided.
4. To obtain identifications and bring back documents, maps, samples of food and clothing and gas masks.
5. To secure machine guns, trench mortars, and other booty.

The raid was entirely successful, seven prisoners being taken while two machine guns and shoulder-straps cut from the enemy dead were brought in. Of the raiding party 2 men were killed, while Second Lieutenants Hollins and Surkitt and 11 other ranks were wounded and 2 men were missing. A wire was received from the General Commanding the 32nd Division congratulating all concerned on their brilliant exploit.

On the 5th March, while at La Bergerie Camp, the Divisional Commander visited the battalion and handed over the divisional monthly cup for having gained most points in the Division in captures during the past month. He also presented the ribbons of the Military Medal to the following for gallantry and devotion to duty during the recent raid : Sergeants J. S. Metcalfe and J. McElroy, Privates C. Lyrett, W. Wood, E. Roebuck, and E. Jones.

The battalion remained in this part of the line during the greater part of the month of March, but on the 27th it was relieved by the 10th Regiment of Belgian Infantry and then moved to Whitehall Camp, Elverdinghe, being there accommodated in huts ; but on the 29th it commenced its move to a new Army Area, proceeding from Elverdinghe by motor-bus, train, and road, by way of Proven and Savy to Hauteville, and thence by march-route to Ayette, where it took over a portion of the front line from the 2nd Battalion Irish Guards, of the 4th Guards Brigade attached to the Cavalry Corps. During the process of relief four men of the Manchesters were wounded.

The battalion was now placed in the reserve trenches and thus was not engaged actively in the operations which the 32nd Division conducted on the 1st and 2nd April, but mention may here be made of what occurred in order that the general situation in the part of the line where the Manchesters now found themselves may be understood. The 32nd Division had been brought up here to relieve the 31st, which had been heavily engaged with five German divisions and was greatly exhausted and reduced in strength.

" On taking over his section of the front, General Shute found before him the village of Ayette, which was strongly held, but was on the forward slope of a hill, so that it could obtain little help from the German guns. He at once determined to attack. The 15th Highland Light Infantry of the 14th Brigade were directed upon the village on the night of 2nd April, while the 96th Brigade continued the attack to the south. The result was a very heartening little success. Three companies of the Highlanders, numbering under 300 in all, carried the village, though it was held by a German battalion. On the right, the 16th Lancashire Fusiliers made the attack, and in spite of one check, which was set right by the personal intervention of General Girdwood of the 96th Brigade, the objectives were reached. The two attacks were skilfully connected up by the 5/6th Royal Scots, while a party of Sappers of the 206th Field Company under Lieutenant Cronin followed on the heels of the infantry and quickly consolidated."[1]

But during the remainder of the month of April, for most of which time up to the 25th (when it was relieved by the 2nd Battalion Scots Guards and went into billets at Barly) the battalion remained in the line, the casualties were sufficiently heavy and were as below stated:

Killed: 3 officers—Second Lieutenants T. S. and W. R. B. Thomas and McSherry—and 11 other ranks.

Wounded: 5 officers—Major Humphreys, Lieutenant Bennett, Second Lieutenants Handley, Berry, and Hollins—and 82 other ranks.

Gassed: 1 officer—Lieutenant Culley—and 15 other ranks.

Missing: 1 man.

During the same month no fewer than 14 officers joined for duty—Major Theobald, Captain Medworth, Lieutenants Prouse, Dennison, and Williams-Green, Second Lieutenants Brownson, Burkett-Gottwaltz, Bramley, Mortiboy, Hayward, Mitchell, Hill, Tait, and Lawrence.

Barly provided a resting-place for the battalion until the 12th May, when a move was made to the neighbourhood of Blairville; here the enemy was more than usually active, and on the very day after arrival Captain Medworth was killed and by the end of May 8 men had been killed and Second Lieutenant Sprowell and 29 men wounded. On the 18th May Lieutenant-Colonel G. McM. Robertson, North Stafford Regiment, assumed command of the battalion.

The month of June was again one of considerable activity in the front line with heavy fatigues of all kinds when the troops, by a pleasant fiction, were considered to be " at rest." The casualties continued among all ranks, and the depleted condition of the senior commissioned ranks of the 2nd Battalion Manchester Regiment may to some extent be gauged from the announcement which appears in the battalion diary under date of the 1st June: "*Lieutenant* J. N. Marshall, M.C., Irish Guards, joined to-day and took over the duties of second-in-command!" Behind the line wiring was carried on and working and carrying parties were constantly provided, while at the front raids and counter-raids took place almost nightly. The strain was great and the casualties in killed, wounded, missing, and gassed increased daily, while seldom does the battalion diary record the arrival of reinforcements to replace wastage.

[1] Conan Doyle, vol. v, pp. 36, 37.

Early in July the battalion went into divisional reserve and was accommodated near Blairville in tents, billets, and shelters, but on the 6th moved by train to La Bazeque, when the diary reads almost as though the days of peace or even home service had returned—bathing, kit inspection, and " recreational training "—even sports. On the 13th there was a further move, via Doullens, to the Proven area, and the month of July came happily to an end without any casualties at all in the battalion.

On the 6th August His Majesty the King inspected representatives of the 96th Brigade at School Camp, Proven, when Captain Taylor and 20 non-commissioned officers and men represented the battalion.

On the day following this inspection the Manchesters left Proven by train for Hangest, marched thence by way of Briquemesnil to Boves, and bivouacked on the night of the 9th–10th August in a field between Mézières and Beaucourt. From here at 4 o'clock on the morning of the 10th the battalion moved up into action and, in support of the 15th and 16th Battalions of the Lancashire Fusiliers, attacked Parvillers and Damery Woods, over three miles, and the day ended with the battalion holding the outpost line and remaining in it until the night of the 11th. In this action Major Marshall and Second Lieutenant Emsley were wounded

On the relief by the Canadians the battalion moved via Le Quesnel and Ignecourt to Harbonnière, which was reached on the 18th, its numbers having been at last brought up to something like establishment by the arrival *en route* of a draft of 300 non-commissioned officers and men. At Harbonnière the Manchesters went into the line again, relieving there an Australian battalion.

The following was the disposal of the companies : right front Company, B ; left, C ; right support, D ; left support, A. About 10.15 a.m. on the 19th the enemy heavily shelled the battalion front- and support-line system with guns of all calibres and trench mortars, and succeeded in penetrating the front line, where, however, they were held up by a party of the Manchesters and hand-to-hand fighting took place in the trenches. Bombing parties of the battalion were then reorganised and the Germans were finally driven back and the front line was completely restored. The enemy left 8 dead in the trenches and was known to have incurred considerable loss by Lewis guns, bombs, and rifle-fire. One prisoner was taken by the battalion, the casualties in which were heavy, Second Lieutenant Mortiboy and 16 other ranks being killed while 53 were wounded and 27 reported missing.

Counter-raids by the British were now the order of the day ; in one carried out on the night of the 21st August Second Lieutenant Hall and 4 men were wounded, while in another undertaken by the 32nd Division on the 23rd, in which 36 German officers and 1,195 other ranks were taken prisoners, the battalion lost 2 men killed, 8 wounded, and 3 missing. The 32nd Division was now commanded by Major-General T. S. Lambert, C.B., C.M.G., and since the 8th August had been attached to the Canadian Corps in the Fourth Army.

The German retreat was now everywhere in progress and the enemy was being pushed back all along the line, fighting desperately and losing men and guns, but hitting back and causing many casualties among the attackers. During the last few days of August the battalion was heavily engaged about Vermandovillers, Ablaincourt, and Cizancourt, receiving during the course of the advance the expression of the admiration of their Brigadier in the following remarks published in Brigade Order No. 478 of the 27th:

"*The work of the 2nd Battalion Manchester Regiment to-day is beyond praise. I am proud to have such a battalion in my brigade, and I thank all ranks for their splendid behaviour to-day. May good fortune attend them to-morrow.*"

Success, however, is not to be won without paying the price, and the losses in the battalion during the four days from the 27th to the 30th August were heavy, being as follows:

Killed: Captain C. W. Eastgate-Smith, 2nd Lieutenant Taylor, and 14 non-commissioned officers and men.
Wounded: Captain McKenzie, 2nd Lieutenants Starkey and Fazackerley, and 40 other ranks.
Missing: 2 men.

On the 30th August the battalion was withdrawn to Berny and was here afforded a welcome opportunity of reorganising the companies and making good deficiencies.

Moving again on the 6th September, the Brigade marched to Ennemain, thence next day to Monchy-Lagache, and then by Villeveque and Marteville to the La Neuville area, where some time was passed and training was carried out under tolerably comfortable conditions. The 32nd Division came on the 11th under the Ninth Corps, remaining with it to the end of the war. This comparatively peaceful existence came, however, to an end on the 28th September, when the 96th Brigade moved to Vendelles, the battalion marching for the line on the afternoon of the 29th, crossing the

St. Quentin Canal about 8.30 p.m., and staying for the night in the old German line of trenches something under two miles E. of the Canal.

Next day the Manchesters moved to positions E. of Magny-La-Fosse near Bellenglise, the battalion headquarters being on the outskirts of the village; losses were incurred in getting into position, 2 men being killed, while Lieutenant Carroll, Second Lieutenants Porter, Macdonald, and Cappock, and 18 non-commissioned officers and men were wounded.

" During the night of September 30th preparations were made for the 14th Brigade to attack Sequehart; for the 96th Brigade to operate against Joncourt in conjunction with the 5th Australian Division and to gain the Beaurevoir–Fonsomme Line round Chataignies Wood in conjunction with the 97th Brigade."[1]

On the morning of the 1st October the 2nd Battalion Manchester Regiment was ordered to attack the enemy line, capture and hold the enemy system and Swiss Cottage on the left flank. Zero hour was 4 p.m., the disposition being as follows: C and D Companies in the front line, A in support, and B Company in reserve.

The attack on Joncourt was successful, but little resistance being encountered; but that on the Beaurevoir–Fonsomme Line and on Sequehart was only partially so, it being found impossible to retain all the ground that had been gained, and some of our men were withdrawn to some distance.

" Complete success crowned the attack of the 96th Brigade on the left. The 2nd Manchester attacked with great gallantry and was assisted by 4 tanks, while 5 tanks followed in rear to clear the trenches to the N. of the objective. The battalion broke through the Beaurevoir–Fonsomme Line, and after stiff hand-to-hand fighting, cleared the line from Swiss Cottage to a point 1,400 yards south of it, capturing 210 prisoners of the 2nd and 241st Divisions. (The wire in front of these trenches was very thick, and the trench itself, though only one foot deep, contained numerous rifle and machine-gun pits.) In this attack the tanks rendered valuable assistance, although unfortunately three were hit just before ' zero.' In one of these tanks the whole crew except the officer became casualties; picking up an officer and a man of the attacking battalion to work the machine guns, the tank went into action and met with considerable success. . . . Repeated counter-attacks were made during the night against the left flank of the 96th Brigade, but the 2nd Manchester successfully maintained

---

[1] Montgomery, *The Story of the Fourth Army*, p. 171.

its position with the assistance of a company of the 15th Lancashire Fusiliers which had been sent forward to reinforce it."[1]

In this day's fighting 4 men of the battalion were killed, 2nd Lieutenant Gregg died of wounds, while Captain Somerville, Second Lieutenants Johnson, Heyward, Potts, Bowden, and Morris, and 78 other ranks were wounded, and 7 men were missing.

On the morning of the 2nd October the commanding officer, Lieutenant-Colonel Robertson, circulated the following message to " all companies " :

"*The G.O.C. desires me to thank on his behalf all ranks for their extremely gallant conduct yesterday and especially last night. He will tell them when they come out what extreme importance was attached to their behaviour, and if to-day's operations are successful their conduct will have led to one of the greatest successes of the war, maybe. They are the only men in the division who did their task and held it. May I be allowed to offer my sincere thanks to all for their work and the honour they have again added to the battalion's credit which is so dear to us all?*"

On the 3rd October, on relief by the 1/8th Battalion Nottinghamshire and Derbyshire Regiment, the battalion moved back into dug-outs on the banks of the St. Quentin Canal near Lehancourt, but in the course of the relief suffered further casualties to the number of 23 killed and 70 wounded, while Second Lieutenant Sprowell was missing. On the 5th a move was made to Hancourt in the Vendelles area, where a certain amount of rest and recreation could be enjoyed and where nine young officers joined the battalion : Second Lieutenants Taylor, Oveston, Winder, Baugh (from hospital), Simpole, Bullen, Jones, Kirk, and Smith.

Later in October the battalion was in turn at Bohain, at Bussigny—where a draft of 85 non-commissioned officers and men joined—and on the 29th at St. Souplet, whence it again went into the line, two companies in the front, one in support, and one in reserve.

The brigade relieved the 56th Infantry Brigade in the line W. of the Oise Canal, N. of Ors, on the night of the 30th–31st October, and it was understood that the battalion would take part in an attack over and beyond the canal at an early date.

" The nature of the country over which the advance was to be made was difficult. On the right there was the obstacle of the Sambre and Oise

[1] Montgomery, p. 173.

Canal which had to be crossed at the outset. This canal runs from La Fère by Mont d'Origny, Vadencourt, and Etreux to Landrécies. From La Fère to Vadencourt it follows the course of the Oise, thence, swinging to the N. near Etreux, it enters the Sambre Valley near Oisy. At Landrécies the canal terminates and the canalised Sambre begins as a separate waterway. The canal is of the ordinary type to be met with in France and Belgium and forms a considerable obstacle, being some 70 feet wide from bank to bank, and 35 to 40 feet broad at water-level except at Lock No. 1 and at the locks at Chatillon, Ors, and Landrécies, where it is 17 feet wide. It contained at that time an average depth of 6 to 8 feet of water and was nowhere fordable except at the bridges, which had been either demolished or prepared for demolition. In addition to the obstacle offered by the canal itself, the low ground on both sides of the canal had been inundated by the Germans and much of it had been transformed into swamp. . . .

" The general configuration of the country, E. of the Sambre and Oise Canal and S. of Mormal Forest, consists of a series of parallel valleys through which run the tributaries of the Sambre, and which are separated by ridges affording excellent successive positions for rear-guard action. The whole area was intersected by wire and hedges, and cavalry or infantry could make only slow progress off the roads, to which the artillery would be entirely confined for any considerable movements or changes of position. . . . There was little or no cultivation, the fields being pasture land. . . .

" For the forcing of the Sambre and the Oise Canal the IX Corps employed the 1st and 32nd Divisions on the right and left respectively. Although the attacks of both divisions were to be simultaneous, they were to be entirely independent as regards their detailed execution, each as it advanced arranging for the protection of its flanks, but establishing connection with the other immediately on crossing the canal. . . . Major-General Lambert, commanding the 32nd Division, arranged that the 14th Brigade should cross the Canal just S. of Ors, and the 96th Brigade immediately S. of the elbow in the canal N. of Ors. Success depended on obtaining complete superiority of fire over the enemy holding the eastern bank of the canal, and arrangements were made for the crossing of the infantry to be covered by a powerful artillery barrage and smoke screen. After effecting a crossing the 14th and 96th Brigades were to reorganise before renewing the advance to the bridgehead line under the creeping barrage. (The barrage was to remain on the E. bank of the canal for 3 minutes; it was then to be lifted 300 yards and remain for 30 minutes, after which pause it was to advance at the rate of 100 yards every 6 minutes.) No barrage was arranged beyond the bridgehead line for the further advance to the first army objective, the arrangements for the necessary artillery support being left to the brigade commanders." [1]

The days prior to " zero " were passed in strong and careful patrolling and initiating all ranks in every detail of the coming advance. Patrols on the nights of the 30th–31st October and 31st October–1st November reported the enemy this side of the canal, but only as occupying alarm posts which were not permanently held or intended as resistance points. The night of the 1st–2nd November was spent on organised clearance of the W. bank and this was completely done by 5 p.m. on the 2nd. The only Germans remaining alive on the battalion front were 4 men who were captured, 3 machine guns being taken at the same time. November 3rd passed without incident, but on that night up to zero hour strong active patrolling took place.

" Zero for the IX Corps attack was fixed for 5.45 a.m. on November 4th. . . . The assembly of the infantry and tanks was carried out during the night of the 3rd without a hitch, and a heavy ground mist in the early morning obscured their movements from the enemy. At 5.45 a.m. the barrage came down in front of the IX Corps along the E. bank of the canal, and the assembled infantry of the 1st and 32nd Divisions moved forward to the attack. . . .
" At 5.45 a.m., on the 32nd Division front, the 14th Brigade moved forward with the 5/6th Royal Scots on the right, the 1st Dorsetshire on the left, and with the 15th Highland Light Infantry in reserve. The 96th Brigade on the left advanced with the 2nd Manchester, 16th Lancashire Fusiliers and 15th Lancashire Fusiliers in line from right to left, and with 2 companies of the 2nd King's Own Yorkshire Light Infantry in reserve. The 97th Brigade, less 2 companies of 2nd King's Own Yorkshire Light Infantry, was held in reserve in the vicinity of St. Souplet."

The 14th Brigade managed to cross by a bridge made of petrol tins which the enemy had failed to locate, and by 8.15 a.m. its two leading battalions were firmly established along the road running parallel to the canal through Rue Verte and the E. outskirts of Ors.
The 96th Brigade was not so successful. The engineers were indeed able to get a bridge across the canal N. of Ors, but the whole area was swept with shell- and machine-gun fire, and it seemed impossible for anyone to live on the bank of the canal.

[1] Montgomery, pp. 242–4.

"Meanwhile 2nd Lieutenant Kirke, of the 2nd Manchester, in a splendid spirit of self-sacrifice, paddled across the canal on a raft and engaged the enemy with a Lewis gun. This gallant act cost him his life, but a bridge was erected and two platoons of his battalion succeeded in crossing. Unfortunately, the bridge was almost immediately destroyed by shell-fire, and, though repeated attempts were made to repair it, the undertaking had to be abandoned, and the remainder of the battalion took shelter from the enemy's fire behind the W. bank of the canal until it received a message from the 1st Dorsetshire that it was possible to cross at Ors."[1]

The original support and reserve companies of the battalion proceeded at once to this bridge with orders to cross rapidly, turn left and push N., keeping in touch with the right brigade, while detailing a special party for protection on the N. flank, where the enemy were offering a stout resistance at La Motte farm. The remaining battalions of the 96th Brigade now crossed by the same bridges and reached the intermediate objective in conjunction with the 14th Brigade.

During the day's fighting the 32nd Division had captured 238 prisoners, 20 guns, and many machine guns, while a bridgehead had been firmly established: by 1 p.m. a bridge at Ors, suitable for the passage of guns, had been made.

The move to the second objective commenced at dawn on the 4th, and here posts were established and consolidated; the 97th Brigade now passed through the 14th and 96th and took up the advance. But during the night of the 4th–5th November the 46th Division moved across the canal, relieving the 1st and 14th Brigades of the 1st and 32nd Divisions respectively astride the main Mézières–Catillon road, and the advance was resumed at 6.30 a.m. on November 5th, and by nightfall the 32nd Division was in occupation of the spur about 2,000 yards E. of Favril and was in touch with the 25th Division S. of Maroilles.

Fighting continued until the 8th and firing was heavy even up to the morning of the 11th November, but for the 2nd Battalion Manchester Regiment its active part in the war came to an end on the 6th, when it went into billets at Sambreton, where at 11 a.m. on the 11th all ranks learnt that an armistice had been declared.

In the final fighting, which actually beginning on the 1st November came to an end on the 6th, the losses of the battalion had been heavy, amounting to 2 officers—Captain A. McKenzie and Second Lieutenant W. E.

---

[1] Montgomery, p. 251. Second Lieutenant Kirke was attached from the 10th Battalion of the Regiment: he was awarded a posthumous V.C.

S. Owen (5th Battalion, attached 2nd)—and 22 other ranks killed, 3 officers—Lieutenant F. G. Hoal (8th Battalion, attached 2nd), Second Lieutenants J. Foulkes and J. D. O'Toole—and 81 other ranks wounded, and 18 non-commissioned officers and men missing.

" In three months the armies of Britain had gained seven victories, each greater than any in her old wars; they had taken some 190,000 prisoners and 3,000 guns; and they had broken the heart of their enemy. To their great sweep from Amiens to Mons was due especially the triumph which Foch had won, and on that grey November morning their worn ranks could await the final hour with thankfulness and pride. . . . Officers had their watches in their hands, and the troops waited with the same grave composure with which they had fought. Men were too weary and deadened for their imaginations to rise to the great moment. . . . Suddenly as the watch-hands touched eleven, there came a second of expectant silence, and then a curious rippling sound which observers far behind the front likened to the noise of a great wind. It was the sound of men cheering from the Vosges to the Sea." [1]

NOTE TO CHAPTER XXV

THE FIRST SEVEN DIVISIONS. COMMEMORATION AT THE ALBERT HALL

From " The Times " of the 17th December, 1917

KHAKI and black were almost the only colours to be seen in the audience that crowded the Albert Hall on Saturday afternoon for the choral commemoration of the First Seven Divisions. The khaki of the 700 officers, N.C.O.'s, and men who represented the survivors of that heroic army could be seen in the boxes and in the galleries above, in masses or patches up to the dizzy heights.

Black was everywhere; for although this was a ceremony of proud commemoration, not of mourning, the civilian audience consisted almost entirely of the relatives of those gallant men, and of them few are not bereaved. Round the tiers hung—richly, not gaily—the regimental and other banners, made for the occasion, embroidered in many instances by women who had travelled from the ends of the kingdom for the honour of putting in a few stitches. If feeling ran high, if at one portion of the ceremony the building rang with shouts and cheers and clapping of hands, the general tone was subdued, grave, and earnest.

There was not, probably, a single unoccupied place, nor even a foot of standing room in the highest gallery, when the King, the Queen, Queen Alexandra, Princess Mary, Princess Alice (Countess of Athlone), and Princess Victoria, with their suites,

---

[1] Buchan, *History of the War*, vol. xxiv, pp. 81, 82.

entered the Royal boxes, the whole audience standing while the National Anthem was played. Field-Marshal Lord French, who commanded the " contemptible little Army," was there. Sir John Jellicoe and other naval officers occupied a box on the right of the Royal party, just beneath a great white ensign ; and among others to be seen in the assembly were Mr. Balfour, Lord Derby, Mr. Fisher (Minister of Education), Brigadier-General Turner, and Brigadier-General Gloster. The programme (performed under the conductorship of Dr. Hugh P. Allen, by an orchestra led by Mr. William H. Reed, and a chorus composed of members of the Bach Choir and members of the Royal Albert Hall Choral Society) consisted of English music only, and followed a scheme of ideas. The first item, Sir Edward Elgar's " Cockaigne (in London Town)," stood for the light-hearted world before the war. Dr. Ralph Vaughan-Williams's song for chorus and orchestra, " Towards the Unknown Region " (Whitman's " Darest thou now, O Soul "), spoke the "challenge to the great adventure." "The cost" was figured by Mr. Howell's " Elegy for Strings," composed in memory of a friend killed in this war ; " the achievement," by Mr. Arthur Somervell's Ode, " To the Vanguard, 1914," composed to the poem by Miss Beatrix Brice—" O little mighty Force that stood for England," which first appeared on the front page of *The Times*. The solo in this was sung by Miss Lillian Stiles-Allen. Next came " Separation," expressed by a motet for unaccompanied voices, which is one of the " Songs of Farewell " written by Sir Hubert Parry for the years 1914–16 ; and Sir C. Villiers Stanford's song for bass solo and chorus (the vocalist being Mr. Plunket Greene), summed up, in the words of Sir Henry Newbolt's poem, " Farewell," the sacrifice, death, reunion, and immortality.

When the concert was over Mr. Balfour and Lord Derby came upon the platform, just in front of which stood a laurel-wreathed replica of Mr. Richard Belt's bust of Lord Kitchener, the original of which, cast from captured cannon, is in the War Office. It was Mr. Balfour's office to read the verses of Ecclesiasticus (xliv. 1–14), beginning " Let us now praise famous men," which are familiar to all public school and university men as the passage commonly read in commemoration of the founders and benefactors of colleges.

" There be of them, that have left a name behind them, that their praises might be reported.

" And some there be, which have no memorial ; who are perished, as though they had never been ; and are become as though they had never been born ; and their children after them. . . .

" But these were merciful men, whose righteousness hath not been forgotten. . . .

" Their seed shall remain for ever, and their glory shall not be blotted out."

This commemoration—ringingly pronounced—of heroes, renowned or nameless, was followed in profound silence and reverence. When it was over, Lord Derby came forward to read the Order of Battle of the First Seven Divisions. First came the names of Field-Marshal Lord French, the principal officers of the General Staff, and the commanders of the four Army Corps ; and loud were the cheers from the khaki-filled boxes and galleries at the names of the great captains. Then the trumpets and drums of the Coldstream Guards, under Major Mackenzie Rogan, broke into the " Fall In," and from the far end of the hall in marched the pipers and drums of the Scots Guards, to swing straight up the centre, playing as they went. Lord Derby then resumed his reading, taking Division by Division, giving the name of the officer commanding and the numbers and titles of the several units of Cavalry, Artillery, Engineers, and Infantry in each. And when the " Regulars " had all been announced, Lord Derby read out the Yeomanry and the Territorial Battalions which had left as reinforcements to the Expeditionary Force before the 23rd November, 1914. Cheering and clapping and crowing came from the gallant 700 ; cries of " Good old this ! " and " Good old that ! " and an interchange of professional banter.

From the liveliness of these moments the gathering passed to a different mood. The singing by all present of the hymn " For all the Saints," to Dr. Vaughan Williams's music, left many eyes filled with tears, which were openly wiped away while the drums and trumpets challenged sorrow with the Reveillé. As their inspiriting clangour died down a voice was heard calling from somewhere below the Royal box for three cheers for the First Seven Divisions ; but the assembly was scarcely in the mood for cheering. The final singing of the National Anthem provided a more appropriate outlet for feeling that was as grave as it was tense.

The music, all by living Englishmen, was wisely chosen and splendidly sung. After the Cockaigne Overture, which gained point by being taken at a brisk pace, came the manliest of English choral works—Vaughan Williams's " Towards the Unknown Region." It goes deep below the show of things to the great thoughts they embody, and in doing that it set the right tone of feeling for the commemoration. Its breadth and stature are realised for the first time in this large space, which, with such an audience and occasion, seemed its natural home. That could not be said of Howell's " Elegy " for strings which followed it, for it was with difficulty audible ; but we should have been sorry to miss hearing a work which so worthily, and with such promise, upholds the true tradition.

With Somervell's " To the Vanguard," now performed for the first time, the appeal was more direct and in so far less deep. The fault lay mainly with the poem, which has no impact, and contains no memorable line. Though the music does all that can be done with it, somehow it never sounded the note we were waiting to hear —that moment which lifts the particular to the universal, the transitory to the eternal. Miss Stiles-Allen made much of her short opportunity with a melodious soprano solo, and the tones of her voice, though tremulous, rang true.

The finest effort of the choir, consisting of the Bach Choir, supported by the Royal Choral Society, was heard in Parry's " There is an old belief." The words offer a sound starting-point, but the motet is a conspicuous instance of the power music has to illumine their message and drive home their meaning, as the setting sun and the incoming tide unite to transfigure a tall ship entering port. It was fitly followed by the song for bass and chorus, " Farewell," on which we did not know whether we were most deeply moved by Newbolt's words or Stanford's tones or Plunket Greene's voice, or by the time and place that made them what they were. Certainly Mr. Greene can seldom have had a more difficult task, or a task have shown more clearly what response the right man can make to it.

If there was anything in which the programme erred it was in a certain uniformity ; we wanted something like the Rondo of Beethoven's Funeral March sonata to cheer us up, and there would have been good military precedent for giving that turn to sad thoughts. Yet, perhaps, it was best as it was, now—and "For all the Saints," to Vaughan-Williams's tune, met the need in the best way. It would have been still better if the audience had noticed the intimation that their help was desired; some day they will sing it, and will realise what it has rescued them from.

The orchestra owned some human imperfections, but atoned for them nobly. Mr. Darke's organ accompaniment was in good taste. Dr. Allen's conducting is a wonderful combination of energy, modesty, and good sense. No one would get the impression that he was "doing it all"—yet he does a great deal, or, more truly, has done it before entering the room. He is there merely as one among others labouring for a cause he has at heart.

The following telegram was sent on Saturday to the Commanders-in-Chief of the British Forces in France, Italy, Egypt, Salonika, and Mesopotamia:

"Those assembled to-day in the Albert Hall, London, at a meeting honoured by the presence of their Majesties the King and Queen and Queen Alexandra to commemorate the heroic deeds of the First Seven Divisions, send their warmest greetings to all absent comrades and wish them good luck and a victorious homecoming."

CHAPTER XXVI

THE 1st BATTALION IN MESOPOTAMIA AND PALESTINE

JULY 1917 — THE ARMISTICE

DURING the summer of 1917, and before the 1st Battalion Manchester Regiment was again called upon to engage in further active operations, a change took place in the command of the Lahore Division, Major-General Keary relinquishing the command which he had held since the commencement of the war. On the 1st July he issued the following farewell order to the 1st Battalion Manchester Regiment :

1917

"*On my leaving the Division I desire to record my very high appreciation of the magnificent work done by your Battalion. From the day on which you saved the right of the British line at Givenchy in December 1914 to the end of my command you have always been in the forefront of the Battle. You have gained renown at Givenchy, at Ypres (2nd Battle), at Fauquissart, at Richebourg St. Vaast, at Loos, at Dujailah, at Beit Aiessa, Mohamed Abdul Hussain and Jebel Hamrin, not to mention numerous other battles of all magnitudes in which you have not perhaps played so prominent a part. Whenever I have had the Battalion in the line of battle I could feel confident that, whatever the odds, I had an unshakable unit to fall back upon.*

"*I believe I am right in stating that in every battle you have invariably gained your objective at whatever cost you have had to pay, and that if you have not always been able to hold on, it has been because there were too few left to do so.*

"*Your battle record must be equal to that of any in the Army.*

"*In addition to the gallantry and devotion shown in action, your discipline, good behaviour and willingness to help others at all times, have been a most marked feature which has done so much to lighten the work of myself and all in command.*

"*I regret I have not been able to say these words of farewell in person as I should have wished, but I shall never forget the services of the Battalion, for which I tender my fullest praise and thanks.*

"*In conclusion let me wish you all a hearty farewell and every good fortune wherever the future may take you.*

"*(signed) H. D'U. Keary, Major-General.
Comdng. 3rd Division.*"

General Keary was succeeded by Major-General Hoskins.

Training was carried out despite the great heat, to which at the end of July several men of the battalion succumbed, for during this month the temperature rose considerably higher than it had done during either of the previous summers passed by Anglo-Indian troops in this part of the world.

At the end of August the battalion moved to a new camp at Istabulat, where perimeter trenches had to be dug as protection in case of attack by hostile aircraft, for the Army Commander at Baghdad had to be ready for a possible active offensive campaign on the part of the enemy, since it was reported that general superintendence over the Ottoman operations was about to be exercised by the well-known German soldier, von Falkenhayn.

" During the closing days of September two important operations were carried out with a view partly to extending the area under control of the Anglo-Indian forces, and partly to depriving the enemy of valuable sources of supply. The first was the occupation of Mendali on the Persian frontier about 50 miles E. of Bakuba, which was effected on the 29th by a cavalry force after a sharp skirmish. The second, a much more serious affair, was a carefully prepared attack by General Brooking with his 15th Division upon Ramadi on the Euphrates above Feluja, where a Turkish force had been in position all the summer. This undertaking proved a signal success. . . . 3,500 prisoners, 13 guns, and 10 machine guns fell into the hands of the victors. . . . Having rendered the position on the Euphrates secure, Maude now turned his attention to his right flank beyond Sharaban, and in the middle of October a number of columns operating in concert succeeded in occupying the whole of the section of the Jebel Hamrin range of hills which is situated to the west of the Diala, and also portions of the range to the E. of that river." [1]

These operations led naturally to others which became necessary for disposing of certain Turkish contingents which all the summer had been assembled on the Tigris to the N. of Samarra, and which would have to be defeated before the British General could advance against Kifri and Kirkuk, his next objectives.

The 3rd Division was employed in the operations against the Turks in

---

[1] Callwell, *Life of Sir Stanley Maude*, pp. 296, 297.

the Samarra direction, and the part played in them by the 1st Battalion Manchester Regiment must now be described in as much detail as possible.

The first intimation that active work was in view was received at 3 p.m. on the 22nd October, when it was reported that a body of the enemy had been located N. of the Al Ajik position N. of Samarra, while later in the day an enemy aeroplane flew low over the camp and dropped several bombs, doing, however, little or no damage.

On the night of the 23rd the battalion marched to a point just west of Mansuriah, where it was learnt that the enemy had evacuated his position; but on the 31st while quartered at Samarra Post orders were received that the 8th Brigade was to concentrate at Samarra in view of operations on the right bank of the Tigris north of that place.

At 1 p.m. on the 1st November the companies moved off independently to the concentration area, and at 6 o'clock the brigade marched to join the 7th Division to which it was to form a reserve, and continued the march throughout the night to a point opposite Daur, 18 miles up-stream from Samarra. Second Lieutenant Hart, Devon Regiment, attached, was detailed to assist the officer guiding the column, Second Lieutenant Oxley acted as liaison officer between brigade headquarters and the R.F.C., Captain Cosgrove was liaison officer with brigade headquarters, and Second Lieutenant Cooper was in charge of the brigade section of the motor convoy.

About 3.30 a.m. on the 2nd November the column halted until dawn, when the 19th and 28th Brigades of the 7th Division marched on, the 8th Brigade moving in an easterly direction towards a point to the S. of Daur about an hour later. The Manchesters formed the rear battalion. Soon after leaving the halting place hostile aeroplanes appeared and dropped some eight bombs near the column, without, however, causing any casualties. The battalion rested until 4 p.m. in a nullah S. of Daur and some three miles from the river, and then moved on a further three miles to another nullah, known afterwards as Jullundur Nullah, where great-coats and rations were issued.

At 7 a.m. on the 3rd the brigade marched to the bivouac of the cavalry and 7th Division near the observation posts behind the first-line trench of the old Turkish position, and remained there throughout the day as divisional reserve. On this day the Turks were driven from the Daur position by the 21st and 28th Brigades, and in the evening the Manchesters were back again at Jullundur Nullah, where orders were received that the 7th Division was moving back to Mukshafa and that the 8th Brigade was to cover its retirement by taking up a picquet line near the Broad Wadi. These orders were subsequently cancelled, the battalion remaining about Jullundur Nullah during the whole of the 4th November, on the evening of which day fresh orders were published regarding further operations to take place on the day following.

The Turks retreating from the Daur position had been followed up by the cavalry and part of the infantry force under General Cobbe and had been shelled in their trenches at Tekrit. This was their river head on the Tigris ever since March, and here they had built an elaborate trench system, seven miles in circumference, with both ends on the river, and with strong rear-guard positions thrown back several miles to the north.

At 7.30 p.m. on the 4th November the 8th Brigade, including the battalion, moved off in the direction of Tekrit. About an hour before dawn on the 5th the column was halted, and then, day having broken, the battalion, and the remaining units of the 8th Brigade, marched in artillery formation to secure the Jibin Wadi. During this advance the battalion came under heavy artillery fire, but though the fire was extremely accurate the Manchesters were fortunate and very few casualties occurred. On arrival at the Jibin Wadi the battalion was held in brigade reserve while the remaining regiments advanced to attack the Turkish positions covering Tekrit.

A historian of the Mesopotamian Campaign [1] writes: " The first assault was delivered by the 8th Brigade on the enemy's centre at 11.30 a.m. The 59th Rifles on the right, the 47th Sikhs on the left, with the 124th Baluchis in support, advanced with great dash over a distance of 1,200 yards and captured the enemy's trenches on the front of attack. The Manchesters went in at 1 p.m."

" About 12.45 p.m.," so it is recorded in the official diary, " the battalion was ordered to attack a portion of the enemy position near Iman Arbain. No. 2 Company led the attack, followed by Nos. 4, 3, and 1 in the order named in the usual attack formation. Battalion headquarters was pushed forward with the rear company and communication was established with brigade headquarters through the headquarters of the 59th Rifles. On the way up Lieutenant Milne was killed and Lieutenant Towers wounded."

" There was some sticky fighting," writes the author of *The Long Road to Baghdad*, " in a complicated warren of trenches for the next three and a half hours. Twice the enemy counter-attacked in force and were driven off. The ground was broken, the trench system irregular, and it was very difficult to know exactly where the Turks were."

At 2 p.m. a message timed 1.50 was received by runner from Major Beadle, 59th Rifles, asking that his Dogra Company, 300 yards to the right,

[1] Candler, vol. ii, p. 241.

might be reinforced. This message was intercepted by Captain Hobkirk, commanding No. 1 Company, and acted upon immediately, and attempts were now made to connect up the companies in the front line with battalion headquarters, and about 3.30 p.m. communication was established with No. 3 Company on the right. In the meantime a message sent off at 3 p.m. was received by a runner from the officer commanding No. 3 Company, stating roughly the situation and saying that further advance was impossible.

At 3.40 it was reported that the Turks were emerging from Tekrit for a counter-attack and artillery support was called for, while ammunition, bombs, and Lewis-gun magazines were collected and sent up to the front line, but the counter-attack was broken up before it could materialise. At 5.30 Captain and Adjutant Adams was wounded and Second Lieutenant Hart was called up to take his place.

To quote here again from Mr. Candler's history : " I found Henderson with a small group of Manchesters holding a forward salient, enfiladed on both sides, with his right flank apparently in the air. He had just driven off a counter-attack, and soon after I came up he received a telephone message that the Seaforths and 125th Rifles were going to attack. The Staff, of course, knew the line we held and our gunners made no mistakes, but an idea of the complicated nature of the ground in front may be gathered from the fact that the Manchesters were expecting the advance of the Seaforths on their right. Henderson put up a blue flag to indicate the end of the line he held in this direction, but while we were waiting for the Seaforths to come up on our right, a heavy barrage opened on an area three-quarters of a mile to the S.W., well behind us on our left at a point we thought clear of the enemy. We saw our line rise from their trenches and walk slowly over the ground, an advance of about 700 yards, while our artillery put in a most effective bombardment. . . . We realised that this was the attack of the Seaforths, very far from the point where we expected it."

At about 5 p.m. a message was received from brigade headquarters that the enemy was retiring in front of the Seaforths and that the battalion was to follow up, but the action was practically over. The Turks in the trenches threw up their hands or fled, the 13th Hussars and 13th Indian Lancers charged and completed the demoralisation of the enemy, and early on the morning of the 6th the town of Tekrit was in our hands ; during the following night the whole enemy force withdrew to Shoreimiya.

Early on the morning of the 6th the 8th Brigade was assembled at the Jibin Wadi, when it was found that the casualties of the battalion totalled 106, made up as follows : *killed or died of wounds*, Lieutenant D. F. Milne, Second Lieutenant W. G. F. Baldry, Essex Regiment, attached, and 12 other ranks ; *wounded*, Captain and Adjutant F. H. Adams, Lieutenant F. Towers, Second Lieutenant G. E. Mann, East Surrey Regiment, attached, and 89 non-commissioned officers and men.

During the operations, and while the battalion was halted during the 7th and 8th November at the Jibin Wadi, many congratulatory messages were received : thus on the 4th General Cobbe sent the following to the G.O.C. 8th Division : "*Good luck! Am confident that the dash and staunchness shown by your brigade since Givenchy 1914 will carry you to brilliant success to-morrow.*" From the general in command of the 7th Division, General Fane,[1] himself an ex-officer of the Manchester Regiment, came on the 6th :

"*8th Infantry Brigade did splendidly yesterday and it is an honour to have had them under my command. The main brunt of the attack fell on them and they broke the backbone of Turkish resistance.*"

The message from the G.O.C. Third Corps ran as follows : "*Hearty congratulations on your splendid success at Tekrit from G.O.C. and all ranks Third Corps*"; while on the 8th the following came from Army Headquarters through the 7th Division : "*General Maude wires well done indeed! My best congratulations on your rapidity of execution and on gallantry and fine tenacity of all ranks. General Cobbe wishes again to convey to all ranks his admiration of their accustomed gallantry which has gained so great a success.*"

On the 10th the 8th Brigade moved to Daur, and on the next day the column marched in very great heat via Huwaislat to Samarra, which was reached about midday on the 12th ; but on the 16th the battalion moved again, to Izakhi, and changed places with the 2nd Battalion Leicester Regiment, finding garrisons for the section of the Samarra defences allotted to the brigade, providing supply train escorts, etc. Here the Manchesters remained until the end of the year 1917, the only excitement during this period being occasional visits from hostile aircraft, which dropped bombs but did no damage and caused no casualties.

There was, however, one dire misfortune which in November overtook the forces in Mesopotamia, and deprived the army operating in that distant theatre of war of the commander under whom the earlier mistakes of the campaign had been rectified and British honour and prestige revived—a commander, moreover, whom every man serving in the Mesopotamia army had learnt to love and respect. On the 16th November General Sir Stanley Maude was taken ill and by the evening of the same day the malady was

---

[1] Appointed Colonel, Manchester Regiment, in January 1920 *vice* Major-General Barnard deceased.

definitely diagnosed to be cholera in a virulent form. The general had been very insistent that his subordinates should be inoculated against this fell disease, but he had omitted this very necessary precaution in his own case, believing that a man of his age was immune. From the outset there was but little hope of recovery, and on the evening of Sunday the 18th November the general passed peacefully away. " Thus our beloved commander," writes the clergyman who was with him at the last, " left us, victor, as always, over the last great enemy."

The command of the army in Mesopotamia was now assumed by Lieutenant-General Sir William Marshall.

The 1st Battalion Manchester Regiment passed the winter months of 1917–18 in camp at Izakhi, going through various forms of military training ; on the 9th January 1918 a reinforcement of 141 non-commissioned officers and men joined the battalion, and on the 23rd Second Lieutenants Heath of the regiment and Jack of the Essex Regiment arrived with a further draft of 48 more. In this month the services of officers and non-commissioned officers were asked for to serve with various levies now being locally raised, and Captain Henderson, a company sergeant-major, and four lance-corporals were posted to the Armenian Irregulars.

In February intimation was received that the battalion would very shortly move to an altogether different and as yet unvisited theatre of war, and on the 15th March it marched to the Samarra Railway station and entrained for Baghdad. While the battalion was entraining the corps commander arrived, said " good-bye " to each individual officer, and before leaving called to the other ranks—" Good-bye, Manchesters ! "

Baghdad was reached at 5 p.m. and the battalion marched about six miles downstream to Hinaidi and occupied the rest camp. Here on the 16th the following officers joined—Captain Shipster and Second Lieutenants McCutcheon and Parsons.

Leaving Hinaidi on the 17th in two parties, the First Manchesters moved by rail and river, via Kut and Amara to Nahr Umar, where the battalion was concentrated between the 6th and 8th April awaiting embarkation orders. These arrived on the 9th, when it was found that the Manchesters were to proceed to their new destination at a strength of 31 officers and 900 other ranks only, with the result that Captain Hobkirk, Second Lieutenant McCutcheon, and 241 non-commissioned officers and men were found to be extra to the required establishment, and these were consequently left behind at the Base Depot at Basra.

The battalion embarked on the morning of the 10th at Nahr Umar in the hired transport *Aronda* and sailed for Koweit; here it was transferred to the transport *Ixion*, sailing on the afternoon of the 12th in company with the following units:

> 372nd, 373rd, and 374th Batteries, R.F.A.
> 72nd Heavy Battery, R.A.
> 2nd Battalion Dorsetshire Regiment.
> 133rd Machine Gun Company.
> Headquarters, 9th Infantry Brigade.

Suez was reached on the 23rd April and, disembarking, the battalion was sent by train to Ismailia, whence it marched some two miles to Moascar, where camp was pitched and where all ranks were employed in various forms of military training.

On the 17th 5 officers—Captain Rigby, Second Lieutenants Lyons, Jones, Blocksidge, and McCutcheon—and 207 other ranks rejoined from Mesopotamia, while on the 20th Captains Fitzpatrick and Minchin, Lieutenants Wilson, Clifford, and Goodman with 75 non-commissioned officers and men arrived from No. 2 British Base Depot at Kantara; these reinforcements once again brought the battalion over the authorised strength, and on the 23rd to 29th May the following were returned to No. 2 Depot: Lieutenant Towers, Second Lieutenants Lyons, Jones, Blocksidge, Clifford, Heath, Wilson, Newbold, and Nicholson, and 179 other ranks.

The 3rd Lahore Division had been ordered to Egypt to take the place of other divisions, and particularly the 74th, which had been sent from Egypt to France; and the consequent reorganisation of the force under General Sir Edmund Allenby's command had, for a time at least, prevented operations of any scope being undertaken, and had rendered necessary the adoption of a policy of active defence. It was not until the middle of June that the last units of the 3rd Division disembarked in Egypt. It was now under the command of Major-General A. R. Hoskins, C.M.G., D.S.O., the 8th Brigade commander being Brigadier-General S. M. Edwards, C.B., C.M.G., D.S.O., and the brigade was composed pretty much as it had now been for many months past, containing the 1st Battalion Manchester Regiment, the 47th Sikhs, the 59th Scinde Rifles, and the 2nd Battalion 124th Baluchistan Infantry.

The battalion remained some time at Moascar, for it was not until the 23rd that it marched by way of El Fedan to Kantara, leaving there on the 24th in three trains for Ludd. Here the division joined the 21st Corps under Lieutenant-General Sir Edward Bulfin, K.C.B., C.V.O., and relieved the 54th Division in the front line from Kh. Umm-el-Ikba to near

Tel-el-Mukhmar, a length of nearly eight miles. The 21st Corps at this time was composed of the 3rd (Lahore), 7th (Meerut), 54th, and 75th Divisions, and there were also attached to it the 60th Division, a French detachment, the 5th Australian Light Horse Brigade, 2 brigades of pack artillery, and 18 batteries of heavy and siege artillery.

On first arrival the brigade was in divisional reserve, the battalion being in bivouac at Wilhelma about Red House Wood, and its duties being mainly confined to training of various kinds, while officers and non-commissioned officers were sent on trips to the front line to obtain information regarding positions to be taken up by the battalion when it should move to the front line, and individuals were detached to attend various courses. All ranks were also by turn inoculated against cholera.

On the night of the 17th July the Manchesters marched up in relief of the Dorsets to the Mejdel Yaba position, coming under a desultory shrapnel fire while the relief was in progress, but no casualties were incurred. There was shelling daily by the enemy and on the 20th two men of the battalion were hit, one, Private Davis, dying of his wounds. Every night patrols, either observation or fighting, went out towards the enemy's lines, and on the night of the 23rd Lieutenant Jack and a fighting patrol encountered a strong Turkish patrol near Bureid Ridge, and the following report of what occurred was forwarded by Lieutenant-Colonel Hardcastle to the G.O.C. 8th Brigade :

" One party of the enemy was first observed about 160 yards away from where the patrol had taken up its position on Bureid Ridge, and moving to the right flank of the patrol, apparently with a view to surrounding it. At least 20 men were observed on this flank and others were still following, but the attention of the sergeant who was counting them was attracted elsewhere when he had counted that number. A party of the enemy, about 30 strong, was also at this time reported 70 yards away and another party of between 50 and 60 men was suddenly observed on the patrol's right flank. This party was about 20 yards away. Apparently our patrol had been observed by the enemy—on the right in the Observation Post—reported by the 59th Rifles.

" One of the patrol who was with Lieutenant Jack states that that officer threw several bombs at a party of the enemy and also emptied his revolver into them. The patrol was then firing at point-blank range, and it is practically certain that several casualties were inflicted on them. The reason one party of the Turks was able to get as near as 20 yards was that the attention of the men at that part of the position was attracted to the party reported to be 60 yards away, and they were waiting to get close up before opening fire, according to Lieutenant Jack's instructions.

"Lieutenant Jack then, seeing one party so close and a larger party further off, and knowing that his right flank was turned, ordered his patrol to withdraw. Lieutenant Jack's orders to the patrol were:

"'Withdraw to the bottom of the hill fighting.' These orders were heard by most of the patrol. Half the patrol returned right to the bottom of the hill; the remainder withdrew slowly. Lieutenant Jack's servant had been wounded and Lieutenant Jack and Private Bullman attempted to carry him away, but owing to the proximity of the enemy, and to the fact that the servant was obviously dead (this was afterwards found to be so) they were unable to take him so far. They were followed down to the gully by the Turks and fired on from the lower slopes of the Harem Ridge, fortunately without any further casualties.

"Lieutenant Jack is reported by all N.C. officers and men of his patrol to have behaved splendidly, and it was greatly owing to his coolness and skill that his party managed to get away so successfully.

"The full particulars of this action have only now been ascertained, owing partly to the reticence of Lieutenant Jack, who is of a somewhat retiring nature and not given to making the most of his own deeds, and partly to his being greatly upset at the death of his servant, who had volunteered to go out on patrol with him.

"Sergeant Woods, who was the N.C.O. with Lieutenant Jack, volunteered to go over the ground in daylight, and with a few men succeeded in bringing in the body of Private Roberts together with his rifle, bayonet, and equipment. As this is the first time that Lieutenant Jack has ever been in action I consider that his behaviour is worthy of special notice.

"I desire to bring to notice the following N.C. officer and men who have been recommended by Lieutenant Jack:

"No. 26740 Sergeant C. H. Woods.
,, 46932 Private L. G. Bullman.
,, 203915 ,, J. Carney.
,, 453 ,, A. E. Simpson.
,, 1277 ,, J. Kelly."

During the remainder of July, the whole of the month of August, and the early part of September, the battalion remained in much the same positions, taking its share of duty in the front line and sending out patrols nightly towards the enemy; and when "resting" in rear being engaged in training of all kinds and making preparations for the final advance which everybody knew could not much longer be delayed. Finally on the 18th September the 1st Battalion Manchester Regiment concentrated at Ras-el-Ain to take part in the general attack and advance arranged for the following day.

To quote from General Allenby's despatch of the 31st October 1918:

" I entrusted the attack on the enemy's defences in the coastal plain to Lieutenant-General Sir Edward Bulfin, K.C.B., C.V.O., commanding the 21st Corps. . . . I ordered him to break through the enemy's defences between the railway and the sea, to open a way for the cavalry, and at the same time to seize the foothills S.E. of Jiljulieh. The 21st Corps was then to swing to the right, on the line Hableh-Tulkeram, and then advance in a N.E. direction through the hills, converging on Samaria and Attara, so as to drive the enemy up the Messudie-Jenin road into the arms of the cavalry at El Afule. I ordered Lieut.-General Sir Harry Chauvel, K.C.B., K.C.M.G., commanding the Desert Mounted Corps, less the Australian and New Zealand Mounted Division, to advance along the coast directly the infantry had broken through and had secured the crossings over the Nahr Falik. On reaching the line Jelameh-Hudeira he was to turn N.E., cross the plains of Samaria, and enter the Plain of Esdraelon at El Lejjun and Abu Shusheh. Riding along the plain the Desert Mounted Corps was to seize El Afule, sending a detachment to Nazareth, the site of the Yilderim Headquarters. Sufficient troops were to be left at El Afule to intercept the Turkish retreat there. The remainder of the Corps was to ride down the Valley of Jezreel and seize Beisan."

On the 18th September a large force of bombing aeroplanes was directed over Nablus, where it was known the enemy had his main telephone and telegraph exchange. This was completely destroyed, a fact which played an important part in enabling our cavalry to reach the Plain of Esdraelon next day, before the enemy G.H.Q. knew they had broken through.

" The Turkish line on the plain consisted of two defensive positions, well constructed and heavily wired. The first, 14,000 yards in length and 3,000 in depth, ran along a sandy ridge in a north-westerly direction from Bir Adas to the sea. It consisted of a series of works connected by a continuous network of fire trenches. The second, or El Tira system, 3,000 yards in the rear, ran from the village of that name to the mouth of the Nahr-el-Falik. On the enemy's extreme right the ground, except for a narrow slip along the coast, was marshy, and could only be crossed in a few places. The defence of the second system did not, therefore, require a large force." [1]

" Before the operations began the 20th Corps took over the extreme right of the 21st Corps line from Berukin to Rafat, reducing the front of the 21st Corps from 25¼ miles to 21¼ miles. The formations taking part in the attack and the frontages allotted to them were:

" French Detachment	5,900 yards.
54th Division	9,500 ,,
3rd Lahore Division	11,300 ,,
75th Division	1,900 ,,
7th Meerut Division	5,500 ,,
60th Division	3,300 ,,
5th Australian Light Horse Brigade.	

" The big differences in the frontages allotted to the divisions were due to the fact that the fronts of the 54th and 3rd Divisions included the wide gap between Mejdel Yaba and Ferekiyeh which was only watched by the two divisions. . . . All the formations were employed in the initial attack and there was no corps reserve." [2]

At 4.30 a.m. on the 19th the four hundred guns concentrated on the front of attack opened an intense fire on the Turkish positions, and the five infantry divisions dashed forward to the assault.

" The 3rd Lahore Division," having the 54th Division on the right and the 75th on the left and attacking on a front of 1,800 yards, " were to advance with their left on the road from Hadrah to El Tira. Two hard nuts to crack lay in their path. One was Brown Hill about 200 yards E. of the road, and the other Fir Hill 2,000 yards farther east. Both were deeply entrenched and connected up by various ways cut into the earth, and behind them the Jewish village of Sabieh had been made a strong place by an elaborate trench system E. and N.E. of the village. After capturing the two hills and the Sabieh defences the 3rd Division were to move eastwards against the villages of Jiljulieh and Kalkilieh, the latter between two and three miles N. of the former. Jiljulieh was covered on the W. by a strongly fortified rise known as the Railway Redoubt, about three-quarters

---

[1] Preston, *The Desert Mounted Corps*, pp. 198, 199.
[2] Massey, *Allenby's Final Triumph*, pp. 126, 127.

of a mile long. Subsequently the 3rd Division was to link up with the 54th Division in the foothills."[1]

In the 3rd Division the 7th Brigade attacked Bir Adas and Fir Hill, while the 8th, held at first in divisional reserve, moved towards Jiljulieh, but in order to avoid casualties only one company of the Manchesters, No. 4 under Captain Minchin, was to be engaged.

In the right attack by the 7th Brigade, the 2/7th Gurkhas captured the trenches N.W. of Bir Adas, the 27th Punjabis those on the W. of Fir Hill, while the 1st Battalion Connaught Rangers carried the main Fir Hill defences against considerable resistance. On the left, the 2nd Battalion Dorsets and 1/1st Gurkhas seized Brown Hill and Hill 283 respectively. The 8th Brigade was now ordered to attack Jiljulieh Village and Railway Redoubt, and the following is the story of the share taken in the action by Captain Minchin's company of the 1st Battalion Manchester Regiment:

"2.30 a.m.—No. 4 Company under Captain Minchin left Ras-el-Ain and proceeded N. along railway to within 600 yards of Turkish picquet post.

"4.35 a.m.—Occupied post with one platoon, 2 shots were fired from it and enemy fled. Platoon pushed 300 yards forward in N.E. direction and consolidated. About 4.30 a.m. enemy shelled mound heavily and continued to do so, also brought a machine gun to bear.

"5 a.m.—Another platoon advanced 150 yards N. of Jiljulieh Bridge, which was swept continuously by two enemy machine guns. Until the mist cleared about 9.30 a.m. it was impossible to locate the machine guns which were in a building in Jiljulieh. A third platoon rushed the small trench and captured 3 prisoners, but in pressing on were caught by a machine gun in some rush huts. Owing to casualties this platoon withdrew to slight cover. Second Lieutenant Raeside was hit at this time together with his platoon sergeant.

"10.15.—Remainder of battalion moved N. along railway embankment in touch with No. 4 company by telephone. Supported the attack on Railway Redoubt," by 2nd Battalion 124th Baluchis, with Lewis gun and rifle fire.

"10.45.—Artillery gave Jiljulieh 5 minutes' bombardment, which drove enemy out. No. 4 Company, supported by No. 1, advanced on Jiljulieh, entering village, after which companies were re-organised.

[1] Massey, p. 129.

"11.40.—Remainder of battalion reached Jiljulieh, and Battalion advanced 11.55 on Hableh Ridge, coming under rifle fire.

"12.45.—In position on Hableh Ridge.

"15.45.—Advanced due E. along ridge to Kh. Ras-el-Tira in support of 59th Rifles, and, 17.45, went into bivouac.

"By nightfall on the 19th the Division held a line about two miles W. of Kh. Kefr Thilth and Azzun on the right, with its left resting on Jiyus."[1]

The casualties this day in the 1st Battalion Manchester Regiment amounted to 3 men killed, Second Lieutenant Raeside and 16 other ranks wounded. But in the day's operations the 21st Corps had captured 7,000 prisoners, over 100 guns, 170 machine guns, and an immense quantity of war material.

"General Bulfin ordered a further general advance eastward to be started at 5 a.m. on the 20th. During the night the 5th Australian Light Horse Brigade had got so far across the hills N.E. of Tulkeram that they were able to destroy half a mile of the Turkish railway about Ajjeh, but there were far too many troops in their path to enable them to reach Jenin and they returned to Tulkeram. . . . When the 8th Brigade of the 3rd Division started their forward movement they were hotly opposed by strong German rearguards, and although the left of the 54th Division gave them assistance, seven hours' fighting only took the brigade to a point one mile E. of Azzun. The opposition against the 7th as well as the 8th Brigade continued to be stubborn until late in the afternoon, when it weakened and both brigades pushed rapidly on to El Funduk, where they captured 250 prisoners, 15 guns, and a large quantity of war material. The 9th Brigade met with less resistance, and passing through Baka at noon got to Kefr Kaddum and Kuryet Jit before it was dark."[2]

Here is the battalion account of the happenings on the 20th September:

"04.30.—Continued advance due E." towards village of Kh. Kefr Thilth.

"05.30.—Enemy opened fire on advance guard.

"07.00.—Held up again by rifle and machine gun (3) fire, also artillery fire from gun posted at cross roads.

"09.00.—59th Rifles passed through battalion and were in turn held up by enemy rearguard holding high ground.

"12.45.—Enemy retreated.

[1] *The Advance of the Egyptian Expeditionary Force*, p. 57. [2] Massey, p. 170.

" 14.00.—Advanced, still supporting 59th Rifles, along, but S., of road to bivouac at 18.00."

The country advanced over was so rugged that artillery support could not be afforded, but the retreat of the enemy was hastened by other brigades working round and threatening the Turkish line of retreat. While passing through Kh. Kefr Thilth Lieutenant Hart, 3rd Battalion Devonshire Regiment, attached, was shot through the heart; while in the course of the day's fighting Captain Shipster was mortally wounded, dying before he could be brought to the field ambulance, and Second Lieutenant Lund and 10 non-commissioned officers and men were wounded.

It had been a very hard and fatiguing day, for the battalion had been continuously in action the greater part of the 19th and 20th, carrying Lewis guns and ammunition all the time over very rough country and through a practically waterless tract. The animals with the brigade were without water for forty-eight hours.

The division halted for the night of the 20th–21st September on the line El Funduk–Kuryet Jit–Kefr Kaddum.

On the 21st the advance was continued in a N.E. direction, the 8th Brigade moving in support of the 7th and Nos. 1 and 2 Companies of the battalion covering the right flank. The advance was over even worse country than that already passed over, while the road was for many miles littered with abandoned guns and material. The day was a very hot and trying one, but the 9th Brigade alone of the 3rd Division encountered any opposition.

The battalion passed through Samaria to the village of Beit Imrin and took up an outpost line from there to the top of the hill of Sheik Beiazid, 2,388 feet above sea-level, and the slopes of which were so steep that it was impossible to get up the mules with rations and water.

This night the 3rd Division occupied a line facing east astride the Tulkeram–Nablus road through Beit Udhen–Zawata–Jennesinia–Nusf Jebil, joining up with the 7th Division near Samaria.

After the 21st September there was no infantry action of importance, and only the mounted troops followed up the retreating Turks, pressing the enemy and consolidating the victories that all along the line had been gained. It must not be thought, however, that the trials of the infantry were over; for some time this arm was busily engaged in clearing the battle-fields, collecting and marching in prisoners, developing the water supply, making roads, and performing the very many other duties which remain to be done after an unprecedentedly rapid and successful advance.

By the 29th September the 3rd Division Headquarters was established at Hableh, while the battalion had marched back to and occupied Jiljulieh. The campaign in Palestine, and the long war, in the course of which the 1st Battalion Manchester Regiment had fought in France, in Flanders, in Mesopotamia, and in the Holy Land, was now drawing to an end. The Turks had realised that for the Central Powers, with whom they had thrown in their lot, victory was impossible ; negotiations were hurriedly opened and as hastily concluded, an armistice was arranged between the Allies and the Turks, and this came into force at noon on October 31st, followed on the 11th of the following month by the conclusion of an armistice with Germany.

Whether as the 63rd or 96th or as the 1st and 2nd Battalions of the Manchester Regiment whose lives are recorded in these pages, these two units of the British Army have fought all the world over, have taken part in almost every one of the many wars in which that army has been engaged, have helped to make and maintain the British Empire, and in so doing have cheerfully paid the inevitable price. In this the greatest of all wars both battalions worthily upheld the good name they had acquired, and if, as some men tell us, there will henceforth be no more war, then surely the Manchester Regiment has done its share to bring about an age of perpetual peace.

The Field-Marshal who commanded the British Armies in France, and under whom at one time or another both battalions of the regiment served, has paid a very noble and a very striking tribute to the men he commanded :

" The long years of patient and heroic struggle," he wrote, " by which the strength and spirit of the enemy were gradually broken down cannot be forgotten. The strain of those years was never ceasing, the demands they made upon the best of the Empire's manhood are now known. Yet throughout all those years, and amid the hopes and disappointments they brought with them, the confidence of our troops in final victory never wavered. Their courage and resolution rose superior to every test, their cheerfulness never failed, however terrible the conditions in which they lived and fought. By the long road they trod with so much faith and with such devoted and self-sacrificing bravery we have arrived at victory, and to-day they have their reward. . . .

" We have been accustomed to be proud of the great and noble traditions handed down to us by the soldiers of bygone days. The men who form the Armies of the Empire to-day have created new traditions which are a challenge to the highest records of the past, and will be an inspiration to the generations who come after us."

NOTE TO CHAPTER XXVI

MEDALS FOR THE WAR

In November 1917 Army Order 350 was published announcing that His Majesty the King had been graciously pleased to signify His pleasure to give a decoration—a Star in bronze—in recognition of the services of such of the military forces of the Crown as had served in France and Belgium under Field-Marshal Sir John French during the earlier phase of the war, from 5th August, 1914, to midnight of the 22nd–23rd November, 1914. No clasp was to be issued with this Star, the riband of which was to be red, white, and blue, shaded and watered.

Rather more than a year later—in December 1918—Army Order No. 20 of 1919 was published, stating that His Majesty was further pleased to recognise the services rendered by others of his military forces who served in theatres of war between the 5th August, 1914, and the 31st December, 1915, both dates inclusive. This decoration was in all respects identical with the "1914 Star," but those eligible for the first were not to receive the second.

Then in July 1919 it was announced in Army Order No. 266 that "His Majesty has been graciously pleased to signify His pleasure that a medal be granted to record the bringing of the war to a successful conclusion, and the arduous services rendered by His Majesty's forces," the medal being in silver and the riband being "centre orange, watered, with stripes of white and black on each side and with borders of Royal blue."

In the following month it was given out in Army Order No. 301 that the services of His Majesty's forces were to be further recognised by the grant of a second medal, to be designated "the Victory Medal," which was to be identical in design with that issued by the other Allied and Associated Powers. The medal was to be of bronze and without any clasps, the riband to be "red in the centre with green and violet on each side, shaded to form the colours of two rainbows."

CHAPTER XXVII

THE 1st BATTALION, 1918–1922

DEMOBILISATION AND RE-FORMATION. THE TROUBLE IN IRELAND

THE 1st Battalion Manchester Regiment remained in bivouac about Jiljulieh until the beginning of November, marching on the 3rd via Tulkeram and Zawata to Burkha, where a few days were spent; but on the 18th the battalion moved back to Tulkeram and entrained on the following day for Ludd, encamping in the Ramleh area and settling down to steady training. During the month 9 officers and 642 non-commissioned officers and men joined the Battalion. The officers were Lieutenants Edwards, Walker, Ingham, Blocksidge, Goodman, Slaney, and Parry, Second Lieutenants Holland and Eastwick.

1918

On the 15th December there was a fresh move, headquarters and Nos. 1 and 2 Companies proceeding by train to Jerusalem, where Nos. 3 and 4 joined two days later, the bulk of the battalion being quartered in the Russian Buildings and No. 3 Company in camp near the railway station, and in or about Jerusalem the battalion remained throughout the rest of its stay in Palestine.

During nearly the whole of the remainder of the month drafts of varying strength, but amounting in the aggregate to one officer and 167 other ranks, joined headquarters; some of these no doubt were men who had been away in hospital or on command, and who rejoined on discharge from hospital or the "shutting down" of the ex-regimental duties upon which they had been employed; but it was not until the last day of the month that an entry occurs in the Battalion War Diary, which shows that the process of reducing the Army was in swing and that demobilisation had actually commenced. The entry runs as follows: "The first demobilisation draft—64 W.O.'s, N.C.O.'s, and men—consisting of coal-miners and men not required in the *post-bellum* army, left for Kantara to await embarkation for the United Kingdom"; and something must now be said in explanation of the steps which had been taken by the authorities for dispersing the many millions of men who had formed the army which the British Government had raised and maintained in the field.

The war had only been six months in progress when the authorities realised that, when peace should again come upon us, very much more must be done than had in any of our previous campaigns been thought of or attempted, to minimise as far as could be the possible distress and inevitable confusion which must result from the sudden disbandment of some millions of men, the majority possessed of but small means and having no immediate prospect of earning money. It would, in fact, be quite impossible simply to " let the people depart, every man unto his inheritance " —for the excellent reason that few of them had an " inheritance " to which to go!

As far back as January 1915 a scheme was prepared and placed before the British Cabinet, containing suggestions for meeting the difficulties likely to be encountered on the conclusion of the war, and it was therein proposed to follow the experience and precedents of earlier wars as far as was desirable, but it was intended to offer a novel advantage in the way of a free insurance against unemployment, and to make use of certain existing organisations, such as the newly-created Labour Exchanges, for helping to provide suitable and congenial employment for the soldiers on final demobilisation. These proposals received Cabinet approval, but since at the time they were made there did not appear to be any immediate prospect of their becoming effective, they were provisionally laid aside. But as the war progressed various committees were set up to deal with the details of the general scheme of demobilisation, and by these it was decided to give each man the following advantages :

    (a) A furlough, with full pay and separation allowances for four weeks from date of demobilisation.
    (b) A railway warrant to his home.
    (c) A twelve-months policy of insurance against unemployment.
    (d) A money gratuity in addition to the ordinary Service gratuity.

Various alternative methods of dispersal were considered, and at first the principle was followed of granting release from army service in an order of priority determined by individual industrial qualifications, bearing in mind at the same time that the reconstruction of the Army must be taken in hand immediately upon the declaration of peace, and that such reconstruction must go hand in hand with demobilisation. The authorities, in fact, had drawn up their scheme with a bias in favour of national rather than of individual interests, and the men composing the Army were to be dispersed in accordance with the needs of the reconstruction of industry, and by individuals rather than by military units.

The scheme as at first announced and originally administered met with no little opposition both in the Army and in the Press, while a system of "Special Releases," which had formed no part of the original scheme, was justly open to the charge of "favouritism"; hopes of early discharge had been raised which it was not found possible to gratify, and men could not easily be made to understand that a large army must for some time to come be retained in being, since there was as yet no peace and there was no more than a cessation of hostilities; as a result of something of the nature of an "agitation," Army Order No. 55 of 1919 was introduced abolishing the principle of release on industrial grounds, and substituting that of demobilisation on the grounds of age and length of service.

Demobilisation actually began in December 1918, and, all things considered, proceeded with really remarkable smoothness and dispatch; before the end of February 1919 one million eight hundred and forty-eight thousand men had been returned to civil life, and of these 85 per cent. had re-entered industrial occupations. At one time between 5,000 and 6,000 men were daily quitting the Army; and in July 1919 the War Minister was able to state that nearly three million soldiers had been demobilised since the Armistice, leaving—inclusive of the 209,000 volunteer regular soldiers—no more than one million two hundred thousand men still in the Army.

A beginning towards complete demobilisation having thus been made, parties of varying strength now left the battalion at short but irregular intervals; thus, on the 6th January 1919, 25 non-commissioned officers and men "having over four years' continuous service with an expeditionary force" left the service companies; on the 19th, 160 more went away; 12 more on the 10th; on the 13th, 34 men left who were over 41 years of age; 40 went away on the 14th, 10 on the 21st, 42 on the 25th, and 18 on the 28th; parties of officers and men also proceeded to the United Kingdom on leave, while "other ranks" who had been for any considerable time in hospital were also evacuated. During February 162 men went home while a small draft came out; in March 372 non-commissioned officers and men were sent down to Kantara to await embarkation to the United Kingdom for demobilisation; and this seems to have temporarily exhausted the numbers of those due to go home, for no more men left during the next two and a half months, until on the 14th June the cadre of the battalion, composed of one officer—Lieutenant H. Ingham—C.S.M. Williamson and seven other ranks, was dispatched from Jerusalem to Transit Camp, Port Said, for embarkation, what was left of the 1st Battalion Manchester Regiment still remaining on in Jerusalem. During the last half of June 37 more men left the Regiment and the Army, and on

MEETING OF THE 1ST AND 2ND BATTALIONS, FARNHAM PARK, OCTOBER 13TH, 1919.

the 30th the day was observed as a general holiday in celebration of the signature of peace.

Some few men remained on in Palestine, their numbers getting gradually smaller, but continuing as a unit for rationing purposes and still known as the 1st Battalion Manchester Regiment, until nothing remained.

On the 9th July 1919 the 1st Battalion Manchester Regiment was re-formed at Blackdown, under the command of Lieutenant-Colonel E. Vaughan, C.M.G., D.S.O., by the transfer to it of officers and other ranks from the 3rd (Special Reserve) Battalion of the Regiment, then commanded by Lieutenant-Colonel C. M. Thornycroft, C.B.E., D.S.O., which then proceeded as a cadre to Ashton-under-Lyne. The following regular officers joined on the re-forming of the 1st Battalion : Lieutenant-Colonel E. Vaughan, C.M.G., D.S.O. ; Majors C. C. Stapledon and C. D. Irwin, M.C. ; Captains E. L. Musson, D.S.O., M.C., G. B. Martin, M.C., and A. W. U. Moore ; Lieutenants C. Cassidy, F. Haywood, M.C., J. R. Nicholson, F. V. Hollingworth, H. Harland, D.C.M., and A. G. Chittenden, with Major and Quartermaster P. O'Brien.

During the next few weeks many officers and men joined, and on the 1st October the battalion moved into Aldershot and occupied Salamanca Barracks ; on the 13th the 1st and 2nd Battalions had a memorable meeting, the Bishop of Winchester lending the grounds of Farnham Castle, whither the 1st Battalion marched from Aldershot and the 2nd from Bordon, and the Regiment spent the day together. On the 2nd November the 2nd Battalion marched into Aldershot for a review of the troops of the Command by the Shah of Persia, and was for this occasion included in the same brigade as the 1st Battalion.

Early in the New Year the Regiment experienced a great grief in the death on the 15th January, 1920, of its Colonel, Major-General W. O. Barnard. He had passed the whole of his regimental life in the Manchester Regiment, had commanded the 2nd Battalion for the full period, and had been Colonel of the Regiment since the 8th January 1904, and always maintained the keenest interest in his old Corps. General Barnard was buried at Twickenham on the 19th January, and his funeral was attended by representatives of all ranks of the Regiment. Major-General Sir V. B. Fane, K.C.I.E., C.B., Indian Army, formerly of the Regiment, was appointed Colonel in place of General Barnard.

During the preceding months the state of Ireland had been wholly deplorable and caused far more anxiety than had ever before been known in the history of the country. At the beginning of this year there were numerous raids by armed men on post offices with the object of obtaining money; there were many murderous attacks upon the police; and a reign of terror gradually became established in Ireland, where it was computed that between the 1st May 1916 and the 31st December 1919 there had taken place 18 murders, 77 armed attacks, numerous attacks upon policemen, soldiers, and civilians, 20 raids for arms and ammunition, 70 incendiary fires, and many other offences, totalling no fewer than 1,529. It was anticipated that the Home Rule Bill, which was introduced in Parliament on February 25th, would bring about " harmonious action between the parliaments of Southern Ireland and Northern Ireland," but its reception by the nationalist party was the reverse of cordial, if not indeed fiercely unfavourable. One Irish paper denounced it as a scheme for " the plunder and partition of Ireland," and as a " betrayal of every principle that was ever professed regarding democracy and nationality " ! In February and March the state of Ireland grew worse rather than better; almost daily fresh murders were reported and policemen were killed in all parts of the country.

The Government now decided to augment the garrison of Ireland, and at the end of March the 1st Battalion Manchester Regiment received orders to proceed thither. An advance party, under Major O'Meara, left Aldershot on the 30th March to take over quarters at Kilworth Camp, County Cork, and on the 1st April the battalion moved by train from Aldershot to Holyhead, embarked there in the *Slieve Gallion*, and, arriving on the 2nd at Dublin, was at once sent on by train via Fermoy to Kilworth, C Company, under Lieutenant-Colonel Evans, providing a detachment at Moore Park, Kilworth.

The following officers accompanied the battalion: Lieutenant-Colonels Vaughan (in command), Dorling, and Evans; Majors Stapledon, O'Meara, and Dearden; Captains Musson (Adjutant), Airy, Martin, and Moore; Lieutenants Grindel, Hollingworth, Moorhead, Pembroke, E. Orgill (Assistant Adjutant), Burkitt, Knibb (Transport Officer), and Morris; and Second-Lieutenant J. Orgill; with Major and Quartermaster O'Brien and Major Howorth, Education Officer.

The Company Commanders were:

    A Company, Major Stapledon.
    B   ,,   Major Dearden.
    C   ,,   Lieutenant-Colonel Evans.
    D   ,,   Major O'Meara.

The battalion now formed part of the 16th Infantry Brigade commanded by Brigadier-General Tyndall-Lucas, C.M.G., D.S.O., the Brigade being in the 6th Division, the commander of which was Major-General Sir

E. P. Strickland, K.C.B., C.M.G., D.S.O., under whom as lieutenant-colonel, the 1st Battalion Manchester Regiment had served during the early days of the Great War.

On the 10th July Headquarters, with B and D Companies, Band and Drums, left Kilworth by march route *via* Fermoy and Cork for Ballincollig, where it joined the 17th Infantry Brigade commanded by Brig.-General H. W. Higginson, C.B.; and on the following day the remaining two companies proceeded under command of Major O'Meara from Kilworth to Macroom, sending out from here detachments to Mill Street, Ballyvourney, and Inchigeela; and almost at once in some of these new garrisons the troops were made to feel as though they were foreign invaders, for at Mill Street the people showed some reluctance to sell articles of food to the soldiers, at Ballincollig the railway authorities refused to carry two truck-loads of military stores, on the 18th a soldier reported having been held up and searched by armed and masked men, while the road from Ballyvourney to Killarney was found to have been blocked and a military lorry travelling on it was burnt.

The state of Ireland during June had become worse rather than better: early in that month a daring raid was carried out in Dublin by a band of nearly 100 armed men; the same night attempts were made to capture three police barracks, two in King's County and another in Tipperary; while fresh difficulties were caused by the refusal of Irish railwaymen to handle munitions, and others declined to take charge of a train carrying a small party of 30 soldiers. Then at the end of the month Brigadier-General Lucas, Colonels Danford and Tyrrell of the Clonmel Military area, were kidnapped while upon a fishing excursion, Colonel Danford being seriously wounded in attempting to evade capture.

In July disorder continued to be rampant, murderous tactics were adopted by the Sinn Feiners, and several particularly brutal outrages were perpetrated in the south and especially in the Cork district. On the 20th July Captain Airy of the Manchester Regiment was wounded by a party of Sinn Feiners during an attack upon a convoy proceeding from Macroom to Ballyvourney, and died next day; three men of the Regiment were wounded at the same time and one of these also died later of his wounds. The following letters were received by the commanding officer in connection with this very sad occurrence: the General Officer Commanding the 17th Infantry Brigade wrote:

"*Please convey to all ranks who were in the lorry which was fired on by rebels between Macroom and Ballyvourney on 20th July my high appreciation of their soldierly conduct and firm discipline under most difficult circumstances. Their behaviour reflects the greatest credit on them and the battalion."*

While the letter from the Major-General Commanding the 6th Division runs :

" The discipline and general behaviour of all ranks on the 20th July in the lorry appears to have been excellent in that they got through with their arms and ammunition intact, in spite of severe casualties. I feel confident that the Battalion will always maintain this high standard of discipline in face of all events."

On the 25th July two officers were held up by armed rebels within three miles of Ballincollig; at least two attempts were locally made this month to induce British soldiers to sell their arms or ammunition; the roads in the vicinity of the English garrisons were repeatedly found to have had trenches dug across them; while on the 18th August an artillery subaltern attached to the battalion and four other ranks were wounded by rebel action during an attack on a bicycle patrol near Ballyvourney, the attacking party being composed of some 40 men armed and disguised.

On the 31st August Colonel Vaughan completed his period of command and was succeeded in command of the battalion by Lieutenant-Colonel F. H. Dorling, D.S.O.

The following day, at a point two-and-a-half miles from Ballincollig on the Dripsey road, a Crossley tender containing an officer and seven men was fired at by a party of rebels; motor patrols were constantly sent round the neighbouring country; on the 2nd October the mailbags were taken from the Cork–Macroom train, and on the same day the Ballyvourney mail was seized by masked men and the letters later returned marked " Censored, I.R.A."; while the military systematically searched the houses of suspected persons, much incriminatory Sinn Fein literature and rebel flags being found. In November the rebels became increasingly active and threatening, and many inquiries were made by them as to the movements of officers in the Ballincollig area, and the inquiries were especially persistent about Captain J. Thompson, who for the last six months had acted as Intelligence Officer with the 1st Battalion Manchester Regiment.

On the 21st November this officer was reported as missing; he had left barracks on his motor-cycle on the afternoon of the 20th: search parties sent out to the destination he had given when leaving barracks failed to trace him, and nothing was heard of him until the 22nd, when his dead body was found in a field $1\frac{1}{2}$ miles from barracks, with seven wounds in the head and two in the body; he had been blindfolded. Several arrests were made, but the murder was not brought home to anybody.

Early in December Martial Law was proclaimed in the following counties:

    The County of Cork (East Riding and West Riding),
    The County of the City of Cork,
    The County of Tipperary (North Riding and South Riding),
    The County of Limerick,
    The County of the City of Limerick,
    The County of Kerry;

while the " generals or other officers " commanding the 6th Division and 16th, 17th, 18th, and Kerry Brigades were appointed Military Governors, the proclamation ending with the somewhat belated announcement that " the Forces of the Crown are hereby declared to be on active service "! The effect of the institution of martial law was for a time good; the district seemed to quiet down and many of the I.R.A. officers were said to be " on the run," while there was a general reluctance to fill their places. Almost daily were motor patrols sent out, houses and hiding-places were searched, and considerable stores of ammunition and explosives were found in small quantities.

On the 28th January 1921, acting on " information received," a party of the battalion, consisting of Lieutenant-Colonel Evans, Lieutenants Sykes, E. Orgill, Tod, and Vining, with 60 non-commissioned officers and men, left barracks at 3.30 p.m. and proceeded in lorries and tenders to Dripsey to round up an ambush reported to be in position in that neighbourhood. The party, on reaching the vicinity, dismounted and advanced in five small bodies. Two of them under Lieutenants Tod and Orgill proceeded north to Peake Station and drove the country in a southerly direction towards the remaining parties which were advancing along the main road to Macroom. A prepared ambush, entrenched and occupied, was found on the north side of the main road. The rebels did not stand their ground on seeing the advance of Colonel Evans and his men, but fired a few rounds and fled across country, their flight being facilitated by the high stone and mud walls dividing the fields. Some 50 rebels here were armed with revolvers, shot-guns, and Lee-Metford rifles, while two of them were dressed in the khaki uniforms of British officers with Sam Browne belts. Two of the rebels were killed, 5 wounded and 5 unwounded men were captured, with some 22 firearms, some ammunition, and bombs. Colonel Evans' party suffered no casualties, and for this, and for the unusual success of the expedition, the officers and men had to thank a brave loyalist woman, Mrs. Lindsay of Coachford, who paid for her loyalty with her life.

Earlier in the day Mrs. Lindsay was motoring to her home with her butler-chauffeur, Joseph Clarke, when she saw a number of men in the distance evidently engaged in preparing an ambush for the police and soldiers, who she knew were that day to pass along the road where the Sinn Feiners were to be seen. Turning back she drove quickly to the Police Barracks and told the Inspector what she had noticed, with the result that Colonel Evans' party made a detour and surprised the rebels with the result above recorded.

A few days later Mrs. Lindsay was missing with her chauffeur, Clarke; weeks wore on and no trace of the two could be found, but it was feared that the rebels had learnt who had caused the failure of their ambush plans, and had kidnapped this brave lady and her equally brave manservant. Finally in July, de Valera, when engaged in conference with Mr. Lloyd George, was induced to inquire into the case, and the result was the receipt of the following remarkable letter by Mrs. Lindsay's sister:

"Dail Eireann,
Department of Defence.
29th July 1921.

"*Madam,*

"*In accordance with instructions from the President, I have made inquiries from our local commanders into the case of Mrs. Lindsay. The information sent us is that she was executed as a spy some months ago. The charge against her was that she was directly responsible for conveying to the enemy information which led to the execution of five of our men by the British authorities, to the death of the sixth from wounds received in action, and to a sentence of 25 years' penal servitude passed upon a seventh.*

"*Mrs. Lindsay wrote a letter to General Strickland pointing out the consequences to herself should our men be executed. They were executed, nevertheless. Five days after their execution in Cork Barracks the sentence which had been passed on Mrs. Lindsay, and suspended pending General Strickland's reply, was duly carried out.*

"*We regret the circumstances and stern necessity to protect our forces which necessitated this drastic action by our local commanders.*

"*(sd.) Cathal Brugha,*
Minister of Defence."

Never, it is to be hoped, will the Manchester Regiment forget Mrs. Lindsay's heroic action. A lady living alone in a rebel district, knowing well the danger she ran in giving information to the troops, did not hesitate to do her duty. It was a great example of courage and devotion to the Empire.

The Officer Commanding the 1st Battalion Manchester Regiment received the following congratulations from the divisional commander:

"*I send you and all ranks my very hearty congratulations on your great success between Coachford and Dripsey. It is such actions as this that bring tangible results and lower the enemy's morale. It reflects the utmost credit on you all.*"

On the 14th February Major and Quartermaster O'Brien, Lieutenants Orgill and Vining, and 24 other ranks were proceeding to Mallow on administrative duties in Crossley cars. Near Mourne Abbey some rebels were come upon preparing an ambush and blocking the road and were immediately engaged; the rebels fled into the arms of a party of the East Lancashire Regiment and Royal Irish Constabulary operating from another direction, and between the two parties the Sinn Feiners suffered some 19 casualties with no loss to the soldiers or R.I.C. On hearing of this smart affair the C.-in-C. telegraphed:

"*The Commander-in-Chief wishes to have conveyed to all concerned his appreciation of the energy displayed and the success gained in the operations at Jordan's Bridge near Mourne Abbey.*"

The O.C. 1st Battalion Manchester Regiment, since arrival of the Battalion at Ballincollig, had been *ex officio* O.C. No. 3 Area, some 240 square miles, the boundaries being roughly:

North: Mill Street–Donoughmore.
South: Waterfall–Inchigeela.
East: Blarney–Leemount Bridge.
West: Ballyvourney–Mill Street.

For some months longer the active operations against the rebels were continued, and daily and nightly parties of the battalion went out on foot or by motor, visiting suspected localities, searching the country for "wanted" men, and combining with mobile columns detailed from other parts to drive the country—duties most harassing to all concerned.

On the 22nd June 1921 His Majesty the King opened the Northern Parliament in Belfast and made a very moving appeal to all Irishmen to join in endeavouring to secure peace; and later the Prime Minister invited the heads of the Northern Government and the leaders of Sinn Fein to meet and discuss matters at a conference in London. An agreement as a basis of discussion was arrived at, and on the 11th July a truce was proclaimed between the Supreme Government and Dail Eireann, all operations against the rebels ceasing on that date. The negotiations which now began were at least once broken off and on another occasion seriously imperilled by the injudicious utterances of de Valera, but finally on the 6th December agreement was reached and Southern Ireland was constituted a Free State under the British Crown.

On the 28th January 1922, the anniversary of the surprise of the rebel ambush near Dripsey, a Memorial Service to Mrs. Lindsay was held in Ballincollig Garrison Church, and the Commanding Officer recalled all the events of the day and, in reminding the officers and men of the battalion of all that they owed to this brave lady, quoted her words to the Inspector of Police—" I came at once in the hope of saving some poor fellows' lives."

It was now possible to make certain reductions in the British garrison of Southern Ireland, and on the 3rd February the 1st Battalion Manchester Regiment embarked at Cork in the S.S. *Glengarriff*, and sailed by way of Fishguard and Weymouth for the Channel Islands at a strength of 23 officers and 380 other ranks. The following are the names of the officers who landed in Guernsey and Alderney with the battalion : Lieutenant-Colonel Dorling, D.S.O. ; Majors Evans (Bt. Lt.-Col.), C.M.G., D.S.O., Stapledon, O'Meara, and Morley ; Captains Humphreys, Burrows, Sheppard, M.C., Hollingworth, and Moorhead, M.C., adjutant ; Lieutenants Luffman, Dyer, Merry, M.C., McKevitt, M.C., Howarth, M.C., Abbott, M.C., Orwin, M.C., Orgill, and Tod, R.F.A., attached ; Second Lieutenants Dobson and Cooper ; Major and Quartermaster O'Brien ; and Captain Sutherland, R.A.M.C.

CHAPTER XXVIII

THE SECOND BATTALION, 1918-1921

IRELAND, MESOPOTAMIA, INDIA

ON the day that hostilities came to an end on the western front, the 2nd Battalion Manchester Regiment was at Sambreton, but that morning it **1918** moved to Prisches, on the afternoon of the 13th November to Avesnes, and next day to Felleries. The stay here was for only a few days, since on the 20th the battalion marched by Liessies and Rance to Froidchapelle, which was reached on the 24th, and here the remainder of the month of November was passed. The Manchesters were now engaged in training and employed on fatigues of all kinds, while six young officers joined—Second Lieutenants Brown, Hey, Hodgetts, O'Grady, White, and Smith.

On the 1st December Major Murphy, D.S.O., and an escort arrived from England with the Colours of the battalion, which they had been sent to fetch; and then on the 12th another move took place, the battalion marching by Philippeville and Stave to Assesse, where it remained for several weeks. During December two batches of officers joined or rejoined —Major Scully, M.C., Lieutenant Barratt, M.C., Second Lieutenants Brownson and Van Heel on the 1st, and Lieutenant Robertson, Second Lieutenants Coppack and O'Toole on the 18th.

The battalion remained in billets in Assesse throughout January, and in this month demobilisation—full details of the general arrangements for **1919** which were given in the last chapter—actually commenced, 4 officers—Captain Kay, D.S.O., M.C., Second Lieutenants Winder, Coleman, and Jones—being the first to go.

Early in February 1919 the battalion moved with the rest of the Division from Assesse in Belgium to Bonn in Germany, and in this town the 2nd Manchesters remained during the whole time that they formed part of the British Army of Occupation, being quartered practically throughout their stay in the German Artillery barracks. While here the duties were not heavy, the main guard, on the Rhine bridge, mounted in turn by the battalions forming the garrison of Bonn, being a more or less ceremonial one, and there were no civil disturbances of any kind, so that the ordinary training routine could be carried on almost as in peace time.

On the 4th April the cadre, consisting of Major C. C. Stapledon, 3 other officers, and some 40 non-commissioned officers and men, left Bonn for England, the remainder of the battalion having been sent home for demobilisation during the two or three weeks previous to the departure of the cadre. This entrained at Cologne for Dunkerque, crossed over from there to Dover, and arrived at Bordon on the 8th April, joining the details of the 1st Battalion there collected in camp, under command of Captain Harrison. Major Stapledon now proceeded on leave and while away was posted to the 1st Battalion, and on the 23rd April Major J. R. Heelis, M.C., arrived and assumed command of the 2nd, which was in process of hasty re-formation in view of proceeding on foreign service at an early date—the destination of the battalion being stated to be North China.

Officers and men now began to come in—12 officers and 333 other ranks joining during the month of May, and 5 officers and 271 other ranks in June, so that when in August Lieutenant-Colonel B. A. Wright, D.S.O., was posted to command, he took over a unit more nearly approaching the strength of a pre-war infantry battalion.

At the beginning of November the orders to proceed to China were cancelled, and instead the battalion was detailed as one of the units providing increased reinforcements for the garrison of Ireland, the state of which was now causing enhanced anxiety to the Government; on the 5th an advance party left Bordon for Tipperary under Lieutenant-Colonel R. N. Hardcastle, D.S.O., and was followed on the 8th by Headquarters, Band and Drums and A and C Companies, and on the 11th by B and D, so that by the afternoon of the 12th November the whole battalion was united at Tipperary in the West Hutments. Here the battalion remained almost exactly three months, and was frequently called out on much harassing and unpleasant duty in aid of the Civil Power.

At the end of the year 1919 orders were received to prepare for embarkation for Mesopotamia, and the advance party, composed of Captain G. M. Glover, M.C., Lieutenant V. D. K. Marley, and 19 other ranks left Ireland on the 1st January 1920. The battalion started some six weeks later, proceeding from Tipperary on the 12th February in two parties to Tilbury, via North Wall and Holyhead, and sailing from the London Docks on the afternoon of the 13th in the *Macedonia*. The Straits of Gibraltar were passed through on the 18th February, Port Said on the 24th, and on the 6th March Bombay was reached, and here the battalion was transhipped from the *Macedonia* to the *Coconada* in No. 4 Alexandra

Dock, sailing the same afternoon. On the 13th Basra was arrived at and, disembarking, the troops were sent by light railway to " A " Camp, Makina, where the battalion was accommodated under canvas.

The following officers landed in Mesopotamia with the 2nd Battalion : Lieutenant-Colonel Wright, D.S.O.; Brevet Lieutenant-Colonel Hardcastle, D.S.O.; Majors Eddowes and Heelis, M.C.; Captains Harrison, Adjutant, Scully (bt. major), M.C., Henderson, D.S.O., M.C., Green, Glover, M.C., and Davidson; Lieutenants Torrance, M.C., Greer, Williams-Green, M.C., Hollins, Pearce, M.C., Henderson, Kelsey, M.C., Marley, Brittorous, Grey, Keightly, M.B.E., and Hawke; and Lieutenant and Quartermaster Carter, D.C.M.

Some account must now be given of the state of the country at this period, explanatory of all that happened during the time that the 2nd Battalion Manchester Regiment remained in Mesopotamia. " After the Armistice, very large numbers of troops and non-combatants were withdrawn from Mesopotamia, and later reductions, some of which appeared to the Arabs to be the result of pressure exerted by the Syrian Government, led the inhabitants to suspect that our military supremacy was at an end. Arabs, like other Eastern peoples, are accustomed to be ruled by the strong hand. Indeed, there is no denying that they respect force and force alone. . . . Amongst other provocative causes were the skilful Turkish and Sharifian propaganda, the delay in settling the future form of government of the country, the prominence given in the West to the subject of self-determination, the attitude of the religious element in the holy cities of Karbala and Najaf, and also a certain amount of local ill-feeling concerning our methods of dealing with the cultivator, who was accustomed to the casual methods of the Turk and disliked the preciseness of the Indian system. These and other incitements to revolt had their effect on a people whose ordinary pastime during the hot summer months has, from time immemorial, been either to squabble among themselves—generally on matters connected with water for irrigation purposes—or with the government that happens to rule the country. The Turkish system of government was such that hostile feeling was encouraged between tribe and tribe; ours, on the other hand . . . directly led to combination, for blood feuds were not only discouraged by us, but even settled by money payments.

" As regards the fighting value of the Arabs, they become formidable only when in large numbers, as the mobility of those on foot, apart from the many mounted men, is extraordinary, while the money which has been poured into the country since 1914, as well as other channels, has served to provide them with hundreds of thousands of rifles, many of which are of modern pattern."[1]

The country wherein all the trouble arose is a flat plain, twice the size of the United Kingdom, traversed by the Tigris and Euphrates, the former river being the main line of communication. Of the railways, there was a metre-gauge single line, 354 miles long, generally running west of the Euphrates, and connecting Basra and Baghdad; another from Baghdad to Quraitu on the Persian border, 130 miles in length; a third, 104 miles long, from Kut to Baghdad; and a fourth, from Baghdad to Shargat, 70 miles south of Mosul, of broad-gauge. All the workshops were at the end of the line at Basra.

On the 20th March the new G.O.C.-in-C. Mesopotamia—Lieutenant-General Sir A. Haldane, K.C.B., D.S.O.—arrived at Basra and was received by a Guard of Honour, detailed from the Manchester Regiment, of 100 non-commissioned officers and men of B Company under Major Heelis, with the Regimental Colour carried by Lieutenant K. S. Torrance.

On the 29th March the battalion embarked in a river steamer and two barges and was conveyed up the River Tigris to Baghdad, where it arrived on the 5th April and went into camp on the right bank. Here some days were spent in getting together equipment, transport, etc., and then on the 16th the battalion left again by train for Tekrit on the Tigris, which was to be its permanent station. This place was reached on the 17th, and the 2nd Manchesters now formed part of the 55th Infantry Brigade of the 18th Indian Division; the commander of the division was Major-General T. Fraser, C.B., C.S.I., C.M.G., and the brigadier was Brigadier-General G. M. Morris, C.B., D.S.O.

Lieutenant Torrance of the battalion joined Brigade H.Q. as officiating staff captain.

Although the men of the battalion were here accommodated in the large Indian E.P. tents, the general arrangements were in other respects uncomfortable and unsatisfactory, there being no wash-houses, dining tents, or recreation-rooms, so that a great deal had to be done to make things "ship-shape," while training was much interfered with by the amount of time spent on camp fatigues of all kinds. Then at the end of April Lieutenant W. T. Williams-Green was sent with a detachment to Karind, a small hill-station on the Persian border, to prepare a camp for one company of infantry and the married families of the British troops in the country. This was only ready just in time, for the married families of the battalion reached Basra early in May and were at once dispatched to

[1] *R.U.S.I. Journal*, February 1923, p. 65. Lecture by Lieutenant-General Sir A. Haldane.

Karind, escorted thither and guarded while there by C Company and the Band and Drums, under Brevet Major A. J. Scully.

At the end of May many attempts by the Arabs occurred at theft from the camp, and early in June the attitude of the people became actively hostile; raids were made upon the railway stations and posts north of Tekrit, the guards had to be increased in size, and night picquets were mounted; while the camp at Tekrit was surrounded by a barbed-wire apron fence and defences were built. Captain Green, Lieutenants Brittorous and Kelsey, and 50 non-commissioned officers and men had been earlier sent to the 17th Machine Gun Battalion at Baghdad for training as the Machine Gun Platoon of the battalion.

At the time when General Haldane assumed command in Mesopotamia that country was divided into three areas, known as the River, the 17th Division and the 18th Division area; the first of these extended roughly as far north as a line from Kut to Nasiriyah, the second included the Upper Euphrates region, Kirkuk, and South Kurdistan, and some 20 miles of railway towards Mosul, while the third comprised the rest of Mesopotamia and ran as far north as Zakho. The infantry in these areas was distributed as under:

> In the River Area there were 3 Indian battalions.
> In the 17th Divisional Area there was a brigade in each of the three sub-areas of Hillah, Kirkuk, and Ramadi.
> In the 18th Divisional Area there was similarly a brigade in each of the three sub-areas of Mosul, Tekrit, and Baiji.

The total force available for holding the country consisted of two divisions, some cavalry, and several lines-of-communication battalions, but all these units were very much below strength, a large proportion of the British infantry was untrained, many men had been withdrawn for temporary duty with departmental services, and all were weak in officers. The total number of units in the country on the 1st July 1920 amounted to:

> Cavalry: 2 British and 6 Indian regiments.
> Artillery: 2 batteries R.H.A., 4 brigades R.F.A., 2 Pack Artillery Brigades, 1 battery R.G.A.
> Infantry: 12 British and 50 Indian battalions.
> R.A.F.: 2 squadrons.
> With Sappers and Miners, Motor Batteries, Signal Companies, Machine Gun Battalions, etc.

But the garrison duties in so large an area were especially heavy: guards amounting to a brigade were required for the Turkish prisoners, some 15,000 in number, while there was the safety to be considered of some 900

British women and children and over 50,000 Assyrian and Armenian refugees, so that actually on the 1st July General Haldane had at his disposal as a mobile force only some 500 British and 2,500–3,000 Indian troops, of which only one battalion was in a position to reach the Middle Euphrates area within twenty-four hours.

The first serious trouble, and the beginning of all that subsequently came to pass, arose at Rumaithah, a small town on the Hillah branch of the Euphrates and 28 miles above Samawah; but the small detachments of troops which were at once sent there became isolated as the railway to north and south was torn up by the Arabs, and the first attempt at relief failed, thereby at once greatly increasing the numbers of the disaffected. General Haldane took all possible steps to meet the situation, and among other measures he ordered Major-General Fraser to send the 55th Infantry Brigade from Tekrit to Baghdad.

The units began to leave Tekrit on the 9th July, but it was not until the 20th that trains could be provided for the 2nd Manchester Regiment, and leaving on this date it arrived at Hillah at midday and marched to Aerodrome Camp. C Company of the battalion had been recalled from duty at Karind and was now with the headquarters of the 55th Brigade, which had pushed on to Diwaniyah, 52 miles nearer Rumaithah; while the party, which had been undergoing instruction with the 17th Machine Gun Battalion, had joined a column detailed for the relief of Rumaithah and was doing duty with it as a Machine Gun platoon under Captain Green.

There was now collected at Hillah, 60 miles from Baghdad and the base of operations against Rumaithah and other places in the vicinity where trouble had arisen, 2 squadrons of the 35th Scinde Horse, the 39th Battery R.F.A. (6 guns), 3 companies of the 2nd Manchesters, 1 company of the 32nd Sikh Pioneers, and other details; and it had been the intention of the General Officer Commanding, so soon as Rumaithah should be relieved, to send a strong force from Hillah to Kufah to effect the relief of a detachment there temporarily stationed. But political pressure was now applied locally to Colonel Lukin commanding at Hillah to send out a small force to reassure the friendly natives and maintain order in the area, and on the 23rd the whole of the troops above enumerated left Hillah under command of Brevet Lieutenant-Colonel Hardcastle, Manchester Regiment, and marched to Imam Bakr, some 6 miles distant. The heat was very great—the shade temperature at this time at Baghdad was 121° Fahrenheit—and the men suffered intensely, and the medical officer with the so-called "Manchester Column" considered that they should not be asked to march further until they had had twenty-four hours' rest.

The Commandant at Hillah, however, ordered the force to advance at dawn next morning to the Rustumiyah Canal. At 9.15 a.m. the head of the column moved off and reached the canal at 12.45 p.m., all ranks greatly affected by the heat. A troop of cavalry was sent out towards Kifl to reconnoitre, and the troops settled down in their camp to the east of the road, in the angle between it and the canal. The position was tolerably strong, for on three sides were banks a few feet above ground level, while beyond were several mounds offering a good field of observation, and these were occupied. A beginning was made of digging a trench on the fourth side. The field of fire was generally good, while there was a plentiful supply of good water close at hand.

Up till nearly 6 p.m. all seemed peaceful, and the political officers were confident that the local inhabitants were friendly inclined and that no enemy was at hand, but then a cavalry patrol came in reporting that a well-armed body of several thousand Arabs was moving against the camp from the direction of Kifl. The guns with the column opened fire as soon as the enemy was visible, fighting then became general, and all seemed for a time to go well.

Neither the O.C. Column nor the political officers with it were aware that within a few hours at most reinforcements would arrive from Diwaniyah, and about 8 o'clock the politicals urged Colonel Hardcastle to commence an immediate retreat on Hillah, declaring that all the Arabs in the area would now rise, and that while some of these held the column to its camp the rest would push on and capture Hillah. These counsels prevailed and the column was directed to be ready to move off within half an hour.

About 8.40 p.m. the retirement began, the battalion finding advance and flank guards, and although the Arabs had by this worked round between the camp and Hillah they were held in check and the retreat began promisingly enough. But while the advance guard was fighting its way through and clearing the flanks, something started a panic among the transport animals and these suddenly stampeded, bolting in all directions but principally through and over the advance and flank guards. The result was that many of the men were knocked over by the runaway carts, cut up into small parties, and temporarily disorganised. The enemy was quick to seize this opportunity and attacked in masses, coming right in among the men and guns. Hand-to-hand fighting ensued and the Arabs were not beaten off until the column had suffered heavy casualties, caused mainly by the men being separated in twos and threes and surrounded by large numbers of the enemy.

However, every officer and non-commissioned officer collected what men he could, some sort of formation was resumed, and the retirement continued; and the Arabs having been at last beaten off, Hillah was reached by the remnants of the Manchester Column in the small hours of the 25th, being met just outside the place by C Company and the Machine Gun platoon of the battalion.

The disaster might have been very much worse than it was but for the steadiness of the men, who were mostly young soldiers, and for the great devotion and gallantry of Captain G. S. Henderson, D.S.O., M.C., of the Regiment. This officer was on the eastern flank when masses of Arabs attacked, and although at once severely wounded, he, time after time, collected what men he could and counter-attacked, finally clearing the flank sufficiently to allow the column to get free. Without doubt he saved the remainder of the column. He continued fighting until he dropped from loss of blood, and even then continued to encourage the men until he was killed by a bullet in the chest.

Captain Henderson was awarded a well-deserved posthumous V.C. in the *London Gazette* of the 29th October 1920, announced in the following words :

"*The late Captain George Stuart Henderson, D.S.O., M.C., 2nd Btn. Manchester Regiment.*

"*For most conspicuous bravery and self-sacrifice.*

"*On the evening of the 24th July 1920, when about fifteen miles from Hillah (Mesopotamia), the Company under his command was ordered to retire. After proceeding about 500 yards a large party of Arabs suddenly opened fire from the flank, causing the Company to split up and waver. Regardless of all danger, Captain Henderson at once reorganised the Company, led them gallantly to the attack and drove off the enemy.*

"*On two further occasions this officer led his men to charge the Arabs with the bayonet and forced them to retire. At one time when the situation was extremely critical, and the troops and transport were getting out of hand, Captain Henderson, by sheer pluck and coolness, steadied his command, prevented the Company from being cut up, and saved the situation.*

"*During the second charge he fell wounded, but refused to leave his command, and just as the Company reached the trench they were making for he was again wounded. Realising that he could do no more, he asked one of his N.C.O.s to hold him up on the embankment, saying, 'I'm done now, don't let them beat you.' He died fighting.*"

The loss in the column amounted to 20 killed, 60 wounded, and 380 missing. Of these last only 79 British and 81 Indians became prisoners with the Arabs, and one of the British soldiers died in captivity. One gun, an 18-pounder, fell into a deep canal during the night retreat, and, despite gallant efforts to recover it, had to be abandoned.

Of the 2nd Battalion Manchester Regiment, besides Captain Henderson, D.S.O., M.C., Captain and Adjutant H. G. Harrison, Captain G. M. Glover, M.C., and 131 non-commissioned officers and men were killed—some of these first reported as missing—and Lieutenant-Colonel B. A. Wright, D.S.O., was wounded.

In his book [1] General Haldane writes, " Among other gallant soldiers who distinguished themselves during the events of this night were Sergeants A. V. Deering, D.C.M., and E. Hinxman of the Artillery, and Sergeant John Willis, 2nd Battalion Manchester Regiment, the first winning a bar to the Distinguished Conduct Medal, and the other two the medal itself."

By the end of July Hillah was strongly garrisoned, but it was somewhat feebly attacked one night, and again on the night of the 31st July–1st August with more determination, but on both occasions the enemy was beaten off with many casualties, while the loss of the garrison was insignificant.

The garrison of Diwaniyah was now withdrawn to Hillah, and on the 8th August a column, in which the battalion was included, went out from Hillah along the Hillah–Jarbuiyah railway line to meet and help in the Diwaniyah troops; and on the 9th orders were received for two columns to move out with the object of securing the Hindiyah Barrage and the town of Musayib, some 8 miles further up the river. The capture of these two places would give the British commander control of the water, and would secure two important crossings over the Euphrates. The larger column contained the 55th Brigade, now under Brigadier-General Walker, C.M.G., D.S.O., and some additional details, and contained the 2nd Battalion Manchester Regiment, while the smaller column was commanded by Lieutenant-Colonel Scott, 10th Gurkhas.

The 55th Brigade Column moved on the 10th August to Khan Mahawil *en route* to Musayib, and on the next day Colonel Scott's force marched out along the railway, repairing it and covering the erection of blockhouses at half-mile intervals.

" The movement of the two columns," wrote General Haldane, " took place during the hottest season of the year—a season, be it remembered, during which no continuous operations in Mesopotamia since our arrival there in 1914 had taken place. But the selection of the season did not lie with us nor could the operations be postponed. These facts were evident

[1] *The Insurrection in Mesopotamia*, p. 102.

to the troops engaged and were accepted in the proper spirit. To add to the discomfort of the columns on the first day of movement, it was found that the Arabs had cut off the water west of Khan Nasiriyah, where the force passed a trying night."

There was some opposition on the 11th and 12th, but a bold advance by the Manchesters forced the enemy to retire with loss and Musayib was then occupied; the Hindiyah Barrage was seized on the 13th, and here the battalion was left as garrison with two 18-pounders. For some weeks now all ranks had a tolerably peaceful time, broken only by intermittent sniping and one or two very half-hearted attacks; and here the battalion remained until the 5th October, when it was relieved by the 45th Sikhs and marched back to Hillah, arriving there on the afternoon of the 8th to find that the Brigade was preparing to move out again against the enemy with the object of relieving Kufah and recovering the British prisoners in the hands of the Arabs. The column was thus composed:

35th Scinde Horse, 2 squadrons.
37th Lancers, 2 squadrons.
2 Batteries R.F.A.
1 Howitzer Battery.
1 Pack Battery.
2 Companies Sappers and Miners.
2nd Battalion Manchester Regiment.
2nd Battalion Royal Irish Rifles.
6 Battalions Indian Infantry.

Operations commenced on the 11th, the Kufah column carrying out the preliminaries necessary to clear its flanks preparatory to the main advance next day. On the 12th and 14th the Kufah Column met with considerable opposition, which was brushed aside, on the 16th the Euphrates was crossed, and next day the outskirts of Kufah were reached, and here the enemy appeared to be in strength and likely to make a stand; they were, however, charged by the Indian cavalry, while the infantry, led by the 108th Native Infantry, followed by the Manchesters and 15th Sikhs, advanced through the palm gardens, low-flying aeroplanes ably co-operating, when the insurgents turned and fled pursued by the British aircraft and cavalry; by 9.30 a.m. Kufah was relieved.

When Kufah fell and the Sheiks in the district surrendered, the 78 British prisoners were brought in from Najaf and handed over to the British on the 19th October. The meeting between these men and their comrades of the battalion was something which no one who witnessed it can ever forget. They had had a very bad time, having been marched from place to place, partly clothed, without helmets and insufficiently clad and in daily danger of their lives; "for their well-being," so General Haldane states, "credit is partly due to Company Sergeant-Major Mutter[1] of the 2nd Battalion Manchester Regiment, the senior non-commissioned officer with them."

But little remains to be said of the closing scenes of this very trying campaign. The column moved for some time longer about the country restoring order without experiencing much serious fighting, and the battalion was present at Najaf in November when the British terms of surrender were finally dictated; then moving back again to Hillah. From this place the battalion went on the 13th December to Baghdad preparatory to departure to India. On the 15th it embarked in a paddle-wheel steamer and two barges for the journey down-stream, reached Basra on the 19th, and embarked on the 27th in R.I.M.S. *Hardinge*, landing in Bombay on the 6th January, 1921. The following officers reached India with the Regiment: Lieutenant-Colonel Wright, D.S.O.; Majors Tillard, D.S.O., Hardingham, Eddowes, and Scully, M.C.; Captains Green and Davidson; Lieutenants Torrance, M.C., adjutant, Greer, Williams-Green, M.C., Hollins, Pearce, Henderson, Kelsey, M.C., Marley, Brittorous, M.C., Hawke, Horner, and Cawley; and Lieutenant and Quartermaster Carter, D.C.M.

On disembarkation the battalion entrained at once for Deolali, where it remained until the 13th February, when it proceeded to Kamptee, its permanent station, one company, under Major Scully, being detached to Fort Sitabuldi, Nagpore.

[1] This Warrant Officer was in possession of the M.M., the D.C.M., and the M.S.M.

NOTE.—Under Army Orders 3 and 4 of January 1923 those of the battalion who served in the above operations became entitled to a new medal, to be known as the "General Service Medal," to commemorate military operations "other than in East, Central, and West Africa, or in India, or on the Indian Frontier." The medal with clasp "Iraq" is issuable to all officers and men who (a) served at Ramadi, or north of a line drawn east and west through Ramadi between 10th December 1919 and 13th June 1920, both dates inclusive; or (b) were present on the establishment of a unit or formation within the boundaries of Iraq between 1st July 1920 and 17th November 1920, both dates inclusive.

CHAPTER XXIX

NOTES ON UNIFORM, COLOURS, BADGES, ETC.

63RD FOOT. NOW THE 1ST BATTALION.

By the late D. Hastings-Irwin, Esq.

It is a difficult matter to say with certainty what the uniform of the Regiment was when raised in 1758; and in the absence, as far as I know, of any definite regulations, or of contemporary pictures, it can only be done "inferentially."

The few papers that can be consulted give little or no information as to details, and the searcher is faced with the further difficulty that Colonels were allowed a very free hand in the way they clothed their regiments.

Indeed, to such an extent had the custom grown, that on September 14th, 1743, it was deemed necessary to issue an order forbidding "*any Colonel for the future putting his Arms, Device, or Livery, on any part of the appointments of his Regiment.*" As this prohibition is repeated in the Clothing Warrant of the 19th December 1768, it would lead one to infer that the previous order had not been very closely observed.

Until the Army Dress Regulations in their present form were first issued in 1822, it was the custom for the Board of General Officers, appointed in 1708, to regulate the clothing of the Army, to decide upon a uniform, and having done so, to have the patterns sealed, and deposited at their office in Pooley Street. The Colonel of the regiment concerned was then informed of what had taken place, and he was requested to call as soon as possible at the office to inspect the uniform selected, and to see that it was taken into wear by his regiment without delay. This only applied in a general way, the Colonel, as mentioned above, being allowed considerable latitude in carrying out the instructions. Hence the reason why so few documents exist describing with any degree of exactitude the uniforms of the period.

Letters however do exist showing that the Colonels were occasionally ordered to show the uniform "*on the men's backs,*" before the Board of General Officers above mentioned.

This was no doubt done with an eye to uniformity, and possibly also to see that the large sum of money with which the Colonel was provided for equipping his regiment was properly laid out, more especially as the amount of his emoluments largely depended upon what he could save out of it. Possibly also the variety of uniform displayed on these occasions gave rise to the order of 1743 quoted above.

The men were clothed out of the "*off-reckonings,*" which were derived as follows: A certain portion (6*d.*) of the daily pay of the soldier (8*d.*) was set aside for subsistence, and the remainder was termed the "gross off-reckonings." After deducting one day's pay per annum for the Chelsea Hospital Fund, and other purposes, the net off-reckonings were handed to the Colonel, out of which he had to clothe his regiment. It was possible to make considerable savings between the amount received and that spent on the uniforms, which was a perquisite of the Colonel. In one regiment in 1743 it amounted to £621, though the average was probably from £400 to £500. This system continued until 1855; but in 1871 it was arranged that all clothing was to be supplied by the Royal Army Clothing Department in Pimlico, and the allowances to Commanding Officers were withdrawn. "*Half-mountings*," another term frequently met with in old documents relating to uniform, are thus described in Gross, *Military Antiquities*: "The black stock and roller (neck cloth) shirt, shoes and stockings are called the *Half-mounting*."

The following Order was issued on April 23rd, 1801: "In every regiment of Infantry of the Line, or Fencibles, serving in Europe, North America, or the Cape of Good Hope (Highland Corps excepted) each Sergeant, Corporal, Drummer, and Privateman, to have annually for clothing, a coat, a waistcoat, or waistcoat-front; a pair of breeches, unlined; a cap made of felt and leather, with a brass plate, conformable to an approved pattern; the felt crown of the cap, cockade and tuft, to be supplied annually; the leather part and brass-plate every two years. And in lieu of the former articles of clothing, called '*Half-mountings*,' two pair of good shoes to the value of five shillings and six pence each pair. Should the price of good shoes at any time exceed five shillings and sixpence each pair, the difference, which is to be declared by the Clothing Board, on, or after, the 25th of April each year, is to be charged to the respective accounts of the N.C.O.'s, or soldier, receiving them.

"When His Majesty approves of the measure, the following sums, being the estimated amount of what the Colonels would have paid to their Clothiers, after a reasonable deduction for incidental charges to which they are liable, are to be given to the men:

	To each Sergeant.	To each Corporal, Drummer, and Private
Clothing	2 18 0	1 5 6
Half-mounting	0 14 0	0 11 0
	£3 12 0	£1 16 6"

Half-mountings, as such, were done away with before 1805.

The earliest reference to the uniform of the Regiment that I have come across is in a Clothing Warrant dated 6th November 1758, in the Public Record Office, wherein the coats are ordered to have buff linings, very deep green facings, white buttons, and white lace, with green and white diagonal stripes. The Drummers' coats are also specified to be of the same shade of green with red facings.

1758

As little or no change took place in the uniforms as laid down in the 1751 Clothing Warrant and that of 1768, it may be reasonably inferred that the uniform of the private soldiers of the Regiment at this period consisted of a full-bodied red coat, with long skirts coming down to the knee, and turned back, to show the buff-lining; the coat lapelled in front with dark-green cloth, and worn open to the waist, thus showing the long red waistcoat. The lapels, and the buttonholes on them, trimmed with regimental braid, and also the deep, wide, green cuffs. The back of the coat quite plain except for three bars of lace on each side of the slit between the turnbacks. At each side of the waist was a button from which to the bottom of the skirt ran a bar of lace with branching arms arranged in the same manner as the lace on the sleeves.

The breeches were red, and long black linen gaiters were worn, coming well up the thigh, and gartered below the knee, with black shoes. Brown gaiters were worn in marching order, when the officers wore boots.

A broad buff leather belt, supporting a large black leather pouch, was worn over the left shoulder, and a wide waist-belt carried the bayonet.

A black felt three-cornered hat bound with broad white braid was worn, with a black cockade and button on the left corner, and a voluminous white neck-cloth, coming almost down to the waist.

The Grenadier Company was similarly clothed, but instead of hats had cloth mitre-shaped caps of the colour of the regimental facings, green, embroidered in front with the Royal Cipher, Crown, and side scrolls; and with the white horse of Hanover on a red flap at the bottom, and the motto " *Nec Aspera Terrent* " in black letters on a white ground edging the top and two sides. The back of the cap was red, divided into three panels by white cloth piping, with a broad dark-green band round the bottom, and with the regimental number in the centre. The Officers' caps were of similar design, but were made of velvet, instead of cloth; and embroidered in gold and silver.

The Grenadiers also wore a brass match-case on their shoulder-belt, laced wings on the shoulders of the coats with a red cloth strap on the left shoulder to keep the belt in position, and short brass-hilted curved swords.

The Drummers wore dark-green coats, with red facings of a similar pattern to that of the Privates ornamented with regimental braid. They had long hanging sleeves, like those worn by the Foot Guards. Their caps were similar to those of the Grenadiers, but with trophies of flags and drums, embroidered in front, instead of the crown and cipher, and with the white horse on the front flap. The back part was not stiffened, but hung down like a bag. They also carried short swords from a waist-belt.

According to Morier's series of paintings of the uniforms of this period in Windsor Castle, when the coat was buttoned across the chest, i.e. with the lapel buttoned over, the waist-belt was worn outside the coat, but under it when worn open, the left skirt hanging over the sword.

The Officers' uniform at this period consisted of a long and wide-skirted coat, coming down to the knees like that of the men, but of scarlet, instead of red cloth. They had lapels in front, from the neck to the waist, of dark-green cloth, with ten loops of silver lace, and silver buttons at the outer ends. The coat was edged with silver lace round the neck, lapels, and to the bottom of the skirts, which were not buttoned back like those of the men. There were cross pockets, edged all round the flap with silver lace, and another row outside the sides and bottom of the flaps, sewn on to the skirts. The cuffs were round, and of dark-green cloth, with a row of silver lace round the top; and with a large scarlet slash, edged with silver, and four silver buttons on it. Outside the flap, and bordering the top and buttoned side, was another row of silver lace. A silver gorget and white cravat were worn, and lace frills showed below the cuffs.

A broad crimson silk sash was worn diagonally over the right shoulder and tied in a large bow on the left side with long tassels at the ends.

The waistcoat and breeches were white, the former coming well below the waist, with silver lace and buttons down the front. The pocket flaps were deep, and edged with silver lace.

The hat was three-cornered, edged with silver lace and with a black silk cockade at the left corner.

A light sword was worn under the skirt of the coat, in addition to the esponton, which was carried when on parade.

White gaiters coming well up the thigh were worn, with black shoes.

1763 Slack, in his history of the 63rd, at this period mentions the uniform as being red, facings *black*, buff linings, yellow lace, but with the exception of the colour of the coat and linings I have found no corroboration of this.

1767 It is not until 1767 that we, for the first time, come across definite instructions as to the length of the infantry coat. In a document of that period it is ordered that " *the men's coats are to be four inches from the ground when kneeling on both knees, and to be of an equal length quite round.*" It is also laid down that the waistcoats of the Grenadiers are to have thirteen holes and buttons on each side from the top of the waistcoat to the point of the pocket ; the centre rank to have eleven holes and buttons ; the remainder twelve.

In the same document the hitherto plain metal buttons were ordered to bear the regimental number on the uniforms of both officers and men.

The Inspection Returns from Dublin, 3rd September 1767, report : "*The 63rd Regiment are a very low body of men. Their hats too much in ye french taste.*" The first remark refers no doubt to their physical, and not to their moral, qualities, and the last probably to the method of cocking their hats.

The *Army List* for this year mentions "*black*" facings ; but this is, I think, a mistake for *very* dark green (nearly black). At any rate, I have found no corroboration of it.

1768 In accordance with the Clothing Warrant of 1768 considerable changes took place in the uniform. The coats were much shorter, and not so full in the skirts as those previously worn, with green lapels, cuffs, and turned-down collars. The lapels were 3 inches wide from top to bottom, and extended from the collar to the waist. There were ten loops of regimental braid and buttons on each lapel, with square ends and four similar loops on each cuff ; one on each side of the collar (which when turned down fastened to the top button on the lapel, and so partly obscured the top loop), and two on each side of the slit behind, with four on the cross-pocket flaps. The cuffs were round (3½ inches deep), and made to unbutton and let down. The coats were lined with white, so that the skirts when buttoned back showed white turnbacks. The lace was white, with a narrow green line down the centre. Every new Colonel could design his own regimental lace. White waistcoats and breeches were worn, also black linen gaiters coming above the knee with black garters below it ; while white stockings drawn well up the thigh showed above the tops of the gaiters.

The waistcoat was much shorter than that previously worn. The hat was of black felt, three-cornered, and bound round the edge with white braid, and with a black cockade and regimental button on the left side. The Sergeants' hats were laced with silver, 1¼ inches wide. A white leather waist-belt, with a brass buckle, was worn under the coat and over the waistcoat and carried the bayonet.

The Grenadiers wore a similar coat but with a red cloth wing on each shoulder, with six loops of regimental braid on it, and with an edging of the same along the bottom. They also wore a white leather cross-belt, with a brass match-case and chain; and carried short swords, and bayonets attached to the white leather waist-belt, and worn under the left skirt of the coat. Their waistcoats, breeches, and gaiters were the same as those of the rank and file.

Their caps were now of black bearskin, mitre-shaped as before with a metal plate with a rounded top below, bearing the King's crest (the Lion of England) on a helmet, with the motto "*Nec Aspera Terrent*" and "*G.R.*" all in white metal on a black ground. The height of the cap (without the bearskin, which reached beyond the top) was 12 inches. On the back, about half-way up, was a circular red cloth patch, in the centre of which was embroidered a white grenade with the number of the Regiment on it.

The Drummers and Fifers still wore dark-green coats with red facings, but without the hanging sleeve previously worn; and the other details of their uniform were similar to those of the men. Their coats were laced according to the Colonel's fancy. They also wore bearskin caps similar to those of Grenadiers, but not so high, and in addition to the King's crest the plate was ornamented with trophies of Colours and drums. For armament they carried short curved brass-hilted swords.

The goat-skin pack, hitherto carried over the right shoulder in Marching Order, was still worn, and a black neck-cloth replaced the white one for all ranks. The coats were hooked, from the neck to below the chest, and the skirts were looped back showing the white lining.

The Officers wore long-tailed scarlet coats, with green lapels to the waist, turned-down collar, round cuffs, and cross-pockets. The lapels were 3 inches wide, from top to bottom, and were fastened back by ten silver buttons, with a corresponding number of silver embroidered loops, placed at equal distances. The skirts were well cut away, and turned back, showing the white lining. White cravats, with embroidered ends, were worn. Officers of Grenadiers wore a silver lace epaulette with bullions, on each shoulder, while Battalion Officers had one on the right shoulder only.

All wore white waistcoats and breeches, and black linen gaiters with black buttons and small stiff tops and shoes. The waistcoats were plain, without either embroidery or lace, but with silver buttons, and cross-pockets, but no flaps. The hats were black felt, three-cornered, bordered with silver lace 1¼ inches wide, and with a black cockade on the left side.

Officers and Sergeants wore crimson sashes round the waist, those of the Officers being of silk, and the Sergeants of worsted with a green stripe down the centre.

Battalion Officers were ordered to carry espontons in addition to their light swords; and those of the Grenadier Company fusils, white leather shoulder belts, 2¾ inches wide, and pouches. Grenadier Sergeants carried fusils and had pouches,

1768 while the Battalion Sergeants had halberds, but no pouches. Corporals were distinguished by a silk epaulette on the right shoulder; and the waist-belts of all ranks were of white leather, 2 inches wide.

All the Sergeants, and the whole of the Grenadier Company, wore small slightly curved swords. The Pioneers wore a distinctive cap with a leather crown and a black bearskin front. The metal front plate was enamelled red, with the King's crest and an axe and saw on it in white enamel. They wore white leather aprons and carried an axe and a saw.

The Officers' button was of bone or ivory, covered with a silver plate, with "63" in the centre, on an eight-pointed star, the rays of which came right up to the edge. The Privates' was the same design—but made of cast pewter.

The Inspection returns from Dublin, dated 27th July 1768, report the Officers' uniform as follows: "*Scarlet, with a silver embroidered buttonhole, lapelled to the waist with deep-green; green cape* [i.e. collar], *small round cuff, silver buttons, numbered: and a green epaulett, embroidered. White linings, white waistcoats, and breeches and silver-laced hats.*"

It is evident from this that the Colonel had availed himself of the choice given in the Clothing Warrant of 1768 to adopt either silver embroidery or lace for the buttonholes on the lapels of the Officers' coats.

A similar report on the Officers' uniform is made from Dublin on the 6th May **1769** 1769; with the addition that "*The Grenadiers and Drummers have black bearskin caps, according to the King's Regulations.*"

Apparently the embroidered buttonholes had not a very long life, as the Inspection Returns from Cork, 30th May 1771, report: "*Officers' Uniforms scarlet, with a* **1771** *silver-laced buttonhole: white lining: lapelled to the waist: small round cuff, and turned-down cape: deep-green. Silvered buttons, numbered. Scarlet epaulettes, silver-laced, white waistcoat, and breeches: silver-laced hats. Black linen gaiters, with small stiff-topps.*" The silver-laced buttonhole with square ends continued to be worn on the lapels as long as it was regulation, i.e. until 1829.

A Light Company was added to the Regiment this year. The officers were, as hitherto, clothed in scarlet, and the men in red; but their coats were very much shorter in the skirts than those of the rest of the battalion. They wore wings on the shoulder like the Grenadiers, white breeches, and stockings, and black half-gaiters, coming half-way up the calf. Their caps were of black, japanned leather (very similar to those worn by Light Dragoons at this period), with a red turned-up peak in front and silk turban, fur crest, and side plume. Their waistcoats were red, and they wore white leather crossed belts with two frogs on the waist-belt, one for the hatchet and the other for the bayonet. When on the march the hatchet was tied on to the goatskin pack.

The Inspection Returns from Dublin, 14th May 1774, report no change in the **1774** Officers' uniform since the last returns, except that instead of scarlet the epaulette was then "*Green; silver-laced.*"

The next Inspection Return which mentions anything about the uniform is from Bury St. Edmunds, and is dated the 3rd May 1784. It states: "*As they were but* **1784** *just arrived from America, where they never made use of Espontons, the Officers saluted with their swords; and although their uniforms were regular,* *and according to orders in point of the colours, and all had silver laced buttonholes; yet they differed most in the make and breadth of the lapels, from the hurry they were in to get them made up. All their regimental books were lost, by the Adjutant being killed in America."*

This year it was ordered that the men's shoulder-straps should be changed from red to green, and the bayonet carriage arranged to slip on and off the belt with two loops. It was also ordered that the belt was to be worn over the right shoulder by way of a cross-belt, instead of round the waist as heretofore. It is curious to note that in Morier's (1751) painting in Windsor Castle some of the regiments are shown as having anticipated this order by about thirty-three years!

On 15th June the powder-horns and bullet-bags of the Light Company were ordered to be laid aside; also the matches, match-cases, and swords of the Grenadier Company. The pouch and bayonet belts were ordered to be 2 inches wide, the flap of the pouch to be plain and to carry 56 rounds of ammunition. A small priming-horn holding about 2 ounces of powder was provided instead of the powder-horn. About this period the Officers' epaulette again had a scarlet cloth strap, with a square top edged all round with silver braid showing a narrow scarlet light outside, with a small regimental button and loop at the top. A silver embroidered crescent, with a rose at each extremity at the shoulder end with silver bullions, and in the centre a silver Fleur-de-lys edged with dark-green cloth.

In April, Infantry Officers were ordered to lay aside the esponton, and to provide themselves with "*a strong substantial uniform sword*," with a straight cut-and-thrust blade 32 inches long instead of the light one hitherto worn. The hilt to be silver, to match the buttons on the uniform. The sword-knot was of gold lace, with crimson stripes. When on duty, and with their sashes on, Officers wore their swords slung over their uniform; and when off duty, and without their sashes, they wore them over their waistcoats, i.e. under their coats. The cross-belt plate worn by the Officers about this time was of elliptical shape, entirely of silver. In the centre was a raised eight-pointed star, with " 63 " engraved in the centre, and round the outside a bold beaded border.

1786

White hats, cocked like the black ones, were ordered to be worn by regiments serving in India.

An Order dated 6th July mentions new hats as having been instituted for Infantry. I can only infer that this has reference to the " cocking " of the existing hat, as I have been unable to trace any new type. It was now cocked nearly vertical, before and behind, instead of being three-cornered.

1787

Halberds for Sergeants were abolished by a General Order of 27th March, and swords were substituted. At the same time brass drums replaced wooden ones.

Towards the end of this year all Field Officers of Infantry were ordered to wear two epaulettes. Grenadier and Light Company Officers, who for some time had worn two, were to be distinguished in future by wearing a Grenade and Bugle respectively on the single epaulette.

1791

On 6th October pikes replaced the halberds abolished in 1787 for Sergeants. They were issued on trial and finally adopted in April 1792.

In December the crown of the Infantry cocked hat was reduced to a depth of 4 inches by 7 inches diameter, the size of the brim, and form of cocking, to remain as heretofore, i.e. with the front and back turned up.

1793

The Officers' silver gorget was discontinued in July, and one of gilt metal, of universal pattern, adopted; this continued until done away with in 1831. It was engraved with the King's Cipher below a crown in the centre, and was suspended by green ribbon from the top buttons on the lapels, with a green rosette at each end. It was worn as a sign that the officer was on duty.

1795

The regimental baggage was this year lost at Helvoetsluis, in Holland.

During this year sundry changes took place in the uniform. On 1st February it was ordered that the coat lapels were to be continued, as then worn, to the waist, but were to be made to button over occasionally, or to clasp close with hooks and eyes all the way down to the bottom (i.e. when the lapels were "buttoned back"). The collar was to be upstanding, instead of lying down, as heretofore, and an opening to be left at the flap, on the outside of the pocket, so as to admit the hand into it, when the lapels were buttoned over. The pocket-flaps of the Light Company to be made oblique, or slashed. The collar to be wide in the neck so as to admit of the large black neck-cloth being worn.

1796

In May a crimson-and-gold cord was added to the bottom of the crown of the Officers' cocked hats, with a crimson-and-gold tassel at each end.

The Officers sword-hilts were ordered to be of brass, with a grip of silver twisted wire, the sword-knot being crimson and gold-striped.

The coats of the rank and file had ten loops of white braid with a narrow green central stripe, square-ended, across the lapels, at equal distance, with a numbered white-metal button, about ⅝ inch diameter, at the outer ends. There were four similar loops on the round green cuffs and one on each end of the stand-up collar.

White-leather crossed belts were worn, one supporting the bayonet, and the other the ammunition pouch, with white waistcoat, and breeches, and black gaiters coming to the knee. The shirt frill was allowed to show from below the black stock to the middle of the chest. Being at this time in the West Indies the Regiment no doubt wore white hats as authorised in 1786.

1797

At this period the Light Company Officers wore a curved sword suspended by two slings from the shoulder-belt.

In October the men's coat-lapels were ordered to be done away with; but the arrangement of the lace and buttons was to be preserved, and to be sewn on the coats, instead of on the lapels as heretofore.

The Officers when on duty were ordered to wear short coats with epaulettes, like those of the N.C.O.s and men, except that they were quite plain, and without lace. When "off duty" and in "Dress," the existing uniform—that is, the long-tailed, lapelled, and braided coat—to continue.

The cap feather was changed to red and white for the Battalion Officers and men, white for the Grenadiers, and green for the Light Company.

The Officers' cross-belt plate worn at this period was silver, oval, and all engraved. In the centre was the regimental number in Roman characters, surrounded by a circular charged garter, and surmounted by a crown. There is in existence a miniature of

Major Johns, who joined the regiment in 1797, which shows the Fleur-de-lys on the epaulette strap. The cross-belt plate also has the same badge engraved on it.

The low-crowned felt hat, so long worn in a variety of shapes, was abolished by a G.O. of the 24th February, for the N.C.O.s and Privates, although the Battalion Officers continued to wear it, as a cocked hat, until 1806. Officers of the Light Company were ordered to wear "*the new Cap*," and Grenadier Officers to wear the cocked hat when their men paraded without their dress-caps.

1800

The new cap was cylindrical, 7 inches deep, with a peak set on at an angle, and was made of lacquered felt. On the front was a large brass plate 6 × 4 inches, with rounded corners, decorated with trophies of arms, etc., with the King's Crest, Cipher, and Garter in the centre. Above it was a small black cockade, with the regimental button in the centre for the battalion men, a grenade for the Grenadiers, and a bugle-horn for the men of the Light Company. The Grenadiers wore this cap when they did not parade in their proper Grenadier caps. A small red and white plume was worn in front of the cap, which had neither chain nor chin-strap. The plumes of the Grenadiers were white and those of the Light Company green. Colonels were allowed to have the number of the Regiment engraved on the cap plate.

The Privates wore at this period a short red jacket, or coatee, with green collar and cuffs. On each side of the breast were ten loops of the regimental braid, with white metal buttons. The loops were 4 inches long with square ends. The shoulder-straps were green, and the battalion men had small white woollen tufts on the ends. The collar was laced all round, and cut away in front, showing the black stock and shirt frill.

Sergeants of flank companies carried swords and fusils on full-dress parades. Sergeants of battalion companies carried silver-mounted Malacca canes, which could be fastened by a buff-leather thong to a button on the left breast of the coatee.

White crossed belts were worn, also white breeches, and black gaiters coming up to the knee. A black leather ammunition pouch was carried behind. The white waistcoat was now completely hidden and was shortly afterwards abolished as an article of full dress; but reappeared with sleeves, as a fatigue jacket, and was so worn until 1830, when it finally disappeared from the Infantry of the Line.

1801 Great-coats were this year provided for the N.C.O.s and private men, and were to last for three years.

Epaulettes and shoulder-knots for N.C.O.s were abolished in July, and chevrons on the right arm were substituted. Sergeant-Majors wore four of silver lace, Sergeants, three, and Corporals, two. The first chevron to be of silver lace, the second of plain white braid, and the third of white braid, with a green central line. The Grenadiers' cap-plate was altered from black-japanned metal to brass.

1802

1805 A regulation black canvas knapsack replaced the goatskin pack worn since the Regiment was raised.

1806 The Infantry cap was slightly altered in construction this year, in that it was not lacquered.

On 27th October 1806 the Sergeants' great-coats were ordered to have green collars and cuffs with chevrons on the right sleeve. Corporals to wear chevrons, without any other distinction on their great-coats.

At this period the Officers' full-dress uniform consisted of a scarlet coatee with dark-green collar, cuffs, and lapels. The lapels were generally worn buttoned over, but with the upper portion turned back, showing the green facing. Two rows of ten silver buttons down the front, set on 2 and 2. One loop and button at each end of the collar, and four similar on each cuff, in pairs, and on the cross-cut pocket-flaps. White turnbacks and linings to the skirts. A white leather sword-belt, with frog, over the right shoulder, on which a silver epaulette was worn. A silver breast-plate in the middle of the belt. White breeches and black Hessian boots, with black tassels at the V in front. A crimson silk sash was worn round the waist and tied on the right side. White gloves. A brass-hilted sword, black scabbard, and gold sword-knot. A black cocked hat with gold tassels at the ends and a red and white plume.

A General Order was issued on 19th February regarding epaulettes, the King having approved of the respective ranks of the officers of Infantry being distinguished by them. Field Officers were ordered to wear two epaulettes; those of a Colonel to have a crown and a star on the strap, a lieutenant-colonel's a crown, and a major's a star. Captains of Flank Companies, who had the brevet rank of Field Officer, wore wings in addition to their epaulettes; the epaulettes of the Grenadiers were to have a grenade on the strap, and those of the Light Company a bugle-horn, below the badges of rank. Company Officers and subalterns wore one epaulette, and that on the right shoulder, excepting those belonging to the flank companies, who wore a wing on each shoulder, with a grenade, or bugle-horn, on the strap, according as they belonged to the Grenadier or Light Company.

Adjutants and Quartermasters wore epaulettes like those of the subaltern officers, but in addition the Adjutant wore an epaulette strap on the left shoulder. On the silver epaulettes of the 63rd the badges of rank were worked in yellow silk.

The Paymaster, Surgeon, and Assistant Surgeon wore neither epaulettes, wings, nor sash, and a waist-belt was now substituted for the shoulder-belt.

The cap was altered. The new one was made of black felt with a gilt oval-shaped plate in front, with the monogram "*G.R.*" reversed, and the regimental number below, a crown surmounting the plate. The front of the cap, representing an upturned peak, was 3 inches higher than the crown, which was 6¾ inches deep and was bound with black braid with a drooping black leather peak 2 inches deep in front. Across the front was a plaited cord, with tassels on the right side. Officers wore crimson and gold cords and tassels, Staff-Sergeants, crimson and silver, and the battalion men, white. Those of the Light Company wore green. A red and white plume, and small black cockade with the regimental button in the centre, were worn on the left side, the Light Company having a green plume. A chin-strap was now worn for the first time.

This cap was worn during the later years of the Peninsular War and until after Waterloo, being replaced in August 1815.

On September 25th an Order was issued, "*that in consequence of the duties to which Trumpeters and Buglers were unavoidably exposed on service, and the inconvenience attendant upon their loss in action, which is attributed to the marked difference of their dress, their clothing is to be of the same colour as that now worn by their respective regiments, and that the distinction which it is necessary to preserve between them and the Privates is to be pointed out by the lace.*"

This doubtless is the date of the institution of special "Bugler's Lace." Henceforward their coats were red, instead of green as hitherto. On 24th December Infantry Officers were ordered to discontinue wearing cocked hats on parade and regimental duties, and to wear a cap similar to that of the men, but with a black beaver body and front instead of felt. Their coats were to be similar to those of the Privates, but to have green lapels to button over the breast and body and with very short skirts.

When the lapels were buttoned over, two rows of buttons were shown down the front of the coat. There was one loop of silver lace and button at each end of the collar, four on each cuff, and a silver epaulette on the right shoulder. A crimson silk sash tied on the left side was worn round the waist, and a white leather sword-belt with frog over the right shoulder with a silver breast-plate.

Officers on service wore grey cloth pantaloons, or overalls, with short boots or shoes, and grey cloth gaiters like the Privates.

They were also ordered to wear a grey cloth great-coat, with a stand-up collar, a cape on the shoulders, and with regimental buttons.

Since 1768 the coats had been gradually shortened, and the skirts cut away in front. They were now worn open at the top to allow the shirt frill to show, but were fastened about half-way down the chest, whence they were gradually cut away to the bottom of the skirts, which were narrow and turned back in front, to show the white lining.

The Officers' full-dress coat had ten loops of narrow silver lace $\frac{3}{8}$ inch wide, with a black central line, square-ended, with silver buttons on the outer end set on in pairs on the lapels, four similar ones on each cuff, four on the pocket-flap, and one on each end of the collar, which was laced all round. A button on each side of the waist behind, with a triangle of silver lace between them, four buttons under the pocket, two half-way down the skirt, and a silver Fleur-de-lys mounted on green as a skirt ornament, on the white turnbacks.

Grey cloth trousers were ordered for the men, with a half-gaiter of the same, instead of the white breeches and gaiters previously worn, thus leaving the knee-joint and the calf of the leg unconfined and so more suitable for marching. It was found that the long gaiters hitherto worn produced sores. The coatees of the Light Company had very short skirts, only a few inches long.

1813 The white hats authorised for wear in the E. and W. Indies were discontinued on 12th October, and the rank of Colour-Sergeant was instituted on 27th July; this rank was abolished in 1914.

1814 The brass chaco-plate was done away with in December for the Light Company and a bugle-horn substituted, with the number of the Regiment below it.

The Privates wore single-breasted red cloth jackets laced across the breast with square-ended loops of regimental lace, 4 inches long set on in pairs, and laced round the collar, which was worn open to show the shirt frill. The shoulder-straps were laced up the sides and had white woollen shoulder tufts. In the flank companies the shoulder-straps terminated in red cloth wings, trimmed with bars of regimental lace, and edged with white worsted fringe.

The Sergeants were dressed like the Privates, but in a finer quality of cloth, having the chevron of their rank on the arm, which, together with their coat lace, was of fine white tape. Their sashes were of crimson worsted with a central green stripe, and they carried a straight sword in a white leather shoulder-belt, with a brass breast-plate. Their other weapon was a halberd, a plain steel spearhead with a cross bar below, not unlike the esponton formerly carried by Officers. The earlier type was a battle-axe-headed weapon, which was abandoned in 1792.

A tailor's book of this period states that the Officers' skirt ornaments were silver Fleur-de-lys, on a dark-green ground.

In August a new pattern cap was introduced. It was of black felt for the rank and file, $7\frac{1}{2}$ inches deep, and bell-shaped, being 11 inches diameter at the top; with white-metal cheek-scales, which could be tied up in front, below the black cockade. It had a black leather sloping peak, and in the centre of the cockade was the regimental button. A white upright feather, 12 inches high, rising from a brass socket was fixed in front. Below the cockade was a round brass plate with the regimental number in the centre surmounted by a crown. A cover of prepared linen was worn in wet weather.

The Light Company wore a green plume and a bugle-horn in front of the cap with the number of the Regiment on the cockade. The Grenadiers still wore their bearskin caps with a gilt plate and leather peak in front, with silver cords and tassels for the Officers and white for the men. The Battalion Companies Officers' cap was of black beaver, and had silver oak-leaf lace $2\frac{1}{2}$ inches wide round the top, and a band of $\frac{1}{2}$ inch silver vellum regimental lace round the bottom. Similar plumes and cockades to those described above were worn by the Officers of Battalion and Light Companies. A silver Star $3\frac{1}{2}$ inches high by $3\frac{1}{8}$ inches wide, of regimental design surmounted by a crown, was worn in front, and the silver cheek-scales could be tied up below the cockade when desired. Gold-looped cap-lines were worn. The Star was encircled by gold lace with a narrow crimson stripe in the centre, and two lines of it, and a scaled white-metal loop, passed upwards to the cockade.

In a contemporary tailor's book "*Silver scale wings*" are mentioned, "*corded on green : gilt grenades, or bugles.*" These were obviously for the Grenadiers and Light Company Officers.

In June it was ordered that regimental badges, or devices, if any, were to be placed on the Star above the regimental number on the officers' caps; but the Star was not to be increased in size by the addition. Battle Honours were to be inscribed on narrow plates, and placed on the scaled loop under the cockade. The caps of N.C.O.s and Privates to be without any badge, device, or inscription. The N.C.O.s and Privates of the Light Company were to have a small bugle-horn only, in front of their caps, with "63" on the cockade as previously mentioned.

The cocked hat which had been retained by Officers since 1806 for full dress when at Court, or on any other occasion, was abolished on 20th June, and it was ordered to be replaced by the regimental cap above described.

At this period the Regiment on parade must have presented a somewhat variegated appearance. The Officers wore scarlet *double-breasted* coats, with dark-green facings, and silver lace on the collar, cuffs, and lapels (when they were not buttoned over, and showed the scarlet underside). The men wore red *single-breasted* coats with white and green striped braid thereon, dark green cuffs and collars also ornamented with the regimental braid. The Grenadiers had white plumes, the Battalion Companies red and white, and the Light Company green. Both Officers and men of the flank companies wore wings ; while in the Battalion Companies the Officers wore epaulettes, and the men white woollen tufts on the ends of the shoulder-straps. The men all wore white breeches and long black gaiters, the Officers grey trousers. To relieve any monotony there was the variegated uniform of the Band ! It is true that the Flank Companies were always kept on the flanks, and not allowed to appear in other parts of the line at different times, but to accomplish this must have necessitated some remarkable complications in drill ; possibly, no doubt, a joy in themselves to the Military Chiefs !

1818 Long-tailed coats for Officers were now universal in the Infantry.

I have come across an order dated 22nd June stating that the waistcoats, breeches, and linings of the 63rd, and of six other regiments were to be altered from buff to **1819** white ; I cannot trace that the 63rd wore anything else but white waistcoats and breeches since 1768 ; and as the other regiments mentioned all wore buff during the intervening period, I can only infer that the 63rd was included in the order in error.

1820 This year short coats were discontinued for all ranks except those of the Light Company.

1822 The following are the regulations laid down this year for the dress of Infantry Officers, modified to suit the 63rd.

FULL DRESS.—*Coatee.*—Scarlet with green lapels, cuffs, and collar, Prussian collar full 3 inches deep, with a loop of silver braid and small button at each end, straight lapels, buttoning back to ten large silver regimental buttons, with silver loops, occupying two-thirds of the space from the outward edge to the front seam of the armhole, tapering to $2\frac{1}{2}$ inches at the bottom, closing in front with hooks and eyes. Cuffs $3\frac{1}{2}$ inches deep, with four loops and large buttons on each, four short loops on the back, coatee skirts with cross flaps and four large silver buttons and loops on each, white kerseymere turnbacks with Fleur-de-lys skirt ornaments. Turnbacks and back skirts laced all round, with a diamond at top, both sides of the skirts turned back, and showing the white lining ; the lace on the skirts edged dark green.

A silver epaulette, on the right shoulder, lace strap $2\frac{1}{2}$ inches wide, with one broad and two narrow beadings round the edges, an embroidered crescent and two rows of bright bullions 3 inches long. Field Officers wore a pair of epaulettes, Colonels to have a crown and star on the strap, Lieutenant-Colonels, a crown, Majors, a star. The Adjutant to wear, in addition to an epaulette, a strap, similar to that of the epaulette, on the left shoulder.

Cap.—Black beaver ; bell shape ; 7 inches deep, 11 inches diameter, as previously described.

Breeches.—White kerseymere, with silver buttons, and buckles at the knee. White silk stockings, and shoes with plated buckles, or white pantaloons with Hessian boots. A brass-hilted sword, with black leather scabbard and gilt mounts ; a gold and crimson sword-knot with a bullion tassel. A white buffalo leather belt, 3 inches wide, with a

1822 frog worn under the coat, diagonally over the right shoulder. A black silk cravat, and white leather gloves.

DRESS.—Only differed in that white kerseymere pantaloons and Hessian boots were worn, or white breeches and leggings when on duty, and that the shoulder-belt with the regimental breast-plate was worn over the coat. The plate was rectangular, of silver, with a raised edge, and with "63," surrounded by laurel-branches, and surmounted by a crown, in gilt mounts in the middle.

A crimson silk net sash with bullion fringe ends was worn, going twice round the waist, and tied on the left side.

UNDRESS.—The lapels on the coatee were worn buttoned over, with blue-grey trousers and ankle-boots.

The Field Officers' horse furniture consisted of a dark-green saddle-cloth 2 feet 10 inches in length, and 1 foot 10 inches in depth, with an edging of silver lace $\frac{5}{8}$ inch wide, with a scarlet cloth edging. The bridle was of black leather, with a bent branch bit with gilt bosses having a Rose, Thistle, and Shamrock in the centre encircled by the words "*Infantry Mounted Officers*," and a crown above. The forehead band and roses were of green leather. A white head-collar and holster covered with black bearskin.

1823 The establishment of the Band was ordered to consist of a Sergeant (Master) and fourteen musicians.

White breeches, leggings, and shoes were discontinued for full-dress parades, and blue-grey cloth trousers and half-boots substituted. N.C.O.'s, Drummers, and Privates of Infantry regiments, at home and abroad, were ordered to have a pair of white linen trousers for full dress parades for summer wear, i.e. between the 1st May and 14th October. On 30th August a sword-belt was instituted for Officers to be worn outside a blue frock-coat. It was of black leather, without any other ornament than the usual brass rings and buckles. The clasp bore the regimental number. The bearskin cap still continued to be worn by Grenadiers in all stations in Great Britain, Ireland, and America.

Instructions were given this year that when the knapsack was not carried, the great-coat was to be folded rectangularly, 17 × 11 inches. In Light Marching Order **1824** it was to be carried in the knapsack; and in Heavy Marching Order it was to be rolled lengthways, and placed over the top of the knapsack, horse-collar fashion, round the mess-tin. The shoulder-belts were increased to $2\frac{3}{4}$ inches in width.

The Officers' waist-clasp was at this period a gilt ring, embossed with burnished **1825** oak-leaves, and in the centre a silver Fleur-de-lys, with the regimental number "*LXIII*" below also in silver on a burnished brass plate.

The Officers' silver button was of the same design as that previously described, but the rays of the Star were shorter, and did not come up to the edge. On 18th **1826** February new sashes were issued to the Sergeants. Instead of as heretofore having a single green central stripe, they had a series of three crimson and two green lines. The short jackets of the Light Company were abolished, and on 28th February alterations were made in the coats of the rank and file. The lace round the front and top of the collar was removed, and a single loop placed at each end. The lace loops on the breast varied in length, tapering from $5\frac{1}{4}$ inches at the top to $2\frac{1}{4}$ inches at the bottom. The lace was removed from the skirts, except the loops on the slashed pockets. This curious proviso is made, that the shoulder-straps shall not touch the lace on the bottom of the collar "*in order to make the men appear as broad as possible*"! Great care was also to be taken that the skirts did not open behind.

The Dress Regulations issued this year made sundry alterations in the Officers' uniform. The size of the cap was increased to 8 inches deep by 11½ inches diameter at the top. The general design remained as heretofore, but the band of silver lace was removed from the bottom, and that round the top was reduced to 2¼ inches wide.

White linen trousers to be worn from 1st April to 30th September, blue-grey, plain, without any stripe of cloth or lace on the outer seam, from 1st October to 31st March with ankle-boots.

The cross-belt plate was authorised to be of regimental design. In "DRESS," trousers, boots, and belt-plate as previously described for "FULL DRESS" were to be worn, and the gorget of gilt metal was ordered to be engraved with "G.R." and the crown, surrounded with laurel. In "UNDRESS" a black leather waist-belt with regimental clasp was authorised, the cap was to be the same as in "FULL DRESS."

The Officers' Levée dress at this period consisted of the chaco, with cap-plate, and coloured plume as laid down for Officers of the different companies, scarlet coatee with wide green lapels, silver-laced, with green collar and cuffs, white turnbacks, laced all round and edged green, silver wings with scarlet centre, green edging, and gold badges of rank (epaulettes for Officers of the Battalion Companies), white breeches, white silk stockings and black shoes with silver buckles. No belt, nor sash. Black scabbard, with gilt mounts.

On 10th April Officers of the Light Infantry Company were ordered to wear coatees corresponding with those of the rest of the Line, their only distinctions being wings, bugle ornaments, and the green cap feather. Whistles and chains were added to their cross-belts.

1827 A new knapsack, smaller, lighter, and easier of access, was introduced for the rank and file.

Another alteration was made in the chaco in December. It was still bell-shaped, but reduced in height to 6 inches, and without lace. It had gilt chin-scales, and a **1828** large gilt Star-plate in front surmounted by a crown, with a silver-cut star in the centre on which was a gilt garter, crown, and "63." Above this was a rich gold festoon, with cap lines and tassels. The Officers' lines and chin-scales were to be of gold throughout the army, irrespective of the colour of the regimental lace or embroidery. Those of all the men were to be white, except in the case of the Light Company, which were to be green. They were only to be worn on parade, and were fastened to the right side of the chaco, coming down below the chest where they were looped, with tassels on the left side. They were abolished in 1830. A white feather plume 12 inches high was worn in front of the chaco.

On 10th February the following orders were issued. The Officers' coats were to be without lapels, and with buttons in two rows of ten, in pairs. The width between **1829** the rows to be 3 inches at the top, and 2½ inches at the bottom. Uniform epaulettes to be worn throughout the Infantry; each officer to wear two. The distinctions in rank were to be by the progressive size of the bullions and devices.

1829

Captains and Subalterns to have a dark-green stripe on the epaulette strap, while Field Officers had no stripes. The Lieutenant-Colonel and Major to have devices on the strap; the Colonel to have them united. Blue-grey trousers were discontinued and those of Oxford Mixture adopted for Officers and men. A blue forage cap with a large flat stiffened top, and peak and a green band, was worn with the frock coat: the chaco only with full dress. Epaulettes not to be worn in future with wings and braided frock-coats were forbidden. A plain blue frock-coat, with regimental buttons, and a small silver shoulder cord to be worn, with a sash and cross-belt.

The black undress waist-belt introduced in 1823 was abolished in April, and a white patent leather cross-belt was ordered to be worn with the frock-coat only.

The brass chin-scales were removed from the Grenadiers' bearskins, and were replaced by a black leather strap.

In June another type of knapsack was adopted. With it, in Light Marching Order, the men's great-coats were carried inside the pack. In Heavy Marching Order they were folded square, and carried on the outside; while on the Line of March they were rolled, and carried on the top of the pack. The knapsack was carried by two shoulder-straps, united by a strap across the lower part of the chest, and crossed belts were worn, one for the bayonet and the other for the ammunition pouch.

On 20th March the then General Officer Commanding-in-Chief (Lord Hill), after having received reports from every regiment in the Service on the articles of clothing and equipment of Officers—"*distinguishing such as are fixed by the King's Regulations, and such as have been introduced without authority*"—issued a confidential circular to General Officers on the Staff, expressing his great surprise at the state of affairs disclosed, "*and the absolute necessity which exists for a decided check being given to the latitude many Commanding Officers have assumed, and the inordinate expenses they have thereby imposed upon the Officers of their respective corps.*" Gold-laced trousers seem to have been a serious cause of offence, and in this respect the 63rd Regiment is mentioned amongst others as transgressing, while the 96th had just reformed by giving them up. With a view to the reduction of expense, quotations were obtained from a number of military tailors for each article of uniform, stating "*ready-money*" prices. These were sent to the Commanding Officers of Regiments, as a check to extravagance; and it was estimated that £53 16s. 6d. should cover the cost of an Infantry Officer's outfit! The observance of the Regulations was to be enforced by frequent inspections and very close inquiry; "*and Lord Hill confidently expects that every means will be adopted by General Officers, and Commanding Officers of Regiments, to give full and complete effect to His Majesty's orders.*"

This year the regimental braid was changed. While still being white with a green stripe, this stripe, instead of as hitherto being in the centre, was now moved to the outside edge, so that when the loop was made up, it had the appearance of being white with a green edge all round.

1830

The Sergeants' pikes were abolished, and in future they were ordered to carry fusils, or short muskets, and bayonets. The cap-lines and tassels on the chacos were done away with, and the upright feather was reduced to 8 inches in height. A green worsted ball was substituted for it on the Light Company's chacos. The men's white undress jacket, which was a survival of the old white waistcoat, was replaced by one of red cloth of similar shape, and the Band was ordered to wear white coatees, with green collar and cuffs. This is the first Order concerning the Band uniforms that I have come across. Hitherto they were dressed according to the fancy of the Colonel, sometimes in the most fantastic fashion.

The Officers' gorgets were finally abolished; and their chaco-plume was ordered to be of hackle-feathers. Their crimson silk sash was ordered to go twice round the waist, and to be tied on the left hip; the pendant being 12 inches in length from the tie. Gold lace and braid this year replaced that of silver wherever worn on the Officers' uniform, and gilt buttons those of silver. The Stars on the epaulettes were to be those of the Order of the Garter. Shoes and buckles were abolished for Levées and Drawing Rooms: Officers to appear in trousers on these occasions. Officers wore a blue cloak lined with scarlet shalloon, of walking length, with clasp ornaments at the bottom of the collar.

On 30th April Field Officers were ordered to provide themselves with a buff leather waist-belt with a gilt plate in front, instead of the shoulder-belt with slings hitherto worn, and a brass scabbard instead of the black leather one. Adjutants to wear steel scabbards. Mounted officers' spurs to be of brass, with necks $2\frac{1}{2}$ inches long, including the rowels.

Oxford Mixture trousers, made perfectly plain, were ordered to be worn from 15th October to 30th April, and white linen from 1st May to 14th October. A narrow red cloth welt, like that of the present day, was ordered to be worn down the outer seams of the trousers.

Apparently "*Full Dress*" was abandoned, as no mention is made of it in the Dress Regulations issued on 1st August. The coatee is ordered to be without lapels, double-breasted, with two rows of gilt regimental buttons down the front, ten in each row, arranged in pairs. The distance between the rows to be 3 inches at the top and $2\frac{1}{2}$ inches at the bottom. A Prussian collar and cuffs of dark green, the latter round and $2\frac{3}{4}$ inches deep. Two loops of gold lace with small buttons at each end of the collar. A scarlet slashed flap on the sleeve, with four loops and small buttons, another on the skirt with four loops and large buttons. Two large buttons and four short twist loops at the waist, white turnbacks, and skirt linings, and Fleur-de-lys skirt ornaments, embroidered in gold and mounted upon green cloth. This skirt ornament was worn until it was done away with, on the introduction of the tunic in 1855.

The double-breasted coatee was worn from 1829 to 1854; the skirts being cut away very much like those of the present day civilian dress-coat.

The buttons which were gilt had a smooth edge, with "63" in the middle of an eight-pointed Star. A gilt mufti button was worn from now until about 1855, having a Fleur-de-lys mounted in the centre.

A new Forage Cap for Officers was authorised on 10th July made of blue cloth with a band of black oak-leaf pattern lace, with the regimental number embroidered in gold in front and fitted with a leather peak.

The shoulder-straps on the blue single-breasted undress frock coat were ordered to be edged with gold regimental lace all round, and with gilt metal crescents at the point of the shoulders.

Chaco-plumes were replaced by white worsted balls, those of the Light Company being green. Mounted Officers' holster caps were ordered to be covered with black leather in tropical climates.

1835 This year new bearskin caps were introduced for the Grenadier Company, the leather peak and brass plate hitherto worn being abolished.

"Regimental lace" was abolished in all regiments of infantry this year, and was replaced by plain white braid, but the square-headed loops in pairs across the breast **1836** of the men's coatees were continued. They were arranged so that when looking at a man from the front, at two yards' distance, the turnbacks of the skirts were not seen. The skirts to be rounded off over the hips and not cut angularly. The cuff to be $2\frac{3}{4}$ inches deep, its upper edge being even with the centre-point of the slashed flap on the sleeve.

The Sergeants wore a double-breasted coatee without loops on the breast with white epaulettes, those of the Flank Companies having wings.

The Drummers' lace, namely, white with three red stripes, was continued on their uniforms.

The undress jacket of the Band was ordered to be white. Side-arms to be worn **1837** on duty only—this, on account of a drunken soldier having killed a civilian in the street with his bayonet. The Jury petitioned the Ministry to order the wearing of side-arms, when off duty in the streets, to be discontinued.

A new cap instituted this year had a leather chin-strap and a linen fall behind. Two years later, however, the strap gave place to a brass curb-chain and the fall was **1839** done away with. The cap-plate was 3 inches in diameter, surrounded by a laurel wreath with "63" in the centre in raised numerals and surmounted by a crown.

The general supply of percussion caps was to be carried in a tin magazine con-**1840** taining 80–100 caps. Those for immediate use in a small patent leather pouch attached to the coat on the right side by a ring, and clear of the belts.

Alterations were again made in the cap. It was increased in depth to $6\frac{3}{4}$ inches, with a lacquered sunk top 11 inches in diameter, communicating by black leather stitched **1842** side-straps $3\frac{1}{4}$ inches apart at the top, with a band of the same which encircled the bottom of the cap, $\frac{7}{8}$ of an inch wide. A black patent leather peak. A gilt star plate, $6\frac{1}{2}$ inches long, surmounted by a crown, as previously described, in front of the cap. Lions' heads on both sides, with a gilt chin-chain attached to the left, and fastened by a hook on the right side. A red and white ball-tuft was worn in front, on top of the cap.

1844 The "Albert Chaco" was introduced; for description see under 1846.

The Officers' cap-plate worn from 1829 until this date was an eight-pointed brass Star about 5 inches wide by $5\frac{1}{4}$ inches high, surmounted by a crown. In the middle **1845** was a silver Maltese cross $3\frac{1}{2}$ inches square with a dead silver edge, and balls at the points of the arms. On the edge of the top arm, the word "*Martinique*"; and "*Guadaloupe*" on the lower one, with a gilt lion between each arm. In the centre, on a green enamelled ground, "63" surrounded by a garter charged "*West Suffolk Regiment*" and with a laurel wreath outside it.

A plain crimson woollen sash 2½ inches wide was introduced for Sergeants, and lavender-coloured trousers for Officers replaced the white ones. Bearskins were abolished for the Grenadiers, and were replaced by the new chaco.

A new chaco plate, for the Officers, was adopted this year. It was an eight-pointed Star, surmounted by a crown, and on the right-hand horizontal ray "*Egmont-op-Zee*," and on the left-hand one "*Martinique.*" On the lower vertical ray "*Guadaloupe.*" In the centre " 63 " surrounded by a garter inscribed "*West Suffolk*," and surrounded by a laurel wreath: the whole in gilded stamped brass.

The badge of the Light Company Officers was a bugle with " 63 " in the middle surrounded by a laurel and palm wreath. That of the Officers of the Grenadier Company was a garter charged "*West Suffolk*," with " 63 " in the middle, and with grenade flames at the top, the whole surrounded by a laurel and palm branches. Both these badges were mounted upon a similar Star and crown to that worn by the Battalion Company Officers.

The Dress Regulations of this year made no alterations in the Officers' coatee as laid down in 1834, except that the four short twist loops at the waist are left off, and that the loops are to be of gold lace; the entire loop not to exceed 1¼ inches in breadth and to be square-ended.

1846

The epaulettes of Field Officers to have a plain gold-lace strap, solid crescent, embroidered badge of the Queen's cipher. The fringe of a Colonel and Lieutenant-Colonel to be 3½ inches deep, and that of a Major 3 inches.

Captains to wear a gold-lace strap with narrow dark-green silk stripes, metal crescent, and fringe 2½ inches deep.

Subalterns' epaulettes to be the same as those of Captains, but with smaller fringe. Officers of Flank Companies to wear wings, the straps having three rows of gold chain, and a gilt centre-plate bearing a bugle in silver (the Grenadiers having a grenade instead); a row of bullion 1¼ inches deep at the centre, diminishing gradually towards the point. The subalterns were distinguished from captains by smaller-sized bullion.

Oxford Mixture trousers with a scarlet welt down the outer seam were worn from 15th October to 30th April, and Grey Tweed from 1st May to 14th October, in the United Kingdom and cold climates. White linen trousers to be worn in hot climates.

The chaco was of black beaver, 6¾ inches deep, and a ¼ inch less in diameter at the top than at the bottom, patent leather top, turned over at the edge to the breadth of ⅝ inch, and stitched round, a band of the same, double-stitched, encircled the bottom, a peak of patent leather 2⅜ inches deep, in front, and another 1¼ inches deep, behind. The cap-plate was a gilt Star of eight points, 4½ inches extreme diameter, surmounted by a crown, and bearing, within a wreath formed of a laurel and a palm-branch, a garter inscribed "*West Suffolk*," in the centre of which was " 63 "; the whole, including the regimental distinction, was of the same metal, without any difference of colour. A gilt chin-chain fastened at the sides with rose-pattern ornaments. A worsted ball-tuft with a gilt socket was worn in front on top. That of the Battalion Companies was two-thirds white and one-third red (at the bottom); that of the Grenadiers being white; and of the Light Company green. This chaco was designed by the Prince Consort, and was known as the " Albert Chaco." The men's chaco

1846 NOTES ON UNIFORMS, COLOURS, BADGES, ETC.

was made of felt, and had a leather chin-strap, and the small brass plate of 1845 was retained on the front.

Ankle-boots were worn, and Mounted Officers had yellow metal spurs.

The sword had a gilt half-basket hilt, with the Queen's cipher inserted in the outward bars, and lined with black patent leather, the grip of black fish-skin, bound with a spiral of three gilt wires, length of blade $32\frac{1}{2}$ inches, solid flat shoulder $1\frac{1}{2}$ inches deep, and the blade hollowed from the flat to within 9 inches of the point, which was spear-shaped. Weight not less than 1 lb. 15 oz. without the scabbard. Regimental field officers wore brass scabbards; other officers on all occasions, and field officers at Levées, Drawing-rooms, and in evening dress, black leather with gilt mountings. The sword-knot was crimson and gold, with a bullion tassel. The sword-belt of Field Officers was of buff leather worn round the waist, $1\frac{1}{2}$ inches wide with slings 1 inch wide. The waist-plate was of burnished gilt metal, rectangular in shape with "*V.R.*" surmounted by a crown, and "63" below all in silver in the centre. Other Officers wore a buff shoulder-belt, 3 inches wide, with a frog, the Adjutant the uniform of his rank, with the sword suspended by a sling from the shoulder-belt, and, in the field, a steel scabbard.

The cross-belt plate was of burnished gilt metal, rectangular in shape, with "63" in the centre with the Battle Honour "*Martinique*" on a scroll above and "*Guadaloupe*" below: a laurel branch on either side, and a crown above all. The mounts were of frosted and burnished gilt metal. The crimson silk sash going twice round the waist and tied in front of the left hip was worn as before, with a black silk stock, and white leather gloves.

For undress a scarlet shell-jacket was worn with Prussian collar and pointed cuffs of dark-green cloth. A row of small regimental buttons down the front in pairs and two on each sleeve, to fasten down the front with hooks and eyes. The shoulder-straps were formed of gold basket cord, twisted double, with a figure at the bottom and a small regimental button at the top. The frock-coat was of blue cloth single-breasted with a plain Prussian collar, eight regimental buttons down the front and two small ones on the cuff. Blue-cloth shoulder-straps edged all round with regimental gold lace, with a metal crescent at the point of the shoulder. The strap was attached to the coat by a brass tongue and a gold lace binder. The different ranks of Field Officers were distinguished by the crown and star. Officers of Grenadiers had a silver grenade, and those of the Light Company a silver bugle inside the crescent. A black patent leather waist-belt with a frog and a snake-clasp was worn with the frock-coat; Mounted Officers wearing slings instead of the frog. The forage cap previously described was continued.

The Band was augmented to a strength of 1 Sergeant and 20 Privates.

A General Order of 30th June abolished the lace loops and buttons on the skirts of the Officers' coatees, the gold Fleur-de-lys being their only ornament. The blue **1848** frock-coat was discontinued, and was replaced by a scarlet shell-jacket with dark-green collar and cuffs, but with no gold lace or other ornament. The Field Officers' badges of rank were worn on the collar. A grey cloth overcoat was introduced for Officers instead of the blue cloth cloak previously worn. A black leather sling waist-belt with a gilt snake-clasp for undress, the white shoulder-belt to be invariably worn in Full Dress.

1848 The undress uniform of an Officer of the Light Company consisted of the blue frock-coat, with eight gilt regimental buttons down the front (two rows), gilt metal epaulette, with blue shoulder pad, a crimson silk waist-sash tied on the left side, dark brown Oxford Mixture trousers with a red welt, and a blue-peaked cap, with "63" in gold embroidery in front. The Field Officers' waist-belt plate was rectangular, of gilt metal, with a crown and "63" below in silver in the centre.

At this period the Band wore a white coatee, with dark-green collar, cuffs, turn-backs, edging, and piping up the back seams; dark-green epaulette, with a white tuft at the shoulder-points; ten white buttons in pairs down the front. The cuffs were round, with two loops of white lace and buttons on them horizontally and two similar loops and buttons above them. A white leather waist-belt with brass buckle was worn, with a white pouch on the right side. Black trousers with a red stripe, and the "Albert Chaco" with a round brass plate numbered and surmounted by a crown. A red and white woollen ball in front on top. A short curved sword with a large brass cross-belt was worn in a black leather scabbard with brass mounts, suspended from the waist-belt by white slings. The undress cap was round, without peak, of red cloth with a blue band, a button in the centre and piping round the top with a brass bugle, and "63" in front. The Drummers wore a white jacket with dark-green facings; black trousers with a red stripe and white belts. Their lace was white with three red stripes. The Drums were brass with green bands round the ends, edged red, and with a white "worm" down the centre.

The men's shoulder-belt with brass plate which had hitherto carried the bayonet was done away with and a plain belt to carry the pouch was authorised, the bayonet **1850** being carried in a frog on the waist-belt. The last brass plate worn by the men was rectangular, of cast brass, with "63" in the centre surrounded by a laurel wreath and surmounted by a crown. Behind this was a Star with sixteen rays—eight long and eight short. On a curved scroll on the lower part of the Star, "*Martinique.*" Above the Star, on a curved swallow-tailed scroll, "*Egmont-op-Zee*"; and below it, on a similar scroll, "*Guadaloupe.*"

The Officers of the Grenadier Company wore the "Albert Chaco" with a white **1852** ball-tuft in front, and with the crimson cords and tassels from their waist-sash looped on the chest to the upper buttons on the coatee.

About this time a scroll inscribed "*Egmont-op-Zee*" was added to the Officers' cross-belt plate and placed above the crown. In all other respects the plate was the same as that worn from 1830 onwards.

The blue frock-coat, discarded in 1848, was reintroduced for undress. It was ordered to be double-breasted, quite plain and with covered buttons. These were later on replaced by gilt ones. Sergeants received sword-bayonets instead of the swords and triangular bayonets previously worn.

The N.C.O.s and men were ordered to wear full-dress uniform when in the streets **1853** on all occasions, between the hours of morning parade and evening roll-call. The shell or undress jacket to be worn within barracks.

Considerable alterations were made in the uniform. The long-tailed coatee, so long worn, was abolished on the 1st April; and the Officers wore a long, double-breasted tunic, with lapels, which folded back at the top, to show the green facing. They were, however, buttoned over on parade or duty. The collar which was rounded off in front **1855** was, like the cuffs, of dark-green cloth. The cuff was round, and 2¾ inches deep, with a dark-green slashed flap 6 inches by 2¼ inches wide, with three loops of ½ inch gold lace and regimental buttons on it. Two rows of nine regimental gilt buttons down the front at equal distances, the rows being 8 inches apart at the top and 4 inches at the bottom. A scarlet slashed flap on the skirt behind 10 inches deep, two buttons on the slash and one on each side of the waist, the two waist buttons being 3 inches apart, with three loops of ½ inch lace on the flap. The coat, collar, cuffs, and slashes edged with white. On the left shoulder a crimson silk cord to retain the sash with a small regimental button at the top.

Dark-blue cloth trousers, with a scarlet welt, were ordered to be worn from 1st May to 14th October in the United Kingdom and cold climates, those of Oxford Mixture at other times.

Field Officers were distinguished by lace round the top and bottom of the collar, down the edge of the skirts behind, also on the edge of the sleeve flaps; two rows of lace round the top of the cuffs, and the following badges embroidered in silver at each end of the collar, viz.:

Colonel	A crown and star.
Lieutenant-Colonel	A crown.
Major	A star.

The other Officers had lace on the top of the collar only, one row round the top of the cuffs, none on the edge of the skirts; the loops only on the skirt-flaps and sleeve flaps, and the following badges at each end of the collar:

Captain	A crown and star.
Lieutenant	A crown.
Ensign	A star.

The buttons were gilt with a raised edge with "63" in the centre of an eight-pointed Star, and the gold lace was not to exceed ½ inch in width.

A lighter and modified form of "Albert Chaco" was introduced. It was of black felt-beaver for the Officers, patent leather sunk top, turned over at the edge to the breadth of ⅜ inch, and stitched round; a band of the same double-stitched, and ⅝ inch wide round the bottom of the cap. A patent leather peak 2¾ inches wide in front, and another 1⅜ inches behind, a chin-strap ¾ inch wide fastened inside to the top of the cap. The cap-plate was a gilt Star of eight points, 3⅝ inches in extreme diameter surmounted by a crown, and having "63" in bright gold on a black ground, within a garter. A bronze gorgon's head at the back for a ventilator. Two rows of gold lace were worn round the top of it by Lieutenant-Colonels and one row by Majors. Similar ball-tufts to those previously worn were retained for the different companies.

A white enamelled leather waist-belt was introduced, 1½ inches wide, to be worn over the coat on all occasions, fitted with slings and gilt hook. The sword when hooked up to have the edge to the rear. The belt was fastened by a round gilt clasp, having on the centre-piece "63" surmounted by a crown both in silver; and on the outer circle "*West Suffolk*" in silver letters above and "*Regiment*" below. This clasp was worn until 1881. The crimson silk sash, with fringe ends, united by a crimson runner, was now to be worn diagonally over the left shoulder, instead of round the waist; the end of the fringe not to hang below the bottom of the coat.

The blue undress frock-coat was double-breasted, with a stand-up collar rounded off in front, cuffs and lapels all blue. Round cuffs $2\frac{3}{4}$ inches deep, slash flap on sleeve $5\frac{1}{4}$ inches long, $1\frac{1}{2}$ inches wide, with three small regimental buttons. Two rows of regimental buttons down the front, nine in each row at equal distances, the distance between the rows 8 inches at top and 4 inches at bottom. Slashed flaps on the skirts behind 10 inches deep, with two buttons on the slash and one on the waist. On the left shoulder a crimson silk cord to retain the sash with a small regimental button at the top. Field Officers to have the distinction of their rank (Crown and Star for Colonels, Crown, Lieutenant-Colonels, Star, Major) embroidered in gold at each end of the collar. The collars of the other Officers to be plain. Epaulettes were abolished, but other details of uniform remained as previously worn. The Officers were ordered to wear a grey cloak-coat according to the pattern, and of the same colour as the great-coats of the men.

The men wore a red double-breasted tunic edged white, dark-green collars and cuffs, and a slashed sleeve with three buttons instead of the four previously worn, while brass buttons replaced the pewter ones. Sergeants wore their sashes over the right shoulder. The men's waist-belt buckle was a round brass plate, with "63" surmounted by a crown in the centre.

The Band wore double-breasted white tunics, with dark-green facings and piping up the back seams and sleeves. The Officers' forage-cap had a straight peak, but did not differ in other respects from that previously worn. The Drummers' lace was white with three red stripes.

The Mounted Officers' saddle-cloth was ordered to be trimmed with one row of $\frac{1}{2}$ inch regimental gold lace, the same as worn on the coat, edged with a small vandyke of scarlet cloth, and the badge of rank embroidered in silver on the corner. The Adjutant's saddle-cloth to be trimmed only with a gold cord, edged with a small vandyke of scarlet cloth. The other details of the horse furniture remained as heretofore.

Pioneers discarded the musket and instead carried a saw-backed sword with **1856** in addition a shovel, pickaxe, and bill-hook. They also wore gauntlets, and the black leather aprons hitherto worn were abandoned in favour of white buckskin.

The double-breasted tunic was comparatively short-lived, and this year a single-breasted one replaced it. This had eight buttons in front set on at equal distances, **1857** dark-green collar and cuffs, the collar rounded off in front, the cuff $10\frac{1}{2}$ inches round, and $2\frac{3}{4}$ inches deep; a green slashed flap on the sleeve, 6 inches long, by $2\frac{1}{4}$ inches wide, with three loops of half-inch gold lace, and three regimental buttons. Scarlet flaps at the plaits behind, 10 inches deep, two buttons on the flap, and one at the waist, the two waist buttons being 3 inches apart, with three loops of $\frac{1}{2}$ inch gold lace. The front of the coat, collar, cuffs, and flaps were edged with white cloth $\frac{1}{4}$ inch wide, and the skirts lined white. On the left shoulder a crimson silk cord to retain the sash, with a regimental button. The trimming on the collars and the badges of rank remained as heretofore.

In other respects the uniform remained practically the same as that worn in 1855, with the exceptions that the Lieutenant-Colonel was ordered to wear two rows of regimental lace (showing a light of ¼ inch between) round the top of the chaco, the Major to wear one row. Wellington boots replaced ankle-boots for all Officers, and a crimson and gold acorn replaced the bullion tassel on the sword-knot. The scarlet shell jacket was allowed to be worn at Mess instead of the coatee hitherto worn. The men's skirts and cuffs were the same as those of the Officers, but had white lace loops on the sleeve slash instead of gold.

Mounted Officers were ordered to have brown leather bridles of cavalry pattern and steel chain-reins. The pattern of Drummers' lace sealed on 19th February this year was white with three red lines down the centre, and the fringe red and white, 1¾ inches long, with ½ inch of red, and the same width of white.

The Sergeants' sashes were ordered to be doubled longitudinally, and passed over the right shoulder under the shoulder-strap, the runner to be level with the waist-belt, and the ends of the tassels to be level with and not to hang below the skirt of the tunic. Staff-Sergeants wore a sash of a finer material and of a darker shade of crimson than the Sergeants.

The Flank Companies were abolished, and with them disappeared the white and green ball-tufts on the chacos ; the whole regiment now wearing them of

1858 the same design, viz. two-thirds white above and one-third red below, introduced in 1846.

1860 The peaks on the men's forage caps were done away with this year.

The Dress Regulations for this year thus describe the new chaco then introduced : Blue cloth with a horizontal peak of black patent leather and chin-strap. Colonels

1861 and Lieutenant-Colonels to be distinguished by two rows of regimental lace (showing a light of ¼ inch between) round the top of the chaco, Majors to wear one row. Brevet rank to be similarly distinguished. The cap was 4 inches high in front, and 6½ inches deep behind, with a black patent leather band round the bottom. The crown was 5½ × 6 inches, with a bronze Gorgon's head ventilator behind. The cap-plate was a gilt Star of eight points, surmounted by a crown, with "63" cut out within a garter, proper ventilating buttons at the sides. A red and white worsted ball-tuft with a gilt socket was worn on top in front.

Officers were ordered to wear black leather leggings 9 inches deep.

The privates wore a small white pouch on the cross-belt for carrying the percussion-caps, and a black leather ammunition-pouch on the waist-belt.

The green slashed cuff was still worn by the N.C.O.s and men. The knapsack was carried by a strap round each shoulder. The lower one across the chest was done away with, as it was found to be detrimental to the men's hearts.

The *Handbook on Equipment* published this year gives the following badges and distinctions of rank : Sergeant-Major, Quartermaster-Sergeant, Sergeant-Instructor

1865 of Musketry, Drum- or Bugle-Major, and Band-Sergeant, chevron on tunic composed of four bars of double ½ inch gold lace. The chevron of the

Sergeant-Major is surmounted by a crown, that of the Sergeant-Instructor of Musketry by a pair of muskets crossed, and that of the Drum- or Bugle-Major by a drum, or bugle, respectively. The Bandmaster-Sergeant has no chevrons, but shoulder-knots of gold cord ; Paymaster-Sergeants and Orderly-room Clerks who have attained the rank and privileges of Colour-Sergeants have three-bar chevrons of double gold lace ; Colour-Sergeants, Colour badge on tunic consisting of one bar of double gold lace surmounted by a device representing a Union flag, embroidered in silk, and cross-swords in silver. On serge frocks and shell jackets, three bars of single gold lace surmounted by a gold crown are worn. Second-class Staff-Sergeants, or Sergeants, and Lance-Sergeants have three bars of $\frac{1}{2}$ inch white worsted lace. Corporals have a chevron of two bars of the same ; Lance-Corporals have one bar ; all these are of double lace for tunics, serge frocks, and jackets. Chevrons to be worn on the right arm between the shoulder and the elbow.

The small pouch for the percussion caps was removed from the cross-belt, and attached to the front of the ammunition pouch, and covered by the flap.

The men's undress coat was a red kersey frock with plain red collar and round cuffs, seven regimental buttons down the front, and one on each red shoulder-strap.

1867 On the 1st April steel scabbards were ordered to replace the black leather ones, Field Officers, however, retaining their brass ones.

In March the double-breasted blue frock-coat was abolished and a blue patrol-jacket substituted. It was rounded off in front, with 1 inch mohair braid all round and up open slits at the sides. Four double drop loops with eyes in the centre, of $\frac{1}{4}$ inch flat plait up the front, top loops $8\frac{1}{2}$ inches, and bottom loops 6 inches long, and one row of knitted olivets. An Austrian knot on the sleeve 7 inches from bottom of cuff to top of knot. Hooks and eyes up front to neck. A stand-up collar with braid on top edge only. Pockets jetted, with flap in and out. Field Officers to have their distinctive badges embroidered in gold on the collar. No sash was worn with it and the sword-belt was worn under it.

The white leather aprons worn by Pioneers were abolished.

1868 Alterations were made in the tunic, which is thus described in the Dress Regulations subsequently issued in November 1874 :

Tunic of scarlet cloth for Officers, with collar and cuffs of dark-green cloth. The collar ornamented with $\frac{1}{2}$ inch gold lace along the top, and with gold Russia braid at the bottom, with the badges of rank, embroidered in silver, at each end. The cuffs pointed instead of slashed as heretofore, with $\frac{1}{2}$ inch lace round the top, and a tracing of gold Russia braid $\frac{1}{4}$ inch above and below the lace, the lower braid having a crow's foot and eye, and the upper an Austrian knot at the top. Eight buttons in front, and two at the waist behind, and a gold square cord loop, with a small button on each shoulder. The skirt closed behind, with a plait at each side, and lined with white. The front, collar, and skirt-plaits, edged with white cloth $\frac{1}{4}$ inch wide.

Field Officers had a row of braided eyes, below the lace on the collar, two bars of lace along the top of the cuff, showing $\frac{1}{4}$ inch of green cloth between the bars, and the braiding on the sleeve in the form of eyes, above and below the lace for Colonels and Lieutenant-Colonels, and above the lace only for Majors.

Captains had no braided eyes on the collars. The lace and braiding on the sleeves

1868 — were the same as those of Field Officers, except that the tracing was plain, without eyes. Lieutenants had one bar of lace only on the cuff.

Sergeants were ordered to wear chevrons of ½ inch gold lace on their tunics and shell-jackets; and Regimental Staff-Sergeants, ranking with the Colour-Sergeants, to be distinguished by a crown over the three-bar chevron.

A Levée dress for the Officers was approved, including gold-laced trousers, the lace 1⅛ inches wide with a crimson silk stripe down the centre of the face ⅛ inch wide; a gold and crimson net sash 2½ inches wide in ½ inch strips of gold and crimson alternately; gold and crimson runners and tassels, and a gold lace sword-belt of the same pattern as the lace on the trousers, with slings of similar pattern ¾ inch wide.

The men's tunic had seven buttons down the front, and was edged with white cloth ¼ inch wide. The shoulder-straps were edged with white braid and the cuffs were pointed, and edged with white cloth along the top with a tracing of white braid below it, showing a green light ¼ inch wide. The Band wore the blue chaco, with brass plate, and red and white ball-tuft, a white single-breasted tunic, with green collar (rounded in front), cuffs, and slash on the sleeve. These parts, as well as the front edge of the tunic, were edged with red cloth. Green and white wings, and green shoulder-straps edged with red cloth. On the slash on the sleeve were three bastion-shaped loops of white braid, and gilt regimental buttons. Bandsmen wore dark-blue trousers with a red stripe.

The Drummers wore a red single-breasted tunic, edged white, with green collar and cuffs, and brass buttons. Their chaco and trousers were the same as those worn by the Band. Their lace was white with two red lines, and there was a line of it down the front of each sleeve and also up the back seams. They wore a white-edged green slash on the cuff and green and white shoulder-straps.

1870 The rank of "*Ensign*" was abolished, being replaced by that of "*Sub-Lieutenant.*"

This year radical alterations were made in uniform. The men's tunics were altered in colour from brick-red to scarlet like those of the Officers. Thus for the first

1871 time the same colour was worn by Officers and men alike. The green cuff was pointed, and was edged with white braid, forming a crow's foot at the top. Only blue trousers are mentioned in the Dress Regulations; cloth in winter, and tartan in summer. The round forage-cap with the regimental number in front, worn previously by the N.C.O.s and men, and known as the "Kilmarnock," was replaced by a Glengarry cap; the old knapsack was withdrawn, and what was known as the "*Valise Equipment*" substituted. The white tunics of the Band were abolished, and they now wore scarlet, being distinguished by a badge of crossed trumpets on the right arm. The Regimental Drummers' lace was done away with, and replaced by one of universal pattern, viz. white, with red crowns, and red and white fringe. Numbers were abolished on the men's buttons; and one of universal pattern, bearing the Royal Arms, was substituted. A plain scarlet serge frock took the place of the red cloth shell jacket for undress, with a line of white braid round the cuff, making a loop in the middle. It had six buttons in front, two pockets with flaps at the hips, and red shoulder-straps with the number of the regiment in white embroidery. A new chaco was introduced, 4 inches high in front and 6½ inches at the back. Gold braid ¼ inch wide round the bottom, up the sides and back, and two rows round the top, ⅛ inch apart. A gilt cap-plate with " 63 " cut out in the centre within a garter bearing the Royal Motto, a laurel wreath round, and a crown above. A burnished gilt chain ½ inch wide, lined with black velvet, gilt rose fastenings at the sides, and a gilt lion's head hook at the back. Colonels and Lieutenant-Colonels had two lines of ½ inch lace round the chaco at the top, instead of braid. Majors had a line of ½ inch lace instead of the upper line of braid. A worsted red and white ball-tuft, divided two-thirds white and one-third red (below), was worn in a brass socket in front, on top of the chaco.

The men's chaco was of the same size and type, but had a red and black striped braid round the top and bottom only, with ventilating buttons on the sides, close to the top.

A puggaree badge worn by the Officers about this time consisted of a silver Fleur-de-lys, with a gilt band at the middle, and a gilt " 63 " below it mounted on the bottom of the emblem.

A universal pattern of Infantry Mess jacket was introduced for the first time, and is thus described in the Dress Regulation for 1874. Scarlet cloth shell jacket, with collar and pointed cuffs of the regimental facings (green). Gold braid edging all round, including the top and bottom of the collar. A loop of gold braid at the bottom of the collar to fasten across the neck. Shoulder cords as on the tunic, i.e. a square gold cord loop, with a small button. A row of gilt studs and hooks and eyes down the front. Scarlet silk lining. Field Officers had a row of braided eyes on the collar below the upper line of braid, and the badges of rank embroidered in silver at each end. Colonels and Lieutenant-Colonels had two chevrons of braid on each sleeve ¾ inch apart, the upper forming an Austrian knot extending to 10 inches from the bottom of the cuff, and the lower braid a crow's foot and eye : a row of braided eyes above and below the chevrons as on the tunic. Majors had the same braiding on the sleeve, omitting the lower row of braided eyes. Captains had similar braiding but without the braided eyes. Lieutenants had a single chevron of braid forming an Austrian knot 8 inches high and a crow's foot and eye below it. The Mess waistcoat was of dark-green cloth with gold braid edging round the top, down the front, and along the bottom to the side seams. The pockets edged with gold braid forming crow's foot and eyes. A row of gilt studs and hooks and eyes down the front. On State Occasions, and at balls, blue cloth trousers with gold lace and crimson silk stripe in the centre, down the side-seam were worn. With the tunic on these occasions a gold and crimson net sash was worn, and sword-belt as described above. The waist-plate was a round gilt clasp with " 63 " surmounted by a crown, in silver, on the centre-piece, and the title " *West Suffolk*," in silver, above on the outer circle and " *Regiment* " below.

The shell jacket of the rank and file was abolished, and a kersey frock substituted with green collar and a plain braided cuff. Brass numerals were added to the shoulder-strap instead of worsted. The men's tunic was edged with white cloth down the front, with a line of narrow white braid along the bottom of the collar. The collar was rounded in front and was 1½ inches deep with plain round green cuffs and seven gilt buttons in front. Two white cloth lines from the waist buttons downwards.

A new great-coat was authorised for the Officers, of grey milled cloth, coming within 12 inches of the ground. It was double-breasted with two rows of gilt regimental buttons down the front; six in each row, and 6 inches apart at the top and 4 inches at the bottom. It was fitted with a detachable cape, coming down to the knuckles, and fastening in front with four small buttons.

In the Dress Regulations for this year two sizes of swords were authorised for Infantry Officers. The full size had a blade 35 inches long, and $1\frac{1}{8}$ inches wide at the shoulder, extreme length, including the hilt, 41 inches, weight, without scabbard, 2 lbs. The blade of the second size was 35 inches long, and 1 inch wide at the shoulder; extreme length, including hilt, $38\frac{1}{4}$ inches, weight without scabbard, 1 lb. 12 oz. In other respects the details were the same as those previously described.

1874

Slight alterations were made in the horse furniture. The dark-green saddle-cloth was ordered to be 3 feet long at the bottom and 2 feet deep; and brown leather holster-caps were to be worn in tropical climates. Mounted Officers were ordered to wear pantaloons, knee boots, and black patent leather sabretaches.

A new Mess jacket with a stand-up collar was adopted, also a new waistcoat. Badges of rank to be worn on the collars: Captains, a crown and star; Lieutenants, a crown; Second-Lieutenants, a star. The peak of the forage caps to be horizontal and the body $2\frac{3}{8}$ inches high.

Chacos were now abolished, and a cork helmet covered with blue cloth was introduced. It is described as follows in the Dress Regulations published in 1883: Cork, covered with blue cloth in four seams, two on each side, peaks, front and back, the front peak pointed, and bound with gilt metal $\frac{3}{8}$ inch wide, the back peak with patent leather $\frac{1}{8}$ inch wide. Above the peaks and going round the helmet a cloth band $\frac{3}{4}$ inch wide. Back peak to centre of crown $10\frac{1}{2}$ inches, front peak to centre of crown $10\frac{1}{4}$ inches, side to centre of crown 8 inches. Gilt curb chain chin-strap $\frac{5}{8}$ inch wide lined with black velvet. Gilt rose fastenings at the sides; gilt convex bar down the centre of the back, and to the bottom of the back peak. At the top of the helmet, a gilt spike, mounted on a cross-piece base. Height of spike $2\frac{3}{4}$ inches, total height of spike and base cross-piece $3\frac{1}{4}$ inches, diameter of spike $\frac{7}{8}$ inch. From front to back the cross-piece was $4\frac{3}{8}$ inches by $3\frac{1}{2}$ inches wide, with a small rose at each of the four terminations which were punctured for ventilation. There was a gilt hook at the back of the base to which the chin-strap could be attached when not worn under the chin. The same plate as that worn since 1871 on the chaco was at first worn on the helmet. It was altered in 1879 to a brass gilt Star of eight points, surmounted by a crown. In the centre, inside a garter charged with the motto, "63," on a black velvet centre. The whole surrounded by a laurel wreath all in gilt brass.

1878

The men's helmets were similar, but with rounded front peaks, bound with leather, and without the convex bar behind. Their helmet plate was of stamped brass.

The valise equipment consisted of an ammunition bag, a waist-belt, a set of braces, two ammunition pouches, each containing twenty rounds, a pair of great-coat straps, a pair of mess-tin straps, a pair of straps for supporting the valise, and a valise of black leather to hold the service kit. All the straps were of buff leather, pipe-clayed. Only one pouch was carried on ordinary occasions in peace, and that on the right side, and the ammunition bag only during rifle practice, or when required for blank ammunition. The braces were attached to the waist-belt when full ammunition was carried, as the weight was then too great for the waist-belt alone. The great-coat was folded about 8 inches high, by 16 inches in width. It was carried behind the shoulders, and the valise at the waist with the mess-tin between it and the great-coat. The haversack was carried on the left side, suspended from a white canvas belt over the right shoulder, and the water-bottle on the right side, by a narrow white leather strap over the left shoulder. The regimental number was painted in white on the flap of the valise. With a view to facilitating exchanges between the "linked battalions," the facings on the collars and cuffs on the men's tunics from now until 1881 were a green tab, somewhat like the present-day staff-pattern. The back of the collars and the cuffs was of the same colour as that of the rest of the coat, and the latter had white braid round them, with a crow's foot at the top. The men wore the regimental number at each end of their collars.

The badges of rank worn by Officers were removed from the collars, and placed on the shoulder cords of the tunic and mess jacket. Cloth straps were added to the shoulders of the patrol jacket, which bore the rank badges. The Officers' **1880** Glengarry ornament was a silver Fleur-de-lys, with a gilt band round the middle.

On the introduction of the Territorial System, and the amalgamation of the 63rd and 96th regiments under the title of "*The Manchester Regiment*," the former lost its **1881** green and the latter its yellow facings. As an English regiment, both battalions were now ordered to wear white facings.

N.B. Henceforward the changes in dress, mentioned in these notes, will apply equally to both battalions.

The helmet plate was now a gilt metal Star surmounted by a crown. On the Star a laurel wreath, within the wreath a garter inscribed with the garter motto, and within the garter the arms of the city of Manchester in silver on a black velvet ground. On the bottom of the wreath a silver scroll inscribed "*The Manchester Regiment.*" The dimensions of the plate were: from the top of the crown to bottom of plate 5 inches; extreme width of Star $4\frac{1}{4}$ inches. The bottom central ray of the Star came half-way over the cloth band of the helmet.

Shoulder-straps of twisted round gold cord, lined with scarlet, and with a small regimental button at the top, were added to the tunic, and "rose pattern" gold lace, $\frac{5}{8}$ inch wide, replaced that previously worn. A Sphinx over "*Egypt*" in gold embroidery; the word "Egypt" embroidered in silver was worn on the collar of the tunic, the buttons had on them the garter with motto, and within it the Sphinx over Egypt, with the crown above. The waist-plate had an eight-pointed Star in silver, on a frosted gilt ground on the Star in dead gilt metal the Sphinx over "Egypt." On the circle "*The Manchester Regiment.*" The waist-plate of the sword-belt worn on State Occasions and at balls was altered to a round gilt clasp, and the Royal Crest, in silver, on a frosted gilt centre, a wreath of laurels forming the outer circle.

A new forage cap of blue cloth was introduced, straight up, 3 inches high, with black patent leather drooping peak, and chin-strap. The peak ornamented with $\frac{1}{4}$ inch, full, gold embroidery. A band of black oak-leaf lace, $1\frac{3}{4}$ inches wide, round the bottom of the cap. Field Officers had a gold French braid welt, instead of blue cloth round the top of the cap. The badge worn in front consisted of the Sphinx over Egypt in gold embroidery, the word " Egypt " in silver embroidery. Below, on a blue cloth gold embroidered scroll "*Manchester Regiment.*"

A blue Glengarry forage cap, of a similar pattern to that worn by N.C.O.s and men but not so deep, was introduced for Active Service and Peace Manœuvres. It was bound with black silk riband an inch wide, with riband ends $1\frac{3}{8}$ inches wide, with a blue tuft on the top. A black silk cockade on the left side, on which was worn, on scarlet cloth, the arms and motto of the City of Manchester, and on a scroll below "*The Manchester Regiment*," all in silver.

Shoulder-straps with badges of rank as for the tunic were added to the mess jacket, and a white mess waistcoat was instituted.

The men's tunics had plain round white cuffs.

1882 The saddle cloths hitherto worn in Review Order by the Mounted Officers were abolished, and a new valise equipment was introduced for the men.

Alterations were made in the badges of rank still worn on the shoulder-straps. Colonels, to wear a crown, and two stars below, Lieutenant-Colonels, a crown and star below, Majors, a crown, Captains, two stars, Lieutenants, one star.

1883 White metal whistles, of the same pattern as those used by Sergeants, were authorised for all Officers.

1890 The serge frock was issued to the men with the shoulder-straps only of the colour of the regimental facings, i.e. white.

1891 Second Lieutenants were ordered to wear no badges of rank, but otherwise to be dressed as Lieutenants.

In the 1st Battalion the Officers' puggaree brooch and field service cap ornament

1892 worn at this time was a silver Fleur-de-lys; this was doubtless a "regimental custom."

1893 The swords to be $32\frac{1}{2}$ inches long, and 1 inch wide at the shoulder, and to weigh, without the scabbard, from 1 lb. 12 oz. to 1 lb. 13 oz.

Brown leather gloves to be worn by Officers, in other than Review Order, when white ones to be worn as heretofore. White buff leather sword-belts to replace those

1896 of white enamelled leather. A scarlet serge patrol jacket was authorised, with white collar, cuffs, and shoulder-straps. A small metal regimental button at the top of the strap with the badges of rank thereon in gold. The collar rounded in front. Five small regimental buttons down the front, and a patch pocket with pointed flap, and small button on each breast. The cuffs were pointed, 5 inches deep in front and 2 inches behind. No badges on the collar. A forage cap for Active Service and Peace Manœuvres of a new type was introduced. It was of blue cloth, "Austrian" pattern, similar in shape to that worn by N.C.O.s and men. It had two small brass buttons in front; and could be turned down on occasion, and buttoned over the chin. The same badge was worn with it as previously with the Glengarry, but the scroll below the Arms was altered from silver to gilt, with the word "*Manchester*" only on it. The steel chains of the Mounted Officers' horse furniture were replaced by head-ropes.

The Mounted Officers' sabretache and bear-skin wallet covers were abolished and also the Levée dress. A new type of sword was adopted, with a straight blade $32\frac{9}{16}$ inches long from shoulder to point, fullered on both sides, and with a steel hilt, pierced with an ornamental device, so arranged as not to permit of a sword point passing through, so as to injure the hand, with "*V.R.*" and Crown near the top. A fish-skin grip bound with silver wire, the length of the grip 5 to $5\frac{3}{4}$ inches. The weight of the sword was 2 lbs. and of the steel scabbard and lining $16\frac{3}{4}$ oz.

The collars of tunics, frock-coats, and jackets were ordered to be cut square at top in front, fastening with two hooks and eyes and not to exceed 2 inches in height.

A new Mess dress was authorised, consisting of a scarlet cloth jacket edged all round with white piping, and with a white roll collar and lapels, white pointed cuffs and cloth shoulder-straps, with badges of rank in gilt metal upon them. Small buttons and button-holes down the front. A white washing waistcoat with lapels, fastened with four $\frac{1}{2}$-inch gilt regimental buttons, on which the regimental device, as on the buttons of the tunic, was mounted in silver.

A universal pattern brown leather "Sam Browne" belt, with two braces, revolver case, ammunition pouch, frog, and brown leather scabbard, was ordered to be worn by all Officers, with yellow metal fittings. When the leather sword-belt was worn under the tunic a web belt was carried over the right shoulder as a support.

A blue serge frock, with collar and cuffs of the same material, in other respects resembling the scarlet frock, was worn, but this was abolished in 1902.

The men's tunics had white pointed cuffs and collars; red shoulder-straps edged white, slashed skirts with white cloth edging, the skirts undivided. The collar was $1\frac{3}{8}$ inches deep, rounded in front. Drummers' and Buglers' tunics were trimmed with white lace with red crowns thereon, down all back and side seams, along the shoulders and down both sides of the arm, with slashed skirts, and wings with fringe.

The Bandsmen wore scarlet tunics with scarlet wings (without fringe), and shoulder straps of the same showing a white cloth edge: a button at the top, and the name of the regiment in brass capitals on the strap. A white collar with the regimental badge an inch from each end. White cloth edging down the front, and pointed white cuffs. The skirts were slashed, and there were seven gilt buttons down the front of the tunic. The back and side seams were piped with white cloth, as well as the seams of the sleeves.

The Sergeant-Drummer and the Sergeant of the Band wore plain broad gold lace on their wings instead of white braid.

In January a new Service Dress was introduced, for wear at home and abroad. It was first supplied to units returning from the South African War. The following is the official description of the men's dress:—

Great-coats.—Made of rainproofed drab mixture cloth, weighing about 27 ounces per yard. Detachable capes are not worn, being replaced by a short cape with shoulder-flaps attached to the coat, and the armholes are made large to facilitate the garment being put on and taken off, an adjustable waist-strap at the back.

Head-dress.—A hat of thick felt with wide brim, the sides perforated about $\frac{3}{8}$ inch from the top with two rows of ventilating holes. Ventilation is also provided at the head band, and clips are provided for fastening up the brim.

Jacket.—Made of a drab mixture serge with a turned-down roll collar, shoulder rifle patches, two patch breast pockets with pleats, two strong side pockets with flaps, and pleated slightly at the waist. It has a wide false pleat down the centre of the back, and the shoulder-straps are removable.

Trousers.—Of drab-mixture tartan, cut narrow as they approach the ankle, and made short, just reaching the top of the ankle-boot. They are not to be worn in public without leggings or puttees. Titles embroidered in white letters on a red ground, on a curved strip on the upper arms of jackets and great-coats. The battalion number embroidered in similar colours on a separate patch close under the title. Chevrons and badges of rank of special colour and material to be worn on both arms. Crowns to be worn by Colour-Sergeants in place of Colours. No collar badges to be worn. Buttons of gilding metal which, when not polished for some time, assumes a dull colour matching the material. For the present, forage, field, or Glengarry caps to be worn at home with the service dress.

OFFICERS.—*Home Service.*—Cap, forage, staff pattern, of material to match the service dress, but of cotton waterproofed; wide peak set at an angle of about sixty degrees, and carried well back to protect the temples, brown leather chin-strap.

Abroad.—Felt hat, Army pattern.

Jacket.—Special mixture serge, of the same colour as that issued to the men, single-breasted, very loose at the chest and shoulders, stand and fall collar fitted with hook and eye. Two cross patch pockets, with flap, and central pleat. Two expanding pockets below the waist, with flaps and buttons. Five large buttons down the front. Shoulder-straps of Melton cloth, the same colour as the garment, edged all round, except at the shoulder seam, with $\frac{1}{4}$ inch scarlet cloth, the top of the strap triangular, with a small button on it. Cuffs pointed. Buttons of "gilding metal," ungilt, die struck of regimental pattern. Rank shown by braiding on the sleeves, with drab braid $\frac{3}{16}$ inch wide. *Second Lieutenant:* Cuffs edged all round, a crow's foot at the point. *Lieutenant:* As above, with double lines of braid added midway between the point of the seams of the sleeves, the lines to be 3 inches long, starting from the braid round the top of the cuff with a crow's foot at the top. *Captain:* As for Lieutenant, with additional double lines 3 inches long from the crow's foot at the point of the cuff, a crow's foot at the top. *Major:* As for Captain, with additional double lines added midway between the two outer and centre lines, $6\frac{1}{2}$ inches long, beginning at the braid at the cuffs, a crow's foot at the top. *Lieutenant-Colonel:* As for Major, with double lines added to the Captain's loop, 5 inches long from the top of the crow's foot; an Austrian knot $2\frac{1}{2}$ inches in length at the top. Khaki knickerbocker breeches and putties or Bedford cord breeches; brown leather leggings and brown leather ankle-boots were worn with steel spurs for Mounted Officers.

The badges were: on the forage cap and felt hat, the Arms of the City of Manchester in brown bronze metal, and the same on the collar of the jacket. On the 1st February the following alterations were made in the Officers' Full Dress uniform: The skirts of the tunic to be made with three-pointed slashes edged with white piping as on the collar, three buttons at the points. A red silk web waist-sash, 2¼ inches wide, with round ends, to be worn with the tassels over the left hip and coming 4 inches below the tunic. The web sword-belt to be worn, under the tunic with gold lace sword slings ⅞ inch wide. No piping, gold lace, or braiding to be worn on the mess jacket or waistcoat; and no buttons on any part of the jacket. The shoulder-straps to be of red cloth, and sewn down. Collar-badges as on the tunic to be worn on the roll collar, with regulation badges of rank in embroidery on the shoulder-strap. All tunics to be laced as laid down for Lieutenants, distinctive rank lacing done away with, and also in all ranks the crow's foot and eye below the lace on the cuffs. The following items of dress were abolished: Crimson silk shoulder-sash; the full-dress sash, sword-belt, and gold and crimson trouser lace; buff sword-belt, slings, and buff sword-knot, brass spurs for Mounted Officers, and "*undress*" clothing and equipment. A universal pattern great-coat, frock-coat, and forage cap was introduced, replacing those previously worn. The great-coat was of drab-mixture cloth, double-breasted, to reach within a foot of the ground; stand and fall collar 5 inches deep, an extending pleat down the back terminating under the back strap, loose turnback cuffs 6 inches deep; two rows of buttons down the front, four in each row, about 6½ inches apart, the rows 8 inches apart at top, and 4 inches at the bottom. A 2-inch cloth back-strap fastened with three buttons. Shoulder-straps as for service dress.

A forage cap of the Staff (or Naval) pattern was adopted, with a plain peak for Officers below field rank, to be of blue cloth with a black band of oak-leaf lace, and a scarlet welt round the crown. The badge in front was the same as that worn already. The frock-coat was of blue cloth double-breasted, with a stand-up collar; plain sleeves, with two small buttons at the bottom; two rows of regimental buttons down the front, six in each row at equal distances, the distance between the rows being 6 inches at the top and 4½ inches at the bottom, flaps behind 10 inches deep, with two buttons on each flap, and one on each side of the waist, the skirt to reach the knees. Shoulder-straps of the same material as the coat with pointed tops and a small button and embroidered badges of rank. On the collar the Sphinx embroidered in gold, over "*Egypt*" embroidered in silver. The crimson silk waist-sash was worn with it, and when the sword was carried the web sword-belt with slings was worn under the silk waist-sash.

The skirt of the men's tunics was made with a slash like those of the Officers.

A new forage cap was introduced for the men. It was similar in shape to that worn by sailors, of blue cloth, and with a semicircular patch of the colour of the regimental facing (white) in front, on which the regimental badge was worn. It was very unpopular; and was nicknamed "*Brodrick*" by the men, after the then Secretary of State for War.

The Dress Regulations for this year make certain alterations in the Officers' Service jacket. The cuffs to be round, with a three-pointed flap edged with ½ inch chevron lace. Badges of rank, in worsted embroidery, to be worn on the flaps. Rings of worsted chevron lace, and tracing braid to be worn round the cuff, according to rank: *Second Lieutenant* and *Lieutenant*: one row of chevron lace. *Captain*: two rows of chevron lace. *Major*: three rows with tracing braid between them. *Lieutenant-Colonels:* three rows of chevron lace and four rows of tracing braid. *Colonel:* four rows of lace and five of braid. The arms of the City of Manchester, with a scroll below inscribed " *Manchester,*" all in bronze, were worn on the collar by the 2nd Battalion, and a bronze Fleur-de-lys by the 1st Battalion.

Badges of rank were restored to *Second Lieutenants,* who were ordered to wear one star ; *Lieutenants,* two ; and *Captains,* three stars, on the tunic and frock-coat, mess and service jackets.

The forage cap was of blue cloth with a top 9¼ inches in diameter, and 3¼ inches deep with a 1¾-inch band round the bottom. A patent leather peak set on at an angle of 45 and 1¾ inches deep. A black patent leather chin-strap ⅜ inch wide, with a ½-inch button at each end close behind the peak. The badge worn in front was the Arms of the City of Manchester in silver, with a gilt scroll below, inscribed " *Manchester.*"

Brown leather bandoliers and pouches were introduced for the men. A forage cap similar to that introduced for Officers in 1902 was adopted for the men. It was

1905 of blue cloth, with a patent leather peak, but without the lace band round the head. It had a patent leather chin-strap, with a small universal type brass button at each side. The cap badge was the Manchester Arms, in white metal, with a brass scroll below.

Web equipment replaced leather for the men. It consisted of a khaki-coloured canvas knapsack, 15 × 13 × 4 inches, carried behind the shoulders, and supported

1908 by khaki canvas straps over the shoulder, with braces to the waist-belt. All the straps and belts were fastened, and adjusted, by brass D buckles. A canvas haversack, 11 × 9 × 2 inches, was carried on the left side. Five ammunition pouches, each holding fifteen rounds, were carried on each side, in front, three below and two above, attached to the knapsack shoulder-straps. A small entrenching tool was carried in a canvas case on the right hip behind, and the short wooden handle, when not in use, was detached, and strapped along the front of the scabbard of the bayonet. The mess-tin was carried in a khaki cover, below the knapsack, and a tin drinking cup on the outside of the haversack. The whole equipment could be put on and taken off together.

This was the equipment worn by the soldier during the Great War, 1914–18.

In the Dress Regulations issued this year *Second Lieutenants on Probation* are ordered to wear no badges of rank. White covers are authorised to be worn on the

1911 blue forage cap in hot weather. The cap to be worn evenly on the head, and not with Service dress unless especially ordered as a distinguishing mark between opposing forces.

White linen collars were authorised to be worn with the Service dress jacket and the undress frock-coat, but not to show more than ⅛ inch above the uniform. Tunic collars to be square in front, and not more than 2 inches high.

Drab flannel shirts to be worn with Service dress, with turn-down collars, and khaki ties. Certain minor alterations were made in the Service dress jacket. A stand

1913 and fall collar was adopted, with four regimental buttons down the front of the jacket, and the false pleat at the back was done away with. Plain cloth shoulder straps were added in place of the twisted drab lace shoulder cords hitherto worn. Brown leather leggings, fastening up the front with laces and six studs were authorised for wear with the drab Service dress for Mounted Officers other than those wearing the brown field boot.

The men's Service jacket was made with a plain back, with a slit at the bottom of each side seam ; there was no demarcation of a cuff, and the shoulder-straps and rolled collar were retained.

By A.O. 279, August 1913, the Officers' jack-spur, or swan-neck pattern spur, was abolished. It was replaced by a light straight hunting spur of sealed pattern, to be worn with Butcher boots, field, and ankle boots, steel chains and black straps with black boots, and brown straps, shields, and steel chains with brown boots. With Wellington boots box spurs with plain rowels as before. Swords to be carried on the saddle by all Mounted Officers, in all mounted orders of dress, other than Review Order.

The web sword-belt with gold slings to be worn under the tunic by all Mounted Officers ; and over it by all other Officers.

The men's tunic had a white collar, 1½ inches deep, cut square in front, with the regimental badge at the ends, white pointed cuffs, and white shoulder-straps, pointed at the top with a button, and "*Manchester*" in brass capitals along the bottom. Seven brass buttons down the front, which was edged white, and slashed skirts.

For some time prior to the Great War the 1st Battalion wore the Fleur-de-lys as a regimental badge, and since its re-formation in 1918–19 the Officers have worn it as a cap-badge and on the collar of the Service jacket ; the men, however, wearing the regulation badge, viz. the Arms of Manchester.

During the Great War (1914–18) the Officers and men wore their Service uniform with trousers and putties. At first the stiff-topped cap was worn, but as it was found to reflect the light, and thus attract the enemy's fire, a soft-topped cap of similar shape was worn instead.

After the first few months of the war, owing to the great preponderance of the injuries being head-wounds, steel "shrapnel helmets" were served out to both officers and men. They were painted khaki colour and in some cases sand was scattered over the paint whilst wet. The men wore the 1908 web equipment as previously described. The shrapnel helmet, when not in use, was carried on the back of the knapsack, the edges being passed under the two narrow straps, which went over, and secured, the pack.

In winter the men wore sleeveless coats made of sheep- or goatskins, over their khaki great-coats (some units wore leather jackets with sleeves), and thick woollen gloves. When in the trenches india-rubber thigh boots were issued.

The Officers carried khaki canvas knapsacks and haversacks like those of the men, and discarded their swords. In some units they carried rifles, and all wore their Sam Browne equipment, with revolvers, electric torches, compasses, etc.

A short wool-lined double-breasted khaki cloth overcoat was worn coming down to the knees, and known as a "British warm." It had a turned-down collar 2½ inches deep, and three large leather buttons on each front and two small ones on each slit cuff. The shoulder-straps were of the same material as the coat, triangular at the top, and fastened with a small leather button, and metal badges of rank were worn on them.

96TH REGIMENT, NOW THE 2ND BATTALION

This Regiment, sometimes spoken of in official documents as "*Monson's*," and nicknamed "*the Backwards*" from the number reading the same when upside down,

1760-3 was when raised ordered to have buff facings, but to wear no lace on their uniform while on service in the East Indies. As apparently it never did any European service its uniform would closely follow that described for the 63rd Regiment during the same period; but without any lace, and with buff, instead of dark-green facings. The order further states that the coats were to be "*lapelled, and by His Majesty's Regulations.*"

I have been unable to trace any record of the colour of the facings of this Regi-

1780-3 ment, but the other details of the uniform would correspond with those described for the same period for the first battalion.

I have come across a letter in the Public Record Office dated Adjutant-General's Office 14.vii.1795, stating that owing to the clothing having been made up in a hurry

1793-8 in Ireland, blue facings had been supplied in error. As the clothing was then "*upon the men's backs*" in the West Indies, His Majesty had on that account been pleased to suffer it to be worn for one year only; after the expiration of which the colour of the facings was to be changed.

What the original colour should have been, or to what it was eventually changed, I have been unable to discover.

With the exception of the facings, the rest of the uniform would agree with that previously described for the 63rd Regiment at this period.

This Regiment was originally the 2nd Battalion of the 52nd Foot, and when renumbered retained the buff facings, and silver lace then worn by it. The uniform,

1803-15 with the exception of the colour of the facings, would be the same as that previously described in the corresponding period. The loops were arranged in pairs; square-ended; of white lace with red, yellow, and blue stripes. The waistcoats and breeches were buff. A tailor's book of the period describes the Officer's coat as having buff cloth facings, cuffs, and collar, ten holes by twos in the lapels, four on the pointed cross-flaps, four on the cuffs. The skirts lined and turned back with buff and buff edging.

The Inspection Return from Antigua, dated 18th June, state that "*The officers wear short coats and round hats.*" These were similar to the present day "wideawake"

1805 with a round top, curved brim, a black fur crest from front to rear over the crown, and with a black silk cockade and red and white plume on the left side.

1814 From Schooten, in Holland, on 26th April 1814, it is reported that "*The officers and men had on the new Regulation Cap.*"

This Regiment retained the blue facings worn when it was the *97th, or Queen's German Regiment*, the rest of the uniform being the same as that described for the 63rd

1815-18 Regiment during this period. The Officers had silver lace on their uniform, and their cross-belt plate was of gilt-metal, rectangular in shape, with rounded corners. In the centre in raised letters "*96th, or Queen's Own*" surrounded by laurel branches, and surmounted by a Sphinx, with a French flag over the left shoulder.

Their chaco-plate was a round silver plate, about 2¼ inches in diameter, with a gilt crown above. At the top of the plate and below the crown was a curved label of gilt metal inscribed "*Peninsula*," and at the bottom another one inscribed "*Queen's Own*." In the middle "96" with a Sphinx with flag, and "*Egypt*" above it, both surrounded by laurel branches, the stalks of which come below the bottom of the silver plate. All the mountings were of gilt metal. The chaco-plate was mounted on a circle of gold lace with a crimson line in the centre.

When the present Second Battalion was raised the facings were yellow, and they were worn until the institution of the Territorial System in 1881. The Officers' lace was silver, and continued so until the general adoption of gold lace in 1830. Their cross-belt plate was of gilt metal, rectangular, with square corners, with "96" in the centre, surmounted by a crown, the device being mounted on the plate.

1824

The regimental lace was white, with a blue, "worm," or wavy line, near each edge, and with a yellow central stripe. It was worn until 1836, when coloured laces were abolished. The loops of lace on the breast of the men's coatees were "square-ended," and 3 inches long.

The various changes in the uniform would closely follow those of the 63rd as previously described from 1824 to 1889, bearing in mind that the facings were yellow, instead of dark-green.

A peculiarity in the dress of this Regiment was that from 1878 onwards, and possibly before, the Officers' crimson silk shoulder sash was of ribbon, instead of net. Their gold lace had a scalloped edge ; and the N.C.O.s and men wore the regimental number, and a Sphinx with "*Egypt*" on the collars of their tunics.

The cross-belt plate worn from 1826 until they were done away with in 1855 was a rectangular gilt frosted plate bearing in the centre an eight-pointed elliptical Star with a bright gilt edging, with a garter in the middle charged with the Royal motto and surmounted by a crown. In the centre of the garter, on a gilt frosted centre, "96" in silver.

The Field Officers' waist-belt plate worn from 1824 to 1832 was rectangular, of frosted silver with a bright bevelled edge, and with "96" surmounted by a crown mounted in bright silver in the centre. The Officers' chaco-plate was an elliptical eight-pointed silver-cut Star. In the centre in silver ornamental numerals "96," surrounded by a gilt pierced garter and motto, and surmounted by a gilt crown ; all on a frosted gilt ground.

The Officers' chaco-plate worn during this period was a gilt elliptical Star of eight points about 5 × 6 inches surmounted by a crown. In the middle was a silver-cut eight-pointed Star, with a bright gilt metal edging, and in the centre a gilt garter inscribed with the Royal motto with "96" in silver, inside it, on a frosted gilt ground. The waist-belt clasp from 1832 to 1840 for Field Officers was of gilt burnished metal with "96" in the centre in silver fancy numerals. From 1840 to 1855 it had "*V.R.*" surmounted by a crown, and "96" below, all in silver.

1829–45

1847 This year the cap-plate worn was a dull gilt eight-pointed Star surmounted by a crown; in the centre, a dull gilt garter charged with the Royal motto in bright raised letters enclosing "96," dull gilt on a bright raised gilt ground. The garter surrounded by a bright gilt laurel wreath. The cap-plates of the Flank Company Officers bore no distinguishing marks.

The other cap-plates worn from 1855 to 1878 were similar to those previously described for the 63rd, during the same periods.

1855-8 The Officers' waist-belt clasp was circular, of gilt metal, with "96" and a crown in the centre in silver, and "*Regiment*" above, on the ring, with laurel branches below also in silver.

1878-81 The Officers' helmet-plate was of the same design as that worn by the 63rd, and previously described; but in the centre was a silver Sphinx, with "*Egypt*" on a label below; and "96" beneath it.

Buttons.—The Officers' coatee button, worn from 1840 to 1855, was of gilt burnished metal with a flat rim. In the centre "96," surrounded by a garter inscribed with the Royal motto and surmounted by a crown. From 1855 to 1881 the design was the same, but the button was larger and had a raised rim. A regimental mufti button worn between 1840 and 1855 was of burnished gilt metal, with "*V.R.*" in the centre surmounted by a crown.

Conclusion.—I should point out that in these notes the dates must be taken as approximate only, as regards the time when the various changes in uniform actually took place in the Regiment.

For example, some of the dates given are those of the General Orders authorising them, and as some time would necessarily elapse between the date of the G.O. and the time when it could be carried out, their adoption by the Regiment would be some time later.

On the other hand, when the dates given are those of the printed Dress Regulations it is more than likely that the alterations had been in many cases made previously in the Regiment; as there would of necessity be a lapse of time between the issue of the G.O. and the printing of the volume of Dress Regulations in which it was included. This, however, only applies in cases where the alterations concerned Officers' uniform. I merely mention this to avoid possible confusion.

THE COLOURS. 63RD REGIMENT

1758 In a communication from the Adjutant-General, dated 6th November 1758, now in the Public Record Office, the Colours for the then newly raised 63rd Regiment are ordered to be as follows:

The King's Colour to be the Union (that was then, of course, only the crosses of St. George and St. Andrew) with the rank of the Regiment in the centre, within a wreath of roses and thistles, the regimental number being surrounded by a shield-shaped border.

The Second, or Regimental, Colour to be deep-green, with the Union in the upper canton, the rank of the Regiment on crimson, within a similar wreath. Similar regulations are laid down in the Clothing Warrant of 19th December 1768, and the size of the Colours is ordered to be 6 ft. 6 in. flying, by 6 ft. 0 in. deep on the staff. The length of the staff, including spear and ferrule, to be 8 ft. 10 in.

The rank of the regiment to be painted, or embroidered, in Roman characters; and the wreath to be treated in the same way. The roses and thistles in the wreath to be on the same stalk. The cords and tassels to be of crimson and gold mixed.

1768 According to the Inspection Returns from Dublin, dated 27th July 1768, the two Colours were in good order, having been presented in 1765. These were doubtless the stand referred to above. They are again reported on as "*good*" in 1774 and 1784.

1801 After the Union of Great Britain and Ireland, the red cross of St. Patrick, "counter charged," was added to the Union Jack, and would consequently appear on the King's Colour; and in the upper canton of the Regimental Colour.

1814 I have come across a drawing of the Regimental Colour of 1814, which might possibly represent that of the second stand carried by the Regiment. It is of dark-green silk with the Union in the upper canton. In the centre upon a crimson ground with an ornamental border, "*LXIII REGT.*," surrounded by a wreath of roses, shamrocks, and thistles on one stalk, and tied below with a white ribbon, the leaves, flowers, etc., being embroidered (or painted) in their proper colours, and surmounted by a crown proper. The portion attached to the staff is of crimson silk. The Inspection Returns from Martinique previously reported "*two Colours bad*"; and doubtless this set replaced them.

1826 A sketch in the Heralds' College, under this date, shows a dark-green flag with the Union in the upper canton. In the centre, on a crimson circle edged yellow, are the words "*West Suffolk*" surrounding "*63 Regiment.*" Outside the circle is a wreath of roses, shamrocks, and thistles in proper colours, on one stalk, tied below with a white ribbon. Above, on a yellow scroll is the word "*Martinique*" in black letters, and below "*Guadaloupe,*" on a similar scroll. The part attaching it to the staff is of crimson silk. The same design, etc., was in the centre of the King's Colour. These Colours are referred to in the Inspection Returns from Madras in 1838 as follows: "*Colours painted, the number also in figures, not Roman letters.*" They were retired in 1842, and were probably the last painted Colours used by any infantry regiment of the Line; size 6 ft. 0 in. × 6 ft. 6 in.

1849 The late Mr. Milne, a well-known authority on regimental Colours, had in his possession a sketch of a set stated to have been presented to the Regiment when in Burma by Brigadier-General Logan on 20th November 1842. The Regimental Colour was dark-green, with "*LXIII*" surrounded by "*West Suffolk,*" on a crimson circle with yellow edgings, in the centre; surrounded by the Union wreath in proper colours, and surmounted by a Royal Crown. On each side of the wreath was a yellow, black-edged scroll, one inscribed in black letters "*Martinique,*" and the other "*Egmont-op-Zee.*" Below the wreath, on a similar scroll, the word "*Guadaloupe.*" The Union was in the upper canton, as usual, with a crimson attachment on the pole. As the Colours were reported "*unserviceable*" from Moulmein on 24th May 1840, this set probably replaced the others, which were stated to be "*painted instead of embroidered.*" The Colours are reported "*serviceable,*" from Preston in June 1850.

1854 There is a sketch in the Heralds' College, dated 28th February 1834, showing a similar Colour to that described above; but with the words "*The West Suffolk*" surrounding the regimental number in the centre. This is probably one of the Colours presented to the Regiment in Dublin on 10th May of that year.

1857 On 27th February the Heralds' College sent to the War Office sketches of a new set of Colours. The Queen's Colour was as usual the great Union, with the regimental number in Roman numerals in the centre, surmounted by the Royal crown. The Regimental Colour was similar to that of 1842, previously described, but in addition to the three original Battle Honours three new ones, "*Alma,*" "*Inkerman,*" "*Sevastopol,*" were added below that for "*Guadaloupe,*" on similar yellow, black-edged scrolls. Size 5 ft. 6 in. × 6 ft. 0 in.

1858 Colours were this year reduced in size to 3 ft. 6 in. × 4 ft. 0 in., and a fringe was added to them. The Lion of England and Crown was fitted to the staves instead of the gilt spearhead hitherto carried.

1870 In the Heralds' College are drawings dated 15th August 1870, which probably represent the stand of Colours presented to the Regiment in Calcutta on 12th February 1872 by Mrs. Vere Hunt Bowles, the wife of the then Lieutenant-Colonel.

The differences between it and that previously described consist of the re-arrangement of the Battle Honours; the replacement of the brass spearhead on the end of the staff by the Lion of England and Crown; and the addition of green and gold fringe round the flag. The Battle Honours are inscribed on yellow scrolls as heretofore, those nearest the pole being "*Egmont-op-Zee,*" "*Guadaloupe 1759–1810,*" and "*Inkerman*"; those on the other side of the wreath being "*Martinique 1809,*" "*Alma,*" and "*Sevastopol.*" An additional scroll with "*Afghanistan 1879–80*" has since been added below "*Inkerman,*" and another with "*Egypt 1882*" below that inscribed "*Sevastopol.*" These Colours were still in use by the 1st Battalion in 1922. They are 3 ft. 6 in. × 4 ft. 6 in., exclusive of the fringe.

96TH REGIMENT

1807 I have been unable to discover any details of the Colours of the earlier regiments numbered 96, but in the Heralds' College I came across a letter dated Gloucester, 26th June 1807, from Lieutenant-Colonel E. Scott, in reply to Sir Geo. Naylor's circular letter to all regiments asking for exact details of the Colours then in use, as follows:

"*The 2nd Battalion of the 96th Regiment has not any Colours. The flags used at exercise have been made up at the Head-Quarters of the Battalion, and are of plain buff.*"

The Colours of the former Regiment carried in 1779 are in the possession of the Officers' Mess of the 2nd Battalion.

1824 The first Regimental Colour issued to what is now the 2nd Battalion of the Manchester Regiment was of yellow silk, with the Union in the upper canton. In the centre, on a crimson circle, was the regimental number XCVI in gold Roman characters, surrounded by a wreath of roses, shamrock, and thistles embroidered in proper colours and surmounted by a Royal crown. The Inspection

Returns for 1825 state: "*Finding that they* (the Colours) *had not been consecrated, I caused this ceremonial to be performed with due solemnity, and I did not omit anything that might contribute to make it properly impressive in the minds of young soldiers. I have reason to expect some good effects from this incident.*"

Subsequently the consecration of Colours on presentation became imperative.

This stand of Colours is now in Manchester Cathedral, and was withdrawn from service in 1861. It was deposited in June 1886.

1861 New Colours were presented by Major-General H. Shirley at the Curragh on 8th May 1861. The Queen's Colour was, as usual, the great Union with the regimental number in Roman numerals embroidered in gold in the centre, surmounted by a Royal crown.

The Regimental Colour was of the same design as its predecessor; but both it and the Queen's Colour were edged with gold fringe, and the Crown and Lion of England replaced the spear-head on the tops of the staves.

1874 There is a sketch in the Heralds' College representing the Regimental Colour with Battle Honours subsequently added. It is of yellow silk, with the Union in the upper canton, and with the regimental number in Roman characters embroidered in gold on a crimson circle in the centre. This is surrounded by a wreath of roses, shamrock, and thistles embroidered in proper colours and surmounted by a crown. The part around the staff is of crimson silk, and between it and the wreath is a blue, gold-edged scroll, with the word "*Peninsula*" thereon in gold letters. On the other side of the wreath is a similar scroll charged "*New Zealand*," added in 1871, and beneath the wreath another scroll inscribed "*Egypt*," granted on 25th June 1874. Below the latter is a Sphinx in white embroidery, with Egyptian characters on the plinth below it and laurel-branch on each side.

These Colours were deposited in Manchester Cathedral in June 1886, at the same time as those withdrawn in 1861.

THE MANCHESTER REGIMENT

1886 On 21st February 1886 the Commander-in-Chief in India, Sir Frederick Roberts, presented new Colours to the 2nd Battalion at Delhi. They were of the post-territorial type, described later on, and were replaced by those presented by H.M. King George V. in Dublin in 1911. They, of course, did not then bear the South African Honours, since added.

When the Territorial System was introduced, the old regimental Colours of the 63rd and 96th (green and yellow respectively) were officially done away with, and the universal regimental Colour for English regiments was substituted.

The Royal, or first Colour is the Great Union, the Imperial Colour of the United Kingdom of Great Britain and Ireland, in which the cross of St. George is conjoined with the crosses of St. Andrew and St. Patrick on a blue field. In the centre is the territorial description, surmounted by the Imperial Crown. The regimental Colour is white, on which is the red cross of St. George with the territorial description in the centre, as on the first Colour; within the Union wreath of roses, thistles, and shamrock, and ensigned with the Imperial Crown.

The regimental Colour presented to the 4th (Line) Battalion by the Duke of Connaught at Cork on 31st July, 1903, was of white silk, with a crimson St. George's Cross in the centre ; in the centre of the cross was the figure " IV " in Roman characters, inside a circle inscribed "*The Manchester Regiment,*" all embroidered in gold ; surmounted by the Imperial Crown and surrounded by the Union wreath of roses, thistles, and shamrock embroidered in proper colours, and tied at the bottom with a yellow ribbon. Below this was a silver Sphinx, with a yellow scroll above inscribed "*Egypt,*" and below it a laurel-branch. On each side of the vertical arm of St. George's Cross was a laurel-branch, which, however, did not cross the horizontal arm ; and on it, in each of the white compartments, were three yellow scrolls, edged black, and inscribed in black letters with the following Battle Honours : "*Guadaloupe 1759,*" "*Egmont-op-Zee,*" "*Martinique 1809,*" "*Peninsula,*" "*Alma,*" "*Inkerman,*" "*Sevastopol,*" "*New Zealand,*" "*Afghanistan 1879–80,*" "*Egypt 1882,*" "*South Africa 1899–02,*" "*Defence of Ladysmith.*" The part encircling the staff was crimson ; and the flag was 3 ft. 9 in. long by 2 ft. 10 in. deep. It was edged with gold fringe, and had the Crown and Lion of England on top of the staff, with gold and crimson tassels and cords.

When the battalion was disbanded in 1906 the Colours were deposited in Manchester Cathedral, those of the 3rd Battalion being hung in the Town Hall, Manchester. The Colours of the 2nd and 3rd Battalions were similar, the only difference being in the numeral in the centre. Size 3 ft. 0 in. × 3 ft. 9 in., exclusive of the fringe.

MEDALS

63RD REGIMENT

When the retrospective Military General Service medal was authorised in 1848, six Officers and fifty-five men were alive to receive it. Two of the officers obtained the clasps for "*Martinique*" and "*Guadaloupe*" ; three, single clasps for "*Martinique*"; and one, the single clasp for "*Guadaloupe.*" Of the men twenty-five received both clasps ; eighteen, the single clasp for "*Martinique*" ; and twelve, that for "*Guadaloupe.*"

The Regiment has also received the Crimean medal, with clasps for "*Alma,*" "*Inkerman,*" "*Balaklava,*" and "*Sevastopol.*"

The Turkish medal for the Crimea to all engaged.

The Sardinian medal for Valour was given to three Officers and one man, during the Crimean War.

The French medal for "*Valeur et Discipline*" was given to six N.C.O.s and two men, during the same war.

The medal for Afghanistan, 1879–80.

The Egyptian medal for 1882.

The Khedive's Star.

The Queen's South African medal for 1899–1902, with clasps.

The King's South African medal for 1901–1902, with clasps.

The King's medal for 1914–18.

The Mons Star for 1914–15.

The Victory medal for 1914–18.

Besides individual awards for gallantry, good conduct, etc.

Thirteen *Victoria Crosses* have, so far, been gained by the combined battalions of the Regiment.

96TH REGIMENT

As this Regiment was granted the Battle Honour "*Egypt*" of one of its predecessors, it is only fair that the medal instituted by Colonel Sir John Stuart in 1801, in commemoration of the capture of the standard of the French "*Invincibles*" at the battle of Alexandria by Private Anthony Lutz, should be credited to it. It was 1¾ inches in diameter, bearing on the obverse a Sphinx, with a Union Jack and the French tricolour on the same staff (the British flag uppermost) sloping over the right shoulder. Above, the word "*Egypt*," and in the exergue the date MDCCCI.

On the reverse "*Queen's German Regiment*," in three lines, within a wreath of palms. It was issued in silver and also in pewter; doubtless as a regimental award.

Other medals issued by the Officers of the Regiment are a silver star inscribed "*To the best Marksman*," and also a silver Temperance Medal. This was a six-pointed star; in the centre "96," inside a circle inscribed "T.A.S." above and "Regt." below. Outside this is another circle with the motto "*Veni, vidi, vici*" upon it. Black enamel is filled in between the letters. Reverse, plain; a ring for suspension.

When the retrospective Military Service medal was authorised in 1848, one Officer and eighteen men received it with a clasp for "*Guadaloupe.*"

When the New Zealand medal was authorised in March 1869, and was made retrospective, two Officers and twenty-five men of the Regiment received it for services in 1845-7. For some reason or other their medals were issued without the date on the reverse, though I have come across instances with the dates engraved, no doubt by the recipients.

The Regiment has also received:

The Egyptian medal for 1882.
The Khedive's Star.
The Indian General Service medal, with clasp for "*Samana*" (to a detachment only).
The Queen's South African medal for 1899–1902, with clasps.
The King's South African medal for 1901–1902, with clasps.
The King's medal for "the Great War," 1914–18.
The Mons Star for 1914–15.
The Victory medal, 1914–18.

Besides awards for individual gallantry, good conduct, etc.

ARMS

The following is a brief summary of some of the fire-arms used from time to time:

"*Brown Bess.*"—Peninsular period. Flint lock smooth bore, ·750 calibre, one-ounce ball, muzzle-loader, triangular bayonet, 18 inches long. Weight, 12 lbs., length with bayonet, 72½ inches, length of barrel, 42 inches. Maximum range about 450 yards; effective range about 150 yards.

1839. "*Brown Bess*," converted to percussion, triangular bayonet.

1840. *Brunswick Rifle.*—Percussion, sword bayonet.

1842.—Percussion; muzzle-loading; smooth bore. Weight, 9 lbs. 14 oz. without the bayonet. Issued to the 96th in 1849.

NOTES ON UNIFORMS, COLOURS, BADGES, ETC.

1851. *Minie Rifle.*—Smaller calibre than "Brown Bess"; triangular bayonet. Barrel thirty-nine inches long, with four grooves, with one turn in 78 inches. Bore ·702; charge of powder, 68½ grains; sighted to 1,000 yards. It is interesting to note that the then Commander-in-Chief, who was always irascible with inventors and their inventions, is reported to have stated that "*We should not be in a hurry to adopt these new-fangled inventions. It was ridiculous to suppose that two armies would fight at a distance of 500–600 yards!*"

1853. *Enfield Rifle.*—Percussion, muzzle-loader, triangular bayonet. Sixteen bullets to the pound, sixty rounds carried on the person. Bayonets, 20¾ inches over all, blade, 17½ inches, weight, 13¼ ounces, curved. Sighted to 1,000 yards, length, 54 inches, weight of rifle, 8 lbs. 14½ oz.; arm complete with bayonet: length, 71½ inches; weight, 9 lbs. 12 oz. Barrel 39 inches long, bore ·577, three rifled progressive grooves making one spiral turn in 78 inches. Bullet 530 grains, length 1·095 inches, charge of powder 2½ drams.

1867. *Snider-Enfield.*—Breech-loader (converted M.L. Enfield); triangular bayonet as above.

1871. *Martini-Henry.*—Breech-loader, ·45 bore, 7 grooves, triangular bayonet, 25⅛ inches over all, weighing 16 ounces; straight blade, 21½ inches long. Weight, 8¾ lbs., the barrel 33 inches long, the bullet a little over 1¼ inches long, weighing 480 grains, 85 grains of powder, sighted to 1,400 yards.

1887.—*Martini-Enfield.*—Weight, 9 lbs. 2 oz.; bore, ·402; length of barrel, 33 1/16 inches, seven grooves, making one complete spiral turn per 15 inches of barrel. The bullet rotated to the right. Sighted to 2,000 yards. Bullet, 1·288 inches long; weight, 284 grains; powder, 85 grains. Sword-bayonet, 18½ inches long; weight, 23½ ounces.

1891. *Lee-Metford.*—B.L., ·303 bore; seven grooves; sword-bayonet.

1896. *Lee-Enfield.*—B.L. Magazine Rifle; very short sword-bayonet, 21½ inches entire length; blade, 17 inches; double-edged with a central rib, gradually vanishing towards the point.

1903. *Lee-Enfield.*—*Mark III.* Short rifle; B.L. magazine; extreme range, 3,500 yards, or two miles (see above notes under 1851); length, 3 ft. 8½ in.; weight, 8 lbs. 10½ oz. Long sword-bayonet, length, 1 ft. 5 in.; weight, 1 lb. 0½ oz. One hundred and fifty rounds of ammunition carried in the man's bandolier and waist-belt.

The pattern of the Officers' revolver was governed only by the order that it must take Government ·455 ammunition. N.C.O.s and men who carried revolvers were armed with the short ·455 six-chambered Webley pistols.

1768–86 The Officers' esponton was 9 feet long over all and had a blade 12 inches long and 1¼ inches wide at the bottom, rounded off below, and capable of revolving above the cross-bar. The latter was 5 inches long, and was fixed 12½ inches below the point. The total length of the steel head was 17 inches, with a strap 9 inches long on each side for attachment to the shaft. The shaft tapered from 1½ inches diameter at the bottom to 1⅜ inches at the top. The lower end was shod with a steel-pointed shoe.

1768–91 The Sergeants' halberd was a battle-axe-headed weapon, with a spear-head 9½ inches long by 2¼ inches wide at the base, and 1¾ inches wide in the middle. Below it, in front, was a rounded axe face 5½ inches long from the central axis, with a downward curved point of the same length behind. The length of the head from the point to where it fitted on to the staff was 11½ inches; and a strap, 14½ inches long, on each side, was provided for attachment to the staff. The staff was of ash, and tapered from 1½ inches in diameter at the bottom to 1¼ inches at the top, and was shod with a pointed steel shoe. The over-all length of the weapon was 8 ft. 6 in.

1791–1830 The Sergeants' pike did not materially differ from the esponton formerly carried by the Officers, and was probably the same weapon re-named.

METHODS OF WEARING THE HAIR

The method of wearing the hair has been the subject of regulations from time to time.

1751 From 1751 Officers wore their hair in queues, without hair powder, on ordinary occasions. The men's hair was cut rather short with large tufts over the ears.

1756 On 15th September 1756 all N.C.O.s and men were ordered to wear their hair "*clubbed,*" and this is shown in Daye's series of military sketches of this period; though some soldiers are shown wearing their queues curled up, like the letter "S."

1760 In 1760 hair powder was only used by the men on Sundays and at reviews; it was abolished in July 1796. Officers, however, continued its use until 1808, when it finally, and fortunately, disappeared.

1770 An Order of 20th April 1770 laid it down that the hair was "*to be plaited, and turned up behind with a black ribbon or tape, ¾ of a yard long, and with a bow-knot at the tye. Those men who have their hair so short that it will not plait, must be provided as soon as possible with a false plait.*" In the *Royal United Service Institution Museum* there is a Grenadier's cap, with the queue sewn on to the back, so that both could be donned at once!

1799 In 1799 Officers and men of Infantry were ordered to wear their hair "*queued except those of the Flank Companies to be tied a little below the upper part of the collar of the coat, and to be ten inches long, including one inch of hair to appear below the binding.*" When "queues" were worn by the Centre Companies the Grenadier and Light Companies wore their hair "*clubbed.*"

1804 In 1804 the queue was ordered to be 7 inches long, bound with ribbon, but without a bow at the top. It was abolished in August 1805, and the hair was then ordered to be cut short in the neck.

1854 Infantry were allowed to grow moustaches and whiskers, previously they had always been clean-shaved.

1856 Pioneers were ordered to wear beards.

1860 Whiskers were abolished throughout the Army in 1870, and in the Queen's Regulations for 1868, moustaches were ordered to be worn, and the chin shaved.

1912 The King's Regulations of 1912 are as follows: "*The hair of the head will be kept short. The chin and underlip will be shaved; but not the upper lip. Whiskers, if worn, will be of moderate length.*"

1916 Upper lip permitted to be shaved.

APPENDIX I

DOCUMENTS RELATIVE TO THE CAPTURE OF THE STANDARD BY ANTHONY LUTZ

THE following is taken from the 4th edition of Colonel R. T. Wilson's *History of the British Expedition to Egypt*.

Extract from the Brigade Orders of General Stuart's Brigade, 25th March 1801.

"It was with the most heartfelt satisfaction that the Brigadier-General contemplated in yesterday's general orders the honourable reward offered to the brigade in the flattering testimony of the Commander-in-Chief's approbation of their conduct in the action of the 21st. Sincerely and warmly attached to each corps from long and peculiar circumstances of connexion, the Brigadier-General acknowledges his own obligations to their exact obedience and discipline, and he cannot but participate with them in the credit of having rendered themselves conspicuous on a day which, independently of the glorious events which have so recently preceded, must ever add lustre to the character of a British army. Regret for the loss of those brave men who fell is a tribute due to their worth, and for none can the Brigadier-General sympathize more fully with the brigade than for that of his late esteemed and valuable Brigade-Major."

Copy of a Certificate, given by the Adjutant-General's Directions to Anthony Lutz, Private Soldier in the Regiment of Minorca, or Stuart.

"I do hereby certify, that Anthony Lutz, private soldier in the regiment of Minorca, or Stuart, did (on the 21st of March, 1801, during the action between the English and French armies, commanded by Sir Ralph Abercrombie and the French General in Chief Menou, on the above day, within three miles of Alexandria) take from the enemy a standard, which bore several marks of honourable distinction, such as the passage of the Piava and Tagliamento, when under Buonaparte in Italy, and in the centre of which is a bugle horn within a wreath of laurel. I do also certify, that the said Anthony Lutz brought the standard to the headquarters of his Excellency Sir Ralph Abercrombie, where he delivered it into my hands, when he, at the same time, received from me, by order, a gratuity of 20 dollars, for so signal an instance of good conduct. And I do farther certify, that I forwarded the standard, thus taken by the above Anthony Lutz, to Sir Ralph Abercrombie, then ill of his wounds in his Majesty's ship *Foudroyant*, that his Excellency received it accordingly, and that it is now in our possession. Given under my hand at the Adjutant-General's quarters, in the camp before Alexandria, this 3d day of April 1801.

"(*Signed*) JNO. DONALD,
　　　　Assist. Adjt. General."

APPENDIX I

Copy of a Regimental Order, in the Regiment of Minorca, or Stuart, now called the Queen's German Regiment, 4th April, 1801.

Private Anthony Lutz, who took the standard from the enemy, on the 21st last month, is directed to wear the representation of a standard (according to the model prescribed by the Brigadier-General) as a mark of his good behaviour, on his right arm [1]; and the Brigadier-General notifies that, as soon as the Regiment is in an established quarter, he will institute a valuable badge, in a certain proportion per company, to be worn by such men as shall have been proved, upon sufficient testimony, to have distinguished themselves, by acts of valour, or by personal instances of meritorious service; and officers are, on this account, to make note of the conduct of individuals.

Copy of Proceedings of a Regimental Committee of Inquiry, held in the Queen's German Regiment, at Gosport, on the 28th August 1802, to examine into the Circumstances which attended the Capture of the Colour, taken in the Action between the English and French Armies, near Alexandria, on the 21st of March, 1801.

Deposition of Corporal John Schmid: "Corporal John Schmid declares, that the Regiment had already taken post in front of the enemy, and had suffered considerably from loss of numbers, when he found himself near Anthony Lutz, who, with Private Wohlwend, himself, and several other men, advanced still nearer the enemy, now greatly dispersed by the heavy fire from the redoubt; that Lutz, notwithstanding the danger of the enterprize, rushed forward, discharging his musket, and presently afterward returned, bearing upon his shoulder an infantry standard. A body of cavalry appearing at this moment, Lutz, in order to secure his prize, threw himself into a hole (or rather hollow place), and lay upon it. Several minutes elapsed before he saw Lutz again, when he found him still in possession of the Colour, and also of a dismounted dragoon, whom he had made prisoner. He further says, that the smoke and confusion of the moment were too great to admit of his distinguishing whether the Colour was in the hands of the infantry or the cavalry; but he positively asserts, that no other than Anthony Lutz captured the standard."

Deposition of Private Wohlwend: "Private Wohlwend corroborates, in every point, the deposition of Corporal Schmid; and he further declares, that he saw Anthony Lutz, as he was retiring to the ranks of the Regiment, closely pursued by two of the enemy's cavalry, one of whose horses he shot and made the rider prisoner: the other horseman escaped."

Separate examination of Corporal Schmid: *Question.* "Did you observe a serjeant, or any other person, of the 42nd Regiment, lying wounded near the spot where the Colour was taken?"

Answer. "None. I saw no red coat whatever (except Lutz, Wohlwend, myself, and a few others of our Regiment) so far in front."

Question. "Did you see the Colour in possession of the enemy?"

Answer. "Yes; I saw it, though indistinctly, through the smoke, wavering over their heads."

Question. "What might have been the space of time, from the moment when

---

[1] The badge was, by a subsequent order, removed from the arm to the left breast.

THE CAPTURE OF THE STANDARD

you saw the standard in the hands of the enemy, to that when it became the property of Lutz ? "

Answer. " Some few minutes, probably seven ; but I cannot now be correct to a minute."

Question. " What might have been the interim, between the instant when Lutz pushed on forward from the place where you were and that when you saw him with the Colour ? "

Answer. " About one or two minutes."

Question. " What distance do you suppose you might have been from the Colour ? "

Answer. " About forty or fifty paces."

Question. " Do you conceive that there was time sufficient, from the moment Lutz left you, to that when he again appeared, to admit of its being taken by any other person previous to the taking of it by Lutz ? "

Answer. " No ; it was too momentary."

The same question being put to Private Wohlwend, he answered nearly to the same effect, except as to the following point, where his testimony is rather more positive than that of Corporal Schmid.

Question. " Did you see the Colour in possession of the enemy ? "

Answer. " Yes ; very distinctly."

APPENDIX II

FLEUR DE LYS

COPY OF APPLICATION FROM THE OFFICER COMMANDING 1st BATTALION ON BEHALF OF ALL BATTALIONS THE MANCHESTER REGIMENT.

No. 108/E/210/2.
2/11/1922.

From : The Officer Commanding, 1st Battalion The Manchester Regiment.
To : Headquarters, 24th (P) Infantry Brigade, Dublin.

DUBLIN,
2nd November, 1922.

SIR,

I have the honour to re-submit a request that application may be made to the Army Council for permission for The Manchester Regiment to use the Fleur de Lys as a Badge.

The application is forwarded by me on the authority and on behalf of the Colonel of the Regiment, Major-General Sir Vere Fane, K.C.B., K.C.I.E., at present Commanding in Burmah.

A previous application was made in 1919 by the Colonel of the Regiment, supported by letters from the Officers Commanding both Regular Battalions, and was replied to by War Office letter No. 20/Infantry/1338 (Q.M.b.7) of 31st October 1919.

It is the unanimous wish of the Officers of both Regular Battalions of the Regiment that the Fleur de Lys should be authorised as one of the Badges of the Regiment.

Letters strongly approving of this application have been received from all the Honorary Colonels and Commanding Officers of the Militia and Territorial Battalions. Further, a resolution of the Manchester City Council was unanimously adopted in August 1922, stating that the application was assented to by the City Council. (A copy of the resolution is attached hereto.)

2. This request is not put forward on the grounds that the Fleur de Lys should be regarded in the light of a Battle Honour. It is forwarded for consideration on the grounds of long usage, custom, and sentiment.

The arms of the City of Manchester as at present worn constitute a Badge of a non-military nature, and they are, moreover, worn at present by every worker in the employment of the City Corporation.

The Badge, therefore, as worn is by no means regarded by all ranks in the Regiment, who mainly come from Manchester, with those feelings which a Regimental Badge should inspire.

3. It is suggested that the Fleur de Lys should be worn as the Badge of the Regiment on the Headdress, and as the Collar Badge of the Service Dress Jacket of Officers.

RESTORATION OF THE "FLEUR DE LYS" BADGE

The Badge of the 63rd Foot would thus be retained and the Badge of the 96th Foot, The Sphinx, would remain on the Officers' buttons and the collar of the tunic, while the Territorial connection with the City of Manchester would be retained by the name of the Regiment.

4. A sample of the Fleur de Lys is enclosed.

I have the honour to be, Sir,
Your obedient Servant,
(Sgd.) F. H. DORLING,
Lt.-Colonel.
Commanding 1st Battalion The Manchester Regiment.

COPY OF THE RESOLUTION OF THE MANCHESTER CITY COUNCIL

TOWN HALL, MANCHESTER,
3rd August, 1922.

SIR,

At the meeting of the City Council held on the 2nd instant I was requested to communicate to you the following resolution, which was unanimously adopted:

FLEUR DE LYS

RESOLVED:

That inasmuch as it is represented to this Council that it is the desire of the Regular and Territorial Commanding Officers of The Manchester Regiment that the Officers and Men of such Regiment shall wear the Fleur de Lys as a Regimental Badge, and that an application in that behalf has or is about to be made to the War Office for authority so to do, and inasmuch as it is represented that if such authority be given, the word "Manchester" will appear on the shoulder straps of all ranks, and upon the buttons of the Officers' tunics, thereby further preserving the connection and association of the City with the Regiment, this Council in so far as it is concerned in such application assents thereto.

I shall be glad if you will submit this resolution to the Army Council.

I am, Sir,
Your obedient servant,
(Sgd.) P. M. HEATH,
Town Clerk.

The Secretary, War Office, London.

COPY OF WAR OFFICE LETTER SANCTIONING RESTORATION OF THE "FLEUR DE LYS" BADGE OF THE 63RD FOOT TO THE MANCHESTER REGIMENT.

WAR OFFICE, LONDON, S.W.1.
31st January, 1923.

20/Infantry/1570 (Q.M.G. 7).

SIR,

With reference to the attached copy of application of the Officer Commanding 1st Bn. The Manchester Regiment, I am commanded by the Army Council to inform you that approval is given for the Manchester Regiment to use the "Fleur de Lys" as a Clothing Badge in place of "The Arms of the City of Manchester."

The proposal that the "Fleur de Lys" should be worn as the headdress Badge for all ranks and as the Collar Badge on the Service Dress Jacket of Officers is sanctioned, on the understanding that no expense to the Public is thereby involved and that provision of the new cap badge for other ranks will not be proceeded with until stocks of the present pattern badge are exhausted.

I am to ask that a report may be furnished whether the enclosed sample "Fleur de Lys" (which was forwarded with the application of the 1st Battalion Manchester Regiment) is of the required design and size for the Service Dress Jackets of Officers, and that a sketch showing the exact dimensions of the cap badge may be forwarded to this Office in order that sealed patterns of the badges may be prepared. The enclosed sample badge should be returned with your reply.

I am to add that copies of this letter are being sent to the Colonel of The Manchester Regiment (Major-General Sir V. B. Fane, K.C.B., K.C.I.E.); to the Officers Commanding the 2nd Battalion and Depot of The Manchester Regiment, and to the Secretary, East Lancashire Territorial Force Association.

I am, Sir,
Your Obedient Servant,
(Sgd.) B. B. CUBBITT.

The G.O.C., Guernsey and Alderney District.

THE FLEUR DE LYS

By Brigadier-General H. C. E. Westropp

THE Fleur de Lys has always been a well-known heraldic device, and there has been much dispute in the past as to its origin.

The late Brigadier-General A. C. Lovett, writing in the Magazine of the 8th Battalion Manchester Regiment, summarised many of the theories which had been broached regarding it, as follows:

"Its division into three parts suggests its ancient meaning as the symbol of life, with its host of forms, and variations, which figure in all the great religions of enormous antiquity.

"In the ancient Hindoo shrine at the source of the Ganges, high up on the Himalayas, I have seen this device in iron of a rude shape fixed in the ground in great numbers, to remind man of his body, soul, and spirit. According to one tradition it was first employed as an Armorial Bearing by Clovis I,[1] and represents the lily presented by an angel to that monarch at his baptism, the three Fleur de Lys of his shield being the sign of the Trinity.

"Newton considers it to be the design of a reed, or flag, in blossom, used in place of a sceptre at the proclamation of the Frankish kings:

---

[1] Clovis I, King of the Franks, born 465, chief of the warlike tribe of Salian Franks, who inhabited Northern Gaul.

RESTORATION OF THE "FLEUR DE LYS" BADGE

"King Louis VII of France is said to have first adopted it as a device, in allusion to his name, Louis Florus. It was, however, an early ornament of Greek, Roman, German, Spanish, and English Kings, and was a symbol employed by many noble families in various parts of Europe in the twelfth and thirteenth centuries. Gioja of Amalfi is said to have marked the north end of the needle of the mariners' compass with a Fleur de Lys in honour of the Kings of Naples. Many compass cards of the present day bear this device, which may originally have been an ornamental cross. Since the twelfth century the Fleur de Lys has been used as the symbol of Royalty in France. After the victory of Agincourt, Henry V married the French Princess Katherine, and in his wooing called her my 'fair flower-de-luce' (Shakespeare). The English Kings adopted on the Royal arms the device as Kings of France, and this may be seen on the Royal Palace of James I, in York, to-day. The Drummers of the Foot Guards still wear the Fleur de Lys pattern lace, as a revival of bygone days." Henry VI granted on the arms of Eton College: "On a field sable three lily flowers argent, intending that our newly founded college (1440), lasting for ages to come, whose perpetuity we wish to be signified by the stability of the sable colour, shall bring forth the brightest flowers redolent of every kind of knowledge."

The History of the 63rd Foot, and the Fleur de Lys badge, which has recently been officially restored to the Regiment, are closely connected, although, so far, no document has been found to prove exactly when the Regiment was granted, or adopted, the badge.

The Regimental tradition regarding its origin is plainly stated in the History of the 63rd by the late Major James Slack, who served with the Regiment for many years, and throughout the Crimean War.

"At Helvoetsluis our baggage was taken by the enemy, on which occasion were lost the attestations and other documents belonging to the Regiment, and it is believed the authority to wear the Fleur-de-Lys was among them."

That documents were lost there is no doubt, as a certificate regarding the loss of attestations, which were sworn before W. Fletcher, and signed by Captain and Paymaster M. N. Johnstone and C. Boyd, Adjutant, 63rd Regiment, is stated by Major Slack to have been as follows:

"We do swear that the attestations were taken with the baggage at Helvoetsluis, and to the best of our knowledge and belief, the date mentioned in the roll is a true date of the attestation which was copied from the regimental books.[1]

"It would be a graceful act, and much appreciated by the Corps, if the authorities would renew the sanction and allow the Regiment *to wear the old badge they prize so highly*; at any rate, it would be no undeserved favour to issue an authority to the Regiment to wear the badge as an emblem to commemorate *the three-fold capture of Guadaloupe, viz., in* 1759, 1810, *and again in* 1815, and that of Martinique in 1809, from the French, with their eagles and flags, etc."; and again: "The distinguished services of the Regiment against the French in capturing so repeatedly these islands creates a belief that on one of these occasions the Fleur-de-lys must have first come as a Badge of Honour into the possession of the Regiment." And on page 163 (1856): "The

[1] The Inspection Report for 1784 states that all the 63rd Regimental books were lost in America by the Adjutant being killed.

uniform of the Regiment was again changed, the old coatee being replaced by a tunic.

"The Fleur-de-lys, which was worn as an ornament on the coatees of the officers and sergeant-major, and the Star which was worn on the buttons were discontinued on the new tunic, as (it was said) written authority sanctioning their wear could not be produced. *There is, however, every probability that sanction to wear the Fleur-de-lys was obtained as a reward for the capture of Guadaloupe from the French in* 1759, when the Regiment suffered heavily in both officers and men.

"There is extant a miniature of an officer of the Regiment (Major Johns), who joined in 1797, which shows the Fleur de lys as an ornament, then worn on the epaulette —also the regimental plate (some of it is very old) has the Fleur de lys engraved on it.

"It seems scarcely credible that these ornaments could, or would, have been taken into wear, by a Regiment having a reputation of so high a character, without first obtaining the sanction of His Majesty the King."

As stated above by Major Slack, the Fleur de Lys badge on this occasion was not then recognised on the grounds that *the Regiment* could produce no written authority for the wearing of the badge. Considering, however, the lapse of time between the date when it was certainly worn (*circa* 1784) and the date when permission to wear it was refused (1856), and considering the many moves and campaigns of the Regiment in its history, this failure to produce written authority is not to be wondered at ; even if the loss of baggage of the Regiment on active service in the year 1795—which may have contained the written authority—is not taken into account.

Major Slack also understood that the Fleur de Lys was probably obtained as a reward for the capture of Guadaloupe from the French in 1759, but, as will be seen below, it had appeared on the drummers' lace in 1758, when the 2nd Battalion 8th " The King's " was constituted a regiment and numbered " 63," before it was sanctioned, or adopted, as a badge. The late Major A. T. P. Hudson, 63rd Regiment, and 1st Battalion Manchester Regiment, who took great interest in this matter, came to the conclusion also that the badge probably dated from 1759.

The late Mr. Milne, the well-known collector and authority on old uniforms, badges, etc., could not trace the actual origin, and in 1895 wrote :

"But it may be that some totally forgotten deed, the taking of a French Standard, or something of the kind, not important enough to be mentioned in despatches, though of sufficient importance to remain in the memory of those present, may have given rise to the adoption of the French badge."

In 1910 he wrote : " I am very sorry to hear that it has not yet been granted to you, for it was a real genuine old badge, and, no doubt, well earned at the time."

Although no document has, so far, been discovered to prove the origin of the badge, there is ample evidence to show that the Regiment has a vested right in the Fleur de Lys from long-continued possession and use.

This evidence may be summarised as follows :

(*a*) On the drummers' lace in 1758, *vide* Mr. Milne's statement.
(*b*) Portraits of officers.
(*c*) Specimens of old uniforms, etc.
(*d*) Extracts from records of Firms who supplied uniforms, badges, etc.

(b) Portraits of Major Johns, mentioned above by Major Slack as being in the officers' mess, 1st Manchester Regiment, and a miniature in possession of Colonel J. Parker, of Browsholme Hall, Clitheroe; of Captain A. W. Barcroft, 63rd Foot, who was drowned whilst in command of the troops on the *Piedmont* transport on the 18th November, 1795. The miniature was taken just before he sailed for the West Indies; *on the cross-belt*, over the number 63, is a Fleur de Lys, quite distinct, but not very elaborately designed, and entirely silver.

In 1895 Mr. Milne wrote as follows: "*At that time* (1759) (*and to this day*) *the drummers of the Foot Guards wear the Fleur de lys pattern lace, so it is pretty well known as a badge.*

"In 1860, when the universal drummers' lace was introduced, the 8th King's Regiment (*N.B., from which the 63rd was formed*) and some eight others were using the Fleur de lys lace of various hues for their drums, and nobody knew its origin. Still the fact remains *that* (*originally*) *the 63rd was the only regiment whose officers wore it at all.*

"There is no doubt that the Fleur de lys was first displayed upon the officers' strap (of the epaulette) towards the end of the last century. My specimen is quite as old as 1790, *if not a little older*.[1] I consider that it was so worn until 1812, when all ornaments were cleared off *epaulette straps* as much as possible, because in that year it was authorised to display field officers' badges of rank, crown or stars, upon the epaulette straps.

"It was then, I believe, placed upon the skirt. I enclose photo (which please accept) of the tails of a light company officer's jacket showing the method of wearing the badge, 1812 to 1820. This garment belongs, or did belong, to Nathans, the costumiers. I did not buy it because the wings were missing, but I did purchase a companion, the long-tailed coat (1820) of a lieutenant-colonel; *the silver epaulettes were attached to it*, rendering it, therefore, more perfect.

"When the lace was changed in 1830 from silver to gold, the Fleur de lys still remained in the same position, until tails and skirt ornaments disappeared with the introduction of tunics in 1855."

The late Mr. Hastings Irwin has stated that in about 1784 the Fleur de Lys appeared in the centre of the epaulette, in silver, edged with dark green, and in 1797 was on the epaulette and cross-belt.

From 1811 the badge was on the "turn backs" of the coatee, in silver, mounted on dark green cloth, and from 1830 to 1856, in gold, when coatees were done away with.

In 1825, he states, it appeared on the officers' waist-clasp, and in 1848 the lace loops and buttons on the skirts of officers' coatees were abolished, and the gold Fleur de Lys *was their only ornament.*

In 1871 it was used as a puggaree brooch, and later on the officers' glengarry, field service cap, mess waistcoat buttons, and, more recently, on the lapels of the mess jacket.

[1] The coatee or jacket of the officer of the *light company*, mentioned above, is now in the possession of Brig.-General H. C. E. Westropp, who also acquired the long-tailed coatee of a lieutenant-colonel, and presented it to the Officers 1st Battalion Manchester Regiment. So far, it has not been possible to trace the epaulettes, which Mr. Milne states were attached to it.

Colonel R. W. Studdy, writing in 1913, stated that when he joined in 1867 in Dublin: "The Field Officers had saddle-cloths, Lincoln green, and gold braiding, and, as far as I can remember, a Fleur de Lys, and crown, in the corner behind the saddle. Mess waistcoats were Lincoln green, with gold cord edging, and gilt buttons, with the Fleur de Lys raised on them. I have a set by me."

In addition to the above, the records of certain tailoring firms afford evidence that the 63rd Regiment wore the Fleur de Lys as a badge. Amongst others the following may be quoted, the entries referring to the 63rd Regiment:

Messrs. Webb & Co.

1812.—"Lace, etc. Silver, dark green, and vellum."

"Skirt ornaments, silver Fleur de Lys on dark green."

Messrs. C. Smith & Co.

January 1824.—"Silver passed and spangled Fleur de Lys on dark green, 1823."

Messrs. Herbert & Co.

1841.—"Skirts, Fleur de Lys on dark green." (The original drawing and description are in possession of Messrs. Herbert & Co.)

Evidence, therefore, is available from old-established firms of tailors, that the Fleur de Lys was in use on the coatees of Officers of the 63rd Regiment in the year 1812 and after.

The records of accoutrement and button-makers have also been searched, and those of Messrs. Jennens & Co.—a firm established since 1760—may be considered as affording the most conclusive evidence.

This firm have in their possession the plate of an officers' waist-clasp, which, according to their records, was approved in July 1825. This clasp was worn until 1840, when the universal "V.R." clasp was introduced. This clasp has the Fleur de Lys on it as the badge, and one has been reproduced.

Mess livery buttons were also made by this firm about 1830, and gilt buttons (such as was the fashion for gentlemen to wear about the period 1820–50) were also made by them. Specimen plates of these buttons are in the possession of Messrs. Jennens.

Neither of these two buttons is official, but it helps to establish the fact that the Fleur de Lys was used by the Regiment. The evidence of the waist-clasp apparently shows that the Fleur de Lys was sanctioned in 1825 for use as a badge by the 63rd Regiment.

It has been engraved on the mess plate for a century and more, and is said to have been cut on the gravestones of those who fell in the American War of Independence. The regimental nickname of "Bloodsuckers" originated (such is the tradition) from the numerous small Fleur de Lys cut on the gravestones in America, which resembled that insect.

It has been painted on the drums, and worn as a badge on the bandsmen's and drummers' pouches. During the South African War it was worn by all ranks on the khaki helmet in green cloth. It is engraved on the monument at Cæsar's Camp, South Africa, and on the memorial panel in the Royal Military College Chapel, Sandhurst.

The restoration of this ancient heraldic device, and badge of the old 63rd Foot, has given immense pleasure to all ranks, past and present.

The inheritors of the Fleur de Lys (the 1st Battalion) could not have passed on to all battalions of "The Manchester Regiment" any badge they hold in such high honour, which, throughout their War and Peace History, has done as much as a badge can do to keep always in the forefront the traditions, services, and esprit de corps which have made this Regiment famous.

"It is the history of Regiments, it is their pride and traditions, which make a Regiment illustrious, which make it formidable in the field, and when weapons and numbers alone will not avail, give the Regiment its glory and its confidence." (Lord Rosebery.)

"I have known many splendid corps in the Army, but not one to beat the 1st Manchesters." (Lieut.-General Sir James Willcocks.)

APPENDIX III

THE BRUNSWICK STARS OF THE 63RD AND 96TH REGIMENTS
By Brigadier-General H. C. E. Westropp.

THE BRUNSWICK STAR OF THE 63RD REGIMENT.

THE regimental tradition concerning the Brunswick Star is stated by the late Major J. Slack in his History of the Regiment to have been as follows: "A tradition was current among the old soldiers of the Regiment that they won the Star by their brilliant services in America from 1775 to 1781, when they frequently rode as mounted infantry under the celebrated cavalry leader Colonel Tarleton." Extract from a letter from Earl Cornwallis to Colonel Tarleton, 10th November 1780: "The 63rd Regiment are well mounted for infantry, and may occasionally ride in your train: they behave vastly well." This was after the action at Fish-dam. One of the names the 63rd was known by was "The Green Horse"—from the colour of their facings. The following is an extract from the short official History of *The Manchester Regiment*:

"The Regiment (63rd) was employed under Tarleton as mounted infantry—a portion was engaged at Blackstocks on the 20th November 1780, and was highly distinguished, but its loss was very severe. The men of the 63rd never lost, and always cherished, the tradition of its exploits as mounted infantry in America, *and it is remarkable that the tradition was maintained, when no published Regimental Record existed, and when the Rank and File were far more illiterate than now.*" The late Mr. Milne's opinion about the Star was as follows: "As far as stars go, I really think your Regiment, the 63rd, was about the earliest to wear it upon the buttons, this pattern being worn by all officers and privates up to 1881. Indeed, only last week, I had a private soldier's button sent me from New York, a relic of the War of Independence, 1775–82, and it was a precisely similar design; as Regimental buttons were only ordered to be numbered in 1768, I think it follows that this particular design, with Star, must have been used from that date until 1881—*a circumstance unequalled in the History of Regimental buttons.*" The eight-pointed Star has also appeared at various dates on the chaco, waist clasp, and helmet.

THE BRUNSWICK STAR OF THE 96TH REGIMENT.

The last Regiment raised and numbered "96"—the present 2nd Battalion Manchester Regiment—also wore the Brunswick Star as a badge. The Regimental tradition is that when re-raised in 1824 an officer, presumably Major-General J. Fuller, from the Coldstream Guards, who by the King's command raised the Regiment in Manchester on 25th January 1824, adopted the Brunswick Star as a badge. The following short

THE BRUNSWICK STARS

descriptions and dates are taken from copies made from the original drawings for the plates cut for the Regiment by Messrs. Jennens & Co., of London. In 1912 I had several of these, and others reproduced exactly like the originals, which are now in a case in the Officers' Mess, 2nd Battalion Manchester Regiment.

From 1824 to 1828 the officer's chaco plate was an elliptical eight-pointed silver-cut Star with gilt edges. In the centre in silver was the number "96," surrounded by a gilt garter charged with the Royal motto, with small crown (gilt) above.

From 1824 to 1855 the breastplate on the officer's cross-belt was gilt and rectangular, with burnished edges. In its centre, a silver-cut eight-pointed Star, with small crown above—the same pattern as described above on the chaco plate of 1824.

From 1828 to 1844 the officer's chaco plate was a very large gilt eight-pointed Star and crown, the centre mount being a silver-cut eight-pointed Star of the same pattern as the 1824 officer's chaco plate.

From 1844 to 1855 the officer's chaco plate was an all-gilt eight-pointed Star, the points of the latter being cut longer and more defined, with large crown above (gilt). There is added to this a note: "No particulars of special plate for Grenadier, or Light, Companies."

From 1855 to 1862 the chaco plate was all gilt as above, but the eight-pointed Star more nearly resembled the original pattern of 1824, with larger crown. This pattern with, apparently, a somewhat smaller Star, was used until 1870, and probably later, with "96" surrounded by a garter containing the Royal motto, and surmounted by a crown. Messrs. Jennens have the drawing of an officer's helmet plate of 1882, an eight-pointed brass-gilt Star in centre, "96" under the sphinx, and "Egypt" surrounded by a garter with the Royal motto, with following note: "Die cut 1882. This plate was worn on the white helmet, no particulars of the date it went out of use." The Star (brass gilt) has been retained on the helmet of the Manchester Regiment.

From 1847 to 1855 it was used as a cap plate—a dull gilt eight-pointed Star, surmounted by a crown. In its centre, a dull gilt garter charged with the Royal motto in bright raised letters, enclosing "96," dull gilt, on a bright raised gilt ground, and the garter was surrounded by a bright gilt laurel wreath.

More recently, a small silver Star, in its centre a Sphinx (silver) over "Egypt," surrounded by a gilt garter charged with "The Manchester Regiment," and surmounted by a gilt crown, has been worn on the forage and fatigue caps, and as a puggaree brooch, also on the lapels of the officer's mess jacket and as a collar-badge of the Field Service Dress Jacket. The Star is engraved on the mess plate, and used as the 96th and 2nd Battalion crests.

APPENDIX IV

SUCCESSION OF COLONELS.

Compiled by Mr. J. J. Holland, R.U.S. Institute.

63RD (WEST SUFFOLK) REGIMENT OF FOOT

DAVID WATSON	21.4.1758
Maj.-Gen. 25.6.1759	
SIR WILLIAM BOOTHBY, Bart.	12.10.1760
Maj.-Gen. 10.7.1762	
RICHARD PIERSON	11.4.1764
Col. 21.7.1760	
CHARLES HOTHAM	13.9.1765
Col. 19.2.1762	
FRANCIS GRANT	6.11.1768
Maj.-Gen. 30.4.1770	
Lt.-Gen. 29.8.1777	
HON. ALEXANDER LESLIE	2.1.1782
Maj.-Gen. 19.2.1729	
GEORGE, EARL OF WALDEGRAVE	4.7.1788
Col. 20.11.1782	
ALEXANDER, EARL OF BALCARRES	27.8.1789
Maj.-Gen. 12.10.1793	
Lt.-Gen. 1.1.1798	
Gen. 23.9.1803	
WILLIAM DYOTT	7.4.1825
Lt.-Gen. 4.6.1813	
Gen. 22.7.1830	
SIR HENRY WATSON, C.B.	17.5.1847
Maj.-Gen. 28.6.1838	
SIR THOMAS KENAH, K.C.B.	25.11.1850
Lt.-Gen. 11.11.1851	
Gen. 26.12.1859	
ARTHUR CUNLIFFE VAN NOTTEN POLE	27.3.1868
Lt.-Gen. 9.4.1868	
THOMAS MAITLAND WILSON	22.8.1873
Lt.-Gen. 23.4.1872	
Gen. 1.10.1877	
SIR RICHARD WADDY, K.C.B.	15.10.1877
Lt.-Gen. 21.11.1876	

96TH REGIMENT OF FOOT

SIR JOSEPH FULLER, G.C.H.	24.1.1824
Maj.-Gen. 4.6.1813	
Lt.-Gen. 27.5.1825	
SIR LIONEL SMITH, K.C.B.	9.4.1832
Maj.-Gen. 12.8.1819	
SIR WILLIAM THORNTON, K.C.B.	10.10.1834
Maj.-Gen. 27.5.1825	
Lt.-Gen. 28.4.1838	
SIR LEWIS GRANT, K.C.H.	9.4.1839
Lt.-Gen. 10.1.1837	
CHARLES EDWARD CONYERS, C.B.	11.2.1852
Maj.-Gen. 9.11.1846	
Lt.-Gen. 20.6.1851	
MILDMAY FANE	11.8.1855
Lt.-Gen. 30.1.1855	
GEORGE MACDONALD	27.12.1860
Maj.-Gen. 7.9.1855	
Lt.-Gen. 29.1.1863	
SIR CHARLES WARREN, K.C.B.	13.2.1863
Maj.-Gen. 26.10.1858	
Lt.-Gen. 29.1.1863	
HON. SIR AUGUSTUS ALMERIC SPENCER, K.C.B.	28.10.1866
Maj.-Gen. 13.2.1860	
Lt.-Gen. 9.5.1868	
GEORGE THOMAS CONOLLY NAPIER, C.B.	14.6.1869
Maj.-Gen. 15.12.1861	
Lt.-Gen. 30.4.1871	
THOMAS CROMBIE	10.5.1872
Lt.-Gen. 25.10.1871	
THOMAS MAITLAND WILSON	15.10.1877
Gen. 1.10.1877	

THE MANCHESTER REGIMENT

EDMUND RICHARD JEFFREYS, C.B.	10.7.1881
Gen. 1.7.1881	
JOHN MCNEIL WALTER, C.B.	18.12.1889
Gen. 1.7.1881	
HENRY RADFORD NORMAN, K.C.B.	25.9.1895
Lt.-Gen. 1.7.1881	
VERE HUNT BOWLES	17.12.1899
Hon. Lt.-Gen. 14.5.1887	
WILLIAM OSBORNE BARNARD	8.1.1904
Maj.-Gen. 10.6.1896	
VERE BONAMY FANE, K.C.B., K.C.I.E.	16.1.1920
Maj.-Gen. 1.1.1917	

APPENDIX V

ALPHABETICAL ROLL (SERVICES COMMISSION REGISTER) OF OFFICERS OF THE 63RD FOOT, 96TH FOOT, AND THE MANCHESTER REGIMENT, 1758—1923

ABBREVIATIONS

Ben. S.C. . . . Bengal Staff Corps	K. in A. . . . Killed in Action.
D. on S. . . . Died on Service.	N.T.A. . . . No trace after.
D. of W. . . . Died of Wounds.	Ret. . . . Retired.
H.P. . . . Half Pay.	Res. . . . Resigned.

ABADIE, George Howard Fanshawe, C.M.G. From R. Scots, Capt. Manch. R. 4.6.1902, Died at Kano 11.2.1904.

ABBOTT, Cecil James Frederick, M.C. From Hon. Art. Coy., Lieut. Manch. R. 25.7.1917, Capt. 26.1.1919.

ABBOTT, Thomas. Lieut. 63rd F. 28.10.1799, H.P. 1802.

ABBOTT, Thomas. From R. Veteran Bn., Lieut. 96th F. 9.4.1825, Capt. R. African Col. Corps 18.8.1830.

ABERCROMBY, George Cosmo. From S. Gds., Capt. Manch. R. 31.8.1887, Ret. 27.6.1888.

ADAIR, William. Chaplain 63rd F. 1.7.1758–24.8.1758.

ADAMS, Frank Henry, M.C. 2/Lieut. Manch. R. 20.8.1915, Lieut. 8.10.1916, Adjt. 4.3.1917, Ret. 14.2.1920.

ADAMS, John Philips. From 8th F., Lieut. 63rd F. 30.8.1756, N.T.A. 1766.

ADAMSON, Joseph Samuel. Ens. 63rd F. 15.3.1831, Lieut. 27.9.1833, Capt. 1.12.1837, 38th F. 15.6.1838.

ADDERLEY, George. Ens. 63rd F. 30.9.1790, Lieut. 28th F. 31.10.1792.

AFFLECK, Gilbert. From 7th F., Capt. 63rd F. 30.4.1781, H.P. 1792.

AGNEW, Quentin Graham Kinnaird, M.V.O., D.S.O. From R. Scot. Fus., Maj. Manch. R. 23.10.1901, Ret. 28.4.1906.

AINSWORTH, Tom Jessop. 2/Lieut. Manch. R. 22.10.1902, Lieut. 25.6.1904, Ret. 24.7.1909.

AIRY, James Osmund. From Essex R., Capt. Manch. R. 15.10.1916, Killed by Sinn Feiners, Ballyvourney, Cork, 21.7.1920.

AKED, Thomas. From H.P. 4th W. India R., Capt. 63rd F. 20.7.1870, 96th F. 28.8.1871, A. Pay Dept. 30.1.1879.

ALBRECHT, Vaudrey Adolph, O.B.E., M.C. 2/Lieut. Manch. R. 8.6.1912, Lieut. 28.4.1914, Capt. 1.10.1915.

ALCOCK, Philip Savage. Ens. 96th F. 12.4.1850, Lieut. 14.9.1852, 95th F. 11.8.1854.

ALIMAN, Frederick Goulburn. Ens. 96th F. 7.8.1846, Lieut. 12.9.1848, Ret. 14.9.1852.

ALLAN, Andrew Timbrell. From 57th F., Capt. 63rd F. 14.6.1842, Maj. 26.12.1851, 81st F. 3.6.1853.

ALSTON, James. From H.P. 42nd F., Lieut. 63rd F. 31.1.1788, Capt. 2.9.1795, Maj. 13.9.1798, Ret. 28.6.1803.

ALT, Daniel. From 3rd Veteran Bn., Lieut. 63rd F. 8.4.1825, H.P. Staff Corps, 6.12.1833.

ALT, William Gerard. From 8th F., Lieut. 63rd F. 4.10.1757, D. on S., W. Indies, 1759.

ANCRAM, William. Ens. 63rd F. 12.10.1760, Lieut. 23.6.1762, H.P. 1763.

ANDERSON, Charles. Ens. 96th F. 20.10.1846, Lieut. 29.12.1848, Capt. 31st F. 20.7.1855.

ANDERSON, Charles Abbot, D.S.O. 2/Lieut. Manch. R. 5.5.1900, Lieut. 20.5.1901, Capt. 7.12.1911, Maj. 1.9.1915, Ret. Lt.-Col. 5.5.1920.

ANDERSON, de Lancy Radcliffe. Ens. 63rd F. 15.6.1855, Lieut. 14.7.1857, 2nd F. 25.8.1857.

ANDERSON, Francis Wyatt Abbot. 2/Lieut. Manch. R. 21.10.1891, Lieut. 14.12.1894, Capt. 11.3.1899, Maj. 1.6.1906, K.O.R. Lanc. R. 22.2.1908, Died at Cairo 1.1.1916.

ANDERSON, George. Ens. 96th F. 10.9.1828, Lieut. 19.9.1834, Capt. 11.8.1837, 22nd F. 20.12.1839.

ANDERSON, John Henry Abbot. 2/Lieut. 96th F. 11.5.1878, Lieut. 21.6.1879, Capt. 12.10.1887, Maj. 2.9.1897, Lt.-Col. 17.2.1904, Brev. Col. 17.2.1907, Comdt. Peking Lega-

tion Guard 4.10.1906–30.5.1911, H.P. 31.5.1911.
ANDERSON, William Robert Le Geyt. Ens. 63rd F. 1.10.1870, Lieut. 28.10.1871, Bom. S.C. 15.6.1875.
ANDREW, David. Ens. 63rd F. 15.7.1783, Lieut. 14.3.1789, Capt. 3.9.1795, Died Aug. 1796.
ANGELO, Frederick William Pakenham. 2/Lieut. 63rd F. 30.1.1878, Lieut. 8.8.1879, Ben. S.C. 5.5.1880.
ANLEY, Barnett Dyer Lempriere Gray, C.M.G. D.S.O. From Essex R., Maj. Manch. R. 20.7.1912, Brev. Lt.-Col. 3.6.1916, Brev. Col. 3.6.1918, Lt.-Col. R. Lanc. R. 6.11.1919.
ANNESLEY, Francis C. Ens. 63rd F. 15.12.1840, Lieut. 13.5.1842, Capt. 26.12.1851, 60th F. 26.12.1851.
ANNESLEY, Stephen Francis Charles. Ens. 63rd F. 6.7.1838, Lieut. 17.8.1841, Capt. 22.10.1847, 37th F. 26.5.1848.
ANSTRUTHER, Basil Lloyd. Sub/Lt. 96th F. 17.7.1872, Lieut. 17.7.1873, Adjt. 7.8.1875–12.6.1879, Capt. 13.6.1879, Maj. 1.8.1883, Lt.-Col. 31.5.1894, Brev. Col. 31.5.1898, H.P. 31.5.1898.
ANSTRUTHER, John. From 8th F., Lieut. 63rd F. 28.8.1756, Capt. 23.7.1762, Maj. 5.11.1766, 62nd F. 21.10.1773.
ARBUTHNOT, Charles G. J. From H.P., Maj. 63rd F. 26.2.1824, Lt.-Col. 1.10.1825, H.P. 1.10.1825.
ARBUTHNOT, William Wedderburn. From 9th L. Drgns., Capt. 63rd F. 7.9.1855, 18th L. Drgns. 26.3.1858.
ARCHER, James Henry. From 29th F., Lieut. 96th F. 18.8.1848, H.P. 9.10.1855.
ARCHER, Richard Halliday. Ens. 63rd F. 29.12.1854, Lieut. 9.3.1855, Ret. 16.8.1861.
ARDOINO, Joseph. 2/Lieut. Manch. R. 21.4.1900, Lieut. 6.5.1901, Ind. S.C. 9.6.1902.
ARMSTRONG, Alexander Moore. From R. Canadian Rifle R., Capt. 63rd F. 2.5.1865, Ret. 25.2.1870.
ARMSTRONG, George. Ens. 63rd F. 10.9.1925, Lieut. 8.5.1828, 60th F. 15.5.1829.
ARMSTRONG, Richard. Capt. 63rd F. 16.6.1808, Brev. Maj. 25.4.1808, Army Depot Staff, 7.9.1809.
ARMSTRONG, William Henry. Ens. 63rd F. 15.9.1807, Lieut. 2nd Garr. Bn. 22.9.1808.
ASHE, ——. Lieut. 63rd F. 6.9.1795, Drowned in shipwreck en route to W. Indies 18.11.1795.
ASHE, Edward. From Clare Militia, Ens. 63rd F. 11.11.1795, Lieut. 57th F. 27.6.1796.
ASHE, Lovet. Capt. 63rd F. 1.3.1782, Maj. 1.3.1794, D. on S., Flanders, 1795.
ATKIN, Benjamin George, D.S.O., M.C. 2/Lieut. Manch. R. 28.7.1909, Lieut. 5.4.1913, Capt. 10.6.1915.
ATKINSON, George. Lieut. 63rd F. 29.10.1799, Capt. 28.6.1800, Ret. 16.3.1805.
ATKINSON, Thomas. Ens. 63rd F. 10.12.1858, Lieut. 16.8.1861, Capt. 28.7.1867, Ret. 2.5.1868.

AUBIN, Francis. Ens. 63rd F. 13.3.1817, Lieut. 7.4.1825, Ret. 1835.
AUBIN, Thomas. Ens. 63rd F. 3.8.1809, Lieut. 12.4.1810, H.P. Nov. 1814.
AUCHINLECK, James A. From Ward's R. of Foot, Capt. 63rd F. 4.9.1795, Res. 28.6.1800.
AUCHINLECK, William Lowry. From 53rd F., Maj. 63rd F. 2.2.1878, Lt.-Col. 18.3.1880, Col. 18.3.1884, H.P. 18.3.1885, Died 13.2.1891.
AULDJO, John. From 34th F., Capt. 96th F. 30.12.1831, Ret. 11.8.1837.
AYTOUN, Marriott. Ens. 96th F. 15.1.1858, Lieut. 14.6.1859, Capt. 18.7.1862, Died 22.4.1866.

BABINGTON, Murray. Ens. 63rd F. 29.2.1816, H.P. W. India R. 1819.
BACK, Edward. Ens. 63rd F., 4.6.1812, H.P. 23rd F. 16.2.1815.
BACON, John. Ens. 63rd F. 4.10.1809, Lieut. 2.2.1811, 9th Drgns. 21.1.1813.
BAGOT, Josceline Fitzroy. Ens. 96th F. 18.3.1874, G. Gds. 21.7.1875.
BAILEY, Geoffrey. 2/Lieut. Manch. R. 26.6.1901, H.P. 27.12.1902, Ret. 27.12.1907.
BAKER, Edward Mervyn. 2/Lieut. Manch. R. 15.5.1897, Lieut. 17.8.1898, Capt. 5.1.1901, R. Fus. 15.2.1908.
BALDWIN, Anthony Hugh. Lieut. Manch. R. 14.5.1884, Adjt. 5.7.1891–4.7.1895, Capt. 3.2.1892, Maj. 15.12.1900, Lt.-Col. 17.2.1908, H.P. 1.6.1914, Killed at Gallipoli 15.8.1915.
BALL, Bent. Ens. 63rd F. 3.5.1770, Lieut. 6.11.1772, Capt. 14.10.1777, N.T.A. 1785.
BALL, George. Ens. 63rd F. 1.5.1801, Ret. 8.6.1803.
BALL, Thomas. From 64th F., Lt.-Col. 63rd F. 20.6.1759, Lieut.-Governor of Jersey 1760.
BAMFORD, Robert Carter. From 2nd F., Capt. 63rd F. 27.6.1854, H.P. 10.11.1856.
BANBURY, William Joseph. Ens. 63rd F. 16.10.1867, Lieut. 26.2.1870, 90th F. 27.7.1870.
BANKES, Edward. Qr.-Mr. and Hon. Lieut. Manch. R. 16.8.1899, Hon. Capt. 29.10.1900, Qr.-Mr. Curragh Camp 16.1.1909.
BANNATYNE, George Augustus. Ens. 63rd F. 13.5.1842, Lieut. 30.6.1844, Died at Clifton 18.1.1850.
BANON, Richard Geo. Davis. From 87th F., Surg. 96th F. 1.7.1853, 87th F. 23.6.1854.
BARCLAY, Edward. Ens. 96th F. 12.7.1827, Lieut. 14.2.1834, Capt. H.P. 3.12.1847.
BARCLAY, Henry Bruce. Ens. 96th F. 13.6.1830, 56th F. 31.8.1830.
BARCLAY, Henry Furguson. From 21st F., Lieut. 63rd F. 16.2.1849, Capt. 23.12.1853, Ret. 9.11.1855.
BARCLAY, James. Ens. 63rd F. 24.8.1785, Lieut. 30.11.1791, N.T.A. 1796.
BARKER, Arthur. 2/Lieut. Manch. R. 10.10.1914, Lieut. 18.12.1914, Capt. 9.2.1918, Ret. 17.8.1920.

ALPHABETICAL ROLL OF OFFICERS

BARKER, Edward Oliver. From 58th F., Lieut. 96th F. 18.8.1848, Died Dec. 1851.

BARKER, James. Ens. 63rd F. 1.9.1804, Lieut. 6.3.1806, Died Aug. 1807.

BARLOW, John Arthur. From 107th F., Capt. 96th F. 12.4.1879, Maj. 14.2.1883, Lt.-Col. 18.3.1892, H.P. 28.7.1895.

BARNARD, John. Ens. 63rd F. 25.9.1761, 4th F. 13.1.1762.

BARNARD, William Arthur M. From G. Gds., Lt.-Col. 96th F. 29.11.1864, Brev. Col. 29.11.1869, Ret. 14.9.1870.

BARNARD, William Osborne. Ens. 96th F. 15.4.1856, Lieut. 21.5.1858, Capt. 18.11.1859, Brev. Maj. 5.7.1872, Maj. 13.3.1878, Lt.-Col. 8.2.1882, Col. in Army, 18.5.1885, H.P. 18.3.1886, Maj.-Gen. 10.6.1896, Col. Manch. R. 8.1.1904, Died 15.1.1920.

BARRATT, James, M.C. 2/Lieut. Manch. R. 3.12.1916, Lieut. 3.6.1918, Res. 18.11.1919.

BARRON, William. From 82nd F., Capt. 96h F. 18.2.1859, Ret. Oct. 1859.

BARROW, Thomas. From H.P. 84th F., Capt. 63rd F. 25.6.1789, Maj. 20.5.1795, W. India R. 20.5.1795.

BARROW, William Warre. From 4th F., Lieut. 63rd F. 18.5.1826, Ret. 19.7.1833.

BARRY, Arthur Gordon, D.S.O., M.C. From Lanc. Fus., Capt. Manch. R. 7.5.1916.

BARWELL, Arthur Ross. Lieut. Manch. R. 25.8.1886, Ben. S.C. 30.1.1888.

BASTOW, Robert W. Ens. 63rd F. 9.3.1866, Lieut. 13.9.1867, Capt. 28.4.1875, Ret. 13.3.1878.

BATES, Henry Cecil. 2/Lieut. Manch. R. 21.4.1900, Lieut. 12.3.1901, Capt. 9.8.1908, K. in A. 7.8.1915, Suvla Bay, Gallipoli.

BATHURST, Arthur Anthony. From R. Berks. R., Capt. Manch. R. 22.3.1902, R. Berks. R. 18.12.1907.

BAWDWEN, Richard. Chaplain 63rd F. 31.5.1788–29.4.1789.

BAXTER, Paul Robert Elmhurst. 2/Lieut. Manch. R. 4.7.1903, Ind. Army 27.2.1904.

BAYLEE, Perry. Ens. 63rd F. 25.4.1805, Lieut. 8.8.1805, Capt. 5.11.1812, Brev. Maj. 22.7.1820, Maj. 17.9.1833, Ret. 16.7.1841.

BAYLEY, William Kercheval. 2/Lieut. Manch. R. 21.4.1900, Lieut. 16.2.1901, Capt. 18.12.1907, R. Berks. R. 20.5.1908.

BAYLIS, John. Ens. 63rd F. 23.10.1775, Lieut. 13.4.1778, Capt. 26.12.1787, Maj. 1.4.1795, Lt.-Col. 7.8.1799, 36th F. 7.8.1799.

BAYLY, Charles. From 41st F., Capt. 63rd F. 31.1.1805, Maj. 3rd Garr. Bn. 2.1.1812.

BAYLY, Henry Nicholas. Ens. 63rd F. 16.8.1861, Lieut. 28.10.1864, 45th F. 24.1.1865.

BEADNELL, Henry Christopher Thomas. Ens. 63rd F. 29.3.1861, Lieut. 11.10.1864, Ret. 22.9.1865.

BEAMISH, George Percival. Ens. 63rd F. 23.6.1854, Lieut. 10.11.1854, Capt. 26.3.1858, 98th F. 1.6.1860.

BEAUMONT, Norman Augustus. 2/Lieut. Manch. R. 25.9.1918, Res. 18.1.1920.

BEDSON, Bernard. 2/Lieut. Manch. R. 2.1.1917, Lieut. 2.7.1918, W. African R. 3.9.1920, Ret. 5.4.1922.

BEECROFT, Ambrose William. Ens. 63rd F. 20.4.1778, Lieut. 22.11.1780, Capt. 14.3.1789, Drowned in shipwreck en route to W. Indies 18.11.1795.

BEERE, William Henry. From 74th F., Lieut. 63rd F. 18.10.1864, Ret. 9.6.1865.

BELL, Charles Harland. Ens. 63rd F. 24.3.1843, Lieut. 2.9.1844, Cape Mounted Rifles 5.5.1848.

BENNETT, Harold Anthony. 2/Lieut. Manch. R. 22.4.1903, Ind. Army 11.6.1904.

BENNETT, Robert. Ens. 63rd F. 17.10.1851, Lieut. 6.6.1854, Capt. 24.4.1855, Adjt. Depot Bn. 3.2.1860.

BENNETT, Thomas Baylis. Lieut. 63rd F. 11.11.1795, D. of W. rec. at Schagerburg, Holland, while carrying the Colours 11.10.1799.

BENNETT, William. Ens. 63rd F. 14.1.1813, H.P. Nov. 1814.

BENNETT, William. Ens. 63rd F. 22.10.1799, Lieut. 23.1.1800, Capt. 14.2.1805, 5th Garr. Bn. 2.4.1809.

BENTLEY, Clarence Leslie. 2/Lieut. Manch. R. 8.8.1914, K. in A. 28.10.1914.

BENYON, Samuel A. Yate. Ens. 63rd F. 24.8.1854, Lieut. 8.12.1854, Died at Nenagh 22.5.1856.

BERDMORE, Vesey. Ens. 63rd F. 9.1.1835, Lieut. 22.8.1836, D. on S., Bellary, India, 15.4.1845.

BERFORD, Michael. Ens. 63rd F. 16.8.1804, Lieut. 6.2.1806, D. on S., Martinique, 20.10.1809.

BERGHEIM, Arthur Cecil. 2/Lieut. Manch. R. 14.9.1901, Res. 19.4.1902.

BERKELEY, Edmund Robert. From 40th F., Lieut. 96th F. 14.9.1870, Capt. 18.6.1877, H.P. 16.2.1878.

BERRY, Robert Gordon John Johnston. 2/Lieut. Manch. R. 20.8.1890, Lieut. 1.6.1893, A.S.C. 30.9.1893.

BERTRAM, William, 2/Lieut. 96th F. 4.9.1878, Lieut. 13.9.1879, Capt. 11.2.1888, Maj. 2.8.1898, Ret. 5.4.1899.

BETTRIDGE, Paul H. Caradoc. From 74th F., Ens. 96th F. 19.7.1864, Ret. 10.11.1865.

BEVERHOUDT, Adam. From 6th W. India R., Lieut. 63rd F. 6.11.1817, H.P. 1818.

BEWICKE, Hugh Bertram Nathaniel. From Welsh R., Maj. Manch. R. 28.8.1890, Ret. 2.8.1898.

BICKNELL, Edward Conduit. Ens. 63rd F. 26.2.1856, Lieut. 31.12.1858, 38th F. 31.12.1858.

BIGG, William. Ens. 63rd F. 4.2.1862, Lieut. 5.2.1866, Capt. 12.6.1869, Ret. 18.10.1871.

BIRMINGHAM, John. Ens. 63rd F. 15.8.1775, Lieut. 7.10.1777, Ret. 29.1.1796.

BLACKWOOD, Robert William. Ens. 96th F. 12.6.1863, 52nd F. 17.7.1863.

BLAKE, Charles Edward. Capt. 63rd F. 2.2.1809, Brev. Maj. 1.1.1805, Brev. Lt.-Col. 1.1.1812, D. on S., Martinique, 23.10.1812.
BLENCOWE, John. Ens. 96th F. 14.2.1828, Lieut. 16.3.1832, 75th F. 6.4.1832.
BLOMER, John. From 8th F. Capt. 63rd F. 29.8.1756, Maj. 27.5.1763, D. on S., Ireland, 21.10.1766.
BOHAN, William. Surgeon 63rd F. 20.5.1824, Died Sept. 1835.
BOILEAU, Charles Lestock. Lieut. Manch. R. 14.5.1884, Capt. 10.9.1890, Res. 8.3.1893.
BOLTON, Charles Arthur, C.B.E. 2/Lieut. Manch. R. 29.1.1902, Lieut. 21.11.1903, Capt. 1.12.1914, Maj. 29.1.1917, Brev. Lt.-Col. 1.1.1919.
BOLTON, Philip. Ens. 63rd F. 17.1.1810, Lieut. 25.7.1811, H.P. 17.1.1822.
BOOKEY, Power Le Poer. From 54th F., Lieut. 63rd F. 9.6.1843, Ret. 10.4.1849.
BOONE, Charles Armel. 2/Lieut. Manch. R. 11.4.1900, Lieut. 1.11.1900, Capt. 3.4.1907, H.P. 18.9.1907.
BOOTHBY, William. Ens. 63rd F. 24.12.1760, 51st F. 22.4.1763.
BORLASE, Charles. From 2nd F., Capt. 96th F. 7.10.1824, Ret. 8.9.1825.
BORRADALE, George Edward. From 19th F., Capt. 63rd F. 9.6.1877, Brev. Maj. 15.3.1879, Ret. Lt.-Col. 26.5.1880.
BORTHWICK, William D. M. Ens. 63rd F. 29.10.1864, Ret. 12.1.1869.
BOSCAWEN, George Evelyn. From 4th F., Ens. 63rd F. 9.5.1774, Lieut. 1.12.1775, Capt. 5th Drgns. 4.11.1777.
BOSTOCK, Lionel Carrington, M.C. 2/Lieut. Manch. R. 19.9.1908, Lieut. 25.5.1912, Capt. 10.6.1915.
BOSWELL, David. From 64th F., Lt.-Col. 63rd F. 14.8.1800, Ret. 19.6.1809.
BOURNE, George. Lieut. 63rd F. 19.12.1799, H.P. 1803.
BOURNE, Harold Edward. 2/Lieut. Manch. R. 4.11.1915, Lieut. 1.1.1917, H.P. 2.7.1918.
BOUTFLOWER, Edward Cyril. 2/Lieut. Manch. R. 28.1.1903, W. Rid. R. 16.2.1907.
BOUVERIE, Duncombe Pleydell. From 22nd F., Capt. 63rd F. 23.11.1855, Died 10.6.1857.
BOWLES, ——. From 14th F., Ens. 63rd F. 4.9.1795, Superseded 15.8.1797.
BOWLES, Vere Hunt. Ens. 63rd F. 10.4.1849, Lieut. 11.8.1853, Capt. 8.7.1855, Maj. 19.12.1861, Lt.-Col. 28.7.1867, Brev. Col. 28.7.1872, 37th F. 8.12.1874, Col. Manch. R. 17.12.1899, Died 7.1.1904.
BOWYER, Thomas. From 67th F., Lt.-Col. 63rd F. 18.2.1761–14.6.1763.
BOXALL, William. From 47th F., Lieut. 63rd F. 4.8.1804, Capt. 13.6.1805, N.T.A. 1821.
BOXER, Hugh Caldwell. 2/Lieut. Manch. R. 22.4.1903, Durh. L.I. 6.3.1907.
BOYD, James Power. From 38th F., Lieut. 63rd F. 28.1.1859, Capt. 28.10.1864, R. Canadian R. Regt. 2.5.1865.
BOYD, John Charles. Ens. 63rd F. 20.8.1794, Lieut. 1.12.1794, Capt. 25.4.1799, Adjt. 2.7.1794–July 1802, 8th R. Veteran Bn. 1805.
BOYLE, Edward. From 69th F., Capt. 96th F. 20.4.1866, A. Pay Dept. 1.4.1878.
BOYLE, George Vere. Sub/Lieut. 96th F. 18.3.1874, 60th F. 14.11.1874.
BOYLE, Gerald Armstrong. 2/Lieut. Manch. R. 22.6.1915, Lieut. 9.6.1916, Res. 4.4.1917.
BOYTON, James. From H.P. 1st Garr. Bn., Lieut. 63rd F. 6.12.1833, Died 1837.
BRADSHAW, James. Lieut. 63rd F. 25.6.1759, N.T.A. 1763.
BRADY, Hugh. Ens. 63rd F. 9.12.1795, Lieut. 1.11.1796, Capt. 57th F. 31.3.1798.
BRADY, Sydney Vincent, M.C. 2/Lieut. Manch. R. 15.4.1917, Lieut. 15.10.1918, Died 4.7.1919.
BRAMLEY, Arthur Henry. 2/Lieut. Manch. R. 9.1.1917, K. in A. 8.6.1918.
BRANSON, Cecil Lugard Smyth. From 15th F., Ens. 96th F. 1.5.1867, Lieut. 21.10.1868, Ret. 19.8.1874.
BRAY, George Frederick Campbell. From 66th F., Lieut. 96th F. 31.12.1847, Capt. 1.2.1855, Maj. 9.12.1862, Lt.-Col. 14.9.1870, H.P. 13.3.1878.
BRERETON, Robert. Qr.-Mr. 63rd F. 1.11.1804, Ens. and Adjt. 24.1.1805, Lieut. 25.6.1806, Capt. W. India R. 17.8.1815.
BRERETON, Robert. From 30th F., Lt.-Col. 63rd F. 27.5.1795, Brev. Col. 29.5.1802, Maj.-Gen. 25.10.1809, Lt.-Gen. 4.6.1814.
BRESLIN, William Irwin. Asst. Surg. 63rd F. 8.3.1827, 9th Drgns. 27.11.1828.
BRIDGFORD, Robert James, D.S.O. 2/Lieut. Manch. R. 21.12.1889, Lieut. 3.12.1891, Capt. 24.1.1898, Maj. 24.2.1904, Shrop. L.I. 16.9.1905.
BRIGGS, James. From 50th F., Capt. 63rd F. 1.10.1825, Maj. 16.11.1832, Ret. Dec. 1837.
BRIGGS, James. From 91st F., Ens. 96th F. 6.7.1852, Lieut. 31.8.1855, Capt. 21.5.1858, Maj. 20.6.1867, Lt.-Col. 13.3.1878, H.P. 18.3.1882, Ret. 18.3.1887.
BRIGHT, Harold Norman. 2/Lieut. Manch. R. 4.1.1916, P. of W.O. York R. 18.7.1917.
BRINDLEY, George Frederick Wallace. 2/Lieut. Manch. R. 9.12.1896, Lieut. 1.11.1897, Capt. 10.10.1900, D. of W., Holland, S. Africa, 19.12.1901.
BRISCO, Horton Coote. From H.P. Bourbon R., Maj. 63rd F. 13.4.1815, Brev. Lt.-Col. 4.6.1814, H.P. 25.5.1818.
BRISSETT, John. Ens. 63rd F. 19.9.1779, N.T.A. 1781.
BRITTOROUS, Francis, M.C. 2/Lieut. Manch. R. 16.9.1916, Lieut. 16.3.1918.
BROMHEAD, Edward Gonville. 2/Lieut. Manch. R. 18.5.1892, Ind. S.C. 8.9.1894.
BROUGH, Redmond William. From H.P. 56th F., Capt. 96th F. 29.1.1824, 2nd F. 7.10.1824.
BROUGHTON, Aubrey Delves. From 15th F., Ens. 96th F. 21.4.1863, Died Sept. 1870.

ALPHABETICAL ROLL OF OFFICERS

BROWN, Charles Bradford. Ens. 63rd F. 15.3.1855, Lieut. 26.2.1856, 8th F. 23.10.1857.
BROWN, Edward. Ens. 63rd F. 22.12.1808, Lieut. 18.1.1810, Capt. 25.10.1827, 73rd F. 10.7.1828.
BROWN, Henry George. 2/Lieut. Manch. R. 4.5.1887, Lieut. Bom. S.C. 23.2.1888.
BROWNE, Edward Poulman. Sub-Lieut. 96th F. 19.6.1872, 10th F. 12.11.1873.
BROWNE, Francis. Ens. 63rd F. 8.8.1799, Lieut. 14.10.1803, Died Mar. 1806.
BROWNE, Henry Ralph. From 37th F., Lt.-Col. 63rd F. 1.12.1874, Brig.-Gen. Bengal 26.6.1875.
BROWNE, Lord Richard Howe. From 7th F., Maj. 96th F. 8.9.1863, Ret. 21.2.1865.
BROWNE, Richard. Ens. 63rd F. 3.5.1770, Lieut. 14.2.1774, N.T.A. 1778.
BROWNE, Robert Geoffrey, D.S.O. 2/Lieut. Manch. R. 19.10.1901, Lieut. 5.2.1903, Capt. 1.12.1914, Maj. 24.10.1916, Died in France 1.11.1918.
BROWNE, Samuel. Lieut. 63rd F. 1.9.1771, N.T.A. 1774.
BROWNING, John Alexander. Ens. 96th F. 27.7.1855, Lieut. 7.7.1857, Ret. Oct. 1859.
BROWNSON, Frank. 2/Lieut. Manch. R. 28.11.1917, Lieut. 28.5.1919, Res. 16.7.1919.
BRUCE, Charles Donald. 2/Lieut. Manch. R. 26.2.1917, Lieut. 26.8.1918, Res. 3.3.1920.
BRUCE, Henry Alexander. Ens. 96th F. 30.4.1841, Died Mar. 1844.
BRUCE, James. Capt. 63rd F. 9.5.1764, Maj. 70th F. 17.4.1769.
BRUCE, Stewart Harvey. Ens. 63rd F. 24.11.1854, Lieut. 2.3.1855, Capt. 19.12.1861, 91st F. 6.11.1863.
BRUEN, Henry. Lieut. 63rd F. 13.2.1765, Adjt. 27.2.1767–29.10.1768, Capt. 29.10.1768, 15th F. 12.7.1777.
BRYAN, Herbert. From Linc. R., Capt. Manch. R. 26.7.1899, Brev. Maj. 29.11.1900, Ret. 17.2.1904.
BRYAN, Marlborough. Ens. 63rd F. 27.9.1757, Lieut. 24.3.1759, D. on S., W. Indies, 1759.
BRYSON, Allen. From 27th F., Surg. 63rd F. 23.3.1870, Staff 5.11.1870.
BUCHAN, Ernest Norman, D.S.O. 2/Lieut. Manch. R. 4.5.1901, Lieut. 27.11.1901, Capt. 1.12.1912, missing, presumed K. in A. 25.9.1915.
BULFIN, Edward Stanislaus. From Yorks. R., Maj. Manch. R. 28.11.1903, Brev. Lt.-Col. 28.6.1902, R. Welch Fus. 15.10.1904.
BULKELEY, James C. From H.P. 3rd F., Lieut. 63rd F. 11.10.1810, Died about 1812.
BULKELEY, William. Lieut. 63rd F. 5.10.1796, N.T.A. 1797.
BULLER, George. From H.P. 23rd F., Ens. 63rd F. 29.8.1822, Lieut. 28.3.1825, Rifle Bde. 9.4.1825.
BULLOCK, Josiah. Lieut. 63rd F. 15.9.1796, Died Mar. 1797.
BUNBURY, Arthur Frank. 2/Lieut. Manch. R. 9.9.1897, Superseded, absent without leave, 12.1.1898.

BUNBURY, Charles. Ens. 63rd F. 15.5.1855, Lieut. 17th F. 10.9.1858.
BUNBURY, Robert Henry. From 94th F., Lieut. 96th F. 17.8.1832, H.P. 22.7.1836.
BURDON, John. 2/Lieut. Manch. R. 13.1.1915, Lieut. 25.6.1915, Wounded and missing 8.3.1916.
BURGHERSH, Lord John. From 7th F., Lt.-Col. 63rd F. 12.12.1811, H.P. Nov. 1814.
BURKE, Edward. From 2nd W. India R., Lt.-Col. 63rd F. 2.5.1822, H.P. 5.2.1829.
BURKE, Theobald. Ens. 63rd F. 11.11.1795, Lieut. 1.6.1796, N.T.A. 1803.
BURKITT, Eric Hammond Beaumont. 2/Lieut. Manch. R. 5.7.1917, Lieut. 5.1.1919, Res. 8.2.1921.
BURKITT, Robert John Paylis. Asst. Surg. 63rd F. 22.8.1811, H.P. 7th F. 18.1.1816.
BURNE, Henry Thomas George. Sub-Lieut. 63rd F. 9.8.1873, Lieut. 9.8.1873, Ben. S.C. 26.4.1876.
BURNE, Jasper. From Militia, Ens. 63rd F. 6.5.1862, Lieut. 17.11.1866, 103rd F. 17.4.1887.
BURRELL, W. G. Asst. Surg. 63rd F. 13.7.1809–13.12.1809.
BURROUGHS, Robert. Ens. 63rd F. 3.7.1765, N.T.A. 1766.
BURROWS, Richard Francis Geoffrey. 2/Lieut. Manch. R. 25.5.1914, Lieut. 25.11.1914, Capt. 1.1.1917.
BURTON, John Pollard Mayers. Ens. 63rd F. 11.1.1859, Lieut. 16.8.1861, Ret. 2.10.1866.
BURTON, Richard Carr F. Ens. 63rd F. 23.8.1864, Lieut. 1.5.1867, Capt. 28.5.1870, Ret. 25.3.1876.
BUSH, Robert. Ens. 96th F. 22.4.1826, Lieut. 26.8.1827, Capt. 23.3.1832, Brev. Maj. 9.11.1846, Maj. 15.6.1849, Ret. 9.8.1852.
BUTLER, Gerald Villiers. From 22nd F., Capt. 96th F. 20.12.1839, Ret. 2.10.1846.
BYRON, George Rochfort. Ens. 63rd F. 30.3.1855, Lieut. 28.10.1855, Ret. Oct. 1864.

CADELL, Alexander. Lieut. Manch. R. 29.8.1885, Ben. S.C. 10.5.1887.
CAIRNCROSS, Alexander, K.H. From R. Veteran Bn., Capt. 96th F. 29.1.1824, Maj. 10.6.1826, Lt.-Col. 19.9.1834, Ret. 22.7.1842.
CAIRNS, William McNeile. Ens. 96th F. 17.3.1863, 43rd F. 22.5.1863.
CALLAGAN, James. Ens. 63rd F. 14.3.1772, Lieut. 22.11.1775, N.T.A. 1778.
CALVERT, Harry. Lieut.-Col. 63rd F. 27.1.1799, Col. W. India R. 6.8.1800.
CAMERON, Aylmer. From W. India R., Capt. Manch. R. 4.3.1903, H.P. 28.7.1905.
CAMERON, Robert Fulton. Ens. 63rd F. 31.12.1839, D. on S., India, 14.6.1841.
CAMPBELL, Alexander. From 74th F., Capt. 63rd F. 12.10.1781, 42nd F. 9.11.1785
CAMPBELL, Colin. Ens. 63rd F. 13.6.1783, H.P. 1784.

CAMPBELL, Colin. From 70th F., Maj. and Brev. Lt.-Col. 63rd F. 13.8.1812, Capt. and Brev. Lt.-Col. C. Gds. 25.6.1814.

CAMPBELL, David. From 26th F., Lieut. 63rd F. 13.6.1778, 99th F. 25.8.1783.

CAMPBELL, David. Ens. 63rd F. 5.3.1806, Lieut. 5.2.1808, Capt. 8.4.1825, H.P. 7.11.1826, Ret. May 1832.

CAMPBELL, Donald. From 40th F., Lt.-Col. 63rd F. 22.12.1808, Ret. 3.6.1810.

CAMPBELL, James. Ens. 63rd F. 30.11.1781, N.T.A. 1794.

CAMPBELL, John. Ens. 96th F. 29.4.1842, Lieut. 2.9.1845, Ret. 11.2.1848.

CAMPBELL, Morris Robinson. Ens. 96th F. 2.7.1829, Lieut. 19.12.1835, Adjt. 30.6.1837–19.8.1841, Paymr. 68th F. 20.8.1841.

CANNON, John Smith. From St. Helena R., Lieut. 96th F. 18.8.1848, Capt. 28.1.1856, H.P. 23.11.1860.

CAREW, William Marcus. Ens. 63rd F. 7.4.1825, Lieut. 16.11.1826, Capt. 22.8.1836, Maj. 16.9.1845, Ret. 21.10.1847.

CAREY, Charles Le Mesurier. Ens. 63rd F. 13.8.1847, Lieut. 18.1.1850, Capt. 6.11.1854, Brev. Maj. 6.6.1856, Maj. 16.11.1860, Ret. 16.8.1861.

CAREY, Geoffrey Newman, M.B.E. 2/Lieut. Manch. R. 7.4.1916, Lieut. 7.10.1917, Ret. 31.7.1922.

CARLAW, John. From Staff, Asst. Surg. 63rd F. 7.12.1867, 101st F. 30.10.1869.

CARLETON, William Napier. From 9th L. Drgns., Lieut. 96th F. 15.1.1861, Ret. 24.3.1863.

CARMODY, John. Ens. 63rd F. 16.5.1811, Cashiered G.C.M. 22.1.1814.

CARNAC, Michael. Surg. 63rd F. 5.10.1785—20.10.1795.

CARNCROSS, H. Ens. 63rd F. 27.3.1806, Lieut. 7.2.1808, D. on S., Martinique, 20.6.1811.

CARNEGY, James A. Ogilvy. Ens. 63rd F. 3.8.1855, Lieut. 10.9.1858, 21st F. 10.9.1858.

CARR, Jonas King, M.D. Asst. Surg. 63rd F. 24.7.1847, 25th K.O. Bord. 9.4.1847.

CARROLL, Herbert Owen. 2/Lieut. Manch. R. 21.4.1900, Lieut. 13.2.1901, Ind. S.C. 30.10.1901.

CART, Robert. From H.P. 84th F., Qr.-Mr. 63rd F. 11.12.1828, H.P. 9.10.1840.

CARTER, David Arthur, D.C.M. Qr.-Mr. and Lt. 15.2.1919.

CARTER, Frederick William. Ens. 63rd F. 1.12.1837, Lieut. 2.4.1841, Capt. 4.6.1847, Brev. Maj. 2.11.1855, Maj. 7.3.1856, Lt.-Col. 16.11.1860, Brev. Col. 11.11.1865, Died at Guernsey 27.7.1867.

CARTER, Victor Wallace. 2/Lieut. Manch. R. 3.12.1916, Res. 20.4.1918.

CARY, Arthur. From 44th F., Capt. 63rd F. 2.9.1845, D. on S., Secunderabad, India, 19.12.1846.

CARY, Hon. Lucius W. C. A. F. From 27th F., Capt. 96th F. 3.3.1857, Ret. 31.12.1857.

CARY, William Lucius. From H.P. 17th F., Lieut. 96th F. 29.1.1824, Capt. 26.5.1825, H.P. 20.1.1832.

CASHALL, Francis. Ens. 63rd F. 9.7.1802, Ret. 2.6.1804.

CASSAN, Edward Sheffield. Ens. 63rd F. 26.12.1834, H.P. German Legion 25.11.1836.

CASSIDY, Christopher. 2/Lieut. Manch. R. 22.4.1917, Lieut. 22.10.1918, Res. 4.2.1920.

CASSIDY, Frederick William Lambert. Ens. 96th F. 22.5.1863, Ret. 1.5.1867.

CATES, Kenneth George Hyde. 2/Lieut. Manch. R. 24.1.1906, Lieut. 24.4.1908, Indian Army 5.3.1909.

CATHCART, Hon. Augustus Murray. From 13th F., Maj. and Brev. Lt.-Col. 96th F. 24.5.1859, Lt.-Col. 9.12.1862, G. Gds. 29.11.1864.

CAULFIELD, James Crosbie. From A.S. Corps, Lieut. Manch. R. 20.10.1914, K. in A., France, 18.11.1914.

CAVENDISH, Godfrey Lionel John. 2/Lieut. Manch. R. 22.4.1903, Ind. Army 5.8.1905.

CHAMBRE, James. From 20th F., Lieut. 96th F. 28.12.1838, 14th L. Drgns. 30.4.1841.

CHAMP, William T. N. Ens. 63rd F. 16.11.1826, Lieut. 18.5.1832, Res. Oct. 1833.

CHAMPION, Guy Bernard. From Connaught Rgrs., Lieut. Manch. R. 9.9.1922, Capt. 1.1.1923.

CHAPLIN, Acton. Ens. 63rd F. 30.1.1796, Lieut. 46th F. 26.3.1796, Capt. 96th F. 9.4.1796, 4th F. 17.8.1799.

CHAPMAN, Gordon Humphrey. 2/Lieut. Manch. R. 4.7.1903, Ind. Army 27.2.1904.

CHAPMAN, Herbert Greenhill. 2/Lieut. Manch. R. 17.2.1900, Lieut. 15.8.1900, Capt. 4.12.1905, Suffolk R. 20.5.1908.

CHAPMAN, John. From 10th Bn. of Res., Capt. 63rd F. 1.8.1804, Maj. 9.7.1812, H.P. Nov. 1814.

CHAPMAN, John Strange. From 16th L. Drgns., Surg. 63rd F. 5.10.1841, 11th F. 24.12.1847.

CHARLTON, John Samuel. Asst. Surg. 63rd F. 1.3.1839, 67th F. 3.9.1847.

CHATOR, Robert. From H.P., R. Afr. Col. C., Ens. 63rd F. 8.4.1832, Res. 24.9.1833.

CHEAPE, Peter. From H.P., Capt. 96th F. 24.4.1828, Brev. Maj. 28.6.1838, Maj. 22.7.1842, Ret. 15.6.1849.

CHEVERS, Hyacinth. From 39th F., Capt. 63rd Foot 26.5.1880, Maj. 29.10.1886, 2nd W. India R. 30.3.1887.

CHICHESTER, Alfred Godfrey de Vaud. 2/Lieut. Manch. R. 16.11.1887, Ben. S.C. 1.4.1888.

CHILD, James Martin, M.C. 2/Lieut. Manch. R. 3.12.1915, Lieut. 2.4.1917, K. in A. 23.8.1918.

CHITTENDEN, Alfred G. 2/Lieut. Manch. R. 26.8.1917, Lieut. 26.2.1919, Res. 5.2.1920.

CHITTENDEN, Arthur Grant Bourne. 2/Lieut. Manch. R. 24.1.1914, D. of W., Marne, France, 9.9.1914.

CHURCH, Arthur George Hay. Ens. 96th F. 5.11.1861, Lieut. 9.1.1863, Capt. 25.12.1867, Maj. 1.7.1881, Lt.-Col. 18.3.1882, H.P. 18.3.1886, Col. in Army 18.3.1886.

ALPHABETICAL ROLL OF OFFICERS

CHURCH, Richard. Ens. 63rd F. 26.8.1807, H.P. 31st F. 17.8.1815.

CHUTE, Richard Aremburg Blennerhassett. From E. Surr. R., Capt. Manch. R. 26.5.1900, Ret. 26.4.1913.

CLARKE, Thomas. From 134th F., Lieut. 63rd F. 10.9.1795, Ret. 4.1.1800.

CLARKE, William Charles. 2/Lieut. Manch. R. 23.4.1902, Lieut. 23.1.1904, Res. 18.11.1908.

CLARKSON, Thomas Hollingworth. From H.P., Depot Bn., Maj. 63rd F. 15.1.1873, 20th F. 26.3.1873.

CLEAVER, Edward. From 8th L. Drgns., Lieut. 63rd F. 31.12.1803, Ret. 23.4.1805.

CLEGG, Eric Calder. 2/Lieut. Manch. R., 28.1.1903, Lieut. Bord. R. 6.2.1907.

CLEILAND, Robert. From 8th F., Capt. 63rd F. 26.8.1756, Maj. 20.6.1759, D. on S., W. Indies, 18.2.1760.

CLELAND-HENDERSON, John Macleod. Lieut. Manch. R. 22.10.1881, Ben. S.C. 10.10.1885.

CLIFFE, Wastell. Ens. 63rd F. 31.8.1781, Lieut. 3.8.1785, H.P. Jan. 1788.

CLIFFORD, John James, M.D. From Staff, Asst. Surg. 96th F. 18.8.1848, 9th Drgns. 27.1.1854.

CLIFFORD, Walter. 2/Lieut. Manch. R. 25.2.1916, Lieut. 16.8.1917, Ret. 30.4.1920.

CLIMO, Verschoyle Crawford. From W. India R., Maj. Manch. R. 19.5.1905, Ret. 11.1.1911.

CLUME, Hamilton Michael. Ens. 63rd F. 21.10.1795, Lieut. 1.5.1796, Capt. 5.8.1804, 55th F. 7.11.1805.

CLUTTERBUCK, George William. Ens. 63rd F. 12.1.1855, Lieut. 1.5.1855, Adjt. 12.11.1858–15.8.1861, Capt. 16.8.1861, Died 26.2.1867.

CLUTTERBUCK, James Alton. From 12th F., Ens. 63rd F. 12.8.1853, K. in A., Inkerman, 5.11.1854, while carrying the Colours.

CLYDE, James. Ens. 96th F. 5.6.1827, Lieut. 23.3.1832, Capt. 18.8.1848, Died 15.7.1850.

COCHRANE, George Henry. From 83rd F., Ens. 96th F. 18.8.1848, Lieut. 13.12.1851, Capt. 8th F. 21.5.1858.

COCKBURN, Ernest Radcliffe. From Wilts R., Capt. Manch. R. 25.12.1901, Wilts R. 18.12.1907.

COCKBURN, John Jeken. Ens. 63rd F. 17.3.1848, Lieut. 9.9.1851, Capt. 29.12.1854, Ret. 10.8.1855.

CODD, Augustus Frederick. Ens. 63rd F. 21.12.1832, Lieut. 21.2.1834, Capt. 14.5.1842, D. on S. 25.3.1844.

CODRINGTON, Edward William. Ens. 63rd F. 14.1.1880, Lieut. 1.7.1881, Ind. S.C. 20.3.1883.

COGHILL, Donald Mackey. 2/Lieut. Manch. R. 4.4.1898, Removed from Service 22.8.1900.

COGHLAN, George. From 8th F., Capt. 63rd F. 26.5.1758, N.T.A. 1760.

COLAN, Harry Norman. 2/Lieut. Manch. R. 27.7.1901, Lieut. 10.11.1902, Ind. S C. 3.3.1903.

COLERIDGE, Edward. Chaplain 63rd F. 30.4.1789, Last of Regtl. Chaplains.

COLES, Charles Andrews. Ens. 96th F. 9.1.1868, 12th F. 25.4.1868.

COLESHILL, William, M.C. D.C.M. 2/Lieut. Manch. R. 19.2.1917, Lieut. 19.8.1918, Res. 28.5.1921.

COLLIER, Edward. From 111th F., Ens. 63rd F. 17.6.1763, N.T.A. 1771.

COLLS, Edward Cooper. From W. Norf. Mil., Ens. 63rd F. 11.4.1811, Lieut. 23.12.1813, H.P. Rifle Bde. 28.12.1820.

COLMAN, Francis. From 8th F., Lieut. 63rd F. 5.6.1758, 3rd F. 25.1.1759.

COLVILLE, Thomas. Ens. 63rd F. 9.3.1860, Lieut. 19.7.1864, 74th F. 18.10.1864.

CONDON, James Knighton. 2/Lieut. Manch. R. 22.8.1888, Lieut. 9.7.1890, Ind. S.C. 30.7.1890.

CONNELL, Sidney Dennis. 2/Lieut. Manch. R. 24.1.1914, Lieut. 30.10.1914, K. in A. near Lacouture 28.11.1914.

CONNERY, James Thomas. 2/Lieut. Manch. R. 19.2.1916, Lieut. 16.8.1917, Ret. 16.2.1922.

CONNERY, William Lawrence, M.B.E. Qr.-Mr. and Hon. Lieut. Manch. R. 27.3.1909, Hon. Capt. 1.7.1917.

CONNINGHAM, William. From H.P. 23rd F., Ens. 63rd F. 16.2.1815, Lieut. 4.4.1816, H.P. 13.3.1817.

CONNOR, George. Ens. 63rd F. 10.6.1778, N.T.A. 1779.

CONOLLY, T. Ens. 63rd F. 2.5.1807, Res. 4.7.1807.

CONROY, Deane Josias. From H.P. 38th F., Lieut. 63rd F. 5.6.1823, Capt. 5.2.1824, 69th F. 25.3.1824.

CONSIDINE, James. From 84th F., Ens. 63rd F. 26.7.1837, Lieut. 31.5.1839, D. on S., Bellary, India, 16.9.1844.

COOK, Herbert Rowley. Ens. 63rd F. 9.4.1870, Lieut. 27.10.1871, Capt. 4.12.1879, Maj. 28.8.1885, Welsh R. 28.8.1890.

COOKSON, Alfred Edward. Ens. 63rd F. 16.10.1855, Lieut. 15.1.1858, Capt. 14.6.1859, Ret. 14.6.1864.

COOMBES, John. Lieut. 63rd F. 2.12.1795, N.T.A. 1797.

COOMBS, Albert Edward, D.C.M. 2/Lieut. Manch. R. 23.5.1915, Lieut. 18.1.1916, Ret. 5.6.1919.

COOPER, Allan Withington. Capt. Manch. R. 4.1.1917, H.P. 17.5.1922.

COOPER, Edward Russell. From 35th F., Ens. 96th F. 24.11.1869, Lieut. 28.10.1871, Ret. 25.4.1874.

COOPER, Geoffrey Danvers. 2/Lieut. Manch. R. 14.7.1921.

COOPER, Harry Ashley. Lieut. Manch. R. 29.8.1885, Ben. S.C. 22.5.1887.

COOPER-KING, George Courtenay, D.S.O. 2/Lieut. Manch. R. 12.3.1892, Lieut. 5.7.1895, Capt. 18.3.1899, Died at Totteridge 27.1.1909.

Cope, Joseph. Ens. 63rd F. 7.10.1777, Lieut. 3.5.1780, N.T.A. 1781.
Cope, William. Ens. 63rd F. 15.5.1776, Lieut. 5.11.1777, N.T.A. 1781.
Copping, S. B. From E. Norf. Mil., Ens. 63rd F. 27.2.1808, Lieut. 16.7.1808, Ret. 6.12.1808.
Cordon, William Ilderton. Qr.-Mr. and Hon. Lieut. Manch. R. 20.6.1900, Camp. Qr.-Mr. (Curragh, Ireland) 4.5.1907.
Corley, James Alma, M.C., M.M. 2/Lieut. Manch. R. 27.2.1918, Lieut. 27.8.1919.
Cosby, Stafford Sydney. Lieut. 63rd F. 11.11.1795, Capt. 20.8.1803, Maj. 15.8.1811, Died about 1813.
Cosby, William. From 60th F., Capt. 63rd F. 31.2.1791, Maj. 10.8.1796, Ret. 24.11.1797.
Cosby, William. Ens. 63rd F. 18.9.1804, Lieut. 8.5.1806, H.P. 5th W. India Regt. 2.4.1818.
Costello, Dudley. From H.P. 34th F., Ens. 96th F. 29.1.1824, H.P. 10.9.1828.
Cottingham, Charles Scarborough. 2/Lieut. Manch. R. 24.4.1889, Lieut. 10.9.1890, Capt. 1.11.1897, D. on S. at Abu Harazon, Blue Nile, 18.10.1898.
Cotton, Lynch Stapleton. From 97th F., Capt. 63rd F. 7.4.1865, Maj. 12.6.1867, Lt.-Col. 26.2.1870, Brev. Col. 1.5.1879, Ret. Hon. Maj.-Gen. 25.3.1885.
Coultman, Humphrey Woodward. From 26th F., Lieut. 63rd F. 20.9.1833, Capt. 2.9.1844, 24th F. 30.1.1847.
Court, John. Ens. 63rd F. 25.8.1809, Lieut. 28.6.1810, 20th L. Drgns. 24.12.1812.
Cowart, Charles. Ens. 63rd F. 3.4.1761, H.P. 1763.
Cowell, Thomas. Ens. 96th F. 17.3.1863, Ret. 9.6.1867.
Cowslade, Christopher. From Yorks. L.I., Vol. Lieut. 63rd F. 4.4.1808, Died Apr. 1810.
Cox, Claude Russell, A.F.C. 2/Lieut. Manch. R. 16.2.1916, Lieut. 16.8.1917, R.A.F. 1.8.1919.
Cox, George Herbert. From 1st W. India R., Lieut. 63rd F. 20.8.1844, 53rd F. 26.11.1847.
Cradock, A. Williamson. From 2nd Res. Bn., Ens. 63rd F. 19.9.1804, Lieut. 21.3.1805, 15th F. 21.3.1805.
Craven, Benjamin. From 22nd F., Lieut. 63rd F. 18.9.1780, Capt. 23.3.1791, Indpdt. Coy. of Invalids 23.3.1791.
Crawford, John Crane. 2/Lieut. Manch. R. 9.4.1888, Lieut. 18.12.1889, Capt. 10.7.1897, Maj. 18.4.1903, Lt.-Col. 10.3.1915, Res. Bn. 1916, Ret. 9.2.1923.
Crawhall, Neil Grant. 2/Lieut. Manch. R. 25.2.1914, Lieut. 1.12.1914, K. in A. 7.7.1916.
Creagh, Charles Douglas Beresford. From 6th Innis. Drgns., Ens. 96th F. 18.12.1867, Ret. 1.4.1868.
Creagh, Leo. 2/Lieut. Manch. R. 4.1.1899, Lieut. 13.9.1899, Capt. 27.11.1901, K. in A. near Bethune, France, 20.12.1914.

Crichton, John Ernest Theodore. 2/Lieut. Manch. R. 5.9.1896, Lieut. 29.10.1897, Capt. 5.9.1900, K. in A. at Schwartz Kopjes, near Belfast, S. Africa, 14.2.1901.
Crisp, Henry. From 64th F., Surg. 63rd F. 22.6.1855, Staff 20.2.1863.
Croker, Edward. From 39th F., Capt. 96th F. 4.8.1848, Maj. 8.7.1856, Ret. 21.5.1858.
Croker, John. Ens. 63rd F. 14.3.1772, Lieut. 11.7.1775, Capt. 20.4.1778, N.T.A. 1781.
Croley, Henry. From 60th F., Lieut. 63rd F. 15.5.1829, Capt. 21.4.1837, Died 16.11.1844.
Crompton, Henry Thomas. From 99th F., Lieut. 63rd F. 16.10.1833, Ret. Dec. 1870.
Croome, John. From 2nd F., Capt. 96th F. 17.3.1863, Died Oct. 1867.
Cross, Richard. From H.P. 11th F., Ens. 96th F. 29.1.1824, Lieut. 7.4.1825, H.P. 17.7.1828, Died 26.2.1842.
Crowther, Richard William Barnardiston. Lieut. 63rd F. 15.1.1856, Capt. 5.2.1866, 1st F. 2.10.1866.
Crowther, William G. L. Ens. 63rd F. 20.10.1840, Lieut. 25.5.1842, Cashiered May 1849.
Crozier, Frank Percy. 2/Lieut. Manch. R. 19.5.1900, Lieut. 13.7.1901, H.P. 14.1.1907.
Cubitt, Henry Archibald. From 36th F., Capt. 63rd F. 2.3.1849, Ret. 12.8.1853.
Cumberland, Bentinck Harry. From H.P., Capt. 96th F. 4.12.1828, H.P. Meuron's R. 9.10.1840.
Cumberland, Charles Brownlow. From 35th F., Lieut. 96th F. 15.10.1825, Capt. 10.6.1826, Maj. 19.9.1834, Lt.-Col. 22.7.1842, Brev. Col. 20.6.1854, Ret. Maj.-Gen. 8.7.1856, Died at Leamington 27.11.1882.
Cumberland, George Bentinck. From 42nd F., Ens. 96th F. 18.8.1848, Lieut. 15.6.1849, Capt. 27.11.1857, Ret. 19.8.1862.
Cumberland, R. F. W. Ens. 96th F. 20.5.1842, Lieut. 25.11.1845, Adjt. 9.4.1847-5.5.1853, Capt. 15.3.1853, 28th F. 26.12.1854.
Cuming, George. Ens. 63rd F. 27.3.1817, Lieut. 9.4.1825, 71st F. 9.4.1825.
Cummings, Henry Jack. Lieut. 96th F. 2.12.1874, 11th Hussars 26.7.1876.
Cummings, William Henry. 2/Lieut. Manch. R. 17.12.1916, Lieut. 17.6.1918, Ret. 24.8.1920.
Cuppage, John Macdonald. From 89th F., Maj. 96th F. 2.5.1865, Ret. 20.7.1867.
Cureton, Edward Robert. Lieut. Manch. R. 30.1.1886, K.O.S. Bord. 20.6.1888.
Curran, Arthur Edward Richards. From W. Riding R., Lt.-Col. Manch. R. 1.6.1898, H.P. 1.6.1902.
Currer, Richard R. Ens. 96th F. 16.9.1836, Lieut. 27.9.1839, Capt. 20.10.1846, Maj. 15.4.1856, 75th F. 27.5.1862.
Curteis, Edward Barrett Hodges. Ens. 96th F. 1.6.1859, Lieut. 23.11.1860, 9th L. Drgns. 15.1.1861.
Curtis, Percival Leopold. From R. Irish R., Lieut. Manch. R. 9.9.1922.

ALPHABETICAL ROLL OF OFFICERS

CURTIS, William. 2/Lieut. Manch. R. 29.12.1914, K. in A. 13/14.3.1915.
CURTOIS, George Charles Widdrington. Ens. 63rd F. 23.3.1847, Lieut. 10.4.1849, K. in A., Inkerman, 5.11.1854.

D'AGUILAR, John Swainson. Ens. 96th F. 9.2.1870, Lieut. 28.10.1871, Hon. Capt. 10.4.1878, A. Pay Dept. 3.2.1879.
DAILEY, George Carlisle, M.C. From N. Zealand Force, Lieut. Manch. R. 1.10.1915, Capt. 1.1.1923.
DAKERS, Colin. Surg. 63rd F. 29.10.1807–7.9.1808.
DALE, Robert. Ens. 63rd F. 25.10.1827, Lieut. 16.11.1832, Ret. 5.11.1835.
DALRYMPLE, John. Ens. 63rd F. 15.1.1762, Lieut. 3.7.1765, K. in A., Bunkers Hill, 17.6.1775.
DALTON, Joseph. Qr.-Mr. 63rd F. 13.11.1775–8.1.1783, Ens. 9.1.1783, H.P. 1784.
DALY, Edward Nugent. Ens. 63rd F. 19.4.1844, Lieut. 16.9.1845, H.P. 29.8.1847.
DALY, Tully. From H.P. 2nd F., Asst. Surg. 63rd F. 11.12.1828, Died Sept. 1829
DALZELL, Hon. Robert Alexander George. From 81st F., Maj. 63rd F. 3.6.1853, Lt.-Col. 6.11.1854, Provsl. Depot Bn., Malta, 7.9.1855.
DANE, Richard, M.D. From 11th F., Surg. 63rd F. 24.12.1847, 29th F. 7.7.1848.
DANIEL, Alexander. From H.P. 88th F., Capt. 63rd F. 19.9.1804, Maj. 4.6.1814, H.P. 1814.
DANKS, Cyril German. 2/Lieut. Manch. R. 15.5.1897, Lieut. 13.4.1898, D. of W. at Aldershot 31.5.1900, received at Elandslaagte, S. Africa.
DANN, William Rowland Harris. 2/Lieut. Manch. R. 19.5.1900, Lieut. 1.7.1901, Bed. R. 8.2.1908.
DARLING, William James. Ens. 63rd F. 5.2.1829, Lieut. 19.9.1833, Adjt. 8.8.1838–19.4.1843, Capt. 20.4.1843, Died en route to England 3.6.1849.
DAVANEY, Parkam Burton. Ens. 96th F. 21.2.1865, Ret. 7.11.1868.
DAVEY, William. Ens. 63rd F. 21.2.1811, Lieut. 12.8.1813, Ret. 9.1.1818.
DAVIDSON, Murdock Ross. 2/Lieut. Manch. R. 15.8.1914, Lieut. 1.12.1914, Capt. 1.1.1917.
DAVIDSON, Ralph Ivan Meynell. 2/Lieut. Manch. R. 18.9.1909, Lieut. 30.7.1913, D. of W. near Locon, France, 24.11.1914.
DAVIES, Herbert Grant. From 83rd F., Lieut. 96th F. 7.4.1863, Ret. 8.6.1867.
DAVIS, Cecil. 2/Lieut. 96th F. 23.4.1881, Lieut. 1.7.1881, Ben. S.C. 15.3.1885.
DAVIS, Richard Christopher. 2/Lieut. Manch. R. 15.8.1915, K. in A. 8.3.1916.
DAWSON, Reginald Harry. 2/Lieut. Manch. R. 21.1.1881, Madras S.C. 3.3.1883.
DAY, Frederick William. Ens. 63rd F. 11.10.1864, Lieut. 12.6.1867, Capt. 31.10.1871, Died Umballa, India, 3.12.1879.
DAY, John. Qr.-Mr. 63rd F. 26.10.1815, H.P. 71st F. 5.7.1821.
DAY, John Robert. Ens. 96th F. 27.2.1852, Lieut. 20.7.1855, Ret. 7.7.1857.
DAY, Robert Ladbroke. Ens. 63rd F. 18.10.1833, Lieut. 7.8.1835, 85th F. 13.5.1842.
DEAKIN, Frederick Farrer. 2/Lieut. Manch. R. 4.5.1898, Lieut. 6.5.1899, Capt. 13.7.1901, 2nd Drgn. Gds. 3.4.1907.
DEAN, Percy Hamilton. 2/Lieut. Manch. R. 28.1.1903, R. Innis. Fus. 15.2.1907.
DEANE, Bonar Millett. Ens. 96th F. 12.3.1853, 22nd F. 15.3.1853.
DEARDEN, John Alfred. 2/Lieut. Manch. R. 28.1.1903, Lieut. 7.2.1907, Capt. 1.12.1914, Maj. 19.5.1917, Ret. 2.7.1921.
DE BURGH, Eric. From Mil., 2/Lieut. Manch. R. 28.1.1903, Ind. Army 6.3.1903.
DE JONGH, Vernon Henry Price. 2/Lieut. Manch. R. 1.1.1917, Lieut. 1.7.1918, Res. 10.2.1919.
DE LA PENHA, Paul David. 2/Lieut. Manch. R. 12.8.1899, Lieut. 16.5.1900, Res. 2.8.1902.
DELHOSTE, D. C. Aug. Ens. 63rd F. 16.9.1845, Lieut. 15.12.1848, 87th F. 16.2.1849.
DE LISLE, Richard Francis Valpy. From Staff, Asst. Surg. 96th F. 24.9.1841, 1st Drgns. 14.11.1851.
DE MEURON, Philip Frederick. Ens. 96th F. 8.4.1825, Lieut. 10.6.1826, Capt. 24.11.1841, Ret. 13.12.1842.
DENHOLME, William. Ens. 63rd F. 25.9.1757, Lieut. 23.3.1759, Capt. 16.9.1768, N.T.A. 1771.
DENIS-DE-VITRE, William Edward. 2/Lieut. Manch. R. 22.8.1888, Died at Agra 28.12.1888.
DENNY, Robert. From 57th F., Capt. 63rd F. 6.1.1814, H.P. 1815.
DENNYS, Hector Travers. Lieut. Manch. R. 29.8.1885, Ben. S.C. 30.5.1887.
DENT, John Ralph Congreve. 2/Lieut. Manch. R. 10.10.1903, Lieut. R. Innis. Fus. 4.5.1907.
DE PUTRON, Hugh. 2/Lieut. Manch. R. 28.8.1901, Lieut. 10.11.1902, Capt. 30.10.1914, Maj. 22.5.1916, Brev. Lt.-Col. 3.6.1918, Ret. Lt.-Col. 7.4.1920.
DE SAUMAREZ, Frederick. Ens. 96th F. 21.10.1862, 71st F. 15.12.1862.
DESBRISAY, Peter. From 11th F., Lt.-Col. 63rd F. 17.4.1758, K. in A., Guadaloupe, 23.3.1759.
DEXTER, Christopher. From H.P. 3rd F., Lieut. 63rd F. 17.3.1825, Died Fort St. George, Madras, 19.5.1834.
DEXTER, William. From 8th F., Lieut. 63rd F. 2.10.1757, D. on S., W. Indies, 1761.
DILLON, Edward Walter. Ens. 63rd F. 21.4.1808, Lieut. 5.10.1809, H.P. 23.12.1819.
DIXON, ——. Ens. 63rd F. 3.9.1795, Superseded 15.8.1797.
DOBBS, Francis. Ens. 63rd F. 30.12.1768, Adjt. 6.6.1770–Apr. 1772, Lieut. 25.7.1771, 51st F. 8.4.1772.

DOBSON, Robert. 2/Lieut. Manch. R. 24.12.1920, Ret. 1.6.1922.
DOLAN, John Joseph, M.C. From R. Dub. Fus., Lieut. Manch. R. 28.5.1919.
DOLAN, Terence Michael. From 2nd W. India R., Lieut. 63rd F. 1.2.1867, Capt. 25.3.1871, 95th F. 31.11.1871.
DOMVILLE, Compton Charles. From 85th F., Lieut. 63rd F. 13.5.1842, Ret. 28.6.1844.
DORLING, Francis. Ens. 96th F. 2.11.1869, Lieut. 15.2.1871, Capt. 13.3.1878, 107th F. 12.4.1879.
DORLING, Francis Holland, D.S.O. 2/Lieut. Manch. R. 9.9.1897, Lieut. 17.8.1898, Capt. 5.1.1901, Maj. 10.3.1915, Brev. Lt.-Col. 3.6.1918, Lt.-Col. 1.9.1920.
DOUGLAS, Rouse Douglas. From 45th F., Lieut. 96th F. 2.11.1855, Capt. 30.4.1858, Ret. 24.11.1863.
DOUGLAS, Sholto. From H.P. 68th F., Lieut. 63rd F. 19.10.1820, Capt. 18.7.1822, Lt.-Col. 23.8.1827, Ret. Nov. 1832.
DOWLING, Joseph. From 1st R. Veteran Bn., Lieut. 96th F. 29.1.1824, H.P. 26.7.1827.
DOWNES, Michael. From 8th F., Lieut. 63rd F. 1.10.1757, D. on S., W. Indies, 23.3.1759.
DOYLE, William S. S. Ens. 63rd F. 20.12.1821, Lieut. 12.2.1824, Capt. 8.4.1826, H.P. 8.4.1826.
DRUMMOND, John William Ainslie. Sub/Lieut. 96th F. 11.2.1875, Scots Gds. 14.6.1876.
DRURY, Edward. Ens. 63rd F. 19.4.1765, Lieut. 29.10.1768, Capt. 16.6.1776, K. in A., Brandywine, 11.9.1777.
DRURY, James. Ens. 63rd F. 18.6.1775, N.T.A. 1777.
DRURY-LOWE, Vincent F. K. Ens. 63rd F. 21.2.1866, Lieut. 21.8.1867, Ret. 1.2.1868.
DUDGEON, William. From 3rd W. India R., Asst. Surg. 63rd F. 29.6.1811, H.P. 25.12.1818.
DUKE, James. From 2nd W. India R., Qr.-Mr. 63rd F. 20.11.1824, H.P. 11.12.1828.
DUMARESQUE, Alexander Macleay. Ens. 63rd F. 1.9.1854, Lieut. 7.2.1855, Capt. 4.12.1857, Died 16.11.1866.
DUMAS, John Craig. From H.P., Capt. 63rd F. 23.8.1827, Ret. Aug. 1830.
DUNBAR, John K. Ens. 63rd F. 20.12.1787, Lieut. 30.9.1790, 69th F. 30.9.1790.
DUNDAS, Donald William. Ens. 96th F. 29.12.1848, Lieut. 8.7.1853, 35th F. 20.6.1854.
DUNDAS, Thomas. Capt. 63rd F. 20.5.1769, Maj. 65th F. 20.1.1776.
DUNDAS, William. From R. Irish R., Qr.-Mr. and Hon. Capt. Manch. R. 16.1.1909, Ret. 27.3.1909.
DUNLOP, Frederick Cleave Strickland. 2/Lieut. Manch R. 1.12.1897, Lieut. 11.3.1899, Capt. 12.3.1901, Adjt. 14.4.1902-13.4.1905, K. in A. near Bethune 8.11.1914.
DUNLOP, James Mair. Ens. 96th F. 2.10.1866, Lieut. 22.1.1868, Adjt. 17.2.1872-21.9.1873, Died at Southampton on P. and O. Steamer *Malun* 24.11.1873.

DUNN, Thomas. From 22nd F., Lieut. 63rd F. 18.9.1780, D. of W., Virginia, 21.10.1781.
DUNN, William. Ens. 63rd F. 28.4.1808, Lieut. 19.10.1809, Res. 1812.
DUPORT, John. Ens. 63rd F. 15.12.1808, Lieut. 17.1.1810, Adjt. 15.10.1812-Nov. 1814, and 7.9.1815-May 1824, Died, Chatham, 27.1.1829.
DURAND, Edward Law. From 25th F., Ens. 96th F. 10.11.1865, Lieut. 4.10.1867, Ben. S.C. 8.10.1868.
DURNFORD, Charles Day. Ens. 63rd F. 11.12.1866, Lieut. 12.2.1870, Ordnance Dept. 13.7.1867.
DURRANT, James Falconer. 2/Lieut. Manch. R. 5.9.1896, Res. 23.6.1898.
DURRANT, William Robert Estridge. Ens. 96th F. 22.6.1858, Lieut. 31.1.1860, 15th F. 21.2.1860.
DYER, John Frederick Cecil. 2/Lieut. Manch. R. 7.1.1916, Lieut. 7.7.1917, Ret. 2.6.1922.
DYNE, John. From 67th F., Capt. 63rd F. 7.12.1797, 3rd F. 23.8.1799.
DYNE, John. From H.P. The Queen's Rngs., Lieut. 63rd F. 26.8.1804, 15th F. 21.6.1810.
DYOTT, Richard. Ens. 63rd F. 11.10.1817, 70th F. 17.9.1827.

EARDLEY, Francis. From 141st F., Lieut. 63rd F. 9.9.1795, N.T.A. 1797.
EASTMEAD, Charles Sidney. 2/Lieut. Manch. R. 11.2.1888, Ind. S.C. 18.7.1889.
EDDOWES, William Black. 2/Lieut. Manch. R. 26.6.1899, Lieut. 7.4.1900, Capt. 5.2.1902, Maj. 1.9.1915, Lt.-Col. 5.11.1921.
EDENSON, James. From H.P. 38th F., Lieut. 63rd F. 31.10.1805, Died about 1813.
EDGAR, Alexander. From 2nd W. India R., Capt. 63rd F. 26.6.1838, Died Moulmein, Burma, 7.4.1839.
EDIE, Robert. Paymaster 63rd F. 14.3.1805, H.P. Nov. 1814.
EDWARDS, George Dall. 2/Lieut. Manch. R. 22.4.1903, Lieut. 15.3.1907, Derby R. 3.8.1908.
EDWARDS, Henry Herbert. Sub/Lieut. 96th F. 28.2.1874, 23rd F. 13.5.1874.
EDWARDS, Justinian Heathcote. Ens. 63rd F. 3.3.1863, Lieut. 2.10.1866, Capt. 26.2.1870, Ret. 28.5.1870.
EGAN, Frederick Charles. 2/Lieut. Manch. R; 27.3.1918, Lieut. 27.9.1919.
ELLERSHAW, Henry. 2/Lieut. Manch. R. 19.10.1901, Lieut. 5.2.1903, Capt. 1.2.1914, Maj. 24.10.1916, H.P. 6.5.1922.
ELLIOTT, Arthur James. 2/Lieut. Manch. R. 14.1.1918, Lieut. 14.7.1919.
ELLIS, John. From 8th F., Capt. 63rd F. 31.8.1756, N.T.A. 1760.
ELLIS, John Oldham. Ens. 96th F. 14.1.1862, Ret. 28.11.1864.
ELTON, John. Ens. 63rd F. 3.8.1830, 4th F. 25.11.1831.
EMERSON, William Henry. From Cape Mounted Rifles, Lieut. 63rd F. 5.5.1848, Ret. 7.9.1852.

ALPHABETICAL ROLL OF OFFICERS

ERSKINE, Archibald. From 48th F., Lieut. 63rd F. 8.5.1828, Capt. 16.11.1832, 45th F. 11.7.1836.
ERSKINE, John David Beveridge. 2/Lieut. Manch. R. 6.6.1896, Lieut. 29.10.1897, Capt. 9.6.1900, Ret. 13.9.1911.
EVANS, Henry Roe. From 10th F., Lieut. 63rd F. 16.6.1848, Capt. 9.9.1851, H.P. 9.9.1851.
EVANS, Ivor Ballantyne. 2/Lieut. Manch. R. 14.7.1915, Lieut. 2.7.1916, Ind. Army 17.10.1917.
EVANS, Wilfred Keith, C.M.G., D.S.O. 2/Lieut. Manch. R. 21.4.1900, Lieut. 13.2.1901, Capt. 18.12.1907, Adjt. 3.5.1906–2.5.1909, and 30.10.1914–1.8.1915, Maj. 1.9.1915, Brev. Lt.-Col. 3.6.1917, Brev. Col. 1.1.1923.
EYKYN, Gilbert Davidson Pitt. 2/Lieut. Manch. R. 4.5.1901, Lieut. 24.12.1901, Ind. S.C. 12.2.1904.
EYRE, Giles. From 20th F., Lieut. 63rd F. 22.8.1837, Capt. 1.12.1840, 39th F. 1.12.1840.
EYTON, William Archibald. Ens. 96th F. 14.2.1834, Lieut. 30.6.1837, Capt. 22.7.1842, Ret. 6.7.1852.

FACER, Walter. Qr.-Mr. 96th F. 13.7.1878, Hon. Capt. 13.7.1888, Ret. 11.9.1889.
FAGAN, Christopher George Forbes. Sub/Lieut. 63rd F. 11.2.1875, Lieut. 11.2.1875, Ben. S.C. 28.2.1879.
FAIR, John. Paymaster 63rd F. 6.6.1798, Died, Barbadoes, 14.2.1808.
FAIRTLOUGH, Charles Edward. Ens. 63rd F. 12.5.1837, Lieut. 31.12.1839, Adjt. 20.4.1843–24.8.1846, Capt. 25.8.1846, Brev. Maj. 17.7.1855, Lt.-Col. 7.3.1856, H.P. 10.11.1856.
FAIRTLOUGH, James. Ens. 63rd F. 8.11.1842, Lieut. 30.7.1844, Ret. 23.8.1850.
FAIRTLOUGH, James William. Ens. 63rd F. 25.8.1802, Lieut. 24.5.1804, Capt. 14.3.1805, Brev. Maj. 12.8.1819, Maj. 26.5.1825, Lt.-Col. 17.9.1833, Ret. 16.9.1845.
FAIRTLOUGH, Samuel. From 3rd F., Lieut. 63rd F. 27.8.1783, Capt. 1.3.1794, Maj. 17.9.1801, Brev. Lt.-Col. 25.4.1808, D. on S., Martinique, 5.8.1810.
FAIRTLOUGH, Samuel. Ens. 63rd F. 8.5.1806, Lieut. 7.5.1807, 90th F. 7.5.1807.
FAIRTLOUGH, Samuel. Ens. 63rd F. 25.8.1846, Lieut. 22.10.1847, H.P. 22.10.1847.
FAIRTLOUGH, Thomas Stephenson. Ens. 63rd F. 12.4.1810, Lieut. 9.4.1812, Capt. 18.11.1819, Maj. 1.10.1825, Died at Windsor 13.11.1826.
FAIRTLOUGH, William Barber. From H.P. 56th F., Ens. 63rd F. 19.9.1833, Lieut. 26.12.1834, D. on S. 15.10.1837.
FANE, Vere Bonamy, K.C.B., K.C.I.E. Lieut. Manch. R. 12.11.1884, Ben. S.C. 30.3.1888, Col. Manch. R. 16.1.1920.
FARIE, George. Ens. 96th F. 14.6.1864, 74th F. 19.7.1864.

FARLEY, Vallie. 2/Lieut. Manch. R. 9.1.1917, Lieut. 9.7.1918, Res. 24.4.1920.
FARRAR, Sidney Gelder. 2/Lieut. Manch. R. 5.7.1917, Res. 16.7.1919.
FARRELL, Charles. Asst. Surg. 63rd F. 5.10.1804, N.T.A. 1807.
FARRINGTON, Douglas McLeod Hunter. 2/Lieut. 63rd F. 11.5.1878, Died Karachi, India, 31.8.1880.
FAWCETT, William Henry, M.M. 2/Lieut. Manch. R. 27.3.1918, Lab. Corps 16.12.1919.
FEAKE, Charles S. Ens. 63rd F. 1.7.1807, Lieut. 17.8.1808, Died 14.9.1809.
FEARSON, Frederick George W. From H.P. 69th F., Capt. 63rd F. 7.7.1854, Ret. 2.11.1855.
FEARSON, John Hodson. From R. Afr. Col. Corps, Lieut. 63rd F. 18.9.1833, Capt. 3.11.1837, H.P. 14.1.1842.
FELLOWS, Francis William. From 56th F., Lieut. 96th F. 15.6.1849, Paymr. 52nd F. 3.6.1853.
FENWICK, Thomas Lyle. From H.P. 71st F., Qr.-Mr. 63rd F. 5.7.1821, Ceylon R. 28.11.1822.
FERNS, William. From H.P. 66th F., Capt. 96th F. 10.8.1826, Brev. Maj. 27.5.1825, Ret. 14.2.1828.
FINNEY, Edward Hamilton. From W. Ind. R., Ens. 96th F. 7.4.1825, Lieut. 62nd F. 13.6.1830.
FINNIS, John Fortescue. 2/Lieut. Manch. R. 21.12.1889, Lieut. 21.10.1891, Ind. S.C. 31.2.1892.
FISH, Joseph. From 8th F., Capt. 63rd F. 28.8.1756, Maj. 23.7.1762, D. on S., W. Indies, 18.3.1763.
FISHER, Basil. From H.P. 3rd Irish Bde., Capt. 63rd F. 16.1.1812, Maj. 4.6.1814, Ret. Apr. 1816.
FISHER, Edward Nelson. 2/Lieut. Manch. R. 24.6.1899, Lieut. 17.2.1900, Capt. 22.3.1902, Died in England 1.6.1909.
FISHER, Harold, D.S.O. 2/Lieut. Manch. R. 4.5.1898, Lieut. 6.5.1899, Capt. 14.7.1901, K. in A. near Bethune 15.12.1914.
FISHER, Henry, M.D. From 7th F., Asst. Surg. 63rd F. 18.1.1816, H.P. 19.1.1826.
FISHER, Robert Arthur. 2/Lieut. Manch. R. 9.1.1917, Lieut. 9.7.1918, Res. 21.4.1920.
FITTON, Guy William. Lieut. Manch. R. 9.9.1882, Capt. 18.3.1890, A. Pay Dept. 1.3.1895.
FITZGERALD, Frederick Lattin. Ens. 63rd F. 14.6.1850, Lieut. 4.11.1853, Ret. 23.11.1855.
FITZGERALD, Henry. Ens. 63rd F. 5.11.1766, Lieut. 12.12.1770, N.T.A. 1771.
FITZGERALD, Jones. Ens. 63rd F. 19.10.1781, N.T.A. 1789.
FITZGIBBON, Victor Nicholas. From Dorset R., 2/Lieut. Manch. R. 15.8.1888, Lieut. 18.12.1889, Res. 21.10.1891.
FITZROY, William. From 83rd F., Capt. 63rd F. 2.11.1855, Maj. 28.7.1867, 47th F. 22.7.1868

FLANAGAN, George. 2/Lieut. Manch. R. 8.11.1915, Lieut. 19.2.1917, Res. 14.1.1922.

FLEMING, Edward James Ingleby. From 24th F., Capt. 63rd F. 30.1.1847, 2nd F. 27.6.1854.

FLEMING, Mungo. Ens. 63rd F. 18.3.1760, Qr.-Mr. 12.10.1760, Lieut. 14.1.1762, H.P. 1763.

FLOWER, William Henry. Asst. Surg. 63rd F. 1854, Res. 1.5.1855.

FLUDER, Alexander. Ens. 63rd F. 30.11.1855, Lieut. 12.11.1858, 17th F. 12.11.1858.

FOLLETT, Thomas. Ens. 63rd F. 29.3.1763, Lieut. 16.9.1768, Capt. 25.7.1771, Ret. 12.7.1775.

FOORD, Alexander Gunning, D.S.O. 2/Lieut. Manch. R. 5.1.1901, Lieut. 30.10.1901, Adjt. 1.12.1906–30.11.1909, Capt. 1.12.1912, Maj. 5.1.1916, Ret. Lt.-Col. 7.12.1922.

FOOT, William Yates. Ens. 96th F. 18.10.1859, Ret. 15.1.1862.

FORD, Alfred John. From 58th F., Ens. 96th F. 12.9.1848, Lieut. 18.7.1851, 35th F. 20.6.1854.

FORD, Robert Penrice. Ens. 63rd F. 16.7.1841, Lieut. 26.1.1844, Died Bellary, India, 24.9.1845.

FORSTER, Hugh Percy. Ens. 63rd F. 24.7.1811, Lieut. 14.12.1815, Paymr. 43rd F. 10.6.1824.

FORTH, Nowell Barnet De Lancy, D.S.O., M.C. 2/Lieut. Manch. R. 19.5.1900, Lieut. 3.7.1901, Capt. 20.7.1911, Maj. 1.9.1915.

Foss, Kenneth Mackenzie. Sub/Lieut. 63rd F. 17.1.1877, Madras S.C. 5.11.1877.

FOSTER, Thomas. Ens. 63rd F. 18.8.1861, Lieut. 28.9.1865, Ret. 31.8.1866.

FOULSTON, John. From 13th F., Capt. 63rd F. 31.12.1839, H.P. 27th F. 26.1.1844.

FOWKE, Mansergh Cuthbert. 2/Lieut. Manch. R. 5.1.1901, Lieut. 7.10.1901, Capt. 1.12.1912, K. in A., Le Cateau, 26.8.1914.

FOWLE, John. From 99th F. Lieut., 63rd F. 5.10.1838, Capt. 14.10.1842, H.P. 14.10.1842.

Fox, Frederick Noel. 2/Lieut. Manch. R. 22.2.1908, Lieut. 1.4.1910, Ind. Army 19.2.1914.

Fox, Peter. From Ceylon R., Qr.-Mr. 63rd F. 22.11.1822, H.P. 20.10.1823.

Fox, Samuel. Qr.-Mr. 96th F. 19.7.1839, H.P. 23.6.1847.

Fox, Thomas. 2/Lieut. Manch. R. 26.6.1918, Res. 19.12.1919.

Fox, Whitney. Ens. 63rd F. 9.9.1758, Lieut. 8.9.1759, N.T.A. 1761.

FRANKLAND, John. From H.P. 24th L. Drgns., Capt. 63rd F. 25.8.1804, Maj. 16.3.1809, 98th F. 4.4.1811.

FRANKLIN, Harry, M.C. 2/Lieut. Manch. R. 10.7.1915, Lieut. 2.7.1916, Ret. 18.3.1920.

FRASER, Adrian William. Ens. 63rd F. 17.12.1852, Lieut. 11.8.1854, Capt. 10.8.1855, Died 1856.

FRASER, Alexander. Ens. 96th F. 11.8.1837, Lieut. 7th F. 12.7.1839.

FRASER, Alister. 2/Lieut. Manch. R. 25.9.1918, Res. 2.7.1919.

FRASER, Reginald Simon. From 24th F., Ens. 63rd F. 7.1.1862, Ret. 28.10.1864.

FREEMAN, Wilfred Rhodes, D.S.O., M.C. 2/Lieut. Manch. R. 22.2.1908, Lieut. 27.3.1912, Capt. 10.6.1915, Brev. Maj. 1.1.1917, R.A.F. 1.8.1919.

FREER, Thomas. Lieut. 63rd F. 1.4.1813, H.P. Nov. 1814.

FREMANTLE, Guy. 2/Lieut. Manch. R. 11.2.1888, C. Gds. 6.2.1889.

FRENCH, Deane. Ens. 63rd F. 29.10.1768, Lieut. 2.5.1770, N.T.A. 1772.

FRENCH, George. From 48th F., Lieut. 63rd F. 2.10.1773, N.T.A. 1778.

FRENCH, John Thomas. Ens. 96th F. 26.7.1855, Lieut. 8.7.1856, Capt. 29.6.1860, 52nd F. 22.10.1861.

FRENCH, Robert. Ens. 63rd F. 29.1.1818, Lieut. 2.1.1823, H.P. 38th F. 5.6.1823.

FRISBY, Henry Guy Fellowes. 2/Lieut. Manch. R. 22.10.1902, Lieut. 20.12.1904, Hampshire R. 18.1.1908.

FRY, Richard. Ens. 63rd F. 26.4.1810, Lieut. 18.6.1812, Capt. 5.6.1830, Ret. 2.4.1841.

FULDA, James Louis. 2/Lieut. Manch. R. 22.10.1902, Lieut. R. Irish R. 6.2.1907.

FULLERTON, James, C.B., K.H. From H.P., Lt.-Col. 96th F. 13.9.1827, Died at Halifax, Nova Scotia, 8.3.1834.

FURLONG, Charles John. From H.P., 43rd F. Paymr. 96th F. 22.4.1824, 2nd Drgn. Gds. 10.8.1826.

GAISFORD, Gilbert. Ens. 96th F. 22.2.1868, Ind. S.C. 2.12.1871.

GAISFORD, James. 2/Lieut. Manch. R. 22.8.1888, Ind. S.C. 9.5.1890.

GALBRAITH, James. From 13th Drgns., Lieut. 63rd F. 28.11.1771, N.T.A. 1772.

GALL, Herbert Reay. From H.P. 5th F., Capt. Manch. R. 12.1.1881, Ret. 1.8.1883.

GALWAY, St. John Dupond. From 73rd F., Capt. 96th F. 11.7.1865, Ret. 10.11.1869.

GARDNER, Charles Amphlett. 2/Lieut. 63rd F. 30.6.1878, Lieut. 6.8.1879, Madras. S.C. 11.1.1882.

GARDNER, Charles Ernest. 2/Lieut. Manch. R. 22.4.1903, Res. 11.11.1905.

GARDNER, Linnæus. Ens. 63rd F. 20.3.1783, N.T.A. 1783.

GARFORTH, Francis. Ens. 63rd F. 2.12.1777, 7th F. 19.9.1779.

GARLAND, George. Qr.-Mr. 96th F. 20.11.1867, Died at Dum-Dum, Bengal, 23.3.1870.

GARLAND, John, K.H. From H.P. 73rd F., Capt. 96th F. 29.1.1824, Maj. H.P. 26.5.1825.

GARNER, Eric Spence. 2/Lieut. Manch. R. 1.5.1917, Lieut. 1.11.1918, Res. 14.9.1920.

GARSTIN, Christopher. From 58th F., Lieut. 96th F. 18.8.1848, 27th F. 16.10.1855.

GARSTIN, George Lindsay. From 33rd F., Ens. 63rd F. 2.8.1871, Lieut. 28.10.1871, Ben. S.C. 3.8.1877.

ALPHABETICAL ROLL OF OFFICERS

GASKILL, William. Ens. 63rd F., 14.11.1805; Lieut. 28.5.1807, Ret. 1.6.1809.
GAUNTLETT, Frederick Edward. Ens. 63rd F. 8.2.1850, Ret. 18.2.1853.
GAUNTLETT, Vincent Cameron. 2/Lieut. Manch. R. 14.3.1900, Lieut. 5.9.1900, Capt. 7.12.1906, King's L'pool R. 20.5.1908.
GEDDES, William Cameron. Ens. 96th F. 15.10.1855, Lieut. 15.4.1856, Ret. 31.1.1860.
GELL, Philip Francis. 2/Lieut. Manch. R. 21.4.1900, Lieut. 15.2.1901, Ind. S.C. 23.5.1901.
GELLIBRAND, John. From S. Lanc. R., Capt. Manch. R. 26.5.1900, Adjt. 23.1.1904–5.5.1905, Ret. 27.4.1912.
GETHIN, John Percy. From Ches. R., Capt. Manch. R. 10.10.1885, Maj. 19.6.1895, Lt.-Col. 17.2.1900, H.P. 17.2.1904.
GETHIN, Richard. From 20th F., Capt. 96th F. 29.1.1824, H.P. 31.1.1834.
GIBBONS, John. Ens. 63rd F. 28.2.1816, Lieut. 8.1.1824, Capt. 17.9.1833, H.P. 23rd F. 29.5.1835.
GIBSON, Charles Herbert. 2/Lieut. Manch. R. 15.9.1915, Lieut. 1.1.1917, Res. 5.6.1919.
GIBSON, Thomas. Ens. 63rd F. 14.12.1774, Lieut. 16.5.1776, Capt. 49th F. 10.8.1778.
GILBERT, William. From 1st W. Ind. R., Lieut. 63rd F. 20.6.1811, H.P. 21st F. 16.5.1822.
GILLAM, William Albert, D.S.O. From R. Garr. R., Capt. Manch. R. 26.8.1905, Bord. R. 20.5.1908.
GILLAND, William. Ens. 63rd F. 29.10.1799, N.T.A. 1800.
GILLESPIE, John. Ens. 96th F. 19.12.1862, Lieut. 14.6.1864, Capt. 9th F. 14.9.1870.
GILMAN, Charles. From 8th F., Capt. 63rd F. 2.9.1756, N.T.A. 1765.
GLASCOTT, James Jocelyn. From 32nd F., Capt. 96th F. 13.9.1879, Ret. Hon. Maj. 15.9.1886.
GLEN, David Alexander. 2/Lieut. Manch. R. 12.5.1915, K. in A. 28.12.1915.
GLOVER, Gerald Mahon, M.C. 2/Lieut. Manch. R. 15.9.1914, Lieut. 1.12.1914, Capt. 1.7.1917, K. in A., Mesopotamia, 24.7.1920.
GODBOLD, George Augustus James. 2/Lieut. Manch. R. 20.2.1895, Lieut. 4.10.1896, Capt. 27.12.1899, Res. 10.6.1905.
GOING, Henry John. Ens. 63rd F. 12.6.1867, Lieut. 24.3.1859, 2/24th F. 1.8.1872.
GOLDFINCH, William Horsman. From N. Staff. R., Capt. Manch. R. 5.10.1898, Brev. Maj. 6.10.1898, Ret. 6.5.1903.
GOLDNEY, Thomas Holbrow. Ens. 96th F. 9.6.1867, 11th F. 16.10.1867.
GORDON, Cosmo. From 94th F., Lt.-Col. 63rd F. 20.7.1809, H.P. 16th Garr. Bn. 8.11.1810.
GORDON, George. Ens. 63rd F. 28.8.1817, 92nd F. 14.1.1819.
GORDON, George Henry. From 12th Drgns., Capt. 63rd F. 22.2.1786, N.T.A. 1789.
GORDON, James. Ens. 63rd F. 8.1.1824, Lieut. 26.5.1825, 4th F. 18.5.1826.

GORDON, James Guy Birnie. 2/Lieut. Manch. R. 4.5.1901, Lieut. 27.11.1901, Ind. S.C. 5.9.1902.
GORDON, John Salmon. From 2nd W. India R., Lieut. 96th F. 18.8.1848, Capt. 93rd F. 31.8.1855.
GORDON, Patrick Robert. Ens. 63rd F. 2.5.1834, Lieut. 20.6.1836, 78th F. 1.5.1840.
GORDON, William. Ens. 63rd F. 10.4.1855, Ret. 19.9.1856.
GORDON, William Fraser Forbes. From 20th F., Maj. 63rd F. 26.3.1873, Lt.-Col. 6.8.1879, Died Bareilly 17.3.1880.
GORGES, Edmund Howard, C.B., C.B.E., D.S.O. 2/Lieut. Manch. R. 14.9.1887, Lieut. 3.7.1889, Capt. 6.10.1896, Maj. 21.12.1901, Brev. Lt.-Col. 26.3.1906, W.Afr.R. 11.1.1912.
GORHAM, Richard. From H.P. 92nd F., Capt. 63rd F. 18.3.1813, H.P. Nov. 1814.
GOULD, Henry Kimberly. Ens. 96th F. 18.7.1862, Lieut. 12.6.1863, 85th F. 28.6.1864.
GOULD, John Stillman. From 31st F., Capt. 63rd F. 27.6.1851, H.P. 10.11.1856.
GOULD, Louis Philip. From 59th F., Lieut. 96th F. 24.3.1863, Capt. 19.5.1869, 77th F. 27.4.1870.
GRACEY, Hugh Malcolm Kirkwood. 2/Lieut. Manch. R. 19.1.1912, Res. 24.9.1913.
GRAHAM, John Scot. From Militia, 2/Lieut. Manch. R. 30.4.1902, Lieut. 5.3.1904, Ind. Army 24.12.1905.
GRAHAM, William. From H.P., Capt. 96th F. 31.1.1834, Ret. 14.2.1834.
GRAHAM, William Bannatyne. Sub-Lieut. 63rd F. 11.9.1876, Lieut. 11.9.1876, Capt. 9.7.1884, Maj. 18.3.1892, Died at Ranikhet, India, 1.9.1897.
GRANT, Francis William Seafield. From 2nd W. India R., Capt. 96th F. 11.9.1875, 32nd F. 13.9.1879.
GRANT, Patrick James John. From 3rd W. India R., Lieut. 96th F. 22.12.1848, Capt. 15.4.1856, Maj. 9.1.1863, 7th F. 8.9.1863.
GRANT, Richard. From 60th F., Lieut. 63rd F. 7.4.1808, Capt. 4.4.1816, H.P. 25.12.1818.
GRANT, Robert. Asst. Surg. 63rd F. 11.4.1800, Surg. 15.10.1803–1807.
GRANT, Thomas Coote. From 16th F., Lieut. 63rd F. 21.9.1855, Ret. 19.12.1861.
GRAVES, William Grogan. Ens. 63rd F. 16.3.1855, Lieut. 23.11.1855, Capt. 23.6.1864, Maj. 17.8.1870, 82nd F. 28.10.1871.
GRAY, Elias William Dixon. Ens. 96th F. 11.5.1855, Lieut. 28.1.1856, Ret. 21.4.1863.
GRAY, Frederick. 2/Lieut. Manch. R.24.6.1916, Lieut. 8.8.1917.
GRAY, John Hardie. Asst. Surg. 63rd F. 3.10.1845, Died at Secunderabad, India, 3.4.1846.
GREEN, Frederick Mason. From Lond. R., Capt. Manch. R. 1.7.1916, Res. 27.3.1919.
GREEN, George. From 38th F., Capt. 63rd F. 15.6.1838, Maj. 19.11.1844, 84th F. 24.12.1847.

GREEN, Herbert Richard Crichton. 2/Lieut. Manch. R. 14.8.1914, Lieut. 1.12.1914, Capt. 1.1.1917.
GREENE, Robert. Ens. 63rd F. 1.3.1778, Lieut. 19.10.1781, N.T.A. 1782.
GREER, Edward. 2/Lieut. Manch. R. 25.12.1917, Lieut. 25.6.1919.
GREGG, Edward Regan. From 26th F., Capt. 96th F. 22.5.1846, Died 31.1.1855.
GREIG, William. Ens. 63rd F. 8.9.1759, N.T.A. 1760.
GREY, Alfred. Ens. 63rd F. 11.1.1855, Lieut. 9.3.1855, Capt. 23.8.1859, 15th F. 23.8.1859.
GREY, Francis Douglas. From 53rd F., Lieut. 63rd F. 26.11.1847, Capt. 4.11.1853, Maj. 17.9.1858, 37th F. 6.5.1862.
GREY, Francis Lennox George. Ens. 96th F. 26.8.1859, Lieut. 14.1.1862, Capt. 14.1.1864, Ret. 25.12.1867.
GRIERSON, Kenneth MacIver, D.S.O., M.C. 2/Lieut. Manch. R. 4.8.1917, Lieut. 4.2.1919, H.P. 29.10.1921.
GRIFFITHS, Arthur George F. Ens. 63rd F. 13.2.1855, Lieut. 27.7.1855, Capt. 12.12.1862, H.P. 20.7.1870.
GRIFFITHS, Edwin. From H.P. 48th F., Paymr. 96th F. 11.1.1833, H.P. 27.7.1855.
GRIFFITHS, Ernest Frederick. Ens. 96th F. 8.7.1842, Lieut. 14.4.1846, Died 27.10.1848.
GRIFFITHS, Theodore Ralph Houghton. From W. India R., Capt. Manch. R. 15.10.1921, Ret. 13.9.1922.
GRIMES, Ernest James. 2/Lieut. Manch. R. 11.4.1917, Lieut. 11.10.1918, Res. 19.2.1920.
GRINDEL, Joseph Harry. 2/Lieut. Manch. R. 20.12.1914, Lieut. 27.4.1915, Ret. 5.1.1921.
GRONOW, William Lettsom. Ens. 63rd F. 14.8.1867, Lieut. 9.2.1870, Capt. 19.4.1879, Maj. 1.1.1884, Lt.-Col. 19.8.1891, Army Pay Dept. 29.7.1886, Ret. 16.9.1891.
GROOMBRIDGE, William. From 53rd F., Capt. 63rd F. 17.12.1812, H.P. 4.5.1820.
GROVE, Thomas. Ens. 63rd F. 8.6.1826, Lieut. 5.2.1829, Res. 1831.
GRUBBE, Thomas Hunt. From 49th F., Capt. 63rd F. 31.8.1826, 9th F. 12.3.1829.
GUINNESS, William Ernest. 2/Lieut. Manch. R. 8.2.1902, Lieut. 3.1.1904, Ret. 3.5.1913.
GUNNING, Orlando George. 2/Lieut. Manch. R. 22.8.1888, Lieut. 9.7.1890, Ind. S.C. 19.2.1892.
GUNTON, Dennis du Moulin. Ens. 96th F. 8.7.1862, Lieut. 21.4.1863, Adjt. 22.3.1864–13.10.1867, Capt. 10.11.1869, Died 11.8.1877.
GURDON, Bertrand Evelyn Mellish. Lieut. Manch. R. 25.8.1886, Ben. S.C. 19.1.1888.
GWATKIN, Willoughby Garnons. Lieut. Manch. R. 10.5.1882, Adjt. 18.4.1888–18.4.1892, Capt. 17.1.1892, Maj. 7.4.1900, Brev. Lt.-Col. 6.1.1904, Brev. Col. 20.11.1907, Col. in Army 7.12.1909.

GWYNNE, Nadolig Ximenes. From 77th F., Capt. 96th F. 27.4.1870, 63rd F. 28.8.1871, Maj. 18.3.1880, Lt.-Col. 1.7.1881, Shrop. L.I. 30.4.1883.
HAIGH-WOOD, Maurice. 2/Lieut. Manch. R. 12.5.1915, Lieut. 1.10.1915, Res. 10.10.1919.
HALFHIDE, Andrew. Ens. 63rd F. 30.1.1807, Lieut. 12.5.1808, 64th F. 7.9.1809.
HALL, Benjamin. Ens. 63rd F. 7.8.1799, N.T.A. 1801.
HALL, William. Ens. 63rd F. 10.8.1799, Lieut. 15.10.1803, Capt. 4.4.1805, 5th Garr. Bn. 31.8.1809.
HALLETT, George Kerr. Ens. 96th F. 30.8.1855, Lieut. 27.11.1857, Capt. 1.4.1859, Ret. 29.6.1860.
HAMILTON, Charles. From 8th F., Capt. 63rd F. 1.9.1756, N.T.A. 1761.
HAMILTON, Charles Frederick. Ens. 63rd F. 24.8.1797, Lieut. 3.1.1798, 5th F. 3.1.1798.
HAMILTON, Edward Chetwood. From 21st F., Ens. 96th F. 14.8.1867, Lieut. 10.11.1869, Ben. S.C. 12.7.1871.
HAMILTON, James. From 15th Bn. of Res., Capt. 63rd F. 24.8.1804, N.T.A. 1805.
HAMILTON, William. Ens. 63rd F. 16.12.1768, Lieut. 14.3.1772, Discharged by G.C.M. 1.12.1775.
HAMMETT, Sydney Jervis. Ens. 63rd F. 7.7.1869, 8th F. 18.11.1869.
HAMMOND, Frederick. 2/Lieut. Manch. R. 29.6.1917, Lieut. 29.12.1918, Res. 18.1.1920.
HANBURY, James Arthur, M.B. From Staff, Surg. 63rd F. 20.2.1863, R. Art. 22.5.1866.
HAND, Charles Augustus. Ens. 63rd F. 11.6.1852, Lieut. 6.6.1854, Capt. 14.7.1857. Died in wreck of transport *Spartan* 11.2.1862.
HANNAH, John Barlow. From 101st F., Asst. Surg. 63rd F. 30.1.1869, Surg.-Maj. A. Med. Dept. 28.4.1876.
HARCOURT, Albert Jackson. Ens. 96th F. 8.7.1856, Ret. 9.4.1861.
HARDCASTLE, Richard Newman, D.S.O. 2/Lieut. Manch. R. 1.12.1897, Lieut. 22.2.1899, Capt. 9.1.1901, Maj. 27.4.1915, Brev. Lt.-Col. 3.6.1916, Ret. 27.4.1921.
HARDIE, John. Ens. 63rd F. 29.3.1839, Lieut. 18.3.1842, Died 2.6.1842.
HARDING, William. From H.P. Rifle Bde., Lieut. 63rd F. 28.12.1820, H.P. 24.10.1821.
HARDINGHAM, Arthur Gatton Melhuish. 2/Lieut. Manch. R. 29.1.1902, Lieut. 19.8.1903, Capt. 1.12.1914, Maj. 29.1.1917.
HARINGTON, Henry Andrew. 2/Lieut. Manch. R. 9.11.1889, Lieut. 14.7.1891, Ind. S.C. 19.5.1892.
HARLAND, Herbert, D.C.M. 2/Lieut. Manch. R. 6.2.1918, Lieut. 6.8.1919, Res. 5.2.1920.
HARPER, James Stuart, M.C. 2/Lieut. Manch. R. 16.8.1905, Lieut. 28.10.1909, Capt. 27.4.1915.

HARRIES, Thomas. Ens. 63rd F. 19.7.1833, Lieut. 2.5.1834, Capt. 26.1.1844, Maj. 6.11.1854, Brev. Lt.-Col. 5.6.1856, Lt.-Col. 17.9.1858, Ret. 16.11.1860.
HARRIS, Harry Thomas Hopkinson. 2/Lieut. Manch. R. 7.5.1902, Lieut. 5.3.1904, Ind. Army 21.4.1904.
HARRIS, William. Ens. 63rd F. 22.10.1799, Lieut. 26.12.1799, 28th F. 9.7.1802.
HARRISON, Gustavus Nicholls. Ens. 63rd F. 5.6.1835, Lieut. 1.12.1837, Capt. 3.4.1846, Brev. Maj. 12.12.1854, K. in A., Sebastopol, 7.7.1855.
HARRISON, Henry. Ens. 63rd F. 9.10.1806, N.T.A. 1808.
HARRISON, Hyde Gwynne. 2/Lieut. Manch. R. 4.6.1904, Lieut. 18.7.1909, Capt. 18.12.1914, Adjt. 27.4.1919, K. in A., Mesopotamia, 24/5.7.1920.
HARRISON, Reginald William Hanson. 2/Lieut. Manch. R. 26.6.1901, Lieut. 17.5.1902, Ind. S.C. 11.12.1902.
HARRISON, Robert Prescott. From 37th F., Maj. 63rd F. 6.5.1862, 80th F. 9.11.1866.
HARRISON, Thomas. From 110th F., Lieut. 63rd F. 5.9.1795, Ret. 23.6.1796.
HART, James. From 8th F., Lieut. 63rd F. 6.10.1757, Indepdt. Coy. 1759.
HART, Thomas Frederick. Ens. 63rd F. 2.1.1823, 13th L. Drgns. 5.2.1824.
HARVEY, Pierce. Ens. 63rd F. 25.3.1759, Lieut. 18.3.1760, Qr.-Mr. 24.8.1763–1765, Qr.-Mr. 18.1.1770–Nov. 1775, Capt. 5.3.1775, N.T.A. 1777.
HASLEWOOD, John (William). Ens. 63rd F. 26.3.1758, Lieut. 26.6.1759, Capt. 25.5.1772, N.T.A. 1778.
HASTINGS, Charles Holland. From 82nd F., Maj. 63rd F. 25.8.1808, Appt. Inspecting F.O. of a Recruiting District in 1809.
HASTINGS, Geoffrey Francis. 2/Lieut. Manch. R. 19.10.1901, Lieut. 5.3.1904, Ind. Army 14.8.1905.
HASTINGS, Marquis of, Paulyn. Ens. 63rd F. 15.2.1850, 52nd F. 14.6.1850.
HASTINGS, Wilfred Charles Norrington, D.S.O. 2/Lieut. Manch. R. 24.6.1899, Lieut. 1.12.1899, Capt. 25.12.1901, Maj. 1.9.1915, Lt.-Col. W. Afr. R. 2.3.1920.
HATELEY, Jeffery. Asst. Surg. 63rd F. 1.10.1808, Surg. 28.7.1814—Nov. 1814.
HATHAWAY, Edwin. Ens. 96th F. 26.7.1827, Lieut. 9.3.1834, Capt. 12.8.1836, Ret. 26.4.1839.
HAULTON, Theodore M. From 38th F., Ens. 63rd F. 16.9.1836, Lieut. 39th F. 20.10.1840.
HAVERTY, John Coghlan. From 40th F., Asst. Surg. 96th F. 14.11.1851, Staff 29.6.1855.
HAWKE, Geoffrey. 2/Lieut. Manch. R. 16.7.1919, Res. 12.4.1922.
HAY, Hon. Arthur. 2/Lieut. 96th F. 24.2.1877, S. Gds. 23.1.1878.
HAY, Patrick. Ens. 63rd F. 13.1.1762, D. on S., W. Indies, 1763.

HAYWARD, Frank, M.C. 2/Lieut. Manch. R. 30.1.1918, Lieut. 30.7.1919, Res. 7.4.1920.
HEATLEY, William. From 8th F., Lieut. 63rd F. 2.9.1756, Adjt. 25.8.1756–1768, Capt. 5.11.1766, N.T.A. 1768.
HEELIS, John Richardson, M.C. 2/Lieut. Manch. R. 4.5.1901, Lieut. 25.12.1901, Adjt. 3.5.1912–26.10.1915, Capt. 1.12.1912, Maj. 8.1.1916.
HEMPHILL, John. Asst. Surg. 63rd F. 8.12.1803–22.6.1804.
HENDERSON, Eric Edward James. 2/Lieut. Manch. R. 22.12.1915, Lieut. 1.7.1917, Res. 9.11.1921.
HENDERSON, George Stuart, V.C., D.S.O., M.C. 2/Lieut. Manch. R. 24.1.1914, Lieut. 9.11.1914, Capt. 24.7.1916, K. in A., Mesopotamia, 24/5.7.1920.
HENDERSON, Ralph Anstruther. 2/Lieut. 96th F. 13.8.1879, Lieut. 18.6.1881, Capt. 2.7.1888, Maj. 5.4.1899, Lt.-Col. 1.4.1904. Ret. 19.3.1910.
HENDRICK, Charles. From H.P. 22nd F., Capt. 96th F. 2.11.1832, Ret. 4.12.1832.
HENNIKER, Frederick. Ens. 96th F. 24.6.1859, Lieut. 14.8.1860, Capt. 24.11.1863, Ret. 29.3.1864.
HENVILLE, Raymond. From 16th F., Lieut. 63rd F. 5.4.1808, Res. 1812.
HERRIES, John. From H.P. 100th F., Lt.-Col. 96th F. 29.1.1824, Ret. 30.12.1826.
HEWETSON, Boyle. Ens. 63rd F. 14.8.1765, Lieut. 30.12.1768, N.T.A. 1775.
HEYWOOD, Herbert. 2/Lieut. Manch. R. 16.8.1915, K. in A., Neuve Chapelle, France, 25.9.1915.
HICKEY, Edward Middleton. 2/Lieut. Manch. R. 23.12.1921.
HICKIE, Frederick Corbett. 2/Lieut. Manch. R. 16.12.1908, Lieut. 1.2.1913, Ind. Army 5.5.1914.
HICKMAN, Henry. Ens. 63rd F. 18.11.1813, H.P. Nov. 1814.
HICKMAN, John Penn. Ens. 63rd F. 19.10.1826, 2nd Drgn. Gds. 30.12.1826.
HICKS, William. Lieut. 63rd F. 30.10.1799, 39th F. 9.7.1803.
HIGGINBOTHAM, Charles. From 48th F., Lieut. 63rd F. 26.9.1833, Capt. 30.6.1844, Maj. 29.12.1854, Brev. Lt.-Col. 26.2.1856, Ret. 26.2.1856.
HIGGINS, Francis. Lieut. 63rd F. 26.9.1795, Died Aug. 1803.
HIGHTON, George. From 8th F., Lieut. 63rd F. 6.9.1756, D. on S., W. Indies, 23.3.1759.
HILDITCH, Charles. Ens. 63rd F. 2.7.1807, Lieut. 15.9.1808, N.T.A. 1810.
HILL, Edward. From 20th F., Capt. 96th F. 15.3.1839, Brev. Maj. 11.11.1851, Maj. 9.7.1852, Ret. 15.4.1856.
HILL, Edward Emburg. From H.P. 28th F., Capt. 63rd F. 3.6.1824, Died at Saleram, Portugal, 31.7.1827.

HILL, Edward Eustace. From R. Veteran Bn., Capt. 96th F. 8.4.1825, Brev. Maj. 22.7.1830, Died at Glasgow 19.12.1835.
HILL, Edward Rowley. From Provsl. Depot Bn., Malta, Lt.-Col. 63rd F. 7.9.1855, H.P. 10.9.1858.
HILL, John Edwin Dickson. From 3rd W. India R., Maj. 63rd F. 6.7.1870, H.P. 1.1.1873.
HILL, Major Dawson. Ens. 63rd F. 3.6.1859, Lieut. 14.2.1862, Capt. 16.10.1867, 99th F. 12.2.1873.
HILL, Richard Ernest. Lieut. Manch. R. 12.5.1883, A.S.C. 24.4.1889.
HIRST, Frederick Christian. 2/Lieut. Manch. R. 20.2.1895, Lieut. 15.7.1896, Ind. S.C. 10.11.1897.
HITCHINS, Henry William Ernest. Lieut. Manch. R. 25.8.1886, Capt. 11.5.1895, Maj. 1.7.1901, Lt.-Col. 10.3.1915, K. in A., Givenchy, 26.4.1915.
HOBKIRK, Stuart William Tatton. 2/Lieut. Manch. R. 23.3.1889, Res. 12.3.1890.
HOBSON, Samuel. Ens. 96th F. 22.11.1839, 10th F. 18.9.1840.
HOEY, Peter J. Asst. Surg. 63rd F. 1.5.1855, Staff 1.8.1856.
HOGG, Edward. Ens. 96th F. 15.4.1858, Lieut. 7.10.1859, Capt. 19.8.1862, Ret. 3.3.1863.
HOLBERTON, Philip Vaughan. 2/Lieut. Manch. R. 9.3.1901, Lieut. 27.11.1901, Adjt. 1.12.1903–30.11.1906, Capt. 1.12.1912, Brev. Maj. 8.11.1915, Maj. 8.1.1916, Brev. Lt.-Col. 3.6.1917, K. in A., France, 26.3.1918.
HOLLEY, Sidney Harry, M.C. 2/Lieut. Manch. R. 16.4.1916, Lieut. 16.10.1917, Adjt. 13.1.1918–26.4.1919.
HOLLINGWORTH, Francis Vernon. 2/Lieut. Manch. R. 15.5.1915, Lieut. 18.1.1916, Capt. 19.11.1921, Ret. 2.6.1922.
HOLLINS, Sidney Ewart. 2/Lieut. Manch. R. 7.4.1916, Lieut. 7.10.1917.
HOLMES, Edward Barclay, M.C. 2/Lieut. Manch. R. 17.9.1914, Lieut. 11.12.1914, Capt. 1.1.1917.
HOLMES, James. Surg. 63rd F. 26.3.1796–1.8.1797.
HOLNESS, Horace Henry James, D.C.M. 2/Lieut. Manch. R. 10.1.1915, Lieut. 25.6.1915, Capt. 21.11.1920.
HOLWORTHY, Mathew. From 7th L. Drgns., Capt. 63rd F. 7.11.1805, Ret. 6.1.1807.
HOOD, Alexander Nelson. 2/Lieut. Manch. R. 21.10.1893, Lieut. 13.7.1896, Ind. S.C. 24.8.1897.
HOPE, Hon. Alexander. Ens. 63rd F. 6.3.1786, Lieut. 30.9.1790, 64th F. 30.9.1790.
HOPE, Falkiner. From 80th F., Lieut. 63rd F. 21.11.1780, N.T.A. 1785.
HOPE, William. From 81st F., Lieut. 96th F. 27.10.1825, Capt. 14.2.1828, 7th F. 2.4.1829.
HOPKINS, Raymond Beechy, O.B.E. From R. Sussex R., Capt. Manch. R. 10.10.1900, Ret. 11.3.1914.

HOPTON, Conan. Ens. 63rd F. 20.2.1835, Lieut. 3.11.1837, Accidentally killed at Moulmein, Burma, 8.9.1838.
HORNE, William. Ens. 63rd F. 6.2.1762, Lieut. 28.7.1768, 48th F. 2.10.1773.
HORNER, Harry, M.B.E. 2/Lieut. Manch. R. 22.9.1917, Lieut. 22.3.1919.
HORSLEY, Nicholas. From 38th F., Lieut. 96th F. 22.7.1836, Capt. H.P. 16.1.1846.
HOSEASON, Henry Sandford. From Connaught Rngrs., Lieut. Manch. R. 5.8.1922.
HOUGHTON, Henry. Ens. 96th F. 13.4.1858, Lieut. 8.7.1859, Capt. 4.10.1867, H.P. 29.4.1874.
HOUGHTON, William. Ens. 63rd F. 6.2.1812, Lieut. 4.5.1815, 15th F. 4.5.1815.
HOUSTON, Arthur Manson. 2/Lieut. Manch. R. 5.12.1891, Lieut. 11.5.1895, Ind. S.C. 15.7.1896.
HOVELL, Orioll Hilton Morden. 2/Lieut. Manch. R. 19.5.1900, Lieut. 1.7.1901, Res. 2.11.1907.
HOWARD, William. From 91st F., Lieut. 63rd F. 11.11.1844, Ret. Nov. 1847.
HOWARTH, Frank, M.C. 2/Lieut. Manch. R. 5.6.1916, Lieut. 5.12.1917, Ret. 1.6.1922.
HOWE, Stephens. From 62nd F., Lt.-Col. 63rd F. 31.7.1789, Col. W. Ind. R. 20.5.1795.
HUDSON, Allen. Ens. 63rd F. 5.10.1809, Res. 3.3.1810.
HUDSON, Anthony Thomas Phillip. 2/Lieut. 63rd F. 30.1.1878, Lieut. 23.6.1879, Adjt. 15.12.1884–17.6.1888, Capt. 2.10.1887, Maj. 1.1.1898, D. of W., S. Africa, 20.12.1901.
HUGHES, Edward Malcolm. 2/Lieut. Manch. R. 24.4.1889, Lieut. 10.9.1890, Ind. S.C. 3.12.1890.
HUGHES, John Carter. Ens. 63rd F. 26.2.1808, Res. 3.8.1809.
HUGHES, Marcus Collingwood. From 69th F., Lieut. 63rd F. 1.11.1842, Died at Secunderabad, India, 31.7.1846.
HUGHES, Robert John, C.B. From 88th F., Lt.-Col. 63rd F. 6.10.1875, H.P. 6.8.1879.
HUGHES, William. Ens. 63rd F. 11.4.1816, Lieut. 18.11.1819, Capt. 3.3.1825, Died at Hobart Town, Tasmania, 5.6.1830.
HUGONIN, Francis James. Ens. 96th F. 12.8.1836, Lieut. 26.6.1839, Capt. 2.10.1846, 39th F. 4.8.1848.
HULME, William. From 7th F., Capt. 96th F. 29.1.1824, Brev. Maj. 23.12.1827, Maj. 9.3.1834, Brev. Lt.-Col. 10.1.1837, Lt.-Col. 18.8.1848, Ret. 15.6.1849.
HULTON, Francis Thomas. Ens. 63rd F. 19.11.1858, Lieut. 21.9.1860, Capt. 22.2.1867, Ret. 14.8.1867.
HUMPHRYS, Nugent Winter. 2/Lieut. Manch. R. 2.3.1904, Lieut. 18.12.1907, Capt. 11.12.1914.
HUNT, Edward Hugh. Ens. 63rd F. 2.1.1817, Lieut. 18.7.1822, Capt. 26.5.1825, 12th F. 6.7.1826.

ALPHABETICAL ROLL OF OFFICERS

HUNT, Edward Joseph. Ens. 63rd F. 17.9.1850, Lieut. 23.12.1853, Capt. 26.2.1856, Ret. 9.11.1866.
HUNT, John Henry. Asst. Surg. 63rd F. 24.8.1860, Staff 10.6.1862.
HUNT, William. Ens. 63rd F. 19.11.1844, 41st F. 14.1.1848.
HUNTER, James. From 42nd F., Capt. 63rd F. 23.1.1812, H.P. Nov. 1814.
HUNTER, Patrick. Ens. 96th F. 15.6.1849, Lieut. 6.7.1852, Maj. 29.12.1857, 82nd F. 18.2.1859, 63rd F. 20.10.1871, Ret. 28.4.1875.
HUNTER, Peter. From 9th F., Capt. 63rd F. 15.6.1809, 2nd Drgn. Gds. 2.11.1809.
HUNTER, William. From 15th F., Lieut. 63rd F. 21.6.1810, H.P. Nov. 1814.
HUNTER, William. From 34th F., Capt. 96th F. 27.11.1828, 28th F. 29.1.1836.
HUNT-GRUBBE, Rupert. 2/Lieut. Manch. R. 1.12.1897, Lieut. 22.2.1899, Capt. 15.2.1901, Died at Secunderabad, India, 14.8.1906.
HUTCHINS, William James. Ens. 63rd F. 2.12.1836, Lieut. 1.12.1840, Capt. 20.12.1846, 12th F. 1.8.1848.
HUTCHINSON, Emanuel. From H.P. 73rd F., Lieut. 63rd F. 3.9.1795, N.T.A. 1797.
HYDE, Henry Barry. From 1st R. Veteran Bn., Capt. 96th F. 29.1.1824, H.P. 13.3.1828.

ILLINGWORTH, Thomas. Ens. 63rd F. 22.9.1808, Lieut. 16.11.1809, Ret. 1817.
IMPETT, John. Ens. 63rd F. 10.8.1778, Lieut. 22.11.1780, Adjt. 11.9.1784–30.10.1789, N.T.A. 1789.
INGLIS, Edward. Ens. 63rd F. 1.10.1812, Lieut. 17.6.1813, 3rd Drgn. Gds. 17.6.1813.
INGRAM, Henry. Qr.-Mr. 63rd F. 16.7.1852, Paymr. 7.12.1855, Hon. Capt. 7.12.1860 Hon. Maj. 16.7.1867, 2nd F. 14.9.1870.
INNES, Alexander. From 70th F., Capt. 63rd F. 13.4.1764, Res. Dec. 1768.
IRVINE, Arthur Henry. From H.P. 3rd F., Lieut. 96th F. 13.1.1837, Ret. 2.11.1838.
IRVINE, Charles. Ens. 96th F. 9.4.1825, Lieut. 38th F. 17.3.1827.
IRWIN, Clinton Delacherois, M.C. 2/Lieut. Manch. R. 22.5.1901, Lieut. 22.3.1902, Capt. 11.12.1912, Maj. 22.5.1916.
IRWIN, Frederick Chidley, K.H. From H.P., Capt. 63rd F. 9.9.1828, Maj. 28.6.1836, H.P. 13.5.1842.
IRWIN, John Robert. From 25th F., Lieut. 63rd F. 28.12.1809, H.P. Nov. 1814.

JACKSON, Frank Gilbert Keatinge. From S. Staff. R., 2/Lieut. Manch. R. 13.7.1892, Res. 16.1.1895.
JACKSON, Halkett Francis. From H.P. 67th F., Capt. 63rd F. 2.2.1881, Brev. Maj. 2.3.1881, Ret. Hon. Lt.-Col. 5.11.1884.
JACKSON, James Henry. From 90th F., Lieut. 63rd F. 27.7.1870, Capt. 19.12.1877, H.P. 19.12.1877.

JACSON, Samuel Fitz-Herbert. From 11th F., Lieut. 63rd F. 2.4.1841, 54th F. 9.6.1843.
JAGGER, Nathaniel A. Ens. 63rd F. 15.9.1807, H.P. 1808.
JAMES, Charles. From 84th F., Brev. Maj. 63rd F. 9.11.1846, Maj. 24.12.1847, H.P. 12th F. 26.12.1851.
JAMES, Charles Owen. From 28th F., Capt. 63rd F. 29.6.1870, Maj. 6.8.1879, Died at Southampton 4.2.1881.
JAMES, Herbert Huleatt. 2/Lieut. Manch. R. 23.12.1914, Lieut. 15.5.1915, Res. 6.5.1920.
JAMES, Herbert Lionel, C.B. Lieut. Manch. R. 6.5.1885, Capt. 18.3.1892, Maj. 13.3.1901, Lt.-Col. 24.2.1908, Ret. 19.2.1919.
JAMES, Thomas. From 7th Bn. of Res., Capt. 63rd F. 2.8.1804, York. L.I. Vol. 30.4.1807.
JAMIESON, James. From 6th F., Qr.-Mr. 96th F. 22.4.1859, H.P. 20.11.1867.
JEBB, Joshua Henry Miles, D.S.O. 2/Lieut. Manch. R. 28.9.1895, Lieut. 19.12.1896, Adjt. 1.12.1899–30.11.1903, Capt. 27.12.1899, Maj. 8.5.1912, Ret. 20.7.1912.
JEFFERSON, Joshua. Surgeon 63rd F. 16.4.1779–5.10.1785.
JENKINSON, Richard. Ens. 63rd F. 6.2.1806, Lieut. 30.1.1807, 56th F. 30.1.1807.
JEPHSON, John Noble, Lieut. Manch. R. 7.2.1885, Ind. S.C. 23.3.1889.
JEPSON, William Holmes, M.D. From 9th L. Drgns., Asst. Surg. 96th F. 27.1.1854, 1st Drgn. Gds. 27.6.1855.
JESSE, Thomas. From 8th F., Lieut. 63rd F. 3.9.1756, Died 1759.
JOHNS, Robert. From 62nd F., Lieut. 63rd F. 5.3.1797, Capt. 13.9.1798, Maj. 25.5.1809, H.P. 135th F. 1810.
JOHNS, Thomas. From 90th F., Lieut. 63rd F. 14.6.1850, Capt. 29.12.1854, Ret. 21.9.1855.
JOHNSON, Arthur Cyril Beaumont. From Lein. R., Lieut. Manch. R. 2.5.1883, Ben. S.C. 20.3.1886.
JOHNSON, Samuel Higgins. From H.P., Ens. 63rd F. 19.9.1833, Died at Fort St. George, Madras, 5.8.1834.
JOHNSTON, Edward. Ens. 96th F. 9.10.1855, Lieut. 30.3.1858, Ret. 17.3.1863.
JOHNSTON, Mathew. Ens. 63rd F. 23.12.1780, Lieut. 26.12.1787, Capt. 27.5.1795, Maj. 15.11.1797, Ret. 13.9.1798.
JOHNSTON, Walter. Lieut. 63rd F. 13.9.1798, N.T.A. 1800.
JOHNSTON, William. Ens. 63rd F. 25.7.1782, Lieut. 20.12.1787, N.T.A. 1794.
JOHNSTONE, James. Ens. 63rd F. 1.5.1801, Lieut. 5.1.1804, Died 23.4.1809.
JONES, Alfred. Qr.-Mr. and Hon. Lieut. Manch. R. 19.3.1890, Ret. 16.8.1899.
JONES, Francis. Ens. 63rd F. 11.1.1760, Lieut. 25.9.1761, Capt. 22.11.1775, D. of W. Oct. 1777, received at Fort Clinton, N. America.
JONES, Frederick Jessop. Ens. 96th F. 2.9.1845, Lieut. 18.8.1848, Ret. 19.8.1853

JONES, Frederick Whitworth Russell. Ens. 63rd F. 8.6.1867, Lieut. 2.5.1868, Capt. 24.11.1879, Maj. 1.7.1881, Highland L.I. 27.8.1884.
JONES, John. Paymr. 63rd F. 14.3.1811, Dismissed the Service, June 1824.
JONES, John Peyton. Ens. 63rd F. 14.5.1829, Lieut. 19.9.1833, Adjt. 18.10.1833, Ret. Nov. 1838.
JONES, Loftus Francis. From 2nd F., Lieut. 96th F. 29.1.1824, Capt. 9.3.1834, Brev. Maj. 9.3.1846, Maj. 9.11.1846, H.P. 14.1.1848.
JONES, Richard. Ens. 63rd F. 28.5.1807, Res. 17.12.1808.
JONES, Roger C. From 5th F., Lieut. 63rd F. 17.8.1785, H.P. 1789.
JONES, R. R. Ens. 63rd F. 20.10.1808, 23rd F. 25.8.1809.
JONES, Thomas William Hathway. From Bed. R., 2/Lieut. Manch. R. 25.3.1896, Lieut. 10.7.1897, Ind. S.C. 29.10.1897.
JONES, Walter. From 9th F., Lieut. 63rd F. 16.3.1775, Capt. 26.10.1777, 8th L. Drgns. 19.11.1781.
JORDAN, Jacob. Lieut. 63rd F. 27.6.1822, Adjt. 20.5.1824–10.8.1825, Capt. 7.11.1826, H.P. 20.3.1827.
JOSSELYN, Frederick John. Ens. 96th F. 29.7.1859, Lieut. 2.7.1861, Adjt. 9.1.1863, Capt. 22.3.1864, Brev. Maj. 1.10.1877, Ret. Hon. Lt.-Col. 16.10.1880.
JOYCE, Edward. Ens. 63rd F. 4.9.1840, Qr.-Mr. 9.10.1840, H.P. 16.7.1852.
JUDGE, George. Ens. 63rd F. 15.2.1810, Lieut. 6.2.1812, H.P. Nov. 1814.

KEATING, John. From 19th F., Qr.-Mr. 63rd F. 5.9.1871, Died at Hazaribagh, India, 21.3.1872.
KEITH, Robert. Ens. 63rd F. 28.3.1758, 1st F. 30.1.1759.
KEITLEY, Cyril Humby, M.B.E. 2/Lieut. Manch. R. 7.9.1915, Lieut. 1.1.1917.
KELL, Francis. Ens. 63rd F. 9.6.1803, Lieut. 18.8.1804, N.T.A. 1806.
KELLY, Luke. Surg. 63rd F. 21.10.1795, Drowned in shipwreck while en route to W. Indies 18.11.1795.
KELSEY, James, M.C. 2/Lieut. Manch. R. 9.1.1917, Lieut. 9.7.1918, Res. 23.7.1921.
KENDALL, Richard. Chaplain 63rd F. 24.8.1758–1.6.1763.
KENNEDY, Hugh Ferguson. From H.P., Capt. 96th F. 2.4.1829, H.P. 31.12.1831.
KENNEDY, John Arthur. Ens. 63rd F. 1.7.1842, Died at Bellary, India, 19.4.1843.
KENNEDY, Thomas. From H.P. W. India R., Lieut. 96th F. 29.1.1824, Capt. H.P. 12.2.1828.
KENNY, William. Ens. 63rd F. 3.11.1837, Lieut. 15.12.1840, 11th F. 8.6.1841.
KEPPEL, Edward George. From Highland L.I., Maj. Manch. R. 27.8.1884, Ret. Hon. Lt.-Col. 10.8.1887.

KER, Thomas. Ens. 63rd F. 18.6.1801, 1st F. 17.9.1801.
KERR, Charles William. From H.P. 62nd F., Capt. and Brev. Maj. 63rd F. 16.9.1824, Ret. 3.3.1825.
KERR, Kenneth Malcolm Eliot. Ens. 96th F. 7.11.1868, Lieut. 16.3.1870, Died at Meerut, India, 15.5.1871.
KERR, Lord Mark. Ens. 96th F. 19.6.1835, Lieut. 14.9.1838, 20th F. 28.12.1838.
KERRY, Arnold John St. Ledgier. 2/Lieut. Manch. R. 4.12.1915, Lieut. 4.4.1917, Died 14.2.1918.
KERSHAWE, James. Ens. 63rd F. 24.6.1819, 13th F. 13.12.1821.
KIDD, Thomas. From 64th F., Surg. 63rd F. 25.7.1799, Staff Corps 20.10.1803.
KIDMAN, William. From 20th F., Lieut. 96th F. 29.1.1824, Capt. 19.12.1835, Ret. 4.3.1836.
KINAHAN, Charles Henry. Ens. 63rd F. 2.11.1855, Lieut. 24.6.1859, Adjt. 16.8.1861–8.11.1866, Capt. 9.11.1866, Maj. 28.4.1875, Ret. H.P. 24.11.1877.
KINCHANT, Richard Caton. From 103rd F., Lieut. 63rd F. 17.4.1867, Ret. 24.3.1869.
KING, George Smyth. From 14th F., Surg. 96th F. 16.8.1864, H.P. 1.5.1867.
KING, Talbot Henry. Ens. 96th F. 16.7.1861, Lieut. 9.12.1862, Ret. 8.6.1867.
KINGSTON, John Lawford. Ens. 63rd F. 9.4.1825, Lieut. 19.9.1826, H.P. 19.9.1826.
KINNEAR, Francis William. From 7th F., Capt. 63rd F. 17.3.1764, Maj. 7.10.1777, N.T.A. 1778.
KINNEER, John. Ens. 63rd F. 25.3.1758, N.T.A. 1759.
KINSLEY, Daniel. From H.P., Lieut. 96th F. 25.11.1828, H.P. 17.8.1832.
KIRK, James Buchanan. Ens. 96th F. 17.10.1851, Lieut. 1.2.1855, Capt. 31.12.1857, Maj. 21.2.1865, 89th F. 2.5.1865.
KIRKPATRICK, Kenneth Eric. 2/Lieut. Manch. R. 7.3.1900, Lieut. 15.8.1900, Ind. S.C. 28.2.1902.
KIRKWOOD, James Morrison. Ens. 96th F. 29.7.1857, Lieut. 1.4.1859, Capt. 5.11.1861, Ret. Aug. 1871.
KIRWAN, George Hastings. 2/Lieut. 96th F. 17.4.1880, Lieut. 1.7.1881, Madras S.C. 1883.
KNAPP, George Wyatville Wynford. Ens. 63rd F. 25.1.1856, Lieut. 14.2.1860, Ret. 19.7.1864.
KNIBB, Ernest Edward, D.C.M. 2/Lieut. Manch. R. 3.12.1917, Lieut. 3.6.1919, Res. 11.9.1920.
KNIGHT, Edward. From 15th Drgns., Capt. 63rd F. 19.7.1811, H.P. 25.12.1816.
KNIGHT, Godfrey Lyon. Ens. 63rd F. 28.2.1845, Lieut. 17.3.1848, Ceylon R. 17.3.1848.
KNOWLES, William Lancelot. Ens. 63rd F. 7.12.1855, Lieut. 25.8.1859, Capt. 17.11.1866, Drowned at sea 12.9.1867.

KNOX, Hubert. 2/Lieut. Manch. R. 18.4.1900, Lieut. 5.1.1901, Capt. 1.4.1909, Maj. 1.9.1915, K. in A., France, 13.10.1916.
KNOX, Lawrence Edward. Ens. 63rd F. 25.8.1854, Lieut. 11.12.1854, Capt. 15.1.1857, H.P. 15.1.1857.

LACY, Gilbert de Lacy. Ens. 63rd F. 14.3.1855, Lieut. 9.12.1855, 12th F. 9.1.1858.
LALER, Mathew. Ens. 63rd F. 14.10.1777, Lieut. 10.8.1778, N.T.A. 1780.
LAMBE, Arthur Francis. Ens. 96th F. 27.5.1862, Lieut. 17.3.1863, Ben. S.C. 26.10.1868.
LAMBERT, Robert Mounsey. Ens. 96th F. 29.1.1841, Lieut. 13.12.1842, Capt. 15.6.1849, Died at sea March 1856.
LANE, Eric Arthur Milner. 2/Lieut. Manch. R. 4.10.1915, K. in A., Mesopotamia, 8.3.1916.
LANE, George Le Mesurier. Ens. 63rd F. 26.10.1841, Died in India 13.5.1843.
LANE, Richard. Ens. 63rd F. 23.6.1826, Lieut. 25.10.1827, Capt. 16.3.1832, Paymr. 29.9.1837, H.P. Oct. 1844.
LANG, Menzies Charles Robinson. 2/Lieut. 63rd F. 13.8.1879, Lieut. 1.9.1880, Res. 27.6.1888.
LASH, Augustus Oliver. 2/Lieut. Manch. R. 1.3.1890, Lieut. 2.3.1892, Ind. S.C. 31.7.1895.
LAVELLE, Sidney Davis. 2/Lieut. Manch. R. 13.6.1916, Lieut. 13.12.1917, Res. 30.3.1920.
LAVENDER, James. Sub/Lieut. 63rd F. 11.9.1876, Died at Solon, Bengal, 22.6.1879.
LAWDER, Thomas Moore-Lane. Ens. 96th F. 14.9.1870, Lieut. 28.10.1871, Adjt. 22.9.1873, Ret. 22.1.1875.
LAWRENCE, John Davies, M.C. 2/Lieut. Manch. R. 20.10.1915, Lieut. 1.1.1917, Res. 20.1.1921.
LAWSON, John Low. 2/Lieut. Manch. R. 18.8.1900, Lieut. 14.7.1901, A.S.C. 18.12.1907.
LEACH, James, V.C. 2/Lieut. Manch. R. 1.10.1914, Lieut. 11.12.1914, H.P. 9.2.1918, Ret. 7.8.1918.
LEAKE, Robert Martin. From 38th F., Capt. 63rd F. 14.2.1811, Maj. 18.7.1822, H.P. 26.2.1824.
LEATHAM, James Birley. Ens. 63rd F. 5.2.1836, Lieut. 9.1.1839, 88th F. 18.3.1842.
LECKIE, William. From 39th F., Lt.-Col. 63rd F. 7.8.1875, Ret. Hon. Col. 1.9.1875.
LEDWARD, Harold Hugh. 2/Lieut. Manch. R. 31.1.1923.
LEE, Henry. Ens. 63rd F. 6.4.1804, Lieut. 16.12.1805, 95th F. 14.5.1807.
LEE, Henry. Ens. 63rd F. 16.2.1849, Ret. 11.6.1852.
LEE, John. Ens. 96th F. 31.8.1830, Lieut. 19.6.1835, Capt. 26.4.1839, 11th F. 7.6.1839.
LEE, Richard. From H.P. 135th F., Maj. 63rd F. 24.5.1810, Died at Martinique 10.6.1811.

LEES, Henry. From 2nd W. India R., Ens. 63rd F. 1.6.1838, Lieut. 8.4.1841, Capt. 15.12.1848, 28th F. 2.3.1849.
LEES, William Munnings. Ens. 96th F. 14.4.1846, Lieut. 18.8.1848, Adjt. 6.5.1853–18.6.1855, Capt. 23rd F. 26.3.1859.
LE GEYT, Charles W. Capt. 63rd F. 8.12.1762, N.T.A. 1765.
LE GEYT, Philip. Lieut. 63rd F. 23.6.1796, Capt. 30.10.1801, Maj. 11.7.1811, Lt.-Col. 12.8.1818, Ret. 26.5.1825.
LE GRAND, Arthur J. Ens. 63rd F. 5.9.1843, Lieut. 16.4.1845, Adjt. 14.12.1849–2.3.1854, Capt. 6.4.1854, 35th F. 7.7.1854.
LEMAN, Arthur Cadell Greenslade. Ens. 96th F. 9.3.1860, Lieut. 18.7.1862, Capt. 14.2.1874, Ret. 26.8.1876.
LEMAN, Reginald Curtis. 2/Lieut. Manch. R. 21.9.1889, Lieut. 26.11.1890, Died at Ashton-under-Lyne 3.10.1896.
LE MESURIER, Sampson. From 27th F., Capt. 63rd F. 11.7.1796, Died Jan. 1797.
LESLIE, Clement Stanley Duncan. 2/Lieut. Manch. R. 25.7.1888, Bom. S.C. 22.3.1889.
LESLIE, Francis Macnaghton. From 105th Madras L. Inf., Lieut. 63rd F. 22.3.1871, Ret. 22.3.1876.
LEVESON-GOWER, J. From 9th F., Lt.-Col. 63rd F. 2.7.1794, Capt. and Lt.-Col. C. Gds. Jan. 1799.
LEVIS, Francis Arthur. From Leinster R., Lieut. Manch. R. 5.8.1922, Capt. 1.1.1923.
LEWES, William Price. Ens. 96th F. 20.4.1832, Lieut. 12.8.1836, Ret. 27.9.1839.
LEWINS, Robert, M.D. From Staff, Asst. Surg. 63rd F. 6.6.1845, Surg. 28.3.1854, H.P. 22.6.1855.
LIDDIARD, Albert James. 2/Lieut. Manch. R. 18.10.1917, Lieut. 18.4.1919, Res. 23.1.1920.
LINDESAY, Patrick. Ens. 63rd F. 21.2.1834, Lieut. 5.2.1836, Capt. 16.9.1845, Maj. 23.12.1853, Lt.-Col. 9.3.1855, Ret. 9.3.1855.
LINDSAY, John Scott. From 1st F., Capt. 63rd F. 7.5.1807, H.P. 3rd Irish Bde. Jan. 1812.
LINFORD, James. Qr.-Mr. 63rd F. 28.12.1855, 19th F. 5.9.1871.
LITTLE, Watkin Tench. From 4th F., Ens. 96th F. 18.8.1848, Died 20.12.1849.
LLOYD, Francis. Ens. 63rd F. 31.3.1792, N.T.A. 1795.
LLOYD, Henry James. Ens. 96th F. 21.7.1825, Lieut. H.P. 22.4.1826.
LLOYD, John William. Ens. 96th F. 22.7.1842, Lieut. 2.10.1846, Died 13.5.1849.
LLOYD, Owen. Ens. 63rd F. 13.4.1778, Lieut. 18.9.1780, N.T.A. 1784.
LLOYD, Richard Cecil. Ens. 96th F. 27.7.1826, Lieut. 3rd F. 29.6.1827.
LLOYD, Thomas William John. Ens. 63rd F. 21.12.1844, Lieut. 20.12.1846, 59th F. 19.11.1847.
LODER, Edward. Ens. 63rd F. 23.11.1826, Ret. 11.10.1828.

LOFTHOUSE, Thomas Robinson. Ens. 96th F. 9.1.1863, Lieut. 21.2.1865, Ret. 16.7.1873.
LOGAN, Joseph. From Rifle Bde., Lt.-Col. 63rd F. 17.12.1829, Brev. Col. 2.11.1841, Died at Dover 7.9.1844.
LORD, John. Ens. 63rd F. 8.5.1828, 88th F. 14.5.1829.
LOUP, Gerald Davis, M.C. From Mach. G.C., Lieut. Manch. R. 25.2.1919.
LOVE, Arnot. Ens. 63rd F. 1.6.1796, Lieut. 5.8.1799, Capt. 26.8.1804, Died Nov. 1812.
LOWMAN, Webb. Ens. 63rd F. 4.7.1811, Lieut. 7.8.1815, H.P. 8.1.1818.
LOWRIE, William Frederick. Ens. 63rd F. 2.4.1841, Lieut. 20.4.1843, Adjt. Recruiting District 24.6.1853.
LOWRY, Henry Macgregor. Ens. 96th F. 31.8.1855, Lieut. 23.3.1858, 12th F. 10.12.1858.
LOWRY, Octavius. Ens. 96th F. 2.10.1846, Lieut. 28.10.1848, Capt. 16.10.1855, Ret. 1.4.1859.
LOWRY, Thomas. Ens. 63rd F. 16.11.1809, Res. 1811.
LUCAS, Edward. Ens. 63rd F. 7.4.1804, Lieut. 17.12.1805, Capt. 14.1.1813, H.P. Nov. 1814.
LUCAS, William. From Ceylon R. Regt., Surg. 96th F. 2.7.1841, Staff Surg. 1.7.1853.
LUFFMAN, Cyril Francis. 2/Lieut. Manch. R. 24.11.1915, Lieut. 19.2.1917.
LUSHINGTON, Charles. From 109th F., Capt. 63rd F. 3.9.1795, Died Jan. 1797.
LUTTRELL, Hugh Courtney Fownes. 2nd Lieut. 96th F. 5.9.1877, Rifle Bde. 25.5.1878.
LUTTRELL, William Hungerford. From H.P. 89th F., Capt. 63rd F. 18.8.1796, Ret. 21.1.1797.
LYNCH, Adolphus. From H.P. German Legion, Ens. 63rd F. 25.11.1836, Ret. 12.5.1837.
LYNCH, John Blake. From York. L.I. Vols., Capt. 63rd F. 30.4.1807, 3rd Veteran Bn. 3.6.1824.
LYNCH, Reginald Francis. 2/Lieut. Manch. R. 18.9.1909, Lieut. 1.12.1913, K. in A., Mesopotamia, 18.3.1916.
LYNN, George. Qr.-Mr. 63rd F. 25.7.1802, Ret. Oct. 1815.
LYONS, Frank Vernon. From Connaught Rngrs., Lieut. Manch. R 5.8.1922.
LYSAGHT, Arthur. Capt. 63rd F. 18.4.1766, N.T.A. 1768.
LYSAGHT, Henry. From 51st F., Lieut. 63rd F. 8.4.1772, Adjt. 15.5.1772-10.7.1775, Capt. 12.7.1775, 22nd F. 30.4.1781.
LYSAGHT, James Richard. Ens. 63rd F. 3.2.1837, Lieut. 6.7.1838, 84th F. 30.8.1840.
LYSTER, Christopher. Ens. 63rd F. 28.4.1774, Lieut. 15.5.1776, D. of W., Virginia, N. America, 18.10.1781.

MABERLY, William Leader. From 72nd F., Lt.-Col. 96th F. 30.12.1826, 76th F. 13.9.1827.
M'ARTHUR, Donald. From Argyleshire Fencibles, Ens. 63rd F. 18.11.1795, Lieut. 23.2.1797, H.P. 1802.
M'ANDREW, Alexander. From H.P. 62nd F., Asst. Surg. 96th F. 19.2.1824, Died 1.3.1832.
McANDREW, William, M.D. Asst. Surg. 96th F. 6.12.1844, Staff Surg. 23.3.1855.
M'CARTHY, Denny F. Ens. 63rd F. 1.11.1810, Lieut. 19.11.1812, H.P. 25.12.1818.
MACCARTHY, Edward Dennis Justin. From 94th F., Lieut. 96th F. 18.8.1848, Capt. 8.7.1856, Ret. 8.7.1862.
MACARTNEY, John Victor. From Lein. R., Capt. Manch. R. 22.7.1922.
MACAULEY, James Shortall. Ens. 63rd F. 18.8.1843, Lieut. 19.11.1844, 1st W. Ind. R. 30.7.1852.
M'CAUSLAND, William. Ens. 63rd F. 26.10.1807, Lieut. 3.10.1809. Died in W. Indies, 4.9.1815.
McCLEARY, Fergus Homersham. 2/Lieut. Manch. R. 31.8.1922.
M'CONNELL, George E. From 64th F., Lieut. 63rd F. 6.4.1808, H.P. 6.11.1817.
M'DONALD, ——. Ens. 63rd F. 19.9.1804, N.T.A. 1805.
M'DONALD, Colin. Lieut. 63rd F. 22.10.1799, Adjt. 1.11.1804, Capt. 5.1.1805, 23rd F. 5.1.1805.
MacDONNELL, Alister Maxwell. 2/Lieut. Manch. R. 17.9.1902, Res. 4.2.1903.
MACDONNELL, Alexander Sheriffe. From 80th F., Surg. 63rd F. 7.7.1848, Staff 3.3.1854.
M'DOWALL, James. Ens. 63rd F. 30.7.1762, N.T.A. 1765.
McERVEL, John Harold. From King's L'pool R., Capt. Manch. R. 2.4.1916, K. in A., France, 8.8.1916.
M'FADDEN, H. Ens. 63rd F. 11.8.1825, Adjt. 11.8.1825, 85th F. 7.6.1827.
M'GRATH, Patrick. Ens. 63rd F. 7.2.1811, Lieut. 14.1.1813, H.P. Nov. 1814.
MacGREGOR, Charles Frederick Murray. Ens. 96th F. 3.9.1870, Lieut. 28.10.1871, Ret. 25.11.1874.
McGREGOR, Charles Reginald. From 83rd F., Ens. 96th F. 25.4.1868, Lieut. 28.10.1871, Ben. S.C. 13.3.1872.
M'INTOSH, James. Lieut. 63rd F. 5.4.1798, K. in A., Schagen Brug, Holland, 6.10.1799.
M'KAY, John. Ens. 63rd F. 15.3.1810, H.P. Nov. 1814.
MACKAY, George. Lieut. 63rd F. 17.11.1813, H.P. Nov. 1814.
MACKAY, James. From 78th F., Capt. 63rd F. 22.3.1810, 53rd F. 17.12.1812.
MACKAY, Roderick. Lieut. 63rd F. 22.9.1808, Died Oct. 1809.
M'KENZIE, Alexander. From H.P. 24th F., Lieut. 96th F. 29.1.1804, Capt. H.P. 20.11.1804.
McKENZIE, Angus, M.C. From W. Ind. R., Capt. Manch. R. 29.4.1916, K. in A., France, 4.11.1918.
MACKENZIE, John. Ens. 63rd F. 20.12.1787, Lieut. 31.3.1793, N.T.A. 1794.
MACKENZIE, Lewis. From 9th L. Drgns., Capt. 63rd F. 30.7.1812, H.P. 92nd F. 18.3.1813.

ALPHABETICAL ROLL OF OFFICERS

MACKENZIE, Roderick. From 98th F., Lieut. 96th F. 9.8.1831, Capt. 19.9.1834, Ret. 30.10.1840.

MACKESY, Vincent. Ens. 96th F. 22.13.1848, Lieut. 7.9.1852, Died Mar. 1855.

McKEVITT, Phillip John, M.C. 2/Lieut. Manch. R. 12.3.1916, Lieut. 12.11.1917.

MACKIE, William George. Ens. 96th F. 2.7.1861, Lieut. 8.11.1862, Capt. 20.7.1867, Ret. 31.8.1872.

M'KINNON, John. From 47th F., Capt. 63rd F., 27.7.1776, N.T.A. 1793.

MACKRELL, Ashton. 2/Lieut. Manch. R. 24.7.1901, Lieut. 25.10.1902, Ind. S.C. 16.3.1905.

MACKWORTH, Arthur. Ens. 63rd F. 5.2.1824, Lieut. 8.12.1825, 48th F. 8.12.1825.

M'LEAN, Alexander. From 1st F., Lieut. 63rd F. 27.10.1786, Capt. 30.9.1787, 8th L. Drgns. 30.9.1787

McLEAN, Hector. Ens. 63rd F. 6.3.1806, N.T.A. 1808.

M'LELLAN, Harold Noble. 2/Lieut. Manch. R. 4.2.1916, K. in A., France, 9.7.1916.

MACLEOD, Donald Hume. Ens. 63rd F. 25.2.1826, Lieut. 17.11.1832, Ret. 19.2.1835.

M'LEROTH, ——, Ens. 63rd F. 20.7.1796, Ret. 29.6.1797.

M'LEROTH, Hugh Lieut. 63rd F. 22.10.1781, Capt. 31.5.1793, Maj. 9.8.1799, N.T.A. 1801.

M'LEROTH, Robert. Lieut. 63rd F. 28.6.1802, Capt. 15.10.1803, Maj. 28.6.1810, Ret. 18.7.1822.

M'LEROTH, Thomas. From 64th F., Lieut. 63rd F. 1.6.1780, Capt. 1.4.1795, Blackness Castle Garrison 1798.

MACLURE, John Edward Stanley. 2/Lieut. Manch. R. 3.5.1890, Lieut. 18.3.1892, A. Pay Dept 15.1.1894.

M'MULLIN, ——, Ens. 63rd F. 1.2.1811, Died 4.8.1811.

M'NAMARA, Arthur From 5th Garr. Bn., Capt. 63rd F. 31.8.1809, Ret. 21.3.1810.

M'NISH, William. Surg 63rd F. 6.7.1809–19.5.1824.

M'NIVEN, Donald. From W. India R., Capt. 63rd F. 6.9.1796, N.T.A. 1801.

M'PHERSON, Duncan. From 105th F., Capt. 63rd F. 1.9.1771, 42nd F. 15.8.1775.

M'PHERSON, James. From 51st F., Ens. 63rd F. 22.4.1763, Capt. 42nd F. 1.9.1771.

MACQUARIE, George William. From 42nd F., Capt. 63rd F. 21.1.1853, Ret. 7.9.1855.

MACQUARIE, John. Ens. 63rd F. 9.3.1809, Lieut. 22.2.1810, Cashiered by G.C.M. 23.6.1813.

McSHERRY, Bernard. 2/Lieut. Manch. R. 27.6.1917, K. in A., France, 13.4.1918.

McVEAN, Donald Archibald Dugald. From King's L'pool R., 2nd Lieut. Manch. R. 17.5.1893, Ind. S.C. 14.8.1896.

MAGILL, John Napier. Ens. 96th F. 18.9.1840, Lieut. 22.7.1842, Died May 1848.

MAGNAY, Christopher James. From 1st W. India R., Lieut. 63rd F. 30.7.1852, Capt. 16.3.1855, 16th F. 24.7.1857.

MAHON, John. Capt. 63rd F. 12.3.1829, Ret. 7.8.1838.

MAHON, Luke. From 77th F., Lieut. 63rd F. 1.11.1842, Died, Secunderabad, India, 1.5.1846.

MAHONEY, Jeffery. Ens. 63rd F. 1.9.1771, N.T.A. 1774.

MAINWARING, Francis George Lawrence. Ens. 63rd F. 30.12.1871, Lieut. 30.12.1871, Ben. S.C. 23.5.1876.

MAIR, Arthur. Ens. 63rd F. 4.3.1780, Lieut. 23.6.1782, 43rd F. 23.6.1782.

MAIR, Brodie Valentine, D.S.O., M.C. 2/Lieut. Manch. R. 22.4.1904, Lieut. 24.4.1907, Capt. 11.12.1914, Maj. 22.4.1918, Died, Waziristan, India, 16.5.1922.

MAIR, Hugh. From 1st F., Qr.-Mr. 96th F. 28.12.1832, Died 11.7.1839.

MAJORIBANKS, Richard. Ens. 63rd F. 9.2.1804, Lieut. 16.5.1805, Res. 1813.

MAKIN, Ernest Llewellyn. 2/Lieut. Manch. R. 17.2.1900, Lieut. 15.8.1900, Capt. 7.2.1904, Wilts. R. 29.12.1906.

MALAHER, David Bryson. 2/Lieut. Manch. R 31.8.1922.

MALLOM, John. From 57th F., Capt. 63rd F. 12.9.1777, N.T.A. 1782.

MANDEVILLE, Theobald. Ens. 63rd F. 31.7.1789, Lieut. 31.1.1792, 18th F. 8.9.1792.

MANERA, Ajax. From 41st F., Ens. 96th F. 9.9.1856, Lieut. 21.5.1858, Ret. 21.10.1862.

MANLEY, Henry. From 3rd F., Capt. 63rd F. 23.8.1799, Ret. 15.6.1805.

MANNERS, Douglas Ernest. From 91st F., Lieut. 63rd F. 18.5.1849, 25th F. 28.3.1851.

MANSELL, Charles Grenville. From 105th F., Lieut. 63rd F. 19.11.1873, Ben. S.C. 30.6.1874.

MANSELL, Rawleigh. From 54th F., Capt. 63rd F. 4.12.1793, Brev. Maj. 31.5.1793, Died Jan. 1797.

MANSELL, Robert Christopher. From H.P. 93rd F., Capt. and Brev. Maj. 96th F. 29.1.1824, Maj. 9.6.1825, Lt.-Col. 10.6.1826, H.P. 10.6.1826.

MANSERGH, Wilmsdorff George. 2/Lieut. Manch. R. 14.9.1901, Lieut. 11.11.1902, Capt. 18.12.14, K. in A., France, 26.8.1915.

MARDELL, Francis Hay. 2/Lieut. Manch. R. 20.4.1910, Lieut. 19.2.1914, Ind. Army 26.2.1914.

MARDEN, Arthur William, D.S.O. 2/Lieut. Manch. R. 11.2.1888, Lieut. 31.7.1889, Adjt. 18.4.1896-1.11.1898, Capt. 6.10.1896, Maj. 1.6.1902, H.P. 7.1.1907.

MARKHAM, William Harold. 2/Lieut. Manch. R. 19.7.1916, Lieut. 19.1.1918.

MARLEY, Vernon Douglas Kenneth. From Spec. Res., 2/Lieut. Manch. R. 15.7.1916, Lieut. 15.1.1918.

MARRYATT, Herbert Charles. From 17th F., Lieut. 96th F. 1.4.1868, Adjt. 15.2.1871-16.2.1872, Capt. 31.1.1877, Maj. 8.2.1882, Lt.-Col. 31.5.1890, Ret. 31.5.1894.

MARSH, Digby Cecil. 2/Lieut. Manch. R. 8.2.1902, Res. 21.2.1903.
MARSHALL, Francis Glasse. From H.P. 13th F., Capt. 96th F. 13.11.1878, Ret. Hon. Lt.-Col. 1.7.1881.
MARSHALL, John. From 91st F., Capt. 63rd F. 1.1.1824, H.P. May 1824.
MARSHALL, William. Lieut. 63rd F. 15.8.1775, Capt. 18.9.1780, H.P. 1789.
MARSON, Walter Samuel. Ens. 63rd F. 5.11.1854, Lieut. and Adjt. 2.3.1855, Capt. 17.9.1858, Died at Aldershot 4.2.1866.
MARTEN, Henry Humphrey. 2/Lieut. Manch. R. 14.2.1915, K. in A., France, 13.8.1915.
MARTIN, Claude. 2/Lieut. Manch. R. 23.5.1900, Lieut. 14.7.1901, Res. 5.3.1904.
MARTIN, George Bellis, M.C. From Ox. and Bucks. L.I., Capt. Manch. R. 21.10.1916.
MARTIN, George Dodd. 2/Lieut. Manch. R. 22.10.1902, Ind. S.C. 6.1.1903.
MASON, Herbert John, M.C. 2/Lieut. Manch. R. 16.4.1917, Died 16.12.1918.
MASSE, Charles Henri. 2/Lieut. Manch. R. 10.12.1913, Lieut. 30.10.1914, A.S.C. 15.5.1915.
MASSEY, Hon. Edward. Ens. 63rd F. 21.9.1789, N.T.A. 1790.
MASSEY, Robert John. Ens. 96th F. 26.5.1825, 4th F. 21.7.1825.
MASTERS, Harcourt. From 8th F., Lieut. 63rd F. 3.10.1755, Qr.-Mr. 25.8.1756, Indpdt. Coy. 12.10.1760.
MASTERSON, Thomas Brisbane. Ens. 63rd F. 16.4.1841, Drowned at sea 30.6.1843.
MAXWELL, Archibald Boyd. 2/Lieut. 96th F., 1.5.1878, Lieut. 19.4.1879, Capt. 20.11.1886, Maj. 28.7.1895, Brev. Lt.-Col. 29.11.1900, Lt.-Col. 1.6.1902, Brev. Col. 30.8.1904, Ret. 1.6.1906.
MAXWELL, Charles. Capt. 63rd F. 1.11.1797, Maj. 15.6.1808, R. African C. 15.6.1808.
MAXWELL, Robert James. From H.P. 80th F., Capt. 96th F. 21.8.1878, H.P. 1.7.1881.
MAYCOCK, Francis Mellowes. From N. Staff. R., Paymr. and Hon. Capt. Manch. R. Apr. 1883, Hampshire R. Jan. 1887.
MAYNE, William. Ens. 63rd F. 17.8.1841, 49th F. 24.6.1842.
MEACOCK, William Richard. Ens. 63rd F. 14.4.1815, Lieut. 21.1.1818, H.P. 20.5.1819.
MEADE, John. From 27th F., Capt. 96th F. 20.3.1857, Ret. 29.12.1857.
MEIN, Frederick Blundell. From 84th F., 2/Lieut. 63rd F. 27.9.1879, Lieut. 1.7.1881, Ind. S.C. 11.4.1882.
MEIN, John Edmund. Ens. 96th F. 6.7.1870, Lieut. 28.10.1871, Ben. S.C. 5.7.1873.
MELDRUM, Thomas. Ens. 63rd F. 22.7.1813, Lieut. 27.3.1817, and 2nd F. 27.3.1817.
MELVILL, Charles Curling. 2/Lieut. 96th F. 13.8.1879, Lieut. 1.7.1881, Adjt. 5.7.1886-4.7.1891, Capt. 12.11.1888, Maj. 6.10.1899, Lt.-Col. 24.2.1904, Brev. Col. 24.2.1907, Ret. 24.2.1908.

MENZIES, Angus. 2/Lieut. Manch. R. 8.11.1890, Lieut. 10.7.1893, Capt. 9.2.1898, D. of W. rec. at Paardeplatz, S. Africa, 22.1.1902.
MENZIES, James. Ens. 96th F. 27.4.1849, Qr.-Mr. Provsl. Bn. 12.3.1853.
MENZIES, Robert. From 42nd F., Lieut. 63rd F. 25.11.1802, Capt. 19.12.1805, H.P. Nov. 1814.
MERCER, John. Ens. 63rd F. 30.6.1788, Lieut. 31.5.1793, N.T.A. 1801.
MERRIMAN, Arthur Drummond Nairne. 2/Lieut. Manch. R. 30.8.1899, Lieut. 16.5.1900, Capt. 5.2.1903, R. Irish Rif. 20.5.1908.
MERRY, Mark Hepper, M.C. 2/Lieut. Manch. R. 12.3.1916, Lieut. 12.9.1917, Adjt. 25.11.1922.
MESSERVEY, George. Ens. 63rd F. 19.10.1809, Died, Martinique, 15.5.1811.
MICHELL, John Basil. 2/Lieut. Manch. R. 19.5.1900, Lieut. 3.7.1901, Comm. cancelled 4.8.1903.
MIDDLETON, Frederick Dobson. From 58th F., Lieut. 96th F. 18.8.1848, Capt. 6.7.1852, 70th F. 27.10.1854.
MILLAR, Arthur George. Ens. 63rd F. 10.2.1869, Lieut. 28.10.1871, Ret. 26.2.1876.
MILLER, Frederick. From 47th F., Lt.-Col. 63rd F. 22.7.1868, H.P. 1.4.1870.
MILLIGAN, William, M.D. From H.P. 60th F., Asst. Surg. 63rd F. 9.7.1829, Surg. 17th F. 1.3.1839.
MILLIKEN, John. From 57th F., Ens. 63rd F. 13.8.1804, H.P. 1805.
MILLS, Thomas Arthur. From H.P. 1st F., Capt. 96th F. 19.1.1876, 101st F. 17.1.1877.
MILLS, William Wilson. Asst. Surg. 63rd F. 28.3.1854, Staff 28.6.1864.
MINOGUE, Martin Joseph. 2/Lieut. Manch. R. 3.9.1902, Lieut. 21.4.1904, E. Surr. R. 26.2.1908.
MITCHELL, Hamilton. From Staff, Asst. Surg. 96th F. 25.5.1855, Surg. 9.3.1867, Staff 1.5.1867.
MITCHELL, Livingstone. From 44th F., Ens. 96th F. 2.11.1838, Lieut. 29th F. 20.5.1842.
MITCHELL, Parry. From 11th F., Capt. 96th F. 8.9.1825, H.P. 66th F. 10.8.1826.
MITCHELL, Patrick. Surg. 63rd F. 2.8.1797, Died 24.7.1799.
MOFFATT, James Williamson Samuel. Ens. 96th F. 3.11.1846, Lieut. 14.5.1849, Capt. 15th F. 9.3.1858.
MOLLAN, William Campbell, C.B. From 57th F., Maj. and Brev. Lt.-Col. 96th F. 27.5.1862, Ret. 9.1.1863.
MÖLLER, Arthur Marquhard. Ens. 96th F. 9.7.1852, 40th F. 25.2.1853.
MOLLOY, William. 2/Lieut. Manch. R. 3.3.1917, Lieut. 3.9.1918, Res. 29.7.1920.
MONEY, John. Ens. 63rd F. 12.7.1773, Adjt. 12.7.1775–May 1780, Lieut. 23.11.1775, D. of W. received at Black Stocks, N. America, Nov. 1780, while A.D.C. to G.O.C.

MONSON, Hon. Debonnaire John. From 52nd F., Capt. 96th F. 22.10.1860, Ret. 18.7.1862.
MONTGOMERY, John. Ens. 63rd F. 7.6.1827, Adjt. 7.6.1827–Oct. 1833, Lieut. 19.9.1833, Ret. 1.5.1834.
MOORE, Alexander William Uredale. 2/Lieut. Manch. R. 8.8.1914, Lieut. 1.12.1914, Capt. 1.1.1917.
MOORE, Cyril Henry. Lieut. Manch. R. 10.5.1882, Capt. 17.1.1890, A. Pay. Dept. 6.7.1896.
MOORE, Stephen. Ens. 63rd F. 15.12.1854, Lieut. 9.3.1855, Capt. 16.11.1860, Ret. Oct. 1867.
MOORES, Samuel. From 17th F., Capt. 63rd F. 8.6.1881, Maj. Devon R. 23.12.1885.
MOORHEAD, Charles Dawson, M.C. 2/Lieut. Manch. R. 11.8.1915, Lieut. 11.8.1915, Adjt. 26.10.1920–25.11.1922, Capt. 19.11.1921.
MORAN, John. 2/Lieut. Manch. R. 23.5.1900, Lieut. 14.7.1901, Ind. S.C. 4.4.1901.
MORGAN, Edward. Ens. 63rd F. 26.6.1806, N.T.A. 1808.
MORGAN, John. Surg. 63rd F. 24.9.1757–2.10.1765.
MORGAN, Thomas Kyd. Ens. 63rd F. 23.12.1853, D. of W., Inkerman, 5.11.1854.
MORLEY, Cecil. 2/Lieut. Manch. R. 17.2.1900, Lieut. 15.8.1900, Capt. 9.8.1908, Maj. 1.9.1915, H.P. 29.4.1922, Ret. 6.11.1922.
MORPHETT, Mars. From 48th F., Lieut. 63rd F. 17.9.1833, Capt. 29.1.1836, 57th F. 22.8.1836.
MORRIS, Arthur Joseph. 2/Lieut. Manch. R. 10.8.1918, Lieut. 10.2.1920.
MORRIS, Charles. 2/Lieut. Manch. R. 16.8.1915, K. in A., Mesopotamia, 8.3.1916.
MORRIS, Evan. 2/Lieut. Manch. R. 18.11.1903, Lieut. R. Innis. Fus. 11.5.1907.
MORSE, Alfred Herbert. Ens. 96th F. 9.4.1861, Lieut. 21.10.1862, Capt. 21.2.1865, 73rd F. 11.7.1865.
MORSHEAD, Charles Anderson. From H.P. 5th F., Lieut. 63rd F. 25.3.1856, 20th F. 23.3.1858.
MOSENTHAL, Alfred. Ens. 96th F. 24.11.1863, Lieut. 8.6.1867, Died at Kasauli, India, 29.7.1872.
MOSTYN, Robert Alges. From 15th F., Capt. 96th F. 3.3.1863, Ret. 19.5.1869.
MOURBAY, James. Ens. 96th F. 28.10.1859, Ret. 27.5.1862.
MULLINGAR, Alfred, D.C.M. 2/Lieut. Manch. R. 22.5.1918, Lieut. 22.11.1919, Res. 28.2.1920.
MULLINS, W. Townsend. Ens. 63rd F. 23.2.1780, Lieut. 9.1.1783, H.P. 1784.
MULOCK, John Joseph. From Staff, Asst. Surg. 96th F. 29.6.1855, 1st Drgns. 25.6.1856.
MUNDELL, Herbert Vaughan. Ens. 96th F. 2.11.1840, Lieut. 65th F. 30.12.1845, 96th F. 3.4.1846, Capt. 13.3.1853, Maj. 21.5.1858, 13th F. 24.5.1859.
MURCHISON, John. Qr.-Mr. 96th F. 5.2.1824, Ret. Dec. 1832.
MURKLAND, James. Ens. 63rd F. 29.8.1807, 25th L. Drgns. 5.10.1808.
MURRAY, ———. Ens. 63rd F. 22.11.1780, N.T.A. 1784.
MURRAY, Adam Walker. Asst. Surg. 96th F. 8.2.1827, Staff Surg. 2.7.1841.
MURRAY, Robert Sherbourne. Ens. 96th F. 21.6.1827, Lieut. 12.7.1833, Capt. 19.6.1835, 20th F. 15.3.1839.
MURRAY, W. H. From 60th F., Lieut. 63rd F. 1.8.1805, Died July 1807.
MUSSON, Edward Lionel, D.S.O., M.C. 2/Lieut. Manch. R. 28.1.1905, Lieut. 12.6.1909, Capt. 18.12.1914, Adjt. 11.8.1919–25.10.1920.
MUSTERS, William Chaworth. Ens. 96th F. 14.4.1858, Ret. 26.8.1859.
MYERS, Arthur. From 1st W. India R., Capt. 63rd F. 23.8.1827, 22nd F. 9.9.1828.
MYERS, Thomas Ricketts. Ens. 63rd F. 8.10.1802, Lieut. 6.8.1804, Capt. 25.7.1811, Ret. 2.1.1823.

NAISH, John. Lieut. 63rd F. 26.7.1797, Ret: 30.12.1800.
NANGLE, Charles. Ens. 63rd F. 6.9.1804, Lieut. 18.4.1805, 62nd F. 18.4.1805.
NAPIER, Gerald Codrington. Lieut. Manch. R. 19.12.1883, Died Devonport 9.9.1887.
NAPIER, John Robert. From 42nd F., Capt. 63rd F. 9.11.1785, Maj. 1.3.1794, Lt.-Col. 10.8.1796, 60th F. 10.8.1796.
NASH, ———. Ens. 63rd F. 20.10.1779, N.T.A. 1783.
NASH, Francis Rowland. From 78th F., Lieut. 63rd F. 1.5.1840, Died at sea 7.4.1841.
NASH, Thomas Llewellyn. From R. Art., Surg. 63rd F. 22.5.1866, 27th F. 23.3.1870.
NASH, William Peel. Lieut. 96th F. 11.2.1875, Capt. 15.9.1881, Maj. 19.8.1891, Ret. 19.6.1895.
NASON, Henry. Ens. 63rd F. 19.9.1811, N.T.A. Apr. 1816.
NASON, Stephen Thomas. Ens. 63rd F. 18.1.1810, Lieut. 19.9.1811, 90th F. 17.11.1813.
NEILLY, William. From H.P., Capt. 63rd F. 16.8.1831, Ret. Oct. 1833.
NEPEAN, Evan Aubrey Ramsay. 2/Lieut. Manch. R. 5.10.1910, Res. 26.4.1913.
NESBIT, Richard. From 8th F., Lieut. 63rd F. 8.9.1757, Capt. 28.7.1768, N.T.A. 1779.
NESHAM, Christopher. Capt. 63rd F. 21.3.1765, N.T.A. 1771.
NEVILLE, Park Percy. From 26th F., Capt. 63rd F. 27.11.1835, Maj. 16.7.1841, H.P. 12th F. 12.11.1844.
NEWBIGGING, William. Ens. 96th F. 17.7.1863, Lieut. 8.6.1867, Adjt. 14.10.1867–14.2.1871, Capt. 15.2.1871, Maj. 1.7.1881, Ret. Hon. Lt.-Col. 5.9.1883.

NEWBIGGING, William Patrick Eric, C.B., C.M.G., D.S.O. 2/Lieut. Manch. R. 23.3.1892, Lieut. 28.7.1895, Adjt. 2.11.1898–1.11.1902, Capt. 18.3.1899, Maj. 22.4.1911, Brev. Lt.-Col. 18.2.1915, Lt.-Col. 1.1.1918, Brev. Col. 1.1.1918, R. Corps of Signals 21.8.1919.

NEWBOLD, William. 2/Lieut. Manch. R. 6.7.1917, Lieut. 6.1.1919, Res. 27.11.1919.

NEWENHAM, William Henry. From 25th F., Lieut. 63rd F. 28.3.1851, Capt. 29.12.1854, Ret. 4.12.1857.

NEWSOM, Gerald Francis. From Rifle Bde., Lieut. Manch. R. 14.2.1923.

NICHOLAS, Francis Mark. 2/Lieut. Manch. R. 15.4.1917, D. of W., France, 28.9.1917.

NICHOLLS, Henry. Ens. 63rd F. 25.7.1811, H.P. Nov. 1814.

NICHOLSON, John Richard. 2/Lieut. Manch. R. 22.3.1917, Lieut. 22.9.1918, Res. 23.4.1920.

NICHOLSON, William Smith. Ens. 96th F. 4.3.1836, Lieut. 19.12.1838, Capt. 2.9.1845, 26th F. 22.5.1846.

NISBET, Frank Scobell. 2/Lieut. Manch. R. 7.5.1898, Lieut. 26.7.1899, Capt. 14.7.1901, Adjt. 1.2.1912, K. in A., Le Cateau, France, 26.8.1914.

NIXON, Henry. From 55th F., Lieut. 96th F. 7.6.1831, Adjt. 14.2.1834–29.6.1837, Ret. 30.6.1837.

NOBLE, Charles John Herbert Hay. From Yorkshire R., Capt. Manch. R. 9.6.1900, D. of W., S. Africa, 12.11.1901.

NORMAN, Stuart Sheridan. 2/Lieut. Manch. R. 8.9.1909, Lieut. 27.8.1913, K.in A., Givenchy, France, 20/21.12.1914.

NORTH, Louis Aylmer. From H.P., Capt. Manch. R. 2.1.1901, Died at Kroonstad, S. Africa, 3.12.1901.

NORTON, Brett. Ens. 63rd F. 31.5.1800, Lieut. 28.9.1801, Capt. 24.5.1804, Died 31.5.1808.

NORTON, Harry Egerton. 2/Lieut. Manch. R. 26.6.1901, 15th Hrs. 25.12.1901.

NORTON, James Roy. From H.P., Capt. 63rd F. 8.11.1844, H.P. 3.4.1846.

NORTON, John. Ens. 63rd F. 17.12.1805, Lieut. 2.7.1807, 34th F. 22.9.1808.

NOTT, John. From 9th L. Drgns., Lieut. 63rd F. 21.1.1813, H.P. 1814.

NUGENT, James. Qr.-Mr. 63rd F. 21.2.1805, Died at St. Christopher, W. Indies, 22.9.1815.

NUGENT, Michael. From 75th F., Asst. Surg. 96th F. 15.6.1832, Staff 6.10.1835.

NUGENT, Pierce Stephen. From H.P. 17th F., Lieut. 96th F. 29.1.1824, H.P. 9.8.1831, Died 18.12.1835.

NUGENT, St. George Mervyn. From 29th F., Capt. 96th F. 26.12.1854, Maj. unattach. 18.11.1855.

NUTHALL, Henry Metcalfe. Ens. 63rd F. 8.1.1868, 38th F. 18.11.1868.

NUTHALL, William Frederick. From 20th F., Ens. 63rd F. 21.8.1867, Lieut. 26.3.1871, Capt. 6.8.1879, Maj. 30.9.1884, Lt.-Col. 3.2.1892, H.P. 3.2.1902.

O'BRIEN, Charles Donatus Corbet. From 48th F., Lieut. 63rd F. 17.9.1833, Capt. 27.9.1842, 94th F. 27.9.1842.

O'BRIEN, Donatus James Thomond. Ens. 63rd F. 25.2.1880, Lieut. 1.7.1881, Ben. S.C. 20.11.1882.

O'BRIEN, Donough. From H.P. 65th F., Ens. 96th F. 29.1.1824, Lieut. 2.7.1829, 72nd F. 29.10.1829.

O'BRIEN, Eugene Robert, M.D. From Staff, Asst. Surg. 96th F. 9.3.1867, Staff Apr. 1873.

O'BRIEN, Patrick. Qr.-Mr. and Hon. Lt. Manch. R. 4.9.1909, Hon. Capt. 3.6.1916, Hon. Maj. 3.6.1918.

O'BRIEN, Richard Serrell. From 31st F., Ens. 96th F. 29.3.1833, Lieut. 19.8.1836, 87th F. 13.1.1837.

O'BRIEN, Theobald Donat. From 17th F., Lieut. 63rd F. 16.10.1867, Ret. 14.6.1873.

O'CONNOR, Ernest Robert. 2/Lieut. Manch. R. 10.1.1915, Lieut. 25.6.1915, Capt. R. Munster Fus. 4.7.1916.

O'DELL, ——. Ens. 63rd F. 30.10.1799, N.T.A. 1800.

O'DELL, Francis. Asst. Surg. 63rd F. 28.7.1854, Staff 24.8.1860.

O'DELL, William. 2/Lieut. Manch. R. 27.1.1904, Connaught Rngrs. 4.5.1907.

O'DONNELL, John Vize. Ens. 96th F. 25.11.1845, Lieut. 11.2.1848, Capt. 15.6.1849, 27th F. 8.11.1850.

O'FARRELL, Thomas. From Staff, Asst. Surg. 63rd F. 19.7.1870, Staff April 1873.

O'HARA, Edward. From H.P. York. L.I. Vols., Lt.-Col. 63rd F. 19.12.1816, 2nd W. India R. 2.5.1822.

OLIVER, John Farquharson. 2/Lieut. Manch. R. 19.5.1900, Lieut. 13.7.1901, Res. 20.1.1912.

OLIVER, Joseph Boyer. From 40th F., Capt. 63rd F. 23.5.1845, Died at Secunderabad, India, 27.4.1846.

O'LOUGHLIN, Joseph Edward. From Staff, Asst. Surg. 63rd F. 30.8.1864, 17th Lancers 17.12.1867.

O'MEARA, Arthur Edward. 2/Lieut. Manch. R. 19.10.1901, Lieut. 11.12.1902, Capt. 1.12.1914, Maj. 24.10.1916.

O'NEAL, John Carter. Ens. 96th F. 22.3.1864, Lieut. 20.7.1867, 6th Innis. Drgns. 18.12.1867.

O'NEILL, ——. Ens. 63rd F. 9.4.1812, N.T.A. Apr. 1816.

ORDE-POWLETT, Amias Christopher Thomas. From R. Welch Fus., Lieut. Manch. R. 23.5.1885, Res. 1.8.1888.

ORGILL, Edward Freer, M.C. From N. Staff. R., Lieut. Manch. R. 25.6.1918, H.P. 11.11.1921.

ORGILL, John Henry. 2/Lieut. Manch. R. 17.2.1919, Lieut. 17.12.1921.

ORR, John Arthur. 2/Lieut. Manch. R. 11.2.1899, Cameron H. 5.4.1899.

ORWIN, Arthur, M.C. 2/Lieut. Manch. R. 22.11.1916, Lieut. 22.3.1919.

ALPHABETICAL ROLL OF OFFICERS

O'SULLIVAN, Edward. From Staff, Asst. Surg. 96th F. 9.6.1865, Staff Apr. 1873.
OSWALD-BROWN, Charles Robert. Sub/Lieut. 96th F. 11.10.1876, Lieut. 11.10.1878, Capt. 28.8.1885, Maj. 31.5.1894, Ret. 1.1.1898.
OTTLEY, Benjamin Wynne. From H.P. 87th F., Lieut. 63rd F. 31.5.1789, N.T.A. 1792.
OUSELEY, Ralph. From A. Depot Staff, Capt 63rd F. 7.9.1809, Maj. 25.11.1813, Staff 25.11.1813.
OUSELEY, William. From 30th F., Lieut. 96th F. 29.1.1825, Capt. 9.6.1825, H.P. 9.8.1831.
OWEN, Francis Mostyn. Ens. 63rd F. 1.11.1833, Lieut. 6.11.1835, Capt. 26.3.1845, 44th F. 2.9.1845.
OXLEY, Henry Hayes. From 19th Hrs., 2/Lieut. Manch. R. 12.1.1917, Lieut. 12.7.1918, Res. 29.7.1919.
OXLEY, Jonas. From 1st R. Veteran Bn., Ens. 96th F. 29.1.1824, R. Afr. Col. Corps 30.6.1824.

PAKENHAM, Hon. Frederick Beauchamp. From 27th F., Capt. 96th F. 8.11.1850, Maj. unatt. list 14.6.1859.
PAKES, Charles Walter Stevenson. 2/Lieut. Manch. R. 31.8.1922.
PALMER, George. Ens. 63rd F. 7.5.1812, Lieut. 28.8.1817, H.P. 25.12.1818.
PALMER, William. From 35th F., Ens. 63rd F. 12.7.1859, Adjt. 6.7.1870–20.6.1879, Lieut. 25.3.1871, A. Pay Dept. 6.7.1880.
PARKE, Charles Johnstone. Ens. 63rd F. 18.3.1842, Res. 24.3.1843.
PARKER, Erasmus Darwin. 2/Lieut. Manch. R. 6.7.1889, Lieut. 10.9.1890, Capt. 25.1.1898, Ret. 2.4.1898, Rejoined 26.11.1914, K. in A., Neuve Eglise, France, 20.3.1915.
PARKERSON, Henry Mount. From 99th F., Capt 63rd F. 12.1.1873, Maj. 6.12.1879, Ret. 6.12.1879.
PARMINTER, Reginald Horace Roger, D.S.O., M.C. 2/Lieut. Manch. R. 5.2.1913, Lieut. 15.9.1914, Capt. 1.10.1915, Adjt. 23.10.1915–3.3.1917, Brev. Maj. 3.6.1919.
PARNTHER, Arthur Sidney. 2/Lieut. Manch. R. 4.5.1916, Lieut. 4.11.1917, Ret. 13.7.1921.
PARRY, Arnold Edward. 2/Lieut. Manch. R. 17.10.1914, Lieut. 22.12.1914, Capt. 9.2.1918, Ret. 30.4.1923.
PARSONS, James Henry. Sub/Lieut. 63rd F. 11.9.1876, Lieut. 11.9.1876, Ben. S.C. 8.8.1879.
PARTRIDGE, Thomas Oliver. Ens. 96th F. 10.4.1825, Lieut. 13.5.1826, 77th F. 7.9.1826.
PATERSON, Falkland Townshend Logan. Ens. 63rd F. 2.6.1848, Lieut. 26.12.1851, Capt. 29.12.1854, Maj. 16.8.1861, Died at Halifax, Nova Scotia, 18.12.1861.
PATERSON, James. Maj. 63rd F. 23.2.1760, Lt.-Col. 15.6.1763, Brev. Col. 29.8.1777, Maj.-Gen. 20.11.1782, 28th F. 13.7.1787.
PATERSON, Thomas. From 8th F., Capt. 63rd F. 10.6.1824, Died at Hobart's Town, Tasmania, 16.2.1831.

PATERSON, Thomas Williams. Ens. 63rd F. 3.4.1846, Died at Manchester, 10.5.1848.
PATERSON, William. From 80th F., Capt. 63rd F. 25.5.1855, H.P. 10.11.1858.
PATON, Donald Robertson. 2/Lieut. Manch. R. 9.9.1893, Lieut. 17.5.1896, Capt. 26.7.1899, Maj. 11.1.1912, H.P. 8.5.1912.
PATY, George William. From H.P., Maj. and Brev. Lt.-Col. 96th F. 29.1.1824, H.P. 9.6.1825.
PAULET, Lord William. From 85th King's L. Inf. R., Capt. 63rd F. 29.3.1827, 21st F. 4.12.1828.
PAULSON, Peter Zacharias, O.B.E. Lieut. Manch. R. 12.11.1902, Capt. 9.11.1914, Maj. 24.10.1916.
PEACH, Thomas Henry. Ens. 96th F. 28.10.1864, Died 8.6.1867.
PEACOCK, William. Capt. 63rd F. 21.3.1765, N.T.A. 1768.
PEACOCKE, George, M.D. Surg. 63rd F. 5.11.1870, Died, India, 5.6.1871.
PEARCE, Graham Ravenhill. 2/Lieut. 96th F. 19.10.1878, Lieut. 6.12.1879, Capt. 27.6.1888, Ret. 29.1.1890.
PEARD, Henry. From H.P. Queen's Rngrs., Lieut. 63rd F. 27.7.1804, Died July 1808.
PEARSE, Denis Colbron, M.C. 2/Lieut. Manch. R. 12.8.1916, Lieut. 12.2.1918, Res. 12.11.1921.
PEARSON, Hugh Frederick Archie. 2/Lieut. Manch. R. 22.8.1888, Ind. S.C. 6.11.1889.
PEARSON, John Edward. 2/Lieut. Manch. R. 9.1.1917, Lieut. 9.7.1918, Res. 12.12.1919.
PEDDER, William. Ens. 63rd F. 8.4.1825, Lieut. 19.12.1826, Capt. 3.8.1830, Died at Madras, 24.6.1837.
PEEL, J. Howorth. From W. India R., Capt. 63rd F. 6.6.1805, 1st Drgn. Gds. 2.3.1809.
PEERS, William. Ens. 63rd F. 23.11.1775, Lieut. 2.12.1777, N.T.A. 1783.
PEIRCE, William Gabriel King. 2/Lieut. Manch. R. 20.5.1899, Lieut. 23.10.1899, Capt. 25.12.1901, Res. 14.11.1911, Rejoined Aug. 1914, K. in A., Festubert, France, 26.10.1914.
PEMBROKE, Sidney Keith. 2/Lieut. Manch. R. 4.10.1915, Lieut. 1.1.1917.
PENNEFATHER, William. Ens. 63rd F. 18.12.1805, Lieut. 28.8.1807, Capt. 7.4.1825, H.P. 31.8.1826.
PENTON, Augustus. Ens. 63rd F. 10.3.1848, 70th F. 22.12.1848.
PERCIVAL, Charles. Ens. 63rd F. 13.6.1811, Lieut. 4.3.1813, H.P. 68th F. 19.10.1820.
PEREIRA, William Duff. From 6th Drgn. Gds., Capt. 96th F. 21.4.1863, Ret. 22.3.1864.
PERRIMAN, J. P. Lieut. 63rd F. 4.5.1809, Res. 1818.
PETRIE, Charles Louis Rowe, D.S.O. 2/Lieut. Manch. R. 5.2.1887, Lieut. 10.4.1889, Capt. 13.7.1896, Maj. 21.12.1901, Ret. 6.5.1907.
PHILBIN, Richard. Ens. 63rd F. 23.2.1797, Lieut. 22.10.1799, N.T.A. 1801.

PHILIPS, Edward. Chaplain 63rd F. 1.6.1763–7.1.1779.
PHILIPS, Ivor. Lieut. Manch. R. 12.5.1883, Ben. S.C. 8.10.1884.
PHILLIPPS, Edward Plantagenet. Ens. 96th F. 10.6.1867, Lieut. 19.5.1869, Capt. 21.4.1877, Maj. 18.3.1882, Ret. 9.7.1884.
PHIPPS, Henry B. From 37th F., Capt. 63rd F. 26.5.1848, 31st F. 27.6.1851.
PICKERING, James. Ens. 63rd F. 19.12.1805, Lieut. 17.12.1807, 96th F. 17.8.1808, H.P. 1813.
PIDCOCK, Henry Henzey Fraser. Ens. 63rd F. 24.3.1869, Lieut. 28.5.1870, 103rd F. 26.12.1870.
PIERCE, Frederick. Ens. 96th F. 18.8.1838, Lieut. 29.1.1841, Capt. 18.8.1848, Ret. 30.5.1858.
PIERS, George. Ens. 63rd F. 27.3.1758, N.T.A. 1759.
PIKE, Francis. Ens. 96th F. 22.4.1853, Lieut. 7.10.1855, 91st F. 25.1.1856.
PILFORD, Medvin R. From 2nd F., Lieut. 96th F. 3.3.1843, Died 5.4.1848.
PILLEAU, Henry. Asst. Surg. 63rd F. 22.1.1836, 16th L. Drgns. 5.10.1841.
PILLING, Oswald. From 2nd W. India R., Capt. 96th F. 4.12.1832, H.P. 17.1.1834.
PIPER, Frederick. From Rifle Bde., Paymr. 63rd F. 14.9.1870, A. Pay. Dept. 1.4.1878.
PIPON, Elias. Lieut. 63rd F. 16.12.1795, Newfoundland Fencibles 20.10.1803.
PLENTY, Edward Pellew. 2/Lieut. Manch. R. 17.4.1915, Lieut. 1.10.1915, Died 21.11.1918.
PLINSTON, George Herbert. 2/Lieut. Manch. R 4.6.1904, Indian Army 29.6.1906.
PLUNKETT, Arthur William Valentine. 2/Lieut. Manch. R. 14.3.1888, Lieut. 6.11.1889, Capt. 13.1.1897, Maj. 1.6.1902, K. in A., Somaliland, 17.4.1903.
PLUNKETT, Christopher. Ens. 63rd F. 27.2.1808, Lieut. 4.10.1808, H.P. 1.7.1819.
POLE, Arthur Gunliffe Van Notten. Ens. 63rd F. 7.11.1826, Lieut. 5.6.1830, Capt. 18.10.1833, Maj. 2.12.1837, Lt.-Col. 2.9.1844, Inspecting Field Officer of Recruiting 23.12.1853.
POLE, Cecil Charles. Ens. 63rd F. 22.10.1847, Lieut. 29.1.1850, 90th F. 14.6.1850.
POLLARD, Benjamin Horatio. Ens. 96th F. 25.12.1867, Lieut. 18.1.1870, Ben. S.C. 23.12.1871.
POUNTNEY, Edward. Capt. 63rd F. 11.5.1763, N.T.A. 1765.
POWELL, Charles Folliott. Ens. 96th F. 9.12.1862, Lieut. 22.3.1864, Ben. S.C. 16.12.1871.
POWELL, Giles. Chaplain 63rd F. 7.1.1778–31.5.1778.
POWER, William. Ens. 63rd F. 19.8.1813, H.P. Nov. 1814.
POWYS, Aubrey Palgrave. Ens. 63rd F. 1.5.1855, Lieut. 7.9.1858, 16th F. 7.9.1858.
PRATT, Egerton James. Asst. Surg. 63rd F. 11.6.1841, 44th F. 6.12.1844.

PRATT, George Brookes. Ens. 63rd F. 31.12.1829, Lieut. 19.7.1833, Capt. 2.4.1841, Died at Bellary, India, 19.4.1843.
PRESTON, Hon. Jenico Edward Joseph. 2/Lieut. Manch. R. 5.1.1901, Res. 3.8.1901.
PRINCE, Alick Lancelot. 2/Lieut. Manch. R. 4.5.1901, Lieut. 24.12.1901, N. Lancs. R. 8.2.1908.
PRINGLE, John. From 21st F., Capt. 63rd F. 29.6.1797, Maj. 1.8.1804, 6th Garrison Bn. 25.8.1808.
PRIOLEAU, Lynch Hamilton, M.B.E. Lieut. Manch. R. 22.10.1881, Capt. 8.11.1889, Maj. 7.4.1900, Ret. 13.3.1901.
PRIOR, John Murray. Ens. 63rd F. 16.9.1768, Lieut. 25.7.1771, N.T.A. 1777.
PROUSE, Richard. 2/Lieut. Manch. R. 13.7.1916, Lieut. 13.1.1918, Ret. 7.8.1919.
PUGH, Walter Barnes. From 2nd W. Ind. R., Lieut. 96th F. 23.3.1858, Adjt. 6.5.1859–1.7.1861, Ret. 5.11.1861.
PURCELL, Goodwin. From 92nd F., Lieut. 63rd F. 13.12.1795, Capt. 29.6.1801, Cape Regt. 29.6.1801.
PURSLOE, James. Ens. 96th F. 28.12.1838, Ret. 29.4.1842.
PYE, Charles Colquhoun. Ens. 63rd F. 14.12.1854, Lieut. 9.3.1855, Capt. 14.2.1860, Ret. 16.8.1861.

QUIN, Thomas. From 41st F., 2/Lieut. 63rd F. 11.9.1880, Lieut. 1.7.1881, Madras S.C. 3.3.1883.
QUINN, Henry Evans. Ens. 63rd F. 24.8.1846, 16th F. 23.3.1847.

RADFORD, Ebenezer. Ens. 63rd F. 6.11.1772, Lieut. 23.11.1775, N.T.A. 1776.
RAE, Gustavus. Ens. 63rd F. 22.9.1865, Ret. 8.6.1867.
RAITT, William Frederick. From 31st F., Ens. 96th F. 13.12.1842, Ret. Sept. 1848.
RALLISON, Victor Edward. 2/Lieut. Manch. R. 24.10.1916, K. in A. 7.4.1917.
RALPH, John. From 8th F., Lieut. 63rd F. 5.9.1756, D. on S., W. Indies, 23.3.1759.
RAMADGE, William. Ens. 63rd F. 11.4.1800, Lieut. 16.11.1800, 58th F. 9.7.1803.
RAMSBOTHAM, John Richard. Ens. 63rd F. 19.1.1855, Lieut. 8.6.1855, Capt. 16.8.1861, 97th F. 7.4.1865.
RAMSBOTTOM, Richard. Ens. 63rd F. 7.8.1835, Lieut. 1.6.1838, 99th F. 5.10.1838.
RANKEN, George Patrick. Ens. 63rd F. 13.8.1879, Lieut. 26.8.1880, Ben. S.C. 2.1.1882.
RATTRAY, David. Lt.-Col. 63rd F. 5.8.1810, H.P. York. L.I. Vols. 19.12.1816.
RAVENSCROFT, Herbert Valentine. 2/Lieut. Manch. R. 28.6.1890, Lieut. 19.5.1892, Capt. 9.2.1898, Brev. Maj. 9.2.1898, Maj. 15.10.1904, Ret. 17.12.1904.
RAVENSHAW, Herbert Edward. Sub-Lieut. 63rd F. 25.6.1873, Lieut. 25.6.1873, Ben. S.C. 27.10.1876.

RAWDON, Lord Francis. Capt. 63rd F. 12.7.1775, Lt.-Col. unatt. 15.6.1778.
RAWDON, Hon. George. From 9th F., Capt. 63rd F. 2.11.1778, Maj. 8.4.1783, 16thF. 8.4.1783.
RAYNES, Frederick Verney M. From 11th F., Lieut. 63rd F. 27.7.1855, Ret. 9.5.1856.
READ, William. From 8th F., Lieut. 63rd F. 5.10.1757, D. of W., Guadaloupe, 23.3.1759.
READE, John Henry Loftus. 2/Lieut. Manch. R. 29.1.1902, Lieut. 3.10.1903, Adjt. 1.2.1909–30.11.1912, K. in A., France, 28.10.1914.
REAY, Charles Tom, C.B. Sub/Lieut. 63rd F. 11.2.1875, Lieut. 11.2.1875, Capt. 18.3.1882, Maj. 24.10.1891, Lt.-Col. 6.10.1899, H.P. 6.10.1903.
REID, Francis. Ens. 96th F. 14.5.1858, Lieut. 7.10.1859, Capt. 9.12.1862, 6th Drgn. Gds. 21.4.1863.
REID, Lestock Hamilton. 2/Lieut. 63rd F. 1.5.1878, Lieut. 4.12.1879, Ben. S.C. 28.2.1883.
REILLY, Rawdon E. Dennys. Sub/Lieut. 63rd F. 31.8.1872, Lieut. 31.8.1872, Ben. S.C. 2.6.1876.
RETALLACK, Francis. From 16th F., Capt. 63rd F. 24.7.1857, Ret. 28.10.1864.
REYNOLDS, Henry. From 50th F., Ens. 63rd F. 1.10.1829, 17th F. 31.12.1829.
REYNOLDS, Montague Lyttleton Varnham. Ens. 63rd F. 2.9.1845, Lieut. 10.3.1848, 94th F. 10.3.1848.
RIACH, John. From H.P., Asst. Surg. 63rd F. 19.1.1826, 10th L. Drgns. 24.8.1826.
RICE, Stephen. Ens. 63rd F. 28.7.1768, N.T.A. 1769.
RICHARDS, Charles. 2/Lieut. Manch. R. 2.11.1916, Lieut. 2.5.1918, Res. 19.11.1919.
RICHARDS, Mark. From 8th F., Lieut. 63rd F. 7.9.1756, N.T.A. 1759.
RICHARDSON, Charles. 2/Lieut. Manch. R. 30.8.1899, Lieut. 16.5.1900, Capt. 8.8.1903, Worcester R. 20.5.1908.
RICHARDSON, John Cottier, D.C.M. 2/Lieut. Manch. R. 20.11.1914, Lieut. 27.4.1915, Capt. 9.2.1918, K. in A., France, 4.10.1918.
RICHARDSON, Marcus. Ens. 63rd F. 24.5.1804, Lieut. 18.4.1805, Capt. 30.3.1809, 45th F. 3.9.1812.
RICHARDSON, Robert Walsh. Ens. 63rd F. 8.1.1807, Lieut. 5.4.1808, Capt. 2.1.1823, 91st F. 1.1.1824.
RICHMOND, Matthew. From 11th F., Capt. 96th F. 7.6.1839, Ret. 2.9.1845.
RICKETTS, Thomas B. Ens. 63rd F. 9.11.1797, Lieut. 5.4.1798, 13th F. 13.9.1798.
RIDGEWAY, Richard Kirby. Ens. 96th F. 22.1.1868, Lieut. 14.2.1870, Ben. S.C. 6.1.1872.
RIDLER, William. Qr.-Mr. 63rd F. 8.6.1872, 37th F. 23.1.1875.
RIDLEY, Charles Parker. Sub/Lieut. 96th F. 9.8.1873, Lieut. 9.8.1873, Capt. 13.9.1879, Maj. 30.9.1884, Lt.-Col. 28.7.1895, Brev. Col. 28.7.1899, Staff 6.10.1899, H.P. 24.6.1902.

RITCHIE, Thomas Fraser. 2/Lieut. Manch. R. 18.4.1900, Lieut. 5.1.1901, Capt. 18.9.1907, Somerset L.I. 20.5.1908.
ROBERTS, John. Ens. 63rd F. 25.7.1771, Lieut. 18.6.1775, Capt. 13.6.1778, N.T.A. 1786.
ROBERTSON, Archibald. From Ceylon R., Lieut. 96th F. 29.1.1824, Capt. 9.1.1835, Ret. 19.6.1835.
ROBERTSON, Charles. From H.P. Meuron's R., Capt. and Brev. Maj. 96th F. 9.10.1840, Ret. 20.10.1846.
ROBERTSON, David. Ens. 63rd F. 12.9.1777, Lieut. 20.4.1778, N.T.A. 1778.
ROBERTSON, Fulton (Waterloo Medal). From H.P., Capt. 96th F. 21.2.1834, Ret. 19.6.1835.
ROBERTSON, William. Ens. 63rd F. 24.11.1775 N.T.A. 1778.
ROBINSON, Edgar Arthur Knott. From Connaught Rngrs., Lieut. Manch. R. 9.9.1922.
ROBINSON, Henry William Stuart. 2/Lieut. Manch. R. 4.10.1899, Lieut. 16.5.1900, Died at Freiburg, Germany, 23.12.1901.
ROBINSON, Herbert Polixfen. 2/Lieut. Manch. R. 15.2.1899, W. India R. 16.8.1899.
ROBINSON, John. From 45th F., Capt. 63rd F. 3.9.1812, H.P. Nov. 1814.
ROBINSON, Richardson G. Ens. 63rd F. 26.1.1816, Died at Antigua, W. Indies, 16.12.1816.
ROBOTHAM, John Harrison. From Staff, Surg. 63rd F. 12.7.1871, Ben. S.C. 1.7.1877.
ROCHE, Frederick Noel Hill. Ens. 96th F. 18.12.1860, Lieut. 19.8.1862, Died 7.11.1862.
ROCHFORT, Lewes. Ens. 96th F. 18.4.1807, Res. 26.5.1807.
ROCHFORT-BOYD, George Warren Woods. Lieut. 96th F. 2.12.1874, Adjt. 5.7.1879–4.7.1886, Capt. 1.7.1881, Maj. 31.5.1890, Died at Manchester 23.10.1891.
ROCKE, Henry Bagshaw Harrison. From 31st F., Capt. 96th F. 26.11.1852, 43rd F. 1.5.1855.
ROE, Humphrey Verdon. 2/Lieut. Manch. R. 1.12.1897, Lieut. 6.5.1899, Res. 3.7.1901.
ROGERS, Henry. From 8th F., Capt. 63rd F. 30.8.1756, N.T.A. 1763.
ROGERS, James. Ens. 63rd F. 19.9.1805, Lieut. 9.4.1807, Died at Martinique 20.10.1809.
ROGERS, William. From 3rd W. India R., Lieut. 96th F. 18.8.1848, Ret. 18.7.1851.
ROLT, Thomas Francis. Ens. 63rd F. 27.10.1846, C. Gds. 28.1.1848.
RONEY, Richard. Ens. 96th F. 14.9.1838, Lieut. 30.4.1841, Adjt. 27.5.1842–8.4.1847, Capt. 16.7.1850, Depot Bn. 3.3.1857.
ROOKE, James. Capt. 63rd F. 15.7.1761, N.T.A. 1761.
ROSE, Alfred Barnes. 2/Lieut. Manch. R. 27.7.1901, Lieut. 25.10.1902, Capt. 25.8.1914, Maj. 22.5.1916, H.P. 8.2.1919.
Ross, Robert. From 7th F., Lieut. 96th F. 9.1.1835, Capt. 14.9.1838, 36th F. 31.12.1839.

APPENDIX V

ROTHBOTHAM, Samuel. From 28th Drgns., Lieut. 63rd F. 1.3.1796, Ret. 8.10.1796.
ROTHNEY, Edward Claude. From 80th F., Sub/Lieut. 63rd F. 13.5.1874, Died at sea 28.11.1879.
ROUNDS, Henry. Ens. 63rd F. 20.8.1807, Lieut. 19.10.1808, 84th F. 19.10.1808.
ROUTH, Gordon Stewart Floyd. 2/Lieut. Manch. R. 16.12.1896, Lieut. 1.11.1897, Ind. S.C. 26.2.1898.
ROUTLEDGE, Henry. Ens. 63rd F. 31.8.1790, Lieut. 1.3.1794, D. of W., Nimeguen, Flanders, 4.11.1794.
ROWBOTHAM, John Gustavus Clifford. Sub/Lieut. 63rd F. 12.11.1873, Lieut. 12.11.1873, Capt. 26.5.1880, A. Pay Dept. 20.4.1883.
ROWLEY, John. 2/Lieut. Manch. R. 29.8.1917, K. in A., France, 23.12.1917.
ROWSE, Thomas. Ens. 63rd F. 29.3.1760, Lieut. 15.1.1762, H.P. 1763.
RUDDY, Thomas. 2/Lieut. Manch. R. 5.1.1915, Lieut. 10.6.1915, Died at Amara, Mesopotamia, 1.7.1916.
RUDOLPH, William. 2/Lieut. Manch. R. 12.9.1917, Lieut. 12.3.1919, Res. 10.2.1920.
RUSSELL, John James. Asst. Surg. 63rd F. 19.10.1826, 73rd F. 22.1.1836.
RUXTON, Samuel. Ens. 63rd F. 30.6.1790, Lieut. 1.3.1794, Capt. 1.11.1796, Died July 1799.
RYAN, Constantine Joseph. Ens. 63rd F. 28.10.1864, Lieut. 28.7.1867, Capt. 6.12.1873, Maj. 1.7.1881, Lt.-Col. 28.8.1885, Col. 28.8.1889, Ret. 31.5.1890.
RYAN, William. From 31st F., Lieut. 63rd F. 17.8.1815, H.P. 25.12.1818.
RYND, Gerald Cleeve. 2/Lieut. Manch. R. 3.5.1890, Lieut. 19.5.1892, Capt. 24.1.1898, Ret. 3.6.1905.

SADLER, Robinson. Ens. 63rd F. 29.6.1809, Lieut. 5.4.1810, H.P. 20.1.1820.
ST. GEORGE, Thomas Bligh. From 90th F., Lt.-Col. 63rd F. 14.3.1805, Inspector of Militia, Canada, Dec. 1808.
ST. LEGER, Hayes. Ens. 63rd F. 12.12.1770, Lieut. 5.3.1775, Capt. 12.6.1777, D. of W., Carolina, N. America, 11.10.1781.
SALT, Thomas. Ens. 63rd F. 14.3.1772, N.T.A. 1775.
SAMPSON, George Dennis. From H.P. Ceylon R., Capt. 96th F. 13.5.1874, 2nd W. India R. 11.9.1875.
SANDYS, Lord Augustus Frederick Arthur. Ens. 96th F. 18.11.1859, Lieut. 8.7.1862, 2nd Life Gds. 12.6.1863.
SANKEY, Charles. From 92nd F., Lieut. 63rd F. 12.12.1795, Capt. 9.7.1803, 67th F. 9.7.1803.
SANKEY, Samuel. Lieut. 63rd F. 8.9.1795, Ret. 13.2.1796.
SAPORTAS, Arnold David. From 95th F., Capt. 63rd F. 31.10.1871, Maj. 4.2.1881, Lt.-Col. 18.3.1885, Col. in Army 18.3.1889, H.P. 18.3.1890.
SAPORTAS, Herbert Arnold. 2/Lieut. Manch. R. 2.5.1914, Lieut. 1.12.1914, K. in A., Flanders, 17.7.1915.
SAUNDERS, Robert. Ens. 63rd F. 24.8.1797, N.T.A. 1797.
SAVAGE, Edmund Sandilands. From 3rd W. India R., Capt. 63rd F. 5.4.1871, H.P. 23.5.1877.
SAVAGE, George William. Ens. 63rd F. 6.7.1804, Lieut. 18.12.1805, Capt. 2.12.1813, H.P. Nov. 1814.
SAWREY, Henry Beckwith. Ens. 63rd F. 6.11.1835, 88th F. 16.9.1836.
SCOTT, Benjamin. From H.P. 25th F., Paymr. 96th F. 5.10.1826, Died at Halifax, Nova Scotia, 24.6.1832.
SCOUGALL, Henry. Ens. 96th F. 8.6.1867, Lieut. 13.1.1869, Ret. 3.7.1872.
SCOVELL, Edmund John. Ens. 96th F. 25.3.1856, Lieut. 30.4.1858, Capt. 7.10.1859, Maj. 14.9.1870, Lt.-Col. 1.7.1881, Col. in Army 1.7.1881, Ret. 8.2.1882.
SCOVELL, Edward William. Ens. 96th F. 29.12.1835, Lieut. 2.11.1838, Capt. 13.12.1842, Brev. Maj. 20.6.1854, Maj. 28.6.1856, Lt.-Col. 8.7.1856, Brev. Col. 8.7.1861, H.P. 9.10.1862.
SCOVELL, Thornton. Ens. 63rd F. 30.12.1858, Lieut. 16.8.1861, Capt. 14.8.1867, H.P. 26.7.1873.
SCULLY, Arthur John, M.C. 2/Lieut. Manch. R. 22.2.1908, Lieut. 12.1.1910, Capt. 10.6.1915, Adjt. 11.2.1916-7.3.1917, Brev. Maj. 3.6.1918, H.P. 14.4.1922.
SEAGRAM, John Henry Stawell. Ens. 96th F. 23.1.1863, 95th F. 17.3.1863.
SEALY, Alfred Edward. 2/Lieut. Manch. R. 8.10.1890, Lieut. 1.6.1893, Ind. S.C. 1.12.1895.
SEDGWICK, Harry. 2/Lieut. Manch. R. 23.10.1916, Lieut. 23.4.1918, Ret. Capt. 25.1.1920.
SEDLEY, Anthony Gardiner. From 45th F., Capt. 63rd F. 11.7.1836, Maj. 2.9.1844, Lt.-Col. 16.9.1845, H.P. 23.10.1847.
SEGRAVE, O'Neil Stewart. From 11th F., Ens. 96th F. 8.10.1850, Lieut. 19.8.1853, 13th F. 11.8.1854.
SERVANTES, William Fraser George. Ens. 96th F. 2.7.1841, Lieut. 6th F. 7.8.1846.
SEYMOUR, Henry R. Ens. 63rd F. 20.9.1833, Lieut. 20.2.1835, Capt. 19.11.1844, 40th F. 23.5.1845.
SHAKESPEAR, Frank. 2/Lieut. Manch. R. 9.11.1887, Lieut. Ben. S.C. 30.3.1888.
SHARLAND, Alan Abbott. 2/Lieut. Manch. R. 22.4.1903, E. Lancs. R. 4.5.1907.
SHARP, Alfred Granville. 2/Lieut. Manch. R. 7.12.1895, Lieut. 6.3.1897, Capt. 9.6.1900, H.P. 15.7.1911.
SHARPE, Edward. Ens. 63rd F. 25.6.1759, Lieut. 2.3.1760, N.T.A. 1771.
SHAW, James. 2/Lieut. Manch. R. 6.2.1909, Lieut. 27.2.1913, Ind. Army 20.2.1914.
SHEERAN, Patrick. Qr.-Mr. 96th F. 27.7.1855, 6th F. 22.4.1859.

ALPHABETICAL ROLL OF OFFICERS

SHELDON, Edward Ralph Charles. From 70th F., Ens. 63rd F. 28.1.1848, Lieut. 23.8.1850, Capt. 12.8.1853, Ret. 4.11.1853.

SHENLEY, Godfrey Harcourt. From H.P. Rifle Bde., Lieut. 63rd F. 29.4.1824, 36th F. 9.4.1825.

SHEPPARD, Claud John Loraine, M.C. 2/Lieut. Manch. R. 12.5.1915, Lieut. 1.10.1915, Capt. 5.11.1921, Res. 3.11.1922.

SHEPPARD, Edgar. 2/Lieut. Manch. R. 27.7.1901, 19th Hrs. 7.12.1901.

SHEPPARD, John. Ens. 63rd F. 25.8.1807, 17th F. 14.1.1808.

SHERER, Moyle. From H.P. 34th F., Capt. 96th F. 9.8.1831, Brev. Maj. 22.7.1830, H.P. 6.7.1832.

SHEWELL, Edward Leslie. 2/Lieut. Manch. R. 31.8.1922.

SHIPSTER, George Cecil, M.C. From R. Fus., Capt. Manch. R. 1.7.1916.

SHIPSTER, Walter Neville, M.C. 2/Lieut. Manch. R. 18.9.1909, Lieut. 3.5.1913, Capt. 18.9.1915, K. in A., Palestine, 20.9.1918.

SHORLAND, James. From H.P. Meuron's R., Surg. 96th F. 16.6.1824, H.P. 20.8.1841.

SHUTER, Reginald Gauntlett, D.S.O. From R. Irish Fus., Capt. Manch. R. 23.11.1901, Adjt. 14.4.1905–23.1.1907, R. Irish. Fus. 8.1.1908.

SILL, Francis Bashill. From 62nd F., Maj. 63rd F. 20.10.1773, K. in A., Fort Clinton, N. America, 6.10.1777.

SIMONET, Francis. Ens. 63rd F. 30.1.1808, N.T.A. 1808.

SIMPSON, Arthur Edmund. Sub/Lieut. 96th F. 21.9.1874, Lieut. 21.9.1874, Capt. 18.6.1881, Maj. 17.1.1890, Ret. 23.9.1903.

SIMPSON, James. Ens. 63rd F. 25.10.1807, Lieut. 29.6.1809, Died at Martinique 30.9.1809.

SINCLAIR, Robert. Ens. 63rd F. 6.9.1759, Lieut. 12.10.1760, N.T.A. 1771.

SINGER, George Hamilton. From 10th F., Paymr. and Hon. Capt. 96th F. 13.11.1880, Norfolk R. Apr. 1883.

SITWELL, Claude George Henry. From Shrop. L.I., Capt. Manch. R. 13.2.1889, Maj. R. Dub. Fus. 19.10.1898.

SKENE, Andrew. Lieut. 63rd F. 8.8.1805, 60th F. 1.10.1807.

SLACK, James. Ens. 63rd F. 15.1.1856, Lieut. 22.4.1859, Qr.-Mr. School of Musketry, 22.4.1859.

SMITH, Henry Sherwood. Lieut. 63rd F. 29.11.1876, Capt. 9.7.1884, Adjt. 15.12.1879–14.12.1884, Maj. 6.12.1893, Ret. 13.1.1897.

SMITH, John Herbert Michael. 2/Lieut. Manch. R. 27.10.1913, D. of W., France, 17.9.1914.

SMITH, Morris Charles. Ens. 63rd F. 21.12.1860, Lieut. 23.8.1864, Ret. 21.8.1867.

SMITH, Peter. 2/Lieut. Manch. R. 22.6.1915, Lieut. 1.7.1916, Ret. 29.8.1918.

SMITH, Ralph William, M.B.E. 2/Lieut. Manch. R. 2.4.1915, Lieut. 1.10.1915, Res. 18.6.1921.

SMITH, Robert. Surg. 63rd F. 2.10.1765–16.4.1779.

SMITH, Thomas Hector. From 72nd F., Qr.-Mr. 96th F. 1.9.1873, 6th R. Lanc. Mil. 15.6.1878.

SMITH, William. Ens. 63rd F. 5.8.1799, Qr.-Mr. 6.11.1800–July 1802, Lieut. 25.6.1803, Capt. 29.6.1809, Died June 1810.

SMITH, William. Ens. 63rd F. 25.7.1802, Adjt. 25.7.1802–Feb. 1810, Lieut. 5.8.1804, Capt. 12.11.1809, 3rd R. Veteran Bn. 16.9.1824.

SMURTHWAITE, Algernon Sidney Thomas. From Middlesex R., Lieut. Manch. R. 20.1.1923.

SMYTH, Algernon Beresford. 2/Lieut. Manch. R. 2.5.1903, York L.I. 20.4.1907.

SMYTH, James Stewart. Ens. 63rd F. 20.11.1858, Lieut. 16.11.1860, Capt. 12.6.1867, H.P. 5.4.1871.

SMYTH, Ralph Montagu. Ens. 63rd F. 10.11.1869, Lieut. 1.11.1871, Ret. 21.8.1872.

SNAPE, William. Ens. 63rd F. 18.4.1805, Lieut. 9.10.1806, Capt. 14.7.1808, Maj. 16.11.1826, Ret. Aug. 1827.

SNODGRASS, John. From 4th F., Capt. 96th F. 12.10.1841, Maj. 15.6.1849, Died at Curragh Camp 27.1.1856.

SNOW, Arthur Henry Cresswell. From 70th F., Capt. 96th F. 27.10.1854, Ret. 26.1.1866.

SOTHAM, Ernest George, M.C. 2/Lieut. Manch. R. 18.11.1903, Lieut. 12.10.1907, Capt. 11.12.1914.

SOUTER, Hugh Maurice Wellesley. 2/Lieut. Manch. R. 18.5.1892, Lieut. 31.7.1895, Ind. S.C. 19.12.1896.

SOUTER, Thomas Alexander. Ens. 96th F. 30.6.1824, 56th F. 21.6.1827.

SOUTHEY, Henry Herbert. 2/Lieut. Manch. R. 5.2.1887, Lieut. Ben. S.C. 28.11.1887.

SOWRAY, Gerald Russell. From Shrop. L.I., Capt. Manch. R. 26.5.1900, Shrop L.I. 18.12.1907.

SPENCE, John. Ens. 63rd F. 5.10.1757, Lieut. 25.6.1759, Died, W. Indies, 1760.

SPENCER, Hon. George Augustus. Ens. 63rd F. 12.2.1824, Lieut. 16.6.1825, 60th F. 15.1.1829.

SPIER, John. Ens. 63rd F. 30.7.1844, Lieut. 1.5.1846, 86th F. 1.5.1846.

SPIER, John. From H.P. 61st F., Lieut. 63rd F. 18.9.1833, Died 24.5.1842.

SPOONER, Reginald Herbert. 2/Lieut. Manch. R. 19.10.1901, Res. 22.11.1902.

SPRAGUE, John Hanmer. From 95th F., Asst. Surg. 63rd F. 31.10.1811, 3rd R. Veteran Bn. 24.12.1812.

SPRATT, Richard. From 8th F., Lieut. 96th F. 29.1.1824, Capt. 7.4.1825, Ret. 7.11.1828.

SPROULE, Robert Edward. Ens. 63rd F. 23.4.1855, Res. 3.4.1857.

STAFFORD, George Ferguson. Ens. 63rd F. 7.9.1804, Lieut. 27.3.1806, Died, Martinique, 12.10.1809.

STAFFORD, John. From 98th F., Maj. 63rd F. 4.4.1811, Brev. Lt.-Col. 4.6.1811, H.P. Bourbon R. 14.1.1815.

STAMER, William John A. Ens. 63rd F. 23.1.1852, Ret. 11.3.1853.
STANDISH, Deacon. From 92nd F., Lieut. 63rd F. 10.12.1795, N.T.A. 1802.
STANFORD, William Luttrell. Ens. 63rd F. 11.7.1769, Lieut. 14.3.1772, N.T.A. 1775.
STANLEY-MURRAY, Harold Evelyn. 2/Lieut. Manch. R. 3.9.1902, Lieut. 1.4.1904, R. Scots. 25.1.1908.
STANSFIELD, Cyril Grey. 2/Lieut. Manch. R. 13.8.1892, Lieut. 1.12.1895, Ind. S.C. 24.8.1896.
STAPLEDON, Charles Cyril. 2/Lieut. Manch. R. 11.8.1900, Lieut. 28.7.1901, Adjt. 3.5.1909–2.5.1912, Capt. 20.7.1912, Maj. 1.9.1915.
STARKE, Henry Bethune. Ens. 63rd F. 29.9.1775, Lieut. 14.10.1777, Adjt. 30.5.1780–Sept. 1784, Capt. 3.8.1785, 60th F. 31.3.1791.
STEELE, John. Ens. 63rd F. 22.11.1775, Lieut. 13.4.1778, N.T.A. 1780.
STEELE, Lawrence Litchfield. From Wilts. R., Lt.-Col. Manch. R. 24.2.1900, H.P. 24.2.1904.
STEELE, Thomas. Ens. 63rd F. 18.12.1777, N.T.A. 1780.
STEPHENS, John. Ens. 63rd F. 27.12.1797, N.T.A. 1806.
STEPHENS, J. Edward, M.D. Asst. Surg. 63rd F. 5.10.1841, 16th F. 3.10.1845.
STEPHENS, W. H. Ens. 63rd F. 31.8.1804, Lieut. 27.6.1805, 45th F. 27.6.1805.
STEVENS, Henry Whitehill. From S. Wales Bdrs., Capt. Manch. R. 22.3.1902, S. Wales Bdrs. 12.2.1908.
STEVENS, John Lucius Cary. 2/Lieut. Manch. R. 30.1.1889, Lieut. 10.9.1890, Ind. S.C. 14.7.1891.
STEVENS, Richard Clavell. Ens. 96th F. 3.3.1863, Lieut. 23.4.1866, Ret. 1.1.1869.
STEVENSON, Walter Wilton Campbell. 2/Lieut. Manch. R. 20.2.1895, Lieut. 19.12.1896, Capt. 27.12.1899, K. in A., Ashanti, 22.9.1900.
STEWART, Albert Fortescue. From W. York R., Capt. Manch. R. 26.5.1900, Adjt. 9.6.1900–29.9.1901, Bed. R. 18.1.1908.
STEWART, Charles. Capt. 63rd F. 15.8.1775, Maj. 20.9.1787, Lt.-Col. in Army 19.2.1783, N.T.A. 1785.
STEWART, Charles Edward. 2/Lieut. Manch. R. 30.6.1916, D. of W. 10.9.1916.
STEWART, Grigor. From Staff, Asst. Surg. 96th F. 29.12.1840, Surg. 18th F. 6.12.1844.
STEWART, Henry William. Ens. 63rd F. 14.1.1819, Lieut. 24.10.1821, H.P. 24.10.1821.
STEWART, James. From H.P. 47th F., Capt. 96th F. 6.6.1832, Ret. 2.11.1832.
STEWART, John Alexander. 2/Lieut. Manch. R. 22.8.1888, Lieut. 9.7.1890, Ind. S.C. 1.6.1893.
STEWART, Thomas. From 77th F., Capt. 63rd F. 15.1.1781, H.P. 1784.
STEWART, William. Ens. 63rd F. 3.7.1765, Res. Dec. 1768.

STEWART-WYNNE, Oscar. Qr.-Mr. and Hon. Lieut. Manch. R. 16.10.1889, Hon. Capt. 16.10.1899, Hon. Maj. 16.10.1904, Ret. 25.8.1909.
STIRLING, James. Ens. 63rd F. 31.3.1793, Lieut. 10.12.1794, Capt. 7.9.1796, Maj. 25.6.1803, Ret. 16.7.1808.
STOCKLEY, Vesey Mangles. Sub/Lieut. 96th F. 5.10.1872, 40th F. 27.8.1873.
STOCKMAN, Sidney. 2/Lieut. Manch. R. 8.5.1918, Res. 27.6.1919.
STOKES, Alfred. Ens. 63rd F. 27.7.1855, Lieut. 12.9.1858, 38th F. 28.1.1859.
STOKES, Henry. From 37th F., Qr.-Mr. 63rd F. 23.1.1875, Died, Bombay, 19.1.1879.
STONEHAM, Thomas. Ens. 63rd F. 10.4.1811, Res. 1813.
STOPFORD, William. Lieut. 63rd F. 21.3.1765, Capt. 30.12.1768, N.T.A. 1775.
STORY, George Walter. From H.P. 17th F., Ens. 96th F. 29.1.1824, Lieut. 26.5.1825, 4th Drgn. Gds. 20.8.1825.
STOURTON, Hon. John Marmaduke. Ens. 96th F. 30.6.1837, Lieut. 30.10.1840, Ret. 14.4.1846.
STOURTON, Marmaduke. From 8th F., Capt. 63rd F. 3.9.1870, Died, Natal, 19.4.1879.
STRACEY, Claude Edward. Lieut. 96th F. 29.11.1876, Capt. 20.8.1885, S. Gds. 31.8.1887.
STRICKLAND, Edward Peter, K.C.B., C.M.G., D.S.O. From Norf. R., Lt.-Col. Manch. R. 1.6.1914, Brev. Col. 18.2.1915, Maj.-Gen. 1.1.1918.
STRONG, Justinian Henry. Ens. 96th F. 30.7.1859, Lieut. 5.11.1861, Ret. 14.1.1862.
STROUD, Henry Wallace. From 98th F., Capt. 63rd F. 1.6.1860, Maj. 1.4.1870, H.P. 1.4.1870.
STUART, Charles Cranfurd. 2/Lieut. Manch. R. 4.4.1900, Lieut. 13.10.1900, Ind. S.C. 6.8.1902.
STUART, Kenneth Bruce. Lieut. 63rd F. 24.6.1853, Capt. 9.12.1855, Ret. 15.1.1857.
STUART, William. From 91st F., Asst. Surg. 63rd F. 6.12.1844, Staff 6.6.1845.
STUBBEMAN, Denis M'Carthy. Ens. 63rd F. 22.3.1827, Lieut. 15.3.1831, Capt. 5.6.1835, 83rd F. 25.12.1835.
STUBBS, Arthur George Bushby. Sub/Lieut. 63rd F. 10.9.1875, Lieut. 10.9.1875, Capt. 1.1.1884, Cheshire R. 10.10.1885.
STUDDY, Robert Wright. Ens. 63rd F. 13.7.1867, Lieut. 12.6.1869, Capt. 13.3.1878, Maj. 1.7.1881, Lt.-Col. 18.3.1886, Col. in Army 18.3.1890, Ret. 18.3.1892.
STURT, Robert Ramsay Napier. Sub/Lieut. 96th F. 9.3.1872, 39th F. 27.8.1873.
SULLIVAN, Cornelius. Surg. 63rd F. 28.4.1808–5.7.1809.
SURKITT, Sidney. 2/Lieut. Manch. R. 26.2.1917, Lieut. 26.8.1918, Res. 28.5.1921.
SUTHERLAND, Edward. From H.P. 100th F., Lieut. 96th F. 29.1.1824, Adjt. 29.1.1824–20.1.1832, H.P. 12.7.1833.

ALPHABETICAL ROLL OF OFFICERS

SUTTON, Henry Godwin. 2/Lieut. Manch. R. 22.4.1903, Ind. Army 30.6.1905.
SWETENHAM, Clement. From 77th F., Ens. 96th F. 27.9.1839, 57th F. 2.7.1841.
SWIFT, Benjamin, M.D. From 87th F., Surg. 96th F. 23.6.1854, Surg. Maj. 8.4.1862, 14th F. 16.8.1864.
SWIFT, William Alfred. Ens. 96th F. 11.2.1848, Lieut. 63rd F. 16.7.1850, 7th F. 10.3.1853.
SWYNY, Exham Schomberg Turner. From 99th F., Lieut. 63rd F. 17.10.1833, Capt. 8.8.1838, Adjt. 30.11.1838, Maj. 22.10.1847, Lt.-Col. 23.12.1853, K. in A., Inkerman, 5.11.1854.
SWYNY, Henry Joseph. Ens. 63rd F. 2.12.1831, Lieut. 18.10.1833, Capt. 16.7.1841, H.P. 8.11.1844.
SYKES, Frank Clifford, M.C. 2/Lieut. Manch. R. 20.10.1915, Lieut. 1.1.1917, Res. 17.9.1921.
SYMONDS, William Cornwallis. From H.P., Capt. 96th F. 31.12.1839, Drowned in Manukao Bay, N. Zealand, 24.11.1841.

TALBOT, Charles Arthur. Ens. 63rd F. 24.3.1854, Lieut. 8.12.1854, Rifle Bde. 8.12.1854.
TARLETON, Banastre Henry. Ens. 96th F. 8.4.1834, Lieut. 11.8.1837, Died 12.12.1838.
TARRATT, Daniel Fox. Ens. 63rd F. 1.7.1859, Lieut. 12.2.1862, Ret. 3.3.1863.
TAUBMAN, Alexander H. Goldie. Ens. 63rd F. 17.8.1861, Lieut. 9.6.1865, Capt. 2.5.1868, Ret. 12.6.1869.
TAYLEUR, Charles E. D. 2/Lieut. Manch. R. 29.1.1902, Lieut. 19.8.1903, Res. 25.5.1912.
TAYLOR, Phillpots Wright. Ens. 96th F. 16.3.1832, Lieut. 4.3.1836, Capt. 30.10.1840, R. Canadian R. 12.10.1841.
TAYLOR, Richard. Ens. 63rd F. 17.8.1843, Lieut. 20.12.1844, 10th F. 16.6.1848.
TAYLOR, Thomas. Ens. 63rd F. 12.7.1777, N.T.A. 1778.
TELFORD, Joseph. From H.P. 9th F., Ens. 96th F. 29.1.1824, Lieut. 8.4.1825, Adjt. 20.1.1832-13.2.1834, Capt. 14.2.1834, Ret. 12.8.1836.
TEMPLE, James Blake. From 61st F., Capt. 63rd F. 25.5.1803, Ret. 2.6.1804.
TENISON, William, P.S.C. Sub/Lieut. 63rd F. 10.9.1875, Lieut. 10.9.1875, Capt. 1.8.1883, Maj. 3.2.1892, Ret. 3.9.1892.
TERNAN, Richard Richards Breffney. From 3rd F., Paymr. 63rd F. 3.3.1880, R. W. Kent R. Nov. 1882.
TERNAN, Trevor Patrick Breffney. From 14th F., 2/Lieut. 63rd F. 27.9.1879, Lieut. 1.7.1881, Capt. 12.11.1888, Maj. 6.4.1898, R. War. R. 6.4.1898.
TERRIL, John. Ens. 63rd F. 24.3.1759, Lieut. 11.1.1760, D. on S., Guadaloupe, 23.3.1760.
TERROT, Charles Ellison. Ens. 63rd F. 18.1.1859, Lieut. 19.12.1861, Adjt. 9.11.1866-12.9.1867, Capt. 13.9.1867, Maj. 24.11.1877, Lt.-Col. 2.5.1883, Died 27.8.1885.

TERRY, Edward Ernest Gregory. 2/Lieut. Manch. R. 8.10.1899, Lieut. 16.5.1900, Res. 16.8.1902.
TERRY, Robert Joseph Atkinson. From R.W. Surr. R., Capt. Manch. R. 9.6.1900, Brev. Maj. 22.8.1902, Adjt. 2.11.1902-2.5.1906, R. Suss. R. 18.1.1908.
THACKER, John. Ens. 63rd F. 30.9.1859, Lieut. 3.3.1863, Ret. 1.5.1867.
THEOBALD, Henry Charles Webb, D.S.O. From Glos. R., Capt. Manch. R. 13.7.1901, Maj. 1.9.1915, Ret. Lt.-Col. 24.10.1919.
THOMAS, Arthur Felex, D.S.O. 2/Lieut. Manch. R. 23.4.1902, Lieut. 17.2.1904, Capt. 1.12.1914, Maj. 23.4.1917, R.C. of Sig. 24.11.1920.
THOMAS, Frederick William. Lieut. 63rd F. 29.11.1876, Capt. 1.7.1885, Ret. 16.1.1889.
THOMAS, Frederick William. 2/Lieut. Manch. R. 1.3.1890, Lieut. 10.2.1892, Ind. S.C. 10.7.1893.
THOMAS, Geoffrey Rittson. 2/Lieut. Manch. R. 15.5.1915, Lieut. 18.1.1916, H.P. 27.1.1920.
THOMAS, Lloyd Henry. From 91st F., Capt. 63rd F. 6.11.1863, Ret. 23.8.1864.
THOMAS, William Godfrey. From K.O. Bord., Maj. Manch. R. 10.1.1883, Lt.-Col. H.P. 17.1.1890.
THOMPSON, George Irwin. Ens. 96th F. 19.8.1853, Lieut. 9.10.1855, Capt. 23.11.1860, Ret. 2.7.1861.
THOMPSON, James. Lieut. 63rd F. 12.8.1795, Ret. 27.1.1800.
THOMPSON, James. Qr.-Mr. 63rd F. 9.1.1783-15.11.1800, N.T.A. 1800.
THOMPSON, Joseph. From 13th Service Bn., Manch. R., Capt. 19.1.1917, Killed by Sinn Feiners at Ballincollig, Ireland, 20.11.1920.
THOMPSON, J. Hamilton. Ens. 96th F. 8.2.1856, Lieut. 2.2.1858, Adjt. 2.2.1858-5.5.1859, Ret. 8.7.1859.
THOMPSON, Robert Thomas. Ens. 96th F. 11.3.1853, Lieut. 56th F. 27.7.1855.
THOMPSON, William. From 1st Garr. Bn., Ens. 63rd F. 3.10.1809, Res. 1810.
THOMPSON, William. Qr.-Mr. 96th F. 23.6.1847, Paymr. 27.7.1855, Hon. Lieut. 27.7.1860, Hon. Capt. 27.7.1865, H.P. 11.8.1874.
THORNE, Edward. From 6th Bn. of Res., Lieut. 63rd F. 6.2.1805, D. on S., Martinique, 21.3.1810.
THORNTON, Thomas William. Ens. 63rd F. 28.11.1811, Lieut. 2.1.1817, H.P. 17.3.1819.
THORNYCROFT, Charles Mylton. 2/Lieut. Manch. R. 12.8.1899, Lieut. 16.5.1900, Capt. 5.2.1902, Ret. 3.6.1911.
THORPE, John. Ens. 63rd F. 27.9.1833, Lieut. 5.6.1835, Paymr. 8.11.1844, H.P. 7.12.1855.
TIGHE, Vincent John, D.S.O. From W. India R., Capt. Manch. R. 22.9.1900, Ret. 13.8.1908.

TILLARD, Arthur George. 2/Lieut. Manch. R. 20.2.1895, Lieut. 24.8.1896, Capt. 13.9.1899, H.P. 8.1.1908, Attacd. 2nd Bn., Aug. 1914, K. in A., La Bassée, 20.10.1914.

TILLARD, Arthur Kenneth Dowell. 2/Lieut. Manch. R. 8.5.1901, Lieut. 25.12.1901, Capt. 11.12.1912, Maj. 8.5.1916, Ret. 24.9.1922.

TOD, Francis. From Indpdt. Coy., Lieut. 63rd F. 27.5.1795, N.T.A. 1796.

TOKE, John Leslie. Ens. 96th F. 2.5.1858, Lieut. 18.11.1859, Adjt. 2.7.1861–8.1.1863, Capt. 9.1.1863, 2nd F. 17.3.1863.

TOOGOOD, Cecil, D.S.O. From Bord. R., Capt. Manch. R. 26.5.1900, Linc. R. 18.1.1908.

TORKINGTON, John Elmsley Bourchier. 2/Lieut. Manch. R. 2.3.1904, Lieut. 3.5.1909, Ind. Army 18.6.1909.

TORRANCE, Kenneth Sanderson, M.C. 2/Lieut Manch. R. 22.1.1915, Lieut. 18.9.1915, Adjt. 24.7.1920, Capt. 21.11.1920.

TORRENS, Henry. From 92nd F., Lieut. 63rd F. 11.12.1795, Capt. 6th W. India R. 28.3.1797.

TOWNSEND, Thomas Edward Brackenbury. Ens. 96th F. 15.1.1862, Lieut. 3.3.1863, 83rd F. 7.4.1863.

TOWZELL, Helier. Lieut. 63rd F. 9.12.1795, Capt. 4.8.1804, Maj. 14.7.1808, Insp. of Jersey Mil. 15.8.1811.

TRAVERS, Robert. From H.P., Lieut. 63rd F. 15.3.1831, Ret. 7.8.1835.

TREFFRY, George Steele. From 45th F., Lieut. 63rd F. 24.1.1865, W. Ind. R. 1.2.1867.

TREVOR, Edward Gapper. From Welch R., Lieut. Manch. R. 20.9.1884, Res. 9.6.1885.

TRIPE, Alfred Polglasse. Ens. 96th F. 8.1.1868, Lieut. 9.2.1870, Ret. 2.2.1875.

TROLLOPE, John. From 8th F., Maj. 63rd F. 30.4.1758, K. in A., Guadaloupe, 23.3.1759.

TRUEMAN, Charles Fitzgerald Hamilton, 2/Lieut. Manch. R. 9.9.1897, Lieut. 17.8.1898, Capt. 9.1.1901, K. in A., Le Cateau, 26.8.1914.

TUELY, Charles Seymour. From R. Irish F., Capt. Manch. R. 27.2.1923.

TUFFNELL, John. From H.P. York. Rngrs., Maj. 63rd F. 1.11.1804, Brev. Lt.-Col. 29.4.1802, Ret. 16.3.1809.

TULLOCH, Alexander Bruce. From 1st F., Capt. 96th F. 29.3.1864, 69th F. 20.4.1866.

TULLOK, William. From H.P., Capt. 63rd F. 31.7.1792, N.T.A. 1794.

TURNER, Dutton. Ens. 63rd F. 9.2.1799, Died Apr. 1799.

TUSON, Harry Dennison. From Bord. R., Maj. Manch. R. 9.12.1905, D. of Corn. L.I. 8.7.1908.

TUTHILL, George. Ens. 96th F. 19.8.1862, Lieut. 24.11.1863, Died 22.10.1867.

TWISTON, Thomas Lewis. Ens. 63rd F. 24.4.1855, Lieut. 21.9.1855, Died Oct. 1859.

TWYSDEN, Heneage Thomas. Ens. 63rd F. 13.3.1853, K. in A., Inkerman, 5.11.1854, while carrying the Colours.

TYLDEN-WRIGHT, Warrington Royds. 2/Lieut. Manch. R. 4.5.1901, Lieut. 30.11.1901, 3rd Hrs. 17.5.1902.

TYNEDALE, Charles Henry Wyndham. From 2nd W. India R., Maj. Manch. R. 30.3.1883, Brev. Lt.-Col. 15.6.1885, Died, Aldershot, 10.2.1888.

TYTLER, Harry Christopher. Lieut. Manch. R. 30.1.1886, Ben. S.C. 9.11.1887.

UNIACKE, Thomas Fane. From 15th F., Lieut. 63rd F. 11.6.1811, 90th F. 1.4.1813.

UTERMARCK, Reginald John Guthrie. Lieut. 96th F. 24.6.1876, Capt. 26.6.1884, A. Pay Dept. 1.4.1885.

VANDERSPAR, Edgar Roland. 2/Lieut. Manch. R. 5.10.1910, Lieut. 20.2.1914, K. in A., Flanders, 24.6.1915.

VAN HEEL, Theodore. 2/Lieut. Manch. R. 1.5.1917, Lieut. 1.11.1918, Res. 1.8.1919.

VANRENEN, Donald Adrian. 2/Lieut. Manch. R. 14.3.1900, Lieut. 13.10.1900, Res. 25.10.1902.

VANSITTART, Eden. Sub/Lieut. 63rd F. 29.8.1876, Madras S.C. 20.7.1877.

VAUGHAN, Edward, C.M.G., D.S.O. 2/Lieut. Manch. R. 10.11.1888, Lieut. 10.9.1890, Adjt. 6.7.1895–30.6.1899, Capt. 1.11.1897. Brev. Maj. 22.8.1902, Maj. 17.2.1904, Lt.-Col. 1.9.1916, Col. 1.9.1920, H.P. 1.9.1920.

VAUGHAN, Edward James Forrester. From Devon R., Capt. Manch. R. 13.7.1901, Devon R. 8.1.1908.

VAUGHAN, William. Ens. 63rd F. 21.1.1778, N.T.A. 1780.

VEITH, Frederick Harris Dawes. Ens. 63rd F. 16.2.1855, Lieut. 27.7.1855, Ret. 21.9.1860.

VICARY, Michael. Ens. 63rd F. 15.11.1809, Lieut. 16.5.1811, Capt. 5.2.1829, Ret. 16.3.1832.

VICKERS, George Edward, D.S.O. From Res. Bn., Qr.-Mr. and Hon. Capt. Manch. R. 5.2.1912, Hon. Maj. 5.2.1917, Lt.-Col. 3.6.1918, Ret. 3.6.1918.

VINCENT, Henry Alexander. From 33rd F., Ens. 96th F. 19.5.1869, Lieut. 28.10.1871, Ind. S.C. 13.2.1872.

VIZARD, Robert Davenport. 2/Lieut. 96th F. 23.4.1881, Lieut. 1.7.1881, Capt. 10.4.1889, Maj. 17.2.1900, Brev. Lt.-Col. 29.11.1900, Lt.-Col. 1.6.1906, Brev. Col. 30.8.1906, Ret. 1.6.1910.

WALKER, Edward John Howard. 2/Lieut. Manch. R. 29.11.1890, Lieut. 15.4.1894, Capt. 2.8.1898, Maj. 4.3.1905, Ret. 3.2.1920.

WALKER, Reginald Fydell. 2/Lieut. Manch. R 12.8.1914, D. of W. 21.10.1914.

WALKLEY, Daniel. Qr.-Mr. and Hon. Lieut. Manch. R. 1.3.1900, Ches. R. 4.5.1907.

WALLER, James Waller Samo. From 31st F., Capt. 96th F. 29.1.1824, H.P. 23.3.1832.

ALPHABETICAL ROLL OF OFFICERS

WALMSLEY, Hugh Mullineux. Ens. 63rd F. 28.6.1844, Lieut. 25.9.1845, Adjt. 8.3.1847, Ret. 18.1.1850.
WALSH, Christopher Joseph. From Connaught Rngrs., Lieut. Manch. R. 6.9.1922, Ret. 5.12.1922.
WALSH, John. From 2nd F., Qr.-Mr. 96th F. 22.6.1870, 72nd F. 1.9.1873.
WALSH, Theodore. From R. Afr. Rifle C., Capt. 63rd F. 25.11.1828, Paymr. Drgn. Gds. 19.3.1829.
WALSHE, Holwell Hely Hutchinson. Ens. 96th F. 6.7.1855, Lieut. 11.3.1856, 2nd W. Ind. R. 23.3.1858.
WALTON, Leslie Arthur, D.S.O., M.C. From Welch R., Lieut. Manch. R. 13.7.1921.
WARBURTON, George Alexander. Ens. 96th F. 15.3.1850, Lieut. 9.7.1852, 19th F. 11.8.1854.
WARD, Edwin Arthur. 2/Lieut. 96th F. 11.8.1880, Lieut. 1.7.1881, Capt. 12.11.1888, Died at Dinapore, 20.10.1894.
WARD, James. From 8th F., Lieut. 63rd F. 4.9.1756, Died, W. Indies, 1760.
WARD, John. Ens. 63rd F. 18.11.1819, Lieut. 8.4.1826, H.P. 103rd F. 8.5.1828.
WARD, Rowland. Ens. 63rd F. 4.4.1761, N.T.A. 1765.
WARD, Walter. Ens. 63rd F. 28.3.1805, Lieut. 26.6.1806, Died at St. Nevis, W. Indies, 22.8.1816.
WARD, Williams Stevens. Ens. 63rd F. 19.7.1864, Lieut. 27.2.1867, Adjt. 5.10.1867–13.5.1870, Died at Kinsale, Ireland, 13.5.1870.
WARDLAW, James. Adjt. 63rd F. 31.10.1789, N.T.A. 1794.
WARDLAW, Sir John, Bart. Capt. 63rd F. 1.3.1794, Maj. 28.8.1800, 64th F. 28.8.1800.
WARDLAW, William. Ens. 63rd F. 18.9.1780, Lieut. 8.12.1784, N.T.A. 1794.
WARNE, Osmund Hornby, M.C. From N. Staff. R., Capt. Manch. R. 1.7.1916.
WARREN, Richard Burke. From H.P. 24th F., Lieut. 96th F. 17.7.1828, Capt. 26.11.1830, Died 1.1.1831.
WASHINGTON, Jonathan Noel. 2/Lieut. Manch. R. 12.5.1915, D. of W. 2.10.1915.
WATERS, Robert Sidney. 2/Lieut. Manch. R. 5.5.1900, Lieut. 23.5.1901, Ind. S.C. 27.7.1901.
WATSON, John Edward. 2/Lieut. 96th F. 11.5.1878, Lieut. 13.6.1879, Capt. 10.8.1887, Maj. 13.1.1897, Brev. Lt.-Col. 29.11.1900, Lt.-Col. 6.10.1903, Brev. Col. 3.5.1905, Col. H.P. 27.11.1907.
WATSON, John William, M.D. From 45th F., Surg. 63rd F. 25.9.1835, Staff 5.10.1841.
WATSON, William. Ens. 63rd F. 30.10.1779, N.T.A. 1782.
WAUCHOPE, John. Ens. 63rd F. 3.8.1785, Lieut. 30.6.1790, Capt. 20.3.1793, 19th F. 20.3.1793.
WEBB, Claud Francis. From Worcs. R., Capt. Manch. R. 1.1.1923.

WEBB, John. Ens. 63rd F. 24.6.1759, Lieut. 1.8.1760, 68th F. 18.7.1766.
WELMAN, Harvey Beauchamp. From Shrop. L.I., Maj. Manch. R. 16.9.1905, Lein. R. 8.7.1908.
WELTON, John. Ens. 63rd F. 28.2.1793, N.T.A. 1795.
WEMYSS, Alexander. Ens. 63rd F. 19.1.1785, Lieut. 21.9.1789, Capt. 2.12.1795, N.T.A. 1798.
WEMYSS, James. Maj. 63rd F. 10.8.1778, Brev. Lt.-Col. 22.8.1783, Lt.-Col. 20.9.1787, Died July 1789.
WEMYSS, William. Ens. 63rd F. 8.12.1784, N.T.A. 1786.
WENTWORTH, D'Arcey. From 73rd F., Capt 63rd F. 10.7.1828, Brev. Maj. 3.11.1837, H.P. 1.12.1837.
WESTON, Christopher. From 8th F., Lieut. 63rd F. 1.3.1758, Engineers 22.2.1760.
WESTON, Reginald Salter, C.M.G., O.B.E. 2/Lieut. Manch. R. 22.8.1888, Lieut. 17.1.1890, Capt. 2.9.1897, Adjt. 9.1.1900–22.9.1903, Maj. 23.9.1903, Ret. Lt.-Col. 19.12.1919.
WESTROPP, Henry Charles Edward. Lieut. Manch. R. 12.5.1883, Capt. 31.5.1890, Adjt. 18.4.1892–17.4.1896, Maj. 15.12.1900, Lt.-Col. 6.10.1907, Ret. 24.2.1912.
WESTROPP, Michael Roberts. Lieut. 63rd F. 8.7.1767, Adjt. 29.10.1768, Capt. 3.5.1770, 1st Troop of Cork Vol. 31.10.1796.
WHEATSTONE, George James. From 22nd F., Lieut. 63rd F. 8.6.1838, Died at Sea 8.1.1839.
WHEELER, Luke Camden. From 27th F., Ens. 63rd F. 25.4.1868, Ret. 1.10.1870.
WHITE, Benjamin. Ens. 96th F. 19.9.1834, Lieut. 28th F. 18.8.1838.
WHITE, Charles. Ens. 63rd F. 14.3.1789, Lieut. 31.1.1794, Capt. 7.7.1795, 22nd F. 7.7.1795.
WHITE, George. Ens. 63rd F. 30.4.1794, N.T.A. 1799.
WHITE, Henry. Ens. 63rd F. 20.9.1844, Lieut. 31.7.1846, H.P. 29.8.1847.
WHITE, Henry. From H.P. 24th F., Maj. 96th F. 27.5.1824, Brev. Lt.-Col. 22.7.1830, Lt.-Col. 9.3.1834, Ret. 19.3.1834.
WHITE, Warren. Ens. 63rd F. 30.5.1800, Lieut. 30.10.1801, 8th Drgns. 31.12.1803.
WHITEHEAD, Edwin Preston, M.C. 2/Lieut. Manch. R. 26.1.1916, Lieut. 20.7.1917, Res. 4.11.1919.
WHITESIDE, John. From 22nd F., Lieut. 96th F. 18.8.1848, Capt. 11.3.1856, 8th F. 3.3.1857.
WHITMORE, Hugh Frederick. 2/Lieut. Manch. R. 7.5.1916, Lieut. 7.11.1917.
WHITTALL, Charles John Sherer. From 28th F. Ens. 63rd F. 14.9.1870, Lieut. 28.10.1871, Ben. S.C. 19.10.1878.
WHITTY, John. Ens. 96th F. 15.10.1852, Lieut. 16.10.1853, Capt. 23.4.1866, Ret. 14.2.1874.

WHYTE, Colin Campbell, M.B.E. 2/Lieut. Manch. R. 25.6.1916, Lieut. 25.12.1917.
WHYTE, Daniel. Qr.-Mr. and Hon. Lieut. 63rd F. 28.3.1879, Hon. Capt. 23.3.1889, Ret. 18.3.1890.
WICKENS, William Henry. Ens. 63rd F. 1.5.1867, Lieut. 1.2.1868, Ret. 15.7.1873.
WICKHAM, Thomas Strange, D.S.O. 2/Lieut. Manch. R. 14.9.1901, Lieut. 12.11.1902, K. in A. 25.8.1914 at Tepe in W. Africa.
WICKHAM, William James Richard. From 103rd F., 2/Lieut. 63rd F. 27.9.1879, Lieut. 1.7.1881, Ind. S.C. 30.11.1881.
WICKHAM, William Thomas Donald. 2/Lieut. Manch. R. 16.6.1915, Lieut. 18.1.1916, D. of W. 10.10.1918.
WIGLEY, George James. From 25th F., Lieut. 63rd F. 25.3.1810, H.P. 20.5.1819.
WILLCOCK, Stephen. From King's L'pool R., Maj. Manch. R. 11.12.1901, Ret. 18.8.1904.
WILLIAMS, Horatio Lloyd. From 12th F., Lieut. 96th F. 10.12.1858, Ret. 18.4.1859.
WILLIAMS, John. Ens. 63rd F. 1.3.1758, Died, W. Indies, 1759.
WILLIAMS, Montagu Stephen. Ens. 96th F. 14.3.1856, 41st F. 9.9.1856.
WILLIAMS, Valentine Albert. 2/Lieut. Manch. R. 20.5.1917, Res. 27.7.1919.
WILLIAMS-GREEN, William Thomas, M.C. 2/Lieut. Manch. R. 4.12.1915, Lieut. 1.1.1918.
WILLIAMSON, Hugh Albert. 2/Lieut. Manch. R. 4.10.1915, Died 2.7.1916.
WILLIAMSON, Thomas Paul. From 48th F., Capt. 63rd F. 12.1.1838, 93rd F. 26.6.1838.
WILLIAMSON, William Herbert. From K.O.S. Bord., Lieut. Manch. R. 20.6.1888, Capt. 28.7.1897, Ret. 10.5.1902.
WILLINGTON, James Arthur. 2/Lieut. Manch. R. 27.11.1895, W. Ind. R. 3.4.1897.
WILLIS, Robert Billopp. 2/Lieut. Manch. R. 19.5.1900, Lieut. 1.7.1901, Res. 7.6.1905.
WILLOUGHBY, Charles Stewart Percival. Ens. 96th F. 15.6.1866, Lieut. 23.10.1867, Capt. 26.8.1876, A. Pay Dept. 1.4.1878.
WILLSON, Selwyn. Ens. 96th F. 12.7.1839, Lieut. 9.4.1842, Ret. 25.11.1845.
WILMOT, Charles Octavius Eardley. Ens. 96th F. 29.5.1844, Lieut. 20.10.1846, Capt. 9.7.1852, 31st F. 26.11.1852.
WILSON, Aristos. From 20th F., 2/Lieut. 63rd F. 11.8.1880, Lieut. 1.7.1881, Ind. S.C. 3.3.1883.
WILSON, Edward. Lieut. 63rd F. 9.2.1808, Capt. 28.6.1810, 57th F. 6.1.1814.
WILSON, Frederick, M.C. 2/Lieut. Manch. R. 10.1.1917, K. in A., France, 25.10.1917.
WILSON, James, M.D. Asst. Surg. 96th F. 30.6.1825, 4th F. 21.12.1826.
WILSON, Joseph. Ens. 63rd F. 5.4.1810, N.T.A. 1811.
WILSON, Samuel. Ens. 63rd F. 7.9.1759, Lieut. 3.4.1761, 70th F. 8.7.1767.
WILSON, Stephen Henry K. From 85th F., Lieut. 96th F. 28.6.1864, Ret. 2.10.1866.
WILSON, Thomas Maitland. From H.P. 78th F., Capt. 96th F. 20.1.1832, Brev. Maj. 9.11.1846, Maj. 18.8.1848, Lt.-Col. 15.6.1849, Brev. Col. 28.11.1854, H.P. 4.4.1856, Col. 63rd F. 22.8.1873, 96th F. 15.10.1877.
WILSON, William. From 48th F., Capt. 63rd F. 16.4.1829, Died, Fort St. George, Madras, 23.6.1836.
WINGROVE, George Frederick. 2/Lieut. Manch. R. 13.7.1916, K. in A., France, 15.7.1916.
WINTER, Noel Norcott. From 13th F., Lieut. 96th F. 27.6.1874, Capt. 6.12.1879, H.P. 22.12.1880.
WITHERINGTON, Henry. Lieut. 63rd F., 1.12.1808, Died at Deal 1809.
WOOD, Adam Alexander. From York. L. Inf. Vols., Lieut. 63rd F. 1.6.1808, Capt. 4.3.1813, 60th F. 4.3.1813.
WOOD, Cuthbert William. From R. Garr. Bn., Lieut. Manch. R. 8.7.1905, Died 27.2.1912.
WOOD, Harry, M.C. From Rifle Bde., Capt. Manch. R. 27.2.1923.
WOOD, William. Ens. 63rd F. 12.5.1808, Died 1811.
WOOD, William. From H.P. 40th F., Lieut. 96th F. 18.1.1818, N.T.A. June 1819.
WOODHOUSE, Henry Geo. Wilkinson. 2/Lieut. Manch. R. 18.4.1900, D. of W. rec. at Vrede, S. Africa, 9.11.1900.
WOODYATT, George. Ens. 63rd F. 26.1.1844, Lieut. 18.4.1845, Ret. 5.10.1847.
WOOLDRIDGE, Thomas. Ens. 63rd F. 2.8.1760, Lieut. 29.4.1762, H.P. 1763.
WOOTTON, Henry. From H.P. 25th F., Lieut. 63rd F. 8.6.1826, 44th F. 2.11.1826.
WRAY, Jackson W. A. Ens. 96th F. 10.6.1826, Lieut. 14.2.1828, Capt. 4.3.1836, Ret. 14.9.1838.
WRIGHT, Bache Allen, D.S.O. 2/Lieut. Manch. R. 28.9.1895, Lieut. 13.1.1897, Capt. 27.12.1899, Adjt. 6.5.1905–15.7.1907, Maj. 24.2.1912, Lt.-Col. 22.8.1919, Ret. 5.11.1921.
WRIGHT, Charles Edward. Ens. 96th F. 27.11.1857, Lieut. 15.11.1859, Capt. 8.7.1862, Ret. Maj. 30.3.1876.
WRIGHT, Henry Thomas Richard Somerset. 2/Lieut. Manch. R. 2.5.1903, Lieut. 26.8.1907, Capt. 11.12.1914, K. in A., Egypt, 21.12.1916.
WRIGHT, John. Asst. Surg. 63rd F. 23.6.1804, Surg. 8.9.1808, H.P. Nov. 1814.
WRIGHT, John. Ens. 63rd F. 10.1.1760, N.T.A. 1760.
WRIGHT, William. Ens. 63rd F. 2.8.1780, Lieut. 3.8.1785, 1st F. 27.10.1786.
WRIXON, Henry. Ens. 63rd F. 5.3.1775, K. in A., Fort Clinton, N. America, 6.10.1777.
WYAT, James. From 8th F., Lieut. 63rd F. 7.9.1757, N.T.A. 1765.
WYBERG, Archibald. Ens. 63rd F. 13.5.1853, Lieut. 6.11.1854, Capt. 21.9.1855, Maj. 27.2.1866, Ret. 6.7.1870.
WYMER, George Petre, D.C.M. 2/Lieut. Manch. R. 5.5.1900, Lieut. 6.5.1901, Capt. 1.4.1909, Maj. 1.9.1915.

WYNNE, Foillet. From 20th L. Drgns., Lieut. 63rd F. 24.12.1812, Died, Antigua, W. Indies, 27.9.1815.
WYNNE, John. Capt. 63rd F. 3.8.1804, Brev. Maj. 4.6.1814, Ret. 18.11.1819.
WYNNE, Thomas William, M.M. 2/Lieut. Manch. R. 8.12.1917, Lieut. 8.6.1919, Res. 13.7.1920.
WYNTER, Arthur Leycester. From 101st F., Capt. 96th F. 17.1.1877, Maj. 1.7.1881, K.O.S. Bord. 10.1.1883.

YARKER, Arnold Francis. Ens. 63rd F. 12.1.1866, Lieut. 14.8.1867, Ret. 9.2.1870.
YATES, William Grandage. 2/Lieut. Manch. R. 24.10.1915, K. in A., Mesopotamia, 9.1.1917.
YEAMAN, James. Ens. 63rd F. 5.10.1807 N.T.A. 1809.

YOUNG, ——. From 110th F., Lieut. 63rd F. 6.9.1795, N.T.A. 1797.
YOUNG, Aretas Sutherland. From 83rd F., Capt. 63rd F. 25.12.1835, Died 22.8.1836.
YOUNG, Colin, M.D. Surg. 63rd F. 15.10.1807-27.4.1808.
YOUNG, Joseph. Asst. Surg. 63rd F. 10.10.1805, Died 1811.
YOUNG, Keith. From H.P. 16th Garr. Bn., Lt.-Col. 63rd F. 8.11.1810, Ret. Dec. 1811.
YOUNG, Montague Sheridan. 2/Lieut. Manch. R. 22.3.1903, Ind. Army 3.6.1906.
YOUNG, W. G. 2/Lieut. Manch. R. 34.4.1902, Res. 12.9.1903.

ZELLER, Henry. Paymr. 63rd F. 8.12.1808, Died, Martinique, W. Indies, 14.9.1810.

APPENDIX VI

DECORATIONS AND HONOURS ROLLS 63RD FOOT, 96TH FOOT, AND 1ST AND 2ND BATTALIONS THE MANCHESTER REGIMENT

Compiled by LT.-COL. H. L. JAMES, C.B., *late commanding 2nd Battalion;* and LT.-COL. D. A. HAILES, R.M.L.I.

VICTORIA CROSS.

RIDGEWAY, Richard Kirby, Capt., Bengal Staff Corps, *London Gazette*, 11 May 1880.

For conspicuous gallantry throughout the attack on Konoma, on the 22 Nov. 1879, more especially in the final assault, when, under a heavy fire from the enemy, he rushed up to a barricade and attempted to tear down the planking surrounding it, to enable him to effect an entrance, in which act he received a very severe rifle shot wound in the left shoulder.

SCOTT, R., and PITTS, J., Ptes., 1st Bn., *London Gazette*, 26 July 1901.

During the attack on Cæsar's Camp, in Natal, on the 6 Jan. 1900, these two men occupied a sangar, on the left of which all our men had been shot down and their positions occupied by Boers, and held their post for fifteen hours without food or water, all the time under an extremely heavy fire, keeping up their fire and a smart look-out though the Boers occupied some sangars on their immediate left rear.

Private Scott was wounded.

LEACH, James, 2/Lieut., 2nd Bn., and HOGAN, John, Sergt., No. 9016, 2nd Bn., 22 Dec. 1914.

For conspicuous bravery near Festubert on the 29 Oct. 1914, when after their trench had been taken by the Germans, and after two attempts at recapture had failed, they voluntarily decided on the afternoon of the same day to recover the trench themselves, and working from traverse to traverse at close quarters with great bravery, they gradually succeeded in regaining possession, killing eight of the enemy, wounding two, and making sixteen prisoners.

SMITH, Issy, A/Corpl., No. 168, 1st Bn., 23 Aug. 1915.

For most conspicuous bravery on the 26 Apr. 1915, near Ypres, when he left his company on his own initiative, and went well forward to the enemy's position to assist a severely wounded man, whom he carried a distance of 250 yards into safety, whilst exposed the whole time to heavy machine-gun and rifle fire.

Subsequently Corporal Smith displayed great gallantry, when the casualties were very heavy, in voluntarily assisting to bring in many more wounded men throughout the day and attending to them with the greatest devotion to duty regardless of personal risk.

Also received Russian Order of St. George (4th Class) 25 Aug. 1915.

FORSHAW, William Thomas, Lieut., 1/9th Bn., 9 Sept. 1915.

For most conspicuous bravery and determination in the Gallipoli Peninsula from the 7 to 9 Aug. 1915.

When holding the north-west corner of the "Vineyard" he was attacked and heavily bombed by Turks, who advanced time after time by three trenches, which converged at this point, but he held his own, not only directing his men, and encouraging them by exposing himself with the utmost disregard of danger, but personally throwing bombs continuously for 41 hours. When his detachment was relieved after 24 hours, he volunteered to continue the direction of the operations.

Three times during the night of the 8-9 Aug. he was again heavily attacked, and once the Turks got over the barricade, but after shooting three with his revolver, he led his men forward and recaptured it.

When he rejoined his battalion he was choked and sickened by bomb fumes, badly bruised by a fragment of shrapnel, and could barely lift his arm from continuous bomb-throwing.

It was due to his personal example, magnificent courage, and endurance that this important corner was held.

STRINGER, George, Pte., No. 15818, 1st Bn., 5 Aug. 1916.

For most conspicuous bravery and determination at Es Sinn, Mesopotamia, 8 Mar. 1916. After the capture of an enemy position he was posted on the extreme right of his battalion to

COL. R. K. RIDGEWAY, V.C., C.B., INDIAN ARMY, FORMERLY 96TH FOOT.

R.Q.M.S. SCOTT, V.C., 1ST BN.

PTE. J. PITTS, V.C., 1ST BN.

2/LIEUT. J. LEACH, V.C., 2ND BN.

guard against any hostile attack. His battalion was subsequently forced back by an enemy counter-attack, but Private Stringer held his ground single-handed and kept back the enemy till all his grenades were expended.

His very gallant stand saved the flank of the battalion and rendered a steady withdrawal possible.

Also received Serbian Gold Medal, 27 Aug. 1917.

COVERDALE, Harry, Sergt., No. 4926, 11th Bn., 18 Dec. 1917.

For most conspicuous bravery in attack on enemy strong points south-west of Poelcapelle, France, on the 4 Oct. 1917. He showed the utmost gallantry in approaching his objective, and when close to it disposed of an enemy officer and two men who were sniping our flank, killing the officer, and taking the two men prisoners. He then rushed two machine-guns, killing or wounding the teams. He subsequently reorganised his platoon in order to capture another position, but after getting within a hundred yards of it, he was held up by our own barrage, and was obliged to return, having sustained nine casualties.

Later, this gallant non-commissioned officer again went out with five men to capture the position, and when he had gone some distance he saw a considerable number of the enemy advancing. He thereupon withdrew his detachment man by man, he himself being the last to retire, when he was able to report that the enemy was forming for a counter-attack.

By his gallant leadership and utter disregard of danger throughout the attack he set a splendid example of fearlessness to his men, and inspired all with a spirit of emulation which undoubtedly contributed largely to the success of the operations.

Also received Military Medal 2 Nov. 1917.

He subsequently was promoted to Second Lieutenant.

MILLS, Walter, Pte., No. 375499, 1/10th Bn., 13 Feb. 1918.

For most conspicuous bravery and self-sacrifice at Givenchy, France, on the 10–11 Dec. 1917.

When after an intense gas attack a strong enemy patrol endeavoured to rush our posts, the garrisons of which had been overcome, and though badly gassed himself, he met the attack single-handed and continued to throw bombs until the arrival of reinforcements, and remained at his post until the enemy's attacks had been finally driven off.

While being carried away he died from gas poisoning. It was solely due to his exertions, when his only chance of personal safety lay in remaining motionless, that the enemy was defeated, and the line remained intact.

KIRK, James, 2/Lieut., 6th, 10th, and (attached) 2nd Bn., 6 Jan. 1919.

For most conspicuous bravery and devotion to duty, north of Ors, on the 4 Nov. 1918, whilst attempting to bridge Oise Canal.

To cover the bridging of the canal he took a Lewis gun, and under intense machine-gun fire, he paddled across the canal on a raft, and at a range of ten yards expended all his ammunition. Further ammunition was paddled across to him, and he continuously maintained covering fire for the bridging party from a most exposed position till killed at his gun.

The supreme contempt of danger and magnificent self-sacrifice displayed by this gallant officer prevented many casualties, and enabled two platoons to cross the bridge before it was destroyed.

WILKINSON, Alfred, Pte., No. 43839, 1/5th Bn., 6 Jan. 1919.

For most conspicuous bravery and devotion to duty on 20 Oct. 1918 during the attack on Marou, when four runners in succession having been killed in an endeavour to deliver a message to the supporting company, Private Wilkinson volunteered for the duty. He succeeded in delivering the message, though the journey involved exposure to heavy machine-gun and shell fire for 600 yards.

He showed magnificent courage and complete indifference to danger, thinking only of the needs of his company and entirely disregarding any consideration for personal safety. Throughout the remainder of the day Private Wilkinson continued to do splendid work.

ELSTOB, Wilfrith, Temp. Lt.-Col., 16th Bn., 9 June 1919.

For most conspicuous bravery, devotion to duty, and self-sacrifice at Manchester Redoubt, near St. Quentin, on the 21 Mar. 1918.

During the preliminary bombardment he encouraged his men in the posts in the Redoubt, by frequent visits, and when repeated attacks developed, controlled the defence at the points threatened, giving personal support, with revolver, rifle, and bombs. Single-handed he repulsed one bombing assault, driving back the enemy and inflicting severe casualties.

Later, when ammunition was required, he made several journeys under severe fire, in order to replenish the supply.

Throughout the day Lt.-Col. Elstob, although twice wounded, showed the most fearless disregard of his own safety, and by his encouragement and noble example inspired his command to the fullest degree.

The Manchester Redoubt was surrounded in the first wave of the enemy attack, but by means of the buried cable Lt.-Col. Elstob was able to assure his Brigade Commander " that the Manchester Regiment will defend Manchester Hill to the last."

Some time after the post was overcome by

vastly superior forces, and this very gallant officer was killed in the final assault, having maintained to the end the duty which he impressed on his men, namely: "Here we fight and here we die."

He set throughout the highest example of valour, determination, endurance, and fine soldierly bearing.

Also received Military Cross, 1 Jan. 1917, and D.S.O., 1 Jan. 1918.

EVANS, George, Co. Sergt.-Maj., No. 10947, 18th Bn., 30 Jan. 1920.

For most conspicuous bravery and devotion to duty during the attack at Guillemont on the 30 July 1916, when under heavy rifle and machine-gun fire he volunteered to take back an important message after five runners had been killed in attempting to do so. He had to cover about 700 yards, the whole of which was under observation from the enemy.

Co. Sergt.-Maj. Evans, however, succeeded in delivering the message, and although wounded, rejoined his company, although advised to go to the dressing station.

The return journey to the company again meant a journey of 700 yards under severe rifle and machine-gun fire, but by dodging from shell-hole to shell-hole he was able to do so, and was taken prisoner some hours later.

On previous occasions at Montauban and Trones Wood this gallant warrant officer displayed great bravery and devotion to duty, and has always been a splendid example to his men.

HENDERSON, George Stuart, Capt., 2nd Bn., 29 Oct. 1920.

For most conspicuous bravery and self-sacrifice.

On the evening of the 24 July 1920, when about fifteen miles from Hillah (Mesopotamia), the company under his command was ordered to retire. After proceeding about 500 yards a large party of Arabs suddenly opened fire from the flank, causing the company to split up and waver. Regardless of all danger, Capt. Henderson at once reorganised the company, led them gallantly to the attack, and drove off the enemy.

On two further occasions this officer led his men to charge the Arabs with the bayonet and forced them to retire.

At one time when the situation was extremely critical and the troops and transport were getting out of hand, Capt. Henderson, by sheer pluck and coolness, steadied his command, prevented the company from being cut up, and saved the situation.

During the second charge he fell wounded, but refused to leave his command, and just as the company reached the trench they were making for, he was again wounded. Realising that he could do no more, he asked one of the N.C.O.'s to hold him up on the embankment, saying: "I'm done now, don't let them beat you." He died fighting.

Posthumous award, killed in action, 24 July 1920.

Also received M.C. (in 1st Bn.), 3 July 1915, and D.S.O., 31 May 1916, bar 3 June 1917.

63RD FOOT

CRIMEAN HONOURS

FRANCE

Legion of Honour

HARRIES, Thomas, Lt.-Col., 5th Class, 2 Mar. 1858.
CARTER, William Frederick, Maj., 5th Class, 2 Mar. 1858.
ELLIOT, Hawthorne Christopher, 2616, Sergt., 5th Class, 2 Mar. 1858.
McGOWAN, John, 3201, Pte., 5th Class, 2 Mar. 1858.

Médaille Militaire

AHERIN, William, 1304, Sergt., 2 Mar. 1858.
BROPHY, John, 1423, Col.-Sergt., 2 Mar. 1858.
HUGHES, Robert, 1560, S.M., 2 Mar. 1858.
McGOWAN, John, 3201, Pte., 2 Mar. 1858.
MORRIS, William, 1200, Col.-Sergt., 2 Mar. 1858.
ROBERTS, Arthur, 2719, Sergt., 2 Mar. 1858.
SULLIVAN, Daniel, 2307, Pte., 2 Mar. 1858.
WARD, James, 2266, Col.-Sergt., 2 Mar. 1858.

SARDINIA

"Al Valore" Medal

DALZELL, Robert Alexander George, the Hon., C.B., Lt.-Col., 2 Mar. 1858.
FAIRTLOUGH, Charles Edward, Lt.-Col., 2 Mar. 1858.
PATERSON, Falkland Logan Townshend, Capt., 2 Mar. 1858.
CEATON, P., 3404, Pte., 2 Mar. 1858.

TURKEY

Imperial Order of the Medjidie

DALZELL, Robert Alexander George, the Hon., C.B., Lt.-Col., 5th Class, 2 Mar. 1858.
FAIRTLOUGH, Charles Edward, Lt.-Col., 5th Class, 2 Mar. 1858.
HARRIES, Thomas, Brev. Lt.-Col., 5th Class, 2 Mar. 1858.
CARTER, William Frederick, Maj., 5th Class, 2 Mar. 1858.

SERGT. J. HOGAN, V.C., 2ND BN.

A/CORPL. ISSY SMITH, V.C., 1ST BN.

LIEUT. W. T. FORSHAW, V.C., 1/9TH BN.

PTE. G. STRINGER, V.C., 1ST BN.

DECORATIONS AND HONOURS ROLLS

PATERSON, Falkland Logan Townshend, Capt., 5th Class, 2 Mar. 1858.
MAGNAY, Christopher James, Capt., 5th Class, 2 Mar. 1858.
BOWLES, Vere Hunt, Capt., 5th Class, 2 Mar. 1858.
WYBERGH, Archibald, Capt., 5th Class, 2 Mar. 1858.
SLACK, James, Ens., 5th Class, 2 Mar. 1858.

SOUTH AND WEST AFRICA (1899-1902) HONOURS

1ST BATTALION

Victoria Cross

PITTS, J., 4858, Pte., Cæsar's Camp, 6 Jan. 1900, 26 July 1901.
SCOTT, R., 4535, Pte., Cæsar's Camp, 6 Jan. 1900, 26 July 1901.

Distinguished Service Order

BRIDGFORD, Robert James, Capt., 19 April 1901.
FISHER, Harold, Lieut., 27 Sept. 1901.
HARDCASTLE, Richard Newman, Lieut., 27 Sept. 1901.
MARDEN, Arthur William, Maj., 31 Oct. 1901.
NEWBIGGING, William Patrick Eric, Capt., 27 Sept. 1901.
SHUTER, Reginald Gauntlett, Capt., 31 Oct. 1901.
PETRIE, Charles Louis Rowe, Maj., 25 April 1902.

Distinguished Conduct Medal

BATEMAN, T., 4629, Pte., 27 Sept. 1901.
BELL, M., 4107, Pte., 27 Sept. 1901.
BROOKS, A., 3635, Sergt. (Mounted Infantry), 27 Sept. 1901.
CARTER, D. A., 4120, Sergt., 31 Oct. 1902.
CUMMINGS, J., 4708, Pte., 19 Apr. 1901.
FINNEY, J. W., 3154, Col.-Sergt., 31 Oct. 1902.
GRANT, E., 4839, Sergt., 27 Sept. 1901.
GRESTY, M. J., 4620, Sergt., 27 Sept. 1901.
FORSHAW, T., 5297, Pte., 19 April 1901.
HADDON, J. T., 2261, Sergt.-Major, 27 Sept. 1901.
HARRIS, J., 3344, L/Cpl., 27 Sept. 1901.
LADLEY, J., 5106, Pte., 19 April 1901.
LLOYD, R., 2699, Sergt., 19 April 1901.
MCKINLAY, C., 1908, Pte., 19 April 1901.
NEWTON, E. F., 4824, Pte., 27 Sept. 1901.
PRESTON, W. J., 4429, L/Cpl., 27 Sept. 1901.
SCOTT, J., 449, Col.-Sergt., 27 Sept. 1901.

2ND BATTALION

Commander of the Bath

REAY, Charles Tom, Lt.-Col., 27 Sept. 1901.

Distinguished Service Order

AGNEW, Quentin Graham Kinnaird, Maj., 26 June 1901.
JEBB, Joshua Henry Miles, Capt., 27 Sept. 1901.
COOPER-KING, George Courtenay, Capt., 27 Sept. 1901.
HASTINGS, Wilfred Charles Norrington, Capt., 31 Oct. 1902.
TOOGOOD, Cecil, Capt., 19 April 1901.
WRIGHT, Bache Allen, Capt., 26 April 1901.
GORGES, Edmund Howard, C.B., C.B.E., Maj., Turkana Punitive Expedition, 25 April 1902.

Distinguished Conduct Medal

ARCHIBALD, J. W., 3293, Pte., 27 Sept. 1901.
COLLIER, E., 668, Pte., 27 Sept. 1901.
KENNEDY, S. E., 2479, Col. Sergt., 27 Sept. 1901.
MORRIS, J., 4073, Sergt., 31 Oct. 1902.
PROSSER, G. T., 1173, Sergt.-Major, 27 Sept. 1901.
WALKER, F., 2562, Col.-Sergt., 27 Sept. 1901.

3RD BATTALION (LINE)

BARTON, J., 2908, Sergt. (Mounted Infantry), 27 Sept. 1901.

4TH BATTALION (LINE)

HALT, J., 2673, Sergt., 31 Oct. 1902.

5TH BATTALION (MILITIA)

FAGAN, F., Sergt., 31 Oct. 1902.

THE MOST HONOURABLE ORDER OF THE BATH

Knight Commander

FANE, Vere Bonamy, Lt.-Gen. Indian Army, Col. of The Manchester Regt., 1 Jan. 1921.
Other Honours: C.B. 1 Jan. 1914, C.I.E. 29 Oct. 1915, K.C.I.E. 24 April 1918, Croix-de-guerre (France) 26 Sept. 1917, Egyptian Order of the Nile (2nd Class) 26 Nov. 1919.

GELLIBRAND, John, Maj.-Gen. Australian Forces (Capt. Reserve of Officers), 9 June 1919.
Other Honours: C.B. 4 June 1917, D.S.O. 2 May 1916, Bar to D.S.O. 18 June 1917, Legion of Honour (Officer) 29 Jan. 1919, Croix-de-guerre (France) 21 Aug. 1919, American Distinguished Medal 12 July 1919.

PHILLIPPS, Ivor, Maj.-Gen. late Indian Army (Civil), 4 June 1917.
Other Honours: D.S.O. 25 July 1901.

STRICKLAND, Edward Peter, Maj.-Gen., 9 June 1919.
Other Honours: C.B. 1 Jan. 1917, C.M.G. 3 June 1913, D.S.O. 1899 (in Norfolk Regt.), Belgian Order of Leopold (Commandeur) and Croix-de-guerre 5 April 1919, Croix-de-guerre (France) 5 Nov. 1920.

Companion

GORGES, Edmund Howard, Lt.-Col. and Brev. Col. W. African Regt. 18 June 1915.
Other Honours: D.S.O. 25 April 1902, C.B.E. 3 June 1919, Legion of Honour (Officer) 22 Aug. 1917.

GWATKIN, Willoughby Garnons, Maj.-Gen. Canadian Army (Civil), 1 Jan. 1916.
Other Honours: C.M.G. 3rd June 1918, K.C.M.G. 7 Jan. 1920, St. Sava (2nd Class, Serbia) 9 Sept. 1918.

JAMES, Herbert Lionel, Lt.-Col. 18 Feb. 1915.

NEWBIGGING, William Patrick Eric, Lt.-Col. and Brev. Col. 1 Jan. 1919.
Other Honours: D.S.O. 27 Sept. 1901, C.M.G. 1 Jan. 1917, Croix-de-guerre (France) 5 Nov. 1920.

WATSON, John Edward, Brig.-Gen. 19 Jan. 1911.

THE MOST DISTINGUISHED ORDER OF SAINT MICHAEL AND SAINT GEORGE

Knight Commander

GWATKIN, Willoughby Garnons, Maj.-Gen. Canadian Army, 7 Jan. 1920.
Other Honours: C.B. (Civil) 1 Jan. 1916, C.M.G. 3 June 1918, St. Sava (2nd Class, Serbia) 10 Sept. 1918.

Companion

ANLEY, Barnett Dyer Lemprière Gray, Maj. and Brev. Lt.-Col., 4 June 1917.
Other Honours: D.S.O., Legion of Honour (Chevalier) (France) 14 July 1917.

EVANS, Wilfred Keith, Maj. and Brev. Lt.-Col. (T/Brig. Gen.), 1 Jan. 1919.
Other Honours: D.S.O. 18 Feb. 1915, Bar. 16 Aug. 1917, Legion of Honour (Officer) (France) 14 July 1919.

NEWBIGGING, William Patrick Eric, Lt.-Col. and Brev. Col., 1 Jan. 1917.
Other Honours: C.B. 1 Jan. 1919, D.S.O. 1901, Croix-de-guerre (France) 5 Nov. 1920.

VAUGHAN, Edward, Lt.-Col. (T/Brig. Gen.), 3 June 1919.
Other Honours: D.S.O. 4 June 1917, Croix-de-guerre (Belgium) 4 Sept. 1919, Legion of Honour (Chevalier) (France) 21 Aug. 1919.

WESTON, Reginald Salter, Maj., 23 June 1915.
Other Honours: O.B.E. (Officer) 3 June 1919.

THE MOST DISTINGUISHED ORDER OF THE BRITISH EMPIRE

ALBRECHT, Vaudrey Adolph, Capt. (A/Maj.), attd. Royal Flying Corps (Officer), 3 June 1919.
Other Honours: M.C. 1 Jan. 1916.

BOLTON, Charles Arthur, Lt.-Col. (Commander), 3 June 1919.
Other Honours: Order of the Nile (3rd Class) (Egypt), 16 Jan. 1920, Order of the Redeemer (Commander) (Greece), 24 Oct. 1919.

CAREY, Geoffrey Newman, Lieut. (Member), 1 Jan. 1919.

CONNERY, William Lawrence, Capt. (Member), 3 June 1919.

GORGES, Edmund Howard, Lt.-Col. and Brev. Col. W. African Regt. (Commander), 3 June 1919.
Other Honours: C.B. 18 June 1915, D.S.O. 25 April 1902, Legion of Honour (Officer) 22 Aug. 1917.

HOPKINS, Raymond Beechey, Capt. Reserve of Officers (Officer), 18 Nov. 1918.

HORNER, Harry, Lieut. (A/Capt.) (Member), 12 Dec. 1919.

KEITLEY, Cyril Humby, Lieut. (A/Capt.) (Member), 3 June 1919.

PAULSON, Peter Zacharias, Capt. (Officer), 9 Sept. 1921.

PRIOLEAU, Lynch Hamilton, Maj. (Member), 3 June 1919.

THORNYCROFT, Charles Mytton, Lt.-Col. (Commander), 3 June 1919.
Other Honours: D.S.O. 14 Jan. 1919.

VIZARD, Robert Davenport, Brig.-Gen. (Commander), 12 Dec. 1919.

WESTON, Reginald Salter, Maj. (T/Lt.-Col.), (Officer), 3 June 1919.
Other Honours: C.M.G. 23 June 1915.

SERGT. H. COVERDALE, V.C., 11TH BN.
Subsequently 2/Lieut.

PTE. W. MILLS, V.C., 1/10TH BN.
(Killed in Action.)

2/LIEUT. J. KIRK, V.C., 6TH, 10TH, AND ATTACHED 2ND BN.

L/CPL. A. WILKINSON, V.C., 1/5TH BN.

DECORATIONS AND HONOURS ROLLS

DISTINGUISHED SERVICE ORDER

1st BATTALION

ATKIN, Benjamin George, M.C., Capt. (T/Maj.), attd. 22nd Bn., Vazzola, 28–29 Oct. 1918, 2 April and 10 Dec. 1919.
BROWN, Robert Geoffrey, Maj. (Capt. and Brev. Lt.-Col.), 29 Aug. 1918 (to date 3 June 1918), Died 1 Nov. 1918.
BRYAN, Herbert, C.M.G. (1906) (T/Lt.-Col.), attd. Labour Corps, 1 Jan. 1918.
HENDERSON, George Stuart, V.C., M.C., Lieut. (T/Capt.), 31 May, 1916; Bar, Mesopotamia, 25 Aug. 1917 (to date 3 June 1917), K. in A. 24 July 1920.
MAIR, Brodie Valentine, M.C., Capt., 26 Sept. 1917 and 9 Jan. 1918.
MUSSON, Edward Lionel, M.C., Capt. (T/Lt.-Col.), 1 Jan. 1918.
PARMINTER, Reginald Horace Roger, M.C., Capt., Mesopotamia, 25 Aug. 1917.

2ND BATTALION

ANDERSON, Charles Abbot, Maj. (A/Lt.-Col.), 1 Jan. 1918.
DORLING, Francis Holland, Maj., 1 Jan. 1918.
ERSKINE, John David Beveridge, Maj.(T/Lt.-Col.), Reserve of Officers, attd. 13th Bn., 3 June 1918.
EVANS, Wilfred Keith, C M.G., Maj. (T/Lt.-Col.), 18 Feb. 1915; Bar, 16 Aug. 1917.
FOORD, Alexander Gunning, Capt., 27 Oct. 1917 and 18 Mar. 1918.
FORTH, Nowell Barnet de Lancy, M.C., Nile (3rd Class), Maj. (A/Lt.-Col.), attd. Egyptian Army, 1 Jan. 1918; Bar, 26 Mar. 1918.
FREEMAN, Wilfred Rhodes, M.C., Chevalier Legion of Honour (France), Capt. (T/Lt.-Col.), and R.F.C., 23 Nov. 1916.
KAY, William, M.C., 2/Lieut. (A/Capt.), 3rd Bn., attd. 2nd Bn., Oise-Sambre Canal, 4 Nov. 1918, 2 April and 10 Dec. 1919.
MURPHY, Joseph Leo, Maj., Fonsomme and Beaurevoir line, 1 Oct. 1918, 15 Feb. and 30 July 1919; Bar, Oise-Sambre Canal, 4 Nov. 1918, 2 April and 10 Dec. 1919.
THOMAS, Arthur Felix, Maj. (Att. Sig. Services), Egypt, 3 June 1918.
THORNYCROFT, Charles Mytton, Maj. (3rd Bn.), 14 Jan. 1916.
VAUGHAN, Edward, C.M.G., Croix-de-guerre (Belgium), Lt.-Col., 4 June 1917.
VICKERS, George Edward, Qr.-Mr. and Hon. Maj., 1 Jan. 1918.

MILITARY CROSS

1st BATTALION

ADAMS, Frank Henry, Lieut. (A/Capt.), Mesopotamia, 11 Jan. 1919.
BOSTOCK, Lionel Carrington, Capt., Egypt, 3 June 1919.
COLESHILL, William, 1015, C.S.M., D.C.M., Italian Bronze Medal for Valour, 25 Aug. 1916.
CROSSLEY, Edwin, T/2/Lieut. (attd. 20th Bn.), 2 Dec. 1918.
FINDLATER, Leslie, 2/Lieut. (3rd Bn.), Neuve Chapelle, 25 Sept. 1915, 29 Oct. 1915.
FINNEY, W., 3154, R.S.M., 23 June 1915 (to date 3 June 1915).
HEELIS, John Richardson, Capt., 23 June 1915 (to date 3 June 1915).
HENDERSON, George Stuart, V.C., D.S.O., Lieut., Ypres, 26 April 1915, 3 July 1915, K. in A. 24 July 1920.
HOLMES, Edward Barclay, Lieut., 11 Mar. and 17 April 1917.
KELSEY, James, 2/Lieut., 17 Dec. 1917.
LAWRENCE, John Davies, Lieut., 1 Mar. 1918.
MAIR, Brodie Valentine, D.S.O., Lieut., 20–21 Dec. 1914, 27 Mar. 1915.
MUSSON, Edward Lionel, D.S.O., Lieut. (attd. 4th (Uganda) Bn., K.A.R.), nr. Mbuvini, German E. Africa, 20 Dec. 1914, 18 Feb. 1915.
PAINTER, Henry Smith, T/Lieut. (attd. 20th Bn.), 2 Dec. 1918.
PARMINTER, Reginald Horace Roger, D.S.O., 2/Lieut., 27 Mar. 1915.
SHIPSTER, Walter Neville, Lieut. (T/Capt.), 14 Jan. 1916.
SYKES, Frank Clifford, Lieut. (T/Capt.), 24 Sept. 1918.

2ND BATTALION

ALBRECHT, Vaudrey Adolph, O.B.E., Lieut., 14 Jan. 1916 (to date 1 Jan. 1916).
ATKIN, Benjamin George, D.S.O., Lieut., 23 June 1915 (to date 3 June 1915).
BOWDEN, Alfred William, T/2/Lieut., 11 Jan. 1919.
BRADY, Sydney Vincent, 2/Lieut., 26 Sept. 1917 and 9 Jan. 1918.
BRITTOROUS, Francis, Lieut. (attd. 8th Bn. L. North Lancs.), 16 Sept. 1918.
BURROWS, Bertie, T/2/Lieut., Fonsomme line, 1–2 Oct. 1918, 15 Feb. and 30 July 1919.
CHILD, James Martin, 2/Lieut. (T/Capt.), Chevalier Order of Leopold and Croix-de-guerre (Belgium), and R.F.C., 4 Feb. and 15 July 1918, K. in A. 23 Aug. 1918.
COOPER, Frederick, T/2/Lieut., 26 July 1917.

FORTH, Nowell Barnet de Lancy, Capt., D.S.O., Nile (3rd Class) (attd. Egyptian Army), Nube Mountains, Sudan, Feb.–April 1914, 10 Mar. 1915.
FOULKES, John, T/2/Lieut., Fonsomme line, 1–2 Oct. 1918, 15 Feb. and 30 July 1919.
FREEMAN, Wilfred Rhodes, D.S.O., Chevalier Legion of Honour (France), Lieut., 27 Mar. 1915, 10 Mar. 1915.
GLOVER, Gerald Mahon, Capt., 26 May 1917, K. in A. 24 July 1920.
GWYTHER, Henry James, Lieut. (3rd Bn., attd. 2nd Bn.), 14 Jan. 1916 ; Bar, 16 Sept. 1918.
HARPER, James Stuart, Lieut., 1 Jan. 1915.
HASTEWELL, George, 5626, Sergt.-Major, 26 May 1917.
HAYWARD, Frank, 2/Lieut., 7 Nov. 1918 ; Bar, 11 Jan. 1919.
HOLLEY, Sidney Harry, Lieut. (A/Capt.), 3 June 1918.
IRWIN, Clinton Delacherois, Capt., 23 June 1915.
JOHNSON, Frederick, T/2/Lieut., Fonsomme line, 1–2 Oct. 1918, 15 Feb. and 30 July 1919.
KAY, William, D.S.O., 2/Lieut. (A/Capt.) (3rd Bn.), 22 April 1918 ; Bar, 11 Jan. 1919 ; 2nd Bar, Joncourt, 2 Oct. 1918, 15 Feb. and 30 July 1919.

MCKENZIE, Angus, Capt., 26 Sept. 1917 and 9 Jan. 1918 ; A/Maj., Bar, 7 Nov. 1918, K. in A. 4 Nov. 1918.
MUTTERS, Charles William, 1175, C.S.M., D.C.M., M.M. and Bar, Croix-de-guerre (Belgium), Fonsomme line, 1–2 Oct. 1918, 15 Feb. and 30 July 1919.
OLDFIELD, Albert Reginald, T/Lieut. (A/Capt.), 2 Dec. 1918 ; Bar, N. of Ors 4 Nov. 1918, 2 April and 10 Dec. 1918.
PEARSE, Denis Colbron, Lieut., N. of Ors 31 Oct.–5 Nov. 1918, 2 April and 10 Dec. 1918.
SCULLY, Arthur John, Lieut., Croix-de-guerre (France), 18 Feb. 1915.
SHEPPARD, Claud John Loraine, Lieut., Alexandrovna, N. Russia, 19 Aug. 1919, 21 Jan. 1920.
SIMPOLE, George Maiden, T/2/Lieut., N. of Ors 4 Nov. 1918, 2 April and 10 Dec. 1919.
SOMERVILLE, Hugh, T/Lieut., 16 Aug. 1917 ; Bar, T/Capt , 2 Dec. 1918.
TORRANCE, Kenneth Sanderson, Lieut. (T/Capt.), Croix-de-guerre (France), 1 Jan. 1919.
WHITEHEAD, Edwin Preston, Lieut. (T/Capt.), 26 Nov. 1917 and 6 April 1918.
WILLIAMSON, George W., 2/Lieut. (3rd Bn.), 18 Feb. 1915.

DISTINGUISHED CONDUCT MEDAL

1ST BATTALION

ARMES, C., 6152, Cpl., Egypt, Jiljulieh, 19 Sept. 1918, 17 April 1919 ; Kafr Thilth, 20 Sept. 1918, 25 Feb. 1920.
BATES, J., 1395, Sergt., Ypres, 29 April 1915, 5 Aug. 1915.
BATLEY, C. H., 1927, L/Cpl., 30 Mar. 1916.
BENSON, R., 824, L/Cpl., 14 Jan. 1916, 11 Mar. 1916.
BEVAN, G. T., 2244, L/Cpl., 14 Jan. 1916, 11 Mar. 1916.
CAIRNS, J. T., 9859, L/Cpl., 4 Oct. 1916.
COLESHILL, W., 1015, A/Sergt., M.C., Medal for Military Valour (Italy), Bronze, Neuve Chapelle, 27 Nov. 1914, 18 Feb. 1915, 1 April 1915.
CRAVEN, W., 1531, L/Cpl., 3 Mar. 1917.
CROOKS, F., 2363, L/Cpl., Neuve Chapelle, 27 Nov. 1914, 18 Feb. 1915, 1 April 1915.
CROSS, W., 9350, Pte., 4 Oct. 1916.
CURRIE, J., 1328, Pte., Neuve Chapelle, 12 Mar. 1915, 3 June 1915.
DAVIES, W., 2227, Pte., 26 Aug. 1917.
DELANEY, T., 1358, Sergt., 14 Nov. 1916.
DERVIN, J., 95, A/Cpl., Ypres, 26 April 1915, 5 Aug. 1915.
DEVONSHIRE, J., 8581, Sergt., Givenchy, 21 Dec. 1914, 10 Mar. 1915, 1 April 1915.
DUFFY, T., 899, Cpl., Order of St. George (3rd Class), Neuve Chapelle, 27 Nov. 1914, 18 Feb. 1915, 11 Mar. 1915 ; Sergt., Bar, 20 Oct. 1916.

EDWARDS, E. J., 2086, Pte., nr. Neuve Chapelle, 25 Sept. 1915, 16 Nov. 1915.
FLANNERY, M., 239, L/Cpl., Givenchy, 20–21 Dec. 1914, 10 Mar. 1915, 1 April 1915.
GAVINS, C. A., 1056, L/Cpl., Givenchy, 20–21 Dec. 1914, 10 Mar. 1915, 1 April 1915.
GLYNN, M., 2393, Pte., M.M., La Bassée Road, 19–20 Feb. 1915, 3 June 1915.
GOODSON, J., 5764, Q.M.S., M.S.M., 20 Oct. 1916.
HARLAND, H., 7280, C.S.M., Givenchy, 20 Dec. 1914, 10 Mar. 1915, 1 April 1915.
HEYWOOD, H., 7624, C.S.M., Givenchy, 21 Dec. 1914, 10 Mar. 1915, 1 April 1915.
HIGGINS, T., Pte., 2179, Neuve Chapelle, 12 Mar. 1915, 3 June 1915.
HUGHES, A. H., 31, C.S.M., M.M., Cross of St. George (Russia), 4th Class, Tekrit (Mesopotamia), 5 Nov. 1917, 16 Jan. 1919.
HUMPHRIES, C. F. G. (formerly 207 (A/Sergt.) A.S.C.), 14000, L/Cpl., Givenchy, 20–21 Dec. 1914, 10 Mar. 1915, 1 April 1915.
HUMPHREY, F. J., 1326, Sergt., Medal for Military Valour (Italy), Bronze, (A/C.Q.M.S.), 29 Aug. 1917.
JUDGES, N., 1498, L/Cpl., Tekrit (Mesopotamia), 5 Nov. 1917, 16 Jan. 1919.
KELLY, J., 101, Pte., Neuve Chapelle, 12 Mar. 1915, 3 June 1915.
LE CRAS, J., 1787, Cpl., La Bassée Road, 21 Feb. 1915, 3 June 1915.
MAGUIRE, E., 9005, C.S.M., Croix-de-guerre (France), 14 Jan. 1916, 11 Mar. 1916.

LT.-COL. W. ELSTOB, V.C., D.S.O., M.C.,
16TH BN. (Killed in Action.)

C.S.M. G. EVANS, V.C., 18TH BN.

CAPT. G. S. HENDERSON, V.C., D.S.O., M.C.,
2ND BN. (Killed in Action.)

DECORATIONS AND HONOURS ROLLS

MAGUIRE, J., 8224, L/Sergt., 30 Mar. 1916.
MARTIN, J., 1118, Sergt., 14 Jan. 1916, 11 Mar. 1916.
METCALFE, A. A., 2016, Pte., Cuinchy, 11–13 Dec. 1914, 18 Feb. 1915, 1 April 1915.
MITCHELL, J., 906, Pte., Neuve Chapelle, 27 Nov. 1914, 18 Feb. 1915, 1 April 1915.
MULLINGER, A., L/Cpl., 1448, 20 Oct. 1916.
NOON, E., 21054, C.Q.M.S., Sept. 1918 particularly, Azzim 20 Sept. 1918, 3 June 1919, 11 Mar. 1920.
O'BRIEN, C., 2047, Cpl., 20 Oct. 1916.
RANKIN, A. V., 2043, Pte., 29 Aug. 1917.
RICHARDSON, F., 1228, Pte., Ypres, 28 April 1915, 5 Aug. 1915.
RYDER, W., 1041, Cpl., M.M., Kut-el-Amara, 9 Jan. 1916, 20 Oct. 1916.
SMITH, F., 2085, Cpl., 20 Oct. 1916.
SMITH, H., 5919, C.S.M., General Work, 17 April 1917.
SUMMERS, A. (attd. Lahore Sig. Co.), 2087, Pte., Neuve Chapelle, 11–12 Mar. 1915, 3 June 1915; Bar, 20 Oct. 1916.
TELLING, W. A., 1874, Sergt., 24 June, 1916.
THIRLWELL, R., 1505, L/Cpl., 20 Oct. 1916.
TIERNEY, P., 1266, L/Cpl., 30 Mar. 1916.
WHITMORE, H., 5254, C.S.M., Croix-de-guerre (France), 20 Oct. 1916.
WILBURN, F., 33268, L/Cpl., 1 May 1918.
WILLIS, A., 1114, L/Cpl., Givenchy, 14–15 and 20 Dec. 1914, 10 Mar. 1915, 1 Apr. 1915.
WILSON, R., 4722, C.S.M., Neuve Chapelle, 27 Nov. 1914, 18 Feb. 1915, 1 April 1915.
WOOD, C. J., 1733, L/Cpl., Medal of St. George (Russia), 4th Class, Givenchy, 21 Dec. 1914, 10 Mar. 1915, 1 April 1915.
WRIXTON, W., 936, Cpl., Cuinchy, 14 Dec. 1914, 10 Mar. 1915, 1 Apr. 1915.
YEO, C., 2838, Pte., 20 Oct. 1916.

2ND BATTALION
COLEMAN, C. D., 1543, C.Q.M.S., 26 May, 1917.
COOK, J., 7885, Sergt., 25 Aug. 1917.
DIXON, H., 8878, Cpl., 14 Jan. 1916, 11 Mar. 1916.
DOMICAN, J., 1488, Sergt., 4 Mar. 1918.
FISHER, M., 22248, Sergt., M.M., 5 Dec. 1918.
GARRARD, H., 46695, L/Cpl., Crossing Oise Canal near Ors, 4 Nov. 1918, 18 Feb. 1919, 10 Jan. 1920.
GLYNN, W., 9025, A/Sergt., M.M. and Bar, Médaille Militaire (France), Crossing Oise Canal near Ors, 4 Nov. 1918, 18 Feb. 1919, 10 Jan. 1920.
HARRISON, F., 232, Sergt., La Petite Douve, 30 June 1915.
HEAP, A. E., 9131, Cpl., 5 Dec. 1918.
JOHNSON, A., 46451, Pte., 15 Nov. 1918.
KELLY, A., 340, Pte. (A/L/Cpl.), 1 Jan. 1918, 17 Apr. 1918.
KENNY, L., 18929, Pte., 5 Dec. 1918.
LAVELLE, E., 1483, Sergt., M.M., near Ors, 4 Nov. 1918, 18 Feb. 1919, 10 Jan. 1920.
LEE, E. S., 16222, Pte., 17 Sept. 1917.
LEMON, J., 7657, C.S.M., M.S.M., 30 June 1915.
McCELLAN, G., 7414, C.S.M., 3 June 1918, 21 Oct. 1918.
McDONALD, T., 582, C.S.M., 3 June 1918, 21 Oct. 1918.
McMULLEN, W., 8673, Pte., 14 Jan. 1916, 11 Mar. 1916.
MANNION, J., 6879, Sergt., M.S.M., 16 Aug. 1916.
MUTTERS, C. W., 1175, C.S.M., M.C., M.M. and Bar, Croix-de-guerre (Belgium), Mending telephone wire, Wulverghem, Oct. 1914, 15 Nov. 1918.
NEWMAN, J. W., 9347, C.S.M., Gallant and consistent good work, 23 Feb.–27 Sept. 1918, Of enormous value to his C.O., 1 Jan. 1919, 3 Sept. 1919.
PARKER, J., 6141, Sergt.-Major, Le Cateau and general work, 18 Feb. 1915, 1 April 1915.
REDIKIN, J., 22016, Pte., Crossing Oise–Sambre Canal, Nov. 1918, 3 June 1919, 11 Mar. 1920.
SHALLIKER, J. E., 8737, Pte., Le Cateau and Festubert, 27 Oct. 1914, 30 June 1915.
SNAPE, J., 8468, Cpl., N. of Ors, 4 Nov. 1918, 18 Feb. 1919, 10 Jan. 1920.
SNOW, F., 888, C.S.M., 14 Jan. 1916, 11 Mar. 1916.
SOUTHERN, H. E., 57983, Pte., N. of Ors, 4 Nov. 1918, 18 Feb. 1919, 10 Jan. 1920.
TANNER, T. J., 89, Sergt., 17 Sept. 1917.
WARD, J., 301, Pte., 14 Jan. 1916, 11 Mar. 1916.
WATERS, H., 7424, Sergt., 9 Dec. 1914, 18 Feb. 1915, 1 April 1915.
WILLIS, T., 1073, L/Cpl., Richebourg l'Avoué, 22 June 1915, 5 Aug. 1915.

MILITARY MEDAL

1ST BATTALION
CASEY, W. M., 1779, Sergt., 26 Mar. 1917.
DANDY, E., 16356, Cpl., 26 Mar. 1916.
FAWCETT, A. H., 39435, Pte. (A/Sergt.), 20 Aug. 1919.
GLYNN, M., 2393, Pte., D.C.M., 26 May 1917.
HUGHES, A. H., 31, Sergt., D.C.M., Cross of St. George (Russia), 4th Class, 26 Mar. 1917.
HYDE, J., 32878, Pte., 10 April 1918.
KELLY, J., 9436, Pte., 26 May 1917.
RYDER, W., 1041, L/Sergt., D.C.M., 26 Mar. 1917.
SCHOFIELD, W., 1818, Pte., 10 April 1918.
SHARPLES, W., 36752, Pte. (A/Cpl.), Egypt, 20 Aug. 1919.
WOODCOCK, J., 7824, Pte., 29 Mar. 1919.

2ND BATTALION

ASHCROFT, E., 351125, Sergt., 23 July 1919.
ATKINSON, J., 31902, Pte. (A/L/Cpl.), 14 May 1919.
BAMFORD, T., 1170, Pte., 4 May 1919.
BATEMAN, T., 352369, Pte., 14 May 1919.
BEADLE, R., 2408, L/Sergt., 7 Oct. 1918.
BENNETT, T. V. R., 24752, Sergt., 19 Feb. 1917.
BEST, E. D., 24086, Pte., 23 July 1919.
BEST, R., 16396, Pte., 26 May 1917.
BIRKS, H., 301177, Pte., 23 July 1919.
BOARDMAN, C., 988, Sergt., 11 Nov. 1916 ; Bar, 24 Jan. 1919.
BRICKNELL, E. H., 302676, Pte., 23 July 1919.
BRIDGE, J., 12678, Pte., 30 Jan. 1920.
BRIDGE, N. E., 251702, Pte. (A/L/Cpl.), 23 July 1919.
BROADBENT, J. E., 2564, Pte., 11 Nov. 1916.
BROWN, T. W., 51295, Pte., 11 Feb. 1919.
CAMPBELL, J., 9089, Pte., 31 Oct. 1916.
CARTER, T., 510, Pte., 26 May 1917 ; Bar, 23 July 1919.
CHAPPELLS, A., 43671, Pte., 11 Feb. 1919.
CLAY, J., 60548, Sergt., 23 July 1919.
CLEAVER, W., 6047, Pte., 11 Nov. 1916.
CLIFFE, T. E., 301115, Pte., 14 May 1919.
COATES, W., 47132, Pte., 14 May 1919.
COCKSEY, J., 29886, Pte., 24 Jan. 1919.
COLEMAN, E., 27923, Pte., 14 May 1919.
COLLINSON, D., 8997, L/Cpl., 21 Oct. 1918.
COLLINSON, W., 23806, Pte. (L/Cpl.), 13 Mar. 1919.
COOPER, H. W., 2332, Pte., 21 Oct. 1918.
CRABBE, J., 41394, Pte., 14 May 1919.
CRANE, T., 9614, Pte., 26 May 1917.
CURTIS, J. W., 52556, Sergt., 24 Jan. 1919.
DAKIN, R., 269, Pte., 11 Nov. 1916.
DALE, H., 32594, Pte., 11 Feb. 1919.
DEMPSEY, C., 1490, Pte. (A/L/Cpl.), 24 Jan. 1919.
DRINKWATER, H., 3338, Pte., 30 Jan. 1920.
EDDLESTON, W., 16910, Pte., 23 July 1919.
FERGUSON, J., 8738, Sergt., 9 Nov. 1916 ; Bar, 19 Feb. 1917.
FISHER, M., 22248, Sergt., D.C.M., 24 Jan. 1919 ; Bar, 14 May 1919.
GARDNER, R., 1028, L/Cpl., 26 May 1917.
GIBSON, W., 4021, Cpl., 23 July 1919.
GILLIGAN, P., 2443, Pte., 11 Nov. 1916.
GLYNN, W., 9025, Cpl. D.C.M., Médaille Militaire, 26 May 1917 ; Bar, Pte. (A/L/Cpl.), 24 Jan. 1919.
GORDON, J. D., 5991, Pte., 19 Feb. 1917.
GRISDALE, G., 43047; Cpl. (A/Sergt.), 23 July 1919.
HALL, A. L., 351177, Pte. (A/Cpl.), 23 July 1919.
HALLIWELL, G., 15631, Pte., 26 May 1917.
HAMMOND, W., 30400, Sergt., 19 Feb. 1917 ; Bar, C.S.M., 14 May 1919.
HARDY, W., 41462, Cpl., 24 Jan. 1919.
HARDY, W. C., 29827, Pte., 14 May 1919.
HIGGINSON, S., 245252, Pte., 14 May 1919.
HIGHAM, W., 28740, Pte., 23 July 1919.
JAMES, T. V., 2856, Pte., 11 Feb. 1919.
JONES, D. W. J., 62367, Pte., 23 July 1919.
JONES, E., 2259, Pte., 10 April 1918.
JORDAN, W., 245324, Pte. (A/L/Cpl.), 23 July 1919.
KENT, E., 1367, Sergt., 11 Nov. 1916.
KENWORTHY, J., 9995, L/Cpl., 16 Aug. 1917 ; Bar, 7 Oct. 1918.
KING, E., 2003, L/Cpl., 19 Feb. 1917.
LACEY, E., 270067, Pte., 24 Jan. 1919.
LAVELLE, E., 1483, Sergt., D.C.M., 24 Jan. 1919.
LEVER, T., 9311, Pte., 30 Jan. 1920.
LEVY, L., 2667, Pte., 11 Feb. 1919.
LOCK, S., 56001, Pte., 4 May 1919.
MANN, C. W., 277790, Pte., 11 Feb. 1919.
MARLAND, J., 3226, Pte., 17 Sept. 1917.
MARTIN, H., 7683, Sergt., 24 Jan. 1919.
McELROY, J., 6255, Sergt., 10 April 1918.
MEREDITH, E. J., 7831, Sergt., 17 Sept. 1917 ; Bar, 23 July 1919.
METCALFE, J., 30351, Pte., 23 July 1919.
METCALFE, J. S., 9561, Sergt., 10 April 1918.
MILLER, A. E., 41496, Pte., 13 Mar. 1919 ; Bar, 20 Oct. 1919.
MONKS, G., 300855, Pte., 11 Feb. 1919.
MOORE, J. E., 252550, Cpl., 23 July 1919.
MORAN, D., 9733, Pte., 14 May 1919.
MULROONEY, F., C.S.M., 9819, 14 May 1919.
MURTON, H., 43149, Pte., 14 May 1919.
MUTTERS, C. W., 1175, Sergt., M.C., D.C.M., Croix-de-Guerre (Belgium), 11 Nov. 1916 ; Bar, 19 Feb. 1917.
NEEDHAM, W., 302926, Pte., 23 July 1919.
NEWTON, R. E., 250137, Pte. (A/L/Cpl.), 20 Oct 1919.
PALIN, E. E., 352521, Pte. (A/Cpl.), 23 July 1919.
PEERS, G., 74952, Sergt., 24 Jan. 1919.
POOLE, H., 2319, Pte., 14 May 1919.
REDMAN, W., 18696, Pte., 14 May 1919.
REED, W., 303361, Pte. (A/L/Cpl.), 23 July 1919.
ROEBUCK, E., 276101, Pte., 10 April 1918 ; Bar, Pte. (A/L/Cpl.), 24 Jan. 1919.
ROEBUCK, H., 59248, Pte., 30 Jan. 1920.
ROSS, J., 245264, Pte., 14 May 1919.
SAVAGE, J. P., 376529, Sergt., 24 Jan. 1919.
SMITH, A., 1422, Sergt., 19 Feb. 1919.
SMITH, A. F., 252156, Pte. (A/L/Cpl.), 23 July 1919.
STACEY, T. G., 53090, Pte. (A/L/Cpl.), 11 Feb. 1919.
STAPLETON, H., 1410, Pte., 19 Feb. 1917 ; Bar, 11 Feb. 1919.
SYRETT, C., 1738, Pte., 10 April 1918.
TAYLOR, E., 2069, Sergt., 11 Feb. 1919.
THOMPSON, F., 29713, Pte., 11 Feb. 1919.
THURKLE, G. H., 2813, Cpl., 23 July 1919.
TOOZE, A. E., 245341, Pte. (A/L/Cpl.), 14 May 1919.
TRIVETT, F., 2321, L/Cpl., 11 Nov. 1916.
WALLWORTH, H., 277636, Pte., 23 July 1919.
WARD, J., 301, Pte., D.C.M., 9 July 1917.
WILKES, S., 34509, Cpl. (A/L/Sergt.), 14 May 1919.
WILLIAMS, T., 27855, Cpl., 14 May 1919.
WILSHAW, J., 41573, Pte., 23 July 1919.
WINTERBOTTOM, A., 9226, C.S.M., 24 Jan. 1919.
WINTERBOTTOM, A., 9226, C.S.M., M.S.M., 24 Jan. 1919.
WOOD, W., 29399, Pte., 10 April 1918.
YOUNG, J. W., 1657, Sergt., 26 May 1917.

DECORATIONS AND HONOURS ROLLS

MERITORIOUS SERVICE MEDAL

1st BATTALION

FINNEY, W., 3154, R.S.M., M.C., 16 Aug. 1917.
GOODSON, J., 5764, R.Q.M.S., D.C.M., 16 Aug. 1917.
KEATING, J., 9107, R.Q.M.S., Mesopotamia, valuable services rendered with forces, 15 Oct. 1918.
LYNESS, A., 6401, C.S.M., Mesopotamia, valuable services rendered with forces, 15 Oct. 1918.
MATTHEWS, W. E., 27558, Cpl. (A/L/Sergt.), 3 Mar. 1919.
O'REGAN, D., 2864, Sergt., Mesopotamia, valuable services rendered with forces, 15 Oct. 1918.
PRESCOTT, J. H., 9071, Pte. (A/C.Q.M.S.), Mesopotamia, 22 Sept. 1919.
ROBINSON, J., 224, Sergt., Siberia, 22 Jan. 1920.
WORDEN, H., 6582, S/Sergt., 20 Oct. 1920.

2ND BATTALION

CRABBE, J., 41394, Pte. (A/L/Cpl.), 17 June 1918.
DAVIES, T., 8912, Cpl. (A/C.S.M.), 29 Aug. 1918.
HART, W., 400723, Cpl., 18 Jan. 1919.
KEELEY, T., 2912, A/L/Cpl., 1 Jan. 1917.
LEMON, J., 7657, S.M., D.C.M., 18 Jan. 1919.
MANNION, J., 6879, C.Q.M.S., D.C.M., 3 June 1919.
MULROONEY, F., 9819, C.S.M., M.M., 18 Jan. 1919.
PENNY, J. W., 2269, Pte., 17 June 1918.
SNOW, F., 888, C.S.M. (A/R.S.M.), D.C.M., 18 Jan. 1919.
WINTERBOTTOM, A., 9226, Sergt., 11 Nov. 1916.
WOODERSON, F., 9972, Sergt., 3 June 1919.

DEPÔT

JACKSON, H., 1037, Sergt., 3 June 1919.
SCOTT, R., 4535, Q.M.S., V.C., 22 Feb. 1919.

DECORATIONS AND MEDALS

Awarded by the Allied Powers, 1914–1920, for distinguished services rendered during the course of the campaign

BELGIUM

BY HIS MAJESTY THE KING OF THE BELGIANS

Ordre de Léopold

STRICKLAND, Edward Peter, K.C.B., Croix-de-guerre (France and Belgium), Maj.-Gen. (Staff), formerly 1st Bn., Commandeur, 5 April 1918.
CHILD, James Martin, M.C., 2/Lieut. (T/Capt.), 2nd Bn. and R.F.C., Chevalier, 24 Sept. 1917, K. in A. 23 Aug. 1918.

Croix-de-Guerre

CHILD, James Martin, M.C., Lieut. (T/Capt.), 2nd Bn. and R.F.C., 11 Mar. 1918, K. in A. 23 Aug. 1918.
STRICKLAND, Edward Peter, K.C.B., Order of Leopold (Commandeur) and Croix-de-guerre (France), Maj.-Gen., formerly 1st Bn., 5 April 1920.
TORRANCE, Kenneth Sanderson, M.C., Lieut. (T/Capt.), 2nd Bn., 4 Sept. 1919.
VAUGHAN, Edward, C.M.G., D.S.O., Legion of Honour (Chevalier), Lt.-Col. (T/Brig.-Gen.), 4 Sept. 1919.
MUTTERS, Charles William, M.C., D.C.M., M.M. and Bar, 1175, C.S.M., 2nd Bn., 12 July 1919.
PEARCE, Albert Edward, 6608, C.S.M., 2nd Bn., 12 July 1918.
PYM, Vivian, 5332, L/Cpl. (A/Cpl.), 2nd Bn., 12 July 1918.

Décoration Militaire

MORRIS, Charles Edward, 302578, Pte., 1st Bn., 15 April 1918.

EGYPT

BY HIS HIGHNESS THE SULTAN OF EGYPT

Order of the Nile

BOLTON, Charles Arthur, C.B.E., Order of the Redeemer (Commander), Maj. (T/Lt.-Col.), 2nd Bn., 3rd Class, 16 Jan. 1920.
FORTH, Nowell Barnet de Lancy, D.S.O. and Bar, M.C., Maj. (Lt.-Col. Egypt. Ex. F.), 2nd Bn., 3rd Class, 6 Nov. 1917.
O'BRIEN, Patrick, Qr.-Mr. and Maj., 1st Bn., 4th Class, 26 Nov. 1919.

FRANCE

BY THE PRESIDENT OF THE FRENCH REPUBLIC

Legion of Honour

EVANS, Wilfred Keith, C.M.G., D.S.O. and Bar, Brev. Lt.-Col. (T/Brig.-Gen.), 2nd Bn., Officer, 14 July 1919.
GELLIBRAND, John, K.C.B., D.S.O., Croix-de-guerre (France), U.S. of A. Distinguished Service Medal, Maj.-Gen. (Com. 3rd Australian Bde.), R.O., formerly 3rd Bn. (Line), Officer, 29 Jan. 1919.

APPENDIX VI

ANLEY, Barnett Dyer Lemprière Gray, C.M.G., D.S.O., Brev. Lt.-Col., 1st Bn., Chevalier, 14 July 1917.
FREEMAN, Wilfred Rhodes, D.S.O., M.C., Brev. Maj. (T/Lt.-Col.), 2nd Bn. and R.F.C., Chevalier, 17 Aug. 1919.
LUXMOORE, Noel, Maj. (T/Lt.-Col.), Devon Regt. (Commander), attd. 2nd Bn., Chevalier, 24 Feb. 1916.
VAUGHAN, Edward, C.M.G., D.S.O., Lt.-Col. (T/Brig.-Gen.), 2nd Bn., Chevalier, 21 Aug. 1919.

Ordre de L'Étoile Noire

MARTIN, George Bellis, M.C., Capt. (T/Maj.), 2nd Bn., Officer, 17 Mar. 1920.

Croix-de-Guerre

FANE, Vere Bonamy, C.B., K.C.I.E., Maj.-Gen., Staff, 26 Sept. 1917.
DE PUTRON, Hugh, Brev. Lt.-Col., 2nd Bn., 17 Aug. 1918.
ERSKINE, John David Beveridge, D.S.O., Capt. (T/Lt.-Col.), R.O., attd. 15th Bn. (formerly 2nd Bn.), 1 May 1917.
GELLIBRAND, John, K.C.B., D.S.O., Legion of Honour (Officer), U.S. of A. Distinguished Service Medal, Maj.-Gen. (Australian Staff), R.O., formerly 3rd Bn. (Line), 21 Aug. 1919.
NEWBIGGING, William Patrick Eric, C.B., D.S.O., Col. (Staff), 1st Bn., 5 Nov. 1920.
SCULLY, Arthur John, M.C., Capt., 2nd Bn., 1 May 1917.
STRICKLAND, Edward Peter, K.C.B., Order of Leopold (Commander) and Croix-de-guerre (Belgium), Maj.-Gen. (Staff), formerly 1st Bn., 5 Nov. 1920.
MASSEY, Herbert, 779, Sergt., 2nd Bn., 24 Feb. 1916.
MAGUIRE, Edward, 9005, C.S.M., D.C.M., 1st Bn., 24 Feb. 1916.
WHITMORE, Harry, 5254, C.S.M., D.C.M., 1st Bn., 31 Aug. 1917.
WILLIS, Thomas, 1073, Cpl., 2nd Bn. (now 27457 M.G.C.), 1 May 1917.

Médaille Militaire

GLYNN, William, 9025, L/Sergt., D.C.M., M.M. and Bar, 2nd Bn., 29 Jan. 1919.
MORRIS, James, 8731, C.Q.M.S., 2nd Bn., K. in A. 14 Aug. 1914 (A.O. 466), 5 Nov. 1914.
PENTLOW, Henry Alfred, 7462, Cpl., 31 Aug. 1917.

GREECE

BY HIS MAJESTY THE KING OF THE HELLENES

Order of the Redeemer

BOLTON, Charles Arthur, C.B.E., Order of the Nile, 3rd Class (Egypt), Maj. and Brev. Lt.-Col. (T/Lt.-Col.), 2nd Bn., Commander, 24 Oct. 1919.

ITALY

BY HIS MAJESTY THE KING OF ITALY

Order of the Crown of Italy

HOPKINS, Raymond Beechey, O.B.E., Maj. (R.O.), 2nd Bn., Officer, 7 Oct. 1919.

Medal for Military Valour

COLESHILL, William, M.C., D.C.M., 2/Lieut. (T/Capt.), 1st Bn., Bronze, 17 May 1919.
HUMPHREY, John, 1326, Sergt., 1st Bn., D.C.M., Bronze, 31 Aug. 1917.

ROUMANIA

BY HIS MAJESTY THE KING OF ROUMANIA

Order of the Crown of Roumania

CAREY, Geoffrey Newman, Lieut., 2nd Bn., Cavalier, 19 Aug. 21.19

RUSSIA

BY HIS IMPERIAL MAJESTY THE EMPEROR OF RUSSIA

Order of St. Anne (with Swords)

HARDCASTLE, Richard Newman, D.S.O., Maj. and Brev. Lt.-Col. (A/Lt.-Col.), 1st Bn., 3rd Class, 15 May 1917.

Cross of the Order of St. George

DUFFY, Thomas, 899, Cpl., D.C.M. and Bar, 1st Bn., 3rd Class, 25 Aug. 1915.
SMITH, Issy, 168, Pte., 1st Bn., V.C., 3rd Class, 25 Aug. 1915.
TALLANTIRE, John Colin, 4884, Sergt., 2nd Bn., 3rd Class, 25 Aug. 1915.

Cross of St. George

HUGHES, Alfred Harry, 31, Sergt., 1st Bn., D.C.M., M.M., 4th Class, 15 May 1917.

Medal of St. George

STOCKDALE, Emanuel, 5865, A/Sergt., 2nd Bn., 1st Class, 25 Aug. 1915.
WHITELY, Arthur, 1745, Cpl., 2nd Bn., 3rd Class, 25 Aug. 1915.
WOOD, Charles John, 1733, Cpl., 1st Bn., D.C.M., 4th Class, 25 Aug. 1915.

Medal of St. George, 3rd Class

BENSON, Robert, 842, L/Cpl., 1st Bn., 25 Aug. 1921.

SERBIA

BY HIS MAJESTY THE KING OF SERBIA

Cross of Karageorge (with Swords)

O'BRIEN, Charles, 2047, Cpl., 1st Bn., 1st Class, 15 Feb. 1917.

Order of the White Eagle (with Swords)

HOLBERTON, Philip Vaughan, Maj. (Adjt. 6th

Bn.), 2nd Bn., 4th Class, 15 Feb. 1917, K. in A. 26 Mar. 1918.

WRIGHT, Bache Allen, D.S.O., Maj. (T/Lt.-Col.) (Comdr. 11th Bn.), 2nd Bn., 4th Class, 15 Feb. 1917.

Gold Medal

STRINGER, George, 15818, Pte., 1st Bn., V.C., 15 Feb. 1917.

Decorations gazetted 15 Feb. 1917 had been awarded Sept.–Nov. 1916.

UNITED STATES OF AMERICA

BY THE PRESIDENT OF THE UNITED STATES OF NORTH AMERICA

Distinguished Service Medal

GELLIBRAND, John, K.C.B., D.S.O., Legion of Honour (Officer), Croix-de-guerre (France), Maj.-Gen. (Australian Forces) (Staff), R.O., 3rd Bn. (Line), 12 July 1919.

APPENDIX VII

THE GREAT WAR, 1914-1918
ROLL OF OFFICERS KILLED IN ACTION

1st Battalion

Lieutenant-Colonel H. W. E. Hitchins, Commanding.

Captain A. B. Close-Brooks, M.C.
Captain L. Creagh.
Captain F. C. S. Dunlop.
Captain H. Fisher, D.S.O.
Captain W. E. Jackson.
Captain W. N. Shipster, M.C.

Lieutenant J. Burdon.
Lieutenant W. Curtis.
Lieutenant R. I. M. Davidson.
Lieutenant F. P. Elliott.
Lieutenant E. C. Graham.
Lieutenant D. F. Milne.
Lieutenant J. Swift.
Lieutenant W. Walker.
Lieutenant W. D. T. Wickham.
Lieutenant W. G. Yates.

Second Lieutenant C. C. Bedford.
Second Lieutenant H. Gaukroger.
Second Lieutenant W. G. Hardman.
Second Lieutenant C. Morris.

2nd Battalion

Lieutenant-Colonel H. Knox.

Captain R. F. Lynch.
Captain A. McKenzie, M.C.
Captain F. O. Mackworth, M.C.
Captain F. M. Nicholas.

ROLL OF OFFICERS KILLED IN ACTION

Captain F. S. Nisbet (Adjutant).
Captain E. D. Parker.
Captain W. G. K. Peirce.
Captain J. C. Richardson.
Captain A. G. Tillard.
Captain C. F. H. Trueman.
Captain H. T. R. S. Wright.

Lieutenant W. Balshaw.
Lieutenant C. L. Bentley.
Lieutenant J. C. Caulfield.
Lieutenant A. G. B. Chittenden.
Lieutenant E. L. Gudgeon.
Lieutenant R. Horridge.
Lieutenant D. F. F. Johnson.
Lieutenant E. F. Lowther.
Lieutenant H. H. Marten.
Lieutenant H. N. McLennan.
Lieutenant B. McSherry.
Lieutenant H. H. O'Leary.
Lieutenant J. H. L. Reade.
Lieutenant H. A. Saportas.
Lieutenant C. W. Eastgate Smith.
Lieutenant J. H. M. Smith.
Lieutenant E. L. Vanderspar.
Lieutenant R. F. Walker.
Lieutenant S. Watts.
Lieutenant T. S. Wickham, D.S.O.

Second Lieutenant J. C. Babbage.
Second Lieutenant W. C. Ball.
Second Lieutenant R. B. Bayliss.
Second Lieutenant A. H. Bramley.
Second Lieutenant G. Dixon.
Second Lieutenant W. H. Howard.
Second Lieutenant V. C. McKeiver.
Second Lieutenant F. W. Mitchell.
Second Lieutenant J. Rowley.
Second Lieutenant L. Taylor.
Second Lieutenant J. B. R. Thomas.
Second Lieutenant G. W. Williamson.

APPENDIX VIII

THE ROYAL MILITARY COLLEGE MEMORIAL

In the years after the termination of the Great War, 1914–1918, the Chapel of the Royal Military College, Sandhurst, was reconstructed to form a General Memorial to all Officers dying in the service of their Country who had been educated as Gentlemen Cadets at the College.

In addition to the General Memorial of the Chapel, the interior has been filled with individual Memorials of all descriptions; Windows, Choir Stalls, Regimental Panels, the Font, Altar, Furniture, etc. etc.

The Manchester Regiment Memorial, which is situated above the pulpit, consists of a marble panel on which the names of our Officers are cut, surmounted by the Regimental Crests, the Fleur de Lys, and the Sphinx. The names and the inscription on the panel are as follow :

THE MANCHESTER REGIMENT.

1914.
CAPTAIN F. S. NISBET.
CAPTAIN C. FITZG. H. TRUEMAN.
2ND. LIEUT. A. G. B. CHITTENDEN.
CAPTAIN A. G. TILLARD.
2ND. LIEUT. R. F. WALKER.
2ND. LIEUT. C. L. BENTLEY.
LIEUT. J. C. CAULFIELD.
LIEUT. R. I. M. DAVIDSON.
LIEUT. S. D. CONNELL.
LIEUT. S. S. NORMAN.

1915.
LIEUT.-COL. H. W. E. HITCHINS.
LIEUT. E. R. VANDERSPAR.
2ND LIEUT. J. N. WASHINGTON.
2ND LIEUT. D. A. GLEN.

1916.
LIEUT. J. BURDON.
CAPTAIN R. F. LYNCH.
CAPTAIN H. T. R. S. WRIGHT.

1917.
2ND LIEUT. W. G. YATES.

THE MANCHESTER REGIMENT

1914
CAPT. F. S. NISBET
CAPT. C. FITZG. H. TRUEMAN
2ND LIEUT. A. G. B. CHITTENDEN
CAPT. A. G. FILLARD
2ND LIEUT. R. F. WALKER
2ND LIEUT. C. L. BENTLEY
LIEUT. J. C. CAULFEILD
LIEUT. P. J. M. DAVIDSON
LIEUT. S. D. CONNELL
LIEUT. S. S. NORMAN

1915
LIEUT. COL. H. W. E. HITCHENS
LIEUT. E. R. VANDERSPAR
2ND LIEUT. J. N. WASHINGTON
2ND LIEUT. D. A. GLEN

1916
LIEUT. J. BUXOON
CAPT. R. F. LYNCH
CAPT. H. T. R. S. WRIGHT

1917
2ND LIEUT. W. G. YATES

1918
BT. LT. COL. P. V. HOLBERTON
CAPT. W. N. SHIPSTER M.C.
LIEUT. W. T. D. WICKHAM
LIEUT. T/MAJ. E. P. PLENTY

WHO WERE CADETS AT THIS COLLEGE
AND TO ALL OTHER OFFICERS, WARRANT
OFFICERS, N.C.Os. AND MEN OF ALL
BATTALIONS OF THE MANCHESTER REGT
WHO GAVE THEIR LIVES IN THE GREAT
WAR 1914-1919

TABLET ERECTED IN THE MEMORIAL CHAPEL, ROYAL MILITARY COLLEGE, SANDHURST,
THE GREAT WAR, 1914-1918.

THE ROYAL MILITARY COLLEGE MEMORIAL

1918.
BT. LT.-COL. P. V. HOLBERTON.
CAPTAIN W. N. SHIPSTER, M.C.
LIEUT. W. T. D. WICKHAM.
LIEUT. (T. MAJOR) E. P. PLENTY.

Who were Cadets at this College, and to all other Officers, Warrant Officers, N.C.O.'s, and Men of all Battalions of The Manchester Regiment, who gave their lives in the Great War, 1914-1918.

The cost of the erection of the Panel was defrayed by subscriptions collected from past and present Officers of the 63rd, 96th, and Manchester Regiments, and relatives of the fallen Officers.

APPENDIX IX

BATTALIONS AND DEPOTS OF THE MANCHESTER REGIMENT IN THE GREAT WAR, SHOWING NUMBERS KILLED IN ACTION OR DIED, AND APPROXIMATE TOTAL CASUALTIES

OFFICERS KILLED IN ACTION

1st Battalion	21
2nd Battalion	44
Service Battalions (11th to 27th)	410
5th Battalion (T.F.)	33
6th Battalion (T.F.)	54
7th Battalion (T.F.)	40
8th Battalion (T.F.)	51
9th Battalion (T.F.)	37
10th Battalion (T.F.)	33
	723

OTHER RANKS

1st Battalion	859.	France, Mesopotamia and Egypt.
2nd Battalion	1,121.	France.
3rd Battalion	82.	Home: Cleethorpes.
4th Battalion	21.	Home: Grimsby.
11th Battalion	698.	M.E.F. and France.
12th Battalion	991.	France.
13th Battalion (converted later to 9th Battalion 9.9.1918	117.	France and Serbia.
14th Battalion	6.	Home: Lichfield.
15th Battalion [1]	0.	
16th Battalion	626.	France.
17th Battalion	677.	France.
18th Battalion	664.	France.
19th Battalion	562.	France.
20th Battalion	646.	France and Italy.
21st Battalion	694.	France and Italy.
22nd Battalion	629.	France and Italy.
23rd Battalion	286.	France.

[1] A 15th Battalion appears in Army List, December, 1915.

UNVEILING GREAT WAR MEMORIAL, ST. ANN'S SQUARE, MANCHESTER, 1924.

CASUALTIES IN ALL RANKS

24th Battalion	162.	France and Italy.
25th Battalion	9.	Home.
26th Battalion	7.	Home.
27th Battalion	7.	Home.
Depot	17.	Home.
28th Battalion (45th Provisional later)	0.	Territorials (A.C.I. 2364, 1916).
1/5th Battalion	480.	Egypt, Dardanelles and France.
2/5th Battalion	245.	France.
5th Reserve Battalion	13.	Home.
1/6th Battalion	637.	Egypt, Dardanelles and France.
2/6th Battalion	261.	France.
6th Reserve Battalion	7.	Home.
1/7th Battalion	566.	Egypt, Dardanelles and France.
2/7th Battalion	315.	France.
7th Reserve Battalion	3.	Home.
1/8th Battalion	543.	Egypt, Dardanelles and France.
2/8th Battalion	125.	France.
8th Reserve Battalion	32.	Home.
9th Battalion	134.	(*vide* 13th Battalion).
1/9th Battalion	274.	Egypt, Dardanelles and France.
2/9th Battalion	238.	France.
9th Reserve Battalion	5.	Home.
1/10th Battalion	453.	Egypt, Dardanelles and France.
2/10th Battalion	120.	France.
10th Reserve Battalion	10.	Home.
196th T.F. Depot	1.	Home.
198th T.F. Depot	1.	Home.
1st Garrison Battalion	22.	India, Hong Kong and Singapore.
2nd Garrison Battalion	3.	Home.
51st Battalion	11.	Home.
52nd Battalion	14.	Home.
53rd Battalion	5.	Home.

13,399.

Total all ranks killed or died—14,122.

Approximate total all ranks killed, wounded, missing, etc.—45,000.

APPENDIX X

CENTENARY CELEBRATIONS

2nd Battalion

At Jubbulpore, Central Provinces, India, the 2nd Battalion celebrated its Centenary, 1824–1924. On Sunday, the 23rd March, 1924, the battalion, with fixed bayonets, and the old Colours of 1779 ("The British Musqueteers") and of 1804 ("The Queen's German Regiment") and the present Colours (1911), marched to the Garrison Church, Jubbulpore, where a special service was held. The Colours were carried by the following officers: King's Colour, Second Lieutenant C. W. S. Pakes; Regimental Colour, Second Lieutenant E. J. H. Moppett; British Musqueteers: King's, Lieutenant E. Greer. Regimental, Second Lieutenant A. L. Alderton; Peninsular Colours: King's, Lieutenant F. C. Egan, Regimental, Second Lieutenant T. A. Hibbard.

The battalion formed up in line outside the Church and the Colours were marched out with the customary honours, after which the battalion filed into Church. The old Colours were placed in the chancel prior to the commencement of the service, which opened with the hymn "Onward, Christian Soldiers," sung as the procession of choir and clergy, preceded by the Cross and the present Colours, carried by the officers named above, moved up the Church from the west door. An impressive service followed. The Lesson, very appropriately chosen, was read by Lieutenant-General Sir Louis Vaughan, Commanding C.P. District, and, in place of a sermon, an address was given by Lieutenant-Colonel W. B. Eddowes, the Commanding Officer, in which he briefly reviewed the history of the battalion during its hundred years' existence, and touched on incidents of which it was especially proud. In conclusion, he asked the congregation to stand with him "while the bugles sound, firstly, 'Last Post,' in memory of those gallant soldiers of the battalion who in the past one hundred years have laid down their lives for their King, their country, their cause, and their comrades. Then 'Reveille' to remind us that we must be up and doing, not resting on past laurels, but going forward to bravely meet whatever the future may have in store, full of cheerful yesterdays and confident to-morrows."

After the Address the buglers of the battalion sounded the "Last Post" and "Reveille." The hymns "For all the Saints" and "Oh God, Our Help in Ages Past" were then sung. The National Anthem was followed by the Benediction and the Recessional hymn, "Soldiers of Christ Arise." The battalion then formed up outside the Church and marched back to barracks, the salute being taken by the District Commander.

On Sunday evening a concert was given by the band of the battalion in the Empire Theatre; the full band appearing for the first time since the war in scarlet.

2ND BATTALION CENTENARY CELEBRATIONS, JUBBULPORE, INDIA, MARCH 1924.

CENTENARY CELEBRATIONS

On Monday, March the 24th, the battalion paraded on the Ridge Barracks parade ground and carried out the " Trooping of the Colour," of which two photographs are given.

The Parade State on this occasion was as follows, and it is interesting to compare it with the " Parade State " of the 24th March 1824, when the battalion was inspected by Major-General Sir John Byng, which is given on p. 210 of Vol. I of this history.

Officers on Strength, the 24th March, 1924

Colonel: Major-General Sir V. B. Fane, K.C.B., K.C.I.E.

Lieutenant-Colonel: Lieutenant-Colonel W. B. Eddowes.

Majors: Majors G. P. Wymer, D.C.M., J. R. Heelis, M.C., A. G. M. Hardingham.

Captains: Captains J. V. Macartney, M.C., J. S. Harper, M.C., H. R. C. Green, M. R. Davidson, E. B. Holmes, M.C., H. H. J. Holness, D.C.M., K. S. Torrance, M.C., C. G. Dailey, M.C., F. A. Levis.

Lieutenants: Lieutenants C. H. Keitley, M.B.E., F. Gray, S. E. Hollins, S. H. Holley, M.C., L. A. Walton, D.S.O., M.C., C. C. Whyte, M.B.E., W. T. Williams-Green, M.C., V. D. K. Marley, F. Brittorous, M.C., J. J. Dolan, M.C., E. Greer, J. A. Corley, M.C., M.M., F. C. Egan, P. L. Curtis, H. S. Hoseason.

Second Lieutenants: Second Lieutenants E. L. Shewell, C. W. S. Pakes, A. L. Alderton, E. J. H. Moppett, T. A. Hibbard.

Adjutant: Captain E. B. Holmes, M.C.

Quartermaster: Lieutenant D. A. Carter, D.C.M.

Regimental Sergeant-Major: F. Snow, D.C.M.

Strength: Officers, 34; Warrant Officers, 8; Colour-Sergeants, 6; Sergeants, 31; Corporals, 40; Privates, 793; Service Companies, 4; " H.Q." Wing, 1.

(Sd.) W. B. Eddowes,
Lieutenant-Colonel Commanding 2nd Battalion,
The Manchester Regiment.

The ceremony was witnessed by a very large number of spectators, detachments from every unit in the station, and most of the officers, including many former officers of the battalion, who came to Jubbulpore to witness the celebrations.

At 8 a.m. a section of the 40th Battery, R.F.A., under the command of Second Lieutenant Shewell of the battalion (attached to the battery) fired a time signal, and the Regimental Colour was " Trooped " through four guards of twenty-five files each which then marched past in slow and quick time.

The officers on duty on this occasion were:

No. 1 Guard.—Captain M. R. Davidson, Lieutenant F. C. Egan, Second Lieutenant E. J. H. Moppett.
No. 2 Guard.—Major A. G. M. Hardingham.
No. 3 Guard.—Captain J. V. Macartney, M.C., Second Lieutenant C. W. S. Pakes.
No. 4 Guard.—Capt. H. H. J. Holness, D.C.M., Lieutenant E. Greer.

The remainder of the battalion kept the ground.

At the conclusion of the ceremony the guards formed line, and General Vaughan addressed them as follows:

"Colonel Eddowes, Officers, Warrant Officers, Non-Commissioned Officers, and Soldiers of the 2nd Battalion The Manchester Regiment. One hundred years to-day your battalion was inspected by Major-General Sir John Byng, a distinguished officer, who commanded the advance guard of Wellington's Army when it advanced on Paris after the victory at Waterloo in 1815. That officer was the uncle of General Sir Julian Byng (now Lord Byng of Vimy), who commanded the Third Army in France in 1917 and 1918, and whose chief staff officer I had the honour to be during the last eighteen months of the Great War. You will, therefore, understand the personal honour and gratification I feel to-day in being associated as Divisional Commander with the Centenary of the 2nd Battalion The Manchester Regiment. I wish to congratulate you upon the accurate and soldierly manner in which you have carried out this ancient, impressive, and intricate ceremony of 'Trooping the Colour'—a ceremony designed to indicate outwardly the veneration and respect in which we hold our Regimental Colours. The Colours themselves are the outward symbol of the duty which we owe to our King and to our country. The record of this battalion in carrying out that duty throughout the last one hundred years is one of which every officer and man of the battalion may justly be proud. That the regimental tradition is safe in the hands of the present generation serving in the battalion I am well assured. I can only offer to you all my best wishes in your endeavour, not only to maintain, but still further to increase, the proud reputation which you happily enjoy."

Mr. Slocock, the Commissioner, also made a brief congratulatory speech, after which the battalion marched back to barracks.

The following order of the day was subsequently published:

ORDER OF THE DAY,

By Colonel-Commandant W. H. Beach, C.B., C.M.G., D.S.O., Commanding 21st Indian Infantry Brigade.

JUBBULPORE,
25th March, 1924.

Ceremonial.—The G.O.C. Central Provinces District has had the honour of attending the Centenary Celebration of the 2nd Battalion the Manchester Regiment, at Jubbulpore, at St. Michael's Church on the 23rd March 1924, and at the "Trooping of the Colour" on the 24th March 1924.

He has already verbally expressed to the battalion his high esteem of the parade work.

He wishes to take further advantage of this occasion to make a permanent record of his appreciation of the perfection of detail attained by all ranks of the battalion throughout this notable ceremony.

(Sd.) W. B. BEACH, Colonel-Commandant,
Commanding 21st Indian Infantry Brigade.

On Monday evening Regimental guest nights were held in the Officers' and Sergeants' Messes, the principal guests being the District Commander, the Commissioner, and the Brigade Commander. On Tuesday another guest night followed, when the officers dined the warrant officers and colour-sergeants of the battalion in the Officers' Mess, when the Sergeants' Mess presented to the officers a photograph of the warrant officers, colour-sergeants, and sergeants of the battalion. The latter occasion is unique, inasmuch as it is the only occasion on record on which the warrant officers and non-commissioned officers have dined in the Officers' Mess. Those present on this historic occasion were :

Officers : Lieutenant-Colonel W. B. Eddowes, Majors J. R. Heelis, M.C., and A. G. M. Hardingham, Captains J. V. Macartney, M.C., J. S. Harper, M.C., M. R. Davidson, E. B. Holmes, M.C., H. H. J. Holness, D.C.M., and F. A. Levis, Lieutenants F. Gray, L. A. Walton, D.S.O., M.C., C. C. Whyte, M.B.E., W. T. Williams-Green, M.C., F. Brittorous, M.C., E. Greer, and F. C. Egan, Second Lieutenants E. L. Shewell, C. W. S. Pakes, A. L. Alderton, E. J. H. Moppett, and T. A. Hibbard, Lieutenant and Quartermaster D. A. Carter, D.C.M.

Warrant and Non-Commissioned Officers : Regimental Sergeant-Major F. Snow, D.C.M., Regimental Quartermaster-Sergeant F. Lewis, Bandmaster J. Nichol, Company Sergeant-Majors J. Redwood, W. Allen, R. M. A. Thomason, C. D. Coleman, D.C.M., Company-Sergeant-Major Instructor in Musketry C. Ward, Company Quartermaster-Sergeants J. Brown, A. Burley, E. Harvey, F. Horsley, and F. Gebhardt, Colour-Sergeant A. Smith, Warrant Officer I. Redhead (A.E.C.), attached, Armourer-Quartermaster-Sergeant J. Duffield (R.A.O.C.).

The remainder of the week was observed as a holiday, and on Wednesday, Thursday, and Friday evenings a Boxing Tournament was held in the quadrangle of the Regimental Institute. On Thursday H.E. Sir Frank Sly, K.C.S.I., Governor of the Central Provinces, and the Divisional and Brigade Commanders dined with the officers, and afterwards witnessed the boxing. On Friday evening the Brigade Commander distributed the prizes at the conclusion of the boxing.

On Saturday the battalion took part in the garrison parade for H.E. the Viceroy, earning his commendation for its steadiness on parade and in marching past.

Many congratulatory messages were received during the course of the celebrations, among others from H.E. Lord Rawlinson, Commander-in-Chief in India, H.E. Sir Frank Sly (who had his address printed and distributed to all ranks), Major-General Sir Vere Fane, Major-General Tytler, Commanding the Burma District in succession to General Fane, and also an old officer of the Regiment, Brig.-General Vizard, General Walker, the Bishop of Nagpur, and many others from past officers of the battalion.

APPENDIX XI
ARMY LIST AUGUST 1881
ON THE AMALGAMATION OF 63RD AND 96TH REGIMENTS AS THE MANCHESTER REGIMENT

443	444	445	446

THE MANCHESTER REGIMENT.

Regimental Dist. No. 63.............. Ashton-under-Lyne.

The Sphinx.

"Egmont-op-Zee," "Egypt," "Martinique," "Guadaloupe," "Peninsula," "New Zealand," "Alma," "Inkerman," "Sevastopol," "Afghanistan, 1879-80."

1st Bn. (63rd Foot) ... *Southern Afghanistan.*		3rd Bn. (6th R. Lancashire Mil.) ... *Ashton.*	
2nd „ (96th „) ... *Malta.*		4th „ (6th R. Lancashire Mil.) ... *Ashton.*	
Depôt ... ... *Ashton-under-Lyne.*			

Uniform.—Scarlet. *Facings.*—White. *Agents.*—Messrs. Cox & Co.

Honorary Colonel.
Wilson, Gen. T. M., *m.c.c.* ... ... 2nd Bn.

Lt.-Colonel Commanding Regtl. Dist. ... ... McGwire, E. T. St. I., *c.*

1st and 2nd Battalions.

Lt.-Colonels. (4)
2Briggs, J., *c.*
1Auchinleck, W. L.
2Scovell, E. J.
1Gwynne, N. X., *p.s.c.*

Majors. (8)
2Barnard, W. O., *l.c.*
1Saportas, A. D.
2Church, A. G. H.
2Newbigging, W.
1Ryan, C. J.
2Wynter, A. L.
1Jones, F. W. R.
1Studdy, R. W.

Captains. (10)
d.2Marryat, H. C.
2Phillipps, E. P.
s.Maxwell, R. J., *l.c., p.s.c.*
d.2Marshall, F. G.
Barlow, J. A.
1Gronow, W. L.
2Anstruther, B. L.
s.1Nuthall, W. P.
2Glascott, J. J
2Ridley, C. P.
1Cook, H. R.
1Chevers, H
1Robotham, J. G. C.
2Gall, H. R.
1Jackson, H. F., *m.*

1Moores, S.
2Simpson, A. E.

Lieutenants. (34)
2Rockfort-Boyd, G. W. W., *adj.*
d.2Nash, W. P.
d.1Reay, C. T.
1Tenison, W., *I. of M*
d. 1Stubbs, A. G. B.
2Utermarck, B. J. G.
1Graham, W. B.

Lieutenants—cont.
1Smith, H. S., *adj.*
1Thomas, F. W.
2Stracey, C. E.
d.2Brown, C. R.
2Maxwell, A. B.
2Watson, J. E.
2Anderson, J. H. A.
1Hudson, A. T. P.
1Gardner, C. A.
Angelo, F. W. P (prob.)
2Bertram, W.
1Reid, L. H.
2Pearce, G. R.
1Ranken, G. P.
1Lang, M. C. R.
2Henderson, R. A.
1Meip, F. B.
2Melvill, C. C.
1Ternan, T. P. B.
1Wickham, W. J. R.
1Codrington, E. W.
1O'Brien, D. J. T.
2Kirwan, G. H.
2Ward, E. A.
1Quin, T.
1Wilson, A.
1Dawson, R. H.
d.2Davis, C.
d.2Vizard, R. D.

Paym.1Ternan, R. R. B., *hon. capt.*
2Singer, G. H., *hon. capt.*

*I. of M.*1Tenison, W., *lt.*

Adj. 2Rockfort-Boyd, G. W. W., *lt.*
1Smith, H. S., *lt.*

*Q.M.*2Facer, W.
1White, D.

3rd and 4th Battalions.

Lt.-Colonel Commandant.
3Chambers, J. H., *hon. c.*

Lt.-Colonel.
4Wray, J. C., *hon. c.*

Majors.
3Mercier, C.
4Piers, Sir E. F., Bt.

Captains. (12)
4Kennedy, J. D.
p.s.3Braybrooke, J.
4Garland-Matthews, H.
4Powell, T. P.
3Trimmer, A. R., Capt. h.p., *hon. m.*
4Taylor, G. E., Capt. h.p.
3Irwin, T. A., Capt. h.p.
3Gray, H. H.
3Burney, W. G. N., *hon. m.*
3Chambers, E. W.
4Dunlop, R. M.

Lieutenants. (18)
4Harper, E. T. M.
3Symonds, H.
4Murphy, J. A.
3Bainbridge, R. B.
3Woodhouse, W. S.
3Gamble, T. A.
4Kershaw, F.
3Foley, A. G. P.
4Elmslie, W. F.
3Waddell-Boyd, J.

Lieutenants—cont.
3Burton, F. V. A.
4Prioleau, C. A.
3Wickham, W. F.
3Balguy, F. N.
3Kay, H.
3Brocklehurst, E. A.
4Guthrie, C. S. J. L.
4Leyden, C. D.

Adj. Wynter, A. L., Maj. 2nd Bn.

Q.M. 3Munro, D. (*temp. Q.M. in Army.*)
4Lofts, W. (*temp. Q.M. in Army.*)

Med. Off.

AUGUST 1881.

ARMY LIST NOVEMBER 1906
THE LAST OF THE FOUR LINE BATTALIONS

995	996	997	997a

THE MANCHESTER REGIMENT.
Regimental District. No. **63** (Lancashire Group).

The Sphinx, superscribed "Egypt."
"Egmont-op-Zee," "Martinique," "Guadaloupe," "Peninsula," "Alma," "Inkerman," "Sevastopol,"
"New Zealand," "Afghanistan, 1879-80," "Egypt, 1882," "South Africa, 1899-1902," "Defence of Ladysmith."

Line and Militia Battalions.

Uniform—Scarlet.   Facings—White.   Agents—Messrs. Cox & Co.

1st Bn. (63rd Foot)	Secunderabad.	*4th Bn.	Aldershot.
2nd ,, (96th ,,)	Guernsey.	5th ,, (6th E. Lancashire Mil.)	Ashton.
3rd ,,	Middelburg, Transvaal, (for Home).	6th ,, (6th E. Lancashire Mil.)	Ashton.
Depôt	Ashton-under-Lyne.	Record Office	Preston.

Volunteer Battalions.

| 1. 1st | Manchester | 3. 3rd | Ashton-under-Lyne. | 5. 5th Ardwick, near Manchester. |
| 2. 2nd | Manchester. | 4. 4th | Manchester. | 6. 6th Oldham. |

1st Cadet Battalion — Manchester.

Colonel — Barnard, Maj.-Gen. W. O. — 5 Jan. 04

1st, 2nd, 3rd and 4th Battalions.

Lt.-Colonels. (2)
- 2 Watson, J. E. 6 Oct. 01, bt. col. 3 May 06
- 3 Anderson, J. H. A. 17 Feb. 04
- 4 Melvill, C. C. 24 Feb. 04
- 1 Vizard, F. D. 1 June 06, bt. col. 10 Aug. 06

Majors. (4) (2nd in Command.)
- 4 Westropp, H. C. E. 28 Mar. 04
- 15 Dec. 00
- 9 Baldwin, A. H. 20 Apr. 04, 15 Dec. 00
- 3 James, H. L. 5 Oct. 05, 19 Mar. 01
- 1 Hitchins, H. W. E. 1 June 06, 1 July 01

Majors. (4)
- 4. 4 Petrie, C. L. R., D.S.O. (Comdg. Depôt) 21 Dec. 01
- r.a. Borges, R. H., D.S.O. 21 Dec. 01, bt. lt.-col. 26 Mar. 06
- 4 Marden, A. W., D.S.O. 1 June 02, 29 Nov. 00
- 2 Crawford, J. O. 18 Apr. 03
- 3 Weston, R. S. 28 Sept. 03
- e.o. Vaughan, E. 17 Feb. 04, 23 Aug. 02
- s. Climo, V. C., p.s.c. 11 Jan. 05, 27 June 00
- 4 Walker, E. J. H. 4 Mar. 05
- 1 Welman, H. R. 16 Sept. 05, 31 July 02
- 3 Tuson, H. D., p.s.c. 5 Dec. 05
- 3 Anderson, F. W. A. 1 June 06

Captains. (13)
- 2 Cooper-King, G. C., D.S.O. 18 Mar. 99
- s. Newbigging, W. P. E., D.S.O. 18 Mar. 99

Captains—contd.
- r. Paton, D. R. 26 July 99
- 4 Tillard, A. G. 18 Sept. 99
- 3 Jebb, J. H. M., D.S.O. 27 Dec. 99
- 3 Wright, B. A., D.S.O., adjt. 27 Dec. 99
- v. Toogood, C., D.S.O. 26 May 00
- 3 Sowray, G. R. 26 May 00
- 3 Chute, R. A. B. 26 May 00
- m. Stewart, A. F. 26 May 00
- s.c. Gellibrand, J. 26 May 00
- 4 Terry, R. J. A. 9 June 00, bt. maj. 22 Aug. 02
- 1 Sharp, A. G. 9 June 00
- m. Erskine, J. D. B. 9 June 00
- s.a. Tighe, V. J., D.S.O. 22 Sept. 00
- Hopkins, R. B. (spec. emp.) 10 Oct. 00
- 1 Baker, E. M. 5 Jan. 01
- s.c. 2 Dorling, V. H. 5 Jan. 01
- 4 Trueman, C. FitzG. H. 5 Jan. 01
- 2 Hardcastle, R. N., D.S.O. 5 Jan. 01
- 1 Dunlop, F. C. S. 19 Mar. 01
- e.a. Vaughan, E. J. F. 12 July 01
- 4 Deakin, F. F. 12 July 01
- 3 Theobald, H. C. W., D.S.O. 13 July 01
- 1 Fisher, H., D.S.O. 14 July 01
- 2 Nisbet, F. S. 14 July 01
- 4 Shuter, R. G., D.S.O., adjt. 23 Nov. 01
- 1 Creagh, L. 27 Nov. 01
- 2 Cockburn, E. R. 25 Dec. 01
- v. Peirse, W. G. K. 25 Dec. 01
- c.o. Hastings, W. C. N., D.S.O. 25 Dec. 01
- c.a. Stevens, H. W. 22 Mar. 02
- 2 Bathurst, A. H. 22 Mar. 02
- 4 Fisher, E. N. 22 Nov. 02
- 1 Eddowes, W. B. 5 Feb. 03
- u. Thorneycroft, O. M. 5 Feb. 03
- 4 Merriman, A. D. N. 8 Feb. 03
- 3 Richardson, C. 5 Aug. 03
- d. Martin, E. L. 17 Feb. 04
- 3 Gillam, W. A., D.S.O. 24 Aug. 03, 16 Aug. 02
- 1 Chapman, H. 4 Dec. 05

Lieutenants. (19)
- (4) Murley, C. 16 Aug. 00
- m. Gauntlett, V. C. 5 Sept. 00
- 2 Boone, O. A. 1 Nov. 00
- 1 Knox, H. 5 Jan. 01
- 1 Ritchie, T. F. 5 Jan. 01
- 1 Evans, W. K. adjt. 12 Feb. 01
- 4 Bayley, W. K. 16 Feb. 01
- d. 4 Bates, H. C. 12 Mar. 01
- 1 Wymer, G. P. 6 May 01
- d. 2 Anderson, C. A. 30 May 01
- 1 Dana, W. R. H. 1 July 01
- 1 Hovell, C. H. M. 1 July 01
- 3 Forth, N. B. de L. 3 July 01
- 2 Crozier, F. P. 13 July 01
- c.o. Oliver, J. F. 13 July 01
- 1 Lawson, J. L. 14 July 01
- 3 Stapledon, C. C. 23 July 01
- 2 Fowke, M. C. 7 Oct. 01
- 2 Foord, A. G. 30 Oct. 01
- 2 Holberton, P. V., adjt. 27 Nov. 01
- 1 Buchan, E. N., D.S.O. 27 Nov. 01
- 1 Prince, A. L. 24 Dec. 01
- 4 Beells, J. R. 25 Dec. 01
- d. 1 Tillard, A. K. D. 25 Dec. 01
- 4 Irwin, C. D. 22 Mar. 02
- 1 Rose, A. B. 25 Oct. 02
- 3 de Putron, H. 19 Nov. 02
- c.o. Mansergh, W. G. 11 Nov. 02
- 2 Paulson, P. Z. 12 Nov. 02
- c.a. Wickham, T. S., D.S.O. 12 Nov. 02
- 1 O'Meara, A. E. 11 Dec. 02
- 1 Browne, H. G. 5 Feb. 03
- 3 Ellershaw, H. 5 Feb. 03
- 1 Tayleur, O. E. 19 Aug. 03
- 2 Hardingham, A. G. R. 19 Aug. 03
- 4 Reade, J. H. L. 30 Oct. 03
- 2 Bolton, C. A. 21 Nov. 03
- 4 Guinness, W. R. 3 Jan. 04
- 1 Clark, W. C. 22 Jan. 04
- 4 Thomas, A. F. 17 Feb. 04
- 2 Stanley-Murray, H. E. 1 Apr. 04
- 3 Minogue, M. J. 21 Apr. 04
- 3 Ainsworth, T. J. 23 June 04
- 4 Frisby, H. G. F. 21 Dec. 04
- 4 Woods, C. W. 5 July 05, 22 Mar. 02

2nd Lieutenants. (12)
- 3 Fulda, J. L. 22 Oct. 04
- 4 Clegg, M. C. 26 Jan. 05
- 4 Dearden, J. A. 26 Jan. 05
- 4 Dean, P. H. 26 Jan. 05
- 4 Boutflower, E. C. 26 Jan. 05
- 1 Edwards, G. D. 21 Apr. 05
- 2 Boxer, H. C. 24 Apr. 05
- 1 Mair, B. V. 22 Apr. 05
- 1 Sharland, A. A. 22 Apr. 05
- 2 Smyth, A. B. 2 May 05
- 2 Wright, H. T. R. S. 2 May 05
- 2 Dent, J. R. C. 10 Oct. 05
- 3 Morris, R. 1 Nov. 05
- 4 Botham, E. G. 18 Nov. 05
- 1 Odell, W. 27 Jan. 04
- 2 Humphrys, N. W. 9 Mar. 04
- 1 Torkington, J. E. B. 9 Mar. 04
- 3 Harrison, H. G. 4 June 04
- i.a. Pinston, P. G. H. 4 June 04
- 1 Musson, E. L. 26 Jan. 05
- 4 Harper, J. S. 16 Aug. 05
- 4 Oates, K. G. H. 24 Jan. 06

Adjutants
- 2 Holberton, P. V. lt. 1 Dec. 05
- 4 Shuter, R. G., D.S.O., capt. 14 Apr. 05
- 3 Wright, B. A., D.S.O., capt. 6 May 05
- 1 Evans, W. K., lt. 1 May 05

Quarter Masters
- 2 Stewart-Wynne, C. 19 Oct. 02, hon. m. 19 Oct. 04
- m. Ormerry, M. H. 7 July 97, hon. capt. 22 Aug. 02
- 1 Bankes, R. 16 Aug. 05, hon. capt. 29 Nov. 06
- 3 Walkley, D. A. u. lt. 1 Mar. 00
- 4 Gordon, W. I., hon. lt. 20 June 05
- m. Vickers, G. E., hon. lt. 5 Feb. 02

*To be disbanded.

APPENDIX XII

THE MANCHESTER REGIMENT GAZETTE

THE *Gazette*, published quarterly, contains, besides matter of general interest, a record of the doings of all battalions of the Manchester Regiment.

Contributions, photographs, and drawings are welcomed, more especially if dealing with events connected with The Manchester Regiment.

All information, and terms of subscription, can be obtained either from the Editor direct, from the Sub-Editors appointed to each battalion, or from the Publishers, Messrs. Sherratt & Hughes, 34 Cross Street, Manchester. The address of the Editor is
       WYECLIFFE HOUSE,
         BREINTON,
          HEREFORD.

APPENDIX XIII
THE MARCHES PAST

THE YOUNG MAY MOON (OLD 63RD FOOT).

THE MARCH PAST OF OLD 96TH FOOT, NOW THE MANCHESTER REGIMENT'S MARCH PAST.

APPENDIX XIV

THE MANCHESTER REGIMENT AID SOCIETY

WHEN the 3rd Battalion (Line) Manchester Regiment was quartered at Middleburg, Transvaal, in 1906, orders were received from England that this battalion and its sister battalion the 4th (Line) were to be disbanded.

Lieutenant-Colonel J. H. Abbot Anderson, Commanding 3rd Battalion, had orders to proceed immediately to Peking to take up the duties of Commandant, British Legation Guard; while Major H. L. James was to take command, and proceed with the battalion to Guernsey, Channel Islands, for disbandment.

A question arose what was to be done with the funds of the battalion? Major James called a meeting of officers and N.C.O.s to discuss the matter. He pointed out that for many years Major-General W. O. Barnard, Colonel of the Regiment, an old Commanding Officer of the 2nd Battalion, and a full-time serving officer with the 96th Regiment and 2nd Battalion Manchester Regiment (which he joined (in the first Regiment) as an Ensign on 15th April, 1856), had wished that the Regiment could have a charitable Fund to be run on the same lines as the "Rifleman's Aid Society."

This disbandment gave the opportunity, and after very careful consideration it was, without one single dissentient, agreed that the Regimental Funds of the 3rd Battalion should be earmarked for this purpose, and sanction was also obtained from the War Office, *vide* W.O. letter 103/Infantry/166 (A.G.3), dated 13th October 1906.

The 4th Battalion Manchester Regiment was similarly asked to join in the scheme, and was willing to give the balance of its funds, on disbandment, for the same object. The sum from the 3rd Battalion was £1,133 1s. 9d., and that from the 4th Battalion £133 13s. 10d., making a total of £1,266 15s. 7d., which formed the commencement of the "Manchester Regiment Aid Society."

Major-General W. O. Barnard was informed that his wish to have an Aid Society for the Regiment was at last a possibility.

The 3rd and 4th Battalions were disbanded in Guernsey, and ceased to exist by 31st December 1906.

In the following year Major-General W. O. Barnard was staying in Guernsey, and a General Meeting was there called on the 10th August, 1907.

Having arrived at some definite conclusion how the funds of the disbanded battalions were to be disposed of, the Officers Commanding 1st and 2nd Battalions were informed of this Society, and they, together with past officers, decided that such a Society was likely to be beneficial to the Manchester Regiment and was a form of Aid Society that had been much needed.

APPENDIX XIV

As the bulk of the funds for starting this Society came from the 3rd Battalion (Line) Manchester Regiment, the following officers offered to be trustees as a temporary measure, viz.: Major H. L. James, Major R. S. Weston, and Captain B. A. Wright. These officers are still the trustees.

A General Committee was formed consisting of Major-General W. O. Barnard as President, together with the Officer Commanding Home Battalion, Officer Commanding Depot, Major H. L. James, and Captain E. D. Parker; the Executive Committee consisting of Major H. L. James, President; Officer Commanding Depot and Captain M. Connery (Hon. Secretary), members.

Rules were drawn up and passed, and are as follows:

(a) To assist men of good character who have served in any of the four Line Battalions of the Manchester Regiment, and who, through sickness or any other cause beyond their own control, are in need of assistance, pecuniary or otherwise.

(b) To obtain suitable employment for men who have served in any of the four Line Battalions of the Manchester Regiment, who either through being discharged, time-expired, or invalided have returned to civil life.

(c) If the amount of available funds subsequently permits:

    (i) To afford relief, or grant pensions, to the widows of men who have served in any of the four Line Battalions of the Manchester Regiment;

    (ii) To assist as far as possible in maintaining orphans till they reach a wage-earning age.

N.B.—Owing to insufficient funds (c) has never become operative.

On Major-General Barnard's death, the Presidency was taken over by Major-General Sir V. B. Fane, K.C.B., K.C.I.E., and the Presidency of the Executive Committee is still in the hands of Lieutenant-Colonel H. L. James, C.B., with Lieutenant-Colonel G. E. Vickers, D.S.O., as Hon. Secretary.

The number of cases dealt with since its formation are 1896, at a cost of £1,539 10s. 9d. The Society has been of much help to the men, and is much appreciated by them. In 1921 and 1923, since the Great War, over 750 calls have been inquired into and assisted where inquiries have proved the case satisfactory.

All applications should be made to Lieutenant-Colonel G. E. Vickers, D.S.O., Hon. Sec., at 62 Victoria Street, Manchester, or O.C. Depot, Ashton-under-Lyne, or Lieutenant-Colonel H. J. James, C.B., 28 Linden Road, Bedford.

INDEX

A

Abbassieh, 108
Abbeville, 99, 129
Abbot-Anderson, Lieut. C., 57, 76, 79, 80, 81, 82
Abbot-Anderson, Capt. J. H., 38, 40; Major, 43; Lieut.-Col. commands 3rd Battalion, 63, 64, 343
Abbott, Lieut., 212
Abbott, Private, wounded, 12
Abdur Rahman, 34
Abercrombie, Lieut., 103
Ablaincourt, 175
Abri Wood, 171
Abu Jisra, 165
Abu Roman, 149, 151; capture of, 154-5
Abu Shusheh, 195
Adams, Second Lieut., 124
Adams, Capt. F. H., Adjutant, wounded, 189, 190
Adams, Rev. J., *V.C.*, consecrates Colours 1886, 35
Adamson, Second Lieut., 158
Address on presentation of Colours to 2nd Battalion 1886, 35-6; to 2nd Battalion 1911, 81
Aden, 41, 42
Adinkerke, 168
Advance to the Aisne begun, 96
Aerodrome Camp, 218
Aeroplane, Maurice-Farman, at Loos, forced to descend by German Aviatik, 121
Agnew, Colonel, 81
Agra, 37
Ainsworth, Lieut., 75
Airy, Capt., 206; mortally wounded, 207
Aisne, Battle of the, ends, 98
Aisne, River, 95, 97, 98
Ajjeh, 198
Al Ajik, 187
Albany, Duchess of, Guard of Honour for, 76
Albert, 132, 134, 137
Albert Hall, Commemoration 1917 "The First Seven Divisions," 181-4
Albertina, 56, 62
Albert Medal, 70
Albrecht, Lieut. V. A., 87; wounded 95, 127; 126
Alderney, 64, 73, 74, 75, 212
Aldershot, 1, 2, 42, 43, 58, 62, 64, 66, 73, 74, 79, 205, 206

Alderton, Second Lieut. A. L., 336, 337, 339
Alexandria, 1st and 2nd Battalions meet 1882, 101, 108
Alexandria, Battle of, 36
Ali Garbi, 147
Aliwal North, 44
Alleman's Nek, capture of, 18
Allen, Co.-Sergt.-Major W., 339
Allenby, Major-Gen., 86, 90, 92; General Sir Edmund, 192, 195
Allenby's Column, 26
Alton, 73
Amara, 147, 159, 191
Ambala, 35
Amersfoort, 19
Amiens, 86, 87, 181
Amir of Afghanistan, 34
Amritsar, 37, 39, 40, 70, 106
Anchor, Private, wounded, 8
Ancre, River, 132, 133, 134, 137, 141
Anderson, Capt., 35
Anderson, Lieut.-Gen., succeeds General Sir J. Willcocks in command of Indian Army Corps, 120
Anderson, Second Lieut., 47
Anley, Major B. L., 86; commands 1st Battalion, 113
Annequin, 99, 137
Annexation Parade and March Past before Field-Marshal Lord Roberts, 32
Ansted, Capt., D.C., 44
Anstruther, Major, 35
Anthony, Capt., wounded, 126, 127
Antwerp, 100
Appreciative Messages, Orders, etc.:
 1st Battalion: action of 6th January 1900, 14; action of 19th December 1901, 23; action of 24th March 1902, 25; on leaving Colonel Park's command May 1902, 27; on conclusion of hostilities in South Africa, 28; on leaving Secunderabad, 68; at Delhi Durbar, 69; on achievements at Givenchy, 20-21st December 1914, 112; fight at Neuve Chapelle 1915, 116-7; specially mentioned for "Great service" performed at 2nd Battle of Ypres, 119; Brig.-Gen. Strickland's letter on relinquishing command of

Jullundur Brigade, 122; on departure of Indian Corps from France, 122-4; action against Dujailah Redoubt 8th March 1916, 153; on capture of Abu Roman position 5th April 1916, 154-5; fighting April 1916, 157; fighting January 1917, 163; fighting 24-25th March 1917, 166-7; Major-Gen. Keary on relinquishing command of Lahore Division, 185; operations at Tekrit, 5th November 1918, 190; lorry incident in Ireland, 207; action between Coachford and Dripsey in Ireland, 211; operations at Jordan's Bridge in Ireland, 211
 2nd Battalion: Miranzai Expedition, 40; manœuvres September 1903, 73; on leaving Channel Isles 1907, 75; manœuvres 1909 and in garrison at Portsmouth, 79; on presentation of Colours 1911, 82; on work with 5th Divisional Artillery 1914, 96; action on Western Front of 29th October 1914, 102; farewell order of General Sir H. L. Smith-Dorrien to 2nd Army Corps, 1st January, 1915, 104-5; address to troops of 14th Brigade on leaving 2nd Army Corps, July 1915, 128-9; raid of 27th February 1918, 172; work in August 1918, 175; operations of 1st October 1918, 177
Army in France: Special Order of the Day by Commander-in-Chief in France, Christmas 1914, 104
Volunteer Service Company: on departure from South Africa for England 1900, 31-3
Arcadia, 17, 32
Archer, Pte., wounded, 10
Archibald, Pte., wounded, 20
Archibald, Pte., promoted for gallantry, 54; Corpl., 55, 58
Armagh Wood, 126, 127
Armentières, 114
Armistice, 200
Armitt, Pte., wounded, 23
Arms used by the Manchester Regiment, 266-8

345

INDEX

Army List, November 1906, last four line battalions, 340; August 1881, amalgamation of 63rd and 96th Regts. into the Manchester Regiment, 341
Army Orders concerning Medals issued for the Great War, 201
Arneke, 168
Ashley, Pte., death, 13
Ashton-under-Lyne, 76, 82; 3rd Volunteer Battalion, 16, 30, 32, 205
Ashtown, 80
Assesse, 213
Assig, Second Lieut., 124
Atherley, Capt., 158
Atkin, Second Lieut., 154, 163; wounded, 166
Attara, 195
Attichy, 95
Aubers, 114
Audruicq, 170
Austin's Drift, 54
Austria, Archduke Franz Ferdinand of, 73
Authuille, 132, 134
Aveluy, 133
Aveluy Wood, 134
Avesnes, 213
Avingdon Park, 73
Ayette, 172
Aylmer, General Sir F., 125, 147, 150, 153; relinquishes command of Tigris Corps, 154
Aziziya, 164
Azzum, 198

B

Babbage, Second Lieut. J. C., death, 331
Badfontein, 20, 21
Badges of the Manchester Regiment, Notes on, 224–268
Baghdad, 158, 164, 167, 186, 191, 216, 217, 218, 223
Baiji, 219
Bailleul, 145
Baka, 198
Baker, Lieut., 44, 58
Baldry, Second Lieut. W. G. F., death, 189
Baldwin, Lieut., 40; Capt. and Adjt., 40
Baldwin, Lieut.-Col., commands 1st Battalion, 69
Baldwin, Major, 73, 75
Ball, Second Lieut. W. C., death, 331
Ball, Pte., death, 31
Ballard, Major, 96
Ballincollig, 207, 208, 211, 212
Ballyvourney, 207, 208, 211
Balshaw, Lieut., 98; missing, 100
Balshaw, Lieut. W., death, 331
Bamboosberg, 51
Bamford, Lieut. P., 31, 33
Bangalore, 68
Bankes, Quartermaster, 3, 29, 81
Baquba, 165, 186
Barberton, 63
Barker, Second Lieut., 154; wounded, 155
Barlow, Colonel, 81

Barlow, Major, 38, 39; Lieut.-Col., 40
Barly, 173
Barnard, Lieut.-Col. W. O., 35, 36; relinquishes command of 2nd Battalion, 37; Major-Gen. Colonel of the Manchester Regiment, 77, 79, 81, 104; death, 190, 205, 343, 344
Barnes, Major-Gen. R. W. R., commanding 32nd Division, 141
Barnes, Pte., death, 20
Barratt, Lieut., 213
Barrett, Pte., wounded, 11
Barrosa Barracks, 2
Barrow, Lieut.-Gen. Sir E., 68
Bartley, Pte., death, 13
Barton, Major-Gen., 32
Barton, Sergt., 58
Basra, 1st Battalion arrives at, 124, 125, 147, 191; 2nd Battalion arrives at, 215, 216, 2nd Battalion embarks at, for India, 223
Bassett, Col.-Sergt., 29
Basuto Hill, 53, 56
Bateman, Pte., 29, 30
Bates, Capt., 69
Bates, Pte., death, 55
Bathurst, Capt., 75
Baugh, Second Lieut., 177
Bavai, 87, 90, 91
Baxter, Lieut., 124; death, 153
Bayley, Hon. Sir Charles, 68
Bayley, Lieut., 75, 76
Bayliss, Second Lieut. R. B., death, 331
Beach, Colonel-Commandant W. H., Commanding 21st Indian Infantry Brigade, 338
Beadle, Major, 188
Beattie, Pte., wounded, 13
Beaucourt, 174
Beaumetz-les-Aires, 124
Beaumont Hamel, 134, 137, 138, 141
Beau Puits, capture of, 100
Beaurevoir–Fonsomme Line, 176
Beauval, 137, 141
Beauvois, 141, 142, 144, 145
Bedford, Second Lieut., 124; death, 153; Second Lieut. C. C., 330
Beisan, 195
Beit Aiessa, 155, 156, 185
Beit Imrin, 199
Beit Udhen, 199
Belfast, 23, 24, 27, 82, 211
Belfield, Brig.-Gen., 73
Bell, Pte., 29, 30
Belle Vue, 169
Bellinglise, 176
Bennett, Lieut., 171; wounded, 173
Bentley, Lieut. C. L., death, 331; memorial, 332
Bentley, Pte., wounded, 13
Bentley, Second Lieut., 98; death, 101
Bergendal Farm, 20, 31
Berguette, 124
Berny, 175
Berry, Pte., wounded, 23
Berry, Second Lieut., 171; wounded, 173

Bertrancourt, 141
Berukin, 196
Bethancourt, 99
Bethel, 24, 26
Bethlehem, 47; distribution of 2nd Battalion in defence of, 50, 51–5, 60, 61
Béthune, 110, 136
Bettington, Second Lieut., wounded, 115
Bhopal, heir-apparent of, 72
Biddulphsberg, 45
Biggarsberg, 4
Bikanir, Maharaja of, 72
Billy-sur-Ourcq, 97
Bir Adas, 195, 197
Bird, Pte., death, 13
Bitry, 95
Black, Surg.-Capt., 44, 48
Blackdown, re-formation of 1st Battalion, 205
Black Horse Shelters, 134
Blairville, 173, 174
Blane, Second Lieut., 100
Blarney, 211
Blocksidge, Second Lieut., 192; Lieut., 202
Bloemfield, 53
Bloemfield Bridge, 56, 62
Bloemfontein, 46, 52, 59
"Bloody Salient," 126
Bluff, The, 126, 127
Boescheppe, 117
Boesinghe, 170
Bohain, 177
Bohin, Pte., death, 23
Boileau, Lieut., 35
Bois de Biez, 114, 115, 116
Bois des Roses, 143, 144
Bois Français, 129
Bolton, Lieut., 75, 80
Bombay, 41, 107; 2nd Battalion arrives at, 214, 223
Bond, Pte., wounded, 13
Bonn, 213, 214
Boone, Second Lieut., 46, 50; specially mentioned for gallantry, 51, 57, 58
Bordon, 205, 214
Borély, 108
Bostock, Pte., death, 13
Bostock, Second Lieut., 69; Capt. 158
Botha's Pass, captured, 18
Bouchoir, 141
Bougincourt, 134, 136, 137
Boulers, 95
Bounds, Pte., 28
Bourne, Second Lieut., 154
Boutflower, Second Lieut., 75
Boves, 174
Bowden, Second Lieut., wounded, 177
Bowers, Pte., wounded, 13
Bowles, Mrs. Vere Hunt, 263
Boyes, Major-Gen., 42, 44, 47
Boyle, Second Lieut., wounded, 126
Boyle, Lieut., death, 13
Brabazon, Colonel, 44
Bradshaw, Pte., wounded, 8; death, 13
Brady, Second Lieut., 171
Braine, 98
Brakspruit, 52
Bramley, Second Lieut., 173

INDEX

Bramley, Second Lieut. A. H., death, 331
Bramwell, Corpl., wounded, 13
Brandreth, Pte., death, 23
Brandwater Basin, 46, 51, 60, 61
Brétigny, 95
Bridgford, Capt., 3, 4, 19, 21, 29
Brielen, 169
Briggs, Second Lieut. D. H., 143, 144
Brindisi Poort, 51
Brindley, Capt., 58
Briquemesnil, 174
"British Musketeers," Representation of, at Army Pageant 1910, 79
Brittorous, Lieut., 215, 217, 223; Lieut. F., 337, 339
Broadbent, Pte., wounded, 19, 21
Broad Wadi, 187
Broadwater, Pte., death, 13
Broadwood, Colonel, 54, 61
Brocklehurst, General, 19
Brodribb, Lieut. R., 86, 87; death assumed, 95
Bronkhartsfontein, 47
Brookes, Corporal, 29
Brooking, General, 186
Brown, Capt., 148; Major, 162
Brown, Capt. R.A.M.C., 87, 98
Brown, Co.-Q.-M.-Sergt. J., 339
Brown, Lieut., 70
Brown, (No. 4100), Pte., wounded, 19
Brown, Pte., wounded, 10
Brown, Pte. A., wounded, 13
Brown, Pte. J., wounded, 13
Brown, Second Lieut., 213
Browne, Lieut., 107; Capt., 115, 116; Major, 124
Brown Hill, 196, 197
Brownhill, Pte., death, 13
Brownlow, Colonel, 39
Brownson, Second Lieut., 173, 213
Bruce-Hamilton, General, 26
Brugspruit–Waterval blockhouse line, 25
Brunswick Stars, 280-1
Buchan, Second Lieut., 29; Capt., 107; commands 1st Battalion, 113; gassed, 118
Bughtie, 56
Bulfin, Lieut.-Gen. Sir Edward, commanding XXI Corps, 192, 195, 198
Bullen, Second Lieut., 177
Buller, General Sir Redvers, 12, 14, 16, 18, 20
Bullman, Pte. L. G., 194
Bulwana, 15
Burdon, Lieut., 124; death, 153; Lieut. J., 330; memorial, 332
Bureid Ridge, 193
Burke, Pte., wounded, 8
Burke, Sergt., 29, 58
Burke, Sergt.-Major, 58
Burkett-Gottwaltz, Second Lieut., 173
Burkha, 202
Burkitt, Lieut., 206
Burley, Co.-Q.-M.-Sergt. A., 339
Burnett, Lieut.-Gen. Sir C., 77
Burrows, Capt., 212
Burrows, Lieut. R. F. G., 87; wounded, 95

Burton, Second Lieut., 171
Busnes, 137
Bussigny, 177
Butler, Lieut. W. E., 86, 87; wounded, 95
Butler, Pte., death, 8
Butterworth, Lance-Corpl., death, 13
Butterworth, Pte., death, 12
Butterworth, Second Lieut., 124; wounded, 149; Lieut., missing, 166
Byng, General Sir Julian, 338
Byng, Major-Gen. Sir John, 337, 338

C

Cadre, 1st Battalion despatched from Jerusalem, 204; 2nd Battalion leaves Bonn for England, 214
Cæsar's Camp, 11-16, 78
Caestre, 128
Cairo, 108
Calais, 129
Caledon Valley, 46
Caledonian Club, 171
Cambridge Barracks, 76
Cambridge, Duke of, 1
Cambrin, 99, 137
Camp Cercottes, 108
Campbell, Brig-Gen. L., commands 9th Brigade, 166
Campbell, Lieut., 124
Campbell, Major-Gen., 42, 51
Canal Bank Trench, 168, 169, 170
Candler, Mr., 189
Cape Colony, 3
Capetown, 3; 1st Battalion arrives at, 28; 2nd Battalion arrives at, 44, 63, 64
Cappock, Second Lieut., wounded, 176
Carey, Pte., wounded, 48
Carlepont, 95
Carnegie, Major-Gen. P. M., 106, 113
Carney, Pte. J., 194
Carr, Lieut., 108
Carroll, Lieut., wounded, 176
Carter, Col.-Sergt., 82
Carter, Pte., 22
Carter, Quartermaster, 215, 223, 337, 339
Carter, Sergt., 29
Cassidy, Second Lieut., 170; Lieut.-Col., 205
Castle, Pte., wounded, 13
Castle Knock, 80
Castletown, Isle of Man, 2
Casualties, In South African campaign, 1st Battalion, 28-9; 2nd Battalion, 57-8; of 1st Battalion in action against Dujailah Redoubt, 152; during the Great War 1914-18, Roll of officers killed in action, 330-1; total numbers killed in action or died, battalions and depots of the Manchester Regiment, 334-5
Cates, Second Lieut., 75
Cathal Brugha, 210
Catillon, 180

Caudry, 94
Caulfeild, Lieut., death, 103
Caulfield, Lieut. J. C., death, 331; memorial, 332
Cawley, Lieut., 223
Centenary Celebrations, 336-9
Chacrise, 97
Chagru Kotal, 39
Chakrata, 41
Chalela, 155
Champagne, 114, 120
Champagne heights, 97
Chandler, Sergt., mortally wounded, 27
Chandler, Sergt., wounded, 12
Chandri Chowk, 69
Chapeau Rouge, 168
Chapigny, 102
Chapman, Lance-Corpl., wounded, 49
Chapman, Pte., wounded, 8
Charlestown, 18
Chase, Sergt., wounded, 23
Chataignies Wood, 176
Château Mazinghem, 123
Château Pomery, 142
Château St. Avoe, 96
Châtillon, 178
Chaundry, Lance-Corpl., wounded, 20
Chauvel, Lieut.-Gen. Sir Harry, 195
Cheatham, Pte., death, 13
Chezy-sur-Ourcq, 97
Chilabagh, 40
Chittenden, Lieut. A. G., 205
Chittenden, Lieut. A. G. B., 87; death, 97, 331; memorial, 332
Chivres, 98
Cholera, outbreak of, August 1894, 41
Christmas Card from the King and Queen, 1914, 104
Church, Colonel, 81
Chute, Capt., 75
Cingolo Hill, 15
Cizancourt, 175
Claber, Pte., prisoner, 20
Clacton, 73
Clark, Corpl., wounded, 45
Clarke, Joseph, 210
Clarke, Lieut., 21, 103
Clarke, Pte., wounded, 20
Clarke, Sergt., 58
Clegg, Second Lieut., 75
Clifford, Second Lieut., 192
Clonmell, 2
Close Brooks, Capt., 158; death, 162; Capt. A. B., death, 330
Cluer, Pte., death, 13
Coachford, 211
Coalin, Pte., wounded, 13
Cobbe, General, commands 1st Indian Corps, 159, 160, 163, 188, 190
Cockburn, Capt., 57
Coggan, Pte., 53
Coghill, Second Lieut., 3, 4
Colchester, 1, 73
Coleman, Co.-Sergt.-Major C. D., 339
Coleman, Second Lieut., 213
Colenso, 17
Collier, Pte., Great gallantry under fire, wounded, 49, 58

INDEX

Collins, Pte., 55
Cologne, 214
Colommiers, 96
Colonels, succession of, 63rd Foot, 96th Foot, and the Manchester Regiment 1758-1920, 282
Colonel's Farm, 171
Colours of the Manchester Regiment, Notes on, 261-8
Colours, consecrated, 35; placed in Manchester cathedral, 37; presented to 4th Battalion, 65; 3rd and 4th Battalions, 66; 2nd Battalion, 80; of 2nd Battalion fetched from England, 213
Comines Canal, 127
Commando Nek, 45, 51
Commemoration 1917 at Albert Hall, The First Seven Divisions, 181-4
Commerford, Pte., death, 20
Compte Calix, Pte., 108
Compton, Brig.-Gen., 141
Condé, bridge at, 97
Connaught, Field-Marshal, Duke of, presents Colours to 4th Battalion, 65, 74
Connell, Lieut. S. D., memorial, 332
Connell, Second Lieut., 107; Lieut., 109; death, 110
Connery, Capt. M., 344
Connery, Col.-Sergt., 29
Connery, Pte., wounded, 55
Connery, Q.-M.-Sergt., 80
Connery, Sergt.-Major, 76; Quartermaster, 80, 81, 87, 92
Connor, Sergt., death, 13
Conroy, Pte., 29
Contay, 137
Contay Wood, 133
Cooper, Second Lieut., 158, 187, 212
Cooper-King, Capt. G., 43, 50, 57, 58, 75
Coppack, Second Lieut., 213
Corbie, 129
Cordon, Sergt.-Major W. I., 44
Cork, 65, 207; 1st Battalion embarks at, for Channel Isles, 212
Corley, Lieut. J. A., 337
Coronation of King Edward VII, 28
Correspondence with 8th (Southland) Regiment, New Zealand, 70-71
Corunna Barracks, 66
Cosgrave, Capt., 124, 187
Couchy à la Tour, 136
Coulter, Pte., death, 10
Cove Redoubt, 10
Coxyde, 168
Crater Barracks, 41
Crawford, Lieut.-Col., commanding 1st Battalion, 120
Crawford, Pte., wounded, 8
Crawhall, Lieut., 86; wounded, 118
Creagh, Second Lieut., 3; Lieut., 4; Capt., 30, 68, 107, 109; death, 112; Capt. L., 330,
Crépy-en-Valois, 95
Crete, 5
Crichton, Capt., 65

Crichton, Lieut., 3, 4; Capt., mortally wounded, 21
Croasdale, Sergt., 29
Cronin, Lieut., 173
Cronje, 15
Cronshaw, Lieut., 53
Crouch, Corpl., wounded, 13
Crozier, Second Lieut., 46, 62
Crucifix Corner, 134
Cuinchy, 99
Culley, Second Lieut., gassed, 173
Cummings, Lance-Corpl., 68
Cummings, Pte., 30
Cummins, Pte., wounded, 20
Curlu, 130, 134
Curragh, The, 82, 83
"Curragh Incident, The," 83-84
Curran, Lieut.-Col., 3, 5, 6; wounded, 8, 11, 13, 16, 19, 21, 24, 25; relinquishes command of 1st Battalion, 28-29
Curtis, Lieut., death, 115
Curtis, Lieut. W., 330
Curtis, Lieut. P. L., 337

D

Dahra Bend defences, 163
Dahra Canal, 164
Dailey, Capt. C. G., 337
Dainty, Pte., wounded, 8
Dalby, Pte., death, 13
Dalhousie, 70, 106
Dalmanutha, 20, 24
Damery Woods, 174
Dance, Pte., wounded, 12
Danford, Colonel, kidnapped in Ireland, 207
Danks, Lieut., 3, 5; death, 8
Dann, Second Lieut., 21
Danvers, Sergt., wounded, 12
Danvers, Sergt., wounded, 22-23
Darband, 38, 40
D'Arcy, Pte., wounded, 11
Dargle Road, 4
Darlington, Lieut. H. C., 16, 31, 33
Darwell, Lieut., 88
Daur, 187, 188, 190
Davenport, Pte., death, 13
Davey, Pte., injured, 21
Davidson, Second Lieut., 98; wounded, 99; Lieut., 107, 108; mortally wounded, 109; Lieut. R.I.M., 330; memorial, 332
Davidson, Capt., 215, 223; Capt. M. R., 337, 339
Davies, Pte., wounded, 20
Davies, Second Lieut., 126
Davies, Sergt., death, 23
Davies, Sergt.-Cook, 29
Davis, Pte., wounded, 8
Davis, Pte., mortally wounded, 193
Davis, Second Lieut., 124; death, 153
Dawson, Pte., 55
Deakin, Second Lieut., 3; Lieut., 6, 21; Capt., wounded, 22-23, 29, 75
Dean, Second Lieut., 75
Dearden, Second Lieut., 75; Lieut., 81; Major, 206

Decorations, etc., South African Campaign, 1st Battalion, 29; 2nd Battalion, 58; 1914 Star to 2nd Battalion, 170; Military Medals to 2nd Battalion 5th March 1918, 172; medals for the Great War 1914-18, 201; V.C.'s, 29, 102, 118, 220; D.C.M.'s, 144, 221; M.M.'s, 172; medals and clasps for Miranzai Expedition 1891, 40; "Samana 1891" clasp to India Medal, 40; medals for operations in Mesopotamia, 223; promotion for gallantry, 54; special mention for gallantry, 51; decorations and honours roll, 63rd Foot, 96th Foot, 1st and 2nd Battalions, The Manchester Regiment, 318-329
Deering, Sergt. A. V., 221
Dehra Dun Brigade, 114
Delagoa railway, 26
de Lancy Forth, Lieut., 75
Delaney, Lance-Corpl., death, 8
de la Penha, Second Lieut. P. D., 43, 47, 58
Delhi, 35, 37, 40, 69, 70
de Lisle, Colonel, 54
Demobilisation, 1st Battalion, commences, 202; 2nd Battalion commences, 213
Dennerley, Pte., 76
Dennison, Lieut., 173
Dennys, Lieut., 35
Deolali, 223
de Putron, Lieut., 75, 82, 96
Derbyshire, Sergt., 22
de Valera, 210, 212
Devonshire Post, 10, 11
De Wet, 44, 45
Dewetsdorp, 44, 45, 59
Dewhurst, Pte., death, 8
Diala River, 164, 165, 186
Dieval, 99
Dinapore, 41
Dirty Bucket Camp, 170
Disbandment, 3rd Battalion, 64, 343; 4th Battalion, 66, 343
Diwaniyah, 218, 219, 221
Dixmude, 114
Dixon, Second Lieut., 86; missing, 100; Second Lieut. G., death, 331
Dobson, Second Lieut., 212
Dolan, Lieut. J. J., 337
Dompierre, 134
Donoughmore, 211
Doran, Sergt., 82
Doran, Pte., wounded, 54
Dorling, Capt., 82
Dorling, Lieut. F. H., 43; Capt., 86; Lieut.-Col. commands 1st Battalion, 206, 208, 212
Dorward, Brig.-Gen. Sir A., inspects 1st Battalion, 67
Doullens, 174
Dours, 90
Dover, 214
Drafts furnished by 4th Battalion 1901-1906, 65
Drakensberg Defence Force, 18
Dranoutre, 103, 126

INDEX

Dripsey, Lieut., 209, 211, 212
Driscoll, Pte., wounded, 23
Dualey, Lance.-Corpl., wounded, 55
Dublin, 42, 80, 86, 206, 207
"Duck's Bill," 120
Duffield, Armourer Q.-M.-Sergt. J., 339
Duffy, Sergt., 152
Dujailah Redoubt, 150; capture of, and withdrawal from, 151-3; 158, 185
Dullstroom, 23
Duncalf, Pte., 55
Duncan, Corpl., 28
Dundee, 9, 18
Dunkerke, 168, 214
Dunlop, Lieut., 3, 4, 16; Capt., 21, 69, 107; death, 109; Capt., F.C.S. 330
Durban, 3, 4, 23, 30, 32, 57
Durbar, Grand, at Rawal Pindi, 34; Coronation, at Delhi, 69
Durham, Pte., 55
Dyer, Lieut., 212
Dyson, Lance-Corpl., wounded, 23

E

Eady, Second Lieut., wounded, 145
Eastgate-Smith, Capt. C. W., death, 175, 331
East Infantry Barracks, 1
Eastwick, Second Lieut., 202
Eaton, Capt., 26
Eddowes, Second Lieut., 3, 10; wounded, 11; Lieut., 21; Capt., 68; Major, 215, 223; Lieut.-Col. W. B., 336, 337, 339
Edenburg, 44, 59
Edmund Candler, 164
Edwards, Brig.-Gen. S. M., commanding 8th Brigade, 166, 192
Edwards, Lieut., 202
Eecke, 145
Egan, Lieut. F. C., 336, 337, 339
Egmont-op-Zee, 36
Egypt, 36, 42
Eikeboom, 26
El Afule, 195
Elandslaagte, 5, 6, 18, 32, 77-78
Eland's River Bridge, 49, 50, 55, 60, 61
Elandspruit, action near, 22
Eldon, Col.-Sergt., 68
El Fedan, 192
El Funduk, 198, 199
El Lejjun, 195
Ellershaw, Second Lieut., 56, 57
Elliot, Lieut., 103; Lieut. F. P., death, 330
Elliott, General, Columns under, 52
Elmsley, Second Lieut., wounded, 174
El Orah, 156
El Tira, 195, 196
Elverdinghe, 170, 172
Embarkation, 1st Battalion for South Africa, 3; 2nd Battalion for South Africa, 43; 2nd Battalion for France, 86
Emile Camp, 170
Ennemain, 175
Entrenchment Barracks, 67
Equipment, Web Infantry, issued, 72

Ermelo, 19
Ermelo-Standerton blockhouse line, 25, 26
Erskine, Lieut. J. D. B., 43; Capt., 50, 57
Esbly, 95
Esdraelon, Plain of, 195
Es Sinn, 149, 150, 151, 158, 159
Establishment, reduction, 3rd and 4th Battalions, 64
Estaires, 108, 109, 114
Etreux, 178
Euphrates, The, 186, 216, 217, 218, 221, 222
Evans, Capt., 98, 101; commands 2nd Battalion, 102; Lieut.-Col., 206, 209, 210, 212
Evans, Pte., wounded, 8, 12; death, 19
Evill, Second Lieut., 131
Ewen, Capt., 153, 155
Eykeyn, Second Lieut., 46

F

Facer, Quartermaster, 35
Fagan, Sergt., 29
Falahiyah, 149, 155, 156
Fallières, 99
Fane, General Sir V. B. Colonel of The Manchester Regiment, vice Major-Gen. Barnard, 190, 205, 337, 339, 344
Farmer, Pte., death, 13
Farnham Castle, 205
Farrar, Lieut., 103
Fatehgarh, 37
Fauquissart, 102, 185
Favril, 180
Fazackerley, Second Lieut., wounded, 175
Felleries, 213
Feluja, 186
Fenton, Pte., wounded, 8
Ferekiyeh, 196
Fergusson, Major-Gen. Sir Charles, commanding 5th Division, 86, 87, 90, 98; commanding II Army Corps, 104, 105
Fermoy, 3, 206, 207
Ferozepore Arsenal, Explosion at, 70, 107
Ferozepore Brigade, 110
Festubert, 1st and 2nd Battalions meet at, 101, 108
Ficksburg, 45, 46, 50, 60
"Fifteen Acres," 80
"Fifth Division in the Great War," 101
Findlater, Lieut., 121
Finney, Col.-Sergt., 29
Fir Hill, 196, 197
Fisher, Capt., 82, 107; death, 110; Capt. H., 330
Fisher, Lieut., 6; Capt., 29
Fisher, Pte., death, 20
Fisher, Second Lieut. E., 3, 12; wounded, 13
Fisher, Second Lieut. H., 3; Lieut., 8; wounded, 12, 21, 29
Fishguard, 212
Fitton, Lieut., 35
Fitton, Pte., wounded, 12

Fitzpatrick, Capt., 192
Flanagan, Pte., wounded, 8
Flanagan, Sergt., wounded, 155
Fleet, Pte., wounded, 23
Fletcher, Corpl., 53
Fletcher, Pte., wounded, 19, 31
Fleurbaix, 114
Fleur de Lys badge, 272-279
Flood, Second Lieut., wounded, 166
Foch, General, 133, 181
Foord, Second Lieut. A. G., 52, 57, 62; Lieut., 76; Adjt., 82; Capt., 87, 88, 90, 94; wounded, 97
Forceville, 135
Ford, Capt., 86
Ford, Sergt., death, 23
Forestier Walker, General Sir F., 3
Forrester, Pte., 19
Forshaw, Pte., wounded, 12, 30
Fort Albert, Alderney, 73
Fort Camden, 2
Fort Château à l'Etoc, 73
Fort George, Guernsey, 73
Fort Napier, 4
Fort Sitabuldi, 223
Foster, Rev. H. K., 108
Foulkes, Second Lieut. J., wounded, 181
Fouriesburg, 46, 51
Fowke, Second Lieut., 52, 57; Capt. M.C., 87; death assumed, 95
Fox, Lieut., 70
Frampton, Pte., death, 13
Francilly-Selency, 142, 143, 144
Francis, Sergt., death, 56
Frankfort Line, 139
Fraser, Major-Gen. T., commanding 18th Indian Division, 216, 218
Freeman, Second Lieut., 81
French, Major-Gen., 5, 6, 9, 10, 59; Lieut.-Gen. Sir John, 73; Field-Marshal, message of appreciation on departure of Indian Corps from France, 122-3
Fresnoy, 141
Fresnoy-la-Rivière, 99
Fricourt, 130, 134
Frisby, Lieut., 75
Frise, 129, 130, 134
Froidchapelle, 213
Frost, Pte., death, 23
Fry, Brig.-Gen. W., 77
Fulda, Second Lieut., 75
Fullwood Barracks, 2

G

Garhwal Brigade, 116, 121
Gaukroger, Second Lieut. H., 124; death, 145, 330
Gauntlett, Capt., 101; wounded, 102
Gazette, The Manchester Regiment, 342
Geary, Lieut., 103
Gebhardt, Co.-Q.-M.-Sergt., F. 339
Gee, Pte., wounded, 11; death, 13
Geluk, 20, 31
Germaine, 142
German Emperor, Guard of Honour for, 76

INDEX

Gethin, Major, commands 3rd Battalion, 43; Lieut.-Col., 62, 63, 64
Gibbon, Pte., wounded, 13
Gibraltar, 2, 3, 41, 214
Giffard, Sir H. A., 75
Gillam, Capt., 75
Gillanders, Rev. R., wounded, 168
Gilligan, Pte., death, 21
Gilligan, Pte., mortally wounded, 54
Girdwood, General, commanding 96th Brigade, 173
Givenchy, 99; capture of, 100; 1st Battalion action at, December 20th–21st, 1914, 110–113, 114, 185
Gleeson, Col.-Sergt., 29
Glen, Second Lieut. D. A., memorial, 332
Glencoe, 5
Glover, Lieut., 131; Capt. G. M., 143; wounded, 144, 145, 214, 215; death, 221
Glyn, Pte., wounded, 13
Gnatong, 41
Godbold, Lieut., 41
Godewaerswelde, 129
Golden Gate, 51
Goldfinch, Capt. and Brevet Major W. H., 43, 50, 58
Gommecourt, 134
Goodman, Lieut., 192, 202
Goodson, Col.-Sergt., 68
Gordon, Lieut., 162
Gordon, Second Lieut., 22; wounded, 23, 28, 29
Gordon Castle, 132
Gorre, 108, 110
Gorringe, Brig.-Gen., 79; Major-Gen., succeeds General Aylmer in command of Tigris Corps, 154, 157
Gough, General, 137
Gough, Pte., wounded, 13; 58
Gourdon, Corpl., 108
Graham, Capt., 37, 38; Major, 40; death, 41
Graham, Second Lieut., 154; death, 162; Lieut. E. C., death, 330
Grand Casemate Barracks, 2
Grand Morin, 96
Granger, Corpl., death, 13
Grant, Sergt., 29
Graskop, 18, 19
Gravesend, 1
Gray, Lieut. F., 337, 339
Green, Lieut., 86
Green, Pte., 55
Green, Pte., death, 13
Green, Pte., wounded, 13
Green, Second Lieut., 103; Capt., 215, 217, 218, 223; Capt. H. R. C., 337
"Green Horse," representation of, at Army Pageant, 79
Greer, Lieut., 215, 223; Lieut. E., 336, 337, 339
Gregg, Second Lieut., mortally wounded, 177
Gregory, Pte., wounded, 13
Gresty, Sergt., 29
Grey, Lieut., 215

Greylingstad, 32
Grierson, Lieut.-Gen. Sir James, 86
Grindel, Second Lieut., wounded, 127, 206
Gudgeon, Second Lieut. E. L., wounded, 126; death, 127, 331
Guernsey, 64, 66, 73, 74, 75, 212, 343
Guinness, Lieut., 75
Guinness, Second Lieut., wounded, 128
Gulistan, 39, 40
Gumbat, 38, 40
Gun Hill, 9
Gunning, Lieut., 38, 40
Guttery, Pte., death, 13
Gwatkin, Colonel W. G., 64
Gwynne, Second Lieut., 158
Gwyther, Second Lieut., 115; wounded, 127; Lieut., 130–1; Capt., 138

H

Hableh, 195, 198, 200
Haddon, Sergt.-Major, 29
Hadrah, 196
Hai, River, 158, 159, 160, 163
Hai (town), 163
Haig, Lieut.-Gen. Sir Douglas, 86
Haigh-Wood, Second Lieut., 131
Haillicourt, 119
Haines, Pte., conspicuous coolness and courage under fire, 48
Hainin, 87
Hainin, River, 88
Hair, method of wearing, 268
Haldane, Lieut.-Gen. Sir A., commanding in Mesopotamia, 216, 217, 218, 221, 223
Hall, Lance-Corpl., injured, 21
Hall, Pte., wounded, 8, 48
Hall, Second Lieut., wounded, 174–5
Hall, Sergt., 29
Haller, 103
Halloy, 141
Hamel, 133
Hamilton, Colonel Ian, 5, 6, 9, 10, 16; General Sir, 77–79
Hammonia, 46
Hancey, Pte., wounded, 13
Hancock, Pte., 28; wounded, 49
Hancourt, 177
Handley, Second Lieut., wounded, 173; Lieut. F., 70
Hangest, 174
Hangu, 38, 39, 40
Hanley, Pte., death, 13
Hannah, see "Umm-el-Hannah"
Hannan, Pte., wounded, 19
Harbonnière, 174
Hardcastle, Lieut., 3, 6; Capt., 29, 57, 79, 80, 81, 82, 86, 98; commanding (temporary) 2nd Battalion, 100; to hospital, 102; Lieut.-Col., commanding 1st Battalion, 124; wounded, 155; resumes command, 157, 193; Lieut.-Col. R. N., 214, 215, 218, 219
Hardecourt, 134
Hardingham, Lieut. A. G. M., 87; Major, 223, 337, 339

Hardman, Lieut., 21
Hardman, Second Lieut. W. G., death, 162, 330
Harem Ridge, 194
Harland, Lieut. H., 205
Harper, Capt. J. S., 337, 339
Harper, Pte., death, 8
Harper, Pte., wounded, 12
Harper, Second Lieut. J. S., 75; Lieut., 81, 87, 88, 94, 95; wounded, 102
Harries, Pte., wounded, 11
Harris, Lance-Corpl., 29, 30
Harris, Lieut., 47
Harris, Pte., wounded, 12
Harrismith, 46, 47, 48, 51, 52, 53; defences taken over by 2nd Battalion, 53, 54, 55, 56, 57, 60, 61
Harrison, Pte., wounded, 13
Harrison, Second Lieut., 53, 75; Lieut., 82, 107; Capt., 214; Adjt., 215, death, 221
Hart, Major-Gen., 44
Hart, Second Lieut., 187, 189; death, 199
Hart, Sergt., wounded, 23
Hartley, Pte., death, 13
Harvey, Co.-Q.-M.-Sergt. E., 339
Hastewell, Sergt.-Major, 135
Hastings, Second Lieut. W. C. N., 43; Lieut. and Adjt., 50; Capt., 57, 58, 69, 70, 107, 108
Hathingsdal, 55
Haucourt, 94
Hauteville, 172
Haut Pommereau, 120
Havre, 87
Hawke, Lieut., 215, 223
Haynes, Lieut., wounded, 169
Hayward, Second Lieut., 173; Lieut. F., 205
Hazebrouck, 128
Headlam, Brig.-Gen., 95
Heath, Pte., death, 8
Heath, Second Lieut., 191, 192
Hébuterne, 134
Heelis, Lieut., 69, 75; Capt., Adjt., 107, 118; Major J. R., commands 2nd Battalion, 214, 215, 216, 337, 339
Heidenkop Redoubt, 138
Helvetia, 20, 21, 23, 24
Hemingway, Pte., wounded, 8
Henderson, Capt., 35
Henderson, Lieut., 215, 223
Henderson, Second Lieut., 107, 126; Capt., 124, 162, 189, 191, 215; Capt. G. S., death, award of posthumous Victoria Cross, 220, 221
Henencourt, 132
Hepworth, Lance-Corpl., 55
Herbert, Corpl., wounded, 131
Hey, Second Lieut., 213
Heydon, Second Lieut. A., 143; death, 145
Heynsberg, 51
Heys, Capt., 21
Heywood, Second Lieut., wounded, 177
Heywood, Capt. B. C. P., 16, 31, 32
Heywood, Col.-Sergt., 110
Heywood, Lieut., death, 121

INDEX

Hibbard, Second Lieut. T. A., 336, 337, 339
Hickie, Second Lieut., 70
Higgins, Drummer, wounded, 12
Higginson, Brig.-Gen. H. W., commanding 17th Infantry Brigade, 207
Hildyard, General, 18, 19
Hill, Second Lieut., 173
Hill, Sergt., 29
Hill 60, 126; battle, 127, 128
Hill 75, 103
Hill 189, 96
Hill 283, 197
Hillah, 217, 218, 219, 220, 221, 222, 223
Hilton, Pte., wounded, 23
Hinaidi, 191
Hindenburg Line, 141
Hindiyah Barrage, 221, 222
Hinges, 99
Hinton's Commando, 24
Hinxman, Sergt. E., 221
Hitchins, Major H. W. E., commanding 1st Battalion, 107; wounded, 112; Lieut.-Col., death, 118, 330; memorial, 332
Hoal, Lieut. F. G., wounded, 181
Hobkirk, Capt., 189, 191
Hodgetts, Second Lieut., 213
Hoffmann, Pte., wounded, 20
Hogan, Sergt., 101; awarded Victoria Cross, 102
Holberton, Brevet Lieut.-Col. P. V., memorial, 333
Holberton, Second Lieut., 52, 53; wounded, 55; Lieut., 57; wounded, 61, 81, 82
Holden, Second Lieut., wounded, 166
Holland, Pte., death, 19
Holland, Second Lieut., 202
Holley, Lieut. S. H., 337
Hollingworth, Lieut., 205, 206; Capt., 212
Hollins, Second Lieut., 171; wounded, 172, 173; Lieut., 215, 223; Lieut. S. E., 337
Holloway, Sergt. Master-Tailor, 76
Holmes, Capt, 124; Capt. E. B., Adjt., 337, 339
Holmes, Lieut., wounded, 162
Holmes, Pte., death, 23
Holmes, Pte., wounded, 20, 31
Holness, Lieut., 115; Capt. H. H. J., 337, 339
Holnon, 142, 143
Holyhead, 42, 206, 214
Honchin, 136
Hooge, 127
Hopkins, Capt., 63, 76
Horby, Second Lieut., death, 168
Horner, Lieut., 223
Horridge, Lieut. R., death, 103, 331
Horsley, Co.-Q.-M.-Sergt. F., 339
Hoseason, Lieut. H. S., 337
Hoskins, Major-Gen., succeeds Major-Gen. Keary in command of Lahore Division, 186, 192
Hospital Farm, 170
Houdain, 91
Houston, Pte., wounded, 8
Houterbek, 24
Houthulst Forest Sector, 171

Houtnek, 45
Hovell, Second Lieut., 21
Howard, Major-Gen., 10, 19
Howard, Pte., 58
Howard, Second Lieut. W. H., death, 331
Howarth, Lieut., 212
Howe, Lieut. E. H., 16, 31, 32, 33
Howick, 4
Howitzer Pits, 168
Howorth, Major, 206
Hoyle, Bandmaster, 82
Hudeira, 195
Hudson, Lance-Corporal, 29
Hudson, Major, 21, 22; death, 23, 29
Hudson, Sergt., 107
Huggard, Second Lieut., wounded, 166
Huggins, Pte., 28
Hughes, Lieut., 38, 40
Hughes, Pte., wounded, 12
Hulme Barracks, 82
Humphreys, Capt., 212
Humphreys, Lieut. N. W., 81, 82, 87
Humphreys, Sergt., 161
Humphreys, Major, wounded, 173
Hunter, Major-Gen., 5
Hunt-Grubbe, Lieut., 3, 4, 6, 13, 16; Capt., 21
Hurst, Sergt., drowned, 147
Huskinson, Lieut., wounded, 118
Hussey, Second Lieut., death, 166
Huwaislat, 190

I

Ignecourt, 174
Imam Bakr, 218
Iman Arbain, 188
Imperani Mountain, 45
Inchigeela, 207, 211
India, 2, 3, 4, 34, 66
India Medal of 1854, "Samana 1891" Clasp, 40
Indian Army Corps, 1st Battalion forming part, transferred from Western Front to Mesopotamia, November 1915-January 1916, 122-125
India's part in the Great War, 72
Ingham, Lieut. H., 202, 204
Intombi, 15
Invincible Standard, 36
Ireland, 2nd Battalion proceeds to, 42, 214; 1st Battalion proceeds to, 206
Irwin, Lieut., 75; Capt., 86, 103, 158; Lieut.-Col. C. D. commands 1st Battalion, 166; 205
Ishmael, Pte., death, 55
Ismaila, 192
Issy Smith, Corpl., awarded Victoria Cross, 118
Istabulat, 167, 186
Ives, Pte., wounded, 20
Izakhi, 190, 191

J

Jack, Second Lieut., 191, 193, 194
Jack Mine, 32

Jackson, Lieut., 154; Capt., death, 162; Capt. W. E., 330
Jackson, Pte., death, 12
Jackson, Pte., wounded, 20
Jackson, Pte., wounded, 55
Jagger, Pte., wounded, 13
James, Lance-Corpl., wounded, 13
James, Lieut. H. L., 35; Capt., 41, 43, 50; Major, 58; commanding 3rd Battalion, 64, 81; Lieut.-Col., commanding 2nd Battalion, 82, 87, 91, 94, 95; to hospital, 100; rejoins 2nd Battalion, 103, 343, 344
James, Second Lieut., 115
Jarbuiyah, 221
Jebb, Capt. J. H. M., Adjt., 43, 50, 58, 75, 76, 82
Jebel Hamrin, 165, 167, 185, 186
Jelameh, 195
Jenin, 195, 198
Jennesinia, 199
Jerusalem, 202, 204
Jezreel, 195
Jibin Wadi, 188, 189, 190
Jiljulieh, 195, 196, 197, 198, 200, 201
Jiyus, 198
Jodhpur, Maharaja of, 72
Johns, Pte., wounded, 48
Johnson, Col.-Sergt., death, 13
Johnson, Lieut., 35
Johnson, Lieut. D. F. F., death, 331
Johnson, Pte., wounded, 20
Johnson, Second Lt., wounded, 177
Jones, Pte., wounded, 8
Jones, Pte., wounded, 13
Jones, Pte., wounded, 23
Jones, Pte. E., awarded Military Medal, 172
Jones, Q.-M.-Sergt., 29
Jones, Second Lieut., 177, 192, 213
Jordan's Bridge, 211
Josephs, Pte., wounded, 12
Joucourt, 176
Joyce, Pte., wounded, 21
Jubbulpore, 336, 338
Jullundur, 68, 70, 106, 107
Jullundur Brigade, 106, 108, 112, 114, 115, 116, 117, 119, 122, 153
Jullundur Nullah, 187
Junono's Kop, 18
Jury, 97, 98, 99

K

Kalkilieh, 196
Kamptee, 67, 68, 69, 223
Kane, Pte., wounded, 13
Kandi Valley, 39
Kantara, 192, 202, 204
Karachi, 106, 107
Karbala, 215
Karind, 216, 217, 218
Kashmir Gate, 70
Kavanagh, commanding X Corps, 128
Kay, Capt., 171, 213
Keary, Major-Gen. H. D'U., commanding Lahore Division, 117, 150, 157, 160, 163, 164, 165, 167; relinquishes command of Lahore Division, Farewell Order, 185-6

INDEX

Keelan, Lance-Corpl., 131
Keetch, Pte., 28
Kefr Kaddum, 198, 199
Keightly, Lieut., 215
Keitley, Lieut. C. H., 337
Kelly, Lance-Sergt., 82
Kelly, Pte., 52
Kelly, Pte. J., 194
Kelly, Pte., death, 13
Kelly, Pte., wounded, 13
Kelsey, Lieut., 215, 217, 223
Kemball, General, 150, 151
Kemmel Hill, 103
Kennedy, Band-Sergt., 68
Kennedy, Col.-Sergt., 58
Kennett, Lance-Corpl., wounded, 13
Kershaw, Pte., injured, 21
Khaidari Bend, 159, 160
"Khanikin Column, The," 164
Khanki Stream, 39
Khanki Valley, 39
Khan Mahawil, 221
Khan Nasiriyah, 222
Kharappa, 39, 40
Kh. Kefr Thilth, 198, 199
Kh. Ras-el-Tire, 198
Kh. Umm-el-Ikba, 192
Khushalgarh, 38, 40
Khusk River, 34
Kifl, 219
Kifri, 186
Kilcoyne, Pte., 28
Killarney, 207
Kilworth, 206, 207
Kimberley, relief of, 15
King Edward VII, Coronation, 28, 57; Review by, June 1903, 73; death, 79
King George V, Accession and Coronation, 79; presents Colours to 2nd Battalion, 80–81; Guard of Honour on visit to Manchester, 82; Message of appreciation on departure of Indian Corps from France, 123–4; Inspects representatives of 96th Brigade, 174; opens Parliament in Belfast, 211
Kinsale, 2, 65
Kirk, Second Lieut., 177
Kirke, Second Lieut., death, 180
Kirkpatrick, Second Lieut. K. E., 44
Kirkuk, 186, 217
Kirwan, Pte., 52
Kitchener, Brig.-Gen., 5, 17; Major-Gen., 20, 21; Lord, 26, 28, 49, 85
Kizil Robat, 167
Klip River, 11
Knibb, Lieut., 206
Knox, Capt. H., 87, 90, 94; wounded, 95; Lieut.-Col., death, 330
Knox, Colonel, 10, 16, 17, 60
Knox, Lieut., 21
Komati River, 19
Koweit, 124, 192
Kufah, 218; relief of, 222
Kurdistan, South, 217
Kuryet Jit, 198, 199

Kut, 125, 147; failure of attempt to relieve, 149, 154; fall of, 157, 158, 159, 160, 164, 167, 191, 216, 217
Kut East Mounds, 162

L

La Bassée, 100, 102, 114, 117, 120
La Bassée Canal, 99, 110, 137
La Bassée Rue, 114, 115
La Bazeque, 174
La Bergerie Camp, 172
La Boisselle, 130, 134, 135
La Brique, 119
La Chaudière, 171
La Cliqueterie Farm, 120
Ladley, Pte., 30
Ladybrand, 60
Ladysmith, 4, 5, 6, 9, 10, 14; end of siege of, 15, 16, 17, 31, 32, 78
La Fere, 178
La Ferté, 96
Lager Alley, 138, 139
Lahore, 106
Lahore Division, arrives region of Ypres, 108, 117, 120, 121; entrains for Marseilles on transfer to Mesopotamia, 122, 123, 160, 185; to Egypt, 192, 193, 196
Laing's Nek, 5, 18
Lajj, 164
Lake, General Sir Percy, 125; General, 154, 157, 158
Lally, Pte., death, 20
Lambert, Major-Gen. T. S., commands 32nd Division, 175, 178
La Motte Farm, 180
Lancer's Nek, 11
Landrecies, 87, 91, 178
Lane, Second Lieut., 121, 124; death, 153
La Neuville, 175
Lang, Capt., 35
Langberg, 55
La Panne, 145, 168
La Petite Douve, 103
La Petite Douve Farm, 126
La Quinque Rue, 109
Laventie, 102
Lawley's column, 26
Lawrence, Second Lieut., 173
Lawson, Second Lieut., 52; Lieut., 57
Leach, Corpl., death, 13
Leach, Pte., wounded, 12
Leach, Second Lieut., 101; awarded Victoria Cross, 102
Le Breuve, 137
Le Cateau, 85, 87, 91, 92–94
Le Couture, 109, 110, 114
Leemount Bridge, 211
Lehancourt, 177
Leicester Post, 11
Leipzig Salient, 135
Le Limon, 96
L'Epinette, 117, 118
Le Préol, 137
Le Quesnel, 174
Le Quesnoy, 99
Le Touret, 99, 109
Le Transloy, 141

Les Trois Maisons, 100
Levis, Capt. F. A., 337, 339
Lewis, Lance-Corpl., wounded, 10
Lewis, Regtl. Q.-M.-Sergt. F., 339
Lewtas, Second Lieut., wounded 131
Lichfield, 42
Liessies, 213
Ligny-le-Grand, 114
Lihons, 134
Lime Street, 16
Limit Hill, 10, 15
Lindley road, 45
Lindsay, Mrs., of Coachford, Heroic action of, 210; memorial service, 212
Lindsay, Pte., death, 13
Lindsay, Sergt., 58; Sergt.-Major, 80, 82
Listergaux, 170
Little Bentley, 73
Liverpool, 2
Lloyd, Col.-Sergt., 29
Lloyd, Sergt., 29
Lloyd George, Mr., 210
Lockhart, Brig.-Gen. Sir William, 37, 39
Locon, 99
Loftus, Pte., death, 13
Logan, Brig.-Gen., 262
Lombard's Kop, 9, 10
Lombartzyde, 168
London, 79, 80, 82
Longbottom, Pte., death, 13
Long Hill, 9
Longpont, 99
"Long Road to Baghdad, The," 188
Longueil, 99
Longworth Camp, 62
Loos, Battle of, 120; offensive, September 1915, 130, 185
Lorette, 133
Lorgies, 100
Loubet, M., President of French Republic, 73
Loupart, 141
Louvignies, 91
Lowther, Second Lieut., 170; Lieut. E. F., death, 331
Ludd, 192, 202
Luffman, Lieut., 212
Lugood, Pte., wounded, 8
Lukin, Colonel, 218
Lumsden, Colonel, V.C., 141
Lumsden, Major, 144
Lund, Second Lieut., 199
Lupton, Capt., 53
Lutz, Pte. Anthony, 36, 266; capture of the standard by, 269–271
Luxmoore, Major, wounded, 130; Lieut.-Col., commanding 2nd Battalion, 134, 135, 142, 169
Lydenburg, 20, 21, 22, 24
Lynch, Lieut., 107; wounded, 112; Capt., 124; death, 153; Capt. R. F., 330; memorial, 332
Lyons, Second Lieut., 192
Lyrett, Pte., C., awarded Military Medal, 772
Lyttelton, General, 5, 18, 20

INDEX

M

Macartney, Capt. J. V., 337, 339
McCabe, Col.-Sergt., 32
McCabe, Pte., death, 12
McCarthy, Pte., wounded, 6, 12
McCarthy, Pte., wounded, 54
McCarthy, Pte., wounded, 55
McCormick, Pte., 55
McCutcheon, Second Lieut., 191, 192
McDermott, Sergt., wounded, 20
Macdonald, Second Lieut., wounded, 176
McDowell, Corpl., 29
McDowell, Lance-Corpl., wounded, 13
McElroy, Sergt., awarded Military Medal, 172
Macgregor, Sir Charles, 34
Machadodorp, 20, 21, 23, 24, 32
Mackay, Second Lieut., 126; wounded, 127
McKeiver, Second Lieut., death, 127; Second Lieut., V.C., 331
McKenzie, Capt., 171; wounded, 175; death, 180; Capt. A., 330
McKenzie, Sergt., 58
Mackenzie's column, 26
McKevitt, Lieut., 212
McKinley, Pte., 30
McLennan, Lieut. H. N., death, 331
McNicholls, Pte., wounded, 48
Macroom, 207, 209
McSherry, Second Lieut., death, 173; Lieut. B., 331
Mackworth, Capt. F. O., death, 330
Madras, 67
Magasis, Turkish Fort, 157
Magny-la-Fosse, 176
Maguire, Assist. Surg., 107
Mahomed Abdul Hassan loop, 162, 185
Mailly-Maillet, 138, 140
Mair, Lieut., 70, 107, 115
Major, Pte., death, 8
Majuba Day, 15
Makin, Pte., death, 21
Makina, 215
Mallow, 211
Maloney, Pte., wounded, 13
Malta, 2, 42
Mametz, 129, 134
Mamuzai Bazar, 39
Manchester, 2nd and 4th Volunteer Battalions, 16, 30, 42, 66; South African memorial, 76, 82
Manchester, Bishop of, 77
Manchester Cathedral, 37
Manchester Quarry, 142, 143
Manchester Regiment Aid Society, 343-4
Manchester Regiment Gazette, 142, 342
Manchester Regiment, 1st and 2nd Battalions meet for first time in 32 years, 101
Mann, Second Lieut. G. E., wounded, 190
Mansergh, Lieut., 46, 49, 57; Lieut. W. G., 87; death assumed, 95
Mansuriah, 187

Marcelcave, 145
Mardall, Second Lieut., 81
Marden, Capt., 3, 5; Adjt., 9; wounded, 13, 21; Major, 25, 28, 29, 75
Maretz, 95
Margharu-Talai Spur, 39
Maricourt, 129, 130, 134
Marley, Second Lieut., wounded, 149, 163; Lieut. V. D. K., 214, 215, 223, 337
Marne Battle, end of, 97
Marne, River, 95, 96
Maroilles, 180
Marryat, Major, 35
Marseilles, 108, 122, 124
Marsh, Lieut., Second Lieut., 56
Marshall, General, commands III Indian Corps, 159, 163, 164; Lieut.-Gen. Sir William, commands Army in Mesopotamia, 191
Marshall, Lieut. J. N., 2nd in command, 2nd Battalion, 173; Major, wounded, 174
Marsland, Pte., wounded, 12
Marten, Lieut. H. H., death, 331
Marteville, 175
Martin, Col.-Sergt., death, 23
Martin, Col.-Sergt., 29
Martin, Lieut., death, 130
Martin, Second Lieut., 103; Capt. G. B., 205, 206
Martin-Smith, Second Lieut., 126, wounded, 127
"Mash" Valley, 136
Masse, Second Lieut., 107; wounded, 109
Masserbock Farm, 59
Mau_, 39, 40
Maubeuge, 85
Maude, Brig.-Gen., commanding 14th Brigade, 104, 129; commands 13th Division 154; Lieut.-Gen. Sir Stanley, 158, 160, 163, 167, 186, death, 190-1
Maud'huy's 10th French Army, 114
Mauquissart, 120
Maxwell, Capt. A. B., 35; Major, 43, 58; Colonel commands 1st Battalion, 75
Maxwell, Lieut.-Col., 30
Mayes, Pte., 82
Medals, 63rd Regiment and 96th Regiment, 265-6
Medals, Army Orders concerning issue of, for the Great War, 1914-1918, 201
Medals, Coronation Durbar, 70
Medals, see "Decorations."
Medworth, Capt., death, 173
Meerut, 37, 40, 41, 106
Meerut Division, 109, 114, 120, 121; entrains for Marseilles on transfer to Mesopotamia, 122
Meerzicht, 19, 31
Mejdil Yaba, 193, 196
Mellor, Pte., wounded, 8
Melvill, Capt., 3, 5; wounded, 8, Major, 29
Melvill, Capt., 35; Major, commands 4th Battalion, 43, 57; Lieut.-Col., C. C., 66

Memorial, Royal Military College, 332-3
Memorial, South African War, unveiling, 76-79
Memorial Tablet, All Saint's Church, Trimulgherry, 68
Mendali, 186
Mentions in Despatches, South African Campaign, 1st Battalion, 29; 2nd Battalion, 58
Menzies, Second Lieut., 38, 40
Menzies, Capt., 3, 11; wounded, 13, 21, 23; mortally wounded, 24, 29
Merriman, Second Lieut, 9; wounded, 12; Lieut., 21, 29; Capt., 75
Merry, Lieut., 212
Merv, 34
Mesopotamia, 1st Battalion to take part in campaign in, 125
Messines, 102, 103
Messines Battle, 145
Messines Ridge, 103
Messudie, 195
Metcalfe, Sergt. J. S., awarded Military Medal, 172
Meteren, 102
Mézières, 174, 180
Middelburg, 20, 63, 343
Middle Hill, 11
Middleton-Stuart, Lieut., 44
Militia Battalions (3rd and 4th) of Manchester Regiment become 5th and 6th Battalions, 43
Mill Post, 132
Mill River Drift, 52
Mill Street, 207, 211
Miller, Lieut. R. T., 87; wounded, 95
Milne, Lieut. D. F., death, 188, 189, 330
Milton, Pte., death, 13
Minchin, Capt., 192, 197
Minogue, Lieut., 75
Minorca, 36
Miranzai Expedition, clasp granted, medals and clasps presented, 40
Miranzai Field Force, 38
Miranzai Valley, 37
Mission Camp, 21
Missy, 98
Mitchell, Pte., wounded, 20
Mitchell, Second Lieut., 173; Second Lieut. F. W., death, 331
Mitlencourt, 132
Moascar, 192
Mobilization, 2nd Battalion for South Africa, 42; for France 86; 1st Battalion for France, 106
Modderspruit, 6, 9
Moncheux, 136
Monchy-Breton, 136
Monchy-Lagache, 175
Monro, General Sir C., commanding Third Army, 129, 136
Monro, Major-Gen., commanding X Corps, 128, 129, 132, 133
Mons, 88, 181
Montauban, 134
Montay, 91
Mont d'Origny, 178
Montreuil, 96

INDEX

Mooi River, 4
Moon, Civil Surgeon, conspicuous bravery, 48
Moore, Lieut., 35
Moore, Second Lieut., 97; wounded, 162; Capt. A. W. V., 205, 206
Moore Park, 206
Moorhead, Second Lieut., 154; Lieut., 206; Capt., Adjt., 212
Moppett, Second Lieut. E. J. H., 336, 337, 339
Moran, Pte., wounded, 8
Morlancourt, 129
Morland, Major-Gen., commanding 5th Division, 104
Morley, Lieut. C., 75; Capt., 87; wounded, 95; Major, 212
Mormal Forest, 178
Morris, Brig.-Gen. G. M., commanding 55 Infantry Brigade, 216
Morris, Second Lieut., wounded, 177; Lieut., 206
Morris, Second Lieut., 75, 124; Lieut., 152; death, 153
Morris, Second Lieut. C., death, 330
Morris, Sergt., 29, 58, 107
Mortiboy, Second Lieut., 173; death, 174
Mosters Hoek, 44
Mosul, 216, 217
Moulin de Fargny, 130
Mound, The, St. Eloi, 126
Mounted Infantry Company, 4, 5, 20, 21, 43, 47, 50, 52, 53, 57, 58, 62, 65
Mountford, Pte., 28
Mouquet Farm, 135
Mourne Abbey, 211
Mukshafa, 187
Muller's Commands, 22
Mullingar, 79, 80, 82
Multan, 34
Munich Trench, 138, 139
Munro, Lance-Corpl., death, 20, 31
Murden, Pte., mortally wounded, 48
Murphy, Lieut., 21, 25
Murphy, Major, 213
Murphy, Pte., death, 8
Murphy, Pte., death, 13
Murphy, Sergt., 29
Murray, Lieut., 103
Murray, Pte., wounded, 55
Musayib, 221, 222
Musson, Lieut., 70; Capt., E. L. 205; Adjt., 206
Mutter, Co.-Sergt.-Major, 223

N

Naauwpoort Nek, 46
Nablus, 195, 199
Nagpore, 223
Nagpur, Bishop of, 339
Nahr Falik, 195
Nahr Umar, 191
Nairne, Major-Gen., presents medals and clasps for Miranzai Expedition 1891, 40
Najaf, 215, 222, 223
Nakhailat, 149, 164
Nanteuil, 95, 99
Napoleon the Great, 36

Nasafieh Canal, 158
Natal, 3, 4, 5, 10
Natal Hills, 53
Natal Spruit, 32
Naylor, Sir Geo., 263
Nazareth, 195
Naziriyah, 217
"Nec Aspera Terrent," 226, 228
Nepal Durbar, 34
Nepal, Prime Minister of, 72
Nepean, Second Lieut., 81
Neuve Chapelle, Battle of, 114-116, 120, 122
Neuve Eglise, 126
Newbigging, Capt., Adjt., 3, 5; wounded, 8, 9, 16, 21, 29
Newbold, Second Lieut., 192
Newbridge, 82
Newcastle, 4, 18
New Denmark, 26
New Parade, 168
Newton, Pte., 58
Newton, Pte., death, 8, 29, 30
Nibbs, Second Lieut., wounded, 145
Niblick, Pte., prisoner, 20
Nichol, Bandmaster J., 339
Nicholas, Second Lieut., 149; Lieut. F. M., Adjt., death, 168, 330
Nicholls, Pte., wounded, 10
Nicholson, Second Lieut., 192; Lieut., death, 103
Nicolson's Nek, 9
Nieuport, 145, 168
Nisbet, Lieut. F. S., 43, 47, 50; Capt., 57, 81, 82; Adjt., 87, 94; death, 95, 331; memorial, 332
Noble, Capt., 47, 48, 49, 50, 52, 53, 54; mortally wounded, 55, 58, 61
Nooitgedacht, 26, 27
Norman, Lieut. S. S., 107; death, 112; memorial, 332
North Wall, 214
Norton, Sergt., 28
Novel Trench, 168
Nusf Jebil, 199

O

Obourg, 88
O'Brien, Quartermaster P., 107, 124, 205, 206, 211, 212
Occupation, British Army of, 2nd Battalion forms part, 213
O'Donnell, Sergt., 55
Officers. Alphabetical Roll, 63rd Foot, 96th Foot and the Manchester Regiment 1758-1923, 283-317
Officers killed in action, 1914-1918, 330-331
Ogden, Col.-Sergt., 80, 82
Ogden, Pte., wounded, 13
O'Grady, Second Lieut., 213
O'Hagan, Lieut. C., 44
Oise, the, 178
Oise Canal, 177-8
O'Leary, Second Lieut., wounded, 128; Lieut. H. H., death, 331
Oliver, Lieut., 57
Olivier's Hoek, 54, 56, 62

O'Meara, Capt., 154; commands 1st Battalion, 155; Major, 206, 207, 212
Onslow, Lieut.-Col., 91
Onvervacht, 24
Oorlog's Poort, 45
Orakzai tribe, primitive expedition against, 37
Organization of 2nd Battalion on four-company basis, 83
Orgill, Lieut. E., Assist. Adjt., 206, 209, 211, 212
Orgill, Second Lieut. J., 206
Orleans, 108
Orwin, Lieut., 212
Ors, 177, 178, 179, 180
O'Toole, Second Lieut., 213
O'Toole, Second Lieut. J. D., wounded, 181
Oudenarde Barracks, 42
Overton, Pte., C. E., awarded the D.C.M., 144
Oveston, Second Lieut., 177
Ovillers, 133, 134, 135, 136
Ovillers Post, 136
Owen, Second Lieut., wounded, 126, 127; Lieut., 149
Owen, Second Lieut. W. E. S., death, 181
Oxley, Second Lieut., 187

P

Paardekop, 19
Paardeplatz, 24
Pageant, Army, June 1910, 79
Page, Pte, wounded, 20
Pakes, Second Lieut. C. W. S., 336, 337, 339
Pan, 24
Paris, 95
Park, Colonel, columns under, 22, 23, 24, 25, 26, 27
Parker, Capt., 126
Parker, Capt. E. D., death, 331, 344
Parker, Col.-Sergt., 81; Sergt.-Major, 82
Parker, Pte., death, 13
Parker, Pte., wounded, 13; wounded, 55
Parker, Second Lieut., 171
Parminster, Second Lieut., 107; Lieut., 115; Capt., Adjt., 124, 156
Parry, Lieut., 202
Parsons, Pte., wounded, 20
Parsons, Second Lieut, 191
Parvillers, 174
Paterson, Lieut., 158
Pathankote, 106
Patiala, Maharaja, 72
Paton, Capt., 4, 5, 7; wounded, 8, 21, 76
Paulson, Lieut., 107; Capt., wounded, 118
Peace signed, South African War, 28
Peacock, Corpl., 52
Peake Station, 209
Pearce, Lieut., 215, 223
Pearce, Sergt.-Drummer, 76
Pearse, Lieut. D. C., 144
Pearson, Pte., 58
Pearson, Lieut.-Gen. Sir A., 69

INDEX

Pegg, Pte., wounded, 8
Peirce, Second Lieut. W. G. K., 43; Capt., 98; death, 102, 331
Peking, 64, 343
Pembroke, Second Lieut, 119; wounded, 162; Lieut., 206
Penjdeh district, 34
Pepworth Hill, 9, 15
Percival, Pte., death, 48
Persia, Shah of, 205
Pertab Singh, Sir, 72
Petite Synthe, 168
Philippeville, 213
Phillips, Capt., 115
Phœnix Park, 80
Picantin, 108, 109
Pickering, Lance-Corpl., wounded, 149
Piet de Wet, 45
Pietermaritzburg, 4, 32
Piggott, Pte., injured, 21
Pike, Q.-M.-Sergt., 29; Sergt.-Major, 68
Pilkington, Pte., wounded, 20
Pill Box, No. 88, 169
Pimm, Lance-Corpl., wounded, 8
Pishin Valley, 34
Pitts, Pte. J., awarded Victoria Cross, 29
Plattberg, 53
Plenty, Lieut. (temporary Major) E. P., memorial, 333
Plumer, General, commanding Second Army, 128
Plunkett, Lieut., 38, 40; Capt., 41
Pomfret, Lieut., 126; Capt., wounded, 127
Pommier Ridge, 130
Pont d'Hinges, 99
Pont Fixe, 110, 111
Pont Moulin, 96
Pontoise, 95
Pont Tournant, 99
Poperinghe, 128, 169
Porle, Pte., death, 13
Portarlington, 82
Port Elizabeth, 44, 46, 59
Porter, Second Lieut., wounded, 176
Portland, 65
Port Said, 124, 204, 214
Portsmouth, 2, 75, 76
Potgieter's Drift, 14
Potts, Second Lieut., wounded, 177
Potts, Sergt., 28
Powell, Major-Gen., 69
Pownall, Pte., wounded, 13
Poyser, Lance-Corpl., death, 8
Presculi defences, 168
Preston, Lance-Corpl., 29, 30
Preston, 64
Pretoria, 31, 32
Price, Pte., 20
Price, Second Lieut., 98; wounded, 100; wounded, 127
Price, Sergt., 58
Prince, Second Lieut., wounded, 23
Prince of Wales, receives German Emperor, 76; reads King's message of appreciation on departure of Indian Corps from France, 123
Princess Mary's present, Xmas 1914, 104
Prinsloo, Commandant, 46, 61

Prioleau, Lieut., 35
Prisches, 213
Prisseloup, 96
Prosser, Sergt.-Major, 58, 76
Prouse, Lieut., 173
Prouse, Second Lieut. R. E., 143
Proven, 172, 174
Prussian Order of the Crown, 76
Purcell, Second Lieut., 158
Pys, 138

Q

Queen of the Belgians Inspects 2nd Battalion, 146
Queen Victoria, Guard of Honour for, 1; death, 49
Queenstown, 2
Quernes, 122
Quinleven, Pte., wounded, 12
Quivères, 145
Quraitu, 216
Qurnah, 147

R

Rackham Bullard, Second Lieut., 52
Raeside, Second Lieut., 197; wounded, 198
Rafat, 196
Railway Redoubt, 196, 197
Raimbert, 137
Raising of 3rd Battalion, 62; 4th Battalion, 64
Ramadi, 186, 217
Ramaithah, 218
Ramleh, 202
Rance, 213
Range Post, 11
Rank of Col.-Sergt., instituted 1813 and abolished 1914, 234
Raphael, Second Lieut., wounded, 127
Ras-el-Ain, 195, 197
Ratcliffe, Pte., wounded, 20
Rawal Pindi, 34, 38, 40
Rawlings, Pte., 52
Rawlinson, General, 133, 137; Lord, 339
Read, Lieut., 75
Reade, Lieut. J. H. L., 76; Adjt., 80, 81, 87, 88; death, 101, 331
Reay, Lieut.-Col. C. T., 43, 45; commands garrison at Bethlehem, 50, 51, 52, 53, 55, 56, 57, 58, 61, 73
Reddersburg, 44, 59
Redford, Pte., death, 23
Redhead, Warrant Officer I, 339
Red House Wood, 193
Redwood, Co.-Sergt.-Major, 339
Re-formation of 1st Battalion at Blackdown, 9th July, 1919, 205
Regiments increased by two line battalions, 43
Regent's Park, 80
Regiments, British:
 Cavalry: 5th Dragoon Guards, 6, 8, 9; 5th Lancers, 6, 8, 18; 8th Hussars, 26; 13th Hussars, 18, 189
 Yeomanry and Mounted Infantry: 1st Battalion Imperial Yeomanry, 42; 4th Battalion Imperial Yeomanry, 42; 11th Battalion Imperial Yeomanry, 42; 62nd Company, Imperial Yeomanry, 54; 4th Mounted Infantry, 25, 26; 18th Mounted Infantry, 26; 19th Mounted Infantry, 26
 Royal Artillery: Brigades: 159th, 145; 161st, 145. Batteries: 2nd, 42; 21st, 6, 7; 39th, 218; 40th, 337; 42nd, 6, 7, 12; 53rd, 13; 72nd, Heavy, 192; 75th, 42; 79th, 42; 96th Trench Mortar, 170; 125th, Heavy, 145; 372nd, 192; 373rd, 192; 374th, 192
 Royal Engineers: 5th Company, 42; 173rd Tunnelling Company, 170; 206th Field Company, 173
 Infantry: Coldstream Guards, 63–64; Grenadier Guards, 42, 53; Irish Guards, 172; Scots Guards, 42, 57, 63, 173; 63rd Regiment at Army Pageant, 79; 96th Regiment at Army Pageant, 79; Argyll and Sutherland Highlanders, 41; Bedfordshire Regiment, 42, 102, 108; Berkshire Regiment, 91; Black Watch, 56; Buffs, the, 80; Cameron Highlanders, 111; Cheshire Regiment, 80, 103, 132; Connaught Rangers, 80, 107, 124, 149, 166, 197; Derbyshire Regiment, 42; Devonshire Regiment, 5, 6, 10, 14, 15, 19, 20, 24, 99, 101, 102, 109, 128, 130, 132, 158, 166, 169, 187, 199; Dorsetshire Regiment, 65, 97, 132, 134, 135, 136, 140, 142, 145, 168, 179, 180, 192, 193, 197; Duke of Cornwall's Light Infantry, 44, 86, 87, 88, 90, 91, 94, 95, 97, 98, 99, 100, 132; Durham Light Infantry, 73; East Lancashire Regiment, 211; East Surrey Regiment, 86, 87, 88, 90, 91, 94, 98, 99, 100, 103, 126, 128, 132, 136, 190; East Yorkshire Regiment, 42, 47, 52, 56; Essex Regiment, 80, 136, 189, 191; Gloucester Regiment, 10, 18; Gordon Highlanders, 5, 6, 7, 11, 13, 15, 18, 19, 128; Highland Light Infantry, 132, 134, 135, 138, 139, 140, 142, 143, 144, 145, 161, 169, 172, 179; King's Liverpool Regiment, 10, 13, 15, 27, 43, 80, 103; King's Own Yorkshire Light Infantry, 86, 138, 139, 140, 179; King's Royal Rifles, 10, 18, 19, 39, 103; Lancashire Fusiliers, 64, 98, 134, 135, 136-7, 169, 170, 172, 174, 177, 179; Leicester Regiment, 10, 19, 103, 190; Leinster Regiment, 42, 53;

London Regiment, 145; Middlesex Regiment, 43; Norfolk Regiment, 108; North Staffordshire Regiment, 103, 173; Northumberland Fusiliers, 43, 64; Notts. and Derby Regiment, 177; Queen's, 103; Rifle Brigade, 5, 11, 13, 20; Royal Dublin Fusiliers, 4; Royal Inniskilling Fusiliers, 18, 63; Royal Irish Fusiliers, 11; Royal Irish Rifles, 222; Royal Lancaster Regiment, 132; Royal Munster Fusiliers, 3, 43, 57, 102; Royal Scots, 24, 132, 134, 137, 142, 169, 173, 179; Royal Warwickshire Regiment, 64; Royal Welsh Fusiliers, 168; Royal West Kent Regiment, 42; Scottish Borderers, 80; Seaforth Highlanders, 189; Shropshire Light Infantry, 80; Somerset Light Infantry, 152; South Lancashire Regiment, 80; South Staffordshire Regiment, 42, 53, 60; Suffolk Regiment, 47, 86, 88, 90, 91, 94, 97, 114, 115, 117, 131, 132; Wiltshire Regiment, 62, 64, 80; Worcestershire Regiment, 42, 43, 50, 60, 80, 126; York and Lancaster Regiment, 98, 100

Colonial and Foreign: Bethune's Horse, 48; Desert Mounted Corps, 195; Dundonald's Cavalry, 18; Imperial Light Horse, 5, 15, 53, 55; Natal Carbiniers, 5, 15, 32; Natal Field Artillery, 5; Natal Volunteers, 11; Natal Police, 13; Queenstown Volunteers, 46; Railway Pioneer Regiment, 32; Royal Canadian Regiment, 64; Royal Irish Constabulary, 211; West African Regiment, 68; Armenian Irregulars, 191; 8th (Southland) Regiment, 70; 10th Regiment, Belgian Infantry, 172; 99th French Infantry Regiment, 129

Indian: 13th Lancers, 165, 189; 35th Scinde Horse, 218, 222; 37th Lancers, 222; No. 2 Mountain Battery, 39; No. 3 Peshawar Mountain Battery, 39; No. 3 Bengal Sappers and Miners, 39; 1st Gurkhas, 147, 148, 197; 2nd Punjab Infantry, 39; 2nd Rajputs, 151, 152; 213 Gurkhas, 116; 3rd Sikhs, 38, 39; 4th Gurkhas, 38; 6th Punjab Infantry, 39; 7th Gurkhas, 197; 8th Gurkhas, 102; 9th Gurkhas, 147; 10th Gurkhas, 221; 15th Sikhs, 106, 109, 114, 222; 19th Bengal Infantry, 39; 27th Punjabis, 197; 28th Punjabis, 69; 29th Bengal Infantry, 38, 39; 32nd Sikh Pioneers, 218; 34th Pioneers, 109, 161, 162; 40th Pathans, 117; 45th Sikhs, 222; 47th Sikhs, 69, 106, 108, 114, 115, 117, 121, 151, 155, 156, 158, 160, 188, 192; 53rd Sikhs, 69; 59th Scinde Rifles, 106, 114, 115, 117, 121, 151, 152, 155, 156, 160, 188, 192, 193, 198, 199; 93rd Burma Infantry, 147, 148, 165; 107th Indian Infantry, 149; 108th Native Infantry, 222; 124th Baluch Light Infantry, 160, 165, 188, 192, 197; 125th Rifles, 189

Reitpan, 48
Reitz, 46, 47, 48, 53, 60
Rening Helst, 128
Retief's Nek, 51
Retreat from Mons ended, 95
Reynolds, Sergt., 107
Rhind, Col.-Sergt., 29
Richardson, Capt. J. C., death, 331
Richardson, Corpl., 29; conspicuous coolness and courage under fire, 48
Richardson, Lance-Sergt., 58
Richardson, Second Lieut. C., 44, 53; Lieut., 57
Richebourg l'Avoué, 99, 100
Richebourg St. Vaast, 114, 116, 123, 185
Richmond, Sergt., wounded, 20
Ridley, Major, 35, 39, 40; Lieut.-Col. commanding 2nd Battalion, 41
"Rifleman's Aid Society," 343
Rifle Association Meeting, Southern India, 112
Rigby, Second Lieut., 158; Capt., 192
Roberts, Lieut., mortally wounded, 118
Roberts, Lord, 14, 15, 32, 44, 45, 49, 62
Roberts, Sir Frederick, 35, 264
Roberts, Pte., 194
Roberts' Drift, 52
Robertson, Lance-Sergt., 58
Robertson, Lieut., 213
Robertson, Lieut.-Col. G. McM., commands 2nd Battalion, 173
Robinson, Lieut., wounded, 118
Robinson, Pte., death, 8
Robinson, Sergt., 68
Rochfort-Boyd, Capt., Adjt., 35
Roe, Lieut., 3, 21
Roebuck, Pte. E., awarded Military Medal, 172
Roellecourt, 137
Rogers, Pte., wounded, 8
Rolt, Brig.-Gen. S. P., commanding 14th Brigade, 86, 104
Roodepoort, 26
Roscoe, Pte., wounded, 20
Rose, Lieut., 75, 81; Capt., wounded, 112
Rosendal, 44, 45, 59
Rosendpel, 168
Rouen, 87
Rougeville, 96
Rounds, Pte., 68
Routley, Lieut., 53
Rowley, Lance-Sergt., 76

Rowley, Second Lieut. J., death, 170, 331
Royal Barracks, 42, 86
Royal Military College Memorial, 332-333
Royston, Colonel, 10
Ruddy, Second Lieut., 119; Lieut., 124, 154
Rue des Berceaux, 115
Rue des Chavettes, 99
Rue d'Ouvert, capture of, 100
Rue L'Epinette, 99, 102
Rue Tilleloy, 102, 109
Rue Verte, 179
Rundle, Lieut.-Gen. Sir H., 42 44, 45, 46, 47, 49, 51, 60
Russian Buildings, Jerusalem, 201
Rustumiyah Canal, 219
Ruz Canal, 165
Rycroft, Major-Gen., Commanding 32nd Division, 132, 141
Rynd, Capt., G. C., 43, 50, 55

S

Saacy, 96
Sabieh, 196
Sablières, 95
Sadarai, 39
Sailly Lorette, 132
St. Eloi, 126, 127
St. George's Chapel, Windsor, 79
St. George's Defences, 168
St. Gratien, 132
St. Helena, 62, 63
St. Jan Capelle, 102
St. Jean, 170
St. Marguerite, 98
St. Mies, 99
St. Pierre Divion, 138
St. Pol, 137, 168
St. Quentin, 95, 141, 143, 145
St. Quentin Canal, 176, 177
St. Souplet, 177, 179
St. Vaast, 87, 90, 91
Salamanca Barracks, 205
Salt, Pte., killed, 21
"Samana 1891" Clasp to India Medal, 40
Samana Ridge, 38, 39, 40
Samaria, 195, 199
Samarra, 186, 187, 190, 191
Samarra Post, 187
Samawah, 218
Sambre, the, 177, 178
Sambreton, 180, 213
Sannaiyat, 149, 155, 158, 159, 160, 163, 164
Saportas, Colonel, 37
Saportas, Second Lieut. H. A., 107; Lieut., death, 128, 331
Sardinière, the, 168
"Sausage" Valley, 136
Savy, capture of, 142, 143, 145, 172
Savy Wood taken, 142, 143, 145
Sayers, Capt., 103
Scarpe, the, 141
Schoeman's Kloof, 20, 31
School Camp, 174
Scott, Col.-Sergt., 29
Scott, Lieut.-Col., 221; Lieut.-Col. E., 263
Scott, Pte., wounded, 13
Scott, Pte., wounded, 20

INDEX

Scott, Pte. R., awarded Victoria Cross, 29
Scully, Lieut. A. J., 68, 86, 87, 95; Major, 213, 215, 217, 223
Sealy, Second Lieut., 38, 40
Seaver, Capt., 107
Secunderabad, 67, 68
Selency, 142, 143, 144
Selle River, 92
Senekal, 45, 47, 48, 60
Senlis, 134, 135, 136
Sequehart, 176
Serre, 134, 137
Serre Trench, 138, 140
Service Companies for South Africa, 17
Seymour, Colonel, 141
Shacklady, Lieut., 131
Shahraban, 165, 186
Shaik Sa'ad, 147, 154, 156
Shargat, 216
Sharkey, Lance-Corpl., wounded, 20
Sharland, Second Lieut., 67
Sharp, Lieut. A. G., 43; Capt., 57
Shatt-el-Arab, 124, 147
Shatt-el-Hai, 150, 160
Shaw, Second Lieut., 69
Shawcross, Pte., death, 49
Shedhaif-ash-Sharqui, 164
Sheik Beiazid, 199
Sheppard, Capt., 212
Shewell, Second Lieut. E. L., 337, 339
Ships, Royal Navy: *Assistance*, 2; *Julnar*, attempts to reprovision garrison in Kut, 157
Shipster, Second Lieut., 70; Lieut., 107; Capt., 149, 154, 191; mortally wounded, 199; Capt. W. N., 330; memorial, 333
Shirley, Major-Gen. H., 264
Shoreimiya, 189
Shorncliffe, 1
Shumran, 164
Shumran Bend, 164
Shute, Major-Gen., commanding 32nd Division, 141, 172
Sialkote, 37, 38, 40
Siegfried Line, 141
Sikkim, 41
Sillifont, Pte., wounded, 8
Simmer, 32
Simpole, Second Lieut., 177
Simpson, Capt., 35
Simpson, Major, 3, 10; wounded, 13
Simpson, Pte. A. E., 194
Singapore, 30, 63, 67
Sinn Aftar Redoubt, 151, 158
Sirhind Brigade, 110, 114, 116
Sitwell, Capt., 37
Slaap Krantz, 46
Slaney, Lieut., 202
Slocock, Mr., 338
Sly, Sir Frank, 339
Smith, Col.-Sergt. A., 339
Smith, Lieut. A. G., 124
Smith, Lieut. J. H. M., 87, 94; death 97, 331
Smith, Lieut. R. W., 124
Smith, Pte., wounded, 23
Smith, Pte. (No. 3512), 28

Smith, Pte., J. 55
Smith, Second Lieut., 213
Smith, Second Lieut., 177
Smith, Second Lieut., wounded, 145
Smith-Dorrien, General Sir Horace, 86, 92, 102; farewell order to II Army Corps, 104; specially mentions 1st Battalion at Second Battle of Ypres, 119
Smyth, Pte., 82
Snelling, Pte., wounded, 13
Snow, Regt. Sergt.-Major F., 337, 339
Snyman's Hoek, 5
Sollesmes, 94
Somerville, Capt., wounded, 177
Somme, The, 128, 129, 130, 134, 137
Sotham, Second Lieut., 75, 76; Lieut., 86
Souchez, 133
Southampton, 2, 31, 32, 42, 43, 57, 64, 73
Sowden, Pte., wounded, 21
Sowray, Capt., 75
Soyecourt, 134
Spackman, Capt. R.A.M.C., 124; wounded, 148
Spencer, Pte., wounded, 20
Spens' Column, 26
Spion Kop, 14
Spithead, 73
Spitz-Kop, 60
Sprowell, Second Lieut., wounded, 173; missing, 177
Standard, Documents relative to the capture of, 269-271
"Standard and Diggers' News," 14
Standerton, 18, 30, 48, 52, 60, 61
Stanley-Murray, Lieut., 75
Stanway, 73
Stapledon, Capt., 75; Major C. C., 205, 206, 212, 214
Starkey, Second Lieut., wounded, 175
Stave, 213
Steamer Point barracks, 41
Steele, Lieut.-Col. L. L., commands 4th Battalion, 64, 66
Steele, Pte., injured, 21
Sterling, Pte., wounded, 20, 31
Stevens, Lieut. (acting Adjt.), 38, 40
Stevenson, Lieut., 21
Stevenson, Pte., 22
Stevenson, Pte., death, 8
Stewart, Pte., wounded, 12
Stewart, Pte., wounded, 21
Stewart-Wynne, Quartermaster O., 38, 40, 44; wounded, 53, 57
Stirke, Sergt., 32
Stirling, Lieut., 21
Straits Settlements, 67
Strathcona's Hill, 21
Strickland, Lieut.-Col. E. P., commanding 1st Battalion, 108; wounded, 109, 110, 111, 112; Brig.-Gen., commanding Jullundur Brigade, 113, 114; relinquishes command of Jullundur Brigade, 122; Major-Gen. Sir, commanding 6th Division, 207
Strydplaats, 52
Stuart, Colonel Sir John, 266
Stuart, Lieut., 21

Stuart, Pte., wounded, 23
Stuart's column, 26
Suez, 108, 192
Sullivan, Lance-Corpl., wounded, 49
Sunken Road, 120
Surkitt, Second Lieut., 171; wounded, 172
Sutherland, Capt., R.A.M.C., 212
Sutton, Sergt., 68
Suwada, 164
Suwaikeh Marsh, 150, 159
Suzanne, 129, 130
Swift, Second Lieut., death, 162; Lieut. J., 330
Swiss Cottage, 176
Sykes, Lieut., 209
Symons, General, 5

T

Table Bay, 3
Tait, Second Lieut., 173
Talana, 5
Talbot, Coke, General, 19
Tambour, The, 129
Tanglin Barracks, 30
Taylor, Capt., 174
Taylor, Pte., death, 8
Taylor, Pte., death, 55
Taylor, Pte., prisoner, 55
Taylor, Second Lieut., 177
Taylor, Second Lieut. L., death, 175, 331
Taylor Smith, Bishop, 62
Tekrit, 188, 189, 190, 216, 217, 218
Tel-el-Mukhmar, 193
Teneriffe, 3
Ten Tree Alley, 139
Tergeden, 145
Terry, Lieut., 21, 22; wounded, 23; Capt., 65, 75
Tetlow, Pte., wounded, 13
Thaba'Nchu, 45, 59, 60
Theobald, Capt. H. C., 81, 87, 88, 94; wounded, 95; Major, 173
Theron's Mill, 51
Thiepval, 133, 134
Thomas, Lieut., 75
Thomas, Lieut. A. F., 81, 87; wounded, 95
Thomas, Lieut. G. R., Adjt., 144
Thomas, Major, 34
Thomas, Second Lieut., 171
Thomas, Second Lieut. J. B. R., death, 331
Thomas, Second Lieut. T. S., death, 173
Thomas, Second Lieut. W. R. B., death, 173
Thomason, Co.-Sergt.-Major, R.M.A., 339
Thompson, Capt. J., death, 208-9
Thornton, Second Lieut., 154
Thornycroft, Second Lieut. C. M., 43; Lieut., 54, 55, 58, 59; Capt., 126; Lieut.-Col., 205
Thornycroft, Mr. Hamo, 76
Thorny Nullah, 151
Thorpe, Pte., prisoner, 20
Thulin, 88
Tigris River, 148, 150, 155, 158, 159, 160, 163, 164, 186, 187, 188, 216

"Tigris Corps," 125; change of command, 154, 159
Tilbury, 214
Tillard, Capt. A. G., death, 331; memorial, 332
Tillard, Lieut., 3; Capt., 21, 75, 98; missing, 100, 107, 109; Major, 223
Tillard, Lieut., 69
Tintwa Pass, 5
Tipperary, 2, 214
Tochi Field Force, 41
Tod, Lieut., 209, 212
Toogood, Capt., 65
Toole, Pte., wounded, 20
Tooley, Second Lieut., wounded, 145
Torrance, Lieut. K. S., 215, 216; Adjt., 223; Capt., 337
Tournan, 95
Tower of London, 1
Towers, Lieut. F., wounded, 188, 190, 192
Townhill, Pte., wounded, 12
Townsend, Pte., 55
Townshend, Major-Gen., 125, 147
Transit Camp, 204
Transports: *Alberta*, 75; *Aronda*, 192; *Avoca*, 67; *Bavarian*, 43, 57, 59; *Bræmar Castle*, 64, 74; *Buteshire*, 86, 87; *Conconada*, 214; *Consuelo*, 73; *Dilwara*, 30, 41; *Dominion*, 62; *Dunera*, 42; *Edavana*, 107, 108; *Englishman*, 32; *Frederica*, 64; *Georgian*, 124; *Glengarriff*, 212; *Goth*, 3; *Greek*, 31; *Hardinge*, 223 *Huntsend*, 124; *Ixion*, 192; *Kinfauns Castle*, 57; *Lützow*, 124; *Macedonia*, 214; *Michigan*, 57; *Nubia*, 2; *Orient*, 57; *Pentakota*, 124; *Plassey*, 63; *St. Andrew*, 57; *Sangola*, 107; *Slieve Gallion*, 206; *Vera*, 75; *Warwick Castle*, 2
Trench, 28, 139
Trenches, Second Battalion complete 87 days in, before relief, 128
Trichardt, Commandant, 22, 24
Trimulgherry, memorial tablet, 68
Troisvilles, 92, 94
Trueman, Capt. C. Fitz G. H., memorial, 332
Trueman, Lieut. C. F. H., 43, 58, 62; Capt. 75, 87, 90, 94; death assumed, 95, 331
Tul Keram, 195, 198, 199, 202
Tumeltz, Pte., wounded, 12
Tunnelling Camp, 169
Turner, Colonel, 39, 40
Turner, Pte., 55
Tweefontein, 55
Twickenham, 205
Tyger Kloof, 55
Tylden-Wright, Second Lieut., 52, 53; wounded, 55
Tyndall-Lucas, Brig.-Gen. commanding 16th Infantry Brigade, of, 206; kidnapped in Ireland, 207
Tyrrell, Colonel, kidnapped in Ireland, 207
Tytler, Major-Gen., 339

U

Uitkyk, 25
Um-al-Tubal, 164
Umbulwana, 9, 11
Umm-el-Hannah, attack on, 147-9, 154, 155
Underberg, 53
Uniform, Colours, Badges, etc., of the Manchester Regiment, 63rd Foot, 1758-1916, 1st Battalion, Notes on, 224-268
Urmston, Colonel, columns under, 24
Urquhart, Pte., wounded, 13

V

Vaal, 26
Vaalbank, 26
Vaal River, 52
Vadencourt, 178
Vailly, 98
Vanderspar, Second Lieut. E. L., 81; Lieut., 87; wounded, 99, 113; death, 128, 331; memorial, 332
Vanderzee, Capt. C. A., 44, 46
Van Dort, Pte., wounded, 20
Van Heel, Second Lieut., 213
Van Reenan's Pass, 5, 56
Vanrenan, Lieut., 21
Vanryne, Pte., wounded, 13
Van Wyk's Vlei, 19
Varney, Lance-Sergt., 76
Vaudrey, Capt., 124, 147; death, 157
Vaughan, Capt., 21, 29
Vaughan, Major, 82; Colonel, commands 2nd Battalion, 168; Lieut.-Col. E. commands 1st Battalion on re-formation, 205, 206; relinquishes command of 1st Battalion, 208
Vaughan, Lieut.-Gen. Sir Louis, 336, 338
Vaux, 130, 134
Vayro, Pte., wounded, 8
Vecquemont, 129
Veldhoek, 171
Vendelles, 175, 177
Venizel, 98
Ventersburg, 47
Venterspruit, 52
Verdun, pressure on French at, 133
Vermando Villers, 175
Vermelles, 99
Viceroy of India, 34
Vickers, Colonel G. E., 344
Victoria Cross. Awards in South African campaign, 29; Second Lieut. Leach and Sergt. Hogan, 102; Corpl. Issy Smith, 118; Capt. George Stuart Henderson, D.S.O., M.C., 220
Villeveque, 175
Vining, Lieut., 209, 211
Violaines, capture of, 100, 101
Vizard, Capt. R. D., 3, 12, 35; Major, 29, 48; commands 2nd Battalion, 50, 51; Lieut.-Col., 54, 57, 68, 69; Brig.-Gen., 339

Vlakfontein, 25
Vlaklaagte, 25
Vlakplaats, 49
Vlamertinghe, 117
Volksrust, 18
Volunteer contingents for South Africa, 16
Volunteer Service companies, 16, 26, 30, 53, 55, 56
Von Falkenhayn, 186
Vrede, 47, 48, 52, 53, 61
Vrischgewaagte, 26

W

Waddington, Band Sergt., wounded, 13
Wadi, 153
Wadi River, 147, 148, 156
Wagon Hill, 11, 12
Wakkerstroom, 45
Walker, Brig.-Gen., commanding 55th Infantry Brigade, 221, 339
Walker, Col.-Sergt., 58
Walker, Lieut., 202
Walker, Lieut. R. F., death, 331; memorial, 332
Walker, Lieut. W., death, 330
Walker, Major, 70, 75, 107
Walker, Pte., wounded, 23
Walker, Second Lieut., 97; death, 100
Walker, Second Lieut., death, 162
Waller, Second Lieut., 98; wounded, 100
Walsh, Lance-Sergt., death, 13
Walsh, Pte., wounded, 20
Walton, Lieut. L. A., 337, 339
War; declared by Transvaal and Orange Free State, 3; European, outbreak of, 1914; 72, 84
Ward, Capt., 37; death, 41
Ward, Co.-Sergt.-Major, Instructor in Musketry C., 339
Ward's Farm, 46
Warley, 1
Warloy, 137
Washington, Second Lieut. J. N., memorial, 332
Wasmes, 88, 90
Waterfall, 211
Waters, Second Lieut., 47, 58
Waterval Boven, 27, 28
Waterval Onder, 27, 28
Watkins, Sergt., 76
Watkis, Lieut.-Gen., 106; Speech to 1st Battalion after Givenchy, 112
Watson, Capt., 38, 39, 40
Watson, Major, 3, 5, 10, 11, 19, 20; Lieut.-Col., 21, 25; commands 1st Battalion, 28, 29; 2nd Battalion, 73, 75
Watson, Major J. E., 71
Watts, Capt., 170
Watts, Lieut. S., death, 331
Wemmershoek Farm, 22
Wemmershoek Valley, 22
Wepener, 44, 59
West Hutments, 214

INDEX

Weston, Lieut., 41; Major 75, 79, 81; Major R. S., 87, 91; wounded, 99, 103; Lieut.-Col., commanding 2nd Battalion, wounded, 130
Westropp, Lieut.-Col., commands 2nd Battalion, 79, 80, 81, 82
Weymouth, 212
White, Colonel, 60
White, Lieut.-Gen. Sir George, 4, 5, 9, 10, 14
White, Second Lieut., 154, 157, 213
Whitehall Camp, 172
Whitehead, Lance-Corpl., death, 12
Whitehead, Pte., wounded, 12, 19, 31
Whittaker, Major, relinquishes command of 2nd Battalion, 168
Whyte, Lieut. C. C., 337, 339
Wickham, Second Lieut., 65
Wickham, Lieut. T. S., death, 331
Wickham, Lieut. W. D. T.; death, 330; memorial, 333
Wieltje, 117
Wigan, 1st Volunteer Battalion, 16, 30
Wilcock, Col.-Sergt., 29
Wildebeestefontein, 27
Wilge River, 46, 52, 56
Wilhelma, 193
Wilkins, Second Lieut., 124; wounded, 145; Lieut., 148; death, 153
Wilkinson, Sergt., wounded, 13
Willcocks, Lieut.-Gen., commanding Indian Army Corps, 106; inspects 1st Battalion, 110; speech to 1st Battalion after Givenchy, 112; address to 1st Battalion after Neuve Chapelle, 116, succeeded by Lieut.-Gen. Anderson in command of Indian Army Corps, 120
Williams, Colonel, column under, 24, 25, 26
Williams, Pte., death, 8
Williams, Pte., death, 20
Williams, Sergt., death, 13
Williams-Green, Lieut. W. T., 173, 215, 216, 223, 337, 339
Williamson, Capt. W. H., 43, 50, 55
Williamson, Co.-Sergt.-Major, 204
Williamson, Second Lieut. G. W., death, 331
Williamson, Second Lieut., 101; Lieut., wounded, 103, 130; wounded, 131
Williamson-Jones, Second Lieut., wounded, 118
Willis, Sergt. John, awarded D.C.M., 221
Willow Farm, 46
Wilson, Brig.-Gen., 80
Wilson, Lieut., 86
Wilson, Pte., wounded, 10
Wilson, Second Lieut., 192
Winburg, 48, 60
Winch, Second Lieut., death, 145
Winchester, Bishop of, 205
Winchester Road, 120
Winder, Second Lieut., 177, 213
Windhoek, 24
Windsor Castle, 79
Wing, Colonel, column under, 24, 25, 26, 27
Witklip, 20, 21, 22
Witklip-Vaal Constabulary, line of posts, 26
Witkopjes, 52
Wittenbergen, 60
"Wolfe-Murray" Cup, 68
Wolseley, Field-Marshal Viscount, 49; funeral, 82
Wonderfontein–Standerton blockhouse line, 26
Wood, Pte., wounded, 20, 31
Wood, Pte. W., awarded Military Medal, 172
Wood, Sergt., 19, 29, 58
Woodhouse, Second Lieut., 46; mortally wounded, 48
Woods, Lieut., 75, 82
Woods, Sergt., death, 15
Woods, Sergt., wounded, 8
Woods, Sergt. C. H., 194
Woormezeele, 127
Worley, Sergt., 76
Wright, Capt. H. T. R. S., death, 331; memorial, 332
Wright, Lieut., 41, 79
Wright, Lieut.-Col. B. A., commands 2nd Battalion, 214, 215; wounded, 221, 223
Wulverghen, 102, 103, 126
Wymer, Capt. G. P., 82, 87, 94; wounded, 95, 337
Wytschaete, 102

Y

Yates, Pte., wounded, 12
Yates, Second Lieut., 158; death, 162; Lieut. W. G., 330; memorial, 332
Yilderim Headquarters, 195
Younghusband, General, 150
Ypres, 102, 108, 114; 1st Battalion meets 2nd Battalion, April 1915, 117, 118; 1st Battalion specially mentioned for "Great Service" at second battle of, 119, 123, 126; 2nd Battalion at second battle of, 127, 129, 185
Ypres Canal, 117
Yser Canal, 169
Yule, Colonel, 9
"Y" Wood ravine, 130

Z

Zakho, 217
Zandspruit, 18, 32
Zawata, 199, 202
Zeur, 164
Zwartelen, 126

Printed in Great Britain for
FORSTER GROOM & CO., LTD.,
by
Hazell, Watson & Viney, Ld., London and Aylesbury.